Cases on Digital Game–Based Learning:

Methods, Models, and Strategies

Youngkyun Baek
Boise State University, USA

Nicola Whitton
Manchester Metropolitan University, UK

Information Science
REFERENCE

Managing Director:	Lindsay Johnston
Editorial Director:	Joel Gamon
Book Production Manager:	Jennifer Yoder
Publishing Systems Analyst:	Adrienne Freeland
Development Editor:	Christine Smith
Assistant Acquisitions Editor:	Kayla Wolfe
Typesetter:	Christina Henning
Cover Design:	Jason Mull

Published in the United States of America by
Information Science Reference (an imprint of IGI Global)
701 E. Chocolate Avenue
Hershey PA 17033
Tel: 717-533-8845
Fax: 717-533-8661
E-mail: cust@igi-global.com
Web site: http://www.igi-global.com

Library of Congress Cataloging-in-Publication Data

Baek, Youngkyun.
  Cases on digital game-based learning: methods, models, and strategies / Youngkyun Baek and Nicola Whitton, editors.
     p. cm.
  Includes bibliographical references and index.
  Summary: "This book analyzes the implementation of digital game applications for learning as well as addressing the challenges and pitfalls experienced, providing strategies, advice and examples on adopting games into teaching"--Provided by publisher.
  ISBN 978-1-4666-2848-9 (hardcover) -- ISBN 978-1-4666-2849-6 (ebook) -- ISBN 978-1-4666-2850-2 (print & perpetual access) 1. Simulation games in education. 2. Educational games. 3. Computer games. I. Whitton, Nicola. II. Title.
  LB1029.S53B34 2013
  371.39'7--dc23
                              2012032518

British Cataloguing in Publication Data
A Cataloguing in Publication record for this book is available from the British Library.

All work contributed to this book is new, previously-unpublished material. The views expressed in this book are those of the authors, but not necessarily of the publisher.

Editorial Advisory Board

Table of Contents

Section 1
Teaching with Commercial Games

Section 2
Teaching with Educational Games

Section 3
Designing Games for Learning

Section 5
Games for Teacher Education

Section 6
Game-Based Learning in Practice

Section 7
Researching Games and Learning

Chapter 26
Racing Academy: A Case Study of a Digital Game for Supporting
Richard Joiner, University of Bath, UK
Ioanna Iacovides, University College London, UK
Jos Darling, University of Bath, UK
Andy Diament, Penwith Further Education College, UK
Ben Drew, University of West of England, UK
John Duddley, Barnfield Further Education College, UK
Martin Owen, Medrus, UK
Carl Gavin, Manchester Business School, UK

Detailed Table of Contents

Section 1
Teaching with Commercial Games

Chapter 1

Maria Velazquez, University of Maryland, USA

Pixie Hollow provides a series of useful, accessible examples for discussing gender, the mechanics of community building, and the interconnections between technological fluency and community norms.

Chapter 2

Mete Akcaoglu, Michigan State University, USA

How some existing classroom factors can substitute or modify the effects of very important game elements is described. Specifically, how virtual teachers can keep the students engaged is explained, even when a very important element of role-playing games, narratives, is missing from a game, and hence, the chapter makes the case for the particularity of playing games in a classroom setting.

Chapter 3

Christina Badman, Sacred Heart Catholic School, USA
Matthew DeNote, Espiritu Santo Catholic School, USA

This chapter describes two years' of work incorporating the Nintendo Wii gaming platform into multiple subjects in our 4th through 8th grade classrooms.

This case study looks at how the retro video game genre of Interactive Fiction was
used with learners of English as a foreign language in order to provide them with
an alternative method of practising reading for fluency in a meaningful, motivating,
and engaging manner.

Section 2
Teaching with Educational Games

This chapter explores how using the digital game Civilization IV could encourage
constructivist learning, target social studies content standards, cultivate 21st century
skills, and increase student engagement.

The focus of this chapter is to introduce mobile learning opportunities, via a mobile
based learning game, at the outset of the learner's academic journey. Its purpose is to
highlight how mobile phone technology could be utilised for educational purposes
and determine if mobile learning could deliver an active and collaborative experience for learners during the induction process.

The case described here demonstrates how the game can be used as a tool for raising
awareness of diet and provide opportunities for meaningful decision-making among
primary school-aged children. The game uses a blend of simulated and pervasive
elements using ubiquitous technologies to enhance children's capacity to make
informed choices with regard to their own eating habits.

This case study relates to a mixed-reality game that aims to provide a highly immersive learning experience to the players and opportunities to enhance their teaching in more creative ways as a result of their engagement and participation. The author shares details about this mixed-reality game and the pedagogical rationale on which it is based with other practitioners.

Section 3
Designing Games for Learning

This chapter discusses the creation of Medicina from inception through to dissemination, detailing the stages, challenges, and lessons learned in the process, in the hope of informing other educators of the level of commitment involved in a digital game-based project. This game familiarizes students with confusable and common medication names. It also aims to improve phonological awareness through a focus on word form.

This chapter considers how Serious Games (SGs) as a digital technology endeavours to support effective lifelong learning. Three fundamental characteristics of the SG ecosystem, namely: game mechanics, interoperability, and assessment, are considered here as strategic elements that impact upon how SGs are to support learning, how they affect the learning environment, and ultimately, the SG development process.

Chapter 11

Scott J. Warren, University of North Texas, USA
Anjum Najmi, University of North Texas, USA

There are two goals for this chapter. The first is it to review existing theoretical models
of game learning and to provide an overview of a new model called Learning and
Teaching as Communicative Actions. The second is to give a detailed description
of the design process for Broken Window, an alternate reality (AltRG) transmedia
game that was developed to support undergraduate learning in a computer applications course.

Section 4
Learning through Game Design

Chapter 12

Brian Herrig, Canon-McMillan School District, USA

Seventh grade students are engaged in digital game-based learning as a method of
introducing them to the concepts of programming. Each student is provided with
an overview of basic programming terminology and is introduced to the functions
of Game Maker, an icon-based, drag-and-drop video game creation software package. Students complete an introductory programming activity in which each student
programs a similar game. A second activity has each student create a more advanced
game of their own design. Rather than digital games being used to deliver content,
in this case, the games become the content.

Chapter 13

Danielle Herro, Clemson University, USA

This case examines the development of a game design curriculum offered to high
school students as an in-school elective course in the Oconomowoc Area School
District (OASD), a Wisconsin suburban school district. The rationale for proposing
the course was based on the overlap of research, trends, and experience studying
game-design and game-based learning environments. To that end, it is important to
note the ITA was simultaneously completing an Educational Technology Doctoral
degree focused on digital media and learning and engaged in research involving Massively Multiplayer Online Games (MMOG) and Augmented Reality Games (ARG).

Chapter 14
Game-Making in a Fourth Grade Art Classroom Using Gamestar
Mechanic 256
> *Michelle Aubrecht, Ohio State University, USA*

This chapter discusses how the author used the free, online video game Gamestar Mechanic in an elementary art classroom and supported the art teacher in learning how to use this tool. Through this professional development experience, the art teacher learned how to use Gamestar Mechanic and how game design and art can be integrated. Players, fourth-grade students in a low-income, urban school, learned basic game design principles and how to design games by playing and fixing them.

Chapter 15
Using Game Design as a Means to Make Computer Science Accessible to
Adolescents 279
> *Roxana Hadad, Northeastern Illinois University, USA*

In this case, the author discusses using game design and community-building as methods for increasing interest and knowledge of computer science for students from underrepresented populations. The game design courses engaged students, developed students' ability to collaborate and utilize critiques, and increased their knowledge of programming.

Section 5
Games for Teacher Education

Chapter 16
3D GameLab: Quest-Based Pre-Service Teacher Education 302
> *Chris Haskell, Boise State University, USA*

This chapter explores the use of game-based pedagogy for a pre-service teacher education course, as well the development of a quest-based learning management system (3D GameLab) to support the class. The chapter is grounded in design-based research, and discusses four phases of development and theory generation.

Chapter 17
Preparing Pre-Service Teachers for Game-Based Learning in Schools 341
> *Soojeong Lee, Kyungnam University, South Korea*

This chapter describes the pre-service teacher's preparation of teaching consumption education to middle school students when using Farmville, a social network-based game. This chapter analyses the consumer education in middle school textbooks. This chapter also describes the possibilities of a student-oriented classroom model using Farmville to teach consumption education.

This chapter presents a case study that used an online game in a pre-service science teacher training course in the context of computer-supported inquiry learning. In this chapter, the authors focused on developing pre-service teachers' skills in using a game to teach students through inquiry-based learning. The game used was Death in Rome, a free-to-access point and click game. Overall, this study showed a positive change in attitudes towards game-based learning in science education.

Section 6
Game-Based Learning in Practice

Chapter 19

This chapter reports on an eco-simulation of a food web in a middle school science classroom. The students were successful in coming to understand the dynamics of complex eco-systems. The authors discuss why the project was successful and describe a design model for teachers to successfully integrate games and simulations in the classroom.

This chapter illustrates a short case in which educational animation and manipulatives were utilized to support communication and learning of mathematical concepts during an after-school program. The authors utilized a computer-based educational animation that involves the concept of length measurement, and a broken ruler as a manipulative to help students learn about measuring objects while communicating mathematically.

The Education Arcade at MIT has worked on design principles that focus on assumptions about play and learning. Lure of the Labyrinth was developed with these principles in mind, requiring teachers to develop a modified perception of their role in the classroom. This chapter describes how teachers implemented the model in real-life classroom settings, and describes the impact of this implementation on students' outcomes.

In this chapter, the authors describe two experiments involving Virtual Worlds and Serious Games in a learning environment. These experiments allowed the readers to understand the real potential of two emerging technologies but also some of the difficulties one can come across. The experiments was to analyse learners' learning styles profile using virtual games and explore if virtual activities are as effective as manual ones to evaluate students efficiently. Some of the pitfalls that should be avoided are described as a set of lessons learnt at the end of the chapter.

Section 7
Researching Games and Learning

This chapter describes some of the work carried out in the MIRROR project, which focuses on reflective learning where adults' motivation to learn and reflect through games is being researched. It introduces the project and the theoretical framework briefly and then describes the serious game that was created for research in detail. The last part of this chapter focuses on users' evaluations and describes some lessons learned about the importance of guidance and of a de-briefing session, thus highlighting the potential of serious games for collaborative knowledge construction.

In this chapter the authors describe the evaluation of the game DOGeometry which was carried out in a classroom environment over a four month period. They report the development process, the design of the evaluation, results, challenges, and problems they faced.

This chapter aims to introduce the case of the eFinance Game (eFG), from the Serious Games' design to an analysis of the learning experience resulting from the use of the game, as well as its use in the context of the Introduction to Finance course in ESADE Law and Business School. After an overall description of the game, the authors turn their attention to the Serious Games learning experience, considering the students' perception of both ease of use and usefulness, but also the implications for teaching and learning assessment that arise with the utilization of this game.

The aim of this chapter is to report a case study where the authors evaluated how effective Racing Academy is at supporting students' learning of science and engineering. They found that after playing Racing Academy there is an increase in students' knowledge and understanding in all five of the courses in which Racing Academy was used. In addition, they found evidence that students found playing Racing Academy motivating.

Foreword

Despite the blossoming interest in the use of games or game elements in educational settings, I often imagine individual teachers or professors getting a spark of interest in this genre, and then sitting down at their laptop - or standing in their local computer game store - and thinking "where do I start?" or "what do I choose?"

For regardless of the recent interest, and the undoubted fact that many games are in use across the world in educational contexts, concrete examples of successful (or, as importantly, failed) implementations are remarkably difficult to find. Local or national press tend to focus on highlights and shadows (the gleeful school treasure hunt, or the worried parents in uproar over the violent video games in their school), and only the larger, well-funded examples tend to make it through to academic journals, with only brief focus on the practicalities of choosing, amending, and implementing games in a classroom context. Evidence for the general efficacy of games in improving learning is currently weak, although there are a number of compelling studies of other benefits and the potential for greater learning (Gee (2003), Salen (2008), Whitton (2009), McGonigal (2011), Whitton & Moseley (2012)).

Key practical questions, therefore, still remain for those starting out in the field: How do you choose a digital game? Should you adapt an existing, or design a new game? How do you fit it into the curriculum? Will it benefit all students and learning styles? How can you assess it? Is it going to be fun? Will it be worth the effort?

It was therefore a great pleasure to hear about Baek and Whitton's idea for this case book. Here, at last is a resource which has spread its feelers across continents to find real examples of digital games in use in real contexts, just like yours or mine. In one place, we can compare the design strategies of teachers at K12/primary level, contrast the efficacy of using Wii consoles in class against designing a simple digital game, and find evidence of increased knowledge/understanding as a result of gameplay to take back to our faculty heads.

Many of the cases here might never be found in journals (or at least, not within realistic timescales and around local access limitations) – these are real examples from real institutions like yours or mine, evidenced by full evaluations in many cases, coalescing to form a picture of current practice across the world.

Youngkyun Baek brings his extensive experience in the use of digital games for learning, both in South-East Asia and the US (in particular his study of Second Life and virtual worlds) together with his long teaching experience in both secondary and tertiary environments; Nicola Whitton draws on her extensive study of the use of digital games for learning and their particular benefits for education, in addition to her experience in designing, implementing and evaluating games within a higher education environment. Together they have formed an astute international team, sourcing case studies which evidence such benefits.

Across seven sections, the editors have selected a wide range of case studies to suit all educational contexts - from primary schooling to teacher education, off-the-shelf games to designs from the ground up, across diverse disciplines from physics to gender studies, and covering small and large budgets.

Armed with this extensive volume, educators no longer have any excuse to put off that spark of interest: a quick dip into here, and they will find a familiar context, a shared problem, or just the idea they need to get started. For every case shared here, another hundred will soon be being written across the classrooms, lecture halls, and online learning spaces of the world.

Alex Moseley
University of Leicester, UK
July, 2012

Alex Moseley *is Educational Designer at the University of Leicester. He is a course designer, and conducts research in games-based learning, subject-based research skills delivery, social media, and museum games for education; he also teaches innovative courses in History and Museum Studies. He was recently awarded the title of University Teaching Fellow.*

REFERENCES

Gee, J. P. (2003). *What video games have to teach us about learning*. New York, NY: Palgrave. doi:10.1145/950566.950595

McGonigal, J. (2011). *Reality is broken: Why games make us better and how they can change the world*. Penguin.

Salen, K. (Ed.). (2008). *The ecology of games: Connecting youth, games, and learning. The John D. & Catherine T. MacArthur Foundation Series on Digital Media and Learning*. Cambridge, MA: MIT Press.

Whitton, N. (2009). *Learning with digital games*. New York: Routledge.

Whitton, N., & Moseley, A. (2012). *Using games to enhance learning & teaching: A beginner's guide*. New York, NY: Routledge.

Preface

An Overview of Digital Game-Based Learning

In recent years, there has been increasing interest in the use of digital games, and in particular, computer games, for learning, among teachers, researchers, policy makers, and other educational practitioners. There are many examples of the effective use of computer games in all stages of formal education, including work in primary schools and secondary schools, as well as post-compulsory education. There are examples of their effective use in a variety of subject areas, from scientific and technical to business and humanities, arts, and languages. As well as in formal education, games have also been used successfully for training, work-based learning, and in informal contexts. Digital games have the potential to create active and engaging environments, which motivate students and support learning in creative ways.

Digital games can also be used to teach a wide variety of different things. This includes specific curriculum content in subject disciplines, but also transferrable skills such as problem-solving, critical thinking, or teamwork. Games can also be used to teach physical skills, cognitive strategies, and change behaviours or attitudes. The value of game-based learning does not stop simply with their use as vehicles for delivering learning, but they can also be used as triggers for discussion or as a design activity where learning takes place through the design process. Game-based learning is not just about teaching with games, but also about learning from games and applying gaming principles to teaching, and understanding the incidental learning that takes place while game play goes on, for example, the collaboration and mentoring that takes place in Massively Multiplayer Online Role Playing Games (MMORPGs). The case studies in this book explore game-based learning from a variety of perspectives, showing a range of different ways in which it can be applied to different teaching and learning contexts.

The application of digital games for learning is also wide ranging, from the use of game consoles and computer platforms, to mobile gaming on phones or tablets, to mixed-media games that incorporate digital and real-world elements. It encapsulates many different game types and genres, from games that take weeks to play to those that are over in minutes, including games played individually or collaboratively. The potential for different types of digital games to be used in different learning situations is vast; and this volume hopes to show this variety through the range of case studies selected.

There are many advantages to using games for learning, both pedagogic and in terms of supporting student motivation and enhancing engagement. They provide active learning environments in which learners can explore problems and test multiple solutions, and create meaningful contexts in which to build on past knowledge and experiences in order to gain a deeper understanding of a subject. Computer games provide a way in which learners can interact with a simulated environment, where they can explore and make discoveries, and they allow players to take part in authentic and purposeful tasks that map on to real world activities. A key goal of many types of game is based around problem-solving – be it strategic planning, lateral thinking, or how to work as a team to defeat a powerful enemy – which provides a motivation and stimulus for learning. Games create mysteries and stimulate curiosity, allowing players to uncover secrets, or journey with a character through a story to discover what happens at the end.

Digital games enable players to take part in active and immersive experiences, not simply to passively receive information, but to explore, try things out, and see the effects of their actions. It is this interaction and feedback that is crucial to learning from games; when a player makes an action it has (a usually immediate) effect and the player can then take further actions based on what has happened and this link between action and immediate, relevant feedback is why games can be so powerful. Making mistakes in computer games is not only seen as an intrinsic part of the game play for many games, but also as an inevitable part of the progress from novice to expert player. In this respect, they provide an ideal forum for practice and reflection on progress. Digital games are particularly good at guiding players as they make the journey from novice to expert, so that new players can make big gains early on, increasing confidence and involvement in the early stages, before they tackle the more difficult challenges or levels later. Goals start small and gradually increase in difficulty as game play progresses, and the support decreases so that as the game becomes harder while the player becomes more independent.

Many games allow learners to work together, be it in an online real-time space, in a face-to-face environment on shared hardware, or though an online gaming community. This ability to share ideas and opinions, clarify and reach shared understandings, is very powerful for learning. It not only allows students to learn about the topic of interest, but also to learn transferable skills such as communication and negotiation. They allow students to work to their strengths while learning from others, developing critical thinking and analytical skills, creative-thinking and problem-solving, testing their ideas, and discovering different learning styles, skills, preferences, and perspectives.

Games provide access to alternative worlds, which are typically safe from the consequences of the real world. Players can experiment, explore, and try out new things without risk of negative outcomes outside of the magic circle of the game. The playful state that games often engender can spark creativity, innovation, and new ideas, as well as allowing players to engage with fictional narratives, characters, and plots. Games allow players freedom and control to create new identities and interact with both the environment and other people in novel and surprising ways. They also create a sense of fun and enjoyment, removing some of the stresses and pressures that are often associated with formal education, and allowing learners to engage with the game activities in a relaxed and light-hearted manner.

Computer games have the potential to be powerful learning tools, particularly when considered beyond the simple arguments that they are motivational when they are used as a reward for learning. Digital games can be rich and interactive, providing context, purpose, authentic activities, meaningful problems to be solved, new experiences, and playful environments to explore, and a forum for social activity. Of course, computer games are not without their disadvantages, and the use of any new technology is likely to have limitations both in terms of its acceptability and practical applications in real world learning and teaching situations. This volume contains a number of real world case studies that addresses some of the issues that occur when using digital games in practice, and considers how they might be overcome.

Digital Game-Based Learning in Context

The field of digital game-based learning is multidisciplinary in nature, drawing on areas as wide-ranging as sociology, psychology, computing, game design, education, learning technology, and interaction design. This means that the field benefits from multiple perspective and approaches, but also presents challenges of opposing philosophies and research paradigms. This volume aims to present case studies from a variety of disciplinary backgrounds, showing how the use and evaluation of games can be approached from different angles.

There are several key challenges in digital game-based learning, which provide a framework for the case studies presented here and, the Editors hope, show ways in which these challenges can be addressed and overcome. Obtaining appropriate games for learning in specific contexts can be difficult, and a primary dichotomy is whether to use games originally designed for entertainment, or those designed for educational purposes. The former option allows learners to play high-end games, designed to be engaging and enjoyable, but they can be expensive, difficult to integrate with curricula or learning situations, technically exclusive, and can focus on gaming objectives at the expense of learning outcomes. The second approach has the advantage of using games that are designed with learning at the key objective, where the designers have considered curricula and the limitations of the educational environment – for example technical, space or teaching time – but can still be expensive to buy or create and may lack the professionalism of design seen in commercial products. Case studies showing the use of entertainment games are shown in Section 1: Teaching with Commercial Games, compared with those in Section 2: Teaching with Educational Games.

Balancing learning design and game design is another important challenge in game-based learning, so that games stand alone as fun and engaging while still meeting the intended learning outcomes of the activity. The whole issue of how to effectively develop bespoke games for learning is addressed in Section 3: Designing Games for Learning. In addition to using games as the vehicle for delivering learning, there is now a greater emphasis on the potential of game design to be used as a means in itself for learning, and examples of this are provided in Section 4: Learning through Game Design.

The way in which the media negatively portrays games, for example in terms of violence, sexualised content, or addictive behaviours, helps to shape negative attitudes towards the use of games for learning, in parents, teachers, and among the learners themselves. One way in which to address this bias and start to question some of the media assumptions is to use games within teacher education, presenting a cascade model in which attitudes towards games for learning become more informed and discussion of games in the media more critical. Examples of games in this context are given in Section 5: Games for Teacher Education. The use of digital games for learning in practice can also be problematic; in particular, many games do not typically lend themselves to supporting collaborative working, or fostering reflection on the learning process. A number of case studies are included that show how issues can be dealt with successfully in order to create effective learning experiences, and these are presented in Section 6: Game-Based Learning in Practice.

Finally, there is a need within the field to provide further evidence of the effectiveness of games for learning, in terms of student enjoyment and engagement, but also in terms of measuring what is being learned, whether it is being retained, and the degree to which learning from games can be transferred to the real world. The case studies in Section 7, Researching Games and Learning, provide excellent examples of how effective research in the field can be carried out.

This book aims to use these case studies to show the wide variety of approaches to the way in which digital games for learning are obtained or created, implemented, supported and evaluation. It is hoped that readers will gain inspiration as well as insights from these examples, and become open to new possibilities, discover ways in which to enhance their own practice, and learn from the experiences of others.

The Target Audience

The intended audience for the book is essentially anyone with an interest in teaching and learning with digital games, who would like to see concrete examples of their application in practice. The case studies in this volume aim to show many different ways in which different digital games can be used in different contexts, providing insights into the drawbacks and limitations of their use, as well as the benefits in a variety of situations.

While this book is designed to have a wide appeal as possible, it is hopes that it will appeal in particular to teachers and lecturers – involved in all phases of education from early years to lifelong learning – who are keen to use game-based learning in their own practice. It will also be of interest to researchers, educational practitioners, and policy makers who are concerned with innovation in teaching and learning, curriculum design, or enhancing learner engagement.

The case studies have purposefully been selected to give an international flavour and are drawn from the USA, Europe, Asia, and Australia, and the book is intended to appeal to an international audience.

Description of Sections and Chapters

Section 1: Teaching with Commercial Games

Within the last few years, we have witnessed growing interest in the potential use of commercial off-the-shelf games for learning. Early studies of these games helped to identify the aspects of games that make them especially engaging and appealing to players of various ages and of both genders. These commercial games have potential as they show many of the inherent strengths of games for learning, as well as their ability to promote collaboration, foster engagement and motivation, and to develop students' thinking skills. Yet, these chapters also detail the difficulties teachers face in incorporating complex, time-consuming, and technically sophisticated games into short classroom hours not intended for use with commercial games.

In the chapter *"Come Fly with us": Playing with Girlhood in the World of Pixie Hollow*, Velazquez introduces Pixie Hollow, which provides a series of useful, accessible examples for discussing gender, the mechanics of community building, and the interconnections between technological fluency and community norms. Pixie Hollow is a useful teaching tool for first and second year college students in women's studies, gender studies, and American studies classrooms because of its incorporation of gender roles into the pre-structuring of the program.

Akcaoglu describes how some existing classroom factors can substitute or modify the effects of very important game elements in the chapter *Using MMORPG's in Classrooms: Stories vs. Teachers as Sources of Motivation.* Specifically, how virtual teachers can keep the students engaged is demonstrated, showing that this is possible even when a very important element of role-playing games, narratives, is missing from a game, and hence, makes the case for particularity when playing games in a classroom setting.

The chapter *Are Wii Having Fun Yet?* describes two years of work incorporating the Nintendo Wii gaming platform into multiple subjects in 4th through 8th grade classrooms (ages 9 to 13 years). Badman and DeNote found that not only were the students learning during the Wii enhanced classes, but they were retaining the information long after the initial lessons.

The case study, *Beyond Hidden Bodies and Lost Pigs: Student Perceptions of Foreign Language Learning with Interactive Fiction*, looks at how the retro video game genre of Interactive Fiction was used with learners of English as a foreign language in order to provide them with an alternative method of practising reading for fluency in a meaningful, motivating, and engaging manner. Pereira found Interactive Fiction to be an engaging way to practice reading, and the majority of students in the sample stated they would use it for autonomous language skills practice.

Section 2: Teaching with Educational Games

Educational games are games that are designed to teach people about certain subjects, expand concepts, reinforce development, shape behaviour or attitudes, understand an historical event or culture, or assist them in learning a skill as they play. Some games may be explicitly designed with educational purposes, while others may have incidental or of secondary educational value, although all types of games may potentially be used in an educational environment. Games can engage learners in ways other tools and approaches cannot, and their value for learning and motivation has been supported through research. We know more about how games work and how to apply them to teaching and learning than we ever have, and that understanding is increasing.

In the chapter *Civilization IV in 7ᵗʰ Grade Social Studies: Motivating and Enriching Student Learning with Constructivism, Content Standards, and 21ˢᵗ Century Skills*, Senrick explores how using the digital game Civilization IV could encourage constructivist learning, target social studies content standards, cultivate 21st century skills, and increase student engagement.

In the chapter *QRienteering: Mobilising the M-Learner with Affordable Learning Games for Campus Inductions*, Horne introduces mobile learning opportunities, via a mobile based learning game, at the outset of the learner's academic journey. Its purpose is to highlight how mobile phone technology could be utilised for educational purposes and determine if mobile learning could deliver an active and collaborative experience for learners during the induction process.

In the case study of *Enhancing Nutritional Learning Outcomes within a Simulation and Pervasive Game-Based Strategy*, McMahon demonstrates how a game can be used as a tool for raising awareness of diet and provide opportunities for meaningful decision-making among primary school-aged children. The game uses a blend of simulated and pervasive elements using ubiquitous technologies to enhance children's capacity to make informed choices with regard to their own eating habits.

"Sell Your Bargains" or Playing a Mixed-Reality Game to Spice up Teaching in Higher Education, describes a mixed-reality game that aims to provide a highly immersive learning experience to the players and opportunities to enhance their teaching in more creative ways as a result of their engagement and participation. Nerantzi shares details about this mixed-reality game and the pedagogical rationale on which it is based with other practitioners.

Section 3: Designing Games for Learning

One of the main shortcomings of using commercial or existing games is that these games are typically designed primarily as entertainment products, without taking into account educational considerations. More often than not, educational software designed to support learning often borrows from game design in an attempt to replicate the levels of engagement and exploit this to facilitate traditional learning; however, this is often done in a superficial or behaviourist way. The chapters in this section are success stories of game designs that managed to apply theories into practice in a more thoughtful and deep manner.

The chapter of *Medicina: Methods, Models, Strategies* discusses the creation of Medicina from inception through to dissemination, detailing the stages, challenges, and lessons learned in the process, in the hope of informing other educators of the level of commitment involved in a digital game-based project. Müller and Mathews indicate that this game familiarizes students with confusable and common medication names. It also aims to improve phonological awareness through a focus on word form.

In the chapter *Strategies for Effective Digital Games Development and Implementation*, Lim and colleagues consider how Serious Games (SGs) as a digital technology endeavour to support effective lifelong learning. Three fundamental characteristics of the SG ecosystem are presented: namely, game mechanics, interoperability, and assessment. They are considered here as strategic elements that impact upon how SGs are used to support learning, and how they affect the learning environment and ultimately the SG development process.

In the chapter *Learning and Teaching as Communicative Actions: Broken Window as a Model of Transmedia Game Learning*, Warren and Najmi review existing theoretical models of game learning and provide an overview of a new model entitled

Learning and Teaching as Communicative Actions. In addition, they describe the design process for Broken Window, an alternate reality transmedia game that was developed to support undergraduate learning in a computer applications course.

Section 4: Learning through Game Design

Game design is becoming a popular strategy for engaging learners' interests in and enhancing skills with computer technology. This can be for purposes ranging from deepening their understanding of scientific principles to fostering critical media literacy, learning about the processes involved in game design and development to their own end, or the transferrable skills that are developed during the creation process, such as teamwork, planning, or negotiation skills.

In the chapter of *Get Your Head in the Game: Digital Game-Based Learning with Game Maker*, Herrig discusses 7th grade students (aged 12-13 years) who are engaged in digital game-based learning as a method of introducing them to the concepts of programming. Each student is provided with an overview of basic programming terminology and is introduced to the functions of Game Maker, an icon-based, drag-and-drop video game creation software package. Students complete an introductory programming activity in which each student programs a similar game. A second activity has each student create a more advanced game of their own design. Rather than digital games being used to deliver content, in this case, the game creation becomes the content.

In the chapter *Elements of Game Design: Developing a Meaningful Game Design Curriculum for the Classroom*, Herro examines the development of a game design curriculum offered to high school students as an in-school elective course in the Oconomowoc area, a Wisconsin suburban school district. The rationale for proposing the course was based on the overlap of research, trends, and experiences studying game-design and game-based learning environments. To that end, it is important to note that one of the development team was simultaneously completing an educational technology doctoral degree focused on digital media and learning and engaged in research involving Massively Multiplayer Online Games (MMOGs) and Augmented Reality Games (ARGs).

In the chapter *Game-Making in a Fourth Grade Art Classroom Using Gamestar Mechanic*, Aubrecht discusses how his use of the free, online video game development toolkit Gamestar Mechanic in an elementary art classroom and how he supported the art teacher in learning how to use this tool. Through this professional development experience, the art teacher learned how to use Gamestar Mechanic and how game design and art can be integrated. Players, fourth-grade students (9-10 years) in a low-income, urban school, learned basic game design principles and how to design games by playing and fixing them.

In the chapter *Using Game Design as a Means to Make Computer Science Accessible to Adolescents*, Hadad discusses using game design and community-building as methods for increasing interest and knowledge of computer science for students from underrepresented populations. The game design courses engaged students, developed students' ability to collaborate and utilize critiques, and increased their knowledge of programming.

Section 5: Games for Teacher Education

One of the biggest obstacles to wide-scale acceptance of game-based learning in classrooms is the lack of proper training for our teachers. In order for game-based pedagogy to really take hold in K-12 (primary and secondary) as well as in higher education, we need teachers who are knowledgeable and skilled in teaching via gaming activities. It is important for teachers to be able to address the inevitable concerns of parents and administrators when the prospect of playing games. Teachers must also be capable of assessing these games and reviews themselves.

In the chapter *3D GameLab: Quest-Based Pre-Service Teacher Education*, Haskell explores the use of game-based pedagogy for a pre-service teacher education course, as well the development of a quest-based learning management system (3D GameLab) to support the class. The chapter is grounded in design-based research, and discusses four phases of development and theory generation.

In *Preparing Pre-Service Teachers for Game-Based Learning in Schools*, Lee describes the pre-service teachers' preparation of teaching consumption education to middle school students when using Farmville, a social network-based game. This chapter analyses the consumer education in middle school textbooks, and also describes the possibilities of a student-oriented classroom model using Farmville to teach consumption education.

In the chapter *Death in Rome: Using an Online Game for Inquiry-Based Learning in a Pre-Service Teacher Training Course*, Kennedy-Clark, Galstaun, and Anderson present a case study that used an online game in a pre-service science teacher training course in the context of computer-supported inquiry learning. In this chapter, the authors focused on developing pre-service teachers' skills in using a game to teach students through inquiry-based learning. The game used was Death in Rome, a free to access point and click game. Overall, this study showed a positive change in attitudes towards game-based learning in science education.

Section 6: Game-Based Learning in Practice

The emergence of game-based learning is offering the learning and teaching community new opportunities to reach and motivate hard-to-engage learner groups.

It supports differentiated and personalized learning, and provides new tools for teaching and learning.

In *Games, Models, and Simulations in the Classroom: Designing for Epistemic Activities*, Ahern and Dowling report on an eco-simulation of a food web in a middle school science classroom. The students were successful in coming to understand the dynamics of complex eco-systems. The authors discuss why the project was successful and describe a design model for teachers to successfully integrate games and simulations in the classroom.

In the chapter *The Role of Animations and Manipulatives in Supporting Learning and Communication in Mathematics Classrooms*, Uribe-Flórez and Trespalacios illustrate a short case in which educational animation and manipulatives were utilized to support communication and learning of mathematical concepts during an after-school program. The authors utilized a computer-based educational animation that involves the concept of length measurement, and a broken ruler as a manipulative to help students learn about measuring objects while communicating mathematically.

In *It's All in How You Play the Game: Increasing the Impact of Gameplay in Classrooms*, Reid, Jennings and Osterweil introduce Lure of the Labyrinth, a digital game for middle school pre-algebra students. The Education Arcade at MIT has worked on design principles that focus on assumptions about play and learning. Lure of the Labyrinth was developed with these principles in mind, which include requiring teachers to develop a modified perception of their role in the classroom. This chapter describes how teachers implemented the model in real-life classroom settings, and describes the impact of this implementation on students' outcomes.

In the chapter *Challenges of Introducing Serious Games and Virtual Worlds in Educational Curriculum*, Ribeiro and colleagues describe two experiments involving Virtual Worlds and Serious Games in a learning environment. These experiments allowed the readers to understand the real potential of two emerging technologies but also some of the difficulties one can come across. The experiment was to analyse learners learning styles profile, using virtual games and explore if virtual activities are as effective as manual ones to evaluate students efficiently. Some of the pitfalls that should be avoided are described as a set of lessons learnt at the end of the chapter.

Section 7: Researching Games and Learning

A common criticism of the field of games and learning is the lack of large-scale, robust, and longitudinal evidence of their value for learning and motivation. Recent research into games and learning are focused on pedagogical effects, design variables, and learning experience of participants. The chapters in this section provide a snapshot of some of the most recent research in the field.

In the chapter *Serious Games for Reflective Learning: Experiences from the MIRROR Project*, Pannese and colleagues describe some of the work carried out in the MIRROR project which focuses on reflective learning where adults' motivations to learn and reflect through games is being researched. It introduces briefly the project and the theoretical framework and then describes in detail the serious game that was created for research. The last part of this chapter focuses on users' evaluations and describes some lessons learned about the importance of guidance and of a de-briefing session, thus highlighting the potential of serious games for collaborative knowledge construction.

In *Evaluating Games in Classrooms: A Case Study with DOGeometry*, Wallner, Kriglstein, and Biba describe the evaluation of the game DOGeometry, which was carried out in a classroom environment over a four month period. The analysis of the gameplay data and the feedback from the children and teachers showed that the pre-evaluation was really important in order to ensure that the game was well-balanced. Although the evaluation went well more effort would be invested in the design of the pre- and post-test for subsequent evaluations to adapt the difficulty better to the target audience.

In *Learning with the Support of a Digital Game in the Introduction to Finance Class: Analysis of the Students' Perception of the Game's Ease of Use and Usefulness*, Romero and Usart introduce the case of the eFinance Game (eFG). They discuss the Serious Games' design, an analysis of the learning experience resulting from the use of the game, as well as its use in the context of the Introduction to Finance course in Esade Law and Business School. After an overall description of the game, the authors turn their attention to the Serious Games learning experience, considering the students' perception of both ease of use and usefulness, but also the implications for teaching and learning assessment that arise with the utilization of this game.

In the final chapter, *Racing Academy: A Case Study of a Digital Game for Supporting Students' Learning of Physics and Engineering*, Joiner and colleagues report a research study where the authors evaluated how effective Racing Academy is at supporting students' learning of science and engineering. They found that after playing Racing Academy, there is an increase in students' knowledge and understanding in all five of the courses, in which Racing Academy was used. In addition, they found evidence that students found playing Racing Academy motivating.

Epilogue

This case book presents twenty-six first-hand accounts of learning with digital games in schools, colleges, and universities. The impact of games in teaching and learning is described, analysed, and synthesized with the objective of offering successful strategies and examples, and addressing challenges and pitfalls experienced during the implementation of digital game applications for learning.

This book serves as a guide to practice for teaching with digital games, highlighting the variety of different ways in which games can be used, looking at different game forms and different contexts. This case book provides methods, models, and applications of digital games for learning in primary and secondary classrooms as well as post-compulsory education. The book provides teachers at all levels with good examples to follow, and advice and context for making decisions about adopting games into teaching. This book holds current models of learning, types of game, and emergent strategies of applications, positioning this book as a crucial reference book in this field at this time.

Digital game based learning will benefit from this case book by the accumulation of authentic cases, which have implications for practical reapplication in new settings. This book is a resource to improve teaching and learning with digital games with well-organized examples categorized by learning model, method, and strategy.

Youngkyun Baek
Boise State University, USA

Nicola Whitton
Manchester Metropolitan University, UK

Section 1
Teaching with Commercial Games

Chapter 1
"Come Fly with Us":
Playing with Girlhood in the World of *Pixie Hollow*

Maria Velazquez
University of Maryland, USA

EXECUTIVE SUMMARY

Pixie Hollow provides a series of useful, accessible examples for discussing gender, the mechanics of community building, and the interconnections between technological fluency and community norms. This game also provides an opportunity to talk about literacy as a fundamentally social act. Also, the overall assignment and its emphasis on journaling as a research tool meant to encourage critical self-reflexivity helps students grasp concepts central to the course as a whole, including race, class, and gender.

INTRODUCTION

Pixie Hollow is a useful teaching tool for first and second year college students in women's studies, gender studies, and American studies classrooms because of its incorporation of gender roles into the prestructuring of the program. This massively multi-player online game centers on the world of the Disney Fairies. Tinkerbell is the most prominent, and she, as well as the other fairies, flit about the Pixie Hollow, helping the seasons, animals, and flora of the Mainland (the world of humans) to flourish. The player designs a character, and embarks on self-selected mini-quests in order to gain points, in-game prizes, and to help the flora and fauna of *Pixie*

DOI: 10.4018/978-1-4666-2848-9.ch001

Hollow. This class looks at the connections between technological evolution and hegemonic structures, so prestructuring here refers to both the technologies of game design and the sociocultural framework surrounding design decisions on the part of the programmers and developers.

Discussing *Pixie Hollow*'s design encourages conversations about a version of femininity centered on consumption, affective labor, and performing acts of kindness. This discussion also provides an opportunity to describe the ways in which girlhood becomes a site of both play and policing. Because this game is designed for younger children, it is very easy for college students with varying degrees of technical competency to master it. *Pixie Hollow* provides a unique opportunity to see how technologies of gender (such as the idea of fairies as feminine and little girls as fragile and in need of protection) impact the technologies of game design. I use this game in the classroom to talk about the prestructuring of gender roles into various types of built environment, the roles of various types of literacies in framing community development.

CASE DESCRIPTION

The course "AMST 260: American Culture in the Information Age" focuses on the use of technology in everyday life. I have taught five iterations, each of which drew on the *Pixie Hollow,* a game hosted on go.Disney.com. I designed this course to help students consider the role information, surveillance, and play take in structuring space online and off. I also placed a particular emphasis on the race, gender, class, and affective labor in the construction of communal space. This is a tall order for a second-year course open to any student at the university. Together, my students and I grappled with a number of theoretically-dense texts, including Hayot and Wesp's "Towards a Critical Aesthetic of Virtual World Geography" (2009), excerpts from Nancy Baym's work on online friendship (2003), Boellstroff's *Coming of Age in Second Life* (2008), and Lisa Nakamura's seminal *Digitizing Race* (2007). Throughout the semesters I have taught these texts, we've struggled with them again and again, particularly their discussions of the built environment of a program's infrastructure and its impact on the emotional experience of community.

We begin discussing these issues in the second week of class, when I introduce the Disney website. For the first six weeks of class, we engage in a series of virtual fieldtrips while in class together, visiting both *Pixie Hollow* and other online games. Our main focus in these initial conversations are the social rituals associated with friendship and community, paying particular attention to the ways in which community as a concept is both amorphous and fraught with emotion. We talk about how the university, for example, refers to students as members of its community, though their membership looks and feels very different from that of faculty and staff. We also talk about the use of the discussion board on Blackboard as a means of fostering a virtual classroom community, where participation is evaluated and enforced through a series of metrics listed in the syllabus. Students continue these conversations on the under-defined nature of community on their own using the discussion board on Blackboard, where I provide weekly links and talking points to guide their participation in this virtual space (See Figure 1).

I first introduce the class to the *Pixie Hollow* website using a laptop and large projector, so that we can discuss the music, the site's layout, and Disney's branding as a large group. Normally, the site's front-page includes references to both the Disney Fairies' movie series (normally emphasizing Tinker Bell) and to a few other Disney properties, including music sung by one of its tween stars. After discussing the site's layout, color scheme, and characters featured, I log in as my fairy, and offer a quick introduction to the world, highlighting how one "flies" by using the mouse as a directional aid and reminding students that the handout associated with the assignment is already in their syllabus. In this discussion, I also model the basics of "close play" (Chang 2008, p. 9), thinking out loud about the accessibility of the website, the coloring of the fairies as reflective of player identities, and the fantasy of girlhood the site describes. Close play is a methodology where the student engages with both in-game and out-game products in order to engage in sociocultural critique. Students primarily rely on journaling and micro-blogging to note their observations while engaged in close play.

Figure 1. A map of Pixie Hollow (© The Walt Disney Company)

Outside of class, students begin their research journal by going to the same home-page. Upon creating their fairy, noting the gendering and racialization of each avatar through customization options, students select a talent (light, water, tinker, garden, and animal), and are greeted, in-game, by their talent-mentor, one of the non-playable characters who provides instructions, quests, and in-game automated companionship to the player. Their talent-mentor introduces them to the mini-games played in-world, and reminds them that "here, work is play!"(*Pixie Hollow*, 2008). In *Pixie Hollow*, to be a good community member is to be of service to the Mainland (the world of humans) and to other fairies. The mentor then instructs the player/student to click on the compass, which folds open into a leather-bound tome, like the gold-limned novels introducing *Masterpiece Theater* or the maps of an animated *Treasure Island*. As the pages flip open, they reveal a flowering, leafy tree whose branches and roots contain all four seasons in glorious exuberance, split into the four quadrants of the original compass. Some sections, mini-game levels, and quests are unavailable to free users, but the rest of the world spreads itself as though eager to be read. The next time the user logs in, they're invited to pick a server, and are then presented with a landscape image of the branches of Pixie Hollow in whatever seasonal section they've selected (See Figure 2 and 3).

Figure 2. Copper's Nook, where Copper will encourage the player to make something for their fairy's home (©The Walt Disney Company)

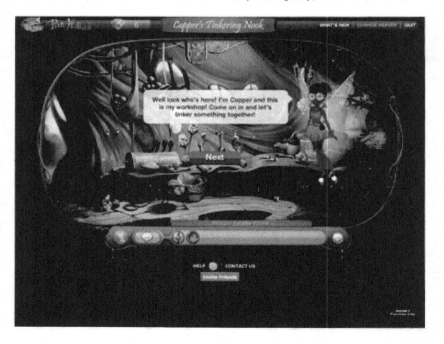

Figure 3. Copper's Nook, with options for tinkering. These options include seedpod fans, leaf blankets, sweet tea lights, and maple mats. (© The Walt Disney Company)

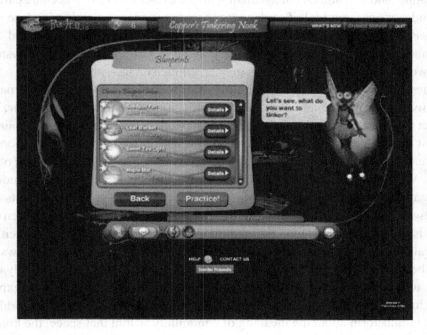

In class, our learning approach draws on close playing *Disney Fairies* as a large group, engaging in a close reading of the game, with multiple pauses for discussion and critical analysis. This challenges students to apply the readings (and their definitions of community, play, friendship, and leisure) to a virtual world the authors have not described. The comments students offer range from a discussion of the types of skin tones available to fairies as a marker of beauty standards already being marketed towards girls to a comparison of the hushed color palette (soft pastels and earth tones) to the bright, saturated world of *Cars*, a movie/partner site also hosted on Disney.com and primarily marketed towards boys. We sometimes use a fishbowl strategy, where a 'working group' (a group of students co-writing a paper due later in the semester on a particular course theme) takes center stage and has an informal, unscripted conversation about the connections between their ongoing research project and game-play. We also begin talking about journaling as a research tool, looking at excerpts from journals kept by researchers, field-notes, and their impact on qualitative research and project design. Throughout, I emphasize the collaborative nature of this kind of project. We are not starting with a set of definitions; instead, we are working towards a shared definition of community with explanatory power for the phenomena they are observing in their own research on virtual worlds and play. Each of these tools – discussion with one's peers, autoethnography through journaling, and a sustained engagement with the extant literature – become parts of the students' research toolkit as they use their experiences engaging in close play in *Pixie Hollow* to analyze the programmatic and social structures associated with community building online and the connections between these structures and systems of power existing off-line, like race, gender, ethnicity, class, and age.

These discussions and activities build towards the 'What is Community?' paper, an individual project centered around the 'built environment' of *Pixie Hollow*. The project components include a 5-8 page paper, as well as a research journal containing at least seven entries. These entries can be in whatever format the student chooses, with many students treating this as an opportunity to docuemt a close playing of the game. Writing out the observations gleaned from close playing requires students to engage in a careful analysis of in-game and out-game cultural products and frameworks (Chang 2008). Basically, because so much of what happens when one plays is unstated and assumed, journaling forces the student to make explicit the cultural connections upon which the game relies. The close play process draws out both the minute observations students might make when exploring an entirely new place, as well their affective/emotional analysis of the initial and ongoing experiences in virtual world. The entries written as students explore their virtual world are used to brainstorm about the meaning of community within that space, the kind of community created by in-game products, and the role that out-game cultural norms take in in-game culture. Most students use their journal entries to talk about their initial impressions of the game, including their own initial thoughts about gender and girlhood. Sometimes these entries are very stream-of-conscious; some will express surprise that even though Tinker Bell and Copper are skilled tinker fairies, their emphasis is on home décor and not mechanics, and that even though some of the non-playable characters like Fairy May are heavy-set, changing one's weight and build to something like hers is not an option. Other students write shorter entries, like brief status messages on Facebook, and still others treat these entries as early drafts of the paper itself. I only see their entries when they turn in the entire assignment, though students will often refer to their entries in their working group meetings and during our large group discussion (See Figure 4).

The assignment goals are to synthesize course materials, engage in critical reflection, and to develop and support a definition of community, drawing on class discussions, the readings, and the student's research journal. Because this assignment is the first stage of a longer, semester-long group project, students may also incorporate their group's meeting notes as well. The overall assignment is designed to challenge students to make the familiar strange, a concept I borrow from Sara Ahmed's *Queer Phenomenology* (2006).This is one of the reasons I use this game.

Figure 4. Copper's Nook, with color choices. Here, Copper is guiding the player through selecting a color for a tenderleaf table (©The Walt Disney Company).

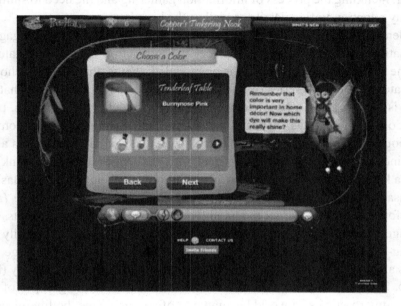

On the one hand, it features character types and genre conventions students are generally familiar with. They're pretty, girly fairies doing 'nature stuff'. As students glibly point out, they've either heard about fairies, read about fairies, or pretended to be a fairy already, so the idea of being a small flying girl collecting acorns and spider webs is not altogether unfamiliar. At the same time, students are analyzing these character types and exploring the world of a game somewhat unfamiliar to them, while engaged in feminist analysis. For many students both the type of analysis and the game itself are somewhat new, as this MMOG was not released until 2008, when college students now would have aged out of its target demographic. Also, this class may be the first where they're encountering a sustained critique of gender and race. So, while the world should resonate and seem familiar because of students' earlier experiences with fairies as a kind of fantasy genre convention, the game itself and their project in that world is not. I also recommend students read "Researchers, Reflexivity, and Good Data: Writing to Unlearn" by Audrey Kleinsasser (2000), available in the Reading/Writing Tools section of our Blackboard site. This article describes the use of writing as a means of engaging in reflexive research, as a tool for revealing researcher biases and theoretical concerns, and for helping students learn some of the methods associated with qualitative research. Finally, I include an MSWord document of a rubric for critical thinking in this same section. This rubric models the different facets associated with critical thinking, including the process of information gathering and the need to simultaneously pay attention to fine details as well as the big picture.

Students are specifically asked to journal the process of logging in, engaging in conversation, moving from place to place, and interaction with both in-game and out-game products. The game itself is open-ended; that is, the user may choose to participate (or not!) in a series of micro-quests suggested by the game. That *Pixie Hollow* is a game set in a larger transmedia universe, with chapter books, picture books, dolls, movies, CDs, websites, and a larger fan community, spurs conversations about the game as a type of boundary object, as well its status as a 'true' game, since its edges and ending are vague. This challenges students to think about play as a kind of pedagogical tool, with multiple sites of reinforcement. Basically, the messages about girlhood and good citizenship disseminated by *Pixie Hollow* are reinforced through a larger media universe, which references concepts, ideas, and imagery extending beyond Disney's brand. Plus, the game itself visually refers to a long-standing tradition in the Western world of representing the large in the small as a kind of imaginative play as well a form of scientific creativity (Hayot & Wesp, 2009). That is, dollhouses as whole households or the glimpse of water through a microscope as a world become part of an immersive, bodily experience where the player/researcher constantly manipulates the "large as small" (by moving the dolls or manipulating the microscope's lens) as well as interacting with the "large as large" (by engaging with the doll house as a real house with real people, or by describing the microbes in the water as real) (Hayot & Wesp, 2009, n.p.). Hayot and Wesp argue that the ways in which these types of play-spaces function relies on nostalgia (medieval fantasy tropes in particular) to make a world that intuitively *feels* like a world because of its affective resonance with other types of media, like movies or fairy tales. Because of this course's commitment to feminist and antiracist analysis, we link this nostalgic resonance to larger histories of conquest, erasure, and fantasies about utopia and racelessness. This also leads into a discussion of one of the readings on technology and power: Donna Haraway's "Situated Knowledges." Haraway (1988) argues that these same mechanisms of visualization (making the large into the small as an imaginative act and an act of scientific research) reflect larger social dynamics where the self "leaps from a marked body and becomes the conquering gaze from nowhere" (p. 581). In this conversation, we return to our discussion of community building and surveillance, discussing the bodiless nature of the university system and its ability to mark student bodies as good or bad, and the role of metrics and surveillance in Blackboard, and my ability to monitor their use without their knowing. We parallel this to the giant's hand moving dolls back and forth in the world of the dollhouse, all powerful, or the ability of the microscope, and the scientist's mind, to penetrate the hidden world of the cell.

We spend a great deal of time in class talking through concepts of literacy, coding bodies, and labor as a means of performing community. In this conversation, we use Barton and Hamilton's definition of literacy, where literacy is both an innately social act, and something that builds community bonds (1998). These conversations in class incorporate assigned readings on virtual communities, particularly Hayot and Wesp's critical aesthetics article, and prestructuring in computer games. These readings are augmented with class discussion focused on the various types of literacy associated with gaming (including technological literacy, genre literacy, medium literacy, etc.) and their connections to the idea of a play-based community. Because the *Pixie Hollow* game seems easy, most students feel free to focus their observations on their interactions with other players as well as their thoughts about the world of the game, instead of focusing on things like strategy. While students sometimes express frustration that we are spending so much time on a game designed for children with no clear rules, this frustration becomes an opportunity for journaling, because it becomes an opportunity to write out the meaning of rules in the context of play and community.

Throughout these first six weeks of the course, we've been talking about the interconnections between histories of race, gender, and technology. At this point in our classroom conversations, I introduce the concept of prestructuring, highlighting that understandings of race, gender, and ethnicity evolve interdependently with technological innovation. Prestructuring refers to the ways in which designers build in particular assumptions about the ideal user and their desires. I introduce this conversation using Jeanette Hoffman's "Writers, Texts, and Writing Acts" (1999), which describes the evolution of word processing software as progressing interdependently with the re-gendering of the office. This article has been difficult for students in the past because many of them cannot imagine a program like MSWord looking any different than it does today. By using *Pixie Hollow*, I am able to illustrate this concept using the design choices of a children's game, and the evolution of these choices over time. For example, we have had really fruitful discussion over the 2010 introduction of Sparrow Men as playable characters is a formerly (female) fairy-only world. Grounding this larger discussion of shifting social and political norms in a children's game provides multiple points of entry for students because they can begin a conversation on prestructuring using visual analysis (a direct comparison of the computer screen to the lens of a microscope or a doll house), spatial analysis (a discussion of the avatar-as-the-student's-body exploring a new space), activity analysis (centered on the events of the world as a whole), and an affective analysis (a discussion of the ways in which the game prompts, encourages, or disrupts feelings of community, confidence, and leisure). Students may move in and out of each type of analysis over the course of playing and analyzing their experiences in-world. We read Richard Dyer's "Making 'White' People White" (1999), as well as Tyler

Pace's "Can an Orc Catch a Cab in Stormwind?" (2008), both of which describe the ways in which whiteness impacts not only technological innovation but what kinds of technologies are considered successful. While Dyer's article focuses on technological innovation, Pace's article provides an opportunity to discuss the ways in which program design in *Pixie Hollow* participates in longer histories of racism and sexism by, for example, limiting skin color choices while providing several in lighter gradations, making blackness and girlhood seem almost like contradictory concepts. Another example would be the types of objects available for collection (flowers, seeds, berries, and webs, with no signs of spiders or bees) as reflective of a fantasy of the forest as idyllic and nurturingly feminine as opposed to a representation of the forest as dirty, wild, and untameable (See Figure 5).

Students as players are invited to explore this massive multiplayer online game, earning points and badges as they gather nuts, berries, flowers, and play games like Bubble Bounce or tinker at Copper's Tinkering Nook. Again, all games are a form of working for the betterment of the Mainland or other fairies. For example, Bubble Bounce is a physics/force game where a fairy bounces a fish in a bubble up a waterfall using a lily pad, earning points for quantity of fish and the bounciness of the bounce, and "tinkering" involves playing a Tetris-like in order to amass matching tools, dyes, and raw "tinkering" materials. Fairies aren't able to keep the items they tinker or tailor without becoming paying members of the site, but are still encouraged to be productive members of the Hollow. In contrast, the student as budding researcher has been reminded to maintain a journal chronicling their adventures in Pixie Hollow, making notes of the moments the familiar no longer feels intuitive, such as navigating the limited conversational capabilities present in game. Players can use SpeedChat, a set of a pre-selected/typed phrases already approved by the designers as appropriate for the Fairy Code of Conduct. These phrases are subdivided into conversational categories (hellos and goodbyes) as well as mood, ranging from happy (including "Flitterific!") to mad (including "Don't be mean!"). In past years, students have offered an analysis of the range of responses, including the quantity of "Happy" mood phrases in comparison to "Mad" mood phrases, describing the number of phrases available to each as suggestive of how much easier it is to be a happy fairy instead of an angry one. Another student also suggested that the types of phrases offered for "Mad" and "Sad" are modeling behaviors, placing an emphasis on reconciliation and using one's words effectively, such as asking "Why did you do that?" when one is frustrated.

In class, we begin talking about social rituals and community norms as channeling behavior, particularly the behavior of women and girls, as part of performing community membership. In order to drive home one of the course's main arguments – that community is a fluid, multi-layered concept – I challenge my students to consider the ways in which technological fluency, genre fluency, and social flu-

Figure 5. The fairy has earned a new badge for collecting spider silk, and is invited to share this accomplishment via Facebook (©The Walt Disney Company)

ency each became unmarked components of the play experience in *Pixie Hollow*. I also ask them to consider the ways in which fantasies of gender, age, labor, and community impacted player experience and the ways in which this Flash-based game is marketed. I asked them to think about what knowledge and skills they had to have in order to fully participate in this community. One of the journal prompts on the assignment handout sheet is: 'What social rituals are present? How do these rituals draw on both real and virtual community histories?' In answering this question, students refer to both the conversational restrictions placed on players (free chat requires parental consent) as well as the practice of inviting other fairies to your bower (decorated, of course, with items one has earned in-game) for a party.

This assignment is part of a semester-long research project. At the start of the semester, students divide themselves into small working groups framed by their self-selected research interests. Students turn in this 'What is Community?' assignment individually, as well as a follow-up research paper meant to further their working group projects. The next two assignments are co-written with their working groups and collectively edited with the class for the class wiki. *Pixie Hollow* and our discussion of the built environment help students talk out the many hegemonic forces framing community participation online. For example, one group discussed the use of nostalgia as an organizing force in some online fandoms, and connected that conversation to our own use of Blackboard and the chalkboard images accompanying its logo. Another group discussed fantasy football as a site where gendered and racialized power dynamics are fetishized, discussing how many fantasy football websites link the consumption of women's bodies to the competitive nature of the game. Each semester, at least one group has brought up conspicuous consumption, and the role of establishing who you are by what you buy. Finally, another group designed their own website discussing the arts and shared creative practices (like story-telling, painting, and avatar-making) as a means of demonstrating friendships online. These conversations change a little each semester, depending on the students enrolled in the class and the ways in which *Pixie Hollow* has itself evolved. However, each semester this game has proven a rich source of discussion material related to gender, community building, and game design.

Technology Components

This game requires Flash, and works best with a high-speed internet connection. The basic levels are free, and do not require any downloads. Some parts of the program require parental consent, like the ability to chat freely, and others are for paying players online. Because all my students were over the age of eighteen, they typically themselves permission to do chat. I do not require them to pay to join, and instead emphasize the site's free content. I sometimes maintain two log-ins, so that students can see any differences between free and pay memberships, but this is not necessary.

The site and its content are updated fairly frequently – sometimes this is a fairly minor content change, like the addition of a new quest or object, and other times it is more major, like the addition of Sparrow Men as playable characters and the incorporation of 'real world' quests, like giving compliments and eating healthily.

Challenges

This popular children's game has limited chat functionality dependent on parental approval. The college students with which I worked provided such approval for themselves. Some male students found it frustrating to play a game involving "fairies." While this concern was a useful jumping off point for discussion, it has also been addressed through Disney's introduction of Sparrow Men as playable characters in April 2010.

REFERENCES

Ahmed, S. (2006). *Queer phenomenology: Orientations, objects, others*. Durham, NC: Duke University Press.

Barton, D., & Hamilton, M. (1998). *Local literacies*. New York, NY: Routledge.

Baym, N. (2003). I think of them as friends: Joining online communities. In Dines, G., & Humez, J. M. (Eds.), *Gender, race, class, and media* (2nd ed., pp. 488–495). Thousand Oaks, CA: SAGE Publications.

Boellstroff, T. (2008). *Coming of age in Second Life*. Princeton, NJ: Princeton University Press.

Chang, E. (2008).Gaming as writing, or, World of Warcraft as world of wordcraft [Electronic version]. *Computers and Composition: An International Journal*. Retrieved February 2, 2012, from http://www.bgsu.edu/cconline/gaming_issue_2008/Chang_Gaming_as_writing/index.html

Dyer, R. (1999). Making 'white' people white. In Mackenzie, D., & Wacjman, J. (Eds.), *The social shaping of technology* (pp. 134–140). Ann Arbor, MI: Open University Press.

Haraway, D. (1988). Situated knowledges: The science question in feminism and the privilege of partial perspective. *Feminist Studies, 14*, 575–599. doi:10.2307/3178066

Hayot, E., & Wesp, E. (2009). Towards a critical aesthetic of virtual world geographies. *Game Studies, 9*. Retrieved February 2, 2012, from http://gamestudies.org/0901/articles/hayot_wesp_space

Hoffman, J. (1999). Writers, texts, and writing acts. In Mackenzie, D., & Wajcman, J. (Eds.), *The social shaping of technology* (pp. 222–228). Philadelphia, PA: Open University Press.

Kleinsasser, A. (2000). Researchers, reflexivity, and good data: Writing to unlearn. *Theory into Practice, 39*(1), 155–162. doi:10.1207/s15430421tip3903_6

Nakamura, L. (2007). *Digitizing race*. Minneapolis, MN: University of MN Press.

Pace, T. (2008). *Can an orc catch a cab in Stormwind?* Conference presentation. Retrieved February 12, 2012, from http://www.chi2008.org/altchisystem/index.php?action=showsubmission&id=156

Silver Tree Media (Design Studio). (2008). *Pixie hollow* [MMOG]. United States: Disney.

KEY TERMS AND DEFINITIONS

Affect: Affect is an emotional/physio response that combines between stimuli, processing, and conscious thought. Affective responses are often meant to be triggered by consumer products.

Epistemology: Epistemology is the study of the organizing surrounding what you know. It focuses on *how* you know what you know.

Habitus: Habitus is the set of habits/ tastes related to thought, action, purchases, etc., that an individual uses to navigate particular social systems. These habits are both the result of individual tastes *and* the larger social structures with which the individual interacts. This definition draws on Pierre Bourdieu's *Distinctions* (1984).

Hegemony: The series of social processes that create social hierarchies. Hegemony strives for its own stability and reinforces itself through a myriad of ways.

Naturalize: To naturalize something is to make it appear to be inevitable or natural. Hegemonic processes generally make themselves invisible by appearing to be natural phenomena, like the idea that girls are naturally nurturing.

Technology: This class draws on phenomenology, particularly the work of Sara Ahmed, to describe technology as a type of world-changing tool. This definition encompasses both technological objects and social structures, including race, class, and gender.

Theory: A system/series of ideas with explanatory power. These ideas provide a "just so story" for particular phenomena in popular culture, and can have implications for the significance and meaning of these phenomena.

Signifying-Function: What an object "does" outside its actual purpose. For example, your clothes keep you from being naked and have a particular social significance.

Chapter 2
Using MMORPGs
in Classrooms:
Stories vs. Teachers as
Sources of Motivation

Mete Akcaoglu
Michigan State University, USA

EXECUTIVE SUMMARY

This case deals with the problem of decision making in allocating resources during an educational game-development process. In educational games, unlike commercial games, there is an added focus on creating learning content, shifting the balance between learning and fun to a degree where essential game elements might be excluded from these games. In some cases, classroom settings, however, are filled with elements that can emulate the role of a missing element. As it was seen in this case, even when some important game elements (i.e., narratives) were missing from a game, the presence of some important classroom elements (i.e., teachers) helped replace them.

OVERALL DESCRIPTION

Although games as educational tools have received a significant amount of scholarly endorsement over the past years (Barab, Gresalfi, & Ingram-Goble, 2010; Gee, 2003; Squire, 2005; Takatalo, Hakkinen, Kaistinen, & Nyman, 2010), the usage of these tools in traditional classroom settings is still rare. One reason for this rare us-

DOI: 10.4018/978-1-4666-2848-9.ch002

age stems from the difficulty of either finding a commercially available game that covers the curricular goals, or developing a game for the specific learning goals at hand. Evidently, the second option is often more costly. Even when the support is found to create such games, the design of these games is often challenging in that they are not being played in a "traditional" manner and the elements that work in commercial games might not work in classroom settings. In this case study, I describe how some existing classroom factors can substitute or modify the effects of very important game elements. Specifically, I will explain how virtual teachers can keep the students engaged, even when a very important element of role-playing games, narratives, is missing from a game, and hence, make the case for the particularity of playing games in a classroom setting.

Compared to playing games at home, when students play educational games in class, there often is a mentor, who is in or outside the virtual world, watching and constraining game experience of the students. Additionally, because during development of educational games teaching certain learning goals gains importance, the developed games may not have some core game elements due to the choices made in apportioning of resources. In this case study, to inform educational game developers and to see the effect of in-game virtual teachers in a Massively-Multiplayer Online Role-playing Game (MMORPG), a quasi-experimental study was conducted to see how episodic narratives and the presence of teachers compare in terms of making students feel engaged. In the results of the study, it was seen that the students (n=19) felt engaged by the presence of a teacher, or narratives equally. In a careful analysis, it was seen that the reason why the students felt engaged in either situation (teacher or narrative) was due to the fact that in both situations they were working on specific goals given by either their virtual teachers or the episodic narratives, making them feel analogously engaged. This finding carries great importance in both usage of games in classrooms and designing educational games, as will be depicted later in this chapter.

LITERATURE REVIEW

Among many game types available, MMORPGs stand out as ideal candidates for language learning for their potential to solve some of the very important challenges to foreign language education: "the lack of the resources, milieu, and incentives to learn and use the target language for real purposes" (Zhao & Lai, 2008, p. 407). Perhaps, one of the most important potential of MMORPGs in language learning is their ability to provide meaningful and authentic contexts for communication and language use, because by definition MMORPGs are played with many other people. This aligns perfectly with the *Communicative Language Teaching* (CLT) approach –the current prominent language teaching theory in second language studies- which sees communication as a fundamental skill a language learner needs to acquire. Hence, communication is a key component of both MMORPGs and current language teaching approaches. Additionally, CLT sees language learning as a social activity (Warschauer, Meskill, & Rosenthal, 2000), and the meaning of the words rather than the grammar is of greater importance (Nunan, 2004). In this sense, being able to use language for communication rather than dealing with grammar is the focus of this approach (Nunan, 2004). MMORPGs, from this perspective, prove to be ideal platforms for language learners to get together and use the language in authentic and meaningful ways, and to communicate with others to accomplish certain game-related tasks.

Player engagement is very important for game designers (Fullerton, 2008; Salen & Zimmerman, 2004) and educators alike. Hence, for game designers and educators, keeping the players or learners in a game, or on a certain task while providing as much guidance as possible without pushing or boring them is a very desirable goal. Apart from its motivational effects, engagement also contributes to success in completing tasks, or learning certain content. According to Dede (2009), when immersed, students benefit from learning activities better. While learning in virtual worlds, where the real-world is simulated, it is suggested that players often feel very engaged and this engagement results in better learning.

One the most important ways of achieving engagement in games is through the presence of strong narratives (Carr, Buckingham, Burn, & Schott, 2006; Fullerton, 2008; Lee, Park, & Jin, 2006; Marsh, 2010). In most games, narratives can be found in two different formats: a) episodic narratives and b) overarching narratives (or narrative arcs). The first narrative types, *episodic narratives*, are short in their duration and are often found as "side missions" in many games. Generally, they help players progress their characters' abilities or gain extra in-game perks, and often require fulfilling a small task for an in-game non-player character (NPC). An example of this can be helping a fellow NPC magician find certain virtual herbs and, upon delivering them, get a special ability to cast a certain spell. Episodic narratives usually conclude with the completion of the task. *Overarching narratives*, on the other hand, are temporally longer, and come to a close only when the game is finished. In a sense, overarching narratives define and contextualize the main goals in games. An example of an overarching narrative can be the story of a protagonist who seeks revenge from a boss character in a game who caused him/her damage in the past; and, usually, until the boss is defeated at the end of the game, the story is not finished.

When used effectively, narratives make games very engaging and motivating, and as previously mentioned, immersion and engagement are important for student success. According to Adams et al. (2011), "[g]ames with compelling story lines are intended to motivate the learner to initiate game play, persist in game play, and exhibit intensity in game play, which in turn result in better learning" (p. 4).

Finally, it should be added that playing games at home is a different activity than playing games in a classroom or laboratory setting (Squire, 2005; Takatalo et al., 2010). When played at home, players have more autonomy as to which game to choose, how long to play and how to play, whereas in a classroom setting, players are usually restrained by the contextual elements of the learning environment/ classrooms. Although it is known that narratives are motivating in games, it is not known if the duty narratives fulfill (giving objectives) can be substituted with elements present in classrooms. In other words, no research has shown if an MMORPG can do without narratives and still be engaging when their role is fulfilled by virtual teachers in a classroom setting. Hence, in this study, the effect of virtual teacher presence in a game is compared against the use of episodic narratives in terms of making students feel engaged.

PRACTICALITIES OF RUNNING THE GAME

Zon[1] is a multiplayer, online learning environment where players assume identities of tourists visiting Beijing and through various activities learn Chinese language and culture (Boyer & Akcaoglu, 2009; Pernsteiner, Boyer, & Akcaoglu, 2010). Since it is a web-based game, players in Zon can connect with others in real-time, interact with various learning activities and other players, and acquire authentic cultural information (Zhao & Lai, 2009; Zon, 2011). In order to provide a safe environment for schools, the game runs on two servers: a public server where everyone can sign up for free, play, and interact with each other; and a private server, created for schools on-demand and hosting only the students of specific schools. In addition, using private servers, students can only interact with each other, creating a safer environment for students.

In Zon, content is mainly provided by non-player characters (NPCs) on both servers. Main activities for the players are going through "Observes" where they get to see, dissect and listen to conversations in Chinese, or "Engages" where the players can role-play a learned conversation with an NPC. Therefore, on the public server, players do not receive in game objectives to fulfill and their persistence in game-play depends mostly on their intrinsic motivation to learn the language. Unlike the public server, however, on school servers, virtual teachers, who are controlled by real Chinese teachers, roam the environment and guide groups of students during their Chinese language classes. On both servers, communicating with other players is done through text or audio chats; while on private servers virtual teachers can also stream their video to the students.

During the implementation of this case study, the students ($n = 19$) were on a private server dedicated to their school. In this special instance of Zon, there was only a specific group of students who were physically sitting next to each other in a computer lab and virtual teachers who were connecting to their Zon server from a different geographical location. At designated times of the week, the students were brought to the computer lab by their classroom teachers, and once they logged on to the game using their lab computers, they were greeted and guided by their virtual Chinese teachers who were physically located in a different state in the US. The virtual teachers both had their avatars, or in-game characters, in the game and they had an audio and video feed window where the students could hear and see them. In each session, like in a regular class, the virtual teachers introduced the topic of the day and then guided the students through activities. The game did not have very many episodic narratives in this implementation, and because narratives are key in MMORPGs, we wanted to see if the game was still engaging for students. Hence, we created another version of the game, a narrative version. In the narrative version, although the "class" session started the same, with the teacher's greeting and introduction of the day's topic, the teacher then left the students on their own for the rest of the class and the students followed the steps of an NPC-initiated episodic narrative.

In order to both guide the game development process and understand the practical importance of narratives in educational games, the researcher sought to understand if narratives and virtual teachers compared in terms of making students feel engaged. While in the episodic narrative version, the students followed the objectives given by NPCs to fulfill a given goal; in the teacher version there were not any episodic narratives, but the teacher provided the students with in-game tasks. Since both narratives in games and the virtual teachers provide tangible objectives for players, there was not a difference in how engaged the students felt, or how much they liked the two different versions of the game. Understanding if the students felt equally engaged with or without narratives or virtual teachers carries a great importance in deciding where to allocate resources during game development.

TECHNOLOGY COMPONENTS

Zon is built using Adobe® Flash® and is a browser-based game. Because of this, advanced hardware is not required in order to run the game. The fact that the game is built using Flash® is a benefit when it comes to running the game on budget computers, which most schools currently have. Therefore, unlike some other free virtual worlds (i.e. Second Life®), running Zon does not require any installations and usually runs smoothly. In addition, due to the fact that private school servers can be installed with ease, the environment is very safe for the students.

As for content creation, although most programming is done by professional computer programmers, there is also a simplified back-end where teachers with some training and computer knowledge can also create and modify in-game activities. This flexibility is also very important for educational games, as modification, maintenance and expansion of content can be something over which the teachers want to have more control.

As is the case with every game, the developers always need to make decisions in determining where to allocate their resources. Developers of educational games face an additional challenge, they need to allocate a considerable amount of their resources to creation and maintenance of learning materials and activities. This sometimes means that other aspects of the game will be comparatively weaker in terms of possessing elements that enhance games. Although on the surface it might seem like a practical decision to make, it becomes a problem when the game is released for the public and players stop playing the game because the elements that satisfy their engagement are left out due to allocation of resources on other elements. Specifically, in Zon, there was neither a strong narrative arc during the implementation of this study, nor any episodic narratives, due to the fact that delivery of strong content was seen to be important. Although this was seen as a problem for the public server, where the players were without objectives due to lack of episodic narratives, in a classroom, the situation was different. The presence of virtual teachers filled the gap of episodic narratives and increased student engagement. Thus the development of games for the classroom, is a very unique phenomenon because the context of classrooms and games can interplay in unimaginable ways.

EVALUATION

The evaluation of the game was made from a motivational perspective, and assessment of learning was beyond the scope of this case study; therefore no evaluation of learning is going to be presented in this section. Specifically, the students' desires to play the game in the future, how engaged they felt and if they liked the game, were measured through cross-sectional surveys. In order to assess if there was a statistical difference between the presence of teachers versus episodic narratives, first two versions of the game were created and students played these two version consecutively. After each game they completed a twelve-item engagement survey.

In order to account for the order effect, the students were divided into two groups and each group played the teacher and episodic narrative versions of the game in different orders.

A paired-samples *t*-test was conducted to see if there were differences in the level of engagement the students reported. The result was not statistically significant[2], indicating that the students felt equally engaged during both the teacher-only and narrative-only versions of the game. Due to the size of the sample ($n = 19$), the power of the study to detect statistical significance was low, and thus generalization of the results should be done with caution. Based on the current data and analyses, however, the result indicate that the students do not necessarily look for or feel more engaged when episodic narratives are present, in comparison to a virtual teacher who evidently provide them with equally engaging tasks.

As part of the evaluation, qualitative data on what the students liked the most about the game was collected through open-ended survey items. The majority of the students indicated that they enjoyed in-game monetary rewards. Considering the fact that the average age of the students was 12.5, it may be correct to argue that students in this case were extrinsically motivated to collect in-game rewards and the origin of the task did not matter so long as they achieved their goals.

CHALLENGES

One particular challenge in creating educational games is that they need to be both tailored for the needs of specific learning situations, and they still need to have the elements that make games engaging (e.g. narratives, social interaction, etc.). The challenge the design team had in this specific case was in deciding how to distribute the limited resources to the two different elements an educational game needs, which are creation and maintenance of content, and creation and maintenance of game elements, specifically episodic narratives in this case.

It should be noted here that this is a challenge unique to using games in a classroom, whereas in a commercial game it is not normal to have virtual teachers who lead groups of people through learning content. In such games, game elements, especially narratives, lead players toward completion of tasks and eventually the games themselves. Therefore, this case study and the evaluation process shed light onto the question of engagement in educational games when used in classroom contexts. As is seen, the presence of virtual teachers seems to be equally engaging for students, and allocation of resources to content creation and maintenance can be justified in this case. It should be reiterated here again that playing the game in a classroom context with virtual teachers is very unlikely in commercial games, but it is probable that it becomes common practice for educational games. Therefore, unforeseen factors as presented in this case need to be given careful consideration while creating educational games, because this might have an important impact on decisions regarding allocation of resources and eventually the created game.

SUMMARY AND CONCLUSION

The purpose of this case study is to evaluate the effectiveness of episodic narratives and virtual teachers in creating an engaging game. It was seen that students feel equally engaged playing the two versions of a game: one with only episodic narratives and a second without episodic narratives but with a virtual teacher, who provided guidance and tasks for students. In this special classroom setting, the students' engagement levels stayed almost the same for both virtual teachers and episodic narratives, as measured by cross-sectional surveys. Despite a body of literature supporting the value of narratives in games (Lee et al., 2006; Marsh, 2010; Salen & Zimmerman, 2004), classroom context seems to modify the lack of narratives when there are other objective providers present. This might hint that classroom usage of MMORPGs, even though they do not have all the features of an MMO, can still be engaging due to the unique classroom conditions. While making investment decisions, these unique usage contexts should be taken into consideration in order to determine resource allocation.

REFERENCES

Adams, D. M., Mayer, R. E., MacNamara, A., Koenig, A., & Wainess, R. (2012). Narrative games for learning: Testing the discovery and narrative hypotheses. *Journal of Educational Psychology*, *104*(1), 235–249. doi:10.1037/a0025595

Barab, S. A., Gresalfi, M., & Ingram-Goble, A. (2010). Transformational play. *Educational Researcher*, *39*(7), 525. doi:10.3102/0013189X10386593

Boyer, D. M., & Akcaoglu, M. (2009). The Zon project: Creating a virtual environment for learning Chinese language and culture. In T. Bastiaens, et al., (Eds.), *Proceedings of World Conference on E-Learning in Corporate, Government, Healthcare, and Higher Education 2009* (pp. 2389-2393). Chesapeake, VA: AACE.

Carr, D., Buckingham, D., Burn, A., & Schott, G. (2006). *Computer games: Text, narrative and play*. Polity Press.

Dede, C. (2009). Immersive interfaces for engagement and learning. *Science*, *323*(5910), 66–69. doi:10.1126/science.1167311

Dickey, M. D. (2006). Game design narrative for learning: appropriating adventure game design narrative devices and techniques for the design of interactive learning environments. *Educational Technology Research and Development*, *54*(3), 245–263. doi:10.1007/s11423-006-8806-y

Fullerton, T. (2008). *Game design workshop: Technology*. Boston, MA: Elsevier.

Gee, J. P. (2003). *What video games have to teach us about learning and literacy*. New York, NY: Palgrave Macmillan. doi:10.1145/950566.950595

Lee, K. M., Park, N., & Jin, S. A. (2006). Narrative and interactivity in computer games. In Vorderer, P., & Bryant, J. (Eds.), *Playing video games: Motives, responses, and consequences* (pp. 259–274). New Jersey: Lawrence Erlbaum Associates.

Marsh, T. (2010). Activity-based scenario design, development and assessment in serious games. In Eck, R. V. (Ed.), *Gaming and cognition: Theories and practice from the learning sciences* (pp. 214–227). Hershey, PA: IGI Global. doi:10.4018/978-1-61520-717-6.ch010

Nunan, D. (2004). *Task-based language teaching*. Cambridge, UK: Cambridge University Press. doi:10.1017/CBO9780511667336

Pernsteiner, S. M., Boyer, D. M., & Akcaoglu, M. (2010). Understanding player activity in a game-based virtual learning environment: A case for data-driven in-structional design. *World Conference on E-Learning in Corporate, Government, Healthcare, and Higher Education 2010* (p. 763). Chesapeake, VA: AACE.

Salen, K., & Zimmerman, E. (2004). *Rules of play*. MIT Press.

Squire, K. (2005). Changing the game: What happens when video games enter the classroom. *Innovate: Journal of Online Education*, *1*(6), 25–49.

Takatalo, J., Hakkinen, J., Kaistinen, J., & Nyman, G. (2011). User experience in digital games: Differences between laboratory and home. *Simulation & Gaming*, *42*(5), 656–673.

Warschauer, M., Meskill, C., & Rosenthal, J. W. (2000). Technology and second language teaching. In Rosenthal, J. (Ed.), *Handbook of undergraduate second language education*. Mahwah, NJ: Lawrence Erlbaum.

Yee, N. (2005). Motivations of play in MMORPGs. *Proceedings of International DiGRA Conference*. Vancouver.

Zhao, Y., & Lai, C. (2009). Massively multi-player online role playing games (MMORPGS) and foreign language education. In Ferdig, R. E. (Ed.), *Handbook of research on effective electronic gaming in education* (pp. 402–421). New York, NY: IDEA Group.

Zon. (2011). *About Zon*. Retrieved January 5, 2012, from http://enterzon.com/#about

ENDNOTES

[1]   http://enterzon.com
[2] $t(19)=1.210, p=.227$

Chapter 3
Are Wii Having Fun Yet?

Christina Badman
Sacred Heart Catholic School, USA

Matthew DeNote
Espiritu Santo Catholic School, USA

EXECUTIVE SUMMARY

Today's students live and thrive in a digital environment, and educators need to help them succeed in the present, as well as their impossible to predict future. Using elements of gaming in the classroom, the authors of this case have provided their students with a challenging and engaging classroom setting where creative and critical thought processes are encouraged and rewarded. This chapter is based on two years' worth of work (still ongoing today) incorporating the Nintendo Wii gaming platform into multiple subjects and grade levels. Since there is no way to know what our world will have to offer when the youth of today graduate from college, it is vital to focus on helping students learn how to think creatively and critically, adapt to different situations, and work collaboratively with others to solve problems and complete tasks. The authors feel gaming in the classroom allows students the opportunity to practice and refine these important life skills.

INTRODUCTION

The chapter is based on two years worth of work beginning in 2009 and continuing on in the present time, incorporating the Nintendo Wii gaming platform into multiple subjects in our 4th through 8th grade classrooms. One of our school goals was to increase the students' aptitude in Math computation and problem solving

DOI: 10.4018/978-1-4666-2848-9.ch003

skills. We had been following an educational blogger out of Australia, Tom Barrett, http://edte.ch/blog/, who was focusing on using the Nintendo Wii in his 4th grade classroom. His primary goal was to increase student engagement during learning experiences. Barrett was using Wii games in a nontraditional way. For example, he was using the golf game in Wii sports to review three digit subtraction with his elementary students. We began by bringing in a personally owned Wii system to a 5th grade classroom with the mission of increasing student engagement, excitement and skills in the subject of Math. The fact that we both were familiar with and owned Wii gaming systems made this opportunity seem perfect.

The first time we utilized the Wii gaming system in the classroom, we just did a little practice with the students so they could see it in the room and in action. One of the games that was purchased was *Are you Smarter than a 5th Grader?* One of the options is called Flashcards where the players (we used four different students) have a question and then get four choices. Each of the questions is worth a different amount of money depending on the grade level. If the student gets the question wrong they lose half of that amount. If they get it correct they get the full amount and if they are the first one to answer the question correctly, they get bonus money. We had all of the students who did not have a controller writing down their answers on paper at their desks. So, it should have been a review for all students and we had several do well. We only had time enough to play two rounds and actively involve eight students, but all in all it was a very successful first installment of the console.

This mission proved so successful that we have expanded the use of the Wii into more grade levels and subject areas.

OBTAINING THE EQUIPMENT

To implement this program, the first thing we needed was the hardware. Due to budgetary constraints, there was no money to make the purchase through the school. So, we brought a Wii in from home on a trial basis. The classroom was already equipped with a ceiling mounted projector which allowed for easy connection to the Wii gaming system. As we utilized the Wii with the students and were impressed and excited with the outcomes and student engagement levels, it became obvious that a school based Wii was needed in the classroom. Fortunately, just such a game system was donated later that year.

OVERVIEW OF NINTENDO WII™ SOFTWARE UTILIZED

See Table 1.

Table 1. Nintendo Wii™ Software

Software Title	Game Played	Subject Integration	Topic Addressed
Wii Sports	Wii Golf	Math	Subtraction/Customary Conversions/Averaging
Wii Sports	Wii Baseball	Math	Averaging
Big Brain Academy: Wii Degree	Balloon Burst	Math	Comparing and Ordering Integers
Wii Sports	Wii Bowling	Math	Identifying and Writing Ratios
30 Great Games Outdoor Fun for the Wii	Internal Clock 2	Math	Using integers in real world situations
Endless Ocean	Endless Ocean	Language Arts/Science	Creative Writing and Study of Marine Habitats
Big Brain Academy: Wii Degree	Relay Game	Various	Team Building and Critical Thinking Skills
Are You Smarter than a 5th Grader?	Are You Smarter than a 5th Grader?	Various	Team Building and Critical Thinking Skills
WordJong Party	WordJong Party	Language Arts	Vocabulary Building
Amazing Race	Amazing Race	Language Arts/Social Studies/Math	Reading/Reading Comprehension/Geography/Critical Thinking Skills/Team Building/Various Math Calculations
Oregon Trail	Oregon Trail	Language Arts/Social Studies/Math	History/Geography/Reading/Reading Comprehension/Critical Thinking Skills/Team Building/Money Skills
Wii Sports Resort	Golf	Math	Subtraction of whole numbers and decimals/ Addition with decimals
Winter Sports, the Ultimate Challenge	Ski Jumping	Math	Metric Conversion/ Using formulas/ Solving Problems using Decimals in Division/ Converting Decimals into Fractions/ Solving Proportions and Ratios
The Amazing Brain Train	The Amazing Brain Train	Various	Team Building and Critical Thinking Skills

ACTION RESEARCH PROJECTS AND BLOG

In conjunction with administration, we decided to continue and expand our use of the Wii in Math and other subject areas and document our activities, successes and challenges in a blog, http://teach-n-learn.blogspot.com/. During the first year of use, our mission of improving the Math computation and problem solving skills, as well as the attitude of our students towards Math, fueled the use of the Wii in the classroom. As the successful implementation continued, we wanted to take this learning experiment one step further and show some evidence of student learning through this game based method. We conducted two action research projects with the fifth grade class at our school that further encouraged our utilization of the Wii with the students. We planned two pre and post assessment activities on comparing and ordering integers and identifying ratios for the fifth graders. These topics are often ones which get pushed to the very end of the year, if taught at all, due to the necessary review of other math standards. We found that not only were the students learning during the Wii enhanced classes, but they were retaining the information long after the initial lessons.

During the 2010-2011 school year, the second year of our Wii implementation, we expanded the use of the Wii to the 6th through 8th grade students and to different subject area focuses. We utilized the Wii in Language Arts, Science and Social Studies as well as a tool to help build teamwork and critical thinking skills in our Middle School students. We found the response from the students to be just as positive as in our 5th grade trials and we began to see how different games could be used across the curriculum to increase student engagement and excitement. As we began the 2011-2012 school year, a change in schools for one of the authors meant an expansion of the Wii experiment in another venue. We have been able to reproduce the level of student interest and engagement as seen in the past and we are also working with new games and a new age level.

WII™ BEGAN IN 5ᵀᴴ GRADE

Our very first experiment in the 5th grade classroom in the winter of 2009 was directly inspired by Tom Barrett. We played *Wii Golf* on the *Wii Sports* game and practiced three digit subtraction with the students for a fifty minute class period. As each student took a turn to come up and swing at the ball, the rest of the class wrote subtraction problems on papers at their desks. Our subtraction problems came from the difference between the total distance to the hole before they hit and then again after the hit. This information is displayed in the Wii game itself. The answers then told the students how far the golf ball had traveled. In the beginning of each lesson, a teacher was at the board showing the students which math problems they should be working on their own at their seats and providing correct solutions and explanations. Once the lessons got going, students were pulled up to the board as well to provide a peer model of the math work to be done at the individual student seats. The students were excited, engaged and enthusiastic to practice subtraction for almost an hour straight!

Next, we decided to create a full lesson plan on using the same *Wii Golf* game focusing on the skill of averaging scores. The students had the distance to the hole divided by the number of strokes to get the ball in the hole to figure out their average distance. We used all four controllers and rotated the students around for each hit until one of the students put the ball in the hole. The math problems were different since, while the total hole distance did not change for any of the four players, the number of strokes it took to put the ball in the hole did vary.

We also utilized a baseball themed activity on the *Wii Sports* game to continue reviewing the averaging skill. We actually used the training portion of *Wii Sports*, not the game itself. The pitcher throws 10 pitches and the computer adds up the total of all the home runs hit at the conclusion. If you do not hit a home run then you do not get any distance added in. But, it is always 10 pitches. First we did a quick oral review of what averaging meant and how to get an average. Next, we brought each student up to get a swing. If they hit a home run then we marked down the distance on the board and the students each did the same on their papers. If they did not get a home run then we marked nothing. After each hit the student would pause the game so the next student could come up and take a swing. At the end of ten swings we have a total (the game gives it to you so the students could check their addition on their papers) distance hit and we averaged that by the number of home run hits to get an average. Then the teacher did the math on the board to have students check their average work. We played four rounds which was enough to let each student get to bat twice. As before, they were interested and excited about getting to play.

WII™ RESEARCH BEGINS

Our first action research project with the Wii began with a lesson on ordering negative numbers. The specific standard that we were targeting was comparing and ordering integers, including integers shown on a number line. First, we gave a pretest to the 5th grade students, because it was a concept that they did not have any experience in. The test was simply to put a set of numbers in order from highest to lowest. We had a total of four students who were able to get the sequences correct. From there, we did an introduction of negative numbers and how they run away from the zero point on a number line. How, even though the number is bigger, it is actually smaller in value. To emphasize this point, we used the Wii game *Big Brain Academy: Wii Degree*, more specifically the game *Balloon Burst*. The point of the game is to burst the balloons by clicking on them with the controller. Each balloon has a number on it and you want to click on the balloons in order from smallest to largest value. If you choose the hardest level, the numbers will come in both positive and negative forms. The balloons are all different sizes and in various locations. They also are different colors and will even rotate back and forth as they appear on the screen.

We gave each student a chance to come around and pop the balloons in order from lowest to highest. While the student was popping balloons in the game, the students at their seats were all writing the numbers down and putting them in order as well. We went around the room to check their seat work and make sure that they were working on the math. Later that day, we gave the students the same test we used in the morning as a posttest. We went from four students getting them correct, to all students passing and 18 of them receiving a perfect score. Needless to say, we were very excited by these results. Two months later, we had the students complete the same post test, just to see if our lesson had stuck with them over time. Over 88% of the class had no problem and received a score of "A" on the post test.

INTEGER ACTION RESEARCH PRE AND POSTTEST RESULTS

See Table 2.

Table 2. Research results

Student/Class	Pretest March 12, 2010	Posttest #1 March 12, 2010	Posttest #2 May 24, 2010
Student 1	100%	100%	100%
Student 2	0%	100%	0%
Student 3	100%	100%	100%
Student 4	0%	100%	100%
Student 5	0%	100%	100%
Student 6	0%	100%	100%
Student 7	0%	100%	100%
Student 8	0%	100%	100%
Student 9	0%	100%	0%
Student 10	0%	100%	80%
Student 11	0%	100%	80%
Student 12	80%	100%	100%
Student 13	100%	100%	100%
Student 14	20%	80%	100%
Student 15	100%	100%	100%
Student 16	80%	100%	100%
Student 17	0%	100%	100%
Student 18	0%	100%	100%
Student 19	60%	100%	100%
Student 20	0%	80%	100%
Student 21	0%	100%	80%
Student 22	0%	60%	100%
Class Average	29.09%	96.36%	88.18%

WII™ RESEARCH CONTINUES

Next, we decided to give another pre and post test to see if we could recreate our success with the Wii and the lesson on integers. We wanted to do a lesson on ratios. All of the students came into the lab and took our pretest. The questions on the pretest asked the students to identify and write ratios. The students' answers were all over the place and by far the majority of students had no concept of ratios. Once the students had taken the test, we began by discussing ratios and the vocabulary involved. We talked about the relationship between the first number and the second and the format which ratios can take (using the word "to", posted with a semicolon or as a fraction). We made a point to remind the students that the relationship that you are asking for will dictate the results of the ratio. It will be wrong if you put the correct numbers down, but in the incorrect order! After this discussion we used the *Wii Sports* game to bowl. We had four players registered and each student was able to bowl one frame. This way we got all the students involved in game play. After each throw, we would ask for a different ratio. For example, the ratio of pins knocked down to total pins, or pins knocked down to pins remaining standing. After a few frames, we increased the difficultly a little and asked questions like the ratio of odd numbered scores to even numbered scores. Each time the students had to write the ratio in multiple ways. We were able to complete several frames (but not a complete game in the time allowed). Bowling lent itself to a lot of varied ratio examples. We were able to stop play in between each bowler and ask a different question without interrupting game play and learning. There were plenty of numbers and plenty of options. Later that day the students retook the post test. Overall, we had much better results, but still had some students who didn't get all aspects of the concept. We had great feedback from the students. They enjoyed bowling and seemed to do a good job with the ratio concepts.

RATIO ACTION RESEARCH PRE AND POSTTEST RESULTS

See Table 3.

WII™ EXTEND THE LEARNING

One of the last games we tried out in the 5th grade Math classroom during this first year was a game called *30 Great Games Outdoor Fun* for the Wii. We used one of the games to continue our work on negative numbers with the students. While the

Table 3. Research results

Student/Class	Pretest May 25, 2010	Posttest May 25, 2010
Student 1	0%	80%
Student 2	0%	100%
Student 3	0%	60%
Student 4	0%	0%
Student 5	0%	20%
Student 6	0%	20%
Student 7	0%	40%
Student 8	0%	20%
Student 9	0%	40%
Student 10	0%	60%
Student 11	0%	40%
Student 12	0%	80%
Student 13	0%	40%
Student 14	0%	60%
Student 15	0%	60%
Student 16	0%	100%
Student 17	0%	80%
Student 18	0%	20%
Student 19	0%	60%
Student 20	0%	20%
Student 21	0%	60%
Class Average	0%	50.47%

reviews of the game were not that favorable, it did have some redeeming qualities for the classroom. The benchmark we were covering was Describe real-world situations using positive and negative integers. The game that we used was called *Internal Clock 2*. Basically, each person gets a time that they have to count up to in their head. The clock begins counting but after about five seconds it goes off and you have to continue to count in your head. When you think you are at the time you push the button. The person closest to the time wins that round. The time is presented in decimal format as seconds, with both tenths and hundredths of seconds. Maybe not the most exciting game around, but the students did like the element of competition, and we actually had one student who hit the time dead on.

We had the students subtract their time from the requested time. The students that hit the button quicker than the requested time were in the NEGATIVE because they were slower than the timer; they still had the amount of time left to get to the correct time. The ones that were over the requested time had to subtract their number from the requested time and they were in the POSITIVE because they were longer than the requested time; they held on too long. For example, during the first round, the students were told to count up to 11 seconds and then hit the button. These were the results:

Student Player One: 10.90
Student Player Two: 12.45
Student Player Three: 11.73
Student Player Four: 11.18

With these results, the answers to the student math problems were:

Student Player One: -.10
Student Player Two: 1.45
Student Player Three: .73
Student Player Four: .18

In the next round, the times are different for each person and in the later rounds the time will change during the actual count, so the students have to pay attention. Also, you can distract the other contestants during the game by waving your controller which causes your person to jump up and down and/or say something. The screen also moves around to other views so you have to make sure you are counting while you are looking at the other things.

As we played the game and completed the math problems, we discussed the use of negative and positive integers and asked the students for other real world situations where negative numbers could be utilized. We received student responses about money issues and (with some help from another adult also in the room) sea level.

Then we asked the students to put the results in order from least to greatest. Now they had to take the negative and positive numbers into account when they placed the results in order. This was a bit of a review from when we played *Big Brain Academy: Wii Degree* where the students had to pop balloons with different integers on them in order from least to greatest. The students did well with this task which made us feel positive that they were retaining the knowledge used during the Wii sessions.

We made what we felt was one slight change during the last round. This slight change ended up being a bit of a bump in the road for the students though and an eye opener for us. During the last round we asked the students to order the numbers not from least to greatest, but from greatest to least. We had four different students who said it was harder for them to group them that way, then it was to group from least to greatest. We asked the students why they thought it was more difficult to go from greatest to least instead of least to greatest, and while we did not really get a complete answer, a couple of students just said it was easier to start with the negative numbers and move up to the positive ones. One or two of the students made the observation that if you were having a problem with the greatest to least ordering, just do least to greatest and reverse it. This helped some of the confused students, but not all.

After we had discussed the difference between ordering greatest to least and least to greatest, we let the students finish up the round and then had the remaining groups compete. We worked out the Math problems, answered the questions and all students had at least 15 math problems completed.

WII™ EXPANDED TO MIDDLE SCHOOL

As we entered the second year of our Wii usage at school, one of the authors moved from teaching 5th grade to Middle School Language Arts, and thus our experiment took a new turn. During the previous year, we had experimented one time with the 6th grade class using the game *Endless Ocean*. This game allows the user to dive into different parts of the world's oceans in search of countless sea creatures. We utilized the game in conjunction with a story the students had read in their Literature textbooks set in an ocean. While the students enjoyed playing the game and discovering different marine animals as they virtually explored the ocean depths, there was not enough action to hold the students' attention for an entire class period. After the interaction with the game, we assigned a narrative writing assignment with only one requirement; the setting was to be in an oceanic environment. The students' creations were wonderfully descriptive, which we believe was a direct effect of the game play.

Over the summer, we made elaborate plans for the use of the *Big Brain Academy: Wii Degree* game with the middle school students. While our plan did not go as we had expected (See Lessons Learned section), the middle school students enjoyed the Wii just as much as the fifth graders had, which gave us enough positive feedback to continue looking for ways to use the Wii with this age group.

PRACTICALITIES OF RUNNING THE GAMES

Big Brain Academy: Wii Degree and Are You Smarter than a 5th Grader?

We played *Big Brain Academy: Wii Degree* in groups using the relay game style. Students would be in teams of four standing in two vertical lines going against each other solving critical thinking puzzles and activities. We also played *Are You Smarter than a 5th Grader?* with the older students who all thought they were definitely up to the challenge. This game works great, because you can play it in small teams, individuals competing against each other or as a whole class with everyone writing down their answer choices at their seats. If you have access to clickers in the classroom, you can have all the students voting for their choice of answer and then use the winning answer choice entered into the game. While both of these games engage the students, work on reading, comprehending and critical thinking skills and allow the students to work cooperatively, we began to search for new games that could be used in a middle school Language Arts classroom effectively.

WordJong Party

First, we found *WordJong Party*, which is a game that is a mix of Scrabble and Mahjongg. We played the game with all the classes. In 7th grade, we played with four teams of three students each. There was a team captain in each group. The captains held the Wii-motes and worked the game board. The team members helped their captains find and create the words. We played in Party mode where the screen is divided into four quadrants. It was user-friendly, because the team's cursor would only become solid in their quadrant; they always knew they were in the right space on the board. You can choose to play 8, 12, or 20 rounds in the Party mode.

Each team is given tiles that are stacked on each other. Each tile has a letter on it. You can see some of the tiles, but some are underneath other tiles so they cannot be used yet. The object is to make the longest word possible with the tiles you have access to. Each time you remove a tile and use it to spell a word, additional tiles become available. You can also hold down the A button and shake the Wii-mote back and forth to receive additional tiles. However, when you do this you cover up some tiles that were on the board and accessible before the shake. Each round brings up the quadrants and tiles and each team tries to make their best word. Once one team completes a word (you set your word by hitting the B button on the Wii-mote) a timer appears in the middle of the screen and begins counting down from 45 seconds. Each of the remaining teams has this amount of time to make the best word they can. This is a great element because it moves the game along and adds a little bit of tension to the game play. Players pull the tiles into spaces in order to spell their words. Once a tile is placed, you can remove it as long as the B button was not pushed. Once all teams have set their final words OR time runs out, you are taken to a screen which shows each team, the word they spelled, the points they were awarded for their word, and their current place (1st to 4th) in the competition. This also adds a little fuel to the fire as at each round they get updates as to the current score. Each round is played the same way until the last round, when a final winner is announced. There are special wild tiles or power-ups earned for various reasons. These wild tiles are located under the team's name in their quadrant. The students love to use these special power tiles and target teams or turn some tiles into ice tiles the other teams cannot use. Sometimes the wild tiles help their team and sometimes they hinder others.

Overall, this game is great and it is easy to play with a large group of students at one time. Teams of two or three work best we found. This game held all students' attention and moved quickly. We also found students working towards trying to put together longer more complicated words to increase their score. We also found this game creates a nice competition for the group, while also providing a bonding experience for teams. Plus, the music in the background is great and relaxing. We unintentionally discovered the students (any age) love the music of the Wii system and games.

Amazing Race

The next game we utilized with the middle school students was the *Amazing Race* game for the Wii. The students really enjoyed this game, and we were impressed with the amount of critical thinking skills needed to play and the increase in cooperative skills the students showed as the game progressed. Listed below are some benefits we found inherent in the game. This game seemed to be able to use competition in a positive way to encourage students to excel and work together to their team's best advantage. For example, students must work together to decide which route choice is both quickest and most cost effective during initial stages of each challenge.

Benefits of the *Amazing Race* Wii game:

- Great for cooperative learning/skills.
- Students learned quickly to work together in order to improve their scores/time/performance.
- Worked on student oral communication with peers.
- Students thought rapid fire challenges were exciting.

- Challenges encouraged students to use critical thinking/ higher order thinking skills.
- Some challenges were physical in nature and allowed students the ability to utilize kinesthetic skills.
- Possible geography/research extension activity in reference to destinations in the game.
- This is a very quick moving game which allows it to maintain student attention throughout game play.

Here are some step by step instructions for implementing this game into the classroom:

1. You can choose two ways to play: individual players against each other or teams of two working together against computer or other teams.
2. You can also choose how many legs of the race you want to play, the more legs the longer the game play.
3. We played with teams of two working together against the computerized teams.
4. Teams choose female or male faces and then the type of team they want to be; for example, sporty, couch fans, military, gothic, etc. Students had a great time in this part of the game and it allowed them to input some of their own personality into the activity.
5. Next there is an introduction to the game and some brief instructions.
6. Teams are given an allowance of money for each leg of the race and then given four options of transportation. Students need to evaluate the best option based on time and money available. The objective of the game is to take the least amount of time to arrive at the chosen destination, so students need to decide which mode of transportation to take and how much money they are willing to spend on it.
7. Once the mode of transportation is chosen, the teams watch as their virtual teams make their way to the given destination and see in which order the teams arrived.
8. There is a brief introduction to the place in which the teams have arrived (some places we have encountered so far: Rome, Rio, New Zealand), accompanied by images from the area.
9. After each challenge of the game, the teams are listed in order by the amount of time they have taken up to that point. This order also lets the teams know how they are ranked in the game.
10. There is a challenge, either physical or mental, at each destination. Students work together to accomplish the tasks in the least amount of time as possible.

Some of the challenges involve both teams at the same time and some have the teams work individually.

11. At the end of all the legs of the race, teams are put in their final order. The last team to arrive to the last destination is eliminated from the race.

The middle school students love this game and while it is not overtly a Language Arts game, the reading, collaborative and oral communication skills practiced in every part of this experience lends its use very well to a literacy based classroom. There are of course many direct connections with Social Studies tied into this game as well. We have found that with many of the games we have used. While we are using the game for one educational goal, there are always additional ways to connect the game to other curriculum areas.

The Oregon Trail

The newest game we have utilized with the middle school students is *The Oregon Trail* game for the Wii. When we were in the fifth grade contained classroom, we had utilized *The Oregon Trail* game for the PC as an interactive way to teach the students about life on the trail. This was always a huge hit each year with the students. When we found *The Oregon Trail* Wii game, we knew the middle school students would love teaming up in a "family" of four and trying to survive across the trail. The Wii game version offers many new features in the game play, including steering the wagon, fishing, forging rivers and trying to out-maneuver obstacles in the water and trail and hunting for food. We were not wrong. The students loved traveling the trail together and making decisions on what to buy, when to stop and rest, who to trade with and how to keep the "family" alive throughout the adventure. There is a lot of textual reading in this game too, which is always welcome in the Language Arts classroom. You may be thinking to yourself at this point, it is great that the kids love the game, but isn't this really a game to be used in the Social Studies classroom? While this game could definitely be utilized in a Social Studies class setting, we are using it in Language Arts as a group experience which leads directly into a historical fiction or expository writing project. Students, after having traveled and hopefully surviving the trail, are asked to write a narrative about their adventures on the trail, or perhaps an expository essay on how to survive the trail. This game served as a fantastic jumping off point for student writing, and the essays the students created were well thought out, interesting, full of knowledge of the trail and amusing anecdotes of trail life. Even more important, the students couldn't wait to start writing and also share their finished projects with their peers who had traveled with them on the trail. Wii gaming system: $200, *The Oregon*

Trail game for Wii: $20, Students engaged and excitedly writing, having no idea they are learning and working the whole time, priceless!

Standards

In looking back to using the Wii in the 5th grade classroom, it was easy to pick out the math standards that the games we were using addressed. In Language Arts, when you do any kind of multi- activity unit, such as The Oregon Trail plan mentioned above, there are many standards addressed and practiced. Depending on what elements of the game and which writing type the teacher chooses to focus on, will decide all the standards which are addressed through this type of unit. Table 4 is a sampling of 8th Grade Language Arts Common Core standards which were addressed through *The Oregon Trail* play and writing unit.

Table 4. 8th grade Language Arts Common Core standards addressed through The Oregon Trail play and writing unit

Reading #1	Cite the textual evidence that most strongly supports an analysis of what the text says explicitly as well as inferences drawn from the text.
Reading #3	Analyze how particular lines of dialogue or incidents in a story or drama propel the action, reveal aspects of a character, or provoke a decision.
Writing #3	Write informative/explanatory texts to examine a topic and convey ideas, concepts, and information through the selection, organization, and analysis of relevant content.
Writing #4	Produce clear and coherent writing in which the development, organization, and style are appropriate to task, purpose, and audience.
Writing #5	With some guidance and support from peers and adults, develop and strengthen writing as needed by planning, revising, editing, rewriting, or trying a new approach, focusing on how well purpose and audience have been addressed.
Writing #6	Use technology, including the Internet, to produce and publish writing and present the relationships between information and ideas efficiently as well as to interact and collaborate with others.
Language #1	Demonstrate command of the conventions of standard English grammar and usage when writing or speaking.
Language #2	Demonstrate command of the conventions of standard English capitalization, punctuation, and spelling when writing.
Language #3	Use knowledge of language and its conventions when writing, speaking, reading, or listening.

WII™ RETURN TO MATH IN NEW WAYS

Since one of the authors moved to a new school during our third year of implementation, 2011-2012, the Wii experiment has spread into this new school too. Fortunately and rather shockingly, this school had a Wii gaming system which had been donated to the PE department. While the PE department uses the game occasionally, this was perfect for continuing the work of using the Wii in the main content classrooms. We are working with a 4th grade Math class to start. When the students came into the classroom the first time with the game set up, they recognized the music and asked about playing the Wii. We had each student get out paper and pencil and take their seats. There was a lot of excitement and even a few "Oohs" and "Ahhs" as we got into the setup for the game.

We decided to begin with the *Wii Sports Resort Golf*. We began by playing three holes on course A. The course doesn't really matter, and there are three to choose from so the students can have different views and starting yardages at least a few times. (Of course, even if they play the same course each time, they will have different yardage because each hit will be a different distance.) The option for holes is 3, 9 or a full 18, so we decided that three would be the way to go. The yardage to the first hole was 396 yards, so we had all the students write down that first number as problem number 1. We gave the controller to our first student (for this time we just started in the front and went in row order) and had him swing away. After he hit, all the students wrote down the distance left to the hole (which is what the computer tells you) and they figured out how far he had hit the ball. This went on two more times until we hit our first snag. The student hit it on the green which changed the distance from yards to feet. At this time the 4th graders do not know how to convert from yards to feet (or vice versa) so we just skipped this problem and went on to the next. Our next problem came in with decimal subtraction and addition. Once you are on the green, it gives you the distance to the tenths place. Again, the 4th graders didn't have much experience with lining up the decimal places, so that took some time to model and work through. They understood the idea of lining up the decimal points and doing the operation well enough.

Then we came to our third different issue of the game. The next person hit the ball and went beyond the cup which makes a new math problem. She had 43.2 feet to go to the cup, but she hit it beyond the cup 18.3 feet (she really got a hold of the club!) so how far did she hit the ball? We asked the students to decide what operation we were going to need to do; and, after a little prodding, we got the correct answer of addition. Again, this was not a problem, but a different task at hand. We had enough time for everybody to hit and since there were still a few minutes left in class, the students wanted the teachers to hit. All teachers in the room took a turn, and the students were all very excited when we hit the ball (we wound up putting it

Figure 1. An example of the math seat work from one of the students; shows the results as well as the work the students complete while not actively interacting with the game

```
1| 396 yrds.            9)12 yrds.
 | -164 yrds left
 |  232               10) 1.9 feet
 |                        -1.9 left
2| 164 yrds.             0
 | -107 yrds left
 |  57               11.) 167 yrds
 |                        37
3| 107 yrds.        12) 37.9 ft
 |  73 yrds left        +7.8
 |  34                  45.7
 |
4| 73 yrds.         13.) 7.8 ft
 |                      /7.8
5| 40.1 FT              0
 | -17.7 FT left
 |  57.8             14) 563 yrds
 |                      -352 yrds left
6| 17.7 ft.             211
 | -55.9 ft left
 |  73.6             15.) 352
 |                      -319
7| 55.9 ft.             33
 |
8| 20 yrds           16. 319 yrds
 | -12 yrds left        -215 yrds left
 |  1.8                 104
```

in the cup). At the end of class, we collected all of the students' sheets so we could review them. All in all, everything went well. The students seemed to get what was going on and all students were engaged and working on math for the entire class period. I heard some good comments, my favorite being "This is the funnest math class ever!" (See Figure 1)

This lesson shows one of the greatest strengths of using the Wii in the classroom: real life application of problem solving skills. The games present the students with situations which allow them to use their understanding of Math computation or other areas of learning to solve real problems. As we played the *Wii Sports Resort Golf* game with additional Math classes, the game play and classroom review continued to engage all the students and the teacher was able to address skills the students lacked.

Recently, we have tried a new game called *Winter Sports, the Ultimate Challenge* with our Math students. We actually found a used copy for only a few bucks at a popular chain store. We had been talking about being able to do ski jumping to work on the formula R = T x D (rate = time times distance). We were discussing using the Wii Fit board because there is a game that allows you to ski jump; but, we decided that one would be more difficult and would require the extra equipment, so we thought we would try this one. It worked great! Basically the students have to go down the hill, pull up on the controllers and keep balance, while you stick the landing - or not!

Because this was the first time we played this game, the students were much more concerned with how to play the game and less concerned about what they were doing when it came to the Math. After the first jump I heard one of the students in the room say "What the heck does any of this have to do with Math?!" "Well, we are so excited that you asked!!" we answered. The teacher led the Math lesson at the front of the room. The student jumped 81.1 meters at a top speed of 83.07kph. The first thing we did was make our formula - 81.1m = T x 83.07kph. The next step was to convert the meters to kilometers. So, 81.1 meters becomes .0811km. From there we divide both sides by 83.07 (which by the way we had the students complete by hand - no calculators for this class). Move your decimals and begin division. We rounded at .001 or 1 thousandths of an hour. Now, that is our answer, but really, how long is that? So we figured out that if we multiply by 3600, we can figure out how many seconds .001 of an hour actually is. Why do we multiply by 3600? We know there are 60 minutes in 1 hour and 60 seconds in 1 minute. And, after all that math, we get to a total of 3.6 seconds. So, if we traveled a distance of 81.1 meters at a speed of 83.07 kph, we were in the air for 3.6 seconds.

One thing that we didn't do (at least this first time we played) that could increase the level of difficulty was cross multiplication. When we had our answer of .001 seconds we could have put it into a problem of 1/1000 times 3600/1. Then have the students do the cross multiplication to get 3600/1000, which can be reduced to 18/5 or 3.6 seconds.

We were able to use the game to introduce a new concept and complete five different standards. The different standards covered in this lesson include:

1. Metric conversion;
2. Use formulas (the already mentioned rate = time x distance);
3. Solve one step problems using decimals in division;
4. Converting decimals into fractions; and
5. Solving proportions and ratios.

WII™ ARE LOOKING TOWARD THE FUTURE

As we look to the future and the continuation of using the Wii in the classroom, our first focus is expanding the use of the gaming system in both of the authors' schools. We look forward to seeing how the 4th and 5th grade Math teacher will continue to find new games and new ways of engaging her students in real or at least virtual world situations using Math concepts, problem solving and computation. There are plans for the PE teacher to utilize the *Just Dance* games with students in preparation for a dance talent show in the spring. We will also strive to find creative ways to integrate the Wii into the Middle School Language Arts curriculum. We are excited by the positive use of *The Oregon Trail* with these classes and will try to connect with additional content area teachers and build cross curricular learning opportunities for our students. We will also look to connecting with new teachers in each building who might have interest in using the games with their students.

Our second focus is on the creation of a website, www.gamingintheclassroom. com, so that we can keep our resources in one public place to share with others. We are posting all the lesson plans we have created on this site, as well as our contact information and a link to our blog about our Wii projects. We would love to hear from other educators who are either already using the Wii in the classroom or who begin on the journey. We would be happy to share what we have learned and also learn new things ourselves.

Finally, there are a few specific projects we have in mind when it comes to using the Wii at our schools. First, the Wii can be connected to the Internet and once this task is accomplished, you can view current news and weather information, buy WiiWare games, and participate in an international poll. The polling and voting element is one of the things we have discussed using with the students as a once a week activity. Wii puts out a random question, such as which would you rather do; watch a movie or read a book? You choose your answer and then in a week or so you can check back and see how everyone around the Wii world voted. After you vote, you are also taken to a screen which asks you to predict the results of the current survey. This exercise could lead into some great class discussions and work on predicting which is a valuable reading comprehension skill. When you come back and check the results of the poll, the results are given in a visual pie chart with the percentages of each choice displayed. This could be an easy way to tie in problem solving with percentages to any class.

As mentioned above, once you are on the Internet with your Wii, you can buy games on the Wii Shop Channel. You need WiiWare points to purchase games this way (gift cards can be found at local gaming stores or points can be bought online), but this opens up a whole new world of gaming options. We have only worked with one of these games so far and it is titled *The Amazing Brain Train*. This game is similar to *Big Brain Academy: Wii Degree* and it offers critical thinking and puzzle activities for the students to solve. The games in this market place are usually much less expensive than the Wii games you buy in stores. One of the games we are also researching through this WiiWare section is called, *TV Show King 2*. This is a jeopardy style game which allows the users to not only play with the game's questions but also to create their own questions. What a fantastic way to do a review for a quiz or test students on vocabulary. We do not know any details about the game or the customizable question feature but we are anxious to find out.

Lastly, as one of our schools is working tirelessly to improve the math computation skills of our students, we are looking to begin an after school Wii Math Computation club for the Middle School students. The school began an after school Math session last year and while the younger students love it and attend regularly, the older students have shown no interest. Our hope is that with the inclusion of the Wii games in these types of sessions, the 5th through 8th graders will be interested and see the value in improving their Math skills.

WII™ TECHNOLOGY COMPONENTS

One of the best things about using the Wii was that there were only a few pieces of equipment necessary to integrate the system into our classrooms, and we already had most of them in the room. The first thing we needed was a Nintendo Wii system. This can be purchased at just about any electronics store and usually costs around $150.00 to $200.00, depending on what bundle is on sale at that time. We also needed something to hook the Nintendo up to so we could see it. We were fortunate enough that our classrooms already had a projector and speaker system, so we were able to easily hook the console up using the cables included and did not have to purchase extra equipment. We now had a 66 inch screen for viewing. Any television could also be used if that is available. You just use the included cable to attach the red, white, and yellow (audio and video) cables to the matching color slots on the back or side of the television.

At the same time that we purchased the system we also purchased extra controllers and extra nunchucks (so we had a total of four), and a wireless sensor bar so we would not be restricted by the placement of the Wii. The extra controllers are essential to have more students at one time involved in game play. The wireless sensor bar proved to be helpful because the plugs to hook the Wii to the projector were in the back of the room, but the board was at the opposite side and we wanted the students to face the board, not the corner of the room. We also purchased a few games to use in the classroom. The standard system comes with one game, Wii Sports, which includes the games we began with: baseball, golf and bowling. As time passes, we continue to purchase additional games (definitely watch for used games at various stores) to integrate into the other subject areas. Lastly, the Wiimotes run on two AA batteries and if you are going to be using the Wii on a regular basis in the classroom, we would highly recommend the purchase of rechargeable batteries.

EVALUATION

We evaluate each game in three ways: before we play with students to see educational value, after we play with students to reflect on objectives reached and through student comments and assessments. One of the biggest things we have learned throughout our work with the Wii is that the most time consuming part of the process is the pre-planning stage. Even when you know that a game has educational value, such as *The Oregon Trail*, or *Wii Sports Golf*, you have to play through the game completely to find out all the appropriate settings to use in order to maximize learning time with the students. While playing the Wii in itself is certainly not a chore, this process can take a lot of time. Games such as *30 Great Games Outdoor Fun* for the Wii take even longer in this pre-planning stage because you are introduced to new types of games that you must play before you even know whether they have educational merit. Out of the 30 games on this disc for example, we only found one which we found meaningful for our curriculum. This does not mean that another teacher might not find others, but for us it was only one. Fortunately, we had a blast playing, learning, and watching for educational possibilities.

Next, through discussions and written reflections in the blog, we always evaluated how classroom sessions had played out. There were often lessons learned and surprising aspects that could not have been predicted, no matter how much time had been spent preparing. Finally, we paid close attention to student comments and opinions during the lessons and afterwards, in order to gain their informal evaluations of the games and the objectives attempted. Student assessments, either formal (pre/post tests or other formative assessments) or observational (students working during the lesson or collected seat work from lesson) were utilized to quantify the learning process as often as possible.

WII™ HAD SOME CHALLENGES

The biggest challenge in implementing the Wii was the time needed to properly evaluate games and how they would best tie to our curriculum standards. We spent multiple hours after school playing different games and making notes on specific game play options that would best suit the classroom environment. Beside purchasing games, we also looked at the many different games available online through the Wii console. These options are constantly updating so there are always new choices available. In the end, time was the biggest challenge but not the only one.

Another challenge was classroom management during game play time. While the games only involved four or fewer active participants, there are fifteen to twenty plus students needing engagement. We find that each game lends itself to different methods of total class involvement, but the teacher needs to plan for this involvement ahead of time for the lesson to be successful. For example, while the few are playing the game, at least one student can be at the board taking notes, doing math problems, etc. while the remainder of the class is at their seats also involved in the note taking and problem solving procedures. This way all students are actively engaged throughout the entire lesson even though they may only play the Wii for a matter of minutes.

Finally, as with all things in education, there is almost always a challenge with the budget needed for programs. First, we found out very quickly that the batteries in the Wii remotes did not last very long. We were going through loads of batteries, two batteries needed for each controller and we have four controllers. We have since remedied this situation through the purchase of rechargeable batteries and chargers. While there was an initial outlay of money, the savings in the long run will be substantial. We have already seen the benefit of this purchase. Second, as we continue to look for new games to incorporate into the classroom, for example *Wii Sports Resort* and *Wii Fit*, there is money needed not only for games but for additional accessories. We would argue that this money would be well spent, as we have seen the positive and lasting results of using games in the classroom. Lastly, there is the ever growing variety of games on the Wii console which are considerably less expensive. As these games are easier on the school wallet to purchase, we are back to our number one challenge of time needed to vet these games and make classroom appropriate lessons. The benefits and excitement these games bring to the students and classroom environment greatly outweigh any challenges mentioned here.

SUMMARY

This chapter has been based on two years' worth of work (still ongoing today) incorporating the Nintendo Wii gaming platform into multiple subjects in our 4th through 8th grade classrooms. In 2008, our school underwent a reaccreditation process which included setting goals for improvement. One of the goals was to increase the students' aptitude in Math computation and problem solving skills. We had been following an educational blogger, Tom Barrett, who was using the Wii to teach Math skills in the primary/elementary classroom. We began by bringing in a personally owned Wii system to a 5th classroom with the mission of increasing student engagement, excitement and skills in the subject of Math. This mission proved so successful that we have expanded the use of the Wii into more grade levels and subject areas.

As our initial classroom implementations of the Wii proved valuable, a Wii system was purchased for the school. During the first year of use, 2009-2010, our mission of improving the Math computation and problem solving skills, as well as the attitude of our students towards Math, fueled the use of the Wii in the classroom. We conducted two action research projects with the fifth grade class at our school that further encouraged our utilization of the Wii with the students. We found that not only were the students learning during the Wii enhanced classes, but they were retaining the information long after the initial lessons.

During the second year of our Wii implementation, 2010-2011, we expanded the use of the Wii to the 6th through 8th grade students and to different subject area focuses. We utilized the Wii in Language Arts, Science and Social Studies as well as a tool to help build teamwork and critical thinking skills in our Middle School students. We found the response from the students to be just as positive as in our 5th grade trials and we began to see how different games could be used across the curriculum to increase student engagement and excitement.

Our mission of using the Wii to increase student engagement and excitement during standards-based lessons continues to drive our work in this field and we are constantly amazed at the results with our students. We look forward to the future possibilities of learning that await us.

REFERENCES

(2008). *Are you smarter than a 5th grader? (Version Wii Platform)* [Computer software]. Agoura Hills, CA: THQ, Inc.

Badman, T., Badman, C., & DeNote, M. (2012, January 3). *Gaming in the classroom.* Retrieved January 14, 2012, from www.gamingintheclassroom.com

Barrett, T. (n.d.). *EDTE.CH inspire connect engage create.* Retrieved January 14, 2012, from http://edte.ch/blog/

Big Brain Academy Wii degree. [Computer software]. (2007). Redmond, WA: Nintendo of America Inc.

DeNote, M. (n.d.). *New ideas?* Retrieved January 14, 2012, from http://teach-n-learn.blogspot.com/

Endless Ocean [Computer software]. (2008). Redmond, WA: Nintendo of America.

30*Great Games Outdoor Fun* [Computer software]. (2009). Los Angeles, CA: D3Publisher of America.

Grubby Games. (2010). *The amazing brain train (Version WiiWare)* [Computer software]. Orem, Utah: NinjaBee.

(2009). *Just Dance* [Computer software]. San Francisco, CA: Ubisoft.

Show King, T. V. *2* [Computer software]. (2009). New York, NY: Gameloft.

(2010). *The Amazing Race* [Computer software]. San Francisco, CA: Ubisoft.

(2011). *The Oregon Trail* [Computer software]. Mechanicville, NY: SVG Distribution.

Wii Fit [Computer software]. (2008). Redmond, WA: Nintendo of America.

Wii Sports [Computer software]. (2006). Redmond, WA: Nintendo of America Inc.

Wii Sports Resort [Computer software]. (2009). Redmond, WA: Nintendo of America.

Winter Sports. (2007). *The Ultimate Challenge* [Computer software]. Santa Monica, CA: Conspiracy Entertainment.

(2008). *WordJong Party* [Computer software]. Plymouth, MN: Destineer.

KEY TERMS AND DEFINITIONS

Clickers: Interactive audience response devices used in the classroom by students as a way of taking attendance, quizzing students, taking a quick survey, etc.

Common Core Standards: The Common Core State Standards Initiative is a state-led effort coordinated by the National Governors Association Center for Best Practices (NGA Center) and the Council of Chief State School Officers (CCSSO). The standards were developed in collaboration with teachers, school administrators, and experts, to provide a clear and consistent framework to prepare our children for college and the workforce. www.corestandards.org.

Composite Plug: Also known as RCA plugs. These are the yellow, red, and white plugs that are needed to hook your Nintendo up to the video source (TV or projector). The plug that comes with the Nintendo fits into the gaming system on one side and into the video source via those three composite plugs.

Mii: A digital avatar used in Nintendo's Wii gaming consoles. They allow users to capture a likeness (or a caricature) of themselves and others. After creating one using the Wii's Mii Channel, they can be used as playable characters in various titles for the console.

Nintendo Wii: A home video game console released by Nintendo on November 19, 2006.

Nunchuck: Is the first attachment Nintendo revealed for the Wii Remote. It connects to the Wii Remote via a cord, and it features an analog stick with one trigger button and one "C" button. It works in tandem with the main controller in many games.

Wiimote: The primary controller for Nintendo's Wii console. A main feature of the Wii Remote is its motion sensing capability, which allows the user to interact with and manipulate items on screen via gesture recognition and pointing through the use of accelerometer and optical sensor technology.

WiiWare: A service that allows Wii users to download games and applications specifically designed and developed for the Wii video game console made by Nintendo. These games and applications can only be purchased and downloaded from the Wii Shop Channel under the WiiWare section on the console. Once the user has downloaded the game or application, it will appear in their Wii Menu or SD Card Menu as a new channel.

Wireless Sensor Bar: This optional bar can be used instead of the wired sensor bar that comes with the console. This is the sensor that you point the Wiimote towards in order to play the game. This wireless sensor allows you to not be restricted with the placement of the Wii system in a classroom setting.

Chapter 4
Beyond Hidden Bodies and Lost Pigs:
Student Perceptions of Foreign Language Learning with Interactive Fiction

Joe Pereira
British Council, Portugal

EXECUTIVE SUMMARY

Interactive Fiction is a text-based genre of video game which blends participatory storytelling, the exploration of virtual worlds, and logical puzzle-solving. As it is a form of electronic literature as well as a form of video game, and it is compatible with the principles of second language acquisition, it can be used for digital game-based language learning. This chapter presents a case study on the perceptions of learners of English as a foreign language on the use of Interactive Fiction to practise language skills, particularly as a means of improving reading for fluency. The games played by the learners were 9:05 and Lost Pig, and the results produced by the study provided positive evidence towards the use of Interactive Fiction as an engaging language learning tool.

DOI: 10.4018/978-1-4666-2848-9.ch004

OVERALL DESCRIPTION

Interest in digital game-based learning (DGBL) from researchers and educators has continued to grow and works such as Gee (2007a), Baek (2010), and Whitton (2010), make a strong case for the potential of video games for learning and how they may be implemented in the classroom. Recent publications on using DGBL for foreign language learning, particularly by De Hann (2005), Purushtoma, Thorne & Wheatley (2009), Reinders & Wattana (2011) and Mawer & Stanley (2011), have shown that despite the existence of challenges, the affordances of video games are in line with modern approaches to language learning pedagogy and are worthy of consideration for classroom application. This case study looks at how the retro video game genre of Interactive Fiction (IF), also known as text-adventures, was used with learners of English as a foreign language in order to provide them with an alternative method of practising reading for fluency in a meaningful, motivating and engaging manner. The research question that guided the study was: "Do learners perceive IF as an engaging way to practise English skills?"

Background Information

The case study took place at the British Council, a private language institute in Porto, Portugal. The sample consisted of a monolingual class made up of six males and four females, between the ages of fifteen and eighteen. The students were at an upper-intermediate level of English and were preparing to do the Cambridge ESOL First Certificate Exam (FCE). As is often the case with exam preparation courses, the actual level of the language proficiency of the students was mixed, with some excellent students in the class and others that would have difficulty in achieving a passing grade on the FCE exam. However, they were for the most part very motivated and interested students based on their attitudes and work in the classroom. Being affluent, a questionnaire given after the gaming session confirmed that all of the students had Internet access at home and owned between three and five computers. Additionally, all but one of the students claimed to own at least one gaming console and every student claimed to own either one or two mobile gaming devices (with the Sony PSP and Nintendo DS being the most cited). It is therefore not surprising that all of the students said that they played video games at home. In comparison, only six of the learners admitted to enjoying reading for pleasure, and only in their native tongue of Portuguese.

The British Council is a well-respected English language-learning organisation with teaching centres in over 100 countries. It caters mostly to learners (children and adults) of upper-class families, who wish to improve their level of English for personal, academic or professional reasons, as well as to prepare for Cambridge

ESOL examinations, which will give them internationally recognised qualifications to further their career prospects or allow them to study abroad. In Portugal, learning English is mostly deemed as a natural, but important step in a child's education. As the English taught in public schools is considered by many parents to be inadequate, those who can afford to do so enroll their children in private language institutes. In these institutes, teachers are usually native speakers and there is a greater focus on oral production rather than the grammar-based instruction of regular schooling.

The official teaching approach adopted by the British Council is the Communicative Language Teaching (CLT) approach, which is based on the following principles (Finocchiaro & Brumfit, 1983; Nunan, 1991; Richards & Rodgers, 2001):

- Language is learned by using it.
- The target language is a vehicle for classroom communication and the speaker's native language is only used as a last resort or to test understanding.
- The use of authentic language and authentic materials is fundamental.
- Students are involved in engaging and meaningful real-world tasks.
- Fluency is strived for over accuracy.
- Intrinsic motivation results from authentic interest in what is being communicated with the language.
- Pair work and group work activities stimulate communication.

There are learning scenarios, however, where aspects of the CLT approach are at odds with what learners need or expect from their language-learning course. The group of students involved in this case study were preparing for an externally assessed exam, which involves becoming familiar with and practising exam techniques and actually spending a great deal of class time doing exam exercises, which strays from the CLT principles of being a meaningful and authentic real-world task. Furthermore, because the CLT approach has a major focus on oral production during class time, for the most part, the development of the reading and writing skills are often not given priority in classroom tasks and are relegated to homework. In the context of this class, instruction in lessons is given in English and students are given ample opportunity to speak English in class. Various types of writing assignments are also done in order to prepare them for the exam and students are encouraged to read as much as possible outside of class time so that they may gain experience in reading a wide variety of texts and genres, useful not only for exam preparation purposes, but also to improve their general fluency in reading extended English texts. However, despite these constant recommendations, most students do not read in English beyond what is set for homework or through casual access to magazine articles, Internet websites or movie subtitles.

Aims

The initial idea behind using IF with these students was to promote the practice of reading for fluency in a more engaging and motivating way, as well as to foster the enjoyment of reading for pleasure by promoting IF as a potential autonomous learning tool. It was my belief that by introducing IF - being a narrative and also a game, students would be more willing to read English outside of the classroom. For this to become a reality, however, it would first be necessary to analyse students' perceptions on whether they believed playing IF to be an engaging activity, if aspects of language learning could be practiced by playing it, and whether they would consider using it as an autonomous learning tool.

The study took place during a three-hour Saturday morning lesson. The lesson was composed of an introduction to IF, the playing of a short IF game (9:05), a twenty minute break, the playing of a more complex IF game (Lost Pig) and the filling out of a questionnaire on the perceived benefits of IF for language learning.

LITERATURE REVIEW

Video Games

Video games, no longer seen as the anti-social pastime of yesteryear, have become a multi-billion dollar industry, played by a wide and varied demographic (ESA, 2011). Why do people spend so much time and money playing video games? Although, the common response to this might be to say they are 'fun', it is precisely the element of 'fun' that is missing in every definition of 'game' (Salen & Zimmerman, 2003; Whitton, 2010). As noted by Michael & Chen (2005, p.20), fun "is not an ingredient or something you put in. Fun is a result ... essentially a positive feedback mechanism to get us to repeat the activity over and over." As 'fun' means different things to different people, the concept of 'engagement', as a combination of mechanisms that produce positive emotional response from the player, might be a more adequate term to describe what makes people want to play video games. To more easily understand why players are drawn to certain games and not others, the Mechanics, Dynamics and Aesthetics (MDA) framework (Hunicke, LeBlanc & Zubek, 2004, p. 2) suggests the following engaging 'pleasures' which can be found in video games:

1. **Sensation:** Game as sense-pleasure
2. **Fantasy:** Game as make-believe
3. **Narrative:** Game as unfolding story

4. **Challenge:** Game as obstacle course
5. **Fellowship:** Game as social framework
6. **Discovery:** Game as uncharted territory
7. **Expression:** Game as soap box
8. **Submission:** Game as mindless pastime

By playing games which trigger the emotional mechanisms that they enjoy, players may become so engrossed in their playing that they enter a state of deep concentration. This state is known as 'the flow experience' (Csikszentmihalyi, 1990), where players' engagement allows them to completely focus on accomplishing their goals, often while being unaware of the passing of time. It is also when experiencing flow that players may unconsciously assimilate content presented in a game. This concept is known as 'stealth learning', which according to Gee (2007a, p. 124) occurs when "learners are not overly aware of the fact that they are learning, how much they are learning, or how difficult it is".

Video games and their potential use in educational contexts have been the growing focus of research in the last decade (de Freitas, 2006a; 2008a; The Horizon Report, 2007; Facer, Ulicsak & Sandford, 2007; Connolly, Stansfield & Boyle, 2009). Research has also shown that video games are intrinsically educational due to their having, amongst many others, the following characteristics (Prensky, 2001; 2006; Foreman, Gee, Herz, Hinrichs, Prensky & Sawyer, 2004; de Freitas, 2006b; Gee 2007a; 2007b):

- They allow players to see things from different perspectives.
- They contextualise and order learning, where you learn to play by playing.
- They activate critical and lateral thinking skills through problem solving.
- They present a conflict that must be overcome, providing unexpected and stressful situations which must be resolved, paralleling real life.
- They provide immediate feedback.
- They encourage players to take risks and evaluate their actions.
- They allow players to make mistakes and learn from them.
- They provide an environment for collaborative and social learning.

Much of the recent research on using DGBL for foreign language learning has focused on this last point, arguing for the affordances of socio-constructivist learning environments for authentic (mostly oral) language practice, more specifically through the use of cutting-edge three-dimensional virtual worlds and massively multiplayer-online games (MMORPGS), such as Second Life and World of Warcraft (Thorne, 2008; Panichi, Deutschmann & Molka-Danielsen, 2010; Pereira, 2011a). However, it is my view that in this age of state-of-the-art 3D graphics and cinematic cut-scenes and soundtracks, the descriptive and immersive power of text should not be overlooked, and completely text-based Interactive Fiction games can still be used as an engaging and meaningful language learning tool.

Interactive Fiction

Interactive Fiction (IF), also called 'text adventures', is a genre of video game, which is completely text-based. The first text adventure game, "Adventure" by William Crowther and Don Woods, was released onto the precursor of the Internet, the ARPANET, in 1976. It would go on to kickstart the upcoming computer games market, where IF would rule the charts for more than half a decade, with the release of "Adventureland" by Scott Adams in 1978 - the first commercial computer game. Today, IF is still created, mostly by members of the online IF community as part of various annual competitions, and it is freely distributed on the Internet at IF repositories such as The Interactive Fiction Database (http://www.ifdb.tads.org). Because nearly all of the IF written today is free, authors no longer have to submit themselves to the pressures of making games for a buying public, and this has led to the emergence of experimental works which have pushed the boundaries of IF and works which have become noted for their high-literary quality. This, in turn, has led to a resurgence of IF in classrooms and as the focus for educational research.

IF is a unique form of electronic literature, blending the narrative qualities of literature and the interactivity and challenge found in video games. Noted narratologist Marie-Laure Ryan (2006, p. 128) describes IF as "a dialogue system in which the user, manipulating a character, interacts with the machine not through the selection of an item from a fixed menu but through a relatively free production of text." Because this interaction requires that the reader/player provide meaningful input in natural language in order for the computer to move the narrative forward, it has been defined as a form of 'ergodic' literature, where "non-trivial effort is required to allow the reader to traverse the text" (Aarseth, 1997, p. 1). This non-trivial effort on the part of the reader involves exploring and interacting with the game-world and not only making choices, but acting upon them in order to shape the flow of the narrative. In this way, the reader becomes a co-creator of the narrative, telling the story together with the author (See Figure 1).

Nick Montfort (2003), author of the first book-length academic study of Interactive Fiction defines IF as being:

1. A text accepting, text generating computer program;
2. A potential narrative;
3. A simulation of an environment or world;
4. A structure of rules, with which an outcome is sought, and played voluntarily: a game.

Figure 1. 9:05 (© 2000, Adam Cadre, Used WITH permission)

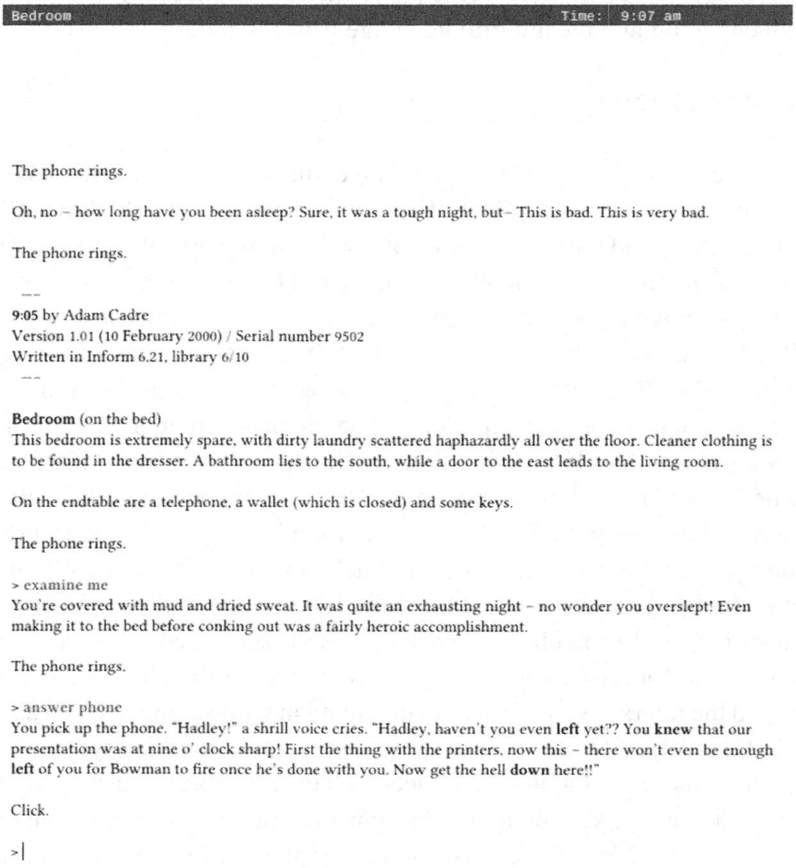

```
Bedroom                                          Time:  9:07 am
```

The phone rings.

Oh, no – how long have you been asleep? Sure, it was a tough night, but– This is bad. This is very bad.

The phone rings.

9:05 by Adam Cadre
Version 1.01 (10 February 2000) / Serial number 9502
Written in Inform 6.21, library 6/10

Bedroom (on the bed)
This bedroom is extremely spare, with dirty laundry scattered haphazardly all over the floor. Cleaner clothing is to be found in the dresser. A bathroom lies to the south, while a door to the east leads to the living room.

On the endtable are a telephone, a wallet (which is closed) and some keys.

The phone rings.

> examine me
You're covered with mud and dried sweat. It was quite an exhausting night – no wonder you overslept! Even making it to the bed before conking out was a fairly heroic accomplishment.

The phone rings.

> answer phone
You pick up the phone. "Hadley!" a shrill voice cries. "Hadley, haven't you even **left** yet?? You **knew** that our presentation was at nine o' clock sharp! First the thing with the printers, now this – there won't even be enough **left** of you for Bowman to fire once he's done with you. Now get the hell **down** here!!"

Click.

>|

The goal of IF, as a game, is to reach the end of the story. Despite this, Keller (2007, p. 290), in his study on player attitudes on IF reports that "readers of IF enjoy trying different actions to find different possible endings, even if those endings are unsuccessful and result in death." He also notes that despite being an important and enjoyable result of playing IF, reaching the end of the story is usually not the player's most memorable experience. For many players, the puzzles, or more correctly, discovering the solutions to these puzzles, is the most pleasurable aspect of IF. As described in Keller (2007, p. 291), "There is nothing quite like the sight of prose coursing down your screen after you did something essential." Logical puzzles in IF bring a level of challenge to the player and serve as obstacles to progress, as well as being pause mechanisms for players to assess their place in the narrative, their understanding of the rules that govern the game-world, and their knowledge of the words that can be used to interact with it. These 'narrative curtains', (O'Brian, 1993) have been described by Ingold (2009) as the author of the IF work "offering the player the chance to have an impact on the game-world and to open up the story through their ingenuity" (p. 230). It is due to the existence of these puzzles that IF is a game and not just a form of non-linear electronic literature like hypertext fiction, and can therefore be used for DGBL.

Using IF for Digital Game-Based Language Learning

In the last 35 years since the inception of the genre, there has been some relevant research into using IF as a learning tool for language learning, mainly focusing on its affordances for improving reading skills (Lancy & Hayes, 1988; Grabe & Dosman, 1988; Desilets, 1989; 1999) and the incidental acquisition of vocabulary (Palmberg, 1988; Cheung & Harrison, 1992; Shelton, Neville, McInnis, 2009). More recent research has looked into incorporating adaptive feedback for language learners (Cornillie, Jacques, De Wannemacker, Paulussen & Desmet, 2011) and authoring IF using software specifically made for its development (Kee, Vaughn & Graham, 2010). This recent research has looked at how IF can be designed and adapted for specific teaching and learning contexts, thus exemplifying that IF can be used as a 'serious game'. Serious games, are games that are created for purposes other than for entertainment. More specifically, Michael & Chen (2005:46) stress their primary goal of facilitating learning by stating that "serious games offer a new mechanism for teaching and training by combining video games with education".

Research by Pereira (in press) has validated IF as an example of appropriate computer-assisted language learning (CALL) material, with one of the main reasons being that it is in line with the principles of the CLT approach to language learning:

- The target language is used to interact with the game (in both input and output);
- The text is authentic and not scripted for language learning;
- Meaningful tasks include solving puzzles and reaching the end of the story;
- Problem-solving requires using language and knowledge, which may be transferable to real-world situations;
- Reading for fluency is seen as a process and not a product.

My main reason for using IF with learners is to provide them with a potentially more engaging reading experience than what can be achieved with traditional text, thus giving them the motivation to become more fluent readers. According to Taguchi, Gorsuch & Sassamoto (2006, p.1) fluent readers "are able to identify words in text quickly and accurately with a minimal amount of attention. Word recognition is done efficiently and effortlessly and consequently, readers can read connected text silently or orally with speed and good comprehension. In addition, fluent readers are able to read aloud with appropriate phrasing and expressiveness." One way in which reading fluency can be achieved is through 'extensive reading'. Hafiz and Tudor (1989) state that "the pedagogical value attributed to extensive reading is based on the assumption that exposing learners to large quantities of meaningful and interesting L2 material will, in the long run, produce a beneficial effect on the learner's command of the L2". It is hoped that by introducing IF, learners may become motivated to play IF (in addition to reading traditional literature) outside of the classroom. However, the potential appeal IF has with young learners may be questioned due to its lack of graphics and sound. Despite this, after some experimentation, most learners are drawn into the game because of the amount of control they are given over the protagonist and because they can influence the direction of the narrative. IF fully embodies Malone and Lepper's (1987) factors of intrinsic motivation, which include the aspects of challenge, fantasy, control and curiosity, and this may go some way toward explaining why readers often persevere in IF, despite the various linguistic and cognitive challenges it provides. Niesz & Holland (1984, p. 122) state that "interactive fiction demands determination and persistence from a reader if she is to overcome the obstacles which confront her". Successfully playing the vast majority of IF requires problem-solving and critical and lateral thinking skills, which not every learner is equally equipped with. While designed to be read individually like a traditional text, in order to give less imaginative or less analytical players a better chance of progressing through the story, IF can easily be made into a collaborative task. By playing IF in pairs or groups, learners can help each other by using these cognitive skills or by applying their own personal knowledge of the world to solve problems. This use of 'schemata', understood as "knowledge structures which the reader brings to the text" (Hudson, 1998, p.185) is an absolute necessity in order to make sense of the texts and to find links between them in order to solve puzzles. As an example of this, Lost Pig includes two puzzles which require the correct manipulation of an object called a 'colour-magnet'. While this object really only exists in the game-world of Lost Pig, if the player knows what a 'magnet' is and how one works in the real-world, she will be able to make more sense of the various bits of information found in the game pertaining to how to use it, and will be better equipped to solve those puzzles.

When playing in pairs or groups, learners are between themselves also engaging in authentic and meaningful language, through giving opinions and making suggestions on how to proceed during game-play. This concept of using a single computer as a mediator between people communicating with each other in order to accomplish a given task is known as computer-mediated collaborative learning (CMCL). Piper (1986) notes the main difference between computers and people as being that computers are not good communicators whereas people are, provided they have something to say. She points out that this difference "underlies a major potential of the computer for language learning, where the machine can provide the 'something to talk about' and the learners can provide the conversation", which she calls 'conversational spin-off' (p. 187). Indeed, IF offers plenty to talk about: the authentic nature of the tasks involved in playing IF - exploring the world, interacting with its objects and characters, and solving puzzles - will often create discussion between players. These discussions include current objectives, how to use objects, where to go, and what to ask in-game characters, amongst others. The text-based nature of IF also raises questions about the meaning of words or passages of text, and as often is the case with the IF genre, on the correct verbs needed to give commands. The use of social language that arises from conversational spin-off, such as asking for repetition and clarification, are also important elements in second language acquisition (SLA) as they facilitate learning "through purposeful dialogic exchange, verbalisation of thought processes, reciprocal understanding and negotiation of meaning" (McLouglin & Oliver, 1998, p.128).

With regards to assessment, IF, like all video games, provides clear and immediate feedback. Learners know when they have been successful in a task - text is produced and the narrative advances, and upon failure, are given an indication of the reason - the game produces replies such as "I do not understand" or "nothing happens", or an attempted action simply does not produce the expected result. Pereira (2011b, p. 94) states that "making progress through the game is clear evidence that the reader is understanding not only the words, but how the words fit into the world model". In this way, reading assessment is built into the game itself, through its 'narrative curtains', as proposed by Desilets (1999, p. 8): "The aesthetically-placed pauses for problems thus become, among other things, compelling and integrated reading comprehension tests, perhaps the only such tests that most kids will take voluntarily."

Furthermore, if straight-forward playing of the game is not 'aligned' (Whitton, 2010, p.90) with required learning objectives, as IF is a form of literature, it can be implemented in the same way that traditional literary texts would be used in the language classroom and in conjunction with pre-reading, while-reading and post-reading tasks, it can then be assessed in a more traditional manner. This opens up the possibility of using IF for literary analysis and as the basis for the implementation of further speaking, listening, and writing tasks, in addition to focusing on discrete language items. (Pereira, 2011b; Hismanoglu, 2005; Bagherkazemi & Alemi, 2010).

PRACTICALITIES OF RUNNING THE GAME

The implementation of using IF was done during a 3-hour lesson in the following phases:

1. Introduction to IF (description, IF vocabulary card, play-through of the first moments of '9:05', pre-reading task) (30 minutes).
2. Participant observation of the learners playing '9:05' (45 minutes).
3. 20 minute break (setting-up of second IF game).
4. Participant observation of learners playing 'Lost Pig' (60 minutes).

1. Introduction to IF

Before playing the first IF game of the session, '9:05', the students were told that they were going to play a type of completely textual video game, called Interactive Fiction. It was explained that they would have to control the protagonist of a story and explore the game-world to discover what the goal of the game is and how it can be achieved, thus creating the narrative in the process. They were warned that they would need to read each passage of text very carefully, many times over, as understanding the meaning of every word and how it fits into the world presented by the game is important in order to create new text and move the story forward. The students were then told that communicating with the game was done via textual input in natural English, albeit usually in a simplified form based on verb + noun collocations. Examples of common actions, such as 'get' and 'drop' and special commands, such as 'examine' and 'inventory' were then presented to the learners. Each student was then given a copy of Andrew Plotkin's (2010) 'IF for Beginners Card', which lists the most common verbs and commands used in IF. After allowing the students to peruse the card for a few minutes, as the classroom is equipped with an interactive whiteboard and a computer, they were shown the start of 9:05 followed by an explanation of the layout of the screen and the user interface. The students were then asked to think of possible commands to give to the protagonist so that they could see the effect of their input, expected and unexpected by the parser, on the game-world. After a few failed attempts at giving commands understood by the parser, the suggestion to 'answer the phone' correctly produced an output of text which gave the learners an idea of who they were and what the immediate goal of the game might be – seemingly, to get the protagonist to his place of work as soon as possible.

As the students were about to encounter an authentic text, unscripted or graded for language learning, they would firstly need to be pre-taught any difficult vocabulary which might hamper their understanding of the text. In language teaching, it is standard procedure to clarify difficult vocabulary as a pre-reading task. Because IF stresses the importance of understanding every word and its relevance to the story in order to progress in the game, this pre-reading phase is even more essential. While it is possible to allow students to guess the meaning of words through context (and they will usually need to do this many times anyway during game-play), clarifying vocabulary before reading eases the burden of encountering new words during the reading process and forces learners to think about words and concepts they may already be familiar with. Although giving the students a list of the words out of context and asking them to write down what they think the words mean is not the best way to introduce new vocabulary to learners, it is the procedure that I followed as part of a planned follow-up study on whether the engagement that IF demands from the reader with the text made the pre-taught vocabulary more memorable, leading to its acquisition. In the case of 9:05, 20 words were found in the text that were above the students' current proficiency level and of some importance to understanding the story. The students were given the word list and asked to write definitions for the words. When finished, we quickly talked through the meanings of the words and the students were given a list with the correct definitions for added support while playing. After having learned some basic commands and conventions of IF and preparing for difficult vocabulary, the students were ready to play 9:05 in the computer-lab.

2. Playing 9:05

Once in the computer-lab, the students were asked to sit in pairs at a computer of their choice. Although the room was set-up with thirteen computers and each student could have had their own computer, they were asked to form pairs, as playing IF collaboratively can bring the gameplay and linguistic benefits previously mentioned and there was an even number of students. I proceeded to install Gargoyle, an IF interpreter and the 9:05 game file on each computer. As expected, however, I was unable to install the program files due to not having administrator rights on those machines. I quickly asked the students to open their web-browsers and type in the URL 'www.iplayif.com' followed by '9:05' and clicking on the link. To the students on machines where it wouldn't load correctly, I asked them to navigate to 'www. adamcadre.ac' and select the option to play 9:05 in a browser window. For the purpose of playing 9:05, the browser versions were perfectly suitable, if perhaps a bit cramped on the second version. For the next 40 minutes, the learners were engaged in playing the game, while I acted as a participant observer, watching their interactions and answering questions if asked and making suggestions when I noticed that the students were unsure of how to proceed or spending too much time in locations without making any progress. Given the nature of most Portuguese teenagers, I had to occasionally remind some of the pairs to speak in English in order for them to benefit from the negotiation of meaning process. Additionally, despite having the 'IF for Beginners card' with them, many learners forgot to look through the verbs listed and only on my suggestion did they think to look for possible synonyms to the rejected commands they were trying.

3. Installing Gargoyle

During the 20 minute break, I proceeded to install the Gargoyle interpreter on the five computers being used, making the playing of the second game, 'Lost Pig', a more visually appealing experience, while at the same time allowing me to save transcripts of the students' game-play.

4. Playing Lost Pig

After their break, the students, back in their pairs, played Lost Pig for one hour. However, an aspect of the game that I called the learner's attention to before playing was the need to draw a map of the geographic locations as they played the game. As Lost Pig has more locations than 9:05 and navigating between them involves the use of more complex compass directions (NE, SW, etc), the classic IF companion activity of drawing a map could offer an extra layer of support and reduce the amount of time players might spend aimlessly wandering around the game environment. I explained that each room should be represented by a box with the description of any seemingly important objects inside it and with exits from the room represented as lines connecting to further boxes, and exemplified how to do this on the whiteboard.

Before leaving the computer lab, I copied the transcripts of the game session from each computer for later analysis and potential use as a post-reading language task.

TECHNOLOGY COMPONENTS

As IF is completely text-based, the computing power needed to run it is minimal – any computer from the last 20 years is easily capable of running the software. It is also extremely portable. The file size of a game and the software necessary to run it is only a few megabytes, therefore it possible to send the required software and game files via email or save them on the smallest-sized USB drives. For the best playing experience, it is first necessary to download the appropriate interpreter for the operating system being used (and they are available for nearly every computer and mobile operating system). An interpreter is a virtual machine that can run specific IF game files. Most IF game files have .z5, .z8., zblorb or .gblorb extensions and some modern interpreters (e.g. Gargoyle, Zoom) can read all of them without any configuration from the user. Most interpreters allow the user to personalise the IF gaming experience by changing the font, font size and background colour as well as having extended control options such as text-to-speech features, useful for implementing listening tasks. As the computers in my institutions run Windows XP and Windows 7, the interpreter I use is Gargoyle, as it is able to read the widest variety of game file types, has a very nice and clean looking interface and respects the typography of each game.

Interpreters can be downloaded for free at the following locations:

1. Gargoyle for Mac OS X, Windows and Linux can be downloaded from http://ccxvii.net/gargoyle/
2. Zoom for Mac OS X can be downloaded from http://www.logicalshift.co.uk/unix/zoom/
3. Frotz for iOS devices (iPhone, iPod Touch & iPad) can be downloaded for free on iTunes
4. Twisty for Android devices can be downloaded from http://code.google.com/p/twisty/

The vast majority of IF games are available for free on the Internet. The best sites to download games, read reviews and see recommendations from other players are:

1. The Interactive Fiction Database – http://ifdb.tads.org/
2. Baf's Guide to the IF Archive – http://wurb.com/if/

Because interpreters are very small and simple programs, they literally take seconds to install. However, in order to install software on many institutional computers, administrator rights are often needed. Thankfully, if one is unable to get authorisation to install these files locally, alternative options can be used to play IF:

1. Use a web-based IF interpreter, such as Parchment, found at http://www.iplayif.com/ and http://parchment.toolness.com.
2. Play IF in a Java or Flash applet window from Internet sites such as 'The Z-Machine Preservation Project' http://zmpp.sourceforge.net/index.html or 'Jay Is Games' http://jayisgames.com/tag/ifiction
3. Run Gargoyle straight from a USB drive. On a machine running Windows, this firstly requires access to a computer that doesn't need administrator rights to install software. This simple procedure involves executing the Gargoyle installer and choosing to save the application files onto a USB drive instead

of the local C: drive. The Gargoyle.exe file can now be run on any computer from the USB drive. On a Mac, simply extract the Gargoyle application from the Gargoyle.dmg file and copy it onto a USB drive.

If it is impossible to install Gargoyle or its files on a USB drive, one of the Parchment web-browser alternatives should be used. The Parchment sites offer a very large library of games to choose from and the interpreter window is full-screen. The Java and Flash sites should only be used as a last resource as they present the games in very small windows and may have publicity or links to other games on the screen, which may be a distraction to learners. The drawback of browser-based interpreters is that they have limitations, such as not being able to produce transcripts or not implementing extended 'save' and 'restore' commands, which enable players to interrupt their playing session and return to the same position in the story at a later time.

Problems Encountered and Solutions

The lesson described in this case study did not take place in the computer lab of the British Council, where Gargoyle had been previously installed, but in the computer room of a nearby school, where classes are held for exam levels on Saturday mornings. As I had neither administrator rights to the workstations nor the possibility of accessing the machines prior to the lesson, I was confident that I would be able to fall back on web-based browsers if I wasn't able to install Gargoyle.

The first obstacle encountered, as expected, was that I couldn't install Gargoyle as I didn't have administrative privileges. As I hadn't previously prepared Gargoyle to run from my USB drive, I quickly asked the students to access http://www.iplayif. com. However, possibly due to an issue with browser plug-ins, the Parchment site only worked on two of the five computers being used. I asked the other pairs to access the official 9:05 site at http://www.adamcadre.ac so they could play the online java version. Unfortunately, the game was presented in a much smaller window than the Parchment site and was not as pleasurable to read. Furthermore, the possibility of creating a transcript file, useful for later analysis on how a game is played by learners and the language they use, is unavailable on browser-based interpreters. As 9:05 was a short game and I didn't want to waste any more time, I decided to move ahead and let the students play in their browsers, which worked without any further issues. However, as I had planned on producing transcripts of the game session for Lost Pig, I would have to find a means of installing Gargoyle on my USB drive during the break. As there is a computer in my classroom that does not require administrator rights, I was able to prepare my USB drive to run Gargoyle and so returned to the computer lab and ran an instance of Gargoyle and lostpig.z8 on the five computers. The learners played Lost Pig without any further issues and Gargoyle's full screen presentation provided a more pleasant reading experience.

EVALUATION

The aim of this study was to learn about students' attitudes towards using IF for practicing English and not on providing empirical evidence of the linguistic benefits of using IF for language learning. In order to evaluate whether IF is an engaging alternative to practise English skills in the classroom, participant observation was employed during the game playing phases, followed by the use of a questionnaire. The questionnaire included a number of Yes/No and open-ended questions on whether the students enjoyed playing IF, if and how they believed IF was useful for learning English and whether they would play IF at home as a leisure activity or as an autonomous means of practising English.

Results from Observations

Results from the observation of the students playing 9:05 were in line with my expectations based on previous experience of using the game with other classes. The students were all completely engaged while playing the game for the total time of the playing session. At no point did I notice any negative feelings towards the activity, nor did any individual learner lose interest altogether. 9:05 was chosen as the game to introduce IF to learners because I consider it to be the best example of IF for beginners, as it includes the following criteria:

- It is short and can be completed in one lesson (our computer room time-slots are 45 minutes long).
- It implements problem-solving (basic object manipulation), but does not have difficult puzzles.
- It is grounded in reality so players are familiar with conventions of the world and schema pertaining to it.
- It isn't a geographically dispersed game and thus avoids the need to make a map, which may be confusing for first time players. Despite having few locations, character movement between them creates the illusion of an actual world that is being explored, and strengthens the sensation of ' being there'.
- It has a memorable ending, which makes a strong initial impression.

As 9:05 is a simple game in terms of puzzles and geography, the only reason for players to get stuck is because they are unable to communicate their thoughts in a way that the parser can understand it. Most pairs did not have many problems with this. However, one pair in particular needed some guidance on choosing the correct commands to give.

This pair was formed by two very weak students by FCE standards, and their difficulty in interacting with the story can be attributed to their basic knowledge of vocabulary and phrasal verbs. Another pair, this one formed by two very communicative and bright students, also lagged behind the others in exploring the 9:05 game-world, but not due to linguistic barriers. The two students seemed to lack the imagination necessary to place themselves in the protagonist's shoes and force exploration of the world from his perspective. Additionally, both pairs had difficulties in understanding that in IF, complex actions (e.g. taking a shower) need to be reduced to their component parts, such as removing each article of clothing and dropping them before attempting to give the command 'take a shower'. This indicates that to successfully play IF without a high-level of support, learners need to have a reasonable level of general English – ideally, strong upper-intermediate. This also shows that linguistic competency is only one-half of the IF equation – above average imagination and problem-solving ability are also required in order to make any kind of progress.

In order to stimulate the students to be persistent in trying to communicate with the game and simultaneously congratulate the pairs that had progressed to certain parts of the narrative, I would occasionally announce that 'pair X' had already 'done Y'. Not only was this a means of giving indirect support, but it also created 'intra-group competition' (Whitton, 2010, p. 174), which effectively indicated to the students that there was indeed a solution to their problem and that somebody else had already discovered it, thus making them make a stronger effort.

After playing 9:05 for 40 minutes, four of the five pairs had managed to finish the game, reaching the expected 'bad' ending and three had explored two (of a possible three) endings and uncovered evidence of the protagonist's shady past, in this way, reaching the alternative 'good' ending and discovering the replay value and ability to take different paths in IF.

Lost Pig proved to be a much larger challenge for the students, as I had imagined it would be given the short time allocated for the playing of the game, coupled with their inexperience in playing IF. I chose Lost Pig as a follow-up game because it drastically contrasts with 9:05 in the ways of setting, difficulty of puzzles, length of time necessary to finish the game, size and layout of the geographic space, existence of non-player characters (NPCs) and even on a linguistic level. All of these elements added a level of complexity and challenge to the game, in addition to potential frustration. One of the reasons I believed Lost Pig would make an interesting game to play in a language learning context is because the protagonist is an Orc and as such, speaks a form of broken English, as demonstrated in the game's introduction in Figure 2.

On its own, this already makes it a unique work of IF, but going even further, instead of the traditional second-person narration, Lost Pig uses Grunk's skewed first/third person perspective to tell the story through his eyes and through his substandard English. It was my view that having to first parse this language and reply using correct English would be a more challenging, but also engaging experiment after having played the more traditional 9:05. This difference in prose did not seem to have any negative effect on the students' ability to play the game, and as expected, produced copious amounts of laughter throughout the session. As the vocabulary used in the majority of the game is basic, as can be expected from an Orc, there was no need to pre-teach any vocabulary. Despite some lapses into Portuguese while playing, learners were often involved in authentic negotiation of meaning in English, indicating that in addition to the reading skill, speaking and listening were also being practised. While some of the pairs did make a map, others chose not to, which had an impact on their more pronounced lack of success and increased frustration in comparison to the pairs that did. As expected, by the end of the hour, none of the pairs had made any significant progress in the game, with two of the five groups unable to discover how to wake the gnome, a question-answering NPC, who would offer help and direction regarding how to approach various puzzles. Unfortunately, of the pairs who did manage to wake the gnome, none of them spent enough time meaningfully conversing with him and were thus confused about what their immediate goals might be. A marked difference was noticed in the students' attitudes between this session and the 9:05 session. Because none of the students were able to solve any of the puzzles beyond waking the gnome, they began to get frustrated with constantly exploring the same rooms and repeatedly trying to catch the pig instead of trying to find a way out of the cave (which should have become their main goal at this point). The students' frustration was mostly identified by comments made between the pairs such as: "I already tried that", "we've already been in that room and there's nothing there" and "what do we do now?". One of the causes leading to frustration was identified as the students' not reading carefully enough and overlooking important words. This was especially apparent during the interactions with the gnome, which required asking questions on things that Grunk had seen throughout the game, in addition to asking for further clarification on words mentioned by the gnome himself.

Figure 2. Lost Pig (© 2007, Admiral Jota, Used with permission)

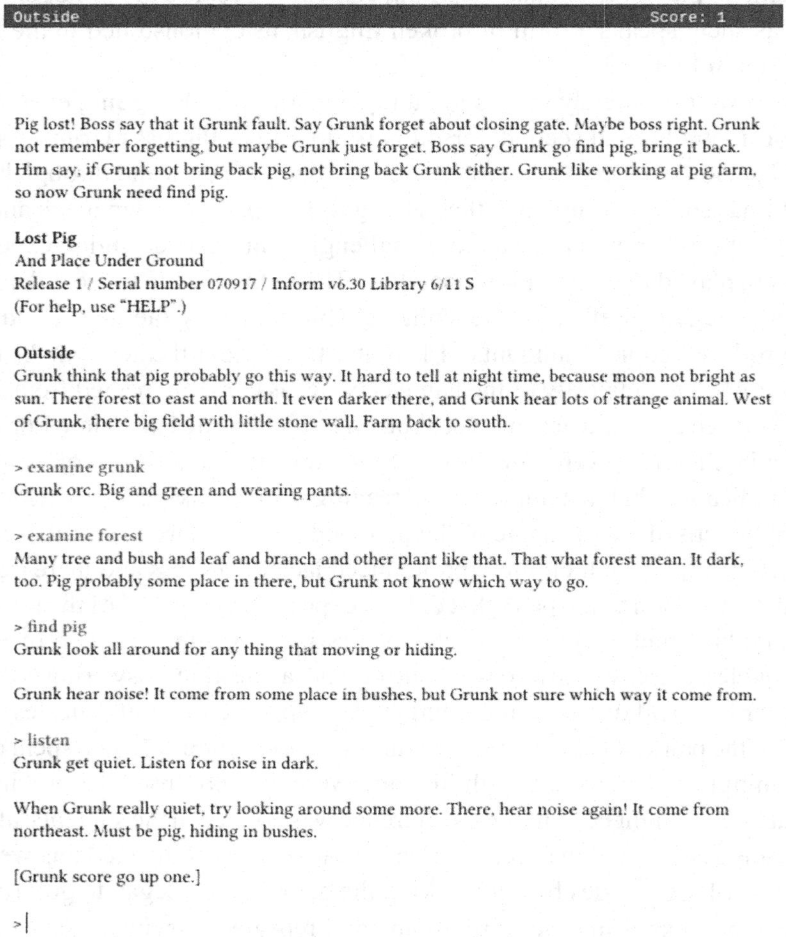

```
Outside                                                    Score: 1

Pig lost! Boss say that it Grunk fault. Say Grunk forget about closing gate. Maybe boss right. Grunk
not remember forgetting, but maybe Grunk just forget. Boss say Grunk go find pig, bring it back.
Him say, if Grunk not bring back pig, not bring back Grunk either. Grunk like working at pig farm,
so now Grunk need find pig.

Lost Pig
And Place Under Ground
Release 1 / Serial number 070917 / Inform v6.30 Library 6/11 S
(For help, use "HELP".)

Outside
Grunk think that pig probably go this way. It hard to tell at night time, because moon not bright as
sun. There forest to east and north. It even darker there, and Grunk hear lots of strange animal. West
of Grunk, there big field with little stone wall. Farm back to south.

> examine grunk
Grunk orc. Big and green and wearing pants.

> examine forest
Many tree and bush and leaf and branch and other plant like that. That what forest mean. It dark,
too. Pig probably some place in there, but Grunk not know which way to go.

> find pig
Grunk look all around for any thing that moving or hiding.

Grunk hear noise! It come from some place in bushes, but Grunk not sure which way it come from.

> listen
Grunk get quiet. Listen for noise in dark.

When Grunk really quiet, try looking around some more. There, hear noise again! It come from
northeast. Must be pig, hiding in bushes.

[Grunk score go up one.]

>|
```

However, despite the difficulty the learners may have experienced playing Lost Pig, they all played the game without demonstrating any vocal intention of stopping or changing activities.

Results from the Questionnaire

The following comments made by the students were written in English and have not been edited. I have added *italics* for my own emphasis.

Feedback from the questionnaire showed that nine of the ten students enjoyed playing IF during the lesson. Being a professed gamer, the sole student who said he didn't enjoy playing IF commented: "I prefer games with images and lots of different sounds. IF is a bit difficult and it takes ten times more time to play the game than if it was on a Playstation." While unfair comparisons to modern graphical games were to be expected, feedback also produced some interesting data regarding the students' perceptions of IF as a game or as an educational activity. Seven students, including the one mentioned previously, stated that they considered IF to be both a game and an educational activity. One student, touching upon the engaging and stealth learning affordances of DGBL eloquently noted:

It's a game because you have fun playing it and because it has the characteristics of a game. It's educational because the educational component is always present during the game. In IF, although you are learning English, you sometimes don't understand it because you are really enjoying the game.

Other students remarked:

- "IF is both, because it is a *game* that interacts with the player and makes us use English (but not any word) – we must think of a strategy to solve the *game*."
- "It's like a *game* – we have to reach a goal by doing things that can be tough sometimes and it is educational as we learn English because we pay more attention to what is written because we want to move on."

The idea of having 'fun' while playing IF was also mentioned numerous times:

- "I had the freedom to make the character do what I wanted him to do and I didn't know what to expect next – that's what makes IF games *fun*."
- "I felt like I was living a random story, which was *fun* and allowed me to use my imagination in order to command my character."
- "When playing the game it *felt very good* when we finally were able to find something important."
- "It's a good way to practise English because you feel the urge to keep playing."

The students' use of the expressions "fun, felt very good" and "urge", can be understood as evidence of IF as being a source of pleasure, and therefore, engaging.

With regards to student perceptions on the aspects of English that were being practised when playing IF, seven of the ten learners mentioned vocabulary, with four of them referring specifically to learning about using verbs.

Some examples of this:

- "You learn new vocabulary while reading IF."
- "We need to think about verbs in order to advance in the game because we are more focused on the text of the game and because in order to finish it we need to pay a lot of attention to find out things that allow us to move on. Besides that, we learn vocabulary."
- "You have to know a lot of verbs (but not like the past or past participle of the verbs), a lot of vocabulary."
- "It could be an important tool to learn new vocabulary and to use different types of vocabulary that is used in more practical situations and not typical classroom behaviour."
- "English is being practised when you command your character and you sometimes have to try to find other words to say the same thing you meant for the computer to understand what you are saying."

Student perceptions on the most practiced skills, were in line with my own thoughts about using IF for improving reading fluency, as can be seen in Figure 3.

The graph shows that the students believe the reading and writing skills are the most practised, followed by speaking and listening. This is interesting for the fact that many of the students were unaware of how much they speak and listen to each other while engaged in CMCL.

Figure 3. Perceptions on skills practised

Perceptions on skills practised

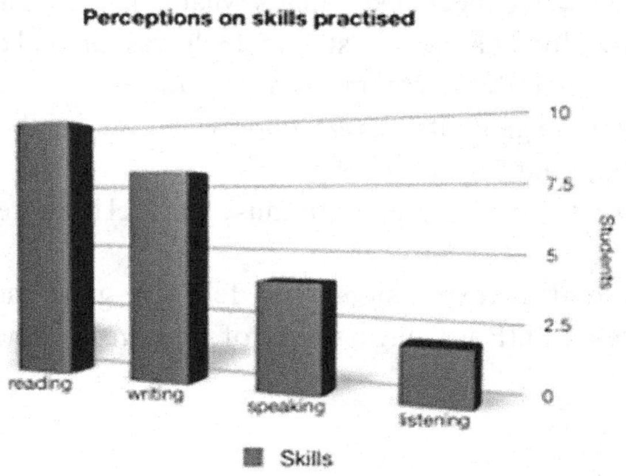

Some examples of students' answers to the question "What skills do you think can be developed by playing IF?":

- "Reading and writing but also a bit of speaking because you try to answer the game really fast, so I think it is helping you to use words and expressions when you're speaking English."
- "Writing and reading and you have to think in English."
- "Reading because we need to play a lot of attention to it and writing because we need to write everything correctly or the game won't accept it."
- "You'll improve your vocabulary, writing, speaking and correct some mistakes that you make."
- "All of them."

In addition to practising English skills, the majority of students commented on how IF was useful for developing problem-solving skills and imagination, as can be seen in the following answers to question "What else can you learn by playing IF?":

- "Our imagination and the ability to build a world in our mind around the games story."
- "Our minds get faster and you can solve more complex problems in the future."
- "Imagination skill, solve puzzles and problems."
- "It improves your capacity to solve problems."
- "You acquire more logical skills and you develop your imagination."
- "The ability to solve problems and learn to use your imagination."

It is interesting to note that the students themselves recognised the need for these qualities when playing IF and later used the exact terminology of 'imagination' and 'solve problems' to answer the open-ended question in the questionnaire. This further shows that the learning affordances of IF can be clearly recognised, even after only playing for a short time.

Several students also mentioned that IF can contribute to learning organisational skills, persistence, and content and cultural knowledge from the story.

From the interpretation of these results, it is possible to conclude that IF is a motivating and engaging way to practise English language skills as part of an English lesson. However, in order to improve their reading fluency, learners need to read large quantities of texts and often, which requires that they be motivated enough to read outside of the classroom. With regards to motivation, which is often reported in DGBL research, Whitton (2007), notes that results of her study showed that "there was no evidence that that there is any relationship between motivation to

71

play a game for leisure and a motivation to use them for learning". Despite focusing on adult learners with different educational aims than the sample in this study, I believe that IF can actually benefit from this fact. Because it is text-based and does not have flashy graphics and control mechanics, to teachers and learners who are unfamiliar with or wary about using video games for learning, IF does not look as intimidating or give as much of an overt idea of leisure as many other graphical genres of video game. It looks serious and its more immediate affordances can be quickly measured. Because of this, even gamers, usually fickle about the games they play for leisure, may well give IF a chance as an educational tool, if not as a pleasurable game.

In order to discover if the engaging and educational characteristics of IF can extend beyond the classroom, the students were asked if they would consider playing it at home in two different scenarios: for leisure (with no specific learning goal) and for practising English (specifically as an autonomous learning activity).

Five of the ten students answered that they would play IF as a leisure activity, while three gave an answer of 'maybe' and two said 'no'. However, all of the 'maybe' answers demonstrate a positive attitude towards IF as a leisure activity:

...not as a first choice to play at home, but I liked it

Maybe, because I had a great time playing it

The two students who answered negatively mentioned that they would rather spend their free time playing other types of games, or doing other kinds of activities, such as playing sports.

When asked if they would consider playing IF as an autonomous learning activity to practice English, the majority of students (seven out of ten) answered affirmatively. One student said "maybe" and two students replied negatively, commenting that they would prefer to do more traditional practice exercises.

Final Results

The results of this research confirm that IF can potentially be used as an engaging and entertaining way for learners of English as a foreign language to practise the four skills as a classroom activity, with a particular focus on reading and vocabulary building. Furthermore, seven of the ten students in this case study stated that they would definitely play IF at home for autonomous language practice, lending some credence to the hypothesis that IF is a valid alternative to traditional text for practicing reading fluency, as posited at the beginning of this case study.

CHALLENGES

Despite the students' universal agreement that IF is an engaging learning tool, some students noted that frustration can easily become a mitigating factor towards their continued engagement and enjoyment of the game. With regards to Lost Pig, some students stated:

If we aren't patient to try everything to solve the puzzle, you can't find out how to move in the game.

It got rather frustrating and although I was trying hard I couldn't move on it takes too much time.

I got frustrated when talking to the gnome and feeling like we're not getting any answers.

When asked what they considered to be the most difficult aspects of IF, most replies were related to knowing the right verbs to use, knowing the best way to express themselves and figuring out what to do.

This shows that like any activity, IF games must be carefully chosen so that they are appealing to the largest number of students in the class and are accessible in terms of difficulty and length. Moreover, giving appropriate support before and during the game (ex. pre-teaching vocabulary, giving verb lists, maps, and hints) is essential in order to avoid frustration, which may result in the students giving up on the game and on IF altogether. Some support in the form of gentle nudges and help with verbs was given to some of the students when they played 9:05, but no specific story-related help was given during the Lost Pig session, as I wanted to document how far the students could get without any guidance. Because of this, the students did not make much progress in the game, leading the majority of them (six out of ten) to prefer 9:05 over Lost Pig citing that Lost Pig was "too long", "too difficult" and "boring". This was an inevitable result of not helping students towards solutions to puzzles as soon as they began to feel frustrated. An additional factor that may have contributed to continued frustration was the constitution of some of the pairs. It is recommended that pairs or groups be a mix of strong and weak students (both linguistically and with regards to imagination and problem-solving skills), so that stronger students can help the weaker ones. For the purpose of this case study, I did not change any of the pairs, despite noting that two of the pairs playing 9:05 were not balanced, and as expected, they did not make very much progress playing Lost Pig and did not enjoy playing it as much as they did 9:05.

SUMMARY

Learners of English as a foreign language need to read large quantities of extended texts in English in order to become fluent readers. However, my experience as a teacher in Portugal has shown that students do not read English texts outside of the classroom. It is my belief that Interactive Fiction, a text-based genre of video game, which is both a participatory form of electronic literature, and a challenging game, can be used as an engaging tool for learners to practise reading for fluency, both in the classroom and as an autonomous learning tool. This case study aimed to analyse a group of learners' perceptions on whether Interactive Fiction is a valid tool for language skills practice and whether they found it to be an engaging gaming experience. Results from participant observation of the students playing 9:05 and Lost Pig and a follow-up questionnaire show that all the learners in the case study perceive Interactive Fiction to be an engaging way to practice reading and the majority of students in the sample stated they would use it for autonomous language skills practice. However, despite positive results, the sample of the case study is small and only focuses on one level of language proficiency. Future studies will involve a larger sample and a wider range of levels. Additionally, a puzzle-focused IF game and a narrative-focused IF game will be used and contrasted, in order to find out if the learners' perceptions on engagement are the same in each case. Beyond studying learner perceptions, there is a real need for empirical research on the actual linguistic benefits of using IF for language learning, specifically with regards to improvement in reading fluency.

REFERENCES

905 [Computer software]. (2000). Retrieved January 8, 2011 from http://adamcadre.ac/content/905.zip

Aarseth, E. (1997). *Cybertext: Perspectives on ergodic literature* (p. 3). Baltimore, MD: Johns Hopkins University Press.

Baek, Y. (2010). *Gaming for classroom-based learning: Digital role playing as a motivator of study*. Hershey, PA: IGI Global. doi:10.4018/978-1-61520-713-8

Bagherkazemi, M., & Alemi, M. (2010). Literature in the EFL/ESL classroom: Consensus and controversy. *LIBRI, 1*(1), 1–12.

Cheung, A., & Harrison, C. (1992). Microcomputer adventure games and second language acquisition: A study of Hong Kong tertiary students. In Pennington, M. C., & Stevens, V. (Eds.), *Computers in applied linguistics: An international perspective*. Clevedon, UK: Multilingual Matters Ltd.

Connolly, T. M., Stansfield, M. H., & Boyle, L. (Eds.). (2009). *Games-based learning advancements for multi-sensory human computer interfaces: Techniques and effective practices*. Hershey, PA: IGI Global. doi:10.4018/978-1-60566-360-9

Cornillie, F., Jacques, I., De Wannemacker, S., Paulussen, H., & Desmet, P. (2011). Vocabulary treatment in adventure and role-playing games: A playground for adaptation and adaptivity. In S. De Wannemacker, G. Clarebout, & P. De Causmaecker (Eds.), *Interdisciplinary approaches to adaptive learning: A look at the neighbours: The First International Conference on Interdisciplinary Research on Technology, Education and Communication, Revised Selected Papers,* ITEC 2010, Kortrijk, Belgium, May 25-27, 2010, (pp. 132-148). Springer.

Csikszentmihalyi, M. (1991). *Flow: The psychology of optimal experience*. Harper Perennial.

de Freitas, S. (2006a). *Learning in immersive worlds*. Joint Information Systems Committee. Retrieved January 8, 2011, from http://www.jisc.ac.uk/media/documents/programmes/elearninginnovation/gamingreport_v3.pdf

de Freitas, S. (2006b). Using games and simulations for supporting learning. In C. Martin & L. Murray (Eds.), *Learning, Media and Technology Special Issue on Gaming, 31*(4), 343-358.

de Freitas, S. (2008). Emerging trends in serious games and virtual worlds. *Emerging Technologies for Learning, 3*.

de Haan, J. W. (2005). Learning language through video games: A theoretical framework, an evaluation of game genres and questions for future research. In Schaffer, S., & Price, M. (Eds.), *Interactive convergence: Critical issues in multimedia* (pp. 229–239). The Inter-Disciplinary Press.

Desilets, B. (1989). Reading, thinking, and interactive fiction. *English Journal, 78*(3), 75–77. doi:10.2307/819460

Desilets, B. (1999). Interactive fiction vs. the pause that distresses: How computer-based literature interrupts the reading process without stopping the fun. *Currents in Electronic Literacy, 1*. Retrieved January 8, 2011, from http://www.cwrl.utexas.edu/currents/spr99/desilets.html

Facer, K., Ulicsak, M., & Sandford, R. (2007). Futurelab. Computer Games in Education. In *Emerging Technologies for Learning,* Vol. 2. Becta. Retrieved January 8, 2011 from http://partners.becta.org.uk/page_documents/research/emerging_technologies07_chapter5.pdf.

Finocchiaro, M., & Brumfit, C. (1983). *The functional-notional approach.* Oxford, UK: Oxford University Press.

Foreman, J., Gee, J. P., Herz, J. C., Hinrichs, R., Prensky, M., & Sawyer, B. (2004). Game-based learning: How to delight and instruct in the 21st century. *EDUCAUSE Review, 39*(5), 50–66.

Gee, J. P. (2007a). *What video games have to teach us about learning and literacy* (2nd ed.). New York, NY: Palgrave Macmillan. doi:10.1145/950566.950595

Gee, J. P. (2007b). *Good video games and good learning: Collected essays on video games, learning and literacy (New literacies and digital epistemologies).* New York, NY: Peter Lang Publishers.

Grabe, M., & Dosmann, M. (1988). The potential of adventure games for the development of reading and study skills. *Journal of Computer-Based Instruction, 15*(2), 72–77.

Hişmanoğlu, M. (2005). Teaching English through literature. *Journal of Language and Linguistic Studies, 1*(1), 53-66. Retrieved January 8, 2011, from http://jlls.org/Issues/Volume1/No.1/murathismanoglu.pdf

Hudson, T. (1998). The effects of induced schemata on the "short circuit" in L2 reading: Non-decoding factors in L2 reading performance. In Carell, P. L., Devine, J., & Eskey, D. E. (Eds.), *Interactive approaches to second language reading* (pp. 183–205). Cambridge, UK: Cambridge University Press.

Hunicke, R., LeBlanc, M., & Zubek, R. (2004). MDA: A formal approach to game design and game research. *Proceedings of the Challenges in Game AI Workshop, Nineteenth National Conference on Artificial Intelligence.* Retrieved January 8, 2011, from http://www.cs.northwestern.edu/~hunicke/MDA.pdf

Ingold, J. (2009). Thinking into the box: On the use and deployment of puzzles. In K. Jackson-Mead & J. R. Wheeler (Eds.), *IF theory reader* (pp. 229-247). Retrieved January 8, 2011, from http://www.lulu.com/items/volume_71/11643000/11643447/1/print/10228464_IFTheoryBookv2.pdf

Kee, K., Vaughan, T., & Graham, S. (2010). The haunted school on horror hill: A case study of interactive fiction in the classroom. In Baek, Y. (Ed.), *Gaming for classroom-based learning: Digital role playing as a motivator of study* (pp. 113–124). Hershey, PA: IGI Global. doi:10.4018/978-1-61520-713-8.ch007

Keller, D. (2007). Reading and playing: what makes interactive fiction unique. In Williams, J. P., & Smith, J. H. (Eds.), *The players' realm: Studies on the culture of video games and gaming* (pp. 276–298). Jefferson, NC: McFarland & Co.

Lancy, D. F., & Hayes, B. L. (1988). Interactive fiction and the reluctant reader. *English Journal, 77*(7), 42-66. Retrieved January 8, 2011, from http://www.jstor.org/stable/818936

Lost Pig [Computer software]. (2007). Retrieved January 8, 2011 from http://www.grunk.org/lostpig/

Malone, T. W., & Lepper, M. R. (1987). Making learning fun: A taxonomy of intrinsic motivations for learning. In Snow, R. E., & Farr, M. J. (Eds.), *Aptitude, learning and instruction: III- Conative and affective process analyses* (pp. 223–253). Hillsdale, NJ: Erlbaum.

Mawer, K., & Stanley, G. (2011). *Digital play Computer games and language aims*. Delta Publishing.

McLouglin, C., & Oliver, R. (1998). Maximising the language and learning link in computer learning environments. *British Journal of Educational Technology, 29*(2), 125–136. doi:10.1111/1467-8535.00054

Michael, D. R., & Chen, S. L. (2005). *Serious games: Games that educate, train, and inform* (p. 46). Muska & Lipman / Premier-Trade.

Montfort, N. (2003). *Twisty little passages: An approach to interactive fiction*. London, UK: MIT Press.

Neville, D., Shelton, B. E., & McInnis, B. (2009). Cybertext redux: Using DGBL to teach L2 vocabulary, reading and culture. *Computer Assisted Language Learning, 22*(5), 409–424. doi:10.1080/09588220903345168

Niesz, A. J., & Holland, N. N. (1984). Interactive fiction. *Critical Inquiry Chicago, 11*(1), 110–129. doi:10.1086/448277

Nunan, D. (1991). Language teaching methodology. London, UK: Prentice Hall International.

O'Brian, P. (1993). *Interactive fiction and reader response criticism.* Unpublished paper, University of Colorado, Boulder. Retrieved January 8, 2011 from http://spot.colorado.edu/~obrian/ifrrc.txt

Palmberg, R. (1988). Computer games and foreign-language vocabulary learning. *English Language Teaching Journal, 42*(4), 247–252. doi:10.1093/elt/42.4.247

Panichi, L., Deutschmann, M., & Molka-Danielsen, J. (2010). Virtual worlds for language learning and intercultural exchange: Is it for real? In Guth, S., & Helm, F. (Eds.), *Telecollaboration 2.0: Languages, literacies and intercultural learning in the 21st century* (pp. 165–195). Bern, Switzerland: Peter Lang.

Pereira, J. (2011a). *The AVALON project and Second Life - The analysis and selection of a virtual world for language learning and teaching.* Retrieved January 8, 2011 from http://avalon.humanities.manchester.ac.uk/wpcontent/uploads/2010/11/AVALON_Second_Life_Report.pdf

Pereira, J. (2011b). A narrative at war with a crossword - An introduction to Interactive Fiction. In H. Görür-Atabaş & S. Turner (Eds.), *Expectations eclipsed in foreign language education: Learners and educators on an ongoing journey* (pp. 87-96). İstanbul, Turkey: SabancıÜniversitesi. Retrieved January 8, 2011, from http://digital.sabanciuniv.edu/ebookacik/3011200000287.pdf

Pereira, J. (in press). Using Interactive Fiction for digital game-based language learning. In Garton, S., & Graves, K. (Eds.), *International perspectives in ELT materials.* Palgrave MacMillan.

Piper, A. (1986). Conversation and the computer. A study of the conversational spin-off generated among learners of English as a foreign language working in groups. *System, 4*(2), 187–198. doi:10.1016/0346-251X(86)90008-4

Plotkin, A., & Albaugh, L. (2010). *IF-for-beginner's card.* Retrieved January 8, 2011, from http://pr-if.org/doc/play-if-card/

Prensky, M. (2006). *Don't bother me mom, I'm learning!: How computer and video games are preparing your kids for twenty-first century success and how you can help!* St. Paul, MN: Paragon House.

Prensky, M. (2007). *Digital game-based learning: Practical ideas for the application of digital game-based learning.* St. Paul, MN: Paragon House.

Reinders, H., & Wattana, S. (2011). Learn English or die: The effects of digital games on interaction and willingness to communicate in a foreign language. *Digital Culture and Education, 3*(1), 4–28.

Richards, J. C., & Rodgers, T. S. (2001). *Approaches and methods in language teaching* (2nd ed.). New York, NY: Cambridge University Press. doi:10.1017/CBO9780511667305

Ryan, M. (2006). *Avatars of story*. Minneapolis, MN: University of Minnesota Press.

Salen, K., & Zimmerman, E. (2003). *Rules of play: Game design fundamentals*. Cambridge, MA: MIT Press.

Schank, R., & Abelson, R. (1977). *Scripts, plans, goals, and understanding: An inquiry into human knowledge structures*. Hillsdale, NJ: Lawrence Erlbaum.

Taguchi, E., Gorsuch, G., & Sasamoto, E. (2006). Developing second and foreign language reading fluency and its effect on comprehension: A missing link. [from http://www.readingmatrix.com/articles/taguchi_gorsuch_sasamoto/article.pdf]. *The Reading Matrix*, 6(2), 1–17. Retrieved January 8, 2011

The Entertainment Software Association (ESA). (2011). *Essential facts about the computer game industry, 2011*. Retrieved January 8, 2011, from http://www.theesa.com/facts/pdfs/ESA_EF_2011.pdf

The Horizon Report. (2007). *EDUCAUSE learning initiative: The New Media Consortium*. Retrieved January 8, 2011, from http://www.nmc.org/pdf/2007_Horizon_Report.pdf

Thorne, S., Wheatley, J., & Purushotma, R. (2009). *10 key principles for designing video games for foreign language learning*. Retrieved January 8, 2011 from http://lingualgames.wordpress.com/article/10-key-principles-for-designing-video-27mkxqba7b13d-2/

Thorne, S. L. (2008). Transcultural communication in open internet environments and massively multiplayer online games. In Magnan, S. (Ed.), *Mediating discourse online* (pp. 305–327). Amsterdam, The Netherlands: John Benjamins.

Whitton, N. (2007). *An investigation into the potential of collaborative computer game-based learning in higher education*. PhD Thesis, Napier University, Edinburg, UK. Retrieved January 8, 2011, from http://playthinklearn.net/?page_id=8

Whitton, N. (2010). *Learning with digital games*. New York, NY: Routledge.

KEY TERMS AND DEFINITIONS

Communicative Language Teaching (CLT): An approach to language teaching that has as its foremost goal the learner becoming competent at basic communication.

Computer-Mediated Collaborative Learning (CMCL): Using a single computer to provide an authentic task for learners to engage in social communication with one another (asking for repetition, giving opinions, agreeing, etc.).

Digital Game-Based Learning (DGBL): Using the learning principles and engaging characteristics of video games for education.

Interactive Fiction (IF): A text-based genre of video game, which is a blend of storytelling and problem-solving.

Interpreter: The software that reads an IF game file and presents it to the player on their screen.

Non-Player Character (NPC): A character in a game that is not controlled by the player.

Parser: The element of an IF game that receives input in natural language from the player, analyses it, and responds with meaningful output.

Schema: The mental images we create of the world, which allow us to link concepts and understand what is communicated.

Section 2
Teaching with Educational Games

Chapter 5
Civilization IV in 7th Grade Social Studies:
Motivating and Enriching Student Learning with Constructivism, Content standards, and 21st Century Skills

Solomon Senrick
American School of Bombay, India

EXECUTIVE SUMMARY

Civilization IV allows a player to experience the development and management of complex components of an empire, like technology acquisition, trade, and diplomacy. It includes a thorough encyclopedia-like reference tool, Civilopedia, which a player can use to inform one's decision making. When the game is broken down into parts and approached with thoughtful, creative pedagogy, students are motivated to learn historical concepts, systems thinking, and skills like information fluency and creativity at their own pace.

OVERALL DESCRIPTION

The purpose of this case was to explore how using the digital game Civilization IV could encourage constructivist learning, target social studies content standards, cultivate 21st century skills, and increase student engagement. In Civilization IV, a player assumes the leadership of a civilization and develops cities and infrastructure, trade and economic policy, government, technology and various other elements. In this case, students played the game in pairs.

DOI: 10.4018/978-1-4666-2848-9.ch005

This case study was of a 7th grade social studies class. There are two enduring understandings of the Beliefs and History unit in which the game was played. The first is that events in history have shaped, and been shaped by beliefs and cultures. The second is that historians use specific tools and thought processes to make sense of the past. To support these enduring understandings, instruction was focused on the American Education Reaches Out (AERO) standards primarily on historical knowledge, skills and concepts, and also other strands. (See Table 1 in Appendix A) The case also targeted 21st century skills, as defined by the American School of Bombay, including creativity, critical thinking, collaboration, information fluency, and managing complexity. The game was played in classes over approximately 20 days. The 80 minute block class structure was divided into segments with approximately half the time dedicated to game play, and the rest to learning specific historical topics in other traditional ways, including readings, research, and discussions.

This case took place in an international school in Mumbai, India with a student population representing at least 20 nationalities. Classes of the case study range from 14-18 students, of which approximately 5-8% receive ESOL support and 5-8% academic support. By 7th grade, nearly all students in the study have used laptops for learning in a 1:1 environment since 6th grade. The school has a very active and supportive tech department, of 8-10 people, who are available to assist students and teachers before, after and throughout the school day. During the case study period, tech support staff was available and present in the classroom to help when needed, approximately 2-4 hours total over the 20 days.

The teacher in this case participated in school taskforces researching and developing best practice in areas like Game Based Learning, Personalized Learning, and 21st Century Skills. At the time of the case study, the teacher had been teaching in a 1:1 laptop program for 3 years.

LITERATURE REVIEW

Various writings focus on digital games in Middle School Classrooms and how they can impact motivation, teach historical skills and concepts, and develop 21st Century Skills. Ray and Coulter (2010) identify authentic learning and active engagement, as well as motivation, as being key to integrating games in the Middle School. They acknowledge in their review of literature that "early studies suggest that carefully selected digital games can support content learning at middle school levels." (Ray and Coulter, 2010, p.94) Ray and Coulter also state that, "digital games provide clear roles for learners to assume, thus motivating students to learn." (2010, p.94) Ray and Coulter's study of pre-service teachers also concludes that "how teacher perceive the efficacy of digital mini-games will determine whether the games will be integrated at all into classroom instruction, and then, if integrated, how effectively they will be used." (2010, p.98) When considering incorporating a complex game like Civilization IV, playing the game and perceiving its value were important for this case study. As the teacher played the game and saw the potential for student learning, the integration level and effectiveness of using the game was improved.

J.V. Bolkan (2010) makes a case for the role that games can play in developing 21st century skills--Creativity and Innovation, Communication and Collaboration, Research and Information Fluency, etc.--as outlined by the National Educational Technology Standards (NETS) for students. In regards to creativity and innovation, Bolkan states, "As [students] become more accomplished [in games], players will often find creative and innovative ways to succeed, based on strategies that have worked well in other games, earlier in that game, or in real life situations." (2010, p. 79) For students developing information fluency skills, Bolkan states that "all but the most basic games have a plethora of resources available" and "guiding students to these and requiring them to research and evaluate the various resources would help them" achieve 21st century skill mastery. (2010, p. 80) Bolkan gives similar rationale and connections to other 21st Century skills. (2010) In addition to linking game based learning to important 21st century skills, Bolkan highlights the important of good pedagogy in using game based learning. For example, Bolkan advocates the importance of teacher support before and after game play to ensure effectiveness. (2010, p. 76)

Betrus and Botturi identify benefits to learning and principles for educators on integrating games in instruction that include increased motivation, complex under-standing, reflective learning, and feedback and self-regulation (2010, p. 43-46). The advantages they identify fit in this case's focus on 21st century skills and construc-tivist learning. For example, they describe Complex Understanding as "Complex processes, especially relationships among systems and system components", which connects to the skill of managing complexity. In games, "players learn to refine their choices and to control their actions" (Betrus and Botturi, 2010, p. 46), emphasizing a constructivist learning environment, with students developing decision making and critical thinking skills.

Civilization's application in teaching and learning has been addressed in previous studies. Betrus and Botturi reference a study of Civilization where, "Squire, Giova-netto, Devane, and Durga (2005) found that students tend to acquire a fundamental understanding of the workings of society, including politics, the military and civilian life." (2010, p. 45) Whelchel identified a number of potential projects and teaching methods to use with civilization simulator games: Hands-on History, Pet Civiliza-tion, and Deconstruction Fun (2003). In Hands-on History, in small groups students played a game for a semester, and kept journals about their progress in decision making and outcomes. The teacher provided prompts that focused on "historical processes such as trade, colonization, or technological development rather than on discrete historical events." (Whelchel, 2003, n.p.) Pet Civilization was suggested as an out of class activity, where students would discuss and write on the "accuracy of the game in its portrayal of the civilization and a narrative describing game play and the actual historical record diverged." (Whelchel, 2003, n.p.) Whelchel also acknowledged that teachers might not have "time to properly prepare students to master the game well enough to gain some historical insight." (2003).

PRACTICALITIES OF RUNNING THE GAME

Executing the game in class is broken down into four stages: (1) Teacher exploration of the game (2) Introduction of the game to students (3) Day to day play, mini-lessons and skill targets (4) Final project work.

Teacher Exploration of Game

As suggested by Betrus and Botturi, the teacher must be both a content expert and a game expert and should "Play the game—a lot" (2010, p. 51). In this particular case, the teacher had played and enjoyed the original Civilization as a middle school student. This was motivational in selecting Civilization IV as a learning tool in a history unit. The teacher spent approximately 15 hours outside of class playing the game in order to understand and master the game itself. The game is quite complex, requiring the understanding of multiple screens, manipulation of various units, modifying allocation of resources, selecting and understanding the progression of technological advancement, etc. In order to facilitate student learning effectively, for instance determining what game aspects to focus on and expect students to fully understand, teacher play of the game was a significant first step. While playing the game, the teacher considered the application to historical knowledge/content as well as 21st century skills. For example, he considered the historical accuracy, potential for historical skill/process development (cause and effect, chronology), opportunities to develop information fluency skills, and others. In this case, a fellow teacher was learning and playing the game concurrently. On numerous occasions, the two teachers met to discuss their game playing experiences, identify teaching applications, trouble shoot potential issues and other relevant topics. After hours of game play spread out over a few weeks, the teacher was ready to integrate the game into the class.

Introducing Game to Students

As suggested by Betrus and Botturi (2011), conducting a briefing before game play is critical to insure learning in the game. When launching game play in this case, sufficient class time was dedicated to discussing the purpose of playing the game, its goal and rules, expectations of student partnerships, intended outcomes from game play, and the various assessments that would take place over the course and at the conclusion of play. Also, the essential questions for the game playing unit were shared: (1) How must history be studied in order to understand how people, cultures and beliefs have changed over time? (2) How have different historical events influenced and been influenced by cultures and belief systems? These questions directed the day to day activities described below.

Students were told that they would be working with a partner to lead a civilization in a simulation game. The partners had to agree on goals for their civilization, for instance whether to be leaders in technology, economics, military, culture or a combination of these. Students then were told that they would be tracking their daily play and game decisions that they believed would help them achieve their Civilization's goal. This approach, of selecting a focus for the civilization and making decisions to achieve the focus, were connected in class discussion to the essential questions of the unit. This also achieved the goal of creating a constructivist learning experience as students directed their learning around their own goals, as opposed to a pre-determined outcome.

After outlining the goals and objectives of the game play, the teacher modeled game play using a wireless projector. In this first modeling, the teacher taught the important basic game features to begin play, including how to: (1) Establish a city and manage it from the city screen (2) Manipulate/move/use units (3) Use various game resources like the technology progression chart (4) Access and understand the Civilopedia pages. During this demonstration, the teacher explained the basic components of each of these, with the expectation that students would be able to explain how they had explored each of the four features after a few days of game play.

After the demo, students logged in to the game computers, and began game play. The first 3-4 class periods were devoted to game play focused more on exploration and understanding how to use the logistical features of the game. During game play, the teacher also circulated and gave feedback to individual partnerships. After each of the first few class periods, the students and teacher debriefed logistical issues of the game and other challenges they had. It was important to master the logistics in order to shift the focus to learning skills and content.

Day to Day Play: Constructivist Learning and 21st Century Skills

After 3-4 class periods where students explored the game and gained a basic understanding of its functionality, students were directed to focus on their civilization goal—political power, military power, trading power, cultural leader, or combination of goals. Some students opted to begin a new game. Students were told that they would track their progress towards their goal, and have to justify how their game decisions aligned with their goal. This approach was intended to allow students to construct learning around their partnership's goals, and develop 21st century skills, like communication and critical thinking. During the remaining days of game play, the teacher incorporated daily mini-lessons prior to play. These mini-lessons taught students how to understand a number of features more in depth that would help them succeed with their goal.

One mini-lesson focused on how to understand and use the technology flow chart. The game provides a flow chart which diagrams the progression of technological advancement. For example, to attain "Metal Casting" technology, first a civilization must acquire "Pottery" and "Bronze Working." When a player acquires a technology in the game, it unlocks certain capabilities for the Civilization. For example, the technology of Metal Casting allows students to build a Workshop, which, when built in a city, speeds up the production of buildings and military units. Students with the goal of having a powerful military would focus on developing such technology. Students had to consider which technologies would help them reach their goals, and then make decisions that would help them acquire such technologies. Not only did this allow students to construct their own learning experience, but it also helped them develop critical thinking skills, as they considered multiple options and determined which technologies would be most useful for their civilization's development. They had to think ahead, in terms of what they wanted their Civilization to achieve, and then reflect later on the decisions that they made and how it impacted their civilization.

Another mini-lesson that facilitated a constructivist experience was on urban planning and unit selection. Again, in order to reach their goals, students had to make decisions about what to build in their cities. For example, students wanting a strong military had to think about what buildings and units to create in order to strengthen their armies. Students might select the development of a barracks, which provided extra attack and defense power for units, over a library, which improved the amount of technology points that the city contributed to the civilization. By focusing in on their cities, students again had to think critically--plan ahead, weigh the outcomes of their building selections, and learn from their decisions on what worked and what didn't in respect to their goal. On the day of this lesson, students blogged on how they justified their gaming decisions that day. In the class Ning, one student wrote, "we decided to build a powerful military that was always prepared for anything, so we're going to build a military academy, since we've just entered the Renaissance Era. A military academy in just one city will improve the experience of all of the units constructed in that afterward. To construct one, you need to have military science, which in turn needs economics and chemistry. We are getting chemistry, and right afterward we will get economics."

Third, and most importantly, students were instructed on the benefits of using the Civilopedia pages. The Civilopedia feature, defined in this case's glossary, provides background and historical information, as well as the game enhancements associated with each particular element of the game. For example, there are Civilopedia pages on military units, technologies, buildings, adversaries, terrain, and all other features of the game. For instance, The Hanging Gardens page explains what technology is required, the special abilities it grants, a historical overview, and its cost and benefits. During game play, students were directed to read Civilopedia pages in order to inform their decision making. Following game play, students were required to reflect on how the Civilopedia was used to help them make their decisions. By using Civilopedia in this way, students' constructed knowledge and information fluency skills based on their own game experiences and needs. Additionally, students implored information literacy skills, as they identified which pages were relevant for their work, determined relevant information for their civilization's goal, and applied their understanding of the resource in their decision making.

Day to Day: Content Standards

In addition to using game play as a way for students to construct learning and build 21st Century skills based on their Civilization goals, game play also targeted specific historical skills and standards. The standards taught and addressed through game play included primary and secondary source analysis, using cause and effect/ chronology to explain history, explaining the role of technology in history, and others. For instance, students must identify and use primary and secondary sources in research. Another example being, students can use chronology and cause and effect to explain patterns of historical change. Periodically throughout the Civilization unit, the teacher did mini-lessons explaining how to understand standards embedded in the game. One such lesson focused on analyzing a Civilopedia page for primary and secondary sources. The teacher began by modeling how the Civilization creators had used primary and secondary sources in their Civilopedia pages. On many, but not all Civilopedia pages, there are references to primary sources, basic primary source quotes from historical figures, as well as the historical descriptions that are secondary sources. In this mini-lesson, the teacher used a think aloud to describe how a particular Civilopedia page could be analyzed for its use of primary and secondary sources. For instance, the class discussed what transition words are associated with chronological writing, and then the teacher read through the historical narrative and asked students to identify transition words related to chronology. The lesson was also used to teach how chronology and cause and effect were used in the Civilopedia page. For example, sections of the Civilopedia page explain how the particular topic being described, for instance, barracks, would have impacts for the player, in this case increasing the defensive strength of units. After the lesson, students were expected to analyze Civilopedia pages during game play, and then blog about it afterwards. Other mini lessons followed, for instance on how and why technology is adopted, and how global interactions and conflict lead to historical change. Pedagogical approaches to these lessons included teacher-directed think-aloud or modeling, followed by student practice and formative assessment through blogging.

TECHNOLOGY COMPONENTS

The minimum system requirements for Civilization IV include Window 2000/XP operating system, 1.2 GHz Intel Pentium processor, 256 MB Ram, 1.7 GB hard disk space, and others. To meet these requirements, the case employed 10 specific game computers to be used. All aspects of setting up the game, like acquiring licensing and uploading software, were completed by the school's tech office staff.

During game play, students relied on two separate computers, the school issued game computer for playing, and their personal computer for tracking and reflecting on their progress. The rationale for this decision was based on cost, efficiency, and focus. First, it was less time consuming and expensive to upload the game onto a set of 10 machines that would be used by multiple classes, as opposed to uploading on to 60 student machines. Also, by uploading on the school's class set of gaming computers, it was more efficient for maintenance and managing game time and use during class. Finally, it focused the game play to class time, as opposed to having students have the game accessible to them at home, which might have led to distractions from other homework.

As there were 10 gaming machines available, students partnered up for game play. In this case, it benefited students communication and decision making skill development, as they had to discuss and evaluate ideas before putting them into action. Students had to listen to the ideas of their partner, resolve conflicts between each other, compromise on decisions, as well as other partner related processes. Each partnership was assigned to one game computer, as well as a respective login and password to access that particular machine. This was necessary as students had to save their game progress and resume play on the same machine each class.

Initially, there were some login issues related to students forgetting their usernames and passwords. This was resolved by the teacher creating a master list of logins and passwords for reference. Another issue that arose was related to the saving of games. Since each gaming computer was being used by students in three separate classes, there were occasions where students inadvertently uploaded the saved games of peers in other classes. To resolve this, a file naming protocol for games was established, with each partnership naming their saved game by their class and last names.

The teacher also relied on a wireless projector to model play and teach various components of the game.

EVALUATION

Game play was evaluated in a number of ways. Formative and summative assessments evaluated student learning of content and skills. Informal observations and a final course evaluation targeted student engagement and thoughts regarding playing the game.

Formative and Summative Assessments of Game Learning

Formative assessments of game learning took place through student blogging or class discussions, which took place daily after game play. Formal blogging questions and prompts targeted skills practiced that day. Sample questions included: What primary sources did you encounter in game play today? What do they mean, and why were they used?; Explain decisions you made in the game today that will help you reach your civilization's goal(s); How did your civilization benefit or falter based on cause and effect relationships that you experienced today? Students reflected on these questions on a class blog. They read the posts of others, and the teacher targeted instruction based on student reflections. In one class period, students discussed the historical narratives in the Civilopedia pages. Specifically, how did the writing in the Civilopedia pages use chronology and cause and effect to describe backgrounds of various game features. Students were given feedback as to whether they met the day's learning targets and how to improve if necessary.

The summative assessment for game play was to propose an addition to the next version of Civilization, and to compose a persuasive email for the suggestion. The assessment included 6 components: a historical narrative, cause/effect game connections, primary source(s), mashed up images, and professional quality. (See Table 2 in Appendix B) This assessment targeted skills and concepts that were addressed by game play, mini-lessons, blog reflections, and class discussions.

Informal Observations

No formal evaluation of students' experiences of playing the game took place; however, there were some observable trends during game play. From teacher observation, engagement level during the game play was generally higher for nearly all students, than it would be for other class activities. Examples of observed engagement include student discussions (on game play, historical content, 21st century skills and their goal attainment), student visual attention to the game computers and their partners, the level of student participation in form of asking questions and sharing successes with the teacher, their partners, and their peers, and the quality and quantity of oral and written reflection regarding their game playing experiences and lessons learned.

Final Course Evaluation

Within two weeks of finishing game play, students completed a class evaluation. The survey, given to all students, did not target Civilization play specifically. Rather, it was an end of the term survey given to evaluate numerous class elements including instruction, assessment, and engagement. Positive feedback for the game experience was prevalent in the survey feedback, indicating a formal acknowledgement of increased engagement and interest in using Civilization in the class. Specific comments included: "I like that we are playing Civilization while we are learning about the history of religions, it helps get an idea of how events such as war influenced the growth of religion." "Civilization is a computer game that helps us learn about primary sources, and a lot of other things." "I like playing civilization because it really shows how we can learn out of it with the questions we had to blog about."

CHALLENGES

Due to the teacher's tech integration experience, as well as a very involved and resourced tech support team, there were few logistical challenges during game play. There were some issues initially with logins and passwords, and saving and retrieving games, which were alluded to earlier in this chapter. By simple record keeping and basic organization instruction, the teacher could have prevented most of those issues. With a strong technical support team, most of the challenges for this case are not with using the technology, but rather with the facilitation of the game and assessing students.

With a game as complex as Civilization, identifying which features to emphasize with students was a challenge. Certain features of the game, like the role of selecting a government and establishing trade partners, were not directly targeted by the teacher. Understanding of these game components would affect students' success in reaching their goals. Students were encouraged to learn more about the game capabilities, and some did research on their own. By playing the game in advance, the teacher was able to identify specific learning targets that corresponded with standards.

While the time frame of 14-18 class days for the study was adequate for most students, it was clear from some blog posts that some students struggled with the complexity of the game. Like all instruction, facilitating the gaming experience required direct differentiation to meet students' needs. Identifying which students were struggling with understanding the game earlier on would have helped the teacher help those students.

Managing student responses and reflections was challenging for the teacher. With students focusing on a plethora of different gaming experiences and Civilopedia page references, it was difficult for the teacher to always assess them accurately. Initially, the teacher asked students to give multiple examples in their learning. For instance, when identifying primary sources, they needed to give 3 quotes and explain them. This proved to be too much for the teacher to manage. Therefore, as the case study progressed, questions for students required fewer examples, and were more specific about what learning they were to reflect.

SUMMARY

The digital game Civilization IV can engage students, personalize their learning, address social studies standards, and develop students' 21st century skills.

The effective facilitation of this digital game required hours of exploration and front loading by the teacher. The complexities of the game needed to be mastered, so that the teacher could troubleshoot with student issues. By playing the game in advance, the teacher also realized which historical standards and 21st century skills could be addressed by the game. It was important for the teacher to introduce the game, teach some of its functions, and provide a few days for students to explore and not be overwhelmed. Only after understanding the practicalities of the game could specific learning goals be targeted.

The facilitation of the game included daily mini-lessons on the various history standards, following which, students explored the topics through their gaming experience. Student blogging and class reflections were crucial to assessing student learning from the game. The summative assessment, based on creating an addition to the game, created an authentic and engaging way of measuring student learning.

Very few problems were encountered in using the technology, as the school in the study has a well-staffed tech support office. Challenges faced had to do with helping students manage the complexities of the game. Also challenging was monitoring the progress of individual students, based on formative assessments that were initially too lengthy to assess in a timely matter.

REFERENCES

AERO Social Studies Curriculum Framework. (n.d.) Retrieved from http://www.projectaero.org/ss/socialstudies.pdf

Betrus, A. K., & Botturi, L. (2010). Principles of playing games for learning. In A. Hirumi (Ed.), *Playing games in school: Video games and simulations for primary and secondary education* (pp. 33-56). Eugene, OR: International Society for Technology in Education

Bolkan, J. V. (2010). Playing games and the NETS. In A. Hirumi (Ed.), *Playing games in school: Video games and simulations for primary and secondary education* (pp. 33-56). Eugene, OR: International Society for Technology in Education

Ray, B., & Coulter, G. A. (n.d.). Perceptions of the value of digital mini-games: Implications for middle school classrooms. *Journal of Digital Learning in Teacher Education, 28*(3), 92-99.

Watson, W. R. (2010). Games for social studies education. In A. Hirumi (Ed.), *Playing games in school: Video games and simulations for primary and secondary education* (pp. 33-56). Eugene, OR: International Society for Technology in Education

Whelchel, A. (2003). Using civilization simulation video games in the world history classroom. *World History Connected, 4*(2), Retrieved from http://worldhistoryconnected.press.illinois.edu/4.2/whelchel.html

KEY TERMS AND DEFINITIONS

21st Century Skills: The key abilities and competencies, identified by the American School of Bombay, that students need for success currently and in the future including creativity and innovation, collaboration, communication, critical thinking, information fluency, global awareness, multicultural literacy, and managing complexity.

Civilopedia: Encyclopedia-like pages in the game Civilization IV intended to aid players in decision making, which include historical descriptions, primary sources, images and other information for the various game elements and topics like buildings, units, technologies, governments, etc.

Collaboration: Cooperative interaction between two or more individuals, with the intent to amplify and build versatility of skills, perspectives, roles, and experience in work towards a common goal.

Constructivism: An educational approach where learners acquire, test and construct knowledge and understanding based on their personal experiences, needs, and interactions with the environment.

Creativity and Innovation: Recognizing, producing, and acting on new ideas or actions that have purpose or relevance for a task, individual, or group.

Critical Thinking: purposeful, disciplined thinking that alters or informs a person's understanding, beliefs or actions.

Information Fluency: The process of locating, understanding, evaluating, and synthesizing information from multiple sources, and then applying findings in a meaningful or significant way.

Managing Complexity: The process of juggling various tasks, goals and inputs, while operating with certain time, resource and system constraints.

Ning: A social networking platform that allows users to share group work, discussions, blogs and other media.

APPENDIX A

AERO Standards and Mini-Lessons

Table 1. AERO Standards and Mini-Lessons

AERO Standard	Game Mini-Lesson
Use key concepts such as chronology, causality, and conflict to identify patterns of historical change	Learning objective: Describe how interactions between cultures/civilizations lead to historical change. (1) Prior to game play, students have learned about the diffusion of Buddhism in Asia through political and economic conditions. (2) Teacher poses questions "How are interactions with other cultures impacting your Civilization?" (3) In game play, students focus on how conflict, trade, and interactions with other civilization's leaders impacts their civilization (4) Class discussion after game play focuses on posed question. Formative Assessment—Students write reflection posts on the class Ning, describing how interactions lead to changes in Civilizations. Summative Assessment—In Civilopedia project, students must demonstrate evidence of the learning objective.
Describe the process whereby adoption of scientific knowledge and use of technologies influence cultures, the environment, economies, and balance of power.	Learning objective: Describe how adopting technology in Civilization impacts culture, environment, economy, etc. (1) Brief discussion on how technology impacts cultures (2) Students read through game technologies, and view the technology flow chart of the game to identify a technology to focus on (3) Using the technology's Civilopedia page, students identify how the selected technology will impact their Civilization's economy, culture, society, foreign affairs, etc. (4) Students play their game and see how the technology impacts their play (5) Class discussion connects readings on historical technology adoption, like science and math in the Islamic empire, to game experiences Summative assessment—Students write reflection paragraph addressing the learning objective.
Identify and use primary and secondary sources in historical research.	Learning objective: Explain how primary and secondary sources can be used purposefully. (1) Brief discussion—What are primary and secondary sources and why are they important in history? (2) Modeling—Teacher shows how and why Civilization game includes primary sources, in forms of quotations. Teacher explains how the game has used secondary sources, by writing historical narratives for the different game elements. (3) Students are directed in game play to identify primary sources and secondary sources in their play that day Formative assessment: Students write reflection on game play that identifies and describes the use of primary and secondary sources in the game. Summative assessment: In Civilopedia project, students must include primary sources and compose a historical narrative for their researched topic.

APPENDIX B

Beliefs and History: Civilization Unit Project

Table 2. Civilopedia page entry rubric

	3	2	1
Historical Narrative	Topic sentence and details are carefully selected to provide a strong overview of the topic. Topic sentence is phrased to address an open-ended question about the topic. Details are of excellent quality including important information such as who/where/when/why/what. Chronological transition words are used consistently throughout the narrative. Narrative includes occasional hyperlinks to find more information.	The paragraph gives a good overview of the topic. The topic sentence and details are clear, but could be improved with better vocabulary or clearer ideas. The topic sentence may address an open-ended question, but it is not fully clear. Details are of good quality regarding important information such as who/where/when/why/what. Chronological transition words are sometimes used in the narrative. Only one or two hyperlinks are added.	The paragraph is of poor quality and not written to address the chronology of the topic. The topic sentence clearly does not address an open-ended question and the details are lacking solid information or are not included at all. Chronological transition words are used incorrectly or are missing. No hyperlinks are added.
Cause/Effect Game Connections	At least 3 cause and effect relationships are used. Each example includes a well-detailed historical fact/connection and explains how/why the game is affected.	At least 2 cause and effect relationships are used. The examples show the historical fact/connection to the game, but may not be as clear. The explanation of how/why the game is affected is included, but could be worded much more clearly.	Only 1 or no cause and effect relationships are used. The examples either do not show the historical fact/connection to the game, or does not make sense. There is a poor explanation of how/why the game is affected, or it is not included at all.
Primary source	Relevant primary source excerpt(s) is/are included. The primary source is thoughtfully included within the narrative or on the proposal.	A primary source relating to the topic is included, but it is not as carefully placed within the narrative. If included on the proposal page it is unclear how it relates to the topic or game.	There is no primary source included or, the source is not relevant or clear to the topic.
Mashed Up Image(s)	Two-three images that relate to the topic, and that would be relevant to the game feature, are combined using Photoshop or another photo mashing tool.	Two images that relate to the topic are included. They both are relevant to the game and show use of a mashing tool. However, they may be a bit unclear.	No images are included or the included images are not mashed-up and do not relate to the game.
Professional Quality	Page is skillfully arranged and organized as in Civilization. Colors, font, headings engage the viewer. Mechanics (spelling, grammar, punctuation, capitalization) are of high standard with minimal errors.	Page is arranged clearly so that the viewer can understand the main ideas of the proposal. A bit more thought is needed to make it engaging. Mechanics (spelling, grammar, punctuation, capitalization) are addressed in some way, but more proofreading is needed.	Page is distracting or unclear. The viewer has a hard time understanding the idea of the proposal. Mechanics (spelling, grammar, punctuation, capitalization) have clearly not been addressed in making this a final copy.

Chapter 6
QRienteering:
Mobilising the M–Learner with Affordable Learning Games for Campus Inductions

Christopher Horne
Forth Valley College, UK

EXECUTIVE SUMMARY

This chapter presents a case study on the use of Quick Response (QR) technologies in learning. It examines how these technologies can be applied to create an affordable learning game, which provides learners with a more active and student-led collaborative approach to campus inductions, whilst also familiarising them with the use of mobile technologies within a learning environment. The study focuses upon the design principles and development of the mobile based game itself and learner response to the effectiveness and validity of the game in enhancing the campus induction process.

OVERALL DESCRIPTION

Introduction

Given the current economic climate and its resulting impact on intensifying operational pressures within educational institutions (IE, 2009; EUA, 2011), a general concern has arisen as to whether educational practitioners can 'afford' to develop and deliver new methods of technology enhanced learning. Are the increasing pressures on teaching, which can include: funding cutbacks, longer class contact time,

DOI: 10.4018/978-1-4666-2848-9.ch006

reduced practitioner development time, to name but a few, hindering any potential desire or progress in embracing and utilising games based technologies for teaching? (Williamson, 2009: p25).

Affordable Games

Three main factors are considered when determining the affordability of introducing a new form of technology driven learning: Development Time: Financial Cost & Technical Skill. These raise the following questions:

- Can practitioners afford the time, or do they possess the technical expertise, to develop and deliver technology driven teaching activities?
- Can the educational establishments financially afford or possess the infrastructure to accommodate emerging technology driven learning at an institutional level?
- Can learners be expected to successfully embrace technology enhanced learning, if they do not possess the technical knowledge and skills, or have access to technology to do so?

In an attempt to address these factors, it was decided to determine whether it was possible to develop and implement a new type of mobile games based learning. The purpose of the game would be to determine if its design could be easily replicated and implemented by practitioners and easily accessed by learners within a campus based educational environment.

Pilot Focus

The focus of this pilot was to introduce mobile learning opportunities, via a mobile based learning game, at the outset of the learner's academic journey. Its purpose was to highlight how mobile phone technology could be utilised for educational purposes and determine if mobile learning could deliver an active and collaborative experience for learners during the induction process.

Why QRienteering and What Does it Mean?

For lack of a better word, I have coined the term '*QRienteering*'; a portmanteau of QR (Quick Response) technology and Orienteering, to describe the mobile learning game for this particular pilot study. The game would adopt the sporting principles of Orienteering, whilst utilising QR code technology as an integral component of the games design.

Objectives of Pilot

The objectives of the 'QRienteering' game were fourfold; Firstly, to enhance campus familiarisation, promote group work and team bonding within the college induction process. Secondly, the game was intended to introduce learners to a more active and experiential approach to mobile learning opportunities and demonstrate to practitioners how electronic games based learning could be blended into real world physical activity. Thirdly, the college involved in the pilot had recently introduced a wireless network and the game was to be utilised as a focal point for creating learner awareness of the network and help promote its adoption by learners early on in the course induction period. Finally, academic staff within the Sport and Fitness department had recently developed QR technology based learning content for inclusion into practical based classes. The purpose of which was to introduce 'anytime learning' within a learning environment that lacked computer terminal access (in this particular case, the college gymnasium). The QRienteering game would be used as a familiarisation activity for new entry students to prepare them for utilising QR code based learning later in the academic year.

Pilot Participants

The learners participating in the pilot were Scottish Further Education students, about to commence study within a Sport and Fitness related course. Given the experiential nature of the study, it was anticipated that this particular student cohort would respond more favourably to a pilot game that had a physical and practical element incorporated into it.

The participants consisted primarily of first year students who were unfamiliar with the campus layout. However, the pilot did also accommodate those students who had studied previously at the college, (on different courses) but who were still unfamiliar with all the services and locations accessible to them during their studies.

In total, 30 learners participated in the pilot. This particular number of learners was chosen to best reflect a standard classroom size within an educational context, be it primary, secondary or tertiary education. Although, the pilot was conducted within a tertiary education environment, the games design can been considered to be operational within all levels of educational levels, where there is an induction need for campus familiarisation and team bonding.

LITERATURE REVIEW

Learner Inductions

Webster's International dictionary defines Induction as "*an initial experience, an exposure that introduces one to something previously mysterious or unknown.*" (Gove, 1986: p1145). This succinctly highlights what the new learner experiences first and foremost during their orientation week in a new educational environment: unfamiliar people and places.

"Early Induction" (Hassanien & Barber, 2007: p35) can be a make or break time for both the learner and the institution. Student retention can be at it most fragile during this period and its success can influence the learner's perception of the institutions value to them, and ultimately determine their decision of whether to continue or not with the education. Cook (2006: p9) claims that the highest levels of student withdrawal occur within the first six to eight weeks. However, withdrawal can also happen much sooner; within a matter of days (McInnes et al, 1995). Therefore, if high retention rates are to be maintained, then positive first impressions do count.

A main factor associated with early learner withdrawal has been linked to the learners experiences of the socialisation process within the institution and lacking of 'a sense of belonging' (Edward, 2004: p228) that can affect them if they do not have the opportunity to socially bond early on with peers and staff.

One of the primary functions of the QRienteering game was that it was designed first and foremost as an ice-breaking and familiarisation activity within the overall induction process. In order for it to be deemed successful, it had to ensure that the game delivered on the key aspects that make a successful induction.

Forrester et al (2004) identify a range of elements that, if successfully implemented during the induction period, would provide the learner with a robust basis for a successful learning experience. These elements, named collectively as STARTOUT (an acronym of: Social, Transitional learner, Academic, Registration, Tutor Support, Orientation, University *identifying with the,* and Tutors). Although, the STARTOUT model was designed for distance learning students, it is felt that given the generic nature of its guidelines, it can also be directly applied to campus based learner inductions. Cook (2006: p8) cites the works of Forrester et al's (2004) STARTOUT model when identifying what needs to be achieved in order to provide a successful induction. The main aspects for effective inductions have been encompassed as (Cook 2006: p8):

- *An encouragement to communicate and socialize both with staff and peers;*
- *Information about administrative procedures, the course and the institution;*

- *Information about support services; and*
- *Support for the transition to new methods of working.*

To achieve the above-mentioned aspects, the QRienteering Game was to be designed to utilise basic core learning skills: Communication, IT, Problem Solving & Teamwork (SQA, 2003) and through game-play, the learner would be offered the opportunity for:

- Peer socialisation through teamwork and collaboration.
- Familiarisation of the campus environment and its associated services through active exploration.
- Transition to mobile learning (considered a new method of learning at the pilot institution).

It has never been the intention of the QRienteering game to replace existing induction methods, but rather add to the overall experience by providing a supplemental method that promotes a more engaging and active learning alternative to the traditional lecturer led campus tour in which the learner passively receives information presented to them.

Defining Game Characteristics

The unique physical nature of the QRienteering game meant it that it possessed an opportunity to provide a more constructivist approach to learning (Wilson and Cole, 1991; Whitton, 2008) and demonstrate how the digital and physical worlds of learning could combine and complement to, quite literally, create an 'active' learning experience. In order to ensure that this experiential element of the QRienteering game was maximised and that it could be truly considered as a game, certain characteristics had to be identified and incorporated within its design.

Much has been written about defining game characteristics, (Narayanasamy et al, 2005; Prensky, 2001; Sauvé et al, 2010) and these can vary depending on the author. However, it was decided to adopt Whitton's (2010) identified game characteristics as a basis for the QRienteering game as they closely relate to games in its most inclusive sense; including traditional, non-digital based game-play along with electronic based gaming. This was deemed an important consideration given that the QRienteering game has is roots based in both forms of game-play.

The characteristics identified were: Competition; Challenge; Exploration; Fantasy; Goals; Interaction; Outcomes; People; Rules & Safety (See Table 1).

Table 1. Whitton's 10 characteristics of Games and their application in QRienteering

Whitton's (2010: p23) Identified game characteristics	Definition	Application to QRienteering game.
Competition	*The goal is to achieve an outcome that is superior to others.*	The goal of the QRienteering game is to locate all campus checkpoints and answer the associated questions correctly within the quickest time possible. Students compete in small groups against each other.
Challenge	*Tasks require effort and are non-trivial.*	The students work collaboratively using basic map reading and problem solving skills to familiarise and orientate themselves with the campus within the context of a competitive game. In addition, a clue word is generated at each checkpoint that contributes to a final phrase, which once solved leads to a final location point. The students must decipher that phrase and find the final location before returning to the start point. Thus, the activity promotes teamwork, communication, problem solving and campus familiarisation. All which are desired elements of an induction activity.
Exploration	*There is a context-sensitive environment that can be investigated.*	The ethos behind the QRienteering game is focused upon physical exploration and familiarisation of the college campus for new students.
Fantasy	*Existence of a make-believe environment, characters or narrative.*	Fantasy, is the one characteristic that is not incorporated into the QRienteering game, and this is intentional. The game is based in a real time, physical world environment, thus maximising the fidelity of the game. Fantasy, in this particular situation would be detrimental as it could affect the quality of knowledge transfer for the learner.
Goals	*There are explicit aims and objectives.*	The overall goal of the game is to familiarise new students to the college campus and the services it offers. This is achieved by the students navigating themselves around different locations of the campus, finding the checkpoints, and familiarising themselves with the student orientated services that each checkpoint locations offers.
Interaction	*An action will change the state of play and generate feedback.*	As the game is based upon a linear route, where each checkpoint reveals a location to the following checkpoint. The learners have to visit and scan each checkpoint in order to find the clue to the next location point, and thus progress through the game.
Outcomes	*There are measurable results from game play (e.g. scoring).*	On completion of the game, students times are recorded and completed answers are scored. These results are then measured against other student's times and scored, to determine the winner.
People	*Other individuals take part.*	Involving other people occurs twofold: The students work collaboratively in groups (though it can be attempted individually, if needed) using basic map reading and problem solving skills to complete the course. Secondly, they are competing against other peer groups.

continued on following page

Table 1. Continued

Whitton's (2010: p23) Identified game characteristics	Definition	Application to QRienteering game.
Rules	*The activity is bounded by artificial constraints.*	Students are briefed on the games rules prior to commencing. These basic rules include start and end checkpoints, use of QR code scanners and recording of answers. The rules are merely included to prevent cheating or collusion with other groups. However, their inclusion also act as technology guidance.
Safety	*The activity has no consequence in the real world.*	The activity occurs intrinsically within campus grounds, thus minimising effects from external environmental factors. Risk assessment of the course is also conducted prior to the game commencing.

Let's Get Physical

In addition to the above identified game characteristics, the QRienteering game incorporates another characteristic; 'Physicality'. With the recent increase in popularity of 'Exergaming' (Bogost, 2005) within mainstream console games based mediums such as the Nintendo Wii, Microsoft Xbox Kinect & Playstation Move, electronic based gaming have started to adopt characteristics normally associated with the traditional physical definition of game-play. However, the physical activity of console based Exergaming still requires the player to be located on one spot, in front of the console. The advantage that mobile technology based games offer over their console based counterparts is unrestricted movement, and the QRienteering game capitalises on this by allowing the participant to physically go beyond the confines of the console sensor bar and actively explore their environment without limitation. This offers the opportunity for not only the technology to be mobile, but also the learner.

DESIGNING THE GAME

Game Development Timescale

As time was an identified affordability factor, it was important that the amount of time required to develop the QRienteering game be kept to a minimum. A time limit of one hour was allocated, as this represented a realistically comparable time for a practitioner to be able to develop the game components within a lunch break or allocated class preparation period. This development time limit would incorporate the inputting, generating, outputting and physical laying-out of checkpoint questions for the QRienteering game. However, it is expected that additional time would be required for preparatory aspects such as the creative thinking process for planning the checkpoint route and question creation for each checkpoints of the QRienteering course.

Checkpoint Selection

The checkpoint locations selected for the QRienteering game, were designed to be generic and specific. Generic in terms of locations that all college learners could use, such as support services; and specific in terms of locations relevant only to the participants chosen subject study area, such as a departmental staff workroom. The idea behind this was not only to ensure that the locations were relevant to the students study, but also to highlight how the QRienteering game could be adapted with minimal effort to accommodate other faculty departments, without having to revise all checkpoint locations (See Table 2).

Table 2. Checkpoint locations for QRienteering game (1) and proposed locations for use in other faculty (2) departments

Checkpoint locations	Proposed alternate checkpoints for other faculty departments.		Subject relevance
Sport & Fitness Department (1)	Hairdressing & Beauty Therapy Department (2)	Hospitality & Catering Department(2)	
Football Pitch	Hairdressing Salon	Training Restaurant	Specific
Sports Hall	Beauty Treatment Room	Kitchen	Specific
Fitness Gym	Massage suite.	Conference Suite	Specific
Sport & Fitness Staff Workroom	Hair & Beauty Staff Workroom	Hospitality & Catering Staff Workroom	Specific
Assembly Hall	Assembly Hall	Assembly Hall	Generic
Learning Resource Centre	Learning Resource Centre	Learning Resource Centre	Generic
Student Finance Office	Student Finance Office	Student Finance Office	Generic
Cafeteria	Cafeteria	Cafeteria	Generic
Learning Development & Equalities Office	Learning Development & Equalities Office	Learning Development & Equalities Office	Generic
Student Union	Student Union	Student Union	Generic

Table 3. Technologies used for creating and running the QRienteering game

Technology	Purpose
Computer with internet access.	To access online QR code generator.
QR code Generator.	To input checkpoint questions and generate QR codes.
Printer.	To create hard copies of generated QR codes.
Mobile smart phone (multiple operating systems are accommodated).	To download QR code scanner application.
QR code scanner application.	To scan and read QR codes.

TECHNOLOGY COMPONENTS

In order to ensure the affordability factor of the QRienteering game was not compromised, emphasis was placed on ensuring that the technologies used were both low tech and low cost, utilising existing technologies wherever possible; typically the types of technologies readily available within an educational institution. This was for a threefold reason

- **Financially:** To alleviate budgetary outlay for the institutions, thus enhancing the probability of activity adoption.
- **Developmentally/Operationally:** To ensure that the associated learning curve with new technologies is minimised for both practitioners and learners, thus reducing activity development time for practitioners and enhancing the learners existing familiarity with personal mobile phone technology.
- **Technologically:** To introduce learners to mobile learning opportunities, allowing them to appreciate how personal smart-phone technology can be also utilised as a learning tool.

The technologies in Table 3 were used to develop and run the QRienteering game.

PRACTICALITIES OF RUNNING THE GAME

The QRienteering game was introduced to the students during the induction week, at the beginning of term one. Students had a short ten-minute briefing presentation on the task set for them. This briefing included a short explanation and demonstration of QR code technology, details on how to download the QR code scanner applications onto their smart-phones, an explanation of the rules of the task, including how to complete each checkpoint task and a quick orientation of the campus grounds via a paper-based map. They were split into groups of three participants. Each participant had a role in the group: Map-reader, Question master and Code reader. These roles were not exclusive to each member and indeed were encouraged to be interchangeable during the game. This allowed each member not only the opportunity to experience the functioning of QR technology, but also to work as a fully collaborative group.

Once every participating group had access to a smart-phone with a working QR code scanner, with the QR reader application downloaded and installed; and had acknowledged that they understood the task and its rules, they were then randomly assigned a starting checkpoint and the game commenced. Each group (ten groups participated) was assigned a different starting checkpoint, in order to ensure that teams could not simply follow other teams. The game was time bound and the rules were simple in the sense that the first team to complete the course, in the fastest time, with the most correct answers from the 10 checkpoints were declared winners.

A final clue-word phrase puzzle was also incorporated into the game, where each group had to decipher clue-words accumulated from each point into a phrase that would lead them to a final checkpoint. This was included to ensure that the groups visited each checkpoint and to promote core skills, problem solving, communication and teamwork (SQA, 2003) within the group.

Upon their return, each of the groups answers were checked and marked, and the winners declared shortly after the return of the final group.

In terms of timescale, the QRienteering game took all participating groups approximately 45 minutes to complete.

POST PILOT QUESTIONNAIRE RESULTS

At the end of the QRienteering game, the participants were also asked, as part of the debriefing process, to access an online survey and individually provide feedback on their experiences of participating in the game, via a series of open and closed questions. The 10 questions that were asked are shown in Table 4.

EVALUATION

Overall, the results gathered showed that 90% of participants involved in the pilot could be categorised as Generation Z, or as 'Net Generation' (Oblinger & Oblinger, 2005) learners. Both these terms are widely used to categorise learners whose birth year falls between chronological ranges of the mid 1990's to late 2000's. Although this learner demographic is frequently assumed to be predisposed with a natural tendency to thrive within 'Neomillennial' (Dede, 2005) learning style environments,

Table 4. QRienteering game questions

Question Number	Question	Response
1	Are you Male or Female?	75% male 25% Female
2	Which age category do you belong to?	15-20: 75% 21-25: 15% 26-30: 5% 31-35: 0% 35+:: 5%
3	Are you a new student or returning student to Forth Valley College's Falkirk Campus?	New: 65% Returning:35%
4	Had you ever heard of QR code technology before taking part in the QRienteering challenge? If yes, where?	Never heard of: 65% Heard of, but never used: 20% Heard of and used before: 15%
	• *In the newspapers to download movie and game trailers.* • *Tried out barcode scanner app on phone.* • *At School.*	
5	Do you think the QRienteering challenge was a useful exercise as part of your induction to the Falkirk Campus?	Yes: 90% No: 10%
	• *It let everyone get talking to one another and get to know each other.* • *I found my way about.* • *It helps getting to know people when you're new to the course.* • *It helped me learn where all the departments were on campus.* • *It got us going all over the college.* • *Walked to places in the college I have never been before.* • *Easier done online.* • *It was a good way to show people the campus and also a good way to meet new members of the class.* • *Allowed everyone to gain experience and knowledge of the software.* • *An excuse to use the phone.* • *It allowed us to work in a team and allowed new students to explore the college.* • *Team building.* • *Get to know your way about the college quicker.*	
6	How do you think the QRienteering challenge performs as a campus familiarisation activity, in comparison to a traditional lecturer-led tour of the campus?	Better: 70% Just as effective: 20% Worse: 10%
	• *It made the induction fun instead of just a tour around the place listening to the one person speaking all the time.* • *I seem to be able to remember certain rooms easier.* • *When you walk about with a lecturer you don't really talk to anyone and it's boring but when you do the orienteering you use team skills to find things so it's much better.* • *You can go at your own pace and visit any department you want first.* • *Because we need to find our ways around ourselves.* • *More enjoyable and good bonding activity.* • *More involved in class.* • *It's better because you have to find things for yourself instead of just following someone around, it's also more enjoyable.* • *Allows you to look around at your own pace.*	

continued on following page

Table 4. Continued

Question Number	Question	Response
	• *Lecturers can show you where to go in less time but the QR means that you have to find it yourself and that takes longer.* • *Allowed students to work out places for themselves instead of just being taken round the college.*	
7	How confident do you now feel in being able to locate rooms and services within Falkirk Campus?	Still not confident: 0% Slightly confident: 25% Comfortably confident: 50% Very confident: 25%
8	How easy was it to understand and take part in the QRienteering challenge?	Very easy: 40% Quite easy: 55% Quite hard: 5% Very hard: 0%
9	What did you like most and/or least about the QRienteering challenge?	
	Most: • *It was better than just walking around the place listening to one person speaking.* • *It was something different.* • *Getting to know people.* • *Trying to find the codes around the college.* • *Working as a team with others on the course.* • *Running around finding the codes.* • *Working in a team.* • *Working as part of a team.* • *It was a laugh.* • *Got talking to different people.* • *Working with technology.* • *The fun it gave finding the rooms instead of just following someone around.* **Least:** • *I think my team lost.* • *I found it difficult to download a good app on Android.* • *Trying to find little things we had to look out for.* • *The phone not picking up the code.* • *The group I was in.* • *Some QR scanners didn't work therefore couldn't complete it all.* • *At times I was just following my group and not understanding where I was or why.* • *I have a smart phone and it did not scan it properly.* • *Went to places that we didn't need to go.* • *Nothing.* • *Nothing to dislike.* • *Consumed too much time.* • *Walking.* • *Singled out those without smart-phones at the start of the year.* • *Walking around the college.* • *Nothing.* • *The map not being specific enough.* • *Sometimes QR scanner didn't work straight away.*	
10	Would you like to see more use of QR code technology within your learning?	Yes: 60% No: 40%
	Do you have any ideas where you would like to see it used? • *Getting jobs in certain places, getting used to where you are working and how things work.* • *On every machine in the gym.* • *Areas around Falkirk, because many don't live in Falkirk so most don't know there way around.*	

where technology plays an integral role within the educational journey, it has to be remembered that the technology itself constantly evolves in the same way that learner demographics evolve through generations X,Y to presently Z. It is therefore inevitable that eventually learners, regardless of what generation they belong to, will encounter an emerging new technology unfamiliar to them. This unfamiliarity factor occurred during this pilot when the participants encountered the QR code technology. It was found that 65% of participants had never heard of QR code technology before, with a further 20% never having actually used them. Therefore, it would be fair to determine that QR codes were a considered new technology to the majority of the group. However, this exposure to new technology did not seem to affect the participant's ability to take part in the QRienteering game, with 95% of the group stating that they found it either very easy or quite easy to understand and participate in the game. This highlighted that the QRienteering game had been successful in achieving one of the affordability factors; Learners quickly familiarised and readily adopted the QR technology driven learning, even though they did not appear to have a perceived technological skill or knowledge prior to exposure to the game.

Following on with the familiarisation theme, and considering physical world familiarisation, it was determined that 65% of the participants were new learners, who were unfamiliar with the college campus. The remaining 35% had been students returning to the college. However, the campus had recently undergone a refit during summer recess with many administrative offices and classrooms changing locations, so the induction still held value in allowing them to re-familiarise with the new locations. This point was reinforced when 90% of all participants responded that the QRienteering game was deemed a useful part of their induction process, citing exploration and familiarisation of the campus as the main benefits. This had an overall positive impact on the participants confidence in being able to locate rooms and offices around campus, with 100% of participants claiming a degree of confidence (from slightly to highly confident) in accessing relevant rooms and services.

In terms of promoting active and experiential learning, the results showed that 70% of the participants felt that the QRienteering game was a preferable method of induction, as opposed to a lecturer-led campus tour, with only 10% feeling that the latter was a better method. Reasons for this preference were varied; some participants found it enjoyable, others liked the sense of self-discovery, whilst other participants liked the element of team bonding and group work. However, the over-riding factor seemed to focus on the sense of control and self-empowerment that the participants felt they gained from the active nature of the game; they did not feel like passive recipients.

In relation to what the students liked and disliked about the QRienteering game, it became apparent that the primary positive factors were problem solving, group work and team bonding, as well as the active and exploratory nature of the game.

This highlights the success in not only the application of core skills learning integration, but also the success of the QRienteering game at promoting peer socialisation, collaborative working and exploration. Overall, however, the positive responses indicated that the participants enjoyed elements that generally would be considered as 'hands-on', thus strengthening that assertion that active and experiential learning methods were preferred method of learning for these participants. It could be argued that a traditional orienteering based induction activity would also promote the abovementioned positive factors. However, by integrating QR code technology into the activity, it made the participants aware of the college wireless network (one of the main objectives of the pilot) and introduced to them the potential for mobile-based learning within the college. This provided the participants with an experiential starting point for future QR code based learning opportunities later in the academic year.

What the participants disliked held equal value as the main concern raised highlighted a technological consideration. Some participants encountered difficulty with the QR software in the phones not scanning the codes correctly. Although, all participants checked that their phones QR scanning apps were operational prior to commencing the game, some participant groups did find that during the game they could not read some of the checkpoint codes and that it took multiple attempts for the application to work correctly. This issue was not related to any particular mobile operating system or any specific checkpoint code, and the issue seemed to occur randomly. However, given that the reading of the QR codes are an integral and essential part of the QRienteering game, it would be prudent to take this potential issue into account for future application and build in safeguards to ensure that this issue does not affect the operational flow of the game. Potential safeguards could be to create larger print-offs of the QR codes, to maximise code readability, or to have a "steward" posted at each checkpoint to resolve any technical code readability issues encountered.

A final dislike that was raised by one participant was that those without mobile phones had been singled out at the beginning of term. Although, this did not impede on their ability to participate as the game was group based, with each group having access to at least one phone, it does highlight a valid perception of feeling technologically excluded should future learning rely upon using mobile driven technologies. It would be naturally understandable and expected that there would be participants who have not yet experienced using QR code technology. This is why the one of the main purposes of the QRienteering activity was to introduce learners to this technology in a fun and non-assessed format, in order to help them familarise with that technology within an informal activity. Also, the activity was designed as a group exercise and therefore there are other non-technologically reliant roles within the group (map reader & question master) where technological ability or input is not required, thus allowing those participants to observe passively how the technology works firsthand, whilst still being an active and included team member.

This point also highlighted a foreseen factor that was realised at the briefing stage of the game. Only 40% of the participants had access to a phone that was able to download a QR code scanning application. However, it is fair to state that smart-phone, and in general mobile technology, is an extremely rapidly expanding market (Gartner, 2011) and that it would be expected that the application of the game during future inductions should naturally be met with an increase in smart-phone ownership, thus minimising the negative impact of technological exclusion.

This last factor may also attribute to the final feedback received from the participants. When asked if they would like to see more usage of QR code technology within learning, 60% stated 'Yes' and 40% stating 'No'. It is unknown why the participant's responses were split on this question, but it is possible to assume that those participants without smart phones may not like to see its future usage in learning, as they may feel unfairly disadvantaged if the mobile learning was focused at an individual level.

CHALLENGES AND SOLUTIONS

Challenges covering a number of areas were encountered during the design, development and implementation of the QRienteering game, many of which were anticipated during the initial design phase. These challenges and how they were addressed, are listed below.

Financial Constraints

One of the affordability factors highlighted during the design phase of the pilot was to acknowledge and find a workable solution for the financial constraints that most educational institutions face today. In order to reflect extreme economic constraints faced by educational institutions, a zero budget limit was applied to the development and implementation process of the QRienteering activity. This limit was achieved through using open source software to develop the activity and utilising existing technologies (software & hardware) during its implementation. As well as working within physical resource limitations, it was also designed to work within human resource limitations. Therefore, only one staff member was assigned to the design, development and implementation of the QRienteering game. It is hoped that this approach taken during the pilot would provide a working model of how to overcome any financial barriers practitioners and institutions could feel were limiting their ability to adopt and implement the QRienteering game.

Development Time

Another of the of the affordability factors highlighted in the aim was to ensure that the core framework for a mobile games based learning model could be easily adapted by practitioners with the most fundamental IT skills. It is hoped that the approach taken would ensure that practitioners could then quickly understand how to create their own QRienteering tasks, thus enhancing their engagement and motivation to adopt it as a new method of teaching and learning. This was achieved by designing the game to be developed using existing technologies such as basic text editor applications, thus not requiring any programming or web development based knowledge. This minimised time intensive learning curves normally associated with technology rich driven applications.

Technological Prior Knowledge and Learning Curve

Although QR code technology has been in existence since 1994, its usage was solely for manufacturing purposes, used the tracking car parts. It has only emerged recently within the past 5 years into public consciousness, firstly through primarily commercial mediums such as product marketing and advertising, but it usage can now be seen in mass consumer orientated sectors including, entertainment and online purchasing. It can be true to say that QR code technology has also been around within education for roughly the same time as its commercial counterparts, but its usage on the whole have been limited to largely non-teaching aspects such as advertising, marketing and administration. Therefore, as a medium for learning, QR code technology usage is currently still in its infancy. (Law & So, 2010) and as such QR codes can be considered an emerging technology within education, as currently so few practitioners or learners are aware of its existence, let alone its potential as an educational tool. This latter point was confirmed during post-pilot feedback questionnaire (Q4) when 65% of responding participants stated that they had never heard of QR codes prior to the pilot commencing, with a further 20% never having actually used them. This raised a practitioner/learner awareness challenge that had to be immediately addressed. Fortunately, the simplicity of the game concept allowed both participants and practitioners to understand the technology via a short ten-minute visual and hands-on demonstration and adoption of the game and its associated technology occurred without hindrance.

Access to Technology and Inclusiveness

Currently, not all students possess mobile phones that can facilitate the downloading of QR code technology. During the preparation phase of the pilot, it was found that only 40% of participants possessed smart-phone technology. However, this challenge was foreseen and is a secondary reason (promoting group work being the primary reason) why the participants were assigned into groups, where at least one participant possessed a QR code technology enabled phone. This group work approach enhanced team bonding and collaboration amongst new students, thus adding value to the overall campus induction process. This was reflected in the participant's responses during the post pilot questionnaire as the most liked factor of the QRienteering challenge (Q9).

Software

Although, all QR code scanning software used was open source and free, many participants did not have the software installed on their mobile phones. This issue was addressed during demonstration and briefing prior to the activity. Given that a number of operating systems had to also be accounted for, including in this study: Google Android, Apple iOS, Blackberry OS & Microsoft Windows Mobile, participants were provided with web-links to download the most appropriate QR scanning software for their particular phone. All QR scanning software downloaded was open source, was neither memory nor storage intensive and free of cost.

Wireless Networks: Online and Offline Modes

Participants who were in mid-enrolment did not, at the time of piloting (August 2011), have access to the institutions newly enabled wireless network, as their wireless network would be granted after the overall college induction process was completed. This challenge was anticipated and the activity was designed to work offline, thus requiring no internet access, or any associated data charges. Data was stored within the QR code technology, which only required scanning in order to access the data. This particular challenge highlighted the versatility of the game by being able to operate in both online and offline modes.

Another advantage of working within offline mode is that it allowed the QRienteering challenge to extend throughout the entire campus, including for example, outdoor sports pitches, and not be limited to areas covered within the campus wireless range, which were limited to allocated hotspots.

FUTURE DEVELOPMENTS FOR QRIENTEERING

A number of potential developments have been considered for future induction applications. They have been included to provide stimulus to the reader or anyone considering adopting the QRienteering game as an induction method.

The first potential development includes making full use of the educational institutions wireless network and providing online interactive checkpoints, allowing participants to watch a streaming induction video for each particular checkpoint location. These videos would contain helpful and detailed information about the visited location and also hold the answer to the clue that the participants would need to answer in order to progress to the next checkpoint. It would be prudent to mention at this point that this would only be practicable if such an accessible network were freely available to learners, otherwise data download cost implications could be incurred upon them.

This media rich approach could be further developed to integrate layers of downloadable Augmented Reality data. This data could provide additional, selective information that new learners may wish to know about their campus environment, information that may not be readily accessible within the real world environment. In a game sense, Augmented Reality could also provide greater challenge and exploration, as it could provide enhanced virtual interaction with the game checkpoints, such as searching for hidden clues.

Another future development could be to allow learners themselves to become involved within the creation of a QRienteering route for future students. Through personal experience as learners they could be the best judges of what services and access they require during induction and then to pass on that experience. By being allowed access and autonomy to design their own route, learner empowerment is being nurtured, and Neomillennial learning styles are being fostered by encouraging the *"co-design of learning experience personalized to individual needs and preferences."* (Dede, 2005: p15).

SUMMARY

In terms of creation and implementation, the QRienteering game was deemed successful at achieving all the above mentioned affordability factors: Development time, Financial and Technical skill. Average development time of the activity was under one hour and required no advanced IT skills on the part of the practitioner. Financially, development outlay costs to the institution were zero as open source software applications were used along with the institutions existing hardware technologies. Finally, all students understood how to utilise the QR code technology after a short demonstration session prior to the activity.

One factor however, that needs to be taken into consideration when using QR code technology in learning was 'access to technology'. Given that only 40% of the participant had personal access to smart-phone, indicated that even with smart-phone technology rapidly increasing its dominance in the mobile technology market, consideration and safeguards have to be taken to ensure that no learner feels isolated from the activity due to not possessing the required technology.

As an induction method, the game was also considered successful when compared to the traditional, lecturer-led campus orientation tour. This was due in most part to the active nature of the game, allowing the participants to self-explore and communicate with each together to achieve the end goal of the game. This naturally created a positive impact on participant's campus familiarisation and socialisation process, allowing them to get to know their surroundings and other each whilst working collaboratively. In support of its success as an induction tool, it would be noteworthy to mentioned that the academic courses on which the participants are enrolled upon have since recorded the highest early student retention rate in recent years, and it has been viewed by staff that the QRienteering game has contributed to these high early retention rates.

It is unclear what the economic climate holds for educational institutions in the near future, and whether there will be further impacts created within educational delivery. Though what has become clear is that affordability and sustainability of technology isnow playing greater importance for educational institutions. However, this does not mean that introducing new methods of technology enhanced learning be avoided, and that creating affordable mobile-based learning games, such as the QRienteering game, which introduce and promote active learning, can be achieved within even the most restrictive of economic conditions.

REFERENCES

Al-Khalifa, H. S. (2011). An m-learning system based on mobile phones and quick response codes. *Journal of Computer Science, 7*(3), 427-430. Retrieved 14th January, 2012, from http://www.doaj.org/doaj?func=abstract&id=803858

Bogost, I. (2005). The rhetoric of exergaming. In *Proceedings of the Digital Art & Culture (DAC) Conference 2005*, Copenhagen, November 30th – December 3rd 2005. Retrieved 14th January, 2012, from http://www.bogost.com/downloads/I.%20 Boogst%20The%20Rhetoric%20of%20Exergaming.pdf

Cook, A. (2006). Induction: A formal initiation into a position or office. In A. Cook, K. A. Macintosh, & B. S. Rushton (Eds.), *Supporting Students: Early Induction* (pp. 7-12). Coleraine, UK: University of Ulster. Retrieved 14th January, 2012, from http://www.ulster.ac.uk/star/resources/%28D%29%20Supporting%20Students%20 -%20Early%20Induction.pdf

Dede, C. (2005). Planning for neomillennial learning styles: Implications for investments in faculty and technology. In D. Oblinger & J. Oblinger (Eds.), *Educating the net generation* (pp. 15.1–15.22). Boulder, CO: EDUCAUSE. Retrieved 14th January, 2012, from http://www.educause.edu/educatingthenetgen

Education International. (2009). *The global economic crisis and its impact on education.* Brussels, Belgium: Education International. Retrieved 14th January, 2012, from http://download.ei-ie.org/Docs/WebDepot/Report_of_the_EI_Survey_on_the_Impact_of_the_Global_Economic_Crisis_on_Education_en.pdf

Edward, N. S. (2003). First impressions last. An innovative approach to induction. *Active Learning in Higher Education, 4*(3), 226–242. doi:10.1177/14697874030043003

European Universities Association. (2011). *Impact of the economic crisis on European universities.* Brussels, Belgium: Author.

Forrester, G., Motteram, G., Parkinson, G., & Slaouti, D. (2004). *Going the distance: Students' experiences of induction to distance learning in higher education.* Paper presented at the British Educational Research Association Annual Conference, University of Manchester, 16–18 September, 2004. Retrieved 14th January 2012 from http://www.leeds.ac.uk/educol/documents/00003849.htm

Gartner. (2011). *Gartner says 428 million mobile communication devices sold worldwide in first quarter 2011, a 19 percent increase year-on-year.* Stanford, CA: Author. Retrieved 14th January, 2012, from http://www.gartner.com/it/page.jsp?id=1689814

Gove, P. B. (Ed.). (1986). *Webster's third new international dictionary of the English language, unabridged.* Springfield, MA: Merriam-Webster.

Hassanien, A., & Barber, A. (2007). An evaluation of student induction in higher education. *International Journal of Management Education, 6*(3), 35-43. Retrieved 14th January, 2012, from http://www-new1.heacademy.ac.uk/assets/bmaf/documents/publications/IJME/Vol6No3/IJME6380pageHassanienBarber.pdf

Law, C., & So, S. (2010). QR codes in education. *Journal of Educational Technology Development and Exchange, 3*(1), 85-100. Retrieved 14th January, 2012, from http://libir1.ied.edu.hk/pubdata/ir/link/pub/7-So.pdf

McInnes, C., James, R., & McNaught, C. (1995). *First year on campus: Diversity in the initial experiences of Australian undergraduates.* Canberra, Australia: AGPS.

Oblinger, D. G. (2003). Understanding the new students: Boomers, Gen-Xers, Millennials. *Educause Review, 38*(4). Retrieved 14th January, 2012, from http://net.educause.edu/ir/library/pdf/erm0342.pdf

Oblinger, D. G., & Oblinger, J. L. (Eds.). (2005). *Educating the net generation.* Washington, DC: Educause. Retrieved 14th January, 2012, from http://www.educause.edu/educatingthenetgen

Scottish Qualifications Authority. (2003). *Core skills framework: An introduction.* Glasgow, UK: Author. Retrieved 14th January, 2012, from http://www.sqa.org.uk/files_ccc/Core%20skills%20combined%20241106.pdf

Whitton, N. (2008). *Alternate reality games for developing student autonomy and peer learning.* Paper presented at LICK 2008. Edinburgh. Retrieved 14th January, 2012, from http://www2.napier.ac.uk/transform/LICK_proceedings/Nicola_Whitton.pdf

Whitton, N. (2010). *Learning with digital games: A practical guide to engaging students in higher education.* New York, NY: Routledge.

Williamson, B. (2009). *Computer games, schools and young people: A report for educators on using games for learning.* Bristol, UK: Futurelab. Retrieved 14th January, 2012, from http://archive.futurelab.org.uk/resources/documents/project_reports/becta/Games_and_Learning_educators_report.pdf

Wilson, B., & Cole, P. (1991). A review of cognitive teaching models. *Educational Technology Research and Development, 39*(4), 47–64. doi:10.1007/BF02296571

KEY TERMS AND DEFINITIONS

Core Skills: A term used by the Scottish Qualifications Authority to describe a group of five key skills required in learning and working environments. The five skills are Communication; Numeracy; Information Technology, Problem solving and Working with others.

Exergaming: A portmanteau of 'exercise' and 'gaming'. Used to describe computer games that are designed primarily to allow the player to physically exercise during play.

Generation X: Generational term used to describe people born between the early 1960's to early 1980's.

Generation Y: Generational term used to describe people born between the mid 1980's to early-mid 1990's. Also known referred to as 'Millennials'.

Generation Z: Generational term used to describe people born mid 1990's to post millennium (2000).

Neomillennial: Used to describe technology influenced learning styles which are closely associated with learners entering post-millennium education.

Physicality: A term used to describe a game characteristic that allows the player to utilise health and skill related components of fitness during play.

QR Code: QR (Quick Response) codes are a type of Two dimensional barcode which is able to store more data than traditional One dimensional barcodes.

QRienteering: A linguistic blend of 'QR' (Quick Response) technology and the outdoor sport 'Orienteering'.

Chapter 7
Enhancing Nutritional Learning Outcomes within a Simulation and Pervasive Game-Based Strategy

Mark McMahon
Edith Cowan University, Australia

EXECUTIVE SUMMARY

The chapter outlines the design of a game to raise nutritional awareness within primary school-aged children. The game uses a blend of simulated and pervasive elements using ubiquitous technologies to enhance children's capacity to make informed choices with regard to their own eating habits. Nute's Adventures in Nomland is a project currently being undertaken at an Australian university to explore the potential of a casual game can be used to help parents and children understand the different nutritional values of the food they eat. The game contains both pervasive and simulation elements. The pervasive nature of the game is evident in the use of mobile phones to scan nutrition labels as part of a shopping activity. This shopping is then brought into a simulation game that allows learners to explore the effects of their decisions on a virtual pet, Nute, and then identify strategies to address shortfalls in that decision-making.

DOI: 10.4018/978-1-4666-2848-9.ch007

BACKGROUND

Australian and international evidence confirms that the early years of a child's life are critical to his or her future development. It is at this time that a child's brain is rapidly developing and the foundations for learning, behaviour and health over the life course are set (FaHCSIA, 2010). While the National Nutrition Survey (NNS) was conducted in 1995 and the last National Physical Activity Survey was in 1985, the intervening decades have seen substantial changes in the Australian physical exercise, food supply and eating habits. These include an increase in technologies that facilitate sedentary behaviour (e.g. video games and mobile phones) and changing family life and structure (e.g. increased participation of both primary and secondary care-givers in the workforce). All of these factors are likely to impact on what children eat and what they do. Indeed, the prevalence of overweight and obesity has rapidly increased since the mid-1980s. State-based surveys indicated that currently 5% of Australian children are obese and a further 20% are overweight using internationally agreed criteria. This trend is not only a national one. In the UK it is estimated that 10% of children between 2 and 10 years old are obese (UK Department of Health, 2011) while USA figures are even more alarming, with the prevalence of childhood obesity at over 17%, almost tripling over the last 20 years (Ogden, Carroll & Flegal, 2008). The World Health Organisation has gone so far as to claim childhood obesity is 'one of the most serious public health challenges of the 21st century' (WHO, 2012).

Effective health communication to young people should be based on a sound understanding of their perceptions of healthy and unhealthy eating habits, their perceptions of the various socialising agents and other sources communicating healthy eating habits to them, and their perceptions of different communication appeals regarding healthy eating. Scholars generally agree that healthy eating habits are developed through a process of socialisation, in which families, schools, the community, the government and international health organizations may all play an active role (Kelly et al., 2006; McGinnis et al., 2006; Raiha et al., 2006). Parents serve as role models and influence adolescents' purchase behaviour directly (McNeal and Ji, 1999). Empirical data supports the notion that parental support for healthy meals and nutrition skills has a positive association with adolescents' healthy food choices and healthy eating habits (Raiha et al., 2006; Young and Fors, 2001). Schools also disseminate nutrition and health information through the formal curriculum as well as extracurricular activities. Schools can support healthy eating by monitoring the nutrition values of the food supplied in lunches and snack shops (Nutbeam, 2000). Interestingly, however, peers have been shown to have a negative influence on healthy eating (Kelly et al., 2006). Conflict between parental influence and peer influence may prompt young consumers to refuse to bring healthy food to school when their friends buy or consume food and beverages that are high in calories and low in nutrients (these foods are sometimes termed 'junk' foods). Peer influence on body weight and body image also triggers unhealthy dieting practices such as vomiting or using laxatives for weight control (McGinnis et al., 2006). With this in mind, a learning environment that helps bridge the gap between formal nutritional education and informal social and recreational activity may offer one approach to reconciling the conflicting messages of peers and the curriculum.

LITERATURE REVIEW

The value of games as learning tools is one that is receiving increasing attention. One of the driving forces behind this growth has been their capacity to give learners a more instrinsically motivating experience than traditional educational curricula (Prensky, 2006). Despite the rhetoric of games-based learning advocates, however, there are still unanswered questions regarding whether learners can actually implement the skills they acquire in games and apply them to real-world problems (Bang, Gustafsson & Katzeff, 2007). Quality games designed explicitly to support learning outcomes are hard to find. Moreover, traditional interactive games seem to result in shallow learning. The frequent approaches of either grafting game elements onto eLearning (the 'chocolate coated broccoli' model) or repurposing commercial games for education both tend to create impoverished applications that are either fun or effective learning, but rarely both.

The goal of any instructional product is to promote learning (Ally, 2004) and increasingly, organisations are adopting digital technologies as the primary delivery method to train employees (Simmons, 2002). There is an ongoing debate as to whether it is the design of the instruction or the use of a particular delivery technology that improves learning (Clark, 2001; Kozma, 2001, cited in Ally, 2004).

It has long been accepted that specialised delivery technologies can provide efficient and timely access to learning materials (Ally, 2004) but Clark (1983) claims that technologies are merely vehicles that deliver instruction, but do not in themselves influence student achievement, with meta-analysis studies on media research have shown:

Students gain significant learning benefits when learning from audio visual or computer media, as opposed to conventional instruction; however, the same studies suggest that the reason for those benefits is not the medium of instruction but the instructional strategies built into the learning materials (Clark, 1983).

Two such strategies that can be used to enhance the development of applied skills are simulations and pervasive games. Simulations provide a virtual representation of a real world system with the goal being to develop knowledge that can be transferred from the representation to the real world (McHaney, 1991; Towne, 1995). To be successful, a simulation must effectively model the real world task (A.L. Alexander, Brunye, Sidman, & Weil, 2005). The assumption is that a faithful representation should enhance the link between the virtual and real environments. This does not require the game activity to necessarily model the real world task in its entirety, however. Every day tasks and problem solving are often mundane and require steps that offer little in the way of challenge or reward. For optimal outcomes, learners need to engage in an intrinsically motivating product. Keller's ARCS theory has been influential tool to guide the design of such environments through the four precepts of Attention, Relevance, Confidence and Satisfaction (Keller, 1987). Visual, auditory and narrative approaches have the potential to support perceptual and inquiry arousal, while such attention is also more easily maintained when the task is perceived as relevant to the learners' goals. Above all, the game needs to provide confidence through an appropriate level of challenge that mitigates both boredom and frustration as well as providing rewards within a system that is perceived as fair. While such elements are inherently design-oriented rather than simply replicating features of the real-world task, they provide a set of useful heuristics that underpin the importance of ensuring that learning activities promote transfer from the game to the actual task to be performed by ensuring some level of fidelity and purposeful activity.

Pervasive games are one way of achieving this in that they bring the real world into the environment itself. Using ubiquitous technologies they are able to integrate the physical and social aspects of the real world, instantiated in forms such as Smart Toys and Affective Gaming, as well as Location Aware and Augmented Reality Games (Magerkurth et al., 2005). Common to all of these is a sense of immediate real world feedback, engagement in the social aspects of an environment and a heightened sense of agency.

This chapter describes the design of a game to raise nutritional awareness within primary school-aged children. The game uses a blend of simulated and pervasive elements using ubiquitous technologies to enhance children's capacity to make informed choices with regard to their own eating habits. By operating in a simulated environment learners are able to make meaningful decisions about a character that acts as a corollary to their own dietary choices. The heart of the game is a shopping activity where players buy the groceries required to keep this character healthy for a typical week. The game has been completed using a simulated shopping activity with the ultimate design goal being the integration of the game into the real supermarket where players will be able to scan actual product barcodes and use the dietary information associated with those foods as the basis of the nutritional energy model within the game. This pervasive approach allows children to interact with peers and parents, raising awareness of nutrition through the use of standard technologies in the form of a smartphone application that uses the camera feature to scan QR codes integrated into the game.

PRACTICALITIES OF RUNNING THE GAME

The game begins with a cut scene that introduces the goals and provides a narrative hook to engage learners. The game concept involves the arrival into the life of the player of a friendly dragon, Nute, who coincidentally has the same dietary needs as the player. Nute becomes the responsibility of the player to ensure that he remains happy and healthy, along the same lines as the familiar virtual pet game genre such as Bandai's Tamagotchi (Bandai, 2012).

The main task is to take Nute shopping. The idea is to do a standard weekly shop, ensuring a diet that is balanced and of adequate quantity to remain healthy (Figure 1). Learners select from a range of food groups including grains, fruit, vegetables, meat, frozen foods, drink and so on which are used as the basis for an aggregated score across a range of dietary variables.

Following the shopping activity, learners witness the effects of the dietary choices on Nute and receive feedback according to the Traffic Light system of food classification (WA Dept of Health, 2011). This feedback remediates food choices according to whether those foods should be eaten rarely, occasionally or regularly. The feedback is based upon a calculation of kilojoules and the sub-components such as fat, carbohydrates, protein and sugars (Figure 2). The effects are directly seen on Nute himself. He can become emaciated or overweight and exhibit sluggish behaviour.

Figure 1. Taking Nute shopping

Figure 2. Nute feedback screen

As both a reward and a tool to highlight the value of exercise within a general nutritional regimen, the game also contains mini-games that allow Nute to work off extra kilojoules to help maintain health (Figure 3). The difficulty of the game is moderated by Nute's current condition. If he has eaten too much bad food, for example, Nute moves across the screen more slowly making it more difficult to keep 'heading' the ball in the soccer min-game. Over a period of shopping instances ('weeks' in the game), players can redress Nute's poor eating habits and bring him back to a good level of dietary health.

TECHNOLOGY COMPONENTS

The game has been prototyped in two forms. The first is through Adobe Flash, enabling the game to be played on any browser that supports it. This version provides an offline mode, where all of the activity is integrated into the game itself. The second version takes the form of a QR enabled Android Application, enabling players select food items by scanning the QR codes using an Android smartphone. While the Flash version contains all of the the nutritional data within the game, the Android iteration uses a series of cards containing food items that are identified via a code that can be scanned as part of a simulated shopping activity. Most converged mobile devices can use their camera facility to take a picture of the code with is then translated into meaningful information through 'app' software. QR Codes are digital representations of information as a pixelated graphic. They can be used as digital business cards or provide information relating to buses at stops and so on. In the initial instantiation of the technology, the information was embedded as a link that updates an online database using PHP/MySQL (Figure 1). Where QR

Figure 3. Soccer mini-game

Codes are presented inline with shopping items such as in pricing information in a supermarket, scanning a code has the potential to update a shopping cart of food items (See Figure 4).

Nute's database contained information not only about the food item itself but also about the nutritional information, drawn from a freely available Australian nutritional database. A further refinement of the Android version of the game embedded the nutritional information in the QR code itself. While this requires visibly larger QR graphics, it reduces the reliance on connectivity to the database (3G or WiFi connection) and enables flexibility in that the range of foods can be easily updated or augmented by anyone implementing the game. All that is required is for an appropriate text string to be integrated into a QR code through freely available QR generators such as that offered by Kaywa (2012). In this case, a sample text string in the form of *product name: energy: weight: unit of measurement: traffic light food type: food category* is parsed within the game and used to calculate the overall balance of elements like the total energy, the nature of foods (grains vs. vegetables etc.) and the general healthiness of foods according to the Traffic Light system (WA Dept of Health, 2011). These QR codes are printed as 'Flash Cards' with illustrative images of the food, which can be pasted around a classroom. The ideal would be to work with a food retailer to incorporate such information into their pricing and barcode systems so the activity could be performed in real life as

Figure 4. Scanning QR codes to update an online shopping cart

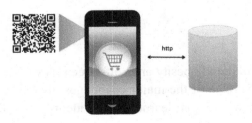

they undertake the weekly shop with their parents. Such an approach would likely require the reintegration of an online database, with the original supermarket barcode being used as a product key field within the database query to access the record with the appropriate nutritional information.

EVALUATION

This project was characterized by a distinct approach to design and development that allowed for low cost development but created challenges in terms of managing and implementing the process. The first of these challenges was a lack of funds to develop it. While the initial concept was broached with a commercial partner, Intellectual Property issues relating to ownership of the product, its implementation for research and the use of a commercial nutritional database hindered its development. Ultimately the product was prototyped as two student projects, each developing one of the Flash or Android versions of the game. This benefitted from the enthusiasm and creativity of a small team of committed developers but was also constrained by the project's focus as a learning experience for the students and the need to set requirements at a Proof of Concept level rather than a refined product.

As a result, a Design-Based Research methodology was implemented. This is a valuable approach to small-scale design and development because of its emphasis on iterative design with the end goal of a specific product or curriculum and acknowledgement of the inherent messiness of educational settings (Design-Based Research Collective, 2003). It is distinctive in its blend of product development and ongoing research, with a focus on developing a class of theories but also putting them in harms way through intervention and using the research as a test bed for innovation (Cobb et al., 2003). The iterative and longitudinal nature of this approach raises issues for any developer in an environment that is constantly changing. Ever evolving technologies and the lack of a stable team of developers in particular provided difficulties in maintaining the development of Nute to the point where it could be applied as a working prototype. Nevertheless, the formative nature of design, development and evaluation allowed for a range of challenges to be identified and addressed throughout the lifecycle of the project.

CHALLENGES

The link between childhood obesity and self-esteem is well documented (French, Story & Perry, 1995). One of the major challenges, therefore, involved the need to create a character with whom learners could identify in order to both enhance motivation for the game as well as provide an embodiment of self, but also one that would not have the potential to be usurped as a tool for bullying or as a negative analogue of the player. Three character concepts were trialed with a focus group (Figure 5) and it was found that the dragon character provided the strongest sense of emotional attachment for the users. A more neutral character, for example, was initially identified as the preferred one for the developers because of its relatively humanoid shape and potential as a 'blank canvas' for users to impart their goals. However, a stronger sense of attachment was felt for a more pet like creature that didn't necessarily promote personal identification but stimulated a desire to nurture the character.

A further challenge was the current state of mobile technologies with regard to development and deployment environments. The Flash prototype, for example would not work on iPhones or other non-flash enabled devices. Android was eventually selected because of its ability to integrate QR Code scanning within the application, use existing elements from the Flash prototype and be distributed in a more open manner than would be available in other mobile operating system environments. Within the life of this project, Flash has diminished as a dominant interactive technology in favour of more compatible but less functional delivery platforms such as HTML 5.

A final challenge related to the extent to which real world characteristics needed to be faithfully modeled within the system to provide an accurate reflection of appropriate dietary decision-making. It would be unlikely that poor nutrition would be visible on a real person from week to week, yet having Nute visibly deteriorate as a result of poor diet was a necessary form of feedback in the game. Similarly, the impacts of diet on health are complex and multivariate. Rather than simply being a function of overall energy, the product needed to integrate the nature of the foods and the balance of essential elements such as fats, protein and so on. The purpose of the game is not to make children experts in nutritional biochemistry but to simply raise awareness of key issues. The use of the Traffic Light approach provided a simple means of communicating dietary messages within the product but belied a more complex algorithm underpinning the simulation.

Figure 5. The three character concepts initially trialed for Nute

SUMMARY

With the growing availability of interactive technologies, in particular the ubiquity of mobile devices among younger learners, there are opportunities to leverage off the casual games market to provide learning experiences. Simulations and Pervasive Games have the potential to provide environments for meaningful decision making that promote transfer of learning and integrate real-world activity to heighten the sense of immediacy and agency with these. Nute has been developed as a casual serious game to promote dietary awareness among a target group of young learners. The case described here demonstrates how the game can be used as a tool for raising awareness of diet and provide opportunities for meaningful decision-making among a vulnerable target market in a fun, non-threatening way. While the game represents ongoing work rather than a final product, the opportunities for formative evaluation and agile decision-making within the design and development process have provided a range of findings and lessons that can be applied to the use of pervasive games and mobile technologies for learning among school-aged children.

ACKNOWLEDGMENT

The authors would like to acknowledge the contributions of students Melissa Cheah, Adolfos Steinenbohmer, Matthew Adams, Sango Cheung, Roy Wagner, and Bastian Pahlke to the development of Nute.

REFERENCES

Alexander, A. L., Brunye, T., Sidman, J., & Weil, S. A. (2005). *From gaming to training: A review of studies on fidelity, immersion, presence, and buy-in and their effects on transfer in pc-based simulations and games.* DARWARS Training Impact Group. Retrieved June 9, 2008, from http://www.darwars.com/downloads/DARWAR%20Paper%2012205.pdf.

Ally, M. (2004). Foundations of educational theory for online learning. In Anderson, T., & Elloumi, F. (Eds.), *Theory and practice of online learning.* Athabasca University.

Australian Government Department of Families, Housing, Community Services and Indigenous Affairs. (n.d.). Retrieved on August 19, 2010, from http://www.fahcsia.gov.au/sa/families/progserv/communitieschildren/Pages/default.aspx

Australian Government Department of Health and Ageing. (n.d.). Retrieved on August 20th 2010 from http://www.health.gov.au/internet/main/publishing.nsf/Content/phd-nutrition-childrens-survey-userguide

Bandai. (2012). *Tamagotchi town.* Retrieved 26 January, 2012, from http://www.bandai.com/tamagotchi/

Bang, M., Gustafsson, A., & Katzeff, C. (2007). Promoting new patterns in household energy consumption with pervasive learning games. *Proceedings of the Second International Conference on Persuasive Technology, Lecture Notes in Computer Science.* Berlin, Germany: Springer.

Clark, R. E. (1983). Reconsidering research on learning from media. *Review of Educational Research, 53*(4), 445–459.

Cobb, P., Confrey, J., DiSessa, A., Lehrer, R., & Schauble, L. (2003). Design experiments in educational research. *Educational Researcher, 32*(1), 9–13. doi:10.3102/0013189X032001009

Design-Based Research Collective. (2003). Design-based research: An emerging paradigm for educational inquiry. *Educational Researcher, 32*(1), 5–8. doi:10.3102/0013189X032001005

French, S. A., Story, M., & Perry, C. L. (1995). Self-esteem and obesity in children and adolescents: A literature review. *Obesity Research, 3*(5), 479–490. doi:10.1002/j.1550-8528.1995.tb00179.x

Kaywa. (2012). *QR-code generator.* Retrieved 27 January, 2012, from http://qrcode.kaywa.com/

Keller, J. M. (1987). Development and use of the ARCS model of motivational design. *Journal of Instructional Development, 10*(3), 2–10. doi:10.1007/BF02905780

Kelly, J., Turner, J. J., & McKenna, K. (2006). What parents think: Children and healthy eating. *British Food Journal, 108*(5), 413–432. doi:10.1108/00070700610661376

Magerkurth, C., Cheok, A., Mandryk, R., & Nilsen, T. (2005). Pervasive games: Bringing computer entertainment back to the real world. *ACM Computers in Entertainment, 3*(3), 1–19.

McGinnis, J. M., Gootman, J., & Kraak, V. I. (2006). *Food marketing to children and youth: Threat or opportunity?* Washington, DC: The National Academies Press.

McHaney, R. (1991). *Computer simulation: A practical perspective*. San Diego, CA: Academic Press.

Nutbeam, D. (2000). Health literacy as a public goal: A challenge for contemporary health education and communication strategies into the 21st century. *Health Promotion International, 15*(3), 259–267. doi:10.1093/heapro/15.3.259

Ogden, C. L., Carroll, M. D., & Flegal, K. M. (2008). High body mass index for age among US children and adolescents, 2003–2006. *Journal of the American Medical Association, 299*(20), 2401–2405. doi:10.1001/jama.299.20.2401

Prensky, M. (2006). *Don't bother me mom—I'm learning. How computer and video games are preparing your kids for 21st century success and how you can help!* St Paul, MN: Paragon House.

Raiha, T., Tossavainen, K., & Turunen, H. (2006). Adolescents' nutrition health issues: Opinions of Finnish seventh-graders. *Health Education, 106*(2), 114–132. doi:10.1108/09654280610650954

Towne, M. D. (1995). *Learning and instruction in simulation environments*. Englewood Cliffs, NJ: Educational Technology Publications.

UK Dept of Health. (2011). *Obesity – Public health*. Retrieved 26 January, 2012, from http://www.dh.gov.uk/en/Publichealth/Obesity/index.htm

WA Dept of Health. (2011). *Healthy options WA: Food and nutrition policy for WA health services and facilities*. Retrieved 15 September, 2001, from http://www.healthyoptions.health.wa.gov.au/visitors/traffic_light.cfm

World Health Organisation. (2012). *Childhood overweight and obesity*. Retrieved 26 January, 2012, from http://www.who.int/dietphysicalactivity/childhood/en/

Chapter 8
"Sell Your Bargains" or Playing a Mixed-Reality Game to Spice-Up Teaching in Higher Education

Chrissi Nerantzi
University of Salford, UK

EXECUTIVE SUMMARY

This case study relates to a mixed-reality game that has been developed and used by the author in the area of Academic Development and specifically within the Learning and Teaching in Higher Education (LTHE) module of the Postgraduate Certificate in Academic Practice (PGCAP). The game aims to provide a highly immersive learning experience to the players and opportunities to enhance their teaching in more creative ways as a result of their engagement and participation. The author shares details about this mixed-reality game and the pedagogical rationale on which it is based with other practitioners. The following also explores how this approach could be adapted and used in different learning and teaching contexts to transform learning in Higher Education into a more playful and creative experience which has potentially the power to motivate and connect individuals and teams combining physical and virtual spaces.

DOI: 10.4018/978-1-4666-2848-9.ch008

ORGANIZATION BACKGROUND

The Academic Development Unit (ADU) at the University of Salford is offering the blended PGCAP to new and experienced academics and other professionals who support learning across the university. The programme consists of the Learning and Teaching in Higher Education (LTHE) module and a selection of optional modules. Students complete two modules in total to gain the PGCAP. The LTHE module is the core module which is normally completed by all students before an optional module is chosen. Successful completion of the PGCAP leads also to Fellowship of the Higher Education Academy (FHEA). The cohort size varies between 20-30 students.

The overall aim of the LTHE module, in which "Sell your bargains", a mixed-reality game is currently used, is to introduce students to Learning and Teaching in HE, including contemporary learning theories and their application as well as to model good and innovative practice and the use of technologies for learning and teaching. The module provides a safe environment and the time to experiment, try new things and learn with and from each other in a multidisciplinary context, face-to-face, online and on the go using no- and low-tech approaches as well as institutional and student-owned technologies. In week 6 of the core module, the focus is creative teaching and learning. Students are encouraged to think and act outside the box and instead of showcasing how creative teaching could look, they are engaged in an immersive gaming experience to discover on their own and with peers what creative teaching and learning could mean through participating in the "Sell your bargains" game. This game is played in the real world and online and players keep their real identities. Mobile technologies owned by the players and freely available social media are used and the physical location is Manchester City Centre which becomes an open classroom.

SETTING THE STAGE

This game has been developed by the author (the game organizer) inspired by the BBC TV series Bargain Hunt and Dragons' Den. The core activity of this game has been carried out before as a field trip which included an individual challenge within initial teacher education in Adult Learning, Further and Higher Education. The approach used has been continuously refined and evolved based on feedback received from players and on self reflections and evaluation. The game organizer has found it more challenging to introduce this game in HE. Whitton (2010) carried out research linked to acceptability of games. Her findings confirm that while students in HE are willing to consider learning through games, they need to be convinced that this is "the most effective way to learning something." (p. 40) Could the same apply not just to students but the individuals who teach students in HE? Also, increasingly the possibilities technologies are providing to transform learning have been considered and have acted as enablers to take the game to the next level and transform into a fun experience and mixed-reality game with player-player and player-technology interactions.

This game in its current form is a mixed-reality game. It takes place in physical and virtual spaces which are seamlessly integrated and interwoven to provide a natural and immersive gaming and learning experience to all players who keep their real professional identities. The game is based on the principal that we are all creative and enjoy learning with and from each other. Learning in the game happens through collaboration and having fun but also on creating novel and immersive learning experiences in multiple locations which resembles Montana's (2011) idea about pervasive games. He says referring to these games that they "expand the magic circle of play socially, spatially or temporally" (p. 4) but he also mentions that for these reasons these games make some feel uncomfortable and awkward. Ramsden (2003) discusses that making a topic interesting has the power to "arouse our interest" and increase our appetite for more and deeper engagement and learning and this can be enabled through game-based learning. Whitton (2010) notes that "the rationale behind the use of alternative reality games is that the use of problem-based, experiential and collaborative activities in alternative reality games makes them ideally suited to teaching in higher education; particularly as they enable players to become involved in both playing and shaping the narrative as it emerges." (p. 87) This observation is also in line with Johnson et al (2011) who in addition states that supporters of game-based learning in HE claim that games enable students to experiment, explore identities and fail in a safe environment.

Players have multiple opportunities to be creative and make artefacts with peers and on their own as well as media-rich digital stories. Stories are part of who we are as humans and it has been shown (Moon, 2010) that they aid understanding of difficult or challenging concepts and deepen thinking, reflection and learning and therefore play a vital role in Higher Education. Through stories we share information, thought processes, research, emotions, entertain and connect with others in the form of lived experiences which are more powerful than the pure transmission of information. Stories bring people together. The narratives are created and shaped throughout the game, alone and in collaboration with peers. Learning is explored through discovery and immersion in authentic experiences, reflection and play.

Gauntlett (2011) talks about the always present "human appetite for making things" (p. 61), how we get pleasure when we create something, love to share it and get some kind of recognition for it too but also how much we learn through the process of making something. Gauntlett also talks about how many more opportunities there are today thanks to easy-to-use, widely available, more affordable and accessible technologies including Web 2.0 which he states "invites users to play" (p. 7). Some of these technologies, social media and player owned mobile media, are used in this game for this purpose but also to connect with each other and wider learning communities. Through these connections, players engage in conversations about teaching, something that Palmer (2007, 148) stresses as being important for teachers. Their conversations focus around their everyday practice: an actual difficulty they are facing when explaining a specific concept to their students in the next few weeks is discussed. This might be a threshold concept (Meyer and Land, 2003) which is vital to be understood by students and will enable them to move their thinking forward and lead to new understanding, but many times is challenging to explain. This concept, and the difficulty it presents, will shape an authentic practice-based Problem-Based Learning scenario (Barrows and Tamblyn, 1980) that will be used as the starting point for conversations with peers to problem solve collaboratively. Palmer (2007) talks about the importance of getting the problems "outside of our heads, into the light of day, where problems often look different than when we recycle them endlessly through our fears and doubts." (p. 157) The link between PBL and game-based learning is also made by Whitton (2010) and de Freitas (2006) who both see problems and problem solving as a vital part of game-based learning. Players were asked using a PBL approach to identify effective and innovative ways using analogies and everyday objects to bring a concept to life for their students or as Gardner (2009) puts it "the teacher is challenged [...] to come up with instructive analogies, drawn from material that is already understood, that can convey important aspects of the less familiar topic." (p. 109). Peer learning (Boud et al, 2001), a more natural, informal and collaborative way of learning through which professional practices can be modelled, is at the heart of this game and used as a powerful driver to increase engagement, motivation and learning and enable players to 'see' with the eyes of others.

In the current format of the game, technologies play an enabling role. They transformed the game into a more creative, participative, collaborative and connected learning experience for all players. Resources are created, adapted and used more effectively to enhance learning through gaming and enable the co-creation and sharing of artefacts. Mobile technology owned by players and freely available social media are used to enable and support a series of tasks, capture the process of the game and also enable the creation of a series of digital artifacts as Open Educational Resources (OER) shared with the whole group but also with the wider academic community at the University and elsewhere. The game is embedded in real-life and players are therefore not asked to change their identity. In fact, their experiences and professional context are vital for the game.

CASE DESCRIPTION

Overview

The current format of the "Sell your bargains" game has been used within the LTHE module of the PGCAP programme with cohort 3 in the academic year 2011/12. It was offered as an option instead of a classroom-based session around creative teaching and learning. Seven (7) out of 32 individuals chose to participate in this game. Each player kept their identity. The PGCAP Wordpress e-portfolios were used by all players to capture their engagement in this game, their reflections, the process as well as the final products and as such the game became part of the reflective journal which was an assessed component of the LTHE module.

The game organizer did not participate in the game but orchestrated the smooth running of the game in the physical and virtual locations, provided instructions and support and guidance to players throughout the game.

The game consisted of three (3) stages which took place in the following chronological order. Instructions about the game were discussed in class and were also made available within the institutional Virtual Learning Environment.

Stage 1: This part of the game took place in online spaces and lasted approximately 1 week. Each player was asked to think about a session they are going to deliver in about two weeks and try and foresee a difficulty explaining something that their students really need to grasp. This might be a threshold concept (Meyer and Land, 2003). Their thoughts about this session and the difficulty they feel they might encounter was captured in their Wordpress e-portfolio in about 100 words, or other media, and formed the authentic PBL scenario that was used during stage 2.

Players were informed about requirements of stage 2. This included the use of their own digital cameras, camcorders, smartphone or mobile phone as well as up to £3 spending money needed per player during stage 2. The exact meeting point and time was also announced to them in advance.

Stage 2: This part of the game took place in a physical location and started a week after stage 1 and lasted 3 hours in total. Players and the game organizer met in Central Manchester and were asked to make their problem scenarios available to their peers.

Shortly after arriving at a shopping area in Central Manchester, all players were briefed about Stage 2. The goal and rules were shared and any questions answered. Stage 2 was played in multidisciplinary pairs competing against eachother. Their challenge was to come up with the most creative and innovative solution to their problem scenarios from Stage 1 and make a hard to grasp concept understandable to students which would be put to the test in a coming week. Working in their pairs, each player was asked to identify and purchase two props, one for each problem scenario, from the surrounding shopping area up to the value of £3 or identify objects that were freely available and could be used to explain creatively a difficult concept.

An hour was given to the pairs to complete this task. Working together, the pairs shared their problem scenarios, discussed the difficulties they anticipated and started generating ideas and problem solving collaboratively. Players used their digital devices to capture their thinking, discoveries and journeys during this stage in a variety of media, some of which were used for Stage 2 and also to create their digital stories during stage 3 of the game.

After one hour, all players got together in a café and participated in the paired "Sell your bargains" competition. They shared their collaborative ideas and the rationale behind them with the group, answered questions and provided feedback to the other pairs. This part of the game lasted about one hour. Their pitches were recorded on a camcorder. Each pair voted for the most innovative idea presented. A point system was used to identify the winning pair. A maximum of three points were given to the most innovative idea. In total six (6) points could be awarded. The pair receiving the most points was announced the winning team and received a prize. The pairs then split and continue playing the game as individual players.

The game organizer captured highlights of the game on still and moving images which were shared with all players online through Flickr and YouTube under a Creative Commons license.

Stage 3: This part of the game took place online and lasted two weeks. The main task during this stage was for individual players to create a digital story linked to their solution showcased in pairs during stage 2 and based on a sound pedagogical rational that was developed by the player. Digital or physical items purchased, created and collected during stage 2, such as photographs, video clips, drawings, conversations and notes could be used during the creative digital storytelling process, including all materials captured by the game organiser that were made available under a Creative Commons licence. Players were also encouraged to take their solution presented during stage 2 one step further and identify opportunities to trial their intervention with their students, reflect on this and include information about their intervention and findings in their digital story which could be made available in their e-portfolios. A variety of media and online tools were used by players to put their stories together.

The digital stories were shared with the rest of the core module cohort and the wider online community. Players competed against each other to be crowned the overall winner of the game through public online voting. A Google docs form was used and made available for one week via Twitter and email to all current and past PGCAP participants to encourage a discussion around the digital stories and enable voting. The player who attracted the majority of votes was announced based on the following criteria, which were

1. Most innovative idea;
2. Rich and deep reflection;
3. Creative storytelling.

The overall winner of the game and received a book prize. All players successfully completed all three stages of the "Sell your bargains" game and received smaller prizes for successful completion, continuous commitment and creative contributions.

Findings

Data was collected from players via a Google docs survey (five out of seven players completed this) as well as through conversations with the game organizer and relevant comments in their e-portfolios. Also, the game organizer monitored the game closely and reflected during and after completion of the game.

Seven individuals out of 32 cohort participants, chose to play this game.

- Findings suggest that all players enjoyed the game. The most common words used describing it as a pleasurable experience were "enjoyable" and "fun". Comments received show that this was due to being engaged in a completely different learning activity, away from the classroom carried out in collaboration with peers but also because it was an opportunity to experiment and be creative.

I must say that I really enjoyed 'Mixed-Reality Game' game! It was great to get away from the lecture room and experience learning in a completely different way. Further, it was also great to be partnered up for the game, as up to that point I had not had chance to meet my partner formally.

I really enjoyed the element of having to think 'on your feet' and develop the ideas as you went along.

- All players found it useful to learn through play with others from different disciplines and saw it as an opportunity for exchange, learning with and from each other.

One participant for example said:

Working with others from other disciplines but finding a lot of common ground. It was beneficial to get different perspectives of a difficult problem. Then coming together to see what others had done & their rationale was also really useful.

While another player commented "The game was a tangible example of the power of social organisation/interaction in learning." which is something Whitton (2010) has also mentioned referring to collaborative games.

- Players also recognized that there was value in having a game with structure. They didn't feel that the structure hindered their experience. On the contrary, they commented that the game gave them the freedom to think outside-the-box, think on their feet, experiment and consider a variety of learning spaces and digital tools and approaches for their practice.

One participant said: "although it had a rigid structure, it didn't have any extrinsic goals, i.e. there was no prescribed learning that ought to have occurred. Thanks to this freedom, or "gaps", learning occurred creatively."

- Players found Stage 3 and the creation of the digital story the most challenging part of the game and this is in line with the game organiser's observations. A small number of players commented that the rationale for Stage 3 wasn't clear enough and some players found it challenging to use the technologies in this stage.

The most challenging aspect of the game was instead the story telling exercise at the end, i.e. the use of learning digital tools such as Flickr or Wordpress.

The last bit of the game creating the digital story was difficult as I wasn't entirely clear as to what was required, the technology was a challenge and I'm still not quite sure what was gained by this part of the game.

While another player recognized that the difficulties experienced presented an opportunity:

It really gave me a boost in experimenting with digital interactive tools for learning and teaching.

I could use this approach with my newer students as I thought that it was a good way of enhancing collaboration within the group, which I think is important for groups of students who do not know each other particularly well. It could also serve as a useful tool for introducing problem-based learning into my degree programme.

While another player stated: "I don't think I would chose to use this experience with my students at the moment. I would feel more comfortable using some of the more traditional techniques that would offer a better learning experience within my limits such as Problem Based Learning.

- At least one of the players shared his eureka moment by stating "I never thought I could exploit our natural curiosity to explore and play as a medium to learn; through my active engagement as a player/learner in the game I realised that I could design this element in my academic modules."

Technology Components

This mixed-reality game took place in real and virtual spaces and connected players, the organizer and their reflections, thoughts, ideas and stories, via freely available social media. These included Wordpress, Twitter, Ipadio, YouTube and Flickr as well as mobile technologies, such as mobile phones and smart phones, camcorders and digital cameras owned by players and the organiser.

The institutional Virtual Learning Environment was also used by the game organizer to make details about the game known, rules and stages in advance and during the game. Technologies were used by the game organizer and the players throughout to capture participation, highlights of the game as well as collect experiences in digital formats that were used to create the digital stories.

Additional digital storybuilding tools, such as LitteBirdTales and Windows Movie Maker, were used to create media-rich digital stories. A Google Docs form was created to enable public digital voting via Twitter and receive feedback from the players at the end of the game.

Technology Concerns

Familiarity with social media varied among players. Only a small minority of players had utilised before some of the technologies used in this game with their students. The majority of players had minimum experience using technologies in their day-to-day practice. Only a small minority were confident users of such technologies. This presented a challenge for the game organizer and the players themselves, especially during Stage 3. However, all players were using Wordpress for their PGCAP e-portfolio and had become familiar with this platform and were using it for over 4 weeks before the start of this game. All players used Stage 3 as an opportunity to develop their stories further and present them in digital format using a variety of media, such as video, images and audio despite the difficulties they experienced. The organizer had suggested a number of digital tools and technologies that could be used making it perhaps more challenging for some players who felt overwhelmed by these.

Despite the difficulties with technology some experienced and concerns shared openly with the organizer during and after completion of the game, all players were keen to learn using these technologies and used the game as an opportunity to develop their understanding of how these could be used for teaching and learning and develop specific skills that would enable them to use such technologies with their own students. Some players required additional support, especially during Stage 3 of the game, which was provided by the game organizer and peers. This lead progressively to the development of confidence in own abilities and the successful completion of the game by all players.

It was noted that players used their own mobile technologies, such as mobile phones, smartphones, digital cameras and camcorders with ease during Stage 2 and collected media-rich evidence of their involvement and engagement. Players felt comfortable and confident in using their own technologies and didn't need any support at all by the game organizer and the transition from using their own technologies in their private lives for teaching and learning happened smoothly.

Management and Organizational Concerns

The game was played for the first time in its current format. It was managed and organized exclusively by the game organizer who also facilitated and supported players during the game which in total lasted three weeks. This was a challenge and required extensive preparation far beyond the preparation required for a three hour classroom session this game was replacing. The game organizer also sourced the prizes for the game well in advance. Players' involvement was monitored through their e-portfolios and support was provided when required, especially during Stage 3 during which players created their digital stories. The small number of players made this game manageable. A larger number of players would require additional resources and support time and a plan needs to be drawn especially linked to the requirements of playing this game with a large group.

CURRENT CHALLENGES FACING THE ORGANIZATION

The "Sell your bargains" game was evaluated by the game organizer. Own observations, reflections and comments were combined with players thoughts and responses provided verbally and through a questionnaire. Conclusions were drawn linked to this particular time the game was played and the players' experience.

- **One Game Organiser:** Mixed-reality games are played in different spaces, physical and virtual. The "Sell your bargains" game took place in Central Manchester and in a variety of virtual spaces. Social and mobile media enabled and enhanced connectivity, creative expression, collaboration and support. However, because of this complexity it was challenging for all activities to be co-ordinated by one game organiser.
- **Technologies:** A variety of technologies, social and mobile media were used. This added to the complexity of the game, and at times led to confusion and became a barrier for some players, especially during Stage 3 that was more demanding pedagogically and technologically despite the fact that some of the technologies were used by players in their personal life. Despite the difficulties experienced with some of the technologies, all players successfully completed all stages of the game.
- **Number of Players:** A relatively small number of players, 7 out of 32, participated in this game, which was provided as an alternative to a classroom-based session around creative teaching and learning.
- **Complexity of Stage 3:** It was noted that the most challenging part of the game was Stage 3 which was carried out individually by the players and included the creation of the digital story using a variety of media and technologies. There was some confusion as to what the requirements were and the pedagogical rationale and benefits.
- **Digital Stories:** The created stories were made available in players' e-portfolios as Open Educational Resources. The game organiser disseminated links to the stories via Twitter and email to encourage a discussion around these. Limited interest was observed from outside the PGCAP programme.

- **Public Voting:** Despite the fact that voting was public and enabled through a Google Docs form distributed via Twitter and also via email to all current and past PGCAP participants, only 16 votes were received.

SOLUTIONS AND RECOMMENDATIONS

Ideas to resolve the main issues experienced during the "Sell your bargains" game during Semester 1 of the Academic Year 2011/12 will inform the framework of the game to be used in Semester 2. The ideas presented in this section will also be useful to others who are considering mixed-reality games for their practice.

- **More Facilitators:** Due to the progressive complexity of the game it is advisable to identify additional facilitators who could support the game organiser, especially if the game would be played with over 10 players. There should be ideally one facilitator per 10 players. The additional facilitators could be players who have successfully completed the game in the past, if for example additional tutors are not available. A briefing session needs to be organised in advance of the game with all facilitators.
- **Technologies and Support:** It would be useful to seek IT support that could be used by the players, in advance of the game and during Stage 3. Staff development and training could be offered during which players would have the opportunity to familiarise themselves with the technologies used and gain a better understanding how these would be useful during the game, boost confidence and enable players to focus on the game itself instead of the technologies. Also, it might be useful to use a buddy system or peer support groups during the game.
- **Mainstream Offer:** Instead of offering this game as an alternative to the more adventurous individuals who are naturally more open to experimentation and out-of-the-box thinking, the game should be offered to a whole cohort to immerse the more traditional and risk-averse individuals into a very different learning experience. There might also be an opportunity to involve students in this game. There is still scepticism in HE about the appropriateness of game-based learning. Therefore, it is advisable to introduce game-based learning in advance of the game, and provide opportunities for discussion and reflection with peers and tutors around game-based research and evidence of its benefits. Also, good organization and communication is needed as well as clear instructions to make playing a fun and meaningful learning activity.

- **Scaffolding Stage 3:** In order to make this task clearer and provide a scaffold approach using a template, digital stories could be developed as media-rich case studies made available in players' e-portfolios. Also digital storytelling should be introduced earlier in the module so that players can familiarise themselves with storytelling in advance of the game.

- **Further Dissemination of Digital Stories:** There is an opportunity and a need to disseminate all digital stories created and made available under Creative Commons among the wider academic community of the institution to showcase innovative teaching and learning ideas and practices. For example, players' with winning ideas and stories could be invited to facilitate a staff development session or write-up their digital story for publication and this might resolve the issue of being under-challenged and act as a motivator especially for players who are already creative practitioners. Also, all digital stories could be deposited in an institutional repository.

- **More Votes:** In order to raise awareness of game-based learning, engage others in this particular game and harvest votes for it, not just for the players and the PGCAP but also the wider academic community, it will be essential to identify suitable channels to promote this game and enable voting from within the Institution. Also, it is considered to give a prize to one lucky voter who would be selected randomly.

CONCLUSION

All players who decided to play this game as described here, enjoyed learning through play but also found it beneficial for their practice. The game was also a break from classroom teaching and learning and the routine, providing a plethora of exciting and stimulating learning opportunities something which is also seen as beneficial by Piatt (2010).

Findings confirm that game-based learning has a place in HE and enables and enhances collaboration, problem solving and communication (Johnson et al, 2011) and transforms learning into an enjoyable and effective learning experience. In mixed-reality games, physical and virtual spaces merge, interaction and interactivity is achieved through the blending of technologies that provide new opportunities for social and collaborative learning through play.

There is a need to be adventurous in our teaching and create and orchestrate stimulating learning experiences through experimentation and out-of-the box thinking. Especially, mixed-reality games bring learners, places, spaces and technologies together and create a rich and multidimensional fabric of learning. It is vital to consider spaces for learning beyond available institutional physical and virtual spaces and explore how these could be used effectively to deepen engagement and learning and enhance the student experience. There is also an opportunity to maximise the use of available technologies and other lo-fi resources owned by institutions, tutors and students for activities based on a clear pedagogical rational that have the power to truly transform learning into something exciting and stimulating.

All learners should be provided with the time and space to be creative using game-based learning approaches and other immersive learning experiences to enable a more natural way of learning through creative expression, collaboration and healthy competition.

A relatively small number, seven out of 32 cohort participants chose to participate in this mixed-reality game. Whitton's (2010) research has shown that many in HE find digital games "frivolous or a waste of time" (p. 37). This game in a previous format has been labelled as a 'patronising' activity. The 'enjoyability' of this game is something the game organizer plans to investigate further when the game is played again in its refined version with the next cohort. There are current thoughts to include students. Further research is required to come to more conclusive findings about this.

REFERENCES

Austin, T. X., & the The New Media Consortium. Retrieved January 8, 2011, from http://wp.nmc.org/horizon2011/

Barrows, H. S., & Tamblyn, R. M. (1980). *Problem-based learning. An approach to medical education*. New York, NY: Springer.

Boud, D., Cohen, R., & Sampson, J. (2001). *Peer learning in higher education: Learning from and with each other*. London, UK: Kogan.

Gardner, H. (2009). Multiple approaches to understanding. In Illeris, K. (Ed.), *Contemporary theories of learning* (pp. 106–115). Oxon, UK: Routledge.

Gauntlett, D. (2011). *Making is connecting. The social meaning of creativity, from DIY and knitting to YouTube and Web 2.0*. Cambridge, UK: Polity Press.

Johnson, L., Smith, R., Willis, H., Levine, A., & Haywood, K. (2011). *The 2011 horizon report*.

Meyer, J. H. F., & Land, R. (2003) Threshold concepts and troublesome knowledge: linkages to ways of thinking and practising, In C. Rust (Ed.), *Improving student learning - Theory and practice ten years on*, (pp. 412-424). Oxford, UK: Oxford Centre for Staff and Learning Development (OCSLD).

Montana, M. (2011). A lulogical view on the pervasive mixed-reality game research paradigm. *Personal and Ubiquitous Computing*, *15*, 3–12. doi:10.1007/s00779-010-0307-7

Moon, J. (2010). *Using story in higher education and professional development*. Oxon, UK: Routledge.

Palmer, P. J. (2007). *The courage to teach. Exploring the inner landscape of a teacher's life*. San Francisco, CA: Jossey-Bass.

Piatt, K. (2010). Who is Herring Hale? In Whitton, N. (Ed.), *Learning with digital games: A practical guide to engaging students in higher education* (pp. 167–171). Oxon, UK: Routledge.

Ramsden, P. (2003). *Learning to teach in higher education*. Oxon, UK: Routledge-Falmer.

Whitton, N. (2010). *Learning with digital games. A practical guide to engaging students in higher education*. Oxon, UK: Routledge.

Section 3
Designing Games for Learning

Chapter 9
Medicina:
Methods, Models, Strategies

Amanda Müller
Flinders University, Australia

Gregory Mathews
Flinders University, Australia

EXECUTIVE SUMMARY

The School of Nursing & Midwifery at Flinders University provides dedicated support for the English language needs of over 500 international students. As part of a strategic plan to deal with communication difficulties among these students, a series of language-learning initiatives are being implemented. One of these is a game called Medicina, which has already undergone the full cycle of development, testing, and release. This game familiarizes students with confusable and common medication names. It also aims to improve phonological awareness through a focus on word form. This chapter discusses the creation of Medicina from inception through to dissemination, detailing the stages, challenges, and lessons learned in the process, in the hope of informing other educators of the level of commitment involved in a digital game-based project.

OVERALL DESCRIPTION

The School of Nursing & Midwifery at Flinders University provides dedicated support for the English language needs of over 500 international students. As part of a strategic plan to deal with communication difficulties among these students, a series of language-learning initiatives are being implemented. One of these is a

DOI: 10.4018/978-1-4666-2848-9.ch009

game called *Medicina*, which has already undergone the full cycle of development, testing, and release. This game familiarizes students with confusable and common medication names. It also aims to improve phonological awareness through a focus on word form. This chapter will discuss the creation of *Medicina* from inception through to dissemination, detailing the stages, challenges, and lessons learned in the process, in the hope of informing other educators of the level of commitment involved in a digital game-based project.

LITERATURE REVIEW

The *Medicina* game has been created in order to support learning and address existing problems with language among international English-as-a-Second Language (ESL) students. The exact cause of the communication difficulties needs to be ascertained before a game could be considered. The identification of the problem can be achieved through a number of means: a needs-analysis, educators' judgments, a literature review, feedback from students, and a review of policy. Before *Medicina* was conceived, a needs analysis was conducted, as described next.

Needs Analysis and a Definition of the Problem Addressed by the Game

As a part of the needs-analysis study of international students' language difficulties, a combination of information sources was used. We did a literature review of nursing journals documenting the language problems found among international ESL students in the health field. We also obtained a personal analysis of the commonalities among struggling students referred for one-on-one assessment. We also combined feedback from the clinical coach who deals with struggling students, feedback from clinical facilitators, and other sources of anecdotal evidence gathered at committee meetings and from students within English classes. This needs assessment was published in Müller (2011).

Among the international students, it was identified that a lack of specialist vocabulary knowledge was found to be a key underlying issue, and listening was found to be a focal skill deficiency. While most international students possess an advanced level of general English, it is specialized medical terminology (including medication names) and the colloquial language used by patients which pose the greatest problems. This is unsurprising because these classes of vocabulary can be considered low-frequency, which means that the student is not often exposed to these words, and there are few opportunities to engage with them before being assessed on their use.

How Serious Was the Problem?

During a literature search of the problematic communicative situations, those that involved medications emerged as a serious issue needing immediate attention. The literature which foregrounds the game points out the level of difficulty students have with interpreting spoken medication names and identifying a specific medication from a range of stored medications. Students report great difficulty in interpreting the names of medications when given by telephone (Blackman & Hall, 2009, p. 179). This is a problem because "nursing is highly dependent on accurate verbal communication and much of the information and many orders are passed on verbally" (Guhde, 2003, p. 113). Less difficult, but still complex tasks are: (1) identifying a specific medication from a range of stored medications; and (2) listening to spoken handovers. The concept of *Medicina* began when we realised that the problems occurred at the level of language encoding and comprehension. Difficulty understanding speech indicates both a lack of automatic vocabulary recognition and an inadequate phonological awareness. Phonological awareness is the ability to process sounds or letters and decode them into recognisable words. Thus, without automatic vocabulary recognition and good phonological awareness, the students' capacity to decode, recognise, and understand a communicative act is substantially hampered.

With regards to difficulties with confusable medication names, clinical facilitators have reported anecdotally the conflation of 'pethidine' with 'betadine' as an example, which is a serious error to make. Since medication dispensing is subject to reporting procedures when an incident occurs, there is a range of publications which list medications which have been confused, often with a number of suggestions about other confusable names to be aware of. In the very least, a game which highlights the problem of confused medications and shows confusable alternatives (this will be explained later in this paper) is in itself an important outcome. When that game also fosters an improvement of reading and listening skills through raising phonological awareness, it is an added benefit.

Acquisition of Vocabulary

Learning vocabulary is not a simple task, and learning low-frequency medication names is even harder to do. Second language learners cannot be expected to hear a word once and have complete mastery over that term. Indeed, when a native speaker hears a medication name for the first time, they may need to hear and use that new word a few times before they feel familiar with it and to 'make it stick' in their mind. Nation (2001, pp. 26-8) provides a theory of vocabulary learning that recognizes three aspects of vocabulary acquisition: form, meaning, and use. The first stage involves gaining familiarity with the form of the word, such as its features, spelling, pronunciation, and the composition of its parts. The second stage involves knowledge of meaning, which for nursing students would involve understanding what type of medication it is, what it does, and associated medications. The third stage involves use, such as appropriate ways to use the word in a sentence, such as constraints on its use, appropriate terms that can be used with the medication name, and how often we would expect to come across the term again.

Another factor involved with learning vocabulary is the number of times a second language learner might need to pass through Nation's first stage of vocabulary acquisition. The research indicates that between eight to ten exposures, where the second language student might read or hear the medication, would establish a sufficient base to then build a solid understanding of meaning and use (Schmitt, 2008, p. 348). The reason for this is that language fluency requires solid skills at the level of form in order to make decoding and recognition become automatized. This means that less time and effort is spent dealing with the processing of the word itself, with more time and effort being devoted to the intended meaning of the communication. When automatization occurs, cognitive resources are freed for other tasks, instead of being concerned with processing the communicative medium itself. This issue is discussed further in the next section.

Cognitive Processes for Optimal Learning

Digital educational games must take into account the same cognitive factors of learning that language educators abide by: information overload is detrimental to learning. The mind can only process a limited amount of information at any given time, and it is important to understand how people learn in order to be an effective teacher and digital game designer. Important concepts that contribute to successful educational gaming are: the role of working memory in learning, the relationship between working memory and long-term memory, the cognitive structures which contribute to information processing, and the optimisation of learning through multimodal input.

A reference which may be useful is Bruning, Schraw, and Norby (2011). Chapter two of their book defines the separate memory system functions, before going on to explain the limitations of attention and perception, and how cognitive processes may be automatic or controlled. They outline the research on two of the sensory registers, visual and auditory, and the effect on learning. For information on processing through the other sensory registers, specifically haptic representations, see Sadoski and Paivio (2004). An excellent article discussing cognitive load and element interactivity is by Sweller (2010).

Practicalities of Creating the Game

Putting forward a compelling case for a digital educational game can be difficult because there are so many other modes of delivery available. A game can be costly, time-intensive, and difficult to design successfully. This section discusses the method by which the *Medicina* game was conceptualised, and implemented.

Is a Game Needed?

The first question an educator must ask is whether the digital game mode of delivery is an effective choice. At times, a computer game is an inefficient method of delivery for educational content. In such situations, it may be better to offer online tutorials, self-test quizzes, checklists, simple board games, and other methods of delivery. The teacher also has to consider the wider curriculum, asking what is already taught, what delivery methods are already used, and how effective these are for student learning. If there many similar online activities, the student may be bored by the lack of variation in format. A digital game needs to address a current gap or replace a presently ineffective means of content delivery. In the case of *Medicina*, both of these factors were present. The latter provided the impetus for the former: it was clear that ESL students experienced considerable communication difficulties which the current curriculum did not address. The educational strategies of expecting students to naturally acquire health terminology while they studied, helped by reading glossaries or dictionaries, had not been particularly effective. A game might be a suitable means to deliver important language items while also motivating students to focus on these important terms.

Conceptualisation and Design of a Digital Game-Based Solution

A search across a number of sources and databases showed that there was no existing medication name game that could be bought, so we decided to create *Medicina* and tailor it to our students' needs. The first thing that we needed to decide upon was what sort of game would be suitable for our educational content. What would it look like and what would it do?

As a part of the formation process for *Medicina*, the team played a wide range of existing games, with the objective of discovering how a particular item or feature gains focus in a game, what are the distractions, what components are motivating for the player, and what are the negative aspects. Just as experience of a good and bad classroom help a teacher to improve their craft, gaming experiences may assist an educator to understand how the digital gaming medium might handle the information exchange needed for educational purposes. A good knowledge of the learning outcomes and the type of tasks you will set can be particularly useful for evaluating the possibility of a particular game's educational suitability. There are a number of other references which can help with the details of game design. Clark and Mayer (2008) provide gaming principles based on research. Dondlinger (2006) reviews the literature, from 1996 to 2006, that identifies elements of design that support learning. Similarly, Pivec and Pivec (2011) discuss how to design a game, what the important game elements might be, and how to support learning. Finally, Van Eck makes some suggestions about which game types might promote particular learning outcomes (2006, p. 22).

Creating the basic concept for the game is essentially a creative process, but it is aided by a clear idea of what one is trying to achieve and the literature in the area. It helps to have a clear idea of what level of educational interaction are needed between the various parts of the game. In *Medicina*, the elements that the player will manipulate are words, in both spoken and written form. We found that Biggs' SOLO taxonomy (1999, pp. 66-7) was particularly useful because it highlights the interactivity of elements within a task and helped define how that task might fit into the curriculum.

Another approach to conceptualising a game is to imagine what the student would need to do in order to demonstrate that they have achieved the educational outcomes. This is normally the task of assessment, since good assessment, according to Biggs (1999, p. 65), is part of a bigger picture where the objectives have already been decided. Assessment both defines what needs to be learned and checks the level of learning the student achieves. In *Medicina*, since the heart of the gameplay is multiple choice assessment tasks, students can self-assess their skills by how well they have matched a spoken word to its written form, and they also get feedback on whether they completed the task quickly enough.

The planned multimodal nature of the digital gaming medium is its strength, because it increases the opportunity to simultaneously present key information that requires player interaction. Games allow the control and release of information in a way that can maximize learning. Games can simulate the important elements of a situation or task, but without overloading the senses as often happens in real life. Keeping this in mind, it was decided that cartoon-styled graphics were suitable for *Medicina*, but the voices of the speakers were real and varied, and were presented while a range of hospital-based noises were present in the background. This is aligned with the notion that realism should be minimized if it is not aligned to instructional objectives (Clark & Meyer, 2008, p. 362). Indeed, too much irrelevant detail can be detrimental to learning (Van Merrienboer & Kester, 2005, pp. 79-80). In order to decide upon the important factors which contribute to completing the instructional objective, we used an ethnographic model of communication to analyse where communicative breakdown was currently occurring. Dell Hymes' 'SPEAKING' model details the components of linguistic interaction that needed consideration (1974, pp. 53-62). Using the model, we were guided through a delineating process of features such as time constraints, physical environment, and social interactions involved in achieving communicative competence.

Overview of the *Medicina* Game

We decided that the heart of the gameplay in *Medicina* would be to answer multiple-choice questions, which are designed to assess successful listening discrimination and spelling identification within minimal pairs-styled tasks. To complete the multiple-choice task, the student listens to the question posed by a character, moves their character to choose a written option among five similar possibilities, receives verbal and written feedback, experiences their avatar responding to their choice, sees the animated consequence on a patient, and is given a score. The continuation of the game depends on the choice made, where the player is forced into choosing, or the game ends. Being much more than a common multiple-choice test, the game has a number of educational interactions, some occurring simultaneously:

- Repeated exposure to spoken and written medication names – which encourages familiarity with terms, their constituent word parts, and their confusable counterparts, supporting the process of automaticity.
- Discrimination between similar words – which improves phonological awareness (including orthographic awareness), and improves word-part familiarity, and again, supporting the process of automaticity.
- Time-limitation on the task – which forces the player to interact (improving focus on task and personal involvement), to encourage faster listening and reading skills, providing the impetus to improve phonological awareness, and development of word-part recognition.
- Immediate visual, written, and spoken feedback – which allows self-monitoring of performance, modification of inefficient or incorrect metacognitive strategies, thereby providing a measure of achievement.

It was expected that the skills gained within the game were expected to impact on wider educational and clinical performance. With greater phonological awareness, the student theoretically was better equipped to deal with the content of lectures and tutorials. It was also anticipated that, with a familiarity with medication names in both spoken and written forms, the student would be more confident in situations where they dealt with medications, such as on the hospital ward.

Practicality of Running the Game

Storyboarding and Scripting

At this point, we charted the game onto a whiteboard, refining and defining the basic game concept and gaming action. This included an outline of what the frames would look like, the artistic directions we would take, and the pathways for action (if 'x' happens, then 'y' pathway is chosen). A formal game development storyboard was then written up. This provided a visual outline of the sequencing of the screens, a set of schematics, and a state diagram for gameplay. It also provided an overview of basic action, detailed description, and information about aspects of the game, such as information displays (HUDs) and the external resources used. The game development storyboard is particularly useful for scripting purposes.

- **Start-Up Screens**
  - ○ Splash Screen
  - ○ Loading
  - ○ Login
  - ○ Create Name
- **Menu Screens**
  - ○ Scores
  - ○ Avatar Choice
  - ○ Aims/Credits/Disclaimer
  - ○ How to Play
- **In-Game Screens**
  - ○ Game Countdown
  - ○ Game Play
  - ○ Game Feedback
  - ○ Game Transition Animation
  - ○ End Game Animation
- **Out-of-Game Cheat-Sheet**
  - ○ Click and play website of all the medication names used in the game

Assets

All elements of the game (assets) were specifically created for *Medicina*. These included text files, audio files, written medication names, art files (including avatars and characters), and animation files. The audio files include the background audio/music, interface audio, incidental audio, and vocal audio. A database was used as a master document to show how each file related to each other element, such as indicating which audio file belongs to each piece of written text. At any given moment during the gameplay of *Medicina*, a multitude of assets are being drawn upon. For each text asset, e.g. for the word 'pethidine', presented during *Medicina* gameplay, four other text assets are also displayed, and for each of these words there is a pronunciation audio file, a request sentence, a negative feedback statement, and a positive feedback statement. Thus, for each group of five words that is presented in each round, there are five text assets and twenty audio assets. The point being made here is that there are many assets being used at any given time and a database is a necessary means of managing all the related elements.

Technology Components: Available Software and Hardware

Most staff in the University have a fairly uniform Microsoft Windows 7 setup with Active Directory and Exchange. A minimum set of desktop applications and utilities are also provided for both student labs and across all staff computers. Flinders University also centrally supports a variety of technologies such as Flinders Learning Online, the set of technologies accessible on the web through a web-based Learning Management system, which enables the creation of online activities such as multiple-choice quizzes, cloze tests, and discussion forums. In each topic, a minimum set of activities and tools are mandated for the student web view. These are asynchronous and mostly text-based – with some images and infrequently, audio. There was no existing protocol for digital game-based learning. As a result, we considered the current software and hardware profile of the university and what we know of how students interact within it, and we decided that a student should not need to install extra software to play the game, nor require access to a particular platform or gaming system. Furthermore, the game needed to reduce any digital overheads incurred in the normal processes of saving gameplay results and other game administration.

Technology Components: Server Load and Download Times

As *Medicina* is a language acquisition game, it requires a lot of audio to work. The complicating factor is that many of our students operate over a variety of internet speeds, and audio files take time to download. Reaction time in these games is often a factor, so streamlined performance is very important. This means as little latency as possible is required when loading and playing audio, which can be a problem when the game uses about 500 compressed audio files. Waiting for sound to be uploaded from the web server during the gameplay itself would seriously interrupt the flow of the game, and thus, the attention of the students. Furthermore, feedback from student surveys in relation to streamed video lectures indicated that students prefer to wait longer for initial uploading, than to have interrupted streaming. We elected to load the audio files from the server when the game itself was uploaded. A special screen was designed to indicate that the game is uploading, in which the student sees a progress bar, watches an animation, and hears jazzy start-up music.

Even though the game has been created and released to the students, we still have to watch for any problems with server load. The choice of server-side technology and database was pre-determined by the School web development server. This contained a Postgres database and a fixed PHP scripting environment. Flinders University provides some development webspace on one of the servers, likely to be on a virtual machine that was on a computer shared amongst other faculties. When the game was running (despite the audio files being loaded already), some dropouts and transfer time lags were noted during high usage periods. The reason for this is that each mouse click by the student is being saved to a database, and rapid file transfer is also required. We are considering cloud hosting, such as Amazon Web Services to insure against this in the future, when there is an increase in users.

Technology Components: Game Engine

Running a game in an internet browser has many advantages. They can be deployed and shared with others using a simple web link. This also makes them easy to distribute from inside a Learning Management System. However, the choice of game engine was the most difficult technological decision. After consideration, the leading contenders for web technologies were HTML5, Java, Adobe Flash and other web-publishable game engines, such as Torque, Unity and Corona. These are described below:

HTML5

At the time when we decided upon the platform, HTML5 technology held much promise. However, comparable examples at the time either ran too slowly, were restricted to working on only particular browsers, or required additional installations. There was also no reliable way to play audio quickly when something happened in the game.

Java

Java has good support across multiple platforms and generally performs rapidly. Unfortunately, we were not unable to find a mature game development environment. We also had mixed student experiences with conflicts between versions of the latest Java Runtime Environment and the older version of the environment required for our Blackboard learning management system to run on. Together, these points dissuaded us from using Java.

Torque, Unity, and Corona

Torque, Unity, and Corona have great cross-platform and mobile support, however they all require plugin software to be installed, in order to run on browsers using MS Windows. Unfortunately, they are not installed on any of the staff Windows desktops or student computing labs across the University, which we were informed would be a large undertaking.

Adobe Flash Player

Flash is easy to prototype rapidly and proceeds smoothly from mock-ups to a full product. Flash has the disadvantage of not running on Apple Mobile devices; however it can be converted into a form that does. Flash has the advantage of being pre-installed on nearly all browsers on PCs and a variety of tablets. It is also already supported on the University desktop environments.

We decided to use Flash as the browser plugin. There is a plan to provide the game for mobile phones. To provide for Apple mobile devices, we have budgeted to have the games converted to the Apple iOS platform. Although Adobe provide a Flash converter, it is possible that the games will be ported to one of the other platforms such as Corona.

Technology Components: Authentication and Security

The server-side scripting and the database are both fairly basic, merely saving and loading student choices, scores, choice of avatar and login names. The login names presented a problem because we had to decide whether to let students use their existing student identification or choose a gaming nickname. All students at Flinders are given a unique Flinders Access Number or FAN, which is recorded in our TechnologyOne Student System. We decided against using this official student login for the game, instead opting for a simple nickname for three reasons: anonymity, potential audience, and security. An individually chosen pseudonym gives students the option of remaining anonymous, since high scores are posted in the game, and the student can safely explore their environment without embarrassment. The potential audience was also a consideration, so it was decided not to use official university login names. This allowed the game to be shown to people outside the University. Finally, a much higher onus on security would be required if Flinders student logins were used, as these are used across all student logins. This presents a security problem, and moreover, any integration with the Student System would unnecessarily increase the scope of the project.

EVALUATION

Three types of evaluation are discussed in this section: the ongoing evaluative process during the development of the game, the evaluation of the effectiveness of the game on learning, and the use of a game for formal assessment purposes.

Evaluation during Game Development

Initially, the game's effectiveness was evaluated according to the game authors' reactions. It was played many times, allowing us to tweak aspects for improvement, such as timing, how difficult it was felt to be for international students, or whether it seemed boring. This was an important phase of the game's development because it is when the tweaking and polishing occurs. After the game was deemed ready to play, it was shown to students on a big screen in class to get their initial feedback. From their comments, the timing was tweaked and the audio was adjusted. The game was then released for a small number of people to use. This was to test if the system could withstand multiple users. Thereafter, a study was run using the game, in preparation for its release. The results of this study would allow us to provide students with research-based information about what kind of results might be gained through playing the game, and how long it took to see this improvement. This is explained in the next section.

Evaluation of Game Effectiveness

After gaining ethics approval, we used an intervention pre-test/post-test design to measure student improvement in phonological awareness (which underpins listening and reading skills). We also conducted a qualitative survey. We did not test to see whether students had memorised the names because, after an average of 688 rounds, or 100 minutes spent within the game, it was highly likely that they were familiar with the bank of medication names. Furthermore, it was also highly likely that the students had an increased awareness of how these medicines could, and have been, confused within the health setting. Instead, we focused on the generalisability of the game in terms of the development of phonological awareness, and improvements in the ability to deal with novel medication names. The results of this study can be found in Mller (2012).

Participants completed the pre-test, played the game (the intervention) as much as they wanted during a two-week period, and then completed the post-test. The same test was used each time. As the test did not use real words, participants were unlikely to learn them, and thus affect the findings. Each test word contained two parts of a real word, either from the game or outside of it. Thus, the word parts 'cele' and 'mide' might be combined to produce 'celemide'. Incorrect distractor answers were variations on this fake word, and incorporated common Asian interference phonemes (most of our students are from China, Korea, India, and South-East Asia). The result was a correct answer of 'celemide', presented next to distractor answers of 'ceremide', 'celemite', and 'ceremite'.

A dependent t-test was conducted on the pre-test and post-test scores. Overall, participants experienced a significant increase in phonological awareness $t(24) = -5.18$, $p < .0001$), as evident in the scores found in the pre-test (M = 36, SE = .87) as compared to the post-test (M = 40, SE = .55) administered after the intervention. The effect size was $r = .73$, which is a substantive finding. Similar results were found for the word parts that the participants were exposed to in *Medicina*, slightly higher than those which were not found in the game. The qualitative survey was quite positive, with some common themes emerging. There was an overall satisfaction with the ability of the game to familiarize participants with Australian accents. Participants also regarded the game as ideal preparation for the fast-paced and noisy environment of the hospital ward. They felt increased confidence to deal with their clinical placement, and were able to engage better in class as a result. They also felt the school had shown concern for them by creating *Medicina* to help them learn.

Use of a Game for Evaluation of Students

Essentially, *Medicina* was intended to support and prepare the students for assessment in the wider curriculum. It will not be used to test the students for formal grading purposes: adding further formal assessment is unnecessarily stressful when there is already a substantial amount of testing in the curriculum. Furthermore, emphasising educational assessment transforms the game from a fun exploration of skill boundaries into a serious test of ability – with a result that stays permanently on your official record. Nonetheless, the game uses formative assessment for each round and a summative assessment score at the end of the game, but these are arguably forms of feedback rather than assessment in the traditional sense. Indeed, the game harnesses a third type of assessment – ipsative assessment – where the student assesses their own progress against their own previous personal-best scores rather than comparing themselves to an institutionally-dictated norm.

CHALLENGES

The two main challenges in creating *Medicina*, which have not yet been discussed, are the wider issues of convincing an educational institution to adopt game-based learning, and finding sources of funding to make the game. This section will present a series of arguments used to show how these two objectives can be achieved.

Compelling an Organization to Adopt Digital Game-Based Learning

It is important to understand the organizational context within which digital game-based learning might be situated, and *Medicina* was no exception to this rule. It was created within Flinders University, a publically-owned institution that provides education and research. The university has faculties within which Schools follow a line-management structure. In financial terms, it is a Commonwealth-funded organisation enacted by state legislation. The Flinders University School of Nursing & Midwifery has around 2,400 students, with approximately 23% being international students. This percentage of international students is higher than the approximately 18% of the remaining 16,000 students in the rest of the university. Within this context, arguments for the funding and approval of the game had to be made. Particular themes arose from the overall argument which successfully convinced various parts of the institution to accept the *Medicina* concept.

Logistics-Based Argument

The School of Nursing & Midwifery has campuses in both city and country areas, and engages in remote education. The school has at least 500 international students, mostly from China, Korea, India, and South-East Asia. Considering the increased need for ESL support for international students, and the use of distance education for remote campuses, any online resource which can independently improve the skills of the students will also help relieve the teaching load of over 140 staff who teach in the School. Thus, if the digital game-based educational medium successfully improves the less than optimal communication skills of students, it will compel its acceptance in the school.

In the case of *Medicina*, it delivers lessons about what medication names sound like, how medication names are spelled, what confusions might, or have, occurred with medication orders, and this is all achieved in an environment in which the student improves their language processing skills and response times to medication orders. The game delivers immediate personalised feedback and allows students to compare personal best scores. The game also allows students to learn at their own pace, in terms of when and where they engage in the task, and when they opt out for rest or further personal investigation. They can engage with the educational content at any time in a 24-hour period. It is physically impossible for a teacher to achieve this kind of one-on-one teaching in an hour-long class which has an average of 30 students. Imagine a situation where you have a minimum of 500 ESL students in your care, undertaking one out of over 25 possible courses with different classes scheduled throughout the week. The ESL students are frequently recognised as being at a disadvantage as compared to native speakers because of their lower language skills, thus such a game, with in-built flexibility and time-efficiency, will be a significant help for this cohort.

Budget-Based Argument

Another argument that can be put forward for an educational game is its value to the budget. This is a variation on the logistics argument that states that there are not enough teaching hours to fulfil the educational needs of the students. A game is useful because it reduces pressure to hire more staff to fulfil this need. The budget-based argument is disliked by teachers who fear they will be replaced by a game. They worry that they will lose their jobs if they are no longer needed. However, this is an unlikely scenario. What must be understood is that a game is an ideal option for skills that require mundane repetition or low-level content learning. When this is removed from the classroom, higher-level cognitive and linguistic development can be encouraged by a teacher who is no longer burdened with teaching the basics. The game will prepare students in advance, and if they are not prepared, the opportunity to engage in the educational content remains open after the class. Indeed, the time to worry is when digital game-based learning is developed as a commercial interest specifically to replace teachers. The market is neither big enough, nor specific enough, to make the kind of money needed to create such a resource, so teachers should have little fear for their employment.

Policy-Based Argument

The policy-based argument was confidently put forward because the Flinders University context is favourable towards innovations in teaching. The notion of forging new directions in the delivery of educational materials aligns with this aim, making favourable conditions for forays into game-based learning. A university with a more traditional educational delivery focus would be much less open to this mode of delivery. It is also fortunate that the School of Nursing & Midwifery itself is placed within a Faculty which is openly committed to flexible learning and distance education. The faculty openly welcomes simulation as an important means of learning. A digital game has a degree of simulation and the task of a game encourages learning by doing, i.e. experiential learning.

When justifying the creation of *Medicina*, the strategic plan of the university was an important reference point. The strategic plan details the aims and intended directions of an institution, and executives and committees refer to it in their decision-making. A strategic plan which explicitly states the desire to move to on-line learning would be more favourable to digital game-based learning than a plan that seeks to improve on-campus participation in the classroom. In the case of the Flinders University Strategic Plan, there are a number of points which can be used to support a request for digital game-based education: to enhance the student experience, to strengthen internationalisation, and to enhance educational opportunities. The student experience is enhanced by *Medicina* in three ways. Firstly, through a diversification of delivery methods (thus increasing motivation to participate); secondly, through the simulation aspect of *Medicina,* which provides a safe practice area for carrying out communicative tasks, and an improvement in language skills through familiarisation with medication names; and thirdly, through the theorised improvement of language skills which will help ESL students engage with educational content (rather than wasting time on the language processing needed to access the educational content). Since the game is aimed at ESL students, it supports the university's aim to strengthen internationalisation. Finally, the desire to enhance educational opportunities is supported by digital game-based education, because this mode of delivery is portable and accessible.

A further source of justification for *Medicina* was found by accessing and examining government policies for education providers. It was established that the national Good Practice Principles required a certain number of English language initiatives for international students at Australian universities (AUQA, 2008; DEWWR, 2007). Furthermore, it was discovered that the aims of *Medicina* would help students meet the national accreditation body's standards ANMC (2006). This is a policy issue that contains liability problems if some effort is not made to address the guidelines, creating possible grounds for complaint and, potentially, legal action against the school or institution.

Student-Based Argument

The student-based argument can be combined with the former arguments by presenting the same issues from a student point of view. Digital games have been an important part of childhood for many people (Kirriemuir & McFarlane, 2004, p. 8).

Considering the interest level in games for learning reported in surveys of primary and secondary students and their teachers, forays into game-based learning seems reasonable (Facer, Ulicsak, & Sandford, 2007, p.48). The research tends to show improved learning outcomes when comparing games to lectures (Mayo, 2008, p. 29). Games are also motivating and provide important learning opportunities, as detailed in Pivec and Pivec (2011, pp. 3-4) Digital games are also viewed as a good drill and practice medium for learning (Van Eck, 2006, p. 22). Finally, games encourage participation and risk-taking (Dickey, 2006).

Applying for Grants/Funding

Once the areas of student need in the curriculum are identified, a literature review conducted of those areas of need, exploration of the availability of existing solutions, an identification of the various policies, and the formation of a possible digital game-based solution have been made, the next step is to find a way to create the game or obtain an existing one. This usually involves applying for funding. The arguments above provided sufficient rationale to successfully attract funding from three sources, greatly facilitating the quality and expertise needed for the creation of *Medicina*.

Disappointment should be avoided if a grant does not get approved, as the creation of a simple game design may not require funding. There are ways to circumvent the need for money, for example, by involving local student programmers and artists looking for experience or a placement as part of their studies. Any audio recordings can be created by the teacher, or sometimes obtained legally online for free or for a small cost. If the educator has a clear idea of a simple game with simple responses to a set task within the game, it can be a laborious, but cheap, process to create. The real cost is on the educators' time. In this case, the only task for the educator is to ensure that the game is approved by the intended institution, and permission is sought (and granted) to have the game hosted on the school website or distributed via memory stick, DVD, or another storage medium. It should also be noted that there are downfalls to making a game without funding. A game produced using volunteer labour cannot be sold without causing a number of legal issues associated with intellectual property, contributor rights, and profit distribution. An educator may find that they cannot alter other people's contributions, or distribute the game to others without all parties consent. This pathway requires careful planning and contracts to be drawn up before work is commenced.

SUMMARY

This chapter has detailed the steps involved in the creation of *Medicina*. It began with an analysis of the problem that was to be addressed through a digital game-based solution. This involved an understanding of the nature of the problem, the processes involved with learning medication names, and the cognitive processes that need to be addressed to optimise learning. The conceptualisation of the game itself was discussed next, and how to support the creative activity involved in educational game design. This lead to a full exploration of the features which might need to be in the game, such as the screens, assets, and game engine. The technological context was seen as a constraining factor which guided the direction of the project, including server load and downloading times.

Next the chapter outlined the feedback and evaluation processes that we undertook. Clearly, evaluation played a key role in deciding the educational content, the ongoing game development, and allowed us to test the effectiveness of the game when used by real learners. The final part of the chapter explored the challenging issue of how to gain approval and funding for a digital game-based project. A number of arguments were presented that might guide others when they promote their own gaming ideas. It was seen that a digital game-based solution has to be considered in terms of logistics, budget, policy, and finally, student needs. Once these factors are successfully identified, application for funding is made easier.

Finally, one issue remains which has not been addressed yet within this chapter. However, it is addressed by the chapter itself, and this is the act of dissemination. Dissemination completes the cycle of development and implementation, for it provides others with important information about what works, why certain elements were chosen, and how the process might be replicated. It is the basis for designing new projects. Hopefully, this chapter has achieved this aim.

REFERENCES

ANMC. (2006). *National competency standards for the registered nurse*. Australian Nursing and Midwifery Council. Retrieved from http://www.anmc.org.au/userfiles/file/competency_standards/Competency_standards_RN.pdf

AUQA. (2008). *Good practice principles for english language proficiency for international students in Australian universities – Final report*. Australian Universities Quality Agency. Retrieved from http://www.deewr.gov.au/HigherEducation/Publications/Documents/Final_Report-Good_Practice_Principles.pdf

Biggs, J. (1999). What the student does: Teaching for enhanced learning. *Higher Education Research & Development, 18*(1), 57–75. doi:10.1080/0729436990180105

Blackman, I., & Hall, M. (2009). Estimating the complexity of applied English language skills. In Matthews, B. (Ed.), *The process of research in education: A Festschrift in honour of John P Keeves AM* (pp. 167–183). Adelaide, Australia: Shannon Research Press.

Bruning, R. H., Schraw, G. J., & Norby, M. M. (2011). *Cognitive psychology and instruction* (5th ed.). Boston, MA: Pearson.

Clark, R., & Mayer, R. E. (2008). *E-learning and the science of instruction* (2nd ed.). San Francisco, CA: Jossey-Bass.

DEEWR. (2007). *National code of practice for registration authorities and providers of education and training to overseas students.* Australian Government Department of Education Employment and Workplace Relations. Retrieved from http://www.aei.gov.au/AEI/ESOS/NationalCodeOfPractice2007/National_Code_2007_pdf.pdf

Dickey, M. D. (2006). *Ninja looting for instructional design: The design challenges of creating a game-based learning environment.* Paper presented at the ACM SIG-GRAPH 2006 Conference, Boston.

Dondlinger, M. J. (2006). Educational video game design: A review of the literature. *Journal of Applied Educational Technology, 3*(1), 21–31.

Facer, K., Ulicsak, M., & Sandford, R. (2007). Can computer games go to school…? *Emerging Technologies for Learning, 2*, 47-63. Retrieved from http://www.mmiweb.org.uk/publications/ict/emerging_tech02.pdf

Guhde, J. A. (2003). English-as-a-second language (ESL) nursing students: Strategies for building verbal and written language skills. *Journal of Cultural Diversity, 10*(4), 113–117.

Hymes, D. (1974). *Foundations in sociolinguistics: An ethnographic approach.* Philadelphia, PA: University of Pennsylvania Press.

Kirriemuir, J., & McFarlane, A. (2004). *Report 8: Literature review in games and learning.* Bristol, UK: Nesta Futurelab Series. Retrieved from http://www.futurelab.org.uk/resources/documents/lit_reviews/Games_Review.pdf

Mayo, M. (2009). Want to truly scale a learning program? Try gaming. *Kaufmann Thoughtbook, 3*. Ewing Marion Kauffman Foundation. Retrieved from http://www.kauffman.org/education/try-gaming.aspx

Müller, A. (2011). Addressing the English language needs of international nursing students. *Journal of Academic Language & Learning, 5*(2), A14–A22.

Muller, A. (2012). Improving the identification of medication names by increasing phonological awareness. In Arnab, S., Dunwell, I., & Debattista, K. (Eds.), *Serious games for healthcare: Applications and implications*. Hershey, PA: IGI Global. doi:10.4018/978-1-4666-1903-6.ch014

Nation, I. S. P. (2010). *Learning vocabulary in another language*. Cambridge, UK: Cambridge University Press.

Pivec, M., & Pivec, P. (2011). Digital games: Changing education, one raid at a time. *International Journal of Game-Based Learning, 1*(1), 1–18. doi:10.4018/ijgbl.2011010101

Sadoski, M., & Paivio, A. (2004). A dual coding theoretical model of reading. In Ruddell, R. B., & Unrau, N. J. (Eds.), *Theoretical models and processes of reading* (5th ed., pp. 1329–1362). Newark, DE: International Reading Association. doi:10.1598/0872075028.47

Schmitt, N. (2008). Review article: Instructed second language vocabulary learning. *Language Teaching Research, 12*(3), 329–363. doi:10.1177/1362168808089921

Sweller, J. (2010). Element interactivity and intrinsic, extraneous, and germane cognitive load. *Educational Psychology Review, 22*(2). doi:10.1007/s10648-010-9128-5

Van Eck, R. (2006). Digital games-based learning: It's not just the digital natives who are restless. *EDUCAUSE Review, 41*(2), 16–30.

Van Merriënboer, J. J. G., & Kester, L. (2005). The four-component instructional design model: Multimedia principles in environments for complex learning. In Mayer, R. E. (Ed.), *Cambridge handbook of multimedia learning* (pp. 71–93). Cambridge, UK: Cambridge University Press. doi:10.1017/CBO9780511816819.006

KEY TERMS AND DEFINITIONS

Assets: The assets are the resources that the game engine or game logic uses to make the game work. Assets may be text, graphics, animations, sounds, icons, textures, etc.

Automaticity: Automaticity refers to a rapid and effortless processing of input which indicates a minimal allocation of cognitive resources. Automaticity of word form refers to an effortless processing of sounds, spellings, and features into whole words, thus enabling more attention to be given to meaning and use of those words.

Game Engine: The game engine is the computational framework, or software platform, that handles the game logic and assets.

Phonological Awareness: Phonological awareness refers to knowledge of the entire phonological system – knowing not only the range of sounds and phonemes used in a language, but also their articulation, permissible sequences and variations, assimilation rules, and more.

Storyboarding: Storyboarding is done pre-production and provides a visual idea of what the game may look like when it is finished. It may be done simply by using graphically depicting the main sequences, but it also can involve more complex descriptions and notes on how the game works.

Chapter 10
Strategies for Effective Digital Games Development and Implementation

T. Lim
Heriot-Watt University, UK

S. Louchart
Heriot-Watt University, UK

N. Suttie
Heriot-Watt University, UK

J.M. Ritchie
Heriot-Watt University, UK

R.S. Aylett
Heriot-Watt University, UK

I. A. Stănescu
"Carol I" National Defense University, Romania

I. Roceanu
"Carol I" National Defense University, Romania

I. Martinez-Ortiz
Universidad Complutense de Madrid, Spain

P. Moreno-Ger
Universidad Complutense de Madrid, Spain

EXECUTIVE SUMMARY

Digital technologies have increased the pace of knowledge creation, sharing, and the way in which learning is being undertaken. This chapter considers how Serious Games (SGs) as a digital technology endeavours to support effective lifelong learning. Three fundamental characteristics of the SG ecosystem, namely, game mechanics, interoperability, and assessment, are considered here as strategic elements that impact upon how SGs are to support learning, how they affect the learning environ-

DOI: 10.4018/978-1-4666-2848-9.ch010

ment, and ultimately, the SG development process. A prospective deconstruction of SGs into its pedagogical elements and its game mechanic nodes is presented to make aware the interoperability modus from which topical (domain) frameworks or architectures can be structured and assessed. To this end, the chapter explores the conceptual underpinnings through a case study on the eAdventure platform and argues that the key elements form the foundation for strategic development and implementation of SGs.

INTRODUCTION

The expansion of technology-enhanced learning coupled with the evolution of the "NET generation" has created new opportunities for immersive and engaging game-based experiences. Serious Games (SGs) represent an enhanced technological platform for complex skills learning (Westera, 2008). The caveat however is the dependence on technology to drive the learning process rather than the learner. Simply transcribing existing material and instructional method into a SG domain can be detrimental if careful consideration is not given to the designs and approaches for learning (Dror, 2008).

Considering the SG ecosystem is a useful way of thinking about structuring a strategy for its design. Serious games are by nature complex environments that need to function perpetually as an ecological unit. The credence to a SG's quality can be measured in terms of its fitness for purpose, utility and effectiveness. For educators SGs are increasingly viewed as an engaging technology to connect the learner. Evidence that learners seek experiential learning suggests learner-generated content to be a principle mechanism for SGs (Derryberry, 2008). That said, the use of games in formal curricula remains limited due in part to facilitator literacy, institutional infrastructure and pedagogical grounding (Zylka & Nutzinger, 2010) and time and monetary constraints of game development. Consequently, SG designers have to consider both the pedagogical practices that meet with the requirements for lifelong learning and one that demonstrates the game's learning objectives. It is in these contexts that this chapter discusses the game-based pedagogical relationships, conflicts and contradictions that exist. Along with exposing the difficulties associated with pedagogical conformance, the authors analyze interoperability as a critical factor to a successful SG development and deployment. This chapter summarizes the characteristics of the serious games field, with special focus on two key areas: (1) the challenges faced when trying to systematize educational game design methodologies that connect learning principles with game mechanics and (2) the need for interoperable ecosystems in which games (or game patterns) can be shared among practitioners to reduce costs and protect the investment. Finally, the chapter proposes a methodology for the creation of successful and interoperable game designs and proposes, as a case study, the employment of the eAdventure educational game design platform to follow the methodology.

BACKGROUND

SGs have evolved from simple, monolithic applications, to assemblies of finer-grained elements that create new value through the composition of high-level capabilities emerging from multiple pedagogical and technical dimensions. We begin with an overview to the SG ecosystem through to its acceptance.

An Overview of the Serious Games Ecosystem

From a pedagogical perspective, SGs are in essence game artefacts developed so as to support learning and should impact a learner on several levels. To begin it is necessary to understand how learners learn. Behaviourists surmise that learning is "the relative permanent change in behaviour brought about as a result of experience or practice." It is an internal event recognised only as learning when overt behaviour is displayed (Ingleby, 2010, pp. 62). Ritterfeld *et al.* (2009) identified Learning, Development and Change as essential dimensions for serious games. Recent developments in learning styles though have illustrated the need to engage student learning in a more psychosocial manner (Roberge, 2011; Boström, 2011). The emphasis here is on the environment used in teaching students how to think and learn (Zollinger, 2010,) and to stimulate individual abilities to learn (Boström, 2011). Then, to generate overt behaviour, learning mechanisms from theories such as contiguity, classical conditioning, and operant conditioning must be present in some manner within the SG's framework. This implies that, in terms of its mechanics and effects, a SG should not only be developed with a clear pedagogical focus, but should also aim to psychologically impact the player and elicit change.

From the standpoint of a game system, game mechanics are mainly used to describe how players interact with game rules and other formal properties such as goals, player actions and strategies and game states. Avedon and Sutton-Smith (1971) first identified a formal structure to games and fixed principles (i.e. courses of action, method of play, and procedure for action) that determined the conduct and behaviour of the game. Bjork and Holopainen (2005) regarded game mechanics as a pattern of rules designed in any part of the rule system of a game covering a unique set of interactions during the game, be it general or specific. Fullerton *et al.*

(2004) regarded game mechanics as rule bounded actions or methods of play, which create interactions and guide player behaviour. Hunicke *et al.* (2004) defined game mechanics at a computational system level and regarded them as actions, behaviours and control mechanisms afforded to the player within a game context. Cook (2006) related game mechanics to user actions and saw them as "rule-based systems/ simulations that facilitate and encourage a user to explore and learn the properties of their possibility space through the use of feedback mechanisms". Rouse (2005) investigated game mechanics from a game design perspective and considered them to be part of the actual game design in the sense that "they describe what the players are able to do in the game world, how they do it, and how that leads to a compelling game experience." Jarvinen (2008) related game mechanics to the role they play in shaping the user's experience, guiding them to elicit a particular behaviour by constraining the space of possible plans to attain goals. Game mechanics are described with verbs to form rule sets that prescribe a causal relationship between game elements and their consequence to particular game states.

The plethora of literature has revealed that there are no concrete accepted definitions of game mechanics. Sicart (2008) concludes succinctly that game mechanics are "Something that connect player's actions with the purpose of the game and its main challenges. But the meaning is not always clear. It is unclear what game mechanics are and how the term can be used in game analysis".

Yet, educational components are expressed through a game artefact and their inherent mechanics are embedded within the actual game mechanics. Gee (2003, 2005) purports that gameplay mechanics comprise repeated elaboration and rehearsal across increasing challenging game levels. Retention of information is increased as a result of the learners' personal experience and their increased ownership of the material (Gee, 2003). Conformances to pedagogical practices mean SGs should have knowledge transference as a core part of its game mechanics (Gredler, 2004; Shaffer, 2005; Shute, 2009). Evidence has suggested that interactivity greatly increases student motivation to learn, retain and apply the information presented to them (Ritterfield & Weber, 2005; Wong, 2007; Foster, 2008). However, interactivity alone is not sufficient to instil learner motivation states Greenwood-Ericksen (2008). He found that even where a game had full narrative and interactivity, learning efficiency was only achieved when the game induce leaner engagement through enjoyable and meaningful play. As a consequence it is difficult to dissociate game mechanics from educational components at implementation level since they form an entity which functions to educate and entertain through a single compelling experience.

The boundaries between entertainment and pedagogy are therefore blurred to the point where both game and learning components serve as the building elements of a single experience. As integral constituents of games for lifelong learning these mechanics form standards fundamental to the planning, prioritisation of objectives, assessment and actions that is the basis of the domain/topical discourse leading to knowledge discovery and acquired skills. These standards are also the avenue to interoperability, which must take into account a learner-centric perspective. Which pedagogical philosophy to use is not the remit of this chapter, rather the methodology taken is that through an experiential curriculum one constructs the cognitive skills to uncover knowledge, the ability to perform social and civic engagements and the attitude of reflection. Consequently, it becomes essential that we understand the means through which pedagogical outcomes are achieved and interpreted through engaging and enjoyable game-play. While the principles of learning and game-play are seemingly contradictory - game-play offers enjoyment, interaction and immersion while learning frequently offers constraints, frustration and may include reflection - they coexist in SGs (Huynh-Kim-Bang, 2011). Game-play expressed through game mechanics concretely describe in-game activities and represent a level of abstraction at which the formal mapping of gaming and learning can be established.

In order to better understand, develop and implement SGs, it is necessary to consider the entirety of the SG ecosystem that enable in-depth and multi facet analyses. The three reference points identified for this analysis are the components included in a digital game, the environment where the digital game will be implemented and external factors that reach beyond the core technical aspects of a digital game (Figure 1), with focus on three specific elements, respectively game mechanics, interoperability and assessment. Standards and interoperability apply to each of the ingredients of the three main topics. This generates a multidimensional model that

Figure 1. The serious games ecosystem

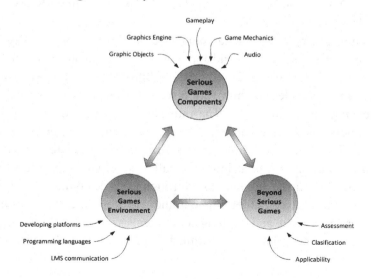

needs to be tailored according to the objectives of the game. Moreover, as some of the ingredients cross the boundaries of the three topics, this multidimensional approach highlights these interconnections.

From Utilitarian to Acceptance

While there is growing acceptance by many institutions on the benefits of SGs for education few have embraced SGs into their formal curriculums. A study by Baek (2008) identified several major issues of which some could be mitigated by a more effective game design strategy. A crucial finding revealed the lack of suitably matched games to current taught material as the primary reason why games were not integrated into the curriculum. The study found that most games were designed to focus on entertainment rather than education. Moreover, those games usually offer a restricted set of assessment instruments that may not fit the instructors' pedagogical model. The findings also indicated teacher's felt at a loss with technicalities of the software and how they could evaluate student performance in the game world. Acceptance therefore relies on games designed to fit the teacher's need and the primary requirements of education along with supplementary material implementation and utilisation of the software. Curriculum inflexibility and time pressure were another two findings which interoperability could resolve.

Acceptance is directly related to the ease of the development and implementation processes. We therefore argue that the successful development and implementation of digital games are critically related to standardisation. Both academic and business entities agree that interoperability enables products to work collaboratively, providing assurance that a product can deliver a certain level of performance and tools, while reducing the Total Cost of Ownership (TCO) for the learning solution. Indeed many open questions have emerged in relation to the following main topics:

- Different standardisation bodies creating different standards result in overheads, such as the format war related to the HTML5 specification that does not specify which video formats browsers should support (H.264 versus WebM and Theora) In addition, standards such as H.264 are only partially open because they are conditioned by various patents and mandatory association membership. Should we reuse existing standards or are new ones required?
- Relevant *de facto* standards are often of a proprietary nature and closely tied to particular pieces of hardware, e.g. game consoles and game controllers, should we adopt them?

- Standards awareness and acceptance does not translate into standards implementation. Some companies find protocols too extensive and complex, performing operations that were not relevant to games and slowing the performance of the system. What are the real benefits of and standard adoption? As a serious games buyer, what are the benefits of requiring standards compliance to serious games developers?
- Some prefer to develop derived protocols that include only those functions needed to support their application; do we need a universal serious games standard? Or, in contrast, do we need a general serious games framework enabling the implementation of the framework with different standards particularly to the application scenario?

Many of these questions have appeared in the technology enhanced learning community particularly on the topic of reusable educational materials and Learning Objects (LOs) (Polsani, 2003; Northrup, 2007; Wiley, 2007). The LO paradigm offers a new perspective on modularisation educational materials. LO adopters have considered interoperability among different VLEs and tools, in order to preserve the investment made in the content development. To achieve LO interoperability several standards and specifications have been developed taking into account aspects including tagging, packaging, deploying, communication, etc. For example, e-learning standards such as IMS Content Packaging (IMS-CP) and ADL Shareable Content Object Reference Model (SCORM) addresses some of the aforementioned issues to avoid specific VLE vendor lock-in/ development tool and to simplify content deployment/interoperability for standard-compliance. Serious games can be seen as a particular type of educational content, thus it is feasible to adopt as an starting point the standards and methodologies that have been put in to practice.

Additionally, serious games can be a practical assessment tool providing a means of communication between games and an external tool (usually a Learning Management System) is available to facilitate assessment, the reporting process and analysis of players' actions. Though there is no widely adopted specification or standard related to the communication between serious games and externals tools, the LO experience can be used as a starting point, for example reusing SCORM communication mechanisms.

PRACTICAL AND TECHNICAL ASPECTS

Digital games have become a reference point in education and training. Unfortunately this rapidly growing domain includes complex software technology with a lack of visibility into its internal architecture and in the context of pedagogical use.

Game Mechanics and Learning Mechanics Interchange

Deconstructing a Serious Game into its pedagogical elements and its game mechanic nodes is often fraught with conflicting arguments of interdependencies. Figure 2 illustrates the relationships of key mechanics present in learning theories and that of games (serious and otherwise). At a glance, the nodes of learning and gaming mechanisms show no obvious direct interchange or relationships between learning theories and actual game mechanics. Hence, the diagram is exemplified by way of mapping a well documented game Re-Mission (available at www.re-mission.net/). The reading of the pedagogy-game mechanic model can be viewed top down for simplicity, with core components running centrally down from the lead nodes of "Learning mechanics" and Game mechanics" respectively. The leaf nodes on either side can be viewed as subsets of the core.

Figure 2. Concept map relating learning mechanics to game mechanics. The illustration abstracts the gameplay loop of Re-Mission. The coded numbers signposts the type and sequential nature of the game and learning mechanics.

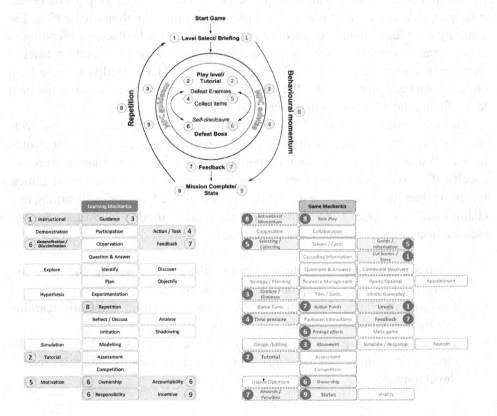

Re-Mission game mechanics follow a third-person shooter genre where the game-play is repetitive and sequential in order. Cut scenes explain the upcoming mission, status and any relevant in-game information at the start of each level. The framework identifies this as an instructional learning mechanism. The player is merely an observer here, much as in a lecture room setting. Once in-game the player must complete the tasks described in the previous cut-scene. This may require additional knowledge of previously unknown mechanics and an NPC (non-player character) will then provide advice and guidance where needed. The framework considers this the layer of understanding. Tutorials act as "safe" learning zones to test the player's understanding tested and guidance is offered when mistakes are made. Having demonstrated the required competency the player enters into the game-play proper. Players subsequently use their acquired knowledge to complete the level. This constitutes the bread and butter of game-play and how the player spends the vast majority of their time. However, occasionally the player will be asked to manipulate taps which send messages to the virtual patient whose body provides the battleground for the current level. Through this mechanism the player's character provides the patient with advice which possibly applies to the user's own treatment. For example, having seen the negative consequences for poor treatment adherence, the player must remind the virtual patient to take their medication. Essentially a protégé effect is created as a consequence of self-disclosure leading to behavioural momentum where the player, motivated by their new conduct, teaches another the correct set of actions. On completing a level basic feedback in the form on level stats are provided and the player can then choose to proceed to the next level, facing the next behavioural outcome.

The game mechanics identified so far only represents a fraction of the wide spectrum of gaming mechanisms that could potentially be pedagogically oriented in SGs. While some are already incorporated many of these mechanics were not specifically developed for SGs but adapted from entertainment and casual games. It is more than likely one game mechanic can be mapped onto various learning mechanics and vice-versa. The proposed approach can be used to investigate Serious Games mechanics over three main dimensions:

- What are the pedagogical theories relevant to serious gaming and more importantly how do they map onto learning mechanics?
- Learning mechanics are commonly structured to target a specific learning experience. How do they map onto a ludic structure?
- In the same way game patterns have been identified so as to explore the structure of games, can these also be used so as to identify strategies for SG development?

Game Mechanics and Learning Mechanics Characteristics

A definition of the concept of Game Mechanics has been provided by several authors (Zimmerman, 2003; Fullerton, 2004; Hunicke, 2004; Bjork, 2005; Sicart, 2008), yet accepted definitions in the field do not provide a single, dominant approach that encompasses all these aspects. The perspective undertaken herein considers that game mechanics (Figure 3) are designed to enable players to interact with rules, and as more formal properties of a game such as game goals, player actions and strategies, and game states to produce an enjoyable gaming experience. Furthermore, interaction of game mechanics determines the complexity of user interaction within a game. A brief summary of elemental game mechanic characteristics is presented here:

- **Rewards:** Feedback a player would receive for a worthy action. Used to incentivise the player to progress in the game. Rewards are designed to sustain engagement and to satisfy the player.
- **Protégé Effect:** Explores learners' tendency to work harder for their teachable agents (i.e. their avatars or alter ego) than for themselves; it has significant benefits for learning and engagement.
- **Resource Management:** Establishing relative values for different types of resources. Games that use this mechanic often have several concurrent transactions and the challenge involves making the best decision given the resources and time constraints.
- **Tokens to Act as Cards or Random Elements:** To add the element of surprise and act as a randomiser, cards and tokens can be used to add a layer of unpredictability to the game and determine game states.
- **Cascading Information, Cut Scene, Story:** Information released in minimal snippets to gain the appropriate level of understanding at each point during a game.
- **Questions and Answers**: Used within the gaming environment as a basic, yet effective means of interacting and engaging with the player to facilitate learning.
- **Behavioural Momentum:** Used to give confidence and motivate players to continue the game.
- **Role Playing:** Rely on mechanics to establish the effectiveness of actions within the game, depending on how well the player assumes and develops their role as a virtual character.
- **Collecting:** Elements of virtual knowledge, competencies, or rewards can be represented by virtual objects, which can be collected by the player.

Figure 3. Game mechanics

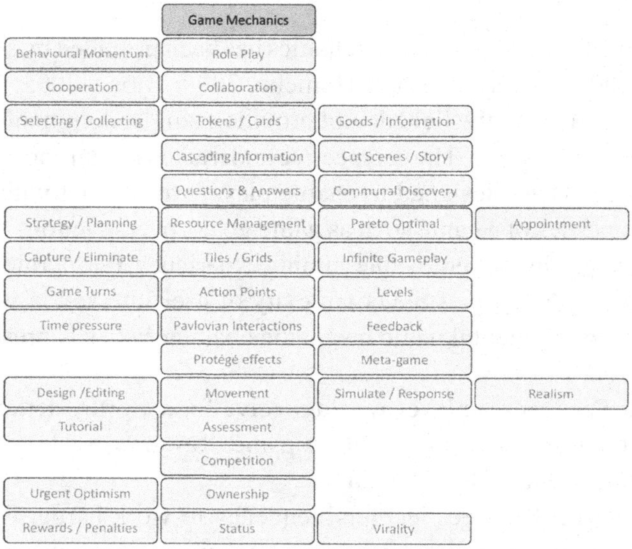

- **Game Turns:** A segment of the game set aside for certain actions to happen before moving on to the next turn, where the sequence of events can largely be repeated.
- **Tile Based and Physical Movement:** Based on how players or elements in games move from one point to another. Tile based movement allow players to move and explore a world which is divided into tiles in turns and amount of tiles moved. Physics based movement provides a greater sense of immersion as players feel as though they are inside the game environment. The focus is no longer about the game tiles but on what players do with them within the limited resources and time.
- **Capture/Eliminate:** The strength of the player is defined by how many points or counters the player has captured. This is most prominent in action, strategic or war based games. Many board games also use this technique.
- **Quick Feedback:** Shows the user what they have just done, and gives them instant gratification (the feel-good factor) of things happening after they have completed a task. Allows the user to feel understood by the game; by giving a user power, the game fulfils a natural human desire.
- **Pavlovian Interactions:** Follows the methodology 'easy to learn, hard to master'. Meaning the game is simple to pick up and play, however, increases its difficulty as the user advances through the game. Used to 'hook' gamers due to its replay value and challenging environment.

- **Action Points:** Control what the user may do during their turn in the game by allocating them a budget of 'action points'. Actions points allow users' time to think of their next and future moves, the game gets the user into a strategical mind set when playing.
- **Tile-Laying:** Often drawn by the player for strategic positioning in order to achieve a set personal objective or game based goal.
- **Appointment:** A mechanic in which to succeed a "player" must return at a predefined time to take a predetermined action. Simple and powerful mechanic to influence the player's behaviour.
- **Communal Discovery:** Involves an entire community working together to solve a problem. Has an incredible opportunity to positively influence the games' usage and acceptance. Essentially crowd sourcing with communal incentives to rapidly create a large, self-propagating network.
- **Urgent Optimism:** Used to elicit a desire to act immediately to tackle an obstacle combined with the belief that it has a reasonable hope of success.
- **Virality:** Mechanics to grow player base which if done right should enrich gameplay. Also designed to reinforce retention.
- **Meta-Game Mechanic:** Rewards or improvements that can be earned during the actual game-play and/or outside of it, that carries over to repeat plays.
- **Status:** Provides a sense of belonging or meaningful empowerment. Multiple forms of status, such as titles, levels, tiers, rank not just globally but also locally within a community.
- **Ownership:** Used to create loyalty of the gaming pool.
- **Infinite Gameplay:** Games that have no explicit end. Most applicable to casual games that can refresh their content or games where a static (but positive) state is a reward of its own.
- **Cooperation/Collaboration:** In cooperative games, the mechanics require players to work with one another but their goals are different, and not all players are guaranteed to benefit equally. In collaborative games, players share common goals and outcomes; players either win or lose together. Cooperative games exist on the spectrum between competitive and collaborative games, where gamers are rewarded for group-oriented strategies only when it is in their own self-interest.
- **Pareto Optimal:** A mechanic where the outcome is one in which no player could be better off without another becoming worse off. The mechanic occurs in a number of conflict, negotiation economic, management and quantum games. Pareto efficiency is reached if the games' outcome is shown to deliver a Pareto optimal allocation of resources.

These are just a myriad of game mechanics that change the dynamics of gameplay and act as the core building blocks used to construct the game layers. By having a deeper understanding of how these game mechanisms work new game dynamics specifically for learning can be discovered.

Brief descriptions of the core learning mechanics (Figure 4) are presented hence:

- **Instructional:** Where a facilitator or teacher provides learner support within a framework determined by the course leader. Specific learning objectives are followed through sequentially. A generic instructional model such as ADDIE (Analysis, Design, Development, Implementation, and Evaluation) can be used.
- **Guidance:** A means to help students see the structure, links and direction of the course material.
- **Demonstration:** A pedagogical method related to problem-based learning.
- **Participation:** A (active learning) process of engaging with the learning task at both the cognitive and affective level.
- **Action/Task:** An approach to learning involving individuals working on real projects, possibly with group support (collaborative/cooperative learning) to assist members reflect on their experience and to plan next actions.

Figure 4. Learning mechanics

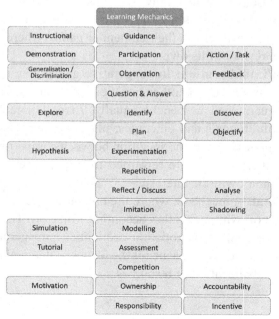

- **Generalisation/Discrimination:** In psychology this relates to the process by which people learn to make different responses to different stimuli. Behaviourists describe this as classical conditioning (also Pavlovian or respondent conditioning, Pavlovian reinforcement). In some ways this can be viewed as induction. Induction (inductive learning/teaching) aims at equipping learners with background information so that they might become effective in their role sooner.
- **Observation:** Observational learning (also referred to vicarious learning, social learning, modelling) is based on the concept that learning occurs as a function of watching, retaining and replicating the behaviour of others.
- **Feedback:** Oral or written developmental advice on performance so that the learner has a better understanding of values, standards, criteria, etc. Linked with formative assessment.
- **Question and Answer:** An active learning mechanism linked with participation that encourages learners to use the questioning strategies to assess what they have learned, to develop their thinking skills.
- **Explore:** A mechanism that encourages the learner to explore and experiment to uncover relationships, with much less of a focus on didactic training (teaching students by lecturing them). Exploratory learning approaches are considered most appropriate for teaching generalised thinking and problem-solving skills, and may not be the best approach for such things as memorisation (or repetition). Is related to constructivist theory.
- **Identify:** A social learning theory (or cognitive theory) that posits learning will most likely occur if there is a close identification between the observer and the model and if the observer also has a good deal of self-efficacy.
- **Discover:** An inquiry-based learning mechanic (from constructivist learning theory) where the learner draws on past experiences and existing knowledge to discover new facts and relationships to solve problems. As a result, learners are more likely to retain concepts and knowledge in contrast to transmissionist learning. Related to: guided discovery, problem-based learning, simulation-based learning, case-based learning, and incidental learning.
- **Plan:** A conditional no-regret learning mechanic associated to Bayesian learning and hypothesis testing. As with a given type of game and a given amount of information, there may exist no learning procedure that satisfies certain reasonable criteria of performance and convergence. The learner has to strategically manage his or her resources to achieve an aggregate learning outcome.
- **Objectify:** Termed behavioural objectives (commonly referred as learning outcomes). Its meaning ranges from exact, measurable outcomes of specific learning experiences to more generalised statements for courses of study.

Learning objectives can be made more difficult or demanding depending on the degree of understanding or levels of experience of learners. One can change the active verb to a more complex one or to add specific conditions or limits.

- **Hypothesis:** Often related to acquisition-learning it is a method to develop competency in a specific subject area. Most contemporary use in education relates to performing a task and being able to debate the underpinning knowledge and understanding.
- **Experimentation:** Typically involves laboratory/practical classes, this type of teaching is often used in curricula in experimental sciences, biomedical and engineering disciplines, which is broadly intended to offer training in techniques and learning how to carry out experimental investigations. Associated to experiential learning.
- **Repetition:** A method that uses traditional curriculum for students to practice at home or onsite. Although significant practice is performed, higher order learning is not involved.
- **Reflect/Discuss:** Consideration of an experience, or of learning, to enhance understanding or inform action. Learners often compile logbooks to record their reflections on learning activities.
- **Analyse:** Related to diagnostic tests to identify weaknesses, and used so that these might be addressed in a more focused manner.
- **Imitation:** This is similar to role-play where a planned learning activity requires participants to take on the role of individuals representing different perspectives (e.g. mock interview) to meet specific learning objectives, such as to promote empathy or to expose participants to a scenario in which they will have to take part in the future.
- **Shadowing:** Often used in medical sciences where the student shadows their mentor during general practice or in operating theatres. Shadowing is also a form of learning through apprenticeships. Associated with experiential learning.
- **Simulation:** Often associated with role-play it is increasingly used with ICT-based learning activities for decision-making to simulate cause and effect.
- **Modelling:** A means to test a hypothesis, to evaluate a concept or as a form of observational learning.
- **Tutorial:** Used with different meanings according to discipline, type of institution, level, and teaching and learning method that involves a tutor or peer.
- **Assessment:** Measurement of the progress and achievement of a learner (typically through quizzes, examinations or even projects). For example, formative assessment allows learners to gauge their proficiency thereby to improve

their self-regulatory skills. Rather than expressed as marks or grades, words are used to convey or reveal information, which can then be used diagnostically (e.g. summative assessment).

- **Competition:** Competitive learning is often used as an extracurricular activity to develop creativity and problem solving skills. Game theory offers techniques for formulating competition between parties that wish to reach an optimal position.
- **Motivation:** In terms of extrinsic motivation, marks and grades are used to target students who are more concerned with the numeric value of their work, and those that seek status. Intrinsic motivation typifies students who enjoy challenge, want to master a subject, are curious and want to learn. They are inspired to achieve high grades even when the task does not inspire interest.
- **Ownership:** Associated to constructivist theory where knowledge is internalised by learners through processes of accommodation and assimilation, they construct new knowledge from their experiences.
- **Accountability:** Can be viewed as autonomy where learners take responsibility for and control of themselves and their learning, including being less spoon-fed. May also include elements of learners taking responsibility for determining and directing the content of their learning. Related with open learning mechanics.
- **Responsibility:** Often related to self-directed learning where the learner has control over educational decisions, including goals, resources, methods and criteria for judging success. Often used as a learning situation where the learner has some influence on some of the learning aspects.
- **Incentive:** Incentive learning is the process via which learners update changes in the value of rewards. Such methods are useful in changing the behaviour of the learner, where a stimulus-response habit mechanism and a goal-directed process are the two learning mechanisms. The first is learning about the instrumental contingency between the response and reward, whereas the second consists of the acquisition of incentive value by the reward.

Assessment and Interoperability

A critical area of interest to the digital game-based learning communities is standards for interoperability. The entertainment industry, to date, has expressed different interests regarding interoperability standards. While the academic community has a strong interest in ensuring that various simulation systems can work together and integrate with the already established e-learning tools in the organization. In contrast, the entertainment industry places strong emphasis on developing proprietary systems and standards that preclude interoperability. Unlike the billion-dollar entertainment video game industry, which has responded to increased product demand by developing increasingly complex and costly games, the SG industry has followed an approach of cost containment and technology simplification (Moreno-Ger, 2010). Commercial *de facto* standards have not sought interoperability between independent systems, but have attempted to allow independently produced software titles to integrate with the same user front-end software such as operating systems, Web browsers, or graphic libraries. Subsequently, these standards enable the same software to run a variety of game applications. However, collaboration of heterogeneous software developers leads to interoperability issues, which represent a major barrier in the software development sector. Obstacles to heterogeneity arise from the fact that software developers seldom share the same semantics for the terminology of their models. Moreover, they use various collaboration scenarios with different organizational constraints.

Eliminating or alleviating fragmentation is the grail of SG development. Fragmentation arises from game domain use and user individual preferences. As with the core content that governs the game's mechanics the SG development and deployment lifecycle must consider portability across software platforms, devices, libraries, and user customization. Importantly, SGs being bespoke learning ecosystems have to cater for the ease of content update and qualified assessment because it has a direct impact on the addressable market share and software development costs.

SCORM (Sharable Content Object Reference Model) makes possible the sharing of distributed learning content across learning management systems that conform to SCORM. Its development and implementation was clearly a vital first step in achieving the long-term vision of providing high quality training and education on demand (Shane, 2010).

SCORM has become an international *de facto* standard in large measure because the goal was the establishment of a consensually negotiated foundation for a community to come together to address community goals: accessible, interoperable, durable, reusable content for learning and performance aiding (Roberts & Gallagher, 2010). In addition, the ADL SCORM 2004 3rd edition has been promoted from simple specification to *technical recommendation* by the ISO/IEC JTC1 SC36 committee in the form of ISO/IEC TR 29163 documents family.

SCORM specification covers two particular topics related to SGs: package and deployment, and communication between a serious game and the Learning Management System (LMS). The serious game is conceived as a SCO object, and considering the SCORM Content Aggregation Model it can be deployed in multiple commercial and open source LMS platforms already available. In addition, SGs can generate a great amount of tracking information that can be used by the instructor to evaluate the student play session. Using the SCORM Runtime Model a SG can set some of the cmi.* properties.

In particular, the following CMI properties have been identified:

- **cmi.completion_status:** This property is used to track if the SG has been finished or not.
- **cmi.success_status:** This property is used to track, once the SG has been completed, if the student has achieved the learning objectives during the game play session or not.
- **cmi.core_score_raw:** In contrast to cmi.success_status, this property can be used to evaluate the overall performance of the student's game play using a numerical scale.
- **cmi.interactions:** This is a collection of properties, that is, multiple values can be collected inside this property. In contrast to cmi_score_raw and cmi. success_status that provide a coarse-grained evaluation of the student's performance, cmi.interactions.* can be used to provide a fine-grained or detailed report of the student game play session and its relation to the SG learning objectives.

These properties (and the rest of SCORM data model) can be used in the eAdventure authoring tool. This way, the internal game state can be translated to a platform neutral data model. Moreover, e-Adventure games sent the information back to the LMS using the SCORM Runtime API, so the game tracking information can be reviewed or used by other tools that are hosted in the LMS.

Strategies for Engineering Serious Games

Serious games development and implementation remain an open challenge within educational environments. Serious game applications are usually complex interactive real-time systems, which are non-trivial to implement. Serious game production has a multi-disciplinary nature, because – in addition to software development – a serious game production process can include, besides areas such as graphics design and implementation, sound engineering, and story design (Stănescu et al., 2011), critical elements that relate to education: game mechanics, learning mechanics, serious game assessment. The research carried herein reveals the challenges that arise at different levels. Monetary and time constraints have been identified among the most relevant impediments in serious game development. Moreover, serious games differ in complexity from commercial games, as they require critical constructs that translate the learning objectives. Corroborating these with the fact that most educators do not possess the advanced IT skills required to develop a game, it becomes mandatory to search for more viable alternatives.

Even if each game is a self-contained entity and its development is a separate and distinct process, an approach were each game is to be built from the ground upward or where no work from one game could possibly be of use for the next, is no longer feasible. Therefore, it has become crucial to generate new strategies that would support a successful development and implementation of serious games through the creation of functionally interchangeable items adapted to the learning environments, the adoption of standards that impact serious games, and of methods that would make game components interchangeable, without having to alter the item to make the new combination work, because each interchangeable part had been designed to have functional characteristics that are equivalent in performance and durability without alteration. It is important to support inter-changeability that considers the position of the development companies and of the educational actors towards standards adoptions in an effort to understand how to create cost-efficient, flexible interoperability solutions. Open systems architecture represents also an alternative because it focuses on a modular design that defines key interfaces within a system using widely supported, consensus-based standards that are available for use by all developers and users without any proprietary constraints.

Under these premises, the authors advance for analysis the use of a standard-compliant graphic editor as a multi-benefit approach for learning based on the belief that many properties and features common to all games and to all platform games can be extracted from their particular context and given an abstract form that has lost all reference to concrete circumstances and applies not only to one game but to all. Generalizable components of a game (such as graphics, sound, game mechanics) can be reused to produce many different games when integrated into a single platform. This approach brings forward a new challenge: the effectiveness of such a platform that integrates serious game development tools.

Even though game development environments will not be able to completely alleviate the need for experiences game developers, they will lower the bar of entry for tech savvy educators, allowing them to customize existing games, and at the same time use these games as a learning tool on how the game development environment works, and how to create new games. Given the digital nature of these games, there will be a great incentive for educators to experiment and learn from them, as they can easily roll back their changes to a previous working copy of the game, as well as share their work with other fellow educators.

CASE-STUDY: E-ADVENTURE PLATFORM

The practicalities of this research are extracted through a case study based on the eAdventure platform (available at: http://e-adventure.e-ucm.es). eAdventure is a platform originally focused on the development of classic point&click adventure computer games with educational purposes. The platform focuses on adventure games because this specific game genre has been previously identified in the literature as the ideal genre for learning (Ju, 1997; Amory, 1999; Amory, 2001; Dickey, 2006). However, eAdventure also supports other types of 2D games based on *point&click* or *drag&drop* interactions, including basic simulations of procedures (Moreno-Ger, 2010).

It provides a teacher-centred framework for the development of educational video games focused on the reduction of the costs and the needed technical background by offering a visual drag & drop interface to create the games (Torrente, 2010) (Figure 5).

To extend the insights of this case study, several sets of interviews have been carried out within three universities: Herriot Watt University in Edinburgh - Scotland, Carol I National Defence University in Bucharest – Romania, and Universidad

Figure 5. The eAdventure game editor

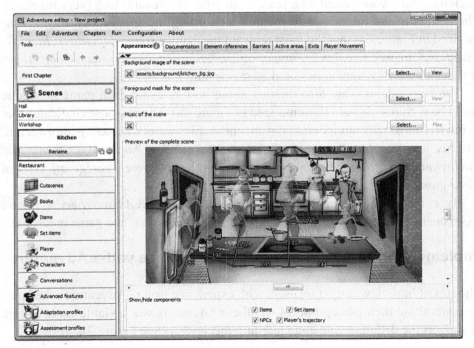

Complutense de Madrid – Spain. In total, nine semi-structured sets of interviews were conducted. The majority of interviews were carried out in person while some were conducted via desktop teleconferencing using Skype®.

This empirical, exploratory study attempts to address the strengths and weaknesses related to a standard-compliant game editor, as well as to identify core learning mechanics and game mechanics that eLearning practitioners consider critical which in turn may provide a basis for the enhancement of the current development practices of game editors.

The participants in this study were selected from various subject areas such as computer science and engineering, military training, medicine, music, maths, and foreign languages. Five sets of interviews were carried out with experts that had no prior experience with eAdventure, while four sets of interviews were carried out with experts that have participated in specialised training for using the eAdventure editor. The following sub-sections describe the results of the case study, with a special focus on measuring to which extent the eAdventure platform may be used to support the requirements identified in the previous section.

Impact of Learning and Game Mechanics

The respondents for all the interviews were asked to report which learning mechanics and which game mechanics they considered especially relevant in their fields. Each mechanic was ranked on a scale from 1 (least relevant) to 5 (very relevant). The results of the interviews in relation to learning mechanics identified (Summarized in Figure 6a) that the most relevant mechanics were: *Repetition; Identify; Question&Answer/Feedback; Simulation/modelling; and Assessment. Competition* and *Accountability* were considered least relevant.

The respondents were also queried about how relevant each game mechanic could be within their field (Summarized in Figure 6b). The responses indicated that as the five most relevant individual game mechanics were: *Cascading information/ Cut Scenes; Simulate/Response; Question&Answer/Feedback; Assessment; and Pavlovian interactions/ Feedback.* The least relevant were *Protégé effects* and *Meta-game.*

By comparison, the analysis revealed that *Question&Answer/Feedback* and *Assessment* were in the top five candidates for both learning and game mechanics.

Implementing Learning and Game Mechanics with eAdventure

The sets of interviews targeting users with experience using eAdventure asked participants about their perceptions of whether eAdventure was a viable game engine to support the different game and learning mechanics (See Figure 7).

Figure 6. Perception of the importance of the individual (a) learning mechanics (b) game mechanics

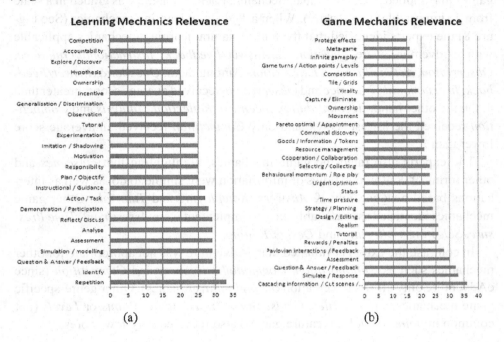

(a)   (b)

Figure 7. Applicability of each learning mechanic in eAdventure

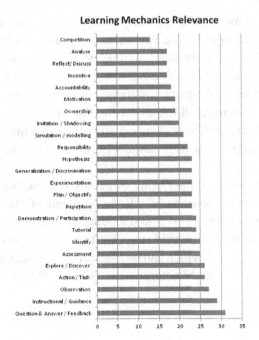

The experts were asked to grade how easy it would be to create eAdventure games that applied each individual mechanic. Each mechanic was graded in a scale from 1 (impossible) to 5 (easily). When asked about learning mechanics (See Figure 8) the experts identified that the 5 most natural learning mechanics applicable with eAdventure were *Question & Answer/Feedback, Instructional/Guidance, Observation, Action/Task* and *Exploration.* Among them, *Question&Answer/Feedback, Instructional/Guidance* and *Observation,* received average scores greater than 4. On the other hand, *Accountability, Incentive, Reflection, Analysis* and *Competition* received the lowest scores, and only *Competition* received an average score lower than 2.

The experts also rated the game mechanics, highlighting that *cutscenes* and other forms of continuous flows of information were simple to do, as well as interactions based on *Questions & Answers, Roleplaying* and *Tutorials.* Other game mechanics identified as reasonably easy to implement were *Assessment, Time Pressure, Selecting/Collecting* and *Design/Editing.*

In contrast, the experts evaluated that eAdventure was not appropriate for other mechanics such as *Collaboration, Communal Discovery* and *Competition* (since eAdventure only allows the creation of *single-player* games). Other genre-specific game mechanics, such as *Tiles, Grids, Game Turns, Action Points* or *Levels* (not common in *point & click* adventure games) also received very low scores.

Support for Assessment and Interoperability

The eAdventure platform was specifically designed to create educational games that could be integrated in Learning Management Systems. It includes assessment mechanisms that allow the identification of relevant game states. These states can be used to generate a human-readable assessment report, assign grades to final states or even compute grades as the game progresses (Moreno-Ger, 2008).

Furthermore, e-Adventure allows exporting the games as standards-compliant Learning Objects adhering different standard, and hence, making possible the deployment of the created games in a wide range VLE or stored them in LO repositories (Torrente, 2009).

In addition to allowing the packaging of games as Learning Objects, eAdventure games can also be exported as SCORM-compliant SCOs, with the ability of opening a connection to the webserver and sending assessment information through this channel. In particular, it is possible to submit values for the fields "Completion Status" and "Success Status", which can be used for assessment or sequencing decisions. Due to eAdventure's architecture, these assessment messages can be sent to

Figure 8. Perception of the importance of the individual game mechanics

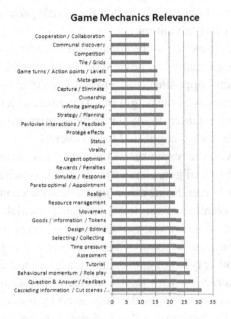

Game Mechanics Relevance

different servers supporting different standards (e.g. SCORM 1.2, SCORM 2004 or LAMS), facilitating interoperability even across systems that comply to different standards or specifications (del Blanco, 2011).

The interviewed experts were also asked about their perceptions of the SCORM-based assessment system, and their responses were mostly positive regarding its effectiveness. Two of the users, however, considered that the strict rule-based assessment system was too restrictive, and did not allow for creative assessment approaches.

Limitations

Working with eAdventure allows practitioners to create their own games, but it also limits them when choosing which learning and game mechanics to apply. Focusing on learning mechanics, the reviewers indicated that eAdventure games were not adequate to exploit learning approaches such as, *Accountability, Incentive, Reflection, Analysis* and *Competition*. Many of the lower graded learning mechanics could be compensated with the context of the games. E.g., even if an eAdventure did not foster *reflection* by itself, the gameplay sessions could be followed by instructor-led debriefing sessions in which reflection could be promoted. However, other mechanics such as Competition do not really match the *single-player* nature and the slow pace of typical *point&click* adventure games.

The limitations become even more apparent when trying to cover the different game mechanics. A single game can never exhibit all possible game mechanics (as some of them are directly opposite), and game genres tend to exhibit well-defined sets of game mechanics. Given the origin of eAdventure as a toolset focused solely on *point&click* adventure games, many game mechanics are not natural within the genre and are therefore poorly supported by eAdventure.

This is consistent with the responses of the expert reviewers, who assigned very low scores to the feasibility of genre-specific mechanics such as *Tiles*, *Grids*, *Game Turns*, *Action Points* or *Levels*. Some other limitations are a consequence of eAdventure allowing only the creation of single-player games, which affects the feasibility of mechanics such as *Collaboration, Communal Discovery* and *Competition*.

These limitations resulted in some of the interviewees suggesting to extend the same type of editor to other types of games, including support for tiled-based games, physics engines or interaction with haptic devices. The addition of collaborative activities or multiplayer options was also requested by the interviewees.

In addition, while the participants that had received previous training using the eAdventure platform considered the system as easy to use, 20% of the participants without prior training considered that the eAdventure Editor was not user friendly and intuitive and some interviewees suggested including step-by-step wizards for different common tasks.

DISCUSSION AND CONCLUSION

The field of digital games is abound with open challenges, in particular learning, and necessitate a critical rethink of the strategic elements that determine their effectiveness for learning. Faced with limited streamlined, interoperability-enabled development processes as a consequence, the gaps in implementation that concern the assimilation and acceptance of digital games into teaching and learning leaves many unanswered questions.

Beginning with these issues, this chapter offers a comprehensive overview of game mechanics investigating relevant concepts such as game patterns, or pedagogical constructs in order to determine a spectrum of activities, practices within which digital game mechanics can be identified. The research analyses the key issues in dissociating game-play mechanisms from pedagogical output in order to facilitate the production of a comprehensive methodology through which digital game mechanics could be abstracted from current digital games and mapped onto pedagogical constructs.

A prospective mapping between educational philosophies and games agenda is presented to make aware the interoperability modus from which topical (domain) frameworks or architectures can be structured. The authors analyze interoperability as a critical factor to a successful development and deployment of digital games. Interoperability is achieved through multiple tools and approaches. This implies collaboration at multidimensional levels that would integrate user communities (such as teachers and developers), software, hardware, standards, etc. The reflection of these interconnections translates into a multidimensional interoperability framework that integrates three key elements: the components included in a digital game, the ecosystem where the game will be implemented and external factors that go beyond the core technical aspects of a digital game.

It is relatively easy to design a game, however, designing a high-quality game is very difficult and designing an effective educational game is extremely difficult. Literature has yet to publish an effective/standard framework or pedagogy guidelines to assist educators identify content most suitable to be translated into a playable game. Even though a number of game engines are available educators may not have the technical ability to create useful applications. An educator may seek the expertise of a game company, however, game developers would not normally be cued to the content or possess the pedagogical knowledge. Games companies would additionally weigh the business incentives over educational games against potential audience numbers.

All games are constructed with a set of activities driven by rules that govern the mechanics. In playing the game the player constantly cycles through these mechanics. The (game) rules restrict the player to the gameplay and consequently the game environment. While most game mechanics are applicable across genres, some genres - particularly content dependent SG - may require several specific set of game mechanics.

The research has identified that pedagogy and learning mechanisms are essential in understanding the relationships between learning outcomes and a digital game experience. Digital games introduce significant new requirements for robustness and interoperability, and encourage game developers to better align their practices with the requirements of the educational domain. In addition to new languages and middleware, developing and adopting standards for interoperability could benefit both the developers and the serious games user communities, and facilitate growth of the genre.

In summary:

- Digital games standardisation needs to be strengthened as digital games standards enable software application to interoperate, enable better management and visibility of digital games assets and ensure quality of digital games products;
- All existing standards that apply to digital games need to be identified and analyzed in collaboration with game developers and teachers, in order to streamline successful development and implementation strategies;
- Industry and all stakeholders should give their feedback for the revision of the current digital games standards considering the current technology needs;
- While considering digital games standards, interoperability should be pursued both for hardware and software;
- Due to the wider and wider use of digital game-based products, user safety and security emerges as an important factor and standards should address these issues.

ACKNOWLEDGMENT

This project is partially funded under the European Community Seventh Framework Programme, through the GALA Network of Excellence in Serious Games (FP7-ICT-2009-5-258169).

REFERENCES

Amory, K. (2001). Building an educational adventure game: Theory, design and lessons. *Journal of Interactive Learning Research, 12*, 249–263.

Amory, K., Naicker, J. V., & Adams, C. (1999). The use of computer games as an educational tool: Identification of appropriate game types and game elements. *British Journal of Educational Technology, 30*, 311–321. doi:10.1111/1467-8535.00121

Avedon, E. M., & Sutton-Smith, B. (Eds.). (1971). *The study of games*. New York, NY: John Wiley & Sons, Inc.

Baek, Y. K. (2008). What hinders teachers in using computer and video games in the classroom? Exploring factors inhibiting the uptake of computer and video games. *Cyberpsychology & Behavior, 11*(6), 665–671. doi:10.1089/cpb.2008.0127

Björk, S., & Holopainen, J. (2005). *Patterns in game design*. Hingham, MA: Charles River Media.

Boström, L. (2011). Students' learning styles compared with their teachers' learning styles in secondary schools. *Institute for Learning Styles Research Journal, 1*, 16–38.

Cook, D. (2006). *What are game mechanics?* Retrieved December 13, 2010, from http://lostgarden.com/2006_10_01_archive.html

del Blanco, Á., Torrente, J., Moreno-ger, P., & Fernández-Manjón, B. (2011). Enhancing adaptive learning and assessment in virtual learning environments with educational games. In Jin, Q. (Ed.), *Intelligent learning systems and advancements in computer-aided instruction: Emerging studies* (pp. 114–163). Hershey, PA: IGI Global. doi:10.4018/978-1-61350-483-3.ch009

Derryberry, A. (2008). *Serious games - Online games for learning*. Retrieved from http://www.adobe.com/resources/elearning/pdfs/serious_games_wp.pdf

Dickey, M. D. (2006). Game design narrative for learning: Appropriating adventure game design narrative devices and techniques for the design of interactive learning environments. *Educational Technology Research and Development, 54*, 245–263. doi:10.1007/s11423-006-8806-y

Dror, I. E. (2008). Technology enhanced learning: The good, the bad, and the ugly. *Pragmatics & Cognition, 16*, 215–223.

Foster, A. (2008). Games and motivation to learn science: Personal identity, applicability, motivation, and meaningfulness. *Journal of Interactive Learning Research, 19*(4), 597–614.

Fullerton, T., Swain, C., & Hoffman, S. (2004). *Game design workshop: Designing, prototyping and playtesting games (Gama Network Series)*. San Francesco, CA: CMP Books.

Gee, J. P. (2003). *What video games have to teach us about learning and literacy*. New York, NY: Palgrave Macmillan. doi:10.1145/950566.950595

Gee, J. P. (2005). Learning by design: Good video games as learning machines. *E-learning, 2*(1), 5–16. doi:10.2304/elea.2005.2.1.5

Gredler, M. (2004). Games and simulations and their relationships to learning. In Jonassen, D. (Ed.), *Handbook of research on educational communications and technology* (pp. 571–581). Mahwah, NJ: Erlbaum.

Greenwood-Ericksen, A. (2008). *Learning African American history in a synthetic learning environment*. Doctoral dissertation, University of Central Florida, Florida.

Hunicke, R., LeBlanc, M., & Zubek, R. (2004). MDA: A formal approach to game design and game research. In *Proceedings of the Challenges in Game AI Workshop, 19th National Conference on Artificial Intelligence AAAI '04,* San Jose, CA. AAAI Press.

Huynh-Kim-Bang, B., Labat, L.-M., & Wisdom, J. (2011). *Design patterns in serious games: A blue print for combining fun and learning.* Retrieved December 13, 2011, from http://seriousgames.lip6.fr/DesignPatterns/designPatternsForSeriousGames.pdf

Ingleby, E., Joyce, D., & Powell, S. (2010). *Learning to teach in the lifelong learning sector.* New York, NY: Continuum International Publishing Group.

Järvinen, A. (2008). *Games without frontiers: Theories and methods for game studies and design.* Doctoral dissertation, Tampere University, Tampere, Finland.

Ju, E., & Wagner, C. (1997). Personal computer adventure games: Their structure, principles and applicability for training. *The Data Base for Advances in Information Systems, 28,* 78–92. doi:10.1145/264701.264707

Moreno-Ger, P., Burgos, D., Sierra, J. L., & Fernández-Manjón, B. (2008). Educational game design for online education. *Computers in Human Behavior, 24*(6), 2530–2540. doi:10.1016/j.chb.2008.03.012

Moreno-Ger, P., Torrente, J., Bustamante, J., Fernández-Galaz, C., Fernández-Manjón, B., & Comas-Rengifo, M. D. (2010). Application of a low-cost web-based simulation to improve students' practical skills in medical education. *International Journal of Medical Informatics, 79,* 459–467. doi:10.1016/j.ijmedinf.2010.01.017

Northrup, P. T. (2007). *Learning objects for instruction: design and evaluation.* Hershey, PA: Information Science Publishing. doi:10.4018/978-1-59904-334-0

Polsani, P. R. (2003). Use and abuse of reusable learning objects. *Journal of Digital Information, 3*(4), 164.

Ritterfeld, U., Vorderer, P., & Cody, M. (Eds.). (2009). *Serious games: Mechanisms and effects.* New York, NY: Routledge.

Ritterfield, U., & Weber, R. (2005). Video games for entertainment and education. In Vorderer, P., & Bryant, J. (Eds.), *Playing video games: Motives responses and consequences* (pp. 399–414). Mahwah, NJ: Erlbaum.

Roberge, G. D., Gagnon, L. L., & Oddson, B. E. (2011). The ideal classroom: A comparative study of education and nursing student learning and psychosocial environmental preferences. *Institute for Learning Styles Research Journal, 1,* 1–16.

Roberts, E., & Gallagher, P. S. (2010). Challenges to SCORM. In Jesukiewicz, P., Kahn, B., & Wisher, R. (Eds.), *Learning on demand: ADL and the future of e-learning* (pp. 49–70). Alexandria, VA: Advanced Distributed Learning.

Rouse, R. (2005). *Game design: Theory and practice* (2nd ed.). Sudbury, MA: Wordware Publishing, Inc.

Shaffer, D. W., Squire, K. D., Halverson, R., & Gee, J. P. (2005). Video games and the future of learning. *Phi Delta Kappan, 87*(2), 104–111.

Shane, G. P. (2010). The development of SCORM. In Jesukiewicz, P., Kahn, B., & Wisher, R. (Eds.), *Learning on demand: ADL and the future of e-learning* (pp. 49–70). Alexandria, VA: Advanced Distributed Learning.

Shute, V. J., Ventura, M., Bauer, M. I., & Zapata- Rivera, D. (2009) Melding the power of serious games and embedded assessment to monitor and foster learning. In U. Ritterfeld, M. J. Cody, & P. Vorderer (Eds.), *Serious games: Mechanisms and effects* (pp. 295-321). Philadelphia, PA: Routledge.

Sicart, M. (2008). Designing game mechanics. *International Journal of Computer Game Research, 8*(2). Retrieved from gamestudies.org/0802/articles/sicart

Stănescu, I. A., Ştefan, S., & Roceanu, I. (2011). Interoperability in serious games. In *Proceedings of the 7th International Scientific Conference "eLearning and Software for Education"*, (pp. 28-29). April 2011, Romania.

Torrente, J., del Blanco, Á., Marchiori, E. J., Moreno-Ger, P., & Fernández-Manjón, B. (2010). <e-Adventure>: Introducing educational games in the learning process. *Proceedings of the IEEE EDUCON 2010 Conference (Special issue e-Madrid)*, 14-16 April 2010, Madrid, Spain.

Torrente, J., Moreno-Ger, P., Martínez-Ortiz, I., & Fernández-Manjón, B. (2009). Integration and deployment of educational games in e-learning environments: The learning object model meets educational gaming. *Journal of Educational Technology & Society, 12*(4), 359–371.

Westera, W., Nadolskl, R. J., Hummel, H. G. K., & Woperels, I. G. J. H. (2008). Serious games for higher education: A framework for reducing design complexity. *Journal of Computer Assisted Learning, 24*, 420–432. doi:10.1111/j.1365-2729.2008.00279.x

Wiley, D. A. (2007). The learning objects literature. In Spector, M. J., Merrill, D. M., & Merrienboer, V. J. (Eds.), *Handbook of research on educational communications and technology* (pp. 345–353). New York, NY: Lawrence Erlbaum Associates.

Wong, W. L., Shen, C., Nocera, L., Carriazo, E., Tang, F., & Bugga, S. Ritterfeld, U. (2007). *Serious video game effectiveness*. Paper presented at the ACE '07.

Zimmerman, E., & Salen, K. (2003). *Rules of play: Game design fundamentals*. Cambridge, MA: The MIT Press.

Zollinger, S. W., & Martinson, B. (2010). Do all designers think alike? What research has to say. *Institute for Learning Styles Research Journal, 1*, 1–15.

Zylka, J., & Nutzinger, H. P. (2010). Educational games in formal education – Results of an explorative study using an educational game in school. *Proceedings of the International Conference on Computer-aided Learning 2010 (ICL 2010)*, (pp. 954-963). 15-17 September, Hasselt, Belgium.

KEY TERMS AND DEFINITIONS

Game Editor: A software tool that enables the creation of games by combining high level constructs instead of coding the game with a programming language.

Game Mechanics: Rules that define the interactions and flow of a game session. They describe interactions, game conditions and triggers in an abstract manner.

Interoperability: The ability of various software components to work with each other in a meaningful and coherent fashion according to their design specifications.

Learning Mechanics: Pedagogical constructs and activities commonly used in education to achieve different types of learning outcomes.

Serious Games: Games that are designed with a primary purpose distinct from entertainment. Usually (and particularly in the context of this work) that purpose is educational.

Serious Game Assessment: The evaluation of the performance while playing a serious game in terms of either in-game achievements or learning outcomes. The assessment may be performed outside the game (with an exam or a debriefing session) or within the game (using the game itself as an evaluation tool).

Serious Game Ecosystem: A set of technical and non-technical elements that define the functionalities of a serious game and impact upon its development and implementation.

Simulation: Replication of real world events, situations, places, etc, in a controlled environment with the purpose of studying interactions and effects between various objects. A simulation could be done either physically (fire drill) or electronically (flight simulator).

Chapter 11
Learning and Teaching as Communicative Actions:
Broken Window as a Model of Transmedia Game Learning

Scott J. Warren
University of North Texas, USA

Anjum Najmi
University of North Texas, USA

EXECUTIVE SUMMARY

Over the last decade, digital games have become important vehicles to support student learning. One form in particular, transmedia games, have shown a propensity to allow instructors, students, and designers to create learning games inexpensively and rapidly, while showing learning improvements and allowing for rapid change as the need arises. There are two goals for this chapter. The first is to review existing theoretical models of game learning and to provide an overview of a new model called "Learning and Teaching as Communicative Actions." The second is to give a detailed description of the design process for Broken Window, an alternate reality (AltRG) transmedia game that was developed to support undergraduate learning in a computer applications course.

INTRODUCTION

Over the last decade digital games, simulations and other complex systems have been at the forefront of the push to support learning in education (Gibson & Baek, 2009b; Squire, 2008). Games and simulations offer learning affordances such as interaction and rapid feedback, autonomous learning opportunities, and a safe place

DOI: 10.4018/978-1-4666-2848-9.ch011

in which to engage in repeated practice of skills that may be too dangerous to do in the real world (Prensky, 2001; Warren & Lin, 2012; Winn, 2002). These tools have also been found to engage students and motivate them in learning especially in areas of science and literacy (Squire, 2008). This chapter examines the educational potential of transmedia games as a means of supporting learning. Transmedia is storytelling through multiple media, information gathering and making connections, and is based on engagement, extended use of technology and collective intelligence (Jenkins, 2006). Each component is experienced individually but makes a valuable contribution to the story as a whole (Jenkins, 2006). In a transmedia learning experience, "[r]ather than listening to lectures, completing practice exercises, and taking frequent multiple-choice tests, students hone their technology skills by solving a series of ill-structured problems posed by fictional clients using the very tools they were expected to learn" (Warren & Lin, 2012, p. 9.) Alternate reality games are a subset of this game genre and are based on digital game based learning students are immersed in a reality similar to their own with fictional elements that direct learners, which "distribute game challenges, tasks, and rewards across a variety of media, both digital and real" (Warren, Dondlinger, McLeod, & Bigenho, 2011, p. 7). As with other game forms, alternate reality games (AltRG) hold the promise of allowing students to interact with real-world situations and engage in problem-solving while addressing core instructional goals (Warren, Dondlinger, McLeod, & Bigenho, 2011). The goal of this chapter is to introduce the core concepts of transmedia as they apply to the development of games and simulations, as well as to outline a process for designing and developing an transmedia supported alternate reality game (AltRG). We further provide an example from our own work with *Broken Window*, an alternate reality game (AltRG) created for undergraduates in an introductory computer applications course.

LITERATURE REVIEW

Learning Game Theory

To begin this section on theories of game and simulation use in education, it is important first to acknowledge that the use of video and computer games to support learning is not new and the research is distributed over a number of disciplines. As with analog technologies like textbooks, computer games are used for different pedagogical purposes to support learning. These have ranged from teacher-directed, memorization-based approaches to situated, social constructivist ones in which the learner uses the game to explore challenging problems with no single correct answer alone or works in small groups with a goal of constructing meaningful knowledge and defensible solutions. Depending on the approach and goals for instruction taken by the designer of the game, the learning outcomes may wildly be different. The following sections explore three different theoretical approaches that have been commonly used to guide the design and development of games and simulations for learning, beginning with those taken from information processing and behaviorist perspectives.

Learning Games for Memory: Information Processing Theories

Some of the earliest games for learning such as typing tutors like *Mavis Beacon Teaches Typing*, included drill-and-practice forms of instruction based on the idea that repetitive practice would improve learner skills and retention of the techniques and knowledge that the student was expected to master. The underlying theory comes from both behaviorist and information processing perspectives, though the two do diverge. Old views of behaviorism foresaw the learner not as truly sentient; instead, they learned the best by associating the desired behavior with some form of reward. In this case, as players correctly typed words, they received points as a reward and competed against the system. As they improved their performance, the system increased the difficulty of play by requiring students to type more difficult words or to type them more quickly. The desired behaviors were linked, moving from the letter level to word and then to sentence as the player displayed mastery of the behavior desired by the system.

Other computer and video games such as *Pong, Pacman,* graphically oriented games like *Mortal Kombat*, and *Doom* were viewed more as edutainment and saw learning to occur when a skill was practiced enough times (Egenfeldt-Nielsen, 2005). As technology and media advanced computer games started to support more cognitive aspects of learning. Games such as *Tetris* (a simple, puzzle game), *The Sims* (a household simulation and story generation game), *Oregon Trail, Math blaster,* and the *Civilization* series chose to target cognitive attributes of learning such as problem solving, narrative, and developing firsthand experiences.

Games and Simulations in Context: Situated and Social Constructivist Theories

The structural characteristics of computer games and the social processes surrounding the educational experiences have been seen for their value to situate student learning (Squire, 2005). Situated learning is the idea that learning occurs and transfers to new settings best when contextualized in activities that reflect how they will be used in real life (Brown, Collins, & Duguid, 1989). Such activities are socially and culturally bound, so the activities in a learning experience are as complex and immersive as when conducted outside of a classroom.

Massively multiplayer online games (MMOGs) such as *World of Warcraft* immerse players in complex visual, social, and interactive digital spaces with strong narratives and goals for play and norms governed by behavior that are both provided by the system as well as emerge through player discourse with peers. Research with current MMOGs such as Blizzard's *World of Warcraft* and older ones such as Sony's *Star Wars Galaxies* and NCSoft's *Lineage,* have been associated with learning, especially in the realms of literacy practices, social discourse, and leadership (Dickey, 2007; Squire & Steinkuehler, 2005; Steinkuehler, 2006, 2008; Yu, 2009). Multi-user virtual environments (MUVEs), which predate these MMOGs, have been designed to social constructivist problem- and inquiry-based learning activities, especially focused on learning scientific concepts by immersing students in rich, detailed contexts that challenge learners to think about ill-structured problems with no one correct answer. For example, in *River City* (Dede, 2006) MUVEs were used to situate the water quality problems within the complex problems of social and economic needs of multiple groups of stakeholders that influence the degradation of the local environment. By embedding learners within spaces that replicate real world challenges along with characters with whom they can interact and question as well as data they can interrogate and understand, students are able to engage in acts of inquiry that allow them to provide defensible solutions to complex problems that face us throughout the world.

Digital games and simulations were seen as conceptual play spaces where users engage in meaningful activity, and construct relevant knowledge by interacting with information, materials, tools, and collaborating with each other (Barab, Warren & Ingram-Goble, 2008). Learning by doing, role-play, cognitive support, socialization and collaboration are perceived as important for education and a way to acquire skills that provide preparation for life beyond school (Prensky, 2001; Gee, 2003; Squire, 2008).

Purely Relative: Learner as Driver

A last, and far less employed approach for using digital games for learning, comes from the relativist or radical constructivist theoretical perspective in which all knowledge is viewed as individual to each learner and therefore learning activities must be designed for each student. As opposed to social constructivist views, knowledge is not built through social interaction and discourse; instead, it is constructed only by each learner, requiring that all learning activities be developed for and with each learner based on their internal motivations and interests. In this perspective, it becomes important to avoid designing *for* learners and to instead view games and the design of games as a tool for allowing the learner to design their own learning experience. The instructor then facilitates learning by engaging in conversation that allows the student to identify their own goals and objectives for the game and what they expect to learn from the process of design. For example, Kodu by Microsoft offered, a game creation tool for children that allowed them to learn programming. Others, such as Gamestar Mechanic, allowed them to establish their own goals and objectives for the game, learn how to use the technology by seeking out their own resources and engage in the literacy practices of game designers (Games, 2009; Torres, 2009).

Researchers found that such environments allowed for cognitive scaffolding, and the rapid feedback and risk free environment invited exploration and experimentation. The game environment intrinsically motivates players "people take on new identity other than their own" (Foreman, 2004), and it allows opportunities for deeper thinking giving players choice and control over their actions (Kirriemuir & McFarlane, 2004; Shaffer, Squire, Halverson & Gee, 2005). Hence, games targeted audience preferences of engagement, interest and learning experience with emphasis on cognitive and social aspects of learning. With theory comes the need to examine the evidence supporting the use of games for learning.

Games and Learning: The Evidence

Digital games are learner centered they promote challenges, cooperation, engagement and encourage the development of problem solving strategies (Gros, 2007). Salen and Zimmerman (2003) defined games as "a system in which players engage in artificial conflict, defined by rules, that result in quantifiable outcomes". Three attributes contribute to this schema *rules*: the organization of the system, *play*: the human experiences, and *culture*: the larger contexts inhabited and influencing the system (Salen & Zimmerman, 2003). Together, they provide a model for understanding. Learning theorists have argued that learning is not a simple process of transfer of information but rather is developed through the learner's active engagement with subject matter, situated within specific contexts (Barab et al., 2007; Brown et al., 1989).

The aim is to prepare learners to encounter problems normally encountered in real life. Such problems are ill defined, usually complex, have multiple solutions, and engage different cognitive processes. Learners engage in story driven tasks, interact amongst each other and the instructor, face artificial conflict and develop defensible solutions. Learning is fundamentally social, as players are collaborative and competitive. Assessment on learning is situated in action, occurring through multiple modalities, in the context of doing. Players solve problems and share their solutions, develop, test, and share strategies, and even maintain identities represented through games and other media. Thus learning goes beyond the acquisition of surface level skills and memorization. Cognitive conflict or puzzlement acts as the stimulus for learning and determines the nature of what is learned (Duffy& Cunningham, 1996).

In *Civilization III*, a real-time, turn-based strategy game (RTS), students were immersed in historical thinking of a civilization that existed in history at some time (Squire, 2004). Students completed game objectives through discourse with each other and shared experiences, reflecting on the curricular tasks, which in turn helps them to understand their own processes of learning and cognitive difficulties encountered during the learning activity. Research on the use of this RTS for learning found that it encouraged historical thinking and provided learning scaffolds that supported acquisition of historical concepts and content (i.e., terminology) encountered in contexts beyond the game-simulation. In the use of *Civilization III,* collaboration, acquisition of strategy-based skills and overcoming frustration through meta-cognitive reflection was also viewed as part of the learning process (Land & Zembal-Saul, 2003; Webb, Nemer, & Ing, 2006).

Similar outcomes have been shown in a different form of game, such as in Quest Atlantis' (QA) *Taiga* (Barab et. al., 2009) and *Anytown* learners engage with fictional characters and situated narratives to confront and develop solutions to ill-structured problems. The digital environment acts as a scaffold for students to work through these problems and engage in metacognitive reflection regarding their actions in the game and how they may apply in other contexts. In the larger QA story, fictional Council members from the distant planet Atlantis ask students to help them develop the ill-structured problems shared by the peoples of both worlds, This parallel resulted in the tag line: "Two Worlds, One Fate" (Barab, Thomas, Dodge, Carteaux, & Tuzun, 2005; Warren, 2005). In both projects technology is used to contextualize subject matter and create interest (Barab et. al., 2007). The focus was to improve writing skills through an ongoing narrative and problem based scenarios i.e., mysterious events, vandalism etc. with students acting as reporters in order to contextualize their findings in a meaningful way based on their age-group and understandings (Warren, Barab & Dondlinger, 2007).

Further in *Environmental Detectives* (Squire & Klopfer, 2007) a game created at The Massachusetts Institute of Technology (MIT) students as environmental scientists investigate a hypothetical toxic spill. Leveraging handheld, mobile devices with global positioning systems (GPS), combined with real world data, students engage in the research of problems central to science in a psychologically safe space where they try out new ideas and identities and can learn through failure. This approach allowed students to discover the interaction and discourse that guided inquiry, and to situate learning in context making the physical environment part of the student's thinking and scientific reasoning. Games such as *Environmental Detectives* helped students make connections between virtual and physical environments, and acquire skills and expertise beyond curricular subject matter (Squire & Klopfer, 2007).

Transmedia: Alternate Reality Games (AltRG)

As described by gamers Alternate reality games (AltRG) are neither solely virtual nor augmented instead they are an alternate reality, fictional in nature that coexist with ordinary life both, spatially and temporally (McGonigal, 2003). Designed for viral marketing purposes, this infectious genre has unique affordances as a problem-based instructional methodology for teaching and learning (Aamodt & Plaza, 1994). The narrative in an AltRG is considerably influenced by the players themselves through solving online puzzles linked to initiatives in the real world that help to advance the story similar to case based reasoning (CBL). Knowledge is constructed with multiple perspectives in a facilitator-led, situated context, and is constructed, both, socially and physically (Unfiction, n.d.).

AltRGs can be viewed as the first narrative art form, native to the Internet, because its storytelling relies on two main activities conducted there the searching and sharing of information (Unfiction, 2008). The game uses any and every application available on the Internet as small parts of the wider game and the real world as a platform (Martin & Chatfield, 2006) A variety of online resources are employed to provide objective information about the ill-structured learning tasks and to spur communications among students, instructors, and game characters. Additionally, a number of different communication tools both synchronous and asynchronous (i.e. chat, instant messaging), podcasts, video clips, wikis, and weblogs are incorporated into the design (Warren et al., 2011). Students use these tools to challenge information offered by the instructor, peers, and even some of the pedagogical agents, which are encountered as digital avatars or e-mail contacts.

Theoretical Models Supporting *Broken Window*

The *Broken Window* alternate reality course game was created to address deficiencies in the original alternate reality course game, *The Door* (Warren et al., 2011). Specifically, research on the original course indicated that the design did not focus students sufficiently on creating an end product that helped them fully synthesize what they had learned, making them mindful of the connections between content and activity. Additionally, *The Door* employed the social constructivist problem-based learning model that students were not prepared to engage with as they entered. As a result, many spent much of their time struggling with self-regulated learning aspects required by *The Door* such as time management, organization, and self-monitoring, all of which were required in the original design. The original study also indicated the use of game throughout the semester was not sufficient to engage and satisfy undergraduates.

In order to address these shortcomings, a new model was created that would include a learning game as an immersive example for students to use as they employed their newly acquired computer literacy skills to build their own alternate reality game. Both *Broken Window* and *The Door* shared an underlying theory stemming from social constructivism (Duffy & Cunningham, 1996), problem-based learning (Barrows, 1986), and situated cognition (Brown et al., 1989) each of which require that for learning to occur, students should be immersed in a context that allows them to struggle with the construction of knowledge that is embedded in a relevant context. These perspectives were merged with game principles indicated by Salen and Zimmerman (Salen & Zimmerman, 2004), revised by Warren, Stein, Dondlinger, and Barab (2009), that was used by Warren, et al (2011) to synthesize and propose a new model of problem-based game design that is depicted in Figure 1.

In addition to employing view of problem based learning and game, the *Broken Window* design employed a theory that emerged from analysis of *The Door*. This theory is called Learning and Teaching as Communicative Actions (LTCA) (Wakefield & Warren, in press; Wakefield, Warren, & Alsobrook, 2012) and is a synthesis of general principles of communication enunciated by Jürgen Habermas (Habermas, 1984, 1987, 1998). From this theory, the game and learning goals were constructed concurrently with a goal of using improved student communication to improve learning.

Figure 1. Merging of PBL and game from Warren et al (2011)

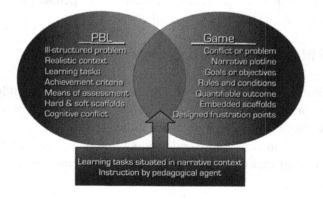

According to this LTCA theory, meaningful discourse around learning and play is normatively bound. The instructor therefore must develop learning activities that have inherent claims to truth and knowledge. Through these, they challenge students to apply what they have learned and defend what they think they know through evidence-supported argumentation. The identity and intersubjectively created products generated through group discourse and actions are open to critique by peers, self, and instructor. This is expected to improve not only the product, but also improve student understanding of the cultural norms that bound these learning discourses. This process helps transform claims to truth from internal experience and relative knowledge into socially valid, defensible claims with evidence that should enable learner growth. LTCA learning expectations for this alternate reality course game were framed in terms of the four types of communicative actions that support such communicative processes. Each is discussed in detail in the following section along with the specific design of the game *Broken Window*.

BROKEN WINDOW INSTRUCTIONAL DESIGN

Learning environments are complex systems and the Broken Window alternate reality game (AltRG) was no exception. It required that students struggle with findings the underlying reasons why a large, ill-structured problem happens, how they can have agency in the development of related solutions, and how to use the cognitive and technology tools available to them. In the case of these cognitive tools, what Jonassen (2011) calls *Mindtools*, are those that support students learning by developing "models…[and] learning *with* the computer, not *from* it (p. 306)." It is either by creating either physical or mental models with these tools that students are able to construct an understanding of the conditions under which a particular set of interactions takes place and develop a defensible solution.

This necessitated an instructional design model that was at once flexible and accommodating of the changing needs of both students and designer. It had to be one that allowed the designer or instructor to cope with the complexities that naturally arise in a classroom. Such a design would allow also for an iterative changing to the environment over time, each supported by research evidence, and that could feed recursively into future designs (Barab, 2006). Thus it was that the *Broken Window* AltRG followed a design-based research model of instructional design to accommodate such needs (Barab, 2006; Barab & Squire, 2004).

As this alternate reality course game employed Re-Examination Theory (Warren & Jones, 2008), its design employed older, well-established tools to support media creation. As such, the development of an AltRG requires less time and energy on the part of the designer than other games. It is also far less expensive to develop such a game than others that employ 3-D engines and high-end graphics. Further, because this game genre uses applications freely available on the Internet they are not device dependent. The narrative contained motivational factors such as,

- A captivating story that extends beyond to make the event dynamic and more appealing.
- The discovery and deciphering of elements of the narrative revealed in a obscure way so people discover information and work together to help the story progress.
- Cross medium interactivity, use of several mediums must be available and accessible using as many as possible i.e. articles, blogs, videos, email, wiki's podcasts etc.
- The progression of the storyline is important as it helps blur the line between reality and fiction; decisions are made instantaneously as the narrative advances (Saleem, 2007).

For the first six weeks (Weeks 1-6), students played the *Broken Window* AltRG and complete core exercises; immersing them in the game, and then, in the latter six weeks (Weeks 7-15), they are expected to construct their own AltRG based on some topic related to the United Nations Millennium Development Goals (UN MDG); applying the skills acquired. In order to provide the reader with a better understanding of how such games are constructed, we provide the following description of the steps individual components of a learning alternate reality game drawn from *Broken Window*. Our goal is not to describe all 15 weeks of the course, but instead to provide a concrete depiction of the steps by which a learning alternate reality game can be constructed in the context of one we have developed and used.

Constructing the Game

An AltRG is made up of several components, many of which follow a normal narrative plot structure. These include the setup, conflict, and resolution. These are not particularly different than what we see in many games in which, as noted earlier by Salen & Zimmerman (2003), there is a set of rules establishing how the game or narrative is expected to progress, an artificial conflict that drives player or protagonist action, and an outcome in which the conflict is somehow resolved. In the case of Broken Window, there was both a narrative within the game that was constructed for the *Broken Window* section of the course that made up the first six weeks, as well as a meta-narrative that governed the entire course and the problems students sought to provide solutions to through their own game construction. In both instances, the game began where narratives often do: at the beginning.

The Setup

During the setup phase, the designer identifies the problem that the instruction seeks to ameliorate, the purpose of instruction, and associated learning goals. In addition, when employing LTCA design, these goals are described in the context of the communicative actions they support. From this point, the designer generates an overall narrative that they feel will support these learning goals as well as related learning activities they feel will best allow them to reach each goal. Based on these activities, the established course goals, and the course time constraints (i.e. 15 weeks), a timeline is established. As with most instructional designs, we began the design of the door through an analysis and establishment of the learning goals we sought to address.

LTCA Theory

In this theory, learning and instructional communicative actions generally have one of four purposes. These include:

- **Strategic Communicative Action:** TLW communicate effectively in a manner that allows for successfully completing personal objectives.
- **Constative Communicative Action:** TLW communicate the validity of their truth claims in a manner that allows for peers and client to accept this validity towards allowing design action.
- **Normative Communicative Action:** TLW communicate with peers and group towards a goal of understanding norms, roles, for functioning as a team in the course and in the real world.
- **Dramaturgical Communicative Action:** TLW communicate through self-expression that allow for others to critique based on elements of individual and group identities that emerge from the communicative process.

As with any curricular material, we began with a series of purposes and overall goals for the course. All goals and other materials created for the course were included in what some game designers call "The Bible," but we, seeking something secular, referred to as "The Codex." Prior to establishing these goals, we established that the problem we sought to address was that *"The Door* does not currently focus students enough on a product and they spend too much time struggling with the requirement of high self-direction." From the Codex (Warren, 2010) and based on this challenge, the general purposes and learning goals are listed in Table 1. For the remainder of the chapter, the initials TLW stands for "The Learner Will."

Table 1. Broken Window purposes and goals

Purpose(s)
The purpose of this course is to prepare students to:
1. communicate effectively using standard technology tools (i.e. MS Office)
2. communicate and function in small groups/teams
3. relate technology tool use to future work, goals and learning
4. synthesize experiences into communicative actions and reflections
5. learn to use technology to think about and work towards solving larger global problems by encouraging collaborative and collective thinking centered on specific problems from United Nations (UN) and others
Goal(s)
The learner will (TLW)
1. be able to communicate effectively using standard business technology tools
2. communicate effectively to create a product using standard computer literacy tools
3. understand how these tools will relate to current and future work
4. reflect on and come to understand how they learn and work best to solve problems
5. generate an effective solution to a global problem
6. show knowledge of and skills with technology applications to generate a product that can help educate others about a particular global problem

Each of these general learning goals were then framed within the context of the types of communicative actions that were expected to foster each.

LTCA Goals

Beyond these general learning goals, we also established a set of learning goals in the context of Learning and Teaching as Communicative Actions Theory. These are presented in Table 2.

Each of these normative communicative actions was intended to provide players with general guidance as to appropriate use of tools, how to function well in the course as students, and how they should generally interact with the game as players. Some of this guidance came through items such as the syllabus, but many more norms were established as students interacted with the characters and one another. As with other norms, those in this course were emergent and were constantly revised based on the discourse that emerged from these interactions as students made normative claims that were rejected by peers or characters, requiring them to be intersubjectively agreed upon anew. Once these norms were tentatively established, the

Table 2. Normative communicative actions for learning

Communicative Action Type	*Broken Window* **Enactments**
Normative	1. Syllabus contained basic outline of class participation expectations (i.e. attendance, discussions, appropriate tools) 2. Rules for game participation that could be changed or broken by learners 3. Expectations for group member roles and participation
	1. Directions and hard scaffolds were embedded in the LMS and web sites 2. Characters role played by instructors provided directives to act in e-mail, blogs, LMS, etc. 3. Directions from the professor in LMS and forums during game construction

instructor used the digital system to establish strategic communications. These were directions that students could either follow or not, accepting or rejecting the validity of the inherent claim made in the order. Examples are presented in Table 3.

These strategic communications came in the form of requirements for participation posted in the learning management systems, directions given by the instructor through characters, and by peers as students self organized. In many instances, students designated a leader, which had been mandated in *The Door*. These leaders gave other students directives to take particular actions to find resources, prepare reports, etc. If another student accepted the validity of the order, they followed it, completing said report. If they rejected the inherent truth of the claim, they did not complete the task, which usually had negative impacts on the group. Such a rejection often created arguments or constative communicative actions as seen in Table 4.

Constative communicative actions have inherent truth claims such as "I think the right way to proceed is to have John e-mail b4xt3r and ask him about c0d4." When another student replies that, "No, we should forward the address to Walter and ask his opinion about how we should move forward," then constative communication has begun. Through the argumentation process, speakers make claims and counter-claims regarding best actions and are then required to provide support for their claims. As each participant provides evidence, intersubjective truths emerge;

Table 3. Strategic communicative actions for learning

Communicative Action Type	*Broken Window* **Enactments**
Strategic	1. Directions and hard scaffolds were embedded in the LMS and web sites 2. Characters role played by instructors provided directives to act in e-mail, blogs, LMS, etc. 3. Directions from the professor in LMS and forums during game construction

Table 4. Constative communicative actions for learning

Communicative Action Type	*Broken Window* **Enactments**
Constative	1. Claims and counter-claims made by fictional characters drove learner discourse towards shared understandings about problems, problem solutions, and approaches to game play 2. Group tasks required collaborative work and discourse regarding the nature of their game construction for the second half of the course to meet course requirements 3. Critiques by instructor and peers on solutions and final products spurred argumentation geared towards meeting shared understandings of what the games should achieve and were expected to engender cognitive conflict

that is to say, speaker and hearer, both learners, come to agree upon the inherent truth of a claim and share an understanding. In this case, such agreement would lead to the best way to proceed based on the information they had at hand. Individual understandings also emerge that student's construct for themselves that result from their communicative actions and internal cognition. Instructors then ask for some form of identity expression that conveys these individual understandings, leading to dramaturgical communicative actions (See Table 5).

In the case of Broken Window, learners were expected not only to construct a shared solution to the problem, but also to create an artifact that reflected their personal understanding. In dramaturgical acts, as with other speech acts, they are not purely relative. Instead, they are open to critique by peers, instructors, and experts and this allows for improvement of the product and helps the learner improve poorly structured cognitive models, similar to the approach used in social constructivist environments. Some students wrote their own story of Broken Window, as they perceived it, others created a poem, while still others created artistic depictions and cartoons of the narrative. While not the focus of this chapter, students were also expected to construct their own game in the last nine weeks that showed their understanding of what an alternate reality learning game is and how it can be used to immerse learners in a complex topic and challenge them to generate solutions to difficult problems.

Developing Instruction with LTCA Theory: The Conflict

From the creation of learning goals, we then sought to create narrative that would support each. This story was established by framing the instruction in the context of the ill-structured problem established in this Setup step. This next piece was the identification and creation of the narrative that would act as The Conflict. Based on the social constructivist and problem-based learning theories that supported this design (Duffy & Cunningham, 1996; Savery & Duffy, 1995), this struggle was

Table 5. Dramaturgical communicative actions for learning

Communicative Action Type	*Broken Window* **Enactments**
	1. Final game products included individual and group claims to truth about the quality of the game, its effectiveness for learning, and their knowledge of what such a game should contain and what form it should take 2. Learner solutions included learner values regarding the projects themselves, their personal identity as an investigator, and how well they participated in constructing knowledge

expected to drive learning in the game space by challenging students to engage in constative communication about the clues, artifacts, and narrative that emerged towards a goal of generating intersubjective, shared understandings that would allow them to generate strong solutions. This Conflict was constructed in *Broken Window* through a set of characters, locations, and in the context of the United Nations Millennium Development Goals (UN MDG) that are ill-structured problems themselves.

Ill-Structured Problems

Problem based learning (PBL) is a learner-centered approach that helps learners to acquire and develop the knowledge and skills needed to solve problems effectively (Engel, 1997). Ill-structured problems encountered in everyday life, and work engage different cognitive processes and require different problem solving skills. They are complex and typically have multiple solutions (Jonassen, 1997). The goal and path constraints are often unknown or open to negotiation and there is uncertainty about which concepts and methods are necessary to solve the problem (Jonassen, 2011, p. 208). Such problems arise through interactions of participants, activity, and context therefore their solutions often are socially and culturally mediated (Kramer, 1986; Roth & Mcginn, 1997). Learners in *Broken Window* AltRG engage in the narrative driven, ill-structured tasks, interact amongst each other and the instructor, face artificial conflict and develop defensible solutions to the problem or conflict. In the first half of the game this is locating the missing associates and finding a solution to preventable disease.

Conflict to Drive Play

As we began, the central narrative Conflict to drive constative communication this took shape under the auspices of the United Nations Millennium Development Goals for the year 2015. These goals were also used to situate Dondlinger's *Global Village Playground* alternate reality game course component (Dondlinger & Warren, 2009). The UN MDG goals are:

- Combat HIV/AIDS
- Maternal Health
- Universal Education
- Environmental Sustainability
- Gender Equality
- Global Partnership
- Child Health
- End Poverty and Hunger

It was decided that it would be too difficult to develop a game that would take place in five or six weeks that could address all eight goals, so the story was narrowed to focus on environmental sustainability for the *Broken Window* AltRG component that students would begin immersed in at the outset of the course. When a problem is as massive as the ill-structured problems identified by the United Nations, ensuring that the problem established for a game is narrow enough to be covered within the course timeline is very important. We do not expect learners to develop easily implemented solutions to such difficult problems. It has been the life work of many to even scratch the surface. Instead, our goal was to have them begin to understand the problem, engage in discourse with peers about it, and use technology tools to support their work.

Cognitive vs. Productivity Tools

In a course focused on learning to use technology applications, as Jonassen suggests, we sought to have them use the tools not to learn from, but as supports to learn with as they sought to solve problems and create new mental models. In order to do this, we identified a series of productivity tools that supported the course goals and could be used to construct the game. Since the course was established to prepare students to be productive with both offline and online technologies, the following tools were included:

- Word Processing
- Spreadsheets
- Presentation Software (i.e. Microsoft PowerPoint)
- Web Browsers and Websites
- Free, Online Email Accounts
- Social Media (i.e. Facebook)
- Video Sharing Tools (i.e. YouTube)
- Virtual Worlds

- Online Games
- Learning Management Systems

The Microsoft Office tools were those we sought to have students master without focusing student attention on them, learning to use them because the game provided them a need to do so. In one case, this was done by requiring the write a professional letter to a UN representative to outline their findings and proposed solution to a particular problem. This required that they use the tool situated in the narrative for a particular purpose rather than just because they were told to so.

Contextualizing Play

As the narrative opened, students were challenged to solve more than one problem by characters from a fictional research think tank. The researchers, friends of their course professor, have gone missing. They were on the verge of developing a collaborative solution that would improve access to clean water around the world and help the UN reach the 2015 Environmental Sustainability goal. It was this UN development goal that would contextualize their play throughout the first five or six weeks of the course. The call for help in finding these researchers came from their professor and through the Moodle learning management system that would organize the resources they would use as they sought to find the think tank researchers and concurrently develop their own solution to the problem using the data each member of the team had left behind.

The name *Broken Window* comes from the social theory known as "broken windows." It states that blight in urban areas leads people to act chaotically and destructively, as they residents do not value their neighborhood and neighbors. It was this that is proposed within the game as a reason for the world continues to fall into disrepair. It is stated by several characters that this theory is the main reason underlying the failure of the industrialized nations to help their neighbors, leading to the need for the UN Millennium Development goals (UN MDG).

The Rabbit Hole

The term, borrowed from Lewis Carroll's book *Alice's Adventures in Wonderland,* is the point of entry through which players engage with the story. It is at this stage that students begin to work with peers and alone to make meaning, construct knowledge and conceptualize reality in an ill-structured space, with an ill-structured problem. As they are immersed in the story, the instructor posts a link to the Havenwyrd Institute public blog, presented in Figure 2.

It is there that they discover a message from the director of the think tank that "it has been recommended that we keep a blog to update the many visitors to our web site. Please check back for details in the weeks to come." Though framed politely, this acts as the first strategic communicative action from a character. They can either do or not do as he asks.

On that blog, there is also a link a negative image of a desktop replete with computer and monitors shown in Figure 3. Exploring the static page reveals information that leads the learner down the "rabbit hole." The hotspots in the image contain different bits of information that build on the narrative. Participants must discover and place them in the correct order in order to advance the story.

Several clues are embedded within this image including the name on a letter that confirms the name of the desktop's owner while the laptop provides an email address of another Associate although the message is intentionally blurred. As they explore, they find that double clicking this message makes the message clear and readable.

Character Interactions to Drive Play

From the email addresses listed on the screen and related clues, students can correctly sequenced each in a way that provides an address a way to contact someone calling themselves "b4xter." Upon contacting him, b4xter's responses are tailored to each student's questions interactively, providing information that should lead to

Figure 2. Havenwyrd Institute blog

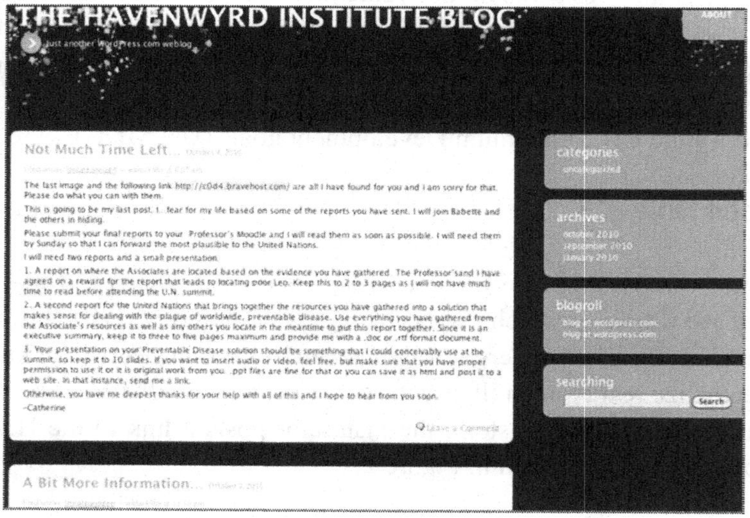

Figure 3. Rybickon's desk in Broken Window (Warren, 2010)

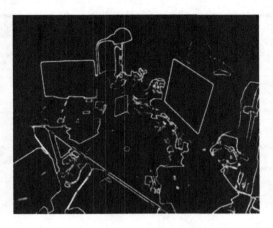

argumentation among group members regarding the next steps to take, challenging them to use evidence to support their views. The narrative unfolds with students shaping their own storyline through their actions as they follow up on the clues. The instructor acts in the role of "Puppetmaster," scaffolding student play and learning through their interactions with students as the fictional characters in the game. Students also share information in forums and through private emails with their small group or the whole class.

For those that fail to catch on to what they are supposed to do in the game, the characters send emails to put them on the right track, reinforcing that they *should* play the game, using normative language. As the weeks of play unfold, the blog is "hacked" by a villain and cryptic messages are posted on the learning management system or the Havenwyrd blog such as that presented in Figure 4.

Each week, new information, clues, and twists in the story are released that help students locate the missing associates and finding a solution to the ill-structured problem. Thus, students are led through the narrative working with uncovering information, working with the curricular objectives moving closer to the final solution. The skills applied are storytelling, information structuring, management and web development - skills far more accessible than those required in other game development.

The Puppetmaster

The instructor's role in an AltRG course game, just as in other social constructivist designs, is that of facilitator. They empower students by playing the characters and changing the narrative in response to discourses with students both as the charac-

Figure 4. Cryptic warning from the villainous c0d4

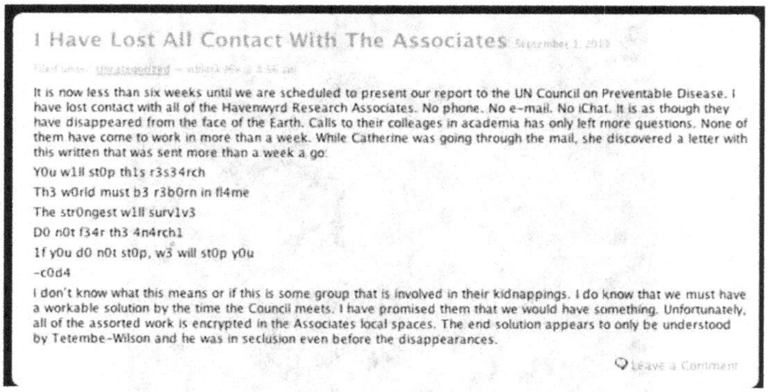

I Have Lost All Contact With The Associates September 1, 2013

It is now less than six weeks until we are scheduled to present our report to the UN Council on Preventable Disease. I have lost contact with all of the Havenwyrd Research Associates. No phone. No e-mail. No iChat. It is as though they have disappeared from the face of the Earth. Calls to their colleagues in academia has only left more questions. None of them have come to work in more than a week. While Catherine was going through the mail, she discovered a letter with this written that was sent more than a week a go:

YOu w1ll stOp th1s r3s34rch

Th3 wOrld must b3 r3bOrn in fl4me

The strOngest w1ll surv1v3

DO nOt f34r th3 4n4rch1

1f yOu dO nOt stOp, w3 will stOp yOu

–c0d4

I don't know what this means or if this is some group that is involved in their kidnappings. I do know that we must have a workable solution by the time the Council meets. I have promised them that we would have something. Unfortunately, all of the assorted work is encrypted in the Associates local spaces. The end solution appears to only be understood by Tetembe-Wilson and he was in seclusion even before the disappearances.

ters and in class. As the instructor scaffolds learning by responding to students in their role play of each character, they help reveal each character's persona and help students engage in suspension of disbelief. These actions broaden the instructor's reach, as the character role-play offers the instructor a metaphorical screen through which to interact and facilitate student learning. Students were encouraged by their instructor to ask questions of the characters or peers. As LTCA theory requires that such communicative actions to be central to the learning process, responses from characters encouraged students to engage in constative communications to help develop their later, personal knowledge constructions. However, these activities alone are not enough to support learning. It was also necessary to include a combination of embedded, static "hard scaffolds" within the digital game environment as well as verbal "soft scaffolds" that are supportive verbal and just-in-time instructional supports to provide a full educational experience (Brush and Saye, 2001).

The Clients: Pedagogical Agents to Pose and Mitigate Problems

In order to maintain some semblance of illusion in the game, instruction and feedback came through a series of fictional characters that appeared and spoke to players, with some only communicating once or twice in the game either through podcast or video. Each character provided a different form of learning support or information that students needed to either solve the game investigation or develop their ill-structured problem solution. Table 6 shows the main characters from *Broken Window,* some of who are shared between *The Door* and *Broken Window*, mainly for the entertainment of the designers. It is important to maintain designer interest in the game, especially when there are many iterations or versions.

Table 6. The clients in Broken Window

Table 6.
The Clients in Broken Window

Character	Role	Description
Walter Black	Protagonist	CEO of Havenwyrd Research Institute
Catherine Felwood	Supporting character	Secretary of Havenwyrd Institute
Leonard Rybickon	Foil character	North American associate taken hostage; his desktop holds many of the initial clues
Jason Baxter	Supporting character	Member of C0d4 whose email is visible on computer screen
Babette Aubuchon Saenz	Foil character	European associate who provides information for solving the larger problem of disease through education
Siri Tanaka	Foil character	Asia associate
Chinua Tetembe Wilson	Foil character	African associate; a mysterious and obscure character that points students to the code that unfolds the mystery. His trail leads students to Second Life
Javier Ochoa Mendez	Supporting character	South American associate but member of C0d4 who has his own solution for solving Global disease. He owns a safe deposit box that has information that also can help defeat C0d4
Red Queen	Antagonist	The all powerful and evil leader of C0d4
Lord Bedlam	Antagonist	Second in command for C0d4
Coda Omega alias C0d4	Antagonist group	Group responsible for all the chaos and anarchy

The person that mainly posed problems in the game was a character named Walter Black and until he disappears, communicated with players through the blog. For those familiar with the game *Bioshock*, he was similar to Atlas; that is, by virtue of being the main contact, he directed players to clues and actions they should take. Upon his disappearance, his secretary Catherine Felwood took on this role. Most of the other characters that support the learner are the Associates, each representing a different continent and were therefore most knowledgeable about the problems there. For example, Siri Tanaka provided players with a Twitter feed late in the game in which the instructor can role play her to rapidly direct students to new resources and reveal more about the game and general player progress. Profiles for each character were also created, an approach similar to that taken with The Council Actors project in Quest Atlantis, which also used a rudimentary form of Learning and Teaching as Communicative Actions theory (Warren & Stein, 2008). These provided the instructor with each character's history and directions on how they should role play each.

Instructors played not only the heroes, but also the villains from a group called c0d4. They have kidnapped the Associate Leo Rybickon in order to put pressure on the Institute to abandon their work. They also confused players by providing misinformation through double agents within the Institute. Such characters are important, because if the narrative is too straightforward, players become bored. If it is too complex, they give up and refuse to play. It is then that the instructor as Puppetmaster uses characters to provide scaffolding and additional information to nudge learners in the right direction. This is similar to the instructor role in any other form of social constructivism, because the instructor mainly supports rather than directs.

In the building game resources, we created Second Life and World of Warcraft accounts or characters that could be used to show up at particular moments to talk to players if they followed the clues. These characters would let slip important information that would be shared among team members and allow for the story to progress. Further, we created our own hand-drawn elements, Adobe Photoshop distortions with text, or used images of friends and family that were willing to participate as shown in Figure 5, with Dr. Warren's grandmother acting in the role of The R3d Qu33n, another allusion to Alice's Adventures in Wonderland.

In this case, we used locations that were familiar to the designers, because it makes it easier to develop a clear sense of place. In this case, parts of the game took place in Detroit while others were in Los Angeles and still others in Houston and locally in Denton. All of these were places that the designers had lived in and created realistic depictions of or embedded relevant images from their own personal stock, rather than paid photographs taken by others.

Job Aid

This is the most important piece of documentation for the instructor to have. Without this, they cannot run the game. This job aid provides each week of the narrative along with a guide to role playing each character. All clues, discourses with players through email, and the specific story of what was happening in the background that players cannot see is included here. For example, the b4xt3r character that appears helpful in week one is revealed to the instructor as being a member of c0d4 and is providing misinformation to players when they contact him through email. The instructor is informed also that this character should let slip clues that he is c0d4 by

Figure 5. Dr. Warren's grandmother as the R3d Qu33n

accidentally using l33t in his email responses, thus tipping them off that he may not be who he seems. From their knowledge of Internet security, they should already be looking for such information as when he asks them for things like their email and password information to leave them special information. All information about the characters, their emails, links to related resources such as podcast logins, were kept in a spreadsheet for easy access.

The job aid should be a living document that changes and is added to as instructors and design team discover things that work and things that do not in the game play. In addition, if an instructor finds hard scaffolds that should be embedded in the learning management system or other spaces, the document should reflect these. All set dialogue pieces and screen shots of online resources such as web sites and images are embedded here with links so that the instructor need not go looking for them. It is also in the job aid that the grading rubrics for assessing learning are located.

The Resolution: Assessing Successful Student Learning and Play

How then is learning assessed in such a game? In this case, we leveraged rubrics that examined two main facets: successful problem solutions and success with the game investigation. Because this part of the game was intended to immerse players in a learning alternate reality game, the focus was not on acquisition of skills, but to provide them with a worked example of the components of such a game and the reasoning skills they would seek to engender in the creation of their own game. Therefore, there were two rubrics. The first identified to what degree players had completed each milestone in the game itself, the degree to which they interacted with characters to gain information, and whether they had generated a defensible set of evidence as to who was responsible for Leo's disappearance to take to the police. The second rubric focused on how defensible each student's solution to the problems of preventable disease and related issues of potable water and education. They were judged on their use of evidence that they either located from the game characters or found on their own from other resources such as the use of Boolean searches, which was another learning goal.

SUMMARY

To conclude, alternate reality games can be used to support student learning. They do require some time commitment to design, though it is generally far less than that required in developing learning games in 3-D environments. In this chapter, we reviewed one design, *Broken Window,* a game designed that challenged undergraduates to use computer applications tools to help them solve large, ill-structured problems. Based on ideas from situated cognition and problem-based learning, we provided interactivity and context that was expected to challenge students to use these productivity tools meaningfully so that the skills they learned would easily transfer to their future work settings their use in that necessitated students to engage in several forms of argumentation.

While games may not always be the best tool for learning, they do act as excellent delivery mechanisms to provide learners with complex tasks that they will be expected to do out in the world of work. By engaging instructors and students in different roles, we can challenge them to think more critically and constructively through learning discourses even as they construct new knowledge and creative solutions to the world's most challenging problems. We hope that anyone choosing to follow our model will be as richly rewarded as we have been.

REFERENCES

Aamodt, A., & Plaza, E. (1994). Case-based reasoning: Foundational issues, methodological variations and system approaches. *AI Communications, 7*(1), 39-59. Retrieved January 26, 2006, from http://www.idi.ntnu.no/emner/it3704/lectures/papers/Aamodt_1994_Case.pdf

Barab, S. (2006). Design-based reearch: A methodological toolkit for the learning scientist. In Sawyer, R. K. (Ed.), *The Cambridge handbook of the learning sciences* (pp. 153–169). New York, NY: Cambridge University Press.

Barab, S., Scott, B., Siyahhan, S., Goldstone, R., Ingram-Goble, A., Zuiker, S., & Warren, S. J. (2009). Transformational play as a curricular scaffold: Using videogames to support science education. *Journal of Science Education and Technology, 18*(4), 305–320. doi:10.1007/s10956-009-9171-5

Barab, S., & Squire, K. (2004). Design-based research: Putting a stake in the ground. *Journal of the Learning Sciences, 13*, 1–14. doi:10.1207/s15327809jls1301_1

Barab, S., Thomas, M., Dodge, T., Carteaux, R., & Tuzun, H. (2005). Making learning fun: Quest Atlantis, a game without guns. *Educational Technology Research and Development, 53*, 86–107. doi:10.1007/BF02504859

Barab, S., Zuiker, S., Warren, S., Hickey, D., Ingram-Goble, A., & Kwon, E.-J. (2007). Situationally embodied curriculum: Relating formalisms and contexts. *Science Education, 91*, 750–782. doi:10.1002/sce.20217

Barab, S. A., Hay, K. E., Barnett, M., & Squire, K. (2001). Constructing virtual worlds: Tracing the historical development of learner practices. *Cognition and Instruction, 19*(1), 47–94. doi:10.1207/S1532690XCI1901_2

Barab, S. A., Warren, S. J., & Ingram-Goble, A. (2008). Academic play spaces. In Ferdig, R. (Ed.), *Handbook of research on effective electronic gaming in education.* Hershey, PA: Idea Group Reference.

Barrows, H. S. (1986). A taxonomy of problem based learning methods. *Medical Education, 20*, 481–486. doi:10.1111/j.1365-2923.1986.tb01386.x

Brown, J. S., Collins, A., & Duguid, P. (1989). Situated cognition and the culture of learning. *Educational Researcher, 18*, 32–42.

Dickey, M. D. (2007). Game design and learning: A conjectural analysis of how massively multiple online role-playing games (MMORPGs) foster intrinsic motivation. *Educational Technology Research and Development, 55*, 253–273. doi:10.1007/s11423-006-9004-7

Dondlinger, M., & Warren, S. J. (2009). *The global village playground: A qualitative case study of designing an ARG as a capstone learning experience*. PhD Dissertation, Denton, Texas: University of North Texas.

Duffy, T. M., & Cunningham, D. J. (1996). Constructivism: Implications for the design and delivery of instruction. In Jonassen, D. H. (Ed.), *Handbook of research for educational communications and technology.* New York, NY: Macmillan.

Egenfeldt-Nielsen, S. (2005). *Beyond edutaiment.* Unpublished dissertation, University of Copenhagen. Copenhagen, Denmark.

Foreman, J. (2004). Game-based learning: How to delight and instruct in the 21st century. *EDUCAUSE Review*, 50–66.

Games, I. (2009). *21st century language and literacy in Gamestar Mechanic: Middle school students' appropriate through play of the discourse of computer game designers.* PhD Dissertation, University of Wisconsin-Madison, Madison, WI.

Gee, J. P. (2003). *What video games have to teach us about learning and literacy.* New York, NY: Palgrave MacMillan. doi:10.1145/950566.950595

Gibson, D., & Baek, Y. (2009a). *Digital simulations for improving education: Learning through artificial teaching environments* (1st ed., p. 514). Hershey, PA: Information Science Reference. doi:10.4018/978-1-60566-322-7

Gibson, D., & Baek, Y. (Eds.). (2009b). *Digital simulations for improving education: Learning through artificial teaching environments* (1st ed.). Hershey, PA: Information Science Reference. doi:10.4018/978-1-60566-322-7

Greenblat, C. S., & Duke, R. (1981). *Principles and practices of gaming-simulation.* Beverly Hills, CA: Sage Publications.

Guetzkow, H. (1963). *Simulation in international relations.* Prentice-Hall.

Habermas, J. (1984). The theory of communicative action: *Vol. 1. Reason and the rationalization of society.* Boston, MA: Beacon Press.

Habermas, J. (1987). The theory of communicative action: *Vol. 2. Lifeworld and system.* Boston, MA: Beacon Press.

Habermas, J. (1998). *On the pragmatics of communication.* Cambridge, MA: The MIT Press.

Horn, R. (1977). *The guide to simulations/games for education and training* (*Vol. 1*). Crawford, NJ: Didactic Systems. doi:10.1177/1046878195264008

Jenkins, H. (2006). *Convergence culture.* New York, NY: New York University Press.

Jonassen, D. H. (2011). *Learning to solve problems: A handbook for designing problem-solving learning environments.* New York, NY: Routledge.

Kirriemuir, J., & McFarlane, A. (2004). *Literature review in games and learning (No. 8).* Bristol, Canada: Nesta Futurelab.

Land, S., & Zembal-Saul, C. (2003). Scaffolding reflection and articulation of scientific explanation in a data-rich, project-based learning environment: An investigation of progress portfolio. *Educational Technology Research and Development, 51,* 65–84. doi:10.1007/BF02504544

Martin, A., & Chatfield, T. (2006). Alternate reality games. In A. Martin (Ed.), *White paper - IGDA ARG SIG* (pp. 82). Mt. Royal, NJ: International Game Developers Association.

Prensky, M. (2001). *Digital game-based learning.* New York, NY: McGraw-Hill.

Salen, K., & Zimmerman, E. (2004). *Rules of play: Game design fundamentals.* Cambridge, MA: MIT Press.

Savery, J. R., & Duffy, T. M. (1995). Problem based learning: An instructional model and its constructivist framework. *Educational Technology, 35,* 31–38.

Shaffer, D. W., Squire, K., Halverson, R., & Gee, J. P. (2005). Video games and the future of learning. *Phi Delta Kappan, 87*(2), 104–111.

Squire, K. (2004). *Replaying history: Learning world history through playing Civilization III. (Ph.D.)*. Bloomington, IN: Indiana University-Bloomington.

Squire, K. (2008). Video game-based learning: An emerging paradigm for instruction. *Performance Improvement Quarterly, 2*(2).

Squire, K., & Steinkuehler, C. (2005). Generating cyberculture/s: The case of Star Wars Galaxies. In Gibbs, D., & Krause, K.-L. (Eds.), *Cyberlines 2.0: Languages and cultures of the Internet* (2nd ed., *Vol. 1*, pp. 177–198). Albert Park, Australia: James Nicholas Publishers.

Steinkuehler, C. (2006). Massively multiplayer online video gaming as participiation in a discourse. *Mind, Culture, and Activity, 13*, 38–52. doi:10.1207/s15327884mca1301_4

Steinkuehler, C. (2008). Cognition and literacy in massively multiplayer online games. In J. Coiro, K. C., C. Lanskear, & D. Leu (Eds.), *Handbook of research on new literacies* (pp. 611-634). Mahwah, NJ: Erlbaum.

Torres, R. (2009). *Learning on a 21st century platform: Gamestar Mechanic as a means to game design and systems-thinking sklils within a nodal ecology*. (PhD Dissertation), New York University, New York.

Wakefield, J. S., & Warren, S. J. (in press). Learning and teaching as communicative actions: Social media as educational tool. In Seo, K. (Ed.), *Using social media effectively in the classroom*. New York, NY: Routledge.

Wakefield, J. S., Warren, S. J., & Alsobrook, M. (2012). Learning and teaching as communicative actions: Tweeting global policy challenges. *Knowledge Management & E-Learning: An International Journal, 3*(4), 563–584.

Warren, S. J. (2005). *Archfall (Vol. 1)*. Bloomington, IN: Quest Atlantis Publishers.

Warren, S. J. (2010). *Broken Window codex* (3rd ed. Vol. 2). Denton, TX: ThinkTankTwo@UNT.

Warren, S. J., Dondlinger, M., McLeod, J., & Bigenho, C. (2011). Opening the door: An evaluation of the efficacy of a problem-based learning game. *Computers & Education, 58*, 1–15.

Warren, S. J., & Jones, G. (2008). Yokoi's theory of lateral innovation: Applications for learning game design. *I-Manager's Journal of Educational Technology, 5*, 32–43.

Warren, S. J., & Lin, L. (2012). Ethical considerations in the design and use of educational games. In Yang, H. H., & Yuen, S. C.-Y. (Eds.), *Handbook of research on practices and outcomes in virtual worlds and environments* (1st ed., Vol. 1, pp. 1–18). Hershey, PA: IGI Global.

Warren, S. J., & Stein, R. (2008). Simulating teaching experience with role-play. In Gibson, D., & Baek, Y. (Eds.), *Digital simulations for improving education: Learning through artificial teaching environments* (*Vol. 1*). Hershey, PA: IGI Global.

Warren, S. J., Stein, R., Dondlinger, M. J., & Barab, S. (2009). A look inside a design process: Blending instructional design and game principles to target writing skills. *Journal of Educational Computing Research*, *40*(3), 295–301. doi:10.2190/EC.40.3.c

Webb, N., Nemer, K., & Ing, M. (2006). Small-group reflections: Parallels between teacher discourse and student behavior in peer-directed groups. *Journal of the Learning Sciences*, *15*, 63–119. doi:10.1207/s15327809jls1501_8

Winn, W. (2002). Current trends in educational technology research: The study of learning environments. *Educational Psychology Review*, *14*(3), 331–351. doi:10.1023/A:1016068530070

Yu, T. (2009). Learning in the virtual world: The pedagogical potentials of massively multiplayer online role playing games. *International Education Studies, 2.*

Section 4
Learning through Game Design

Chapter 12
Get Your Head in the Game:
Digital Game–Based Learning with Game Maker

Brian Herrig
Canon-McMillan School District, USA

EXECUTIVE SUMMARY

This chapter discusses the development and implementation of an introductory programming unit within a seventh grade technology education course. The goal of this unit was to introduce the concepts of programming to middle school students in a way that was accessible and unintimidating. Digital games provide an inherent level of engagement not present in other programming activities, and the digital game environment provides a safe platform for experimentation without concern for safety or equipment. The curriculum described in this chapter provides many practical examples of how digital games can be incorporated into a technology education classroom to engage students in the world of programming.

OVERALL DESCRIPTION

Seventh grade students at Canonsburg Middle School, a public middle school located in Canonsburg, Pennsylvania are engaged in digital game-based learning as a method of introducing them to the concepts of programming. Each student is provided with an overview of basic programming terminology and is introduced to

DOI: 10.4018/978-1-4666-2848-9.ch012

the functions of Game Maker, an icon-based, drag-and-drop video game creation software package. Students complete an introductory programming activity in which each student programs a similar game. A second activity has each student create a more advanced game of their own design. Rather than digital games being used to deliver content, in this case, the games become the content.

LITERATURE REVIEW

Digital Games in the Classroom

The use of digital games in the classroom should be considered because of the student engagement that can follow and the academic benefits that can be promoted. "Digital games are user-centered; they can promote challenges, co-operation, engagement, and the development of problem-solving strategies" (Gros, 2007, p.23). According to Dede, Ketelhut & Nelson (as cited in Sardone & Devlin-Scherer, 2010), the use of games within the classroom can encourage student participation. Student engagement when using digital games in the classroom is not only influenced by the game play. When they are used for educational purposes within the classroom, some of the engagement may come from the relevance of learning new things within the context of the digital game itself (Van Eck, 2006). Jackson (as cited in Devaney, 2008) states that, "gaming and simulations are highly interactive, allow for instant feedback, immerse students in collaborative environments, and allow for rapid decision making" (para. 2). Additionally, the use of digital games in the classroom can benefit students' tendencies towards multiple intelligences other than traditional verbal delivery of information. "Many computer applications, especially computer games, have design features that shift the balance of required information-processing, from verbal to visual" (Gros, 2007, p. 29). According to Gee (as cited in Ray & Coulter, 2010), "digital games promote critical thinking, reasoning, and problem-solving skills along with decision-making and strategizing skills" (p. 94).

Teachers' Decisions to Use Digital Games in the Classroom

Many factors may affect a teacher's decision to use a particular instructional strategy within their classroom. Factors that may affect the incorporation of digital games in the classroom include the nature of the digital games themselves and their perceived value in an educational setting. When secondary pre-service teachers were asked if increased student motivation would compel them to include digital games in their classrooms after graduation, many responded that, "motivation alone was not sufficient reason to influence them to use digital game-based instruction in their future classrooms" (Sardone & Devlin-Scherer, 2010, p. 421). When middle level pre-service teachers participated in a study to determine their perceptions on the value of digital mini-games (limited challenges, short play time) in the middle school classroom, the majority of participants agreed that there was the potential for digital games to promote learning (Ray & Coulter, 2010, p. 97). Other factors that may affect a teacher's decision to include digital games in the classroom may include funding and student safety. According to Settles (2011), "Using well-structured games is cost-effective, accessible, and safe for students and the organizations that employ the games to teach" (p. 70).

Designing and Programming Digital Games in the Classroom

One reason that the creation of digital games within the classroom should be considered is the ease with which our current students can create and modify digital content. According to Lenhart & Madden (as cited in Gershenfeld, 2011), more than half of all teens are currently involved in the creation and modification of digital content ranging from videos to music to blogs. Digital game creation and modification is a natural extension of this. The design and creation of a digital game requires students to think on a much larger scale than they would if they were simply viewing content and making minor changes. "Designing a digital game requires one to think systematically and holistically about games as systems, to experiment and test out theories, to solve problems, to think critically, and to effectively create and collaborate with peers" (Gershenfeld, 2011, p. 55). Unlike experimentation in the real world, testing out theories in the world of a digital game contains much less risk (Settles, 2011). Providing opportunities for students to design and create their own digital games may also promote a new type of literacy, "programming literacy, the ability to make digital technology do whatever, within the possible one wants it to do – to bend digital technology to one's needs, purposes and will, just as in the present we bend words and images" (Prensky, 2008, para. 4).

Practicalities of Programming and Running the Game

Digital game-based learning is a practical method for introducing students of varied ability levels to the concepts of programming in the technology education lab setting. The initial game that the students are presented with at the beginning of this unit is simple enough that there is a very shallow learning curve to be overcome prior to the students engaging with the content. As the students work on the later portions of the instructional unit, they are creating and programming a game of their own design, so the difficulty of each game varies according to each student's ideas and abilities. If a student determines that the game they are designing and programming is too complicated for their own abilities, they are free to modify their design during the process, eliminating the components of the game that are causing difficulty and replacing them with components that fit their ability level. The programming concepts of logic and sequence can be addressed through the application of a variety of different game components. Varying the difficulty of the game components being programmed does not have a major detrimental effect on the learning outcomes desired for this instructional unit.

In addition to the ease of transition into the digital game environment, the design and function of the software being utilized also allows students to become acclimated very quickly to its interface. Although most students have not used this software prior to this instructional unit, and although the menus do not match those of more common software packages, the layout of the software is very intuitive and is not intimidating for most students. Minimal instruction is needed on the software itself prior to engaging the students in the programming content directly.

TECHNOLOGY COMPONENTS

While a variety of free and low cost software packages are available that allow users to program their own digital games, this curriculum used Game Maker. One reason that this software was chosen over others is the large amount of resources available at no cost. Forums exist covering a variety of different game components and online videos and tutorials abound. The extent of these resources provides a support system for curriculum development as well as independent student enrichment outside of the classroom. A second reason that Game Maker was selected is the range of concepts that can be covered with it. Simple games can be programmed using only the drag-and-drop features and more advanced games can be programmed using the built-in code editor.

There are currently versions of Game Maker available for both Mac and PC. For this instructional unit, the PC version of the software was used. Game Maker can be run in Simple Mode or Advanced Mode. The introductory programming activity is completed with the software in Simple Mode. This allows more advanced features that are not needed to be hidden from view, helping to reduce anxiety in students who were less confident. Advanced Mode can be accessed by any student at any time while working on the individual game. All features available in Simple Mode are still available in Advanced Mode, and additional features are now accessible. A lite version of Game Maker that contains only the more basic functions is currently available for free download by individuals wishing to pursue video game programming independently. This provides an excellent enrichment opportunity for students wishing to explore content beyond the scope of the instructional unit and outside of the classroom. Currently, site license pricing is available for schools wishing to purchase Game Maker for multiple computers or labs. Stand-alone license pricing is available for anyone wishing to purchase Game Maker for a single computer.

When students are creating Sprites and Sounds to represent the visual and auditory components of their games, a variety of different image and audio file types can be used. There is a collection of sample sounds that is provided with the install of Game Maker and there are a variety of Internet resources available that provide royalty free sound effects and music that can be used when programming games. Game Maker also provides a collection of image files that can be used as Sprites and it contains a built in image editor that allows users to modify existing images or even draw their own from scratch. The use of Icon (.ico) files when creating Sprites has several benefits. There are a variety of Internet resources that provide royalty free Icon files. Icon files are typically smaller in size and are able to be more readily used as Sprites within Game Maker. Any image file can be resized using the image editor within Game Maker or any other image editing software available.

For the case being described here, a variety of sound and image files were made available to the students through the use of the school's internal computer network. The resource files were saved to an area of the network to which all users have access to view, but only teachers have access to save. This ensures that all students can access the resources at any time, but cannot accidentally delete or modify them. Most school networks should be able to restrict access to network folders to allow all users to view files but only allow teachers to modify or delete them.

Details of Using Digital Games to Learn Programming

At the beginning of the unit of instruction, the students are given an overview of basic programming terms and components of the software they will be working with. Students are provided with a definition of programming as well as an explanation of the connection between True/False and the 1/0 of binary code. The concepts of Relative and Absolute programming are presented with examples to help differentiate between them. Definitions and examples are provided for Sprites, Sounds, Backgrounds, Objects and Rooms, the five game resources in the Simple Mode of Game Maker. Students are also presented with an explanation of the Game Information and Global Game Settings areas of the Game Maker software (Herrig, 2009).

This unit involves two separate components: the basic game and the individual game. The basic game serves as an introduction for the students. It introduces them to the concepts of programming and helps them to become acclimated to the software they will work with throughout the instructional unit. The individual game helps the students to take their knowledge to the next level. The knowledge gained from the basic game serves as a foundation for the students to build and grow from.

Initially, each student is given a playable version of the basic game and is asked to reverse engineer it. Each student is provided with two pages of direct questions that ask them to observe the game they are playing and take note of what is being seen and heard throughout. This section of the instructional unit is important in helping the students to be successful in mastering the concepts of programming. In learning to be critical observers, the students begin to make connections between something happening in the game (an Event) and the way that the game reacts to it (Actions) (Herrig, 2009). These concepts are the basis for the way Game Maker games are programmed, following what is referred to as "an event driven approach" (Overmars, 1999-2009, Game Maker Help, Events section, para. 1). The connection between Events and Actions in Game Maker will greatly help the students during the programming stage and will make any troubleshooting that becomes necessary much easier to complete.

Following the reverse engineering, each student works to recreate the basic game by following a set of teacher-created technical directions. These directions contain a combination of text and images taken directly from the Game Maker software. The students begin by creating the Sprite and Sound resources they will need to use for the game. Each is given a name by the student and a file is selected to represent it within the game. In the case of Sprites, this will be an image file that provides a visual representation of the Object. For Sounds, this will be an audio file that can be cued to play within the game. Next, the game Objects must be programmed. Each game Object is given a name by the student and is assigned a Sprite to visually represent it within the game. Objects within Game Maker are programmed by assigning them Events and Actions. An Event is something that occurs in the game, like two Objects colliding or a given Object being clicked on. Actions are the way that game Objects respond or react to an Event. Actions within Game Maker can serve a variety of functions, including causing a sound to play, increasing or decreasing the score or affecting change on the movement or speed of a game Object (See Figure 1).

Throughout the directions, the level of detail provided for each step is progressively reduced. The first time that a new process is presented, all necessary details are listed. If the procedures for a later step are similar to a previous one, reference is simply made to complete the step. This method is designed to help the students increase their technical knowledge and to immediately begin drawing from their newly created knowledge base. If a student is not ready to complete later steps without all necessary details being provided, they can review the earlier sections of their directions where all steps are listed (Herrig, 2009).

The next step of the introductory portion of the activity provides the students with a sheet of enhancements that must be added to the basic game. The students have not seen these enhancements in action and this sheet only provides a text description

Figure 1. Object properties

of what needs to be done, with no Game Maker images provided. The enhancements contain Events and Actions that the students have not used previously, further requiring them to explore the software and learn its capabilities and limitations.

Following the introductory portion of the unit, the students draft a Proposal for a game they would like to create of their own design, their individual game. The Proposal provides the name of the game and the game description, as well as the Objects, Sounds, controls and levels (Rooms) that will be present in the game. The individual game that the students will create must have a purpose, at least two sounds (one music, one sound effect), at least two rooms and at least one object that is controllable with either a keyboard or USB game controller. The requirements for the individual game build upon the foundation that the students developed during the introductory portion of the unit. The process of creating a proposal helps the students to organize their thoughts about what each area of their game will involve. Each student presents their Proposal to their peers. This allows each student to receive validation for their ideas and to benefit from the ideas of other students. There is no penalty if a student decides to modify their individual game during the programming process. The Proposal serves as an initial rough draft of ideas and the process provides the opportunity for progression throughout.

As a resource while programming their individual game, the students have access to a teacher-created instruction manual that explains how individual game components work and how they can be programmed. This manual contains a combination of text and images taken directly from the Game Maker software. A class set of binders containing a print version of this manual is available to the students throughout the lab time for this portion of the unit. This manual does not explain how to program a game from start to finish. The students must determine which components are needed for their game and how to combine them together. This part of the instructional unit helps the students to begin thinking independently about the logic and sequence of programming. Students begin to evaluate what they would like their game to do and then attempt to determine how they can program it to function that way. Throughout this instructional unit, peer assistance is encouraged.

In addition to the benefits associated with using digital games in the classroom, such as student engagement and visual stimulation, having students program their own games brings additional advantages. Programming a digital game helps students to understand cause and effect. Problem solving and critical thinking skills are strengthened by their application in an authentic environment. A real-world work atmosphere is created as the students are encouraged to use classroom reference materials and peer assistance before addressing problems with the instructor. The virtual world of a video game is an excellent place for students to apply concepts such as the Cartesian coordinate system and variables. Having students program their own digital games is an authentic way to apply the concepts of Science, Technology, Engineering and Math (STEM) in way that is meaningful for students.

Differentiation of Instruction

The content covered by this instructional unit inherently lends itself to differentiation. Students who hold an Individualized Education Plan (IEP) that requires reduced assignments can be assessed on the basic game with or without enhancements using the same criteria. The modest requirements for the individual game can be met by most students with minimal difficulty. Students who require reduced assignments can meet the requirements with an extremely simple game. Advanced students can meet the requirements for the individual game and have the opportunity to continue exploring possibilities beyond them. Both simple and advanced individual games, as well as those that fall in between can be evaluated using the same criteria.

Evaluation

The introductory portion of this unit is evaluated by watching the students play their version of the basic game with enhancements and comparing the accuracy of the Sprites, Sounds, Backgrounds, Objects, Rooms, Events and Actions to the directions provided to the students. Students are not evaluated on their ability to succeed while playing the game. If a student is having difficulty in game play during the evaluation, the remaining sections can be completed by having the students exit the game and show the Object Properties windows for their game Objects. The visual nature of the Game Maker interface makes such an evaluation an easy task (See Figure 2).

Figure 2. Game evaluation

Name			Period	
Computer #	**Big Mac Attack Rubric**			
	Criteria			
	2	**3**	**4**	**5**
Sprites	3 or more errors.	2 errors.	1 error.	No errors.
Sounds	3 or more errors.	2 errors.	1 error.	No errors.
Backgrounds	3 or more errors.	2 errors.	1 error.	No errors.
Objects	3 or more errors.	2 errors.	1 error.	No errors.
Rooms	3 or more errors.	2 errors.	1 error.	No errors.
Events	3 or more errors.	2 errors.	1 error.	No errors
Actions	3 or more errors.	2 errors.	1 error.	No errors.
			Total	/35

The individual game portion of this instructional unit is evaluated in three separate but related areas (See Figure 3). Near the beginning of the unit, the first component of the evaluation, the individual game Proposal is conducted. For this evaluation, each student presents their individual game proposal to their peers. During the presentation, the students are simply explaining each of the required areas of the game they plan to design. Each student has a printed copy of their proposal with them during the presentation and no points are deducted if a student chooses to read the information directly from their printed copy.

At the end of this instructional unit, the second and third components of the evaluation are completed as each student presents their completed game to their peers. The student who is presenting selects a peer who will play their game during the presentation. The entire class is able to see the game being played with the use of an LCD projector. Prior to the game play beginning, the student who is present-ing tells the class the name of their game and describes it, detailing how the main character is controlled. The student is also asked to identify any differences in the final game from what was described in the initial Proposal. Points are not deducted for making changes after the Proposal is written and presented, but the student should be able to identify the reasons why the changes occurred. These four ele-ments make up the Final Presentation section of the evaluation.

The third component of the evaluation is the Final Game. For this component, the criteria are based on those used during the evaluation of the basic game in the introductory portion of the activity that all of the students completed previously. The Final Game is evaluated on its Sprites, Sounds, Objects, Controls, Rooms, Purpose and Overall Quality. These areas are evaluated during the Final Presentation, as the game is played by the selected student.

Figure 3. Areas of evaluation

<table>
<tr><td colspan="5">Proposal</td></tr>
<tr><td></td><td>0</td><td>1</td><td>2</td><td>3</td></tr>
<tr><td>Name of the Game</td><td>No Name of Game given.</td><td>Minimal detail given.</td><td>Moderate detail given.</td><td>Full detail given.</td></tr>
<tr><td>Game Description</td><td>No Game Description given.</td><td>Minimal detail given.</td><td>Moderate detail given.</td><td>Full detail given.</td></tr>
<tr><td>Game Objects</td><td>No description of Game Objects given.</td><td>Minimal detail given.</td><td>Moderate detail given.</td><td>Full detail given.</td></tr>
<tr><td>Sounds</td><td>No description of Sounds given.</td><td>Minimal detail given.</td><td>Moderate detail given.</td><td>Full detail given.</td></tr>
<tr><td>Controls</td><td>No description of Controls given.</td><td>Minimal detail given.</td><td>Moderate detail given.</td><td>Full detail given.</td></tr>
<tr><td>Levels</td><td>No description of Levels given.</td><td>Minimal detail given.</td><td>Moderate detail given.</td><td>Full detail given.</td></tr>
<tr><td>Presentation</td><td>No presentation given.</td><td>Minimal detail given.</td><td>Moderate detail given.</td><td>Full detail given.</td></tr>
<tr><td colspan="4">Proposal Total</td><td>/21</td></tr>
</table>

Computer #   Name _____   Period _____

<table>
<tr><td colspan="4">Game</td></tr>
<tr><td></td><td>1</td><td>3</td><td>5</td></tr>
<tr><td>Sprites</td><td>Sprites NOT appropriate to represent game objects.</td><td>Reasonably appropriate sprites to represent game objects.</td><td>Completely appropriate sprites to represent game objects.</td></tr>
<tr><td>Sounds</td><td>Game has NO sounds.</td><td>Game has only 1 sound.</td><td>Game has at least 2 sounds. (1 music, 1 sound effect)</td></tr>
<tr><td>Objects</td><td>Game objects are NOT appropriate for game.</td><td>Game has reasonably appropriate game objects.</td><td>Game has completely appropriate objects.</td></tr>
<tr><td>Controls
(Keyboard or controller)</td><td>Game does NOT have an object that is controlled.</td><td>Game has at least 1 object that is not controlled correctly.</td><td>Game has at least 1 object that is correctly controlled.</td></tr>
<tr><td>Rooms</td><td>Game has NO rooms.</td><td>Game has only 1 room.</td><td>Game has at least 2 rooms.</td></tr>
<tr><td>Purpose</td><td>Game has NO purpose.</td><td>Game has a reasonably appropriate purpose.</td><td>Game has a completely appropriate purpose.</td></tr>
<tr><td>Overall Quality</td><td>Overall game quality is poor.</td><td>Overall game quality is fair.</td><td>Overall game quality is excellent.</td></tr>
<tr><td colspan="3">Game Total</td><td>/35</td></tr>
</table>

<table>
<tr><td colspan="4">Final Presentation</td></tr>
<tr><td></td><td>1</td><td>3</td><td>5</td></tr>
<tr><td>Game Description</td><td>Minimal detail given.</td><td>Moderate detail given.</td><td>Full detail given.</td></tr>
<tr><td>Goal or Purpose</td><td>Minimal detail given.</td><td>Moderate detail given.</td><td>Full detail given.</td></tr>
<tr><td>Controls</td><td>Minimal detail given.</td><td>Moderate detail given.</td><td>Full detail given.</td></tr>
<tr><td>Differences from proposal</td><td>Minimal detail given.</td><td>Moderate detail given.</td><td>Full detail given.</td></tr>
<tr><td colspan="3">Final Presentation Total</td><td>/20</td></tr>
</table>

CHALLENGES

A significant challenge in implementing this instructional unit is its progressive nature: the more information that is provided to the students, the more information the students request. As students work to create and program their individual games, they often ask questions related to more advanced game components that are not in the teacher-created manual. Students are often excited to go beyond what is expected of them to produce a more advanced product. In order to provide all students with the tools they need to succeed and reach their maximum potential, the teacher-created instruction manual for the individual game components is a perpetual work-in-progress. As students ask questions relating to content not present in the manual, a list of future additions is developed. As new components of the manual are completed, updated versions are printed and made available to the students. Instructional materials for a unit containing digital game-based instruction must be progressive.

SUMMARY

As seventh grade students at Canonsburg Middle School are presented with content that may be familiar to few of them, the concepts of programming, they are given the opportunity to work with something that is routine for many of them, digital gaming. Students are given the opportunity to see playable games, recreate them and then add enhancements. The ideas of each individual student are cultivated as they create a proposal for a game of their own and the students are given the opportunity and resources needed to see their idea come to life on the screen.

ACKNOWLEDGMENT

The author would like to thank Amy Barbarino, René Kruse and Greg Taranto for their assistance in preparing this chapter.

REFERENCES

Devaney, L. (2008, April 22). *Gaming helps students hone 21st-century skills.* Retrieved November 28, 2011, from http://www.eschoolnews.com/2008/04/22/gaming-helps-students-hone-21st-century-skills/

Gershenfeld, A. (2011, September/October). Leveling up from player to designer. *Knowledge Quest, 40*(1), 55–59.

Gros, B. (2007, Fall). Digital games in education: The design of games-based learning environments. *Journal of Research on Technology in Education, 40*(1), 23-38. ERIC database (EJ826060).

Herrig, B. (2009, Winter). Thinking like a programmer. *TEAP Journal*, *57*(4), 9–17.

Overmars, M. (1999-2009). *GameMaker* (Version 8.0 Pro) [Computer software and manual]. YoYoGames Ltd.

Prensky, M. (2008, January 13). *Programming is the new literacy*. Retrieved April 9, 2012, from http://www.edutopia.org/programming-the-new-literacy

Ray, B., & Coulter, G. A. (2010, Spring). Perceptions of the value of digital mini-games: Implications for middle school classrooms. *Journal of Digital Learning in Teacher Education, 26*(3), 92-100. ERIC database (EJ881731).

Sardone, N. B., & Devlin-Scherer, R. (2010). Teacher candidate responses to digital games: 21st-century skills development. *Journal of Research on Technology in Education, 42*(4), 409-425. ERIC database (EJ895055).

Settles, D. (2011, September/October). Gaming and core content: Conjoined twins. *Knowledge Quest, 40*(1), 70–72.

Van Eck, R. (2006, March/April). Digital game-based learning: It's not just the digital natives who are restless. *Educational Review, 41*(2), 16–30.

KEY TERMS AND DEFINITIONS

Action: The behavior of an Object as a reaction to an Event within a Game Maker game.

Background: A large image seen behind the Objects in a Room.

Event: Something that happens to an Object within a Game Maker game.

Object: An entity within a game that can be programmed to do something.

Room: A level where the game takes place (contains Objects, and often Backgrounds).

Sound: An audio representation of music or a sound effect within a game.

Sprite: A visual representation of an Object within a game.

Chapter 13
Elements of Game Design:
Developing a Meaningful Game Design Curriculum for the Classroom

Danielle Herro
Clemson University, USA

EXECUTIVE SUMMARY

This case examines the development of a game design curriculum offered to high school students as an in-school elective course in the Oconomowoc Area School District (OASD), a Wisconsin suburban school district of 5,200 students. Elements of Game Design (EOGD) was created by an Instructional Technology Administrator (ITA), Technical Education (TE) teacher, and Visual Arts (VA) teacher in 2010, and implemented 9 times during the 2011-12 school year. The rationale for proposing the course was based on the overlap of research, trends, and experience studying game-design and game-based learning environments. To that end, it is important to note the ITA was simultaneously completing an educational technology doctoral degree focused on digital media and learning and engaged in research involving Massively Multiplayer Online Games (MMOG) and Augmented Reality Games (ARG).

DOI: 10.4018/978-1-4666-2848-9.ch013

REVIEW OF THE LITERATURE INFLUENCING COURSE PROPOSAL AND DESIGN

The last decade has seen social and behavioral science theorizing game-based environments motivate, engage, and incorporate good learning principles (Gee, 2003; 2004; 2005; Shaffer, Squire, Halverson & Gee, 2005; Squire & Jenkins, 2004; Squire & Steinkuehler 2005; Squire 2008). Digital media and learning research clearly supports game design curricula as a viable method of teaching complex and collaborative problem solving, strategizing, and emulation of real-world processes and system thinking (Gee, 2003; 2007; Shaffer, Squire, Halverson, & Gee, 2005; Squire, 2008). Significant bodies of research suggest games have the potential to increase learning, yet many of these studies have been based on out-of-school or after-school programs (Squire & Durga, 2008; Steinkuehler & King, 2009; Ito, Horst et al., 2009). The few existing authentic in-school opportunities are typically relegated to charter school programs as curriculum requirements, attitudes, logistics, support for teachers and social and cultural structures present barriers in adopting gaming in-school (Klopfer, Osterweil, & Salen, 2009, p. 18). Built on principles of collaborative play, inquiry-based learning, systems thinking and creative problem solving, schools such as Quest to Learn and ChicagoQuest apply successful game-based learning principles to understandable frameworks for learning (Salen, Torres, Wolozin, Rufo-Tepper, Shapiro, 2011).

Moreover, recent guidelines and standards for literacy suggests games and game design are a powerful way to adopt New Media Literacies (Jenkins et al., 2006), meet the International Society for Technology in Education (ISTE) National Educational Technology Standards (NETS) for students (ISTE, 2007), and address technology trends expected to impact teaching and learning (Johnson, Smith, Levine, & Haywood, 2010). According to the annual Horizon Reports:

K-12 students are interested in experiencing and modifying game-like spaces accessed on the web (Johnson, Levine, Smith & Smythe, p. 6, 2009).

Based on the success in industry, the military, online play, and emerging research on the cognitive benefits of game play, *interest in game-based learning has accelerated considerably in recent years* (Johnson et al., p. 8, 2010). The report further avers, *"Developers and researchers are working in every area of game-based learning, including games that are goal-oriented; social game environments; non-digital games that are easy to construct and play; games developed expressly for education; and commercial games that lend themselves to refining team and group skills"* (p. 17).

The National Education Technology Plan 2010 (NETP), specifically points to games as a conduit to "provide immediate performance feedback so that players always know how they are doing" maintaining "they are highly engaging to students and have the potential to motivate students to learn," and "They also enable educators to assess important competencies and aspects of thinking in contexts and through activities that students care about in everyday life" (U.S. Department of Education, p. 37). Games and simulations promote a broader, multimodal definition of literacy (Gee, 2003), one necessary to compete in the modern world.

Finally, effective game play and design in the context of a meaningful project offer a means towards future employability as they advance skills such as: communication, teamwork, collaboration, problem-solving, organization and analysis (Klopfer, Osteweil & Salen, 2009) as well as encouraging reflective and creative practices (Hill, Morton, Lawton, & Hemingway 2007).

A SCHOOL DISTRICT CULTURE SUPPORTING INNOVATION

Building a culture of understanding and participation with digital media and learning was instrumental in establishing support for this innovative gaming curriculum. Within the Oconomowoc Area School District case described in this paper, the Horizon Reports, ISTE standards and Jenkins et al., "new media literacies" directed technology planning; the year before Elements of Game Design was formally proposed, ongoing discussions surrounding game-based learning occurred during on-site graduate courses, administrative, and instructional technology meetings. The district administrative team read *Disrupting Class: How Disruptive Innovation Will Change the Way the World Learns* (Christensen, Horn & Johnson, 2008), excerpts of *Rethinking Education in the Age of Technology* (Collins & Halverson, 2009), and The Horizon Report (Johnson et al., 2010), was embedded in a graduate course with K-12 teaching and administrative participants. Moreover, *Confronting the Challenges of Participatory Culture: Media Education for the 21st Century* (Jenkins et al., 2006) was staple reading in many professional development offerings. An increasing group of teachers, site and district-level administrators realized the potential of games to provide interactivity, immediate feedback, multimodal, and engaged learning environments.

The Beginnings

In the winter of 2009, a team of four Oconomowoc educators and two technical support staff met with graduate students involved with Games+Learning+Society (GLS) at the University of Wisconsin, Madison. The meeting was arranged by the district's ITA, preceded by numerous in-district conversations and research-based presentations detailing the potential of games in education. Purposefully, the stage was set to consider possibilities for in-school game design curricula. The GLS meeting offered credibility, curriculum-writing direction, and concrete examples of games previously made by students during a week-long summer camp at UW-Madison. Driving fifty miles home, the team's discussion centered on brainstorming the curriculum, and considering ways to engage students with physical, board, and digital game-play and design. The technicians were both gamers and proposed ways to engage students, two of the teachers suggested surveying students to gauge interest before creating a new elective, and the ITA contemplated the type of instructor, curriculum-writing team, and process necessary to get a gaming course off the ground. The insight from GLS and feedback from the OASD team was instrumental in moving *Elements of Game Design* forward.

PRACTICALITIES OF WRITING AND IMPLEMENTING THE CURRICULUM

Approval of a game design curriculum in a public high school, especially during an economic downtown with increasingly limited resources, entails building a culture of participation (Jenkins et al., 2006) with digital media and learning to support necessary structures, policies, and allocation of resources. In all likelihood the proposal for *Elements of Game Design* would have fallen short without philosophical agreement and intellectual understanding of games capacity to impact learning. To that end, numerous research-based articles regarding the impact of social media, games, and emerging technologies on learning (Gee, 2003; 2007; Squire, 2006; 2008; Jenkins et al., 2006) were presented to the Director of Curriculum and Instruction, Superintendent, teaching staff, and technical support. The District was heavily steeped in integrating Web 2.0 technologies into existing curriculum, and an entity called "Tech Cabinet" was established to bring together administration, technical support and instruction to vet and implement technology-embedded initiatives. For game-play and game-design to thrive in the context of traditional schooling, these supportive structures and culture are essential.

Purpose and Objectives of the Course

While the course is not explicitly intended to prepare students for careers in game design, significant college and career readiness skills are addressed throughout the curriculum. Beyond exposing students to new media litercies and 21st Century skills, the course assists in building critical thinking, logic, computational thinking, and technical skills. The course meets or exceeds many state level Model Academic Standards for Technical Education, Informational and Technology Literacy, and Language Arts. In fact, it is housed in the Technology Education Department within the high school. Interdisciplinary standards are met as the course utilizes a cycle of design and development, and relies on open-ended, problem-based individual and collaborative work. Perhaps the most important aspect of this curriculum is the propensity to build high-level cognitive skills as stated by Klopfer, Osterweil and Salen who argue:

Video games provide a practice space where players hone high-level cognitive skills like literacy, storytelling, collaboration, analysis, and leadership. These skills, while not always rewarded in standardized curricula, comprise a toolkit of 21st century competency that will serve students well whatever path they take and that employers increasingly emphasize in recruiting. Not surprisingly, these same skills provide the bedrock for effective civic participation in any democracy (2008, p. 47).

The process bringing the curriculum forward after the initial visit with GLS is summarized in these steps: (1) a general syllabus was created by the ITA and high school students were surveyed to gauge interest in the course, (2) the Districts' Curriculum Coordinating Council reviewed research, the course proposal and the syllabus before approval, (3) the ITA, TE and VA teachers met multiple times over 6 months to write and revise the curriculum, (4) equipment, materials, and logistical considerations were addressed the summer before the course was offered, and (5) and students were surveyed during the fall implementation to offer improvements. The next section of this case details four of the five steps; student revisions are addressed in a later section.

Surveying Students with a Mock Syllabus

During spring registration, 2010, students entering grades 9-12 were presented a simple mock syllabus surveyed to assess their interest in electing to take a half-credit course, entitled "Elements of Game Design". If affirmed by students, administration, and OASD's Curriculum Coordinating Council during the fall of 2010, the course would be written in early 2011 and offered to students the following academic year. The course and abbreviated mock syllabus is shown in Exhibit 1.

Ultimately 481, or roughly 1/3 of the high school students, took the survey with the results shown in Table 1. The question asked was:

Elements of Game Design

Exhibit 1. Course and abbreviated mock syllabus

Oconomowoc High School
Elective Course: Elements of Game Design
Instructor: TBA

Course Description: Elements of game design will introduce students to basic concepts of gaming including their history, elements, purpose, and usefulness.

Students in this course will: (1) study games and their usefulness to business, military, science and education, (2) play games (physical, board, and video) in order to understand the elements of what makes them successful (or unsuccessful), (3) purposefully design a simple board game or computer game using Scratch or Alice, (4) modify their game after others have played it, and (5) read about, write about, and discuss items 1-4 above.

Week 1-3 What are games?
Week 1: History of games.
Week 2: Why study them? Who uses games?
Week 3: The Video Game Industry
Week 4 Game Play
Playing Games
- Physical games
- Board games
- Video/online games

Week 5-6 Unpacking the games: Mechanics, Dynamics, Aesthetics
Difference between games and other entertainment – consumption is unpredictable. Content of the game is actually its behavior, not the media itself.
Mechanics – **components** of the game and data representation
Dynamics – **behavior** of players based on their inputs and outputs
Aesthetics – desirable **emotional responses** in the player after interacting with the game
Week 7-8 Build a game: Design a simple game in Alice
What is fun? Vocabulary of gameplay:
1) Sensation, fantasy, narrative, challenge, fellowship, discovery expression, submission
2) The role of a game designer vs. game player.
Week 9: Playing games again
Charades – fellowship, expression, challenge
The Sims – Discovery, Fantasy, Expression Narrative
Rockband or Guitar Hero
Kongregate
Week 10-15 (5 weeks, 45 min per day) Collaboratively designing a game
Purposefully designing a game: who is your audience?
Choice of: board game, or computer game using Scratch or Alice
Groupwork
Elements of Gaming:
Storyboard, scripting, narrative
Week 16-17-18 Game play of student-made games, Modding
4 day cycle: a day of play, a day of feedback
Play testing and tuning
Improving the game
First and Second Pass

Table 1. Student responses indicating interest in enrolling in a gaming course

	Female	Male	Response totals
Would enroll in gaming course	10.4%	55.2%	36.4% (175)
Would NOT enroll in gaming course	54.5%	19.0%	33.8% (163)
Might enroll in course	35.1%	25.8%	29.7% (143)

Would you enroll in a gaming course (described/given tentative syllabus) if offered by Oconomowoc High School?

Administration believed there was enough interest to move forward and propose the course. The mock syllabus served as a starting point for curriculum writing, though the final syllabus and curriculum presented to students contained only rudimentary elements of its predecessor.

Presenting Elements of Game Design for Course Approval

In OASD, Curriculum Coordinating Council (CCC) exists to direct the District in necessary curriculum revisions, additions, or deletions. Advisory in nature, it consists of multidisciplinary teachers and administrators. After completing the standard 8-page course proposal outlining the description, rationale, relationship to district initiatives, guidelines of practice, intended evaluation, infusion of standards and fiscal implications, the ITA reviewed the proposal with the council where it was unanimously approved.

Writing the Curriculum

Over 6 months, the Instructional Technology Administrator (ITA), a Technical Education (TE) and Visual Art (VA) teacher met formally on four occasions to write the curricula. Since the course was introductory, the team agreed an examination of gaming history, elements, and process was foundational to building the course. Existing "canned" game design courses were quickly eliminated as they felt too prescribed; they appeared stifling when considering creativity and innovation. Instead, fundamental works, articles, and books including *MDA: A Formal Approach to Game Design and Game Research* (Hunicke, LeBlanc, & Zubek, 2004), *What video games have to teach us about learning and literacy* (Gee, 2003) and *Game Design for Teens* (Pardew, Nunamaker, & Pugh, 2004) guided the course outline. At the outset, three general gaming projects were determined: creation of board game, digital game, and mobile game. The syllabus was fleshed out into a framework of potential units and projects for students encompassing criteria, rubrics, assignments and assessment documents. Between meetings the team parceled out tasks and worked on portions of the curricula. The final syllabus and curricula bore a resemblance to the mock syllabus but was much richer with projects, media, assessments and creative tasks. A list of resources to access or purchase was compiled including board game-making supplies, game-controllers, headsets, and technical requirements for download, installation and unblocking.

Ordering Equipment and Testing Technical Requirements

Many materials and resources for the course exist in open source or at minimal cost on the web. No formal text was purchased, instead free or low-cost websites, videos and game-based platforms such as *The Game Crafter, Kodu, Scratch, ARIS* and *Daqri* provided much of project-based, collaborative work. Peripherals and board-game making supplies cost less than $1,000. The largest cost was procuring mobile devices for *ARIS* and *Daqri* - for this, the ITA wrote a matching grant, funded by a local computer company and the school district, for 6 Samsung Galaxy Tablets and 12 iPod Touches. *Scratch* and *Kodu* were uncomplicated downloads performed by OASD's technical support staff. *The Game Crafter* and *Daqri* had to be unblocked for students to access, as did a number of gaming websites, Frontline's Digital Nation, and TED.com. Opening the web-filter to access and download Daqri and ARIS to mobile devices proved difficult for two reasons (1) traditional educational web-filtering security systems are designed to prevent entertainment and gaming use, and (2) developers often chose non-standard ports. In the end, even after contacting developers, some applications had to be downloaded outside of school.

CURRICULUM DETAILS: TEACHING, LEARNING, ASSESSMENT, AND EVALUATION

Elements of Game Design is taught in both a block (90 minutes for 9 weeks) and skinny (45 minutes for 18 weeks) format each term. The course intentionally allows students to critically examine the history, usefulness, elements, and process of game design. Three iterations of game design are embedded in the course; students collaboratively create a board, digital, and mobile game and repeatedly explore the mechanics, dynamics, and aesthetics of game design. Awareness of gaming culture and authentic expertise is integrated in the course as students research the value or insignificance of gaming and create a TED Talk filmed on iPod Touches. Game designers Skype with students to talk about game play, game design, and the gaming industry. Students pose questions ahead of time for the guest gamer to discuss and follow-up with additional questions after the talk. Within the curriculum are opportunities to review *Games for Change, Globaloria, Games for Heath*, and *Play Value* videos. In addition, participants read short articles, watch videos and examine websites of gaming experts such Jane McGonigal, Jim Gee, and Katie Salen as they consider the value of games in society. Assignments are geared to creative tasks, concept practice, reflection, and game design and iteration. Formative assessments are designed to provide analysis and critical feedback and allow for ongoing self-improvement. Summative assessments include (1) instructor and *peer* reviewed student-produced games or media and (2) project work demonstrating conceptual understanding of the history, elements, and process of game design. Plans are underway to extend the culture and learning within *Elements of Game Design* by creating a "Game Jam Club" open to all high school students with opportunities to design Apps, create mobile games, and further draw on interest-based game design.

Technology Components

The course is presented in a Learning Management System (LMS) to retrieve, guide, and discuss assignments and assessments. Technology is seamlessly embedded in course work and necessary for assignment and project completion. Students utilize (1) an online site to design a board game complete with QR codes, (2) MicroSoft Research's Kodu to play and dissect an immersive gaming environment, (3) Augmented Reality for Interactive Storytelling (ARIS) to build a game on a mobile device, and (4) video and Google Docs to create, reflect, and share assignments. Visual and multimodal representations of content or knowledge construction are encouraged. The instructor uses YouTube, Prezis, and constructed examples to scaffold learning, and students are continually offered opportunities for responses in various modalities.

Currently the course is taught locally as a face-to-face, web-enhanced class in Blackboard. Future plans include offering *Elements of Game Design* in blended or fully online environment to students outside the school district. Expansion for a second level course offering will be considered after studying participant feedback, artifacts, and achievement.

Surveying Students and Revising Curriculum

At present, four sections of Elements of Game Design have been successfully taught, with another five to be completed by the academic year's end. The instructor, Patrick, is a Technical Education teacher by training and identifies himself as a gamer. While there is no specific empirical data to support this claim, it appears this identity is critical to the early success of the course. He speaks the same "gamer" language as his students, and knows the value of learning through game play and game design.

Midway through the first 18 week EOGD course, thirty-five (n=35) participants, 26 boys and 9 girls, elected to answer 6 questions shared via a Google Form. The responses provide insight into student interests and goals and critical feedback aiding in course revision slated for the end of the academic year. Respondents ages were as follows: one was 18, seven were 17, five were 16, thirteen were 15, and nine reported being 14. Seven students choose not to participate in the questionnaire.

All (35) students completing the survey answered each the following questions:

1. In two or three sentences, tell me how you'd describe yourself and tell me what you are most interested in (hobbies, interests, and/or future goals).
2. How would you describe the class to someone who hasn't taken it yet?
3. What do you like about the class?
4. What, if anything, do you think you've learned?
5. What tools do you think have helped you learn the content in this class?
6. What don't you like about the class, what would you change, or what could be improved?

For the purpose of better understanding the type of student and their perceptions of value towards an in-school gaming course, answers to questions 1, 4 and 6 are discussed in greater detail.

General Interests of Students in the Course

Analysis of the responses resulted in a general profile of the type of student interested in taking the course. Students' self-described main interests included playing video games (17 responses), physical activities (21 responses) such as snowboarding, sailing, Parkour, dancing, dirt biking, baseball, football, track, cross-country, hunting, horse-back riding, and creative activities (13 responses) consisting of drawing, reading, writing, dancing, painting, playing music, photography, or building things. A few students described themselves as smart, curious, or outgoing, and one student described herself as "straight A".

Of seventeen who described themselves as "gamers", eight professed to be heavily into sports and six detailed their creative outlets. Only one gamer described his interests as "slacking off, hanging out with friends and eating a lot." Many expressed future plans to attend a 4 year college or described career goals including: police officer, game artist and designer, criminal justice major, dietary nutritionist, F.B.I agent, technologist, author, storeowner of tabletop games, businessman, or "something with computers".

Student Perceptions of Learning within the Course

Some students wrote brief, one-sentence answers, and others responded with multiple ideas about their learning within the class. Student assessment of learning can be grouped in 8 categories depicted in Table 2. Representative responses illustrate the replies.

Student Responses to "What, if anything, do you think you've learned?"

Table 2. Student perceptions of learning fostered in Elements of Game Design

Category	Number	Examples
Game Process and Design	10	"I've learned a ton about how to design a game, including a board game, html, and video game.", "I've learned about the process of making a game.", "How to build your own games with your own rules and thoughts."
Technical Skills	9	"how to code in HTML", "new picture editing software", "how to make a site on Google Apps"
Complexity of Games	9	"I've learned how hard it is to create a trivia board game somewhat similar to the board game Scene It.", "I've learned it takes time and planning it takes to create a game."
Teamwork	6	"You have to work together with your team if you want a game to be successful." "I've actually learned to feel comfortable working in groups."
History of Games	5	"Some history on gaming and where they came from.", "I've learned about all sorts of games and their history."
Time Management	2	"I think I've definitely learned better time management as well as how to program a game."
Educational Value	2	"Video games are not only fun because of the entertainment part, but they can also be educational."
Nothing	1	"I don't think I've learned anything besides the fact that how hard the gaming bissness is."

Student Suggestions for Course Improvements

Students responded the course could be improved by allowing them to choose their own partners for group projects (9 responses) and playing more video games each week (5 responses). Three students stated the technical level of some work was too difficult, two students felt the HTML game was boring or had little value, two students suggested purchasing better graphic cards, and two students said they wouldn't change a thing about the course. One student suggested we form an after-school gaming club to offer more opportunities.

Initial Course Revisions

Formal evaluation of this new curriculum will take place after the first full year of implementation. However the instructor is already responding to student, technical, and methodological concerns through minor revisions. Self-selecting partners or collaborative groups, eliminating an HTML game that students deemed trivial and planning for more intensive mobile game development are underway. Admittedly, exergaming and intense physical game-play is absent within this course; student and instructor evaluations may eventually dictate its inclusion in this, or a future course. To that end, a second, advanced course focused on more sophisticated game play, design, and programming is being considered for the 2013-14 school year.

CHALLENGES

Garnering support for in-school, for-credit gaming curricula is challenging in today's educational climate. Educational games are fraught with barriers and challenges making them a risky enterprise (Klopfer, Osterweil, Salen, 2009). The pace of innovation requires on-going training for instructors if they are to effectively keep up with improvements and advancements in game design tools and platforms. Educator understanding of the potential for game design and game play affecting learning must be included in high-quality professional development programs. These programs are often non-existent or lack skilled instructors. Administrative, teacher, and community support for innovative curricula is fostered over time, and schools with high staff turnover rates struggle to maintain pedagogical consistency. Infrastructure issues supporting wireless and mobile devices pose a challenge, as does time and expertise to test and unblock necessary sites. Welcoming participant and expert critique, while finding time for revision and refinement, involves conscious effort and planning. The many challenges schools face often impede progress and stifle innovation, underscoring reasons why schools are notoriously slow in their ability to adopt expansive transformation (Collins & Halverson, 2009). Admittedly, *Elements of Game Design* is proving successful because of the absence of, or response to, many above-mentioned challenges.

SUMMARY

After two years of researching, proposing, surveying students, curriculum writing and refinement, *Elements of Game Design* is in its first year of implementation. By carefully considering all of the stakeholders, including community members and students, and remaining open to critique and refinement, the district believes this offering will help students succeed. Offering an in-school, rigorous, engaging game design curriculum holds promise for educators wishing to realize the potential of digital media and learning, and for students preparing for a future rich in 21st Century Skills (Partnership for 21st Century Skills, 2004). Games and game design present an engaging, exciting, and clear path towards challenging students and embedding New Media Literacies (Jenkins et al., 2006), meeting the International Society for Technology in Education (ISTE) National Educational Technology Standards (NETS) for students (ISTE, 2007), and addressing technology trends expected to impact K-12 teaching and learning (Johnson, Smith, Levine, & Haywood, 2010). In this instance, students were presented, through game play and design, a viable method to solve complex and collaborative problems, strategy, and emulation of real-world processes and system thinking (Gee, 2003; Squire, 2011). Detailing the efforts of this public school district to build a sustainable framework supporting games and learning environments offers administrators and practitioners a roadmap to consider their own transformation.

REFERENCES

Christensen, C., Johnson, C. W., & Horn, M. B. (2008). *Disrupting class: How disruptive innovation will change the way the world learns.* New York, NY: McGraw-Hill.

Collins, A., & Halverson, R. (2009). *Rethinking education in the age of technology.* New York, NY: Teachers College Press. doi:10.1007/978-3-540-69132-7_1

Gee, J. P. (2003). *What video games have to teach us about learning and literacy.* New York, NY: Palgrave Macmillan. doi:10.1145/950566.950595

Gee, J. P. (2004). *Situated language and learning: A critique of traditional schooling.* London, UK: Routledge.

Gee, J. P. (2005). Learning by design: Good video games as learning machines. *E-learning, 2*(1), 5–16. doi:10.2304/elea.2005.2.1.5

Gee, J. P. (2007). *Good video games + Good learning: Collected essays on video games learning and literacy.* New York, NY: Peter Lang.

Hill A., Morton N., Lawton R., & Hemingway A. (2007, January). *Enhancing employability through games and simulations.* Creativity or Conformity? Building Cultures of Creativity in Higher Education Conference, University of Wales Institute, Cardiff.

Hunicke, R., LeBlanc, M., & Zubek, R. (2004). *MDA: A formal approach to game design and game research.* Retrieved from http://www.cs.northwestern.edu/~hunicke/MDA.pdf.

International Society for Technology in Education (ISTE). (2007). *Standards for students.* Retrieved August 10, 2010, from http://www.iste.org/Content/NavigationMenu/NETS/ForStudents/2007Standards/NETS_for_Students_2007_Standards.pdf

Ito, M., Baumer, S., Bittanti, M., Boyd, D., Cody, R., & Herr-Stephenson, B. … Tripp, L. (2009). *Hanging out, messing around, and geeking out: Kids living and learning with new media* (John D. and Catherine T. MacArthur Foundation Series on Digital Media and Learning, 1 edition). Cambridge, MA: The MIT Press.

Jenkins, H., Clinton, K., Purushotma, R., Robison, A., & Weigel, M. (2006). *Confronting the challenges of participatory culture: Media education for the 21st century.* Chicago, IL: The MacArthur Foundation. Retrieved April 16, 2007, from http://digitallearning.macfound.org/atf/cf/%7b7e45c7e0-a3e0-4b89-ac9c-e807e1b0ae4e%7d/jenkins_white_paper.pdf

Johnson, L., Levine, A., Smith, R., & Smythe, T. (2009). *The 2009 horizon report: K-12 edition.* Austin, TX: The New Media Consortium. Retrieved March 12, 2011, from http://www.nmc.org/pdf/2009-Horizon-Report.pdf

Johnson, L., Smith, R., Levine, A., & Haywood, K. (2010). *The 2010 horizon report: K-12 edition.* Retrieved March 12, 2011, from http://www.nmc.org/pdf/2010-Horizon-Report-K12.pdf

Klopfer, E., Osteweil, S., & Salen, K. (2009*). Moving learning games forward: Obstacles, opportunities and openness.* Cambridge, MA: The Education Arcade. Retrieved November 14, 2011, from http://education.mit.edu/papers/MovingLearningGamesForward_EdArcade.pdf

Pardew, L., Nunamaker, E., & Pugh, S. (2004). *Game design for teens. Premier Press Game Development Series.* Premier Press.

Partnership for 21st Century Skills (2004). *The intellectual and policy foundations of the 21st century skills framework.* Retrieved July 9, 2009, from http://www.21stcenturyskills.org/route21/images/stories/epapers/skillsfoundationsfinal.pdf

Salen, K., Torres, R., Wolozin, L., Rufo-Tepper, R., & Shapiro, A. (2011). *Quest to learn: Developing the school for digital kids.* Cambridge, MA: MIT Press.

Shaffer, D. W., Squire, K. D., Halverson, R., & Gee, J. P. (2005). Video games and the future of learning. *Phi Delta Kappan, 87*(2), 105–111.

Squire, K. (2011). *Video games and learning: Teaching and participatory culture in the digital age.* New York, NY: Teachers College Press.

Squire, K., & Durga, S. (2008). Productive gaming: The case for historiographic game play. In Ferdig, R. (Ed.), *Handbook of research on effective electronic gaming in education.* Hershey, PA: Information Science Reference.

Squire, K., & Jenkins, H. (2004). Harnessing the power of games in education. *Insight (American Society of Ophthalmic Registered Nurses), 3*(1), 5–33.

Squire, K., & Steinkuehler, C. (2005, April 15). Meet the gamers. *The Library Journal.* Retrieved March 14, 2010, from http://www.the library journal.com

Squire, K. D. (2008, Mar-Apr). Video games and education: Designing learning systems for an interactive age. *Educational Technology Magazine: The Magazine for Managers of Change in Education, 48,* 17–26.

Steinkuehler, C., & King, B. (2009). Digital literacies for the disengaged: Creating after school contexts to support boys' game-based literacy skills. *Horizon, 17*(1), 47–59. doi:10.1108/10748120910936144

U.S. Department of Education, Office of Instructional Technology. (2010). *Transforming American education: Learning powered by technology.* Washington, DC: Author. Retrieved December 16, 2011, from http://www.ed.gov/sites/default/files/netp2010.pdf

KEY TERMS AND DEFINITIONS

ARIS: An acronym meaning Augmented Reality and Interactive Storytelling created by educational researchers at University of Wisconsin, Madison, and the University of New Mexico. ARIS is an open-source authoring platform allowing users to design place-based narrative games.

Canned Game Design Courses: The reference in this paper refers to educational games with accompanying premade curriculum and teacher resources offering little room for customization or modification. They are typically purchased as time and expertise to write the curricula in-house is absent.

Daqri: A platform that can be used to make augmented reality games expressed in QR codes. For game creation, developers can customize content within the code and download an App to a mobile device enhancing the experience for players in board or mobile games.

Games, Learning, and Society (GLS): An organization of academic researchers, game developers, and industry leaders who investigate the impact of games and game-like environments on society.

Kodu: A 3-D immersive environment developed by Microsoft Research encouraging participants to use a visual programming language to create digital games.

Model Academic Standards: Content and performance standards which specify what students should know and be able to do. Benchmarks at grades 4, 8, and 12 guides the adoption and dissemination of the standards used to develop curricula and learning paths. Recently, Common Core Standards have updated, replaced, and aligned standards across disciplines and states.

New Media Literacies: A list of eleven skills and practices identified by Henry Jenkins and fellow researchers outlining skills necessary for success to fully participate in new media landscapes. Research, technical, critical analysis, and traditional literacy skills provide the basis for these skills which encompass much broader cultural competencies and social skills.

The Game Crafter: A web-based application providing necessary steps, design materials, a publication space, and peer review when creating board games.

Chapter 14
Game–Making in a Fourth Grade Art Classroom Using Gamestar Mechanic

Michelle Aubrecht
Ohio State University, USA

EXECUTIVE SUMMARY

Making a game can be a creative act for students—much like writing a novel, making artwork, or designing a science experiment, it is a way to "play" with ideas. Game making is a creative and iterative process, and it may help students develop the ability to think non-linearly, create and understand systems, and hone such 21st century skills as critical and analytical thinking skills, while allowing deeper explorations of social issues that afford avenues for storytelling, allowing both game players and game makers to engage in meaning-making experiences. In the art classroom, students can explore design considerations, such as color, shape, balance, composition, rhythm, and meaning making. Game making is an iterative, multi-disciplinary mode of self-expression and communication, and it is a demonstrable example of student learning.

OVERALL DESCRIPTION

The computer is the new tool, the new medium which links the concept of information and art together.... Due to the computer's complexity and its capability of being used for such diverse possibilities, it is a tool and a medium with its own built-in agenda. Electronic tools have a hidden point of view far more complex than that built into a brush, printing press, or a camera (Lovejoy, 1992, p. 139, 142, as cited in Rogers, 1995, p. 17).

DOI: 10.4018/978-1-4666-2848-9.ch014

This chapter discusses how this researcher used the free, online video game *Gamestar Mechanic* (http://gamestarmechanic.com/) in an elementary art classroom and supported the art teacher in learning how to use this tool. Through this professional development experience (done as part of graduate research), the art teacher learned how to use *Gamestar Mechanic* and how game design and art can be integrated. Players (fourth-grade students in a low-income, urban school) learned basic game design principles and how to design games by playing and fixing them. Students can use *Gamestar Mechanic* to make their own games, post them online, receive feedback from classmates, teachers, and other players, and then revise and repost. Because game making is an iterative process, it is like the scientific method of stating a hypothesis, creating an experiment, testing, reworking, and retesting. It is also the method used by professional game designers.

Students spent time making a comic strip prior to using *Gamestar Mechanic*. Each student made a three-panel comic that functioned as a storyboard, helping them grasp the concept of avatar, obstacle, and goal. This experience gave both the researcher and the teacher feedback allowing for formative assessment so that future lessons could be redesigned. An alternative practice that could enhance lessons and learning outside the art classroom might occur if teachers collaborated in using *Gamestar Mechanic* to support learning math, science, reading, writing, spelling, and story composition.

Literature Review

In 1938, Dutch sociologist Johan Huizinga put forward the idea that playing games evokes a "Magic Circle." Interpreting Huizinga, Brown (2008) describes this phenomenon:

All play moves and has its being within a playground marked off beforehand either materially or ideally... All are temporary worlds within the ordinary world, dedicated to the performance of an act apart (p. 97).

Brown explains that "play is something outside the province of moral reasoning, neither moral nor amoral." Provoking contemplation, Salen and Zimmerman (2003) ask, "Does the magic circle enframe a reality completely separated from the real world? Is a game somehow an extension of regular life? Or is a game just a special case of ordinary life?" (p. 96). Salen and Zimmerman (2003) assert that games encompass agreed-upon rules, a common understanding of the game system, and identification with the representation of oneself within the game as a token or avatar. These rules and the immersion within the game are what create the magic circle.

Video games have the potential to change the way that students and teachers think about learning (McLellan, 1996; Jenkins, Clinton, Purushotma, Robison, & Weigel, 2006; Prensky, 2006; Annetta, 2008; Gee & Hayes, 2010). According to Thai, Lowenstein, Ching, and Rejeski (2009).

Educational digital games offer a promising and untapped opportunity to leverage children's enthusiasm and help transform teaching and learning in America. These games allow teachers to tap into their students' existing enthusiasm for digital games to engage, expand, and empower them as learners (as cited in Wellings & Levine, 2009, p. 10).

Game making can be a collaborative, interdisciplinary effort or part of a single subject, such as art; making games offers myriad ways to express understanding of academic subjects while providing significant opportunities for meaning-making. Keifer-Boyd (2005) suggests that when older students make games for younger students, it maximizes learning. "When children create games for children, they form educational theories, test their pedagogy, and make changes based on peer responses to their games" (p. 117).

Because students grow up in a visual culture, it is imperative that they be able to understand and navigate within it. Discussion in the art education literature suggests that video games are a significant aspect of visual culture, even when they are not explicitly identified. For example, Keifer-Boyd, Amburgy, and Knight (2003) state that:

In creating, one needs to consider the cultural use of symbols and recognize how culture shapes our preferences for design, colors, and subject, or content. Creativity is not only the expression of personal feelings; it communicates cultural values and social meanings (p. 50).

They conclude by stating, "perception is active interpretation, or making meaning. In other words, what we SEE (sic) is not primarily based on sense stimulus, but on past knowledge, situational contexts, and cultural narratives" (p. 51). This was written in 2003, when video games had not yet been accepted as an art form (some would still dispute that point). Games were also not considered valued as classroom teaching tools. Video games, both as something to be played and created, are an essential part of our visual culture. They allow for individual narratives and meaning-making. According to Freedman (1997), understanding visual literacy requires "a broad view of creative production and interpretation in relation to multiple meanings and visual qualities … if we are to understand and teach about the use of images in contemporary life" (p. 7).

As video games mature as a medium, conventions for the user-interface and in-game navigation have begun to use symbols that shape contemporary culture and provide an ongoing exploration of how to communicate visually, through interacting with a computer or game console. For example, Microsoft's Xbox Kinect has radically altered the game interface by removing the hand-held controller. Players interact with the game space by using gesture control, voice commands, and face recognition.

In the past, much of the discussion about video games in art education has been about technology use. Several aspects of making games in the art classroom are relevant to the use of technology in art education. Making video games is an art form that uses technology. Game-making software is much like other software tools that art educators have been using for years, such as Photoshop, Paint, and iMovie, among others. When people make games, creative thinking, image making, gathering multiple perspectives, making connections, and reflective thinking are facilitated (Keifer-Boyd, 2005). Game-making inherently requires a multi-disciplinary approach utilizing different skill sets, such as programming, artwork, design, sound, and communicating in a multi-media environment.

Use of technology allows a teacher to act as a facilitator (Morrison, Lowther, & DeMeulle, 1999), partner (Prensky, 2010), and coach and advisor (Squire, 2011). In these roles, the teacher guides students' thinking and research while also allowing for peer teaching. Students thus have the opportunity to become active producers instead of remaining in the traditional role of passive receivers of knowledge (Jenkins, 2006; Gee & Hayes, 2010; Prensky, 2010; Squire, 2011). A white paper from the Joan Ganz Cooney Center cites numerous benefits of using technology with students, among which are building 21st century skills, engaging students in content creation, providing access to virtual communities and expertise, supporting STEM fields and differentiated instruction, and reducing the dropout rate (Wellings & Levine, 2009).

Children can learn from playing, critiquing, and making games. *Gamestar Mechanic* is an excellent first exposure to game-making, which can otherwise be complicated and time intensive. By engaging in game-making, students become novice game designers who use specialist language and participate in a community of game designers. Students may use games to engage in real-world, simulated activities, participate in communities of practice, and become producers. In so doing, students become game literate. Gaming literacy involves systems thinking, meaning making, meaning production (Games, 2008; Buckingham, 2007; Salen, 2007; Squire, 2008), digital literacy (Squire, 2008; Steinkuehler 2010), and visual literacy. Digital video games are a cultural product in our society that is both interactive and visual.

Before students can benefit from playing or making games, support materials (Baek, 2008) and training for teachers are needed so that games can be integrated into the curriculum (Becker, 2010; Oblinger, 2006; Thai, et al., 2009). According to Oblinger (2006), "integration requires an understanding of the medium and its alignment with the subject, the instructional strategy, the student's learning style, and intended outcomes" (p. 7). Through training and support, teachers can gain understanding, confidence, and the ability to use games with students (Becker, 2007).

Challenges that teachers must overcome to use arts integration methods are similar to those necessary for game integration methods. Several similar barriers to arts integration methods or new curriculum materials and teaching methods have been identified by several researchers (Probart, McDonnell, Lachterberg, & Anger 1997; Werner & Freeman, 2001). Baek (2008) identified several barriers to using games in the classroom, including teacher concerns about the negative effects of gaming, student uneasiness, fixed class schedules, inflexible curriculums, and limited budgets. In addition to perceived negative effects of gaming, Rice (2007) also identified lack of adequate computer hardware, fixed class schedules, and a lack of alignment to state standards as barriers to integrating games into the curriculum. Other factors inhibiting the use of games include objections from those who consider games to be inappropriate for education (Charsky & Mims, 2008; Oblinger, 2006). Additionally, non-gamer students may feel concerned about their ability to figure out how to use games (Baek, 2008; Charsky & Mims, 2008).

Constraints vary from school to school and teacher to teacher, including availability of computers, internet access and speed, and IT policy and negotiation. Teachers may not have time to play a game long enough to feel confident in using it with students, creating a lesson or unit based on it, or adapting a pre-written game lesson to meet specific curricular needs. Because games differ widely, assessing student learning depends upon the teacher defining learner outcomes clearly and understanding that learning through game play and game making develops complex skill sets. Such learning cannot be assessed using multiple choice questions, as is common on standardized tests, because the student is not learning through memorization; instead, they are integrating analytical and critical thinking, systems thinking, problem solving, and evidence based reasoning (Boyce & Barnes, 2010; Chaffin & Barnes, 2010; Gee & Shaffer, 2010).

PRACTICALITIES OF RUNNING THE GAME

Gamestar Mechanic provides both a clear pathway through learning the elements of game design (See Figure 1) and all of the necessary components, such as avatars, background images, built-in game rules, and mechanics, and lots of design options, such as sound, backgrounds, and sprite selection and settings. It is necessary to understand these elements in order to grasp the complexity of making a game. Each of these elements must support the narrative and what it is teaching or communicating.

Figure 1. Five elements of game design (© Robert Torres, 2009, Used with permission)

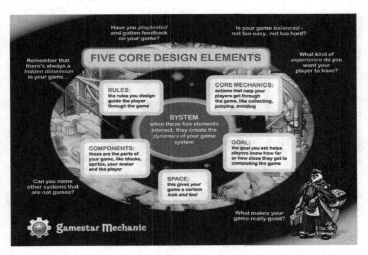

It is important that the instructor be very clear about what learning outcomes are expected from game making and how they meet state-mandated standards (See Table 1). It is also helpful to contemplate how games teach and why they are both valuable teaching tools and an expressive medium. In so doing, the instructor will be able to articulate these concepts to administrators, other teachers, and parents, and rethink how lessons can be learned through students making games (See Figure

Table 1. Ohio Department of Education standards for art

From the Ohio Department of Education standards, this researcher identified the following standards for art education that could be met using *Gamestar Mechanic*:
Creative Expression and Communication **Benchmark B** – Use the elements and principles of art as a means to express ideas, emotions and experiences. (p. 220) **Benchmark C:** Develop and select a range of subject matter and ideas to communicate meaning in two- and three-dimensional works of art. (p. 221) **Benchmark D:** Recognize and use ongoing assessment to revise and improve the quality of original artworks. (p. 221)
Connections, Relationships and Applications **Benchmark A:** Demonstrate the relationship the visual arts share with other arts disciplines as meaningful forms of nonverbal communication. (p. 242) **Benchmark B:** Use the visual arts as a means to understand concepts and topics studied in disciplines outside the arts. (p. 243) **Benchmark C:** Create and solve an interdisciplinary problem using visual art processes, materials and tools. (p. 243) **Benchmark D:** Describe how visual art is used in their communities and the world around them and provide examples. (p. 244)

(Ohio Department of Education, 2010)TECHNOLOGY COMPONENTS

Figure 2. Gamestar Mechanic user interface

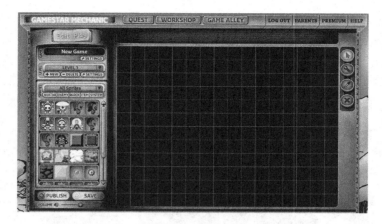

2). This is especially important as schools look to cut costs and downsize, sometimes eliminating academic subjects, such as social studies, music, art, and physical education, that do not directly appear to support student success on achievement tests.

Practicalities of Running the Game

Before beginning a game-making lesson using Gamestar Mechanic with students, there are a few questions to consider:

1. Do you have access to a computer lab?
2. Do you have a computer projector in the computer lab or your classroom?
3. Will students need to share computers or will each student have his or her own?
4. Do the computers have headphones?
5. Do the computers have Flash Player 10 installed?

Knowing one's options allows the one to decide the best way to configure the classroom space, distribute technology resources, and download the latest Flash Player.

Administrators and IT

1. Determine whether or not you need your school administrator's permission in order to use a game. Your IT professional will be able to lift any blocks to specific game websites (e.g., *Gamestar Mechanic*).

2. Determine whether you will use the free or the premium version. For a comparison of all of the features, see the *Gamestar Mechanic* website. The primary benefit of the premium version is that students can upload their own background images. In addition, teachers have more options for managing student accounts. In either case, student accounts are created by using the teacher's email address, so students are not required to have a personal email account. Any reports of inappropriate language or games are sent to the teacher's email account.

3. If you want to use the premium version, consider what resources you might have to pay for it (e.g., school funds, PTO support, etc.).

Teacher Preparation

Teachers should use the teacher guide and resources provided on the *Gamestar Mechanic* website and play the teacher's quest (under "New to *Gamestar Mechanic*/ How do I use it as a teacher"). Insight into what sorts of games students might make can be gained from playing student-created games in both the teacher's section and Game Alley. See a brief overview of how to play *Gamestar Mechanic*.

Gamestar Mechanic takes time. For this reason, it is important to generate understanding and support from other teachers and parents. If they understand the value of playing through the Episodes, they will allow students to play through the levels during indoor recess and other free times before or after school. This will speed up the process of learning how to make games within *Gamestar Mehcanic* (See Table 2).

Students

Students should have a general knowledge of how to use a computer and browser. Students are generally excited to use *Gamestar Mechanic* because it allows them to create sophisticated games without knowing how to program (Barry Joseph, personal communication, May 25, 2010). In the classrooms this author worked in, some students progressed more quickly than others, and these students were valuable partners in helping other students allowing them to assume a leadership role. This researcher observed several students who regularly and enthusiastically responded to peer questions and requests for assistance.

Once players have completed Episode 5, they may publish their games in Game Alley. Because students will progress at varying rates, it may be useful to group students into teams in which the team leaders publish games. In this way, a small group can design and make a game and then publish it for peer review. Once a

Table 2. How to play Gamestar Mechanic overview by author

Overview of How to Play *Gamestar Mechanic*

Through game play, students learn the concepts of game design: space, rules, core mechanics (jumping, collecting, avoiding), goals, and components (sprites, images, and sounds/music). There are five episodes to play, with several missions within each episode as well as a few bonus missions. After successful completion of each mission, the player earns sprites (images and animations) and background environments that can be used to make games. Each episode moves the player through games, which builds their knowledge of the different options for making games as well as the core principles of game design. Episode 3 scaffolds the learning about how space, rules, and goals are essential to good game design by requiring players to repair games and thereby learn to use the toolbox to design their own games (see image).

(© E-Line Media, Used with permission)

In the workshop area, players use the sprites (located in the left hand toolbox) that they have earned to make games. Players may create multiple levels; write directions, instructions, and a title; make choices about the game environment; and adjust settings on components and backgrounds. Using the toolbar on the right, players can select, delete, copy, and adjust settings on the sprites.

After completing Episode 5, players are allowed to publish their games in Game Alley, where any *Gamestar Mechanic* registered player can play them. After playing through all five episodes, players will have earned several game components, giving them a range of choices when they design their own games. Extra game components can be earned by playing bonus games offered in Game Alley.

game is published in Game Alley, other students can comment and write reviews. By using this feedback, students may rework their games.

Parents

Sending a letter to parents introducing the idea of using video games to teach can help overcome negative parental preconceptions. Parents may be concerned about violence in games and may think that children already spend too much time playing video games. An informative letter could include a link to the website and the parent materials provided there (http://gamestarmechanic.com/parents). A review of *Gamestar Mehcanic* can also be found on Common Sense Media that addresses common parental concerns about violence and online safety. A clear statement of the learning objectives and suggestions for how parents can support their children, such as allowing them time to play the game at home and playing the games their children make, asking the children to explain how their games work, their games' goals, and so on, will help parents understand the value of the learning process. A culminating event could include a demonstration and presentation night showcasing the students' work and demonstrating student learning.

UNDERSTANDING AND ADDRESSING VIOLENCE AND SHOOTING IN GAMES

Understanding and addressing concerns regarding violent games may be necessary. To avoid controversy, some teachers may elect not to allow student game designers to use shooting in *Gamestar Mechanic*. However, because it is an option, the teacher will do well to consider what shooting represents and why it can be an important game action, thus gaining the ability to justify it to other teachers, administrators, and parents. Denying the option to use shooting limits the student game designer in creating certain game mechanic patterns. In essence, it is like removing some of the colors from an artist's palette. The point is, an obstacle must be overcome to make a game challenging. Obstacles can be avoided, gone around, moved, or removed. Removing "shooting" eliminates the option to remove the obstacle during game play. On the other hand, constraints can foster creativity and provide challenges.

Prensky (2006) explains that "kids don't even see the violence for what adults think it represents. They see it rather as just a form of window dressing to what they are really doing, which is trying to achieve goals and beat the game" (p. 21). *Gamestar Mechanic* has options to design games that allow players to use weapons and shoot or be shot at, but it is not done in a graphically violent or aggressive way (See Figure 3). There is also an option to use a "freeze blaster" that briefly immobilizes the enemy. Using shooting to remove "bad guys" is a way of removing "obstacles." In designing games, player challenges can be created by adjusting the speed of the avatar and enemy movement and intervals for "gun fire" – such as traversing a path at specific speed without being "hit" so often that one "dies." This is analogous to tag; when a child is tagged, he must sit out until the next round. Removing obstacles is simply a part of the player's strategy, achieved by identifying underlying patterns or rhythms of "gun fire" that can be understood as an obstacle to

Figure 3. Shooting is represented by a short animation. The enemy disappears and a cog blows up and disintegrates (© E-Line Media, Used with permission).

overcome. Game designer Raph Koster (2005) explains that games can be reduced to the essential game play and stripped of the narrative layer. In this way, one can understand shooting in games as "dressing" and, at the game play level, irrelevant to core game mechanics. It is the overlay of narrative that makes a game fun and different from other games.

Outside of games played in the classroom, it is likely that children are being exposed to myriad forms of violence through movies, novels, television, and games, despite ratings that inform parents so that they may regulate their children's exposure (National Center for Children Exposed to Violence Website, 2012). However, according to Lenhart, et al. (2008), it is evident that while some teens play violent video games, violent video games are not the majority of video games played by teens. The two most widely played game genres were "racing" and "puzzle games", which were played by nearly three-quarters of teens in the sample. These genres are noteworthy because they have little to no violent content. However, two-thirds of teens reported playing "action" or "adventure" games, some of which contain considerable levels of violence. In 2010, 76% of games sold were rated "E" for everyone, "E10+" for people 10 and older, or "T" for teen, as opposed to those rated "M" for mature (Entertainment Software Association website).

Gee argues (2008) that teaching people to think critically and reflectively about all the forms of the media that they consume would go a long way toward addressing violent and aggressive behavior. Williams (2006) suggests that the focus on video games as a corrupting influence stems from societal tensions over hidden or unspoken social ills. In some respects, this controversy may be focusing our collective attention on something other than the real problems we face as a society, such as poverty, health care inequity, access to services, or lack of a political voice. Kutner and Olsen (2008) argue that focusing on video games as the cause of violence in our society, "causes parents, social activists and public policy makers to ignore the much more powerful and significant causes of youth violence that have already been well established, including a range of social, behavioral, economic, biological, and mental health factors" (p. 190). Likewise, Gee (2008) asserts that "politicians who get hot and heavy about violence in video games usually don't want to worry about such contexts … like poverty, bad parenting, and a culture that celebrates greed, war, and winning" (p. 11).

Using the Game with Students: Process and Evaluation

Gamestar Mechanic was used over a four-week period during the winter, in a low-income, urban school. Two fourth-grade classes with about 25 students in each met with the art teacher two times a week for 40 minutes each. The comic strip lesson was taught prior to using *Gamestar Mechanic*.

Figure 4. Gamestar Mechanic. Eight slides that were part of the introductory presentation to the fourth grade students (© E-Line Media, Used with permission).

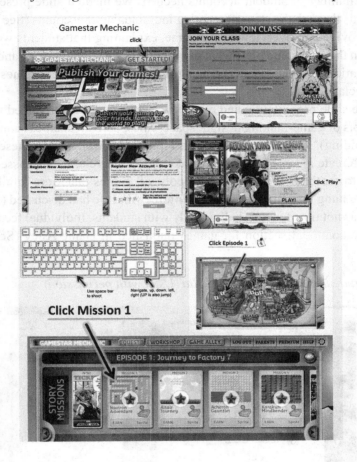

The classroom art teacher (hereafter referred to as Brooke) had used a comic strip lesson with her students in the past. Brooke adapted this lesson to support the student's learning about game design and *Gamestar Mechanic* by restructuring it so that it would lead into game design and teach the students three specific game design terms: avatar, obstacle, and goal. A simple example would be to design a comic strip of three cells: a dog (avatar) wants to get past the fence (obstacle) to get a bone (goal). Brooke planned to introduce the lesson by discussing and illustrating cartoon drawing techniques, such as using shapes to draw figures. The three-cell comic strip was intended to serve as the narrative for their game. However, as discussed below in the challenges section, students largely ignored the comic strip lesson once they began using *Gamestar Mechanic*.

We began the game design lesson by contacting *Gamestar Mechanic* and setting up the number of student accounts needed. We made a slide presentation to walk students through the steps of creating individual user accounts (See Figure 4). Then we provided an overview of the game, explaining that students would learn game design through game play, what game choices they would have, and the basic game navigation. The classroom account groups published student games in an area called "my class."

After the slide presentation and overview, students were introduced to the five core concepts of game-making design: space, rules, core mechanics (jumping, collecting, avoiding), goals, and components (sprites), as well as how these elements combine to create a game system. To make these concrete, we discussed them as they relate to football, chess, and Monopoly, all games that were familiar to the students. We hung up a small poster to reinforce what we had discussed (Figure 1).

There was not time to work individually with students. Individual feedback was given in the comment section for games published in Game Alley (See Figures

Figure 5. Student game (© E-Line Media, Used with permission)

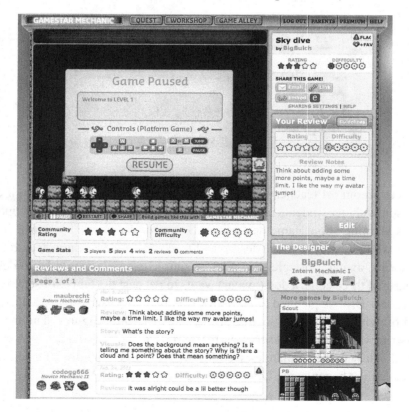

Figure 6. Game Alley's feedback area allows both the teacher and other players to give comments and reviews (© E-Line Media, Used with permission)

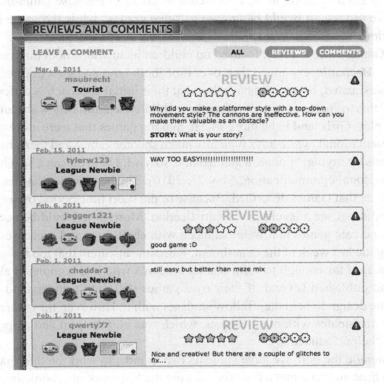

5 and 6). Teachers may log in to student accounts to view unpublished games; however, unlike Game Alley there is no feedback system provided, which requires teachers to provide comments elsewhere. Examples of teacher feedback include: "think about adding some more challenges like time, stationary obstacles, points" or "nice job! – Why don't you make a new level?" and "seems too easy, what can you add to make it more challenging?" More detailed messages were also left, like this one (See Figure 5):

Think about adding some more points, maybe a time limit. I like the way my avatar jumped!

Story: What's the story?

Visuals: Does the background mean anything? Is it telling me something about the story? Why is there a cloud and 1 point? Does that mean something?

As the instructor, I indicated difficulties but declined to rate the games because I did not want that rating to be interpreted as grading. Because game-making is an iterative process, it would be unwise to "give grades" while the game is under construction.

Alex Games, whose Ph.D. focused on children in an afterschool program using *Gamestar Mechanic*, explained that, over time, both boys and girls grasped how to make sophisticated, balanced games, but that their initial approach is different. He attributed this to "patterns of use" referring to children's familiarity with games they typically play. Girls tend to be more social, making games that were more strategic and representational, while boys typically make shooter games and then challenged their friends by saying, "I made a game that is so hard, I bet you can't beat it" (Alex Games, personal communication, May 25, 2010). The boys in our classes had the same attitude that Games described. Because of the short time period of our experiment, we did not see a leveling of sophistication. More time would be needed for students to create games that were balanced with challenges and successes.

During the last week of the experiment, it became apparent that too few students had progressed far enough to form teams. Students who had completed all of the games and published several of their own games still didn't understand enough about game design to help their fellow students with it. However, they were able to help their classmates with other aspects, which was very helpful and empowering for those "helper" students.

To conclude the unit, we gave students two months to work on their games on their own time and then met a final time during the last week of school. Two games from each class were selected and the student designers were asked to talk about their games while a fellow student played the game that was simultaneously projected using a SMART board. One student was at first reluctant to speak in front of his peers, but soon became very excited as he discussed his game (See Figure 7).

Below is a screen shot of "Food and Water." This student in particular made a lot of games and worked on them at home. His games demonstrate his growth, as he began to develop a deeper understanding of game making. He explained why he made this game in Game Alley (quoted directly, including misspellings and poor punctuation):

normaly I whould just edit the defalt but no not this time I have a message people are out on the streats with no shelter no food and no water there are kids out there with no home and japan is horrible to so if you see something that says donate plase do.

While the game maker's spelling and punctuation do interfere with the message, he communicates a desire to express something that had deeply affected him. He is clearly disturbed by the events following the tsunami in Japan and the result-

Figure 7. Ensposuble. The student titled the game, wrote tips and tricks, and the goals and rules for game play (© E-Line Media, Used with permission).

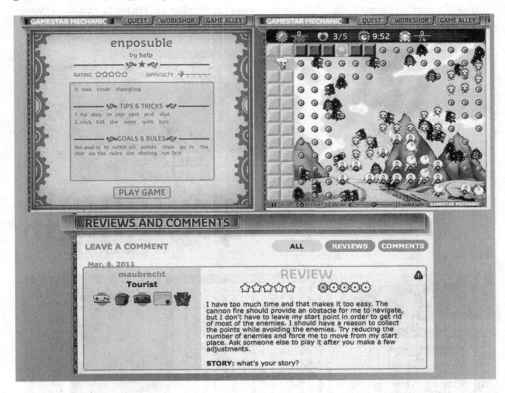

ing homelessness, and perhaps by seeing homeless people in his own town. One reviewer wrote, "I like it because it is hard and you tried to help poor people in a way" (http://gamestarmechanic.com/game/player/124604). Without any prompting on the teacher's part, this student used game making as a way to express his ideas using symbols of water, plants, and bread. The game play could be improved and the theme could be developed further, but it is impressive nonetheless (See Figure 8). It is clear that he did attempt to develop a narrative and understood game making as a vehicle or medium for self-expression and social commentary.

In this case, the teacher chose not to implement a formal evaluation because she was not sure what to expect from the students. However, using a rubric tied to standards would provide a way to evaluate student effort, understanding, and accomplishment.

From this researcher's observation of the students' work and classroom behavior, it is clear that the students were highly motivated and excited about their tasks. While there were a handful of students who were not progressing to the stage of making

Figure 8. Screen shots from Food and Water grouped together. This student made four levels and wrote a title and description. Realizing the importance and necessity of food and water to human life, this student used Gamestar Mechanic to make a game about a social issue about which he cared (© E-Line Media, Used with permission).

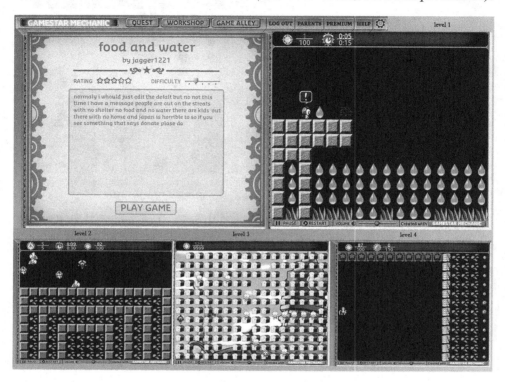

games, most were enthusiastic and looked forward to the class. The students were glad to see me and wanted to discuss and demonstrate their games; they didn't want to leave class and gave me high-fives on their way out.

Because this was a district with 85% of students on free and reduced price lunches, and we encountered several children who moved in or out of the district during this time,, doing work outside of school may have been difficult. We did not track the amount of work done outside of school because the research was focused on how to support the teacher in teaching game making in the art classroom. Looking at the Game Alley classroom postings, however, there are 74 games posted by 17 students. (Please realize that if students do not complete all five episodes, they can make the games, but they cannot publish them.) Of those, one student bought the premium access and continued posting games after the school year ended. To date, this student has posted 35 games. Almost no games were revised by the students. The researcher attributes this to lack of direction by the primary classroom teacher.

In another school the author consulted in, the classroom teacher required students to revise their games at least once. Some students worked outside of class and at home. They had support from classroom teachers, and found the experience to be very successful. In that district, those students used *Gamestar Mechanic* for a total of 6 hours, split over two three-week periods, one in the fall and one in the spring.

Challenges

Time constraints, compounded by absenteeism and school closings, were the largest challenge. Because students progressed at different rates we changed our plans and allowed the students time to work on their projects independently and then had a final class during the last week of school as described above.

Another challenge was student user names and passwords. The students created their own so that they could choose an online identity. However, some students couldn't remember their names or passwords and others had incorrectly recorded them, making it time-consuming to help them log into their accounts. In retrospect, using a naming convention and identical passwords would have solved this problem. However, once the accounts were created, we could not change there usernames.

One day, the block to *Gamestar Mechanic* that had previously been lifted by IT had been reapplied. That required us to change our lesson for the day quickly. Using graph paper, we asked students to sketch their game designs. Some students had difficulty understanding how the paper graph corresponded to the Workshop grid used to design games.

The only negative aspect to using Gamestar Mechanic is the time it takes to allow students to play through the Episodes so that they can publish their games. There were a few students that were less enthusiastic than the others, but this may be because they were unfamiliar with video games or computers. Allowing them to partner with someone who is familiar with these technologies might have ameliorated some of the frustration or apprehension.

Summary

The classroom teacher reflected that using *Gamestar Mechanic* was life-changing for some of the students. She explained that two students in particular had been helping their classmates solve problems, using the knowledge that they had gained and their newfound creativity to teach others. She also said that they both commented that they might want to work with computers as a profession; it is "really powerful … for a fourth grader to connect like that" (Personal communication, April 15, 2011). Since she often asks students to help one another on class projects, it was easy for her to allow the students who were excelling in the game play to help their classmates. The students who were most engaged began to see how game making could be used as a vehicle to comment on social issues that were important to them. Game making need not be limited to the art classroom—it could be used by a group of teachers for collaborative, interdisciplinary student projects.

Making a game combines many ways of knowing and understanding. It requires an understanding of design, storyboard creation and artwork. One must combine visual images to represent ideas, and demonstrate relationships, connections, and influences. A game gives the game player a way to manipulate those variables, thereby making his or her own meaning. While many discussions about using video games for teaching and learning focus on how games support STEM areas, integrating socio-emotional intelligence and art as part of the educational experience is integral to the process (Gee and Hayes, 2010). "There is no real divide between technology and art." Gee and Hayes explain that the arts "drive us to see things in new ways leading to new solution" (2010, p. 15).

Gamestar Mechanic is an easy way for students to make games, and neither teachers nor students need to understand programming. At first glance, making games may seem irrelevant to the business of learning. However, this researcher believes that game making affords students a complex learning task that can be done individually or in groups. Game making can be undertaken by students as an avenue not only for self-expression or commentary, but also as a way to demonstrate learning about content areas requiring research, such as science. Game making requires thinking about narrative, timing, consequences, strategy, and non-linear choices, as well as artistic considerations and multimedia components, such as sound and artwork. It would best be used as a cross-disciplinary project in English, math, science, music, and art class.

CONCLUSION

Begin by introducing *Gamestar Mechanic* during the first weeks of the school year. Require students to use a naming convention and all have the same password. Coordinate the project among several teachers, (including specialist teachers, such as reading) creating learner outcomes and rubrics for each subject area. Use an expanded comic strip lesson as described above. Prior to asking students to make their 3-cell comic, give them an overview of the options they will have in the *Gamestar Mechanic* workshop area. Allow them to see what sprites will be available to them after they earn them through game play. In addition, create a guide for students to think through their game design using the options in the workshop.

REFERENCES

Annetta, L. A. (2008). Video games in education: Why they should be used and how they are being used. *Theory into Practice, 47,* 229–239. doi:10.1080/00405840802153940

Baek, Y. K. (2008). What hinders teachers in using computer and video games in the classroom? Exploring factors inhibiting the uptake of computer and video games. *Cyberpsychology & Behavior, 11*(6), 665–671. doi:10.1089/cpb.2008.0127

Becker, K. (2007). Digital game-based learning once removed: Teaching teachers. *British Journal of Educational Technology, 38*(3), 478–488. doi:10.1111/j.1467-8535.2007.00711.x

Becker, K. (2010). Distinctions between games and learning: A review of current literature on games in education. In Van Eck, R. (Ed.), *Gaming and cognition: Theories and practice from the learning sciences* (pp. 22–54). Hershey, PA: Information Science Reference. doi:10.4018/978-1-61520-717-6.ch002

Boyce, A., & Barnes, T. (2010). BeadLoom Game: Using game elements to increase motivation and learning. In *Proceedings of the Fifth International Conference on the Foundations of Digital Games* (FDG '10), (pp. 25-31). New York, NY: ACM.

Brown, H. J. (2008). *Videogames and education.* New York, NY: M.E. Sharpe.

Buckingham, D., & Burn, A. (2007). Game literacy in theory and practice. *Journal of Educational Multimedia and Hypermedia, 16*(3), 323–349.

Chaffin, A., & Barnes, T. (2010). Lessons from a course on serious games research and prototyping. In *Proceedings of the Fifth International Conference on the Foundations of Digital Games* (FDG '10) (pp. 32-39). New York, NY: ACM.

Charsky, D., & Mims, C. (2008). Integrating commercial off-the-shelf video games into school curriculums. *TechTrends, 52*(5), 38–44. doi:10.1007/s11528-008-0195-0

Entertainment Software Association Website. (2012). Retrieved, January 2, 2012 from http://www.theesa.com/facts/index.asp

Freedman, K. (1997). Visual art/virtual art: Teaching technology for meaning. *Art Education, 50*(4), 6–12. doi:10.2307/3193647

Games, I. A. (2008). Three dialogs: A framework for the analysis and assessment of twenty-first-century literacy practices, and its use in the context of game design within *Gamestar Mechanic. E-learning, 5*(4), 396–417. doi:10.2304/elea.2008.5.4.396

Gee, J. P. (2008). *Good video games + good learning.* New York, NY: Peter Lang.

Gee, J. P., & Hayes, E. R. (2010). *Women and gaming: The Sims and 21st century learning*. New York, NY: Palgrave Macmillan.

Gee, J. P., & Shaffer, D. W. (2010). Looking where the light is bad: Video games and the future of assessment. *Edge, 6*(1), 1–19.

Jenkins, H. (2006). *Convergence culture: Where old and new media collide*. New York, NY: New York University Press.

Jenkins, H., Clinton, K., Purushotma, R., Robison, A. J., & Weigel, M. (2006). *Confronting the challenges of participatory culture: Media education for the 21st century* [White Paper]. MacArthur Foundation.

Keifer-Boyd, K. (2005). Children teaching children with their computer game creations. *Visual Arts Research, 31*(160), 117–128.

Keifer-Boyd, K., Amburgy, P. M., & Knight, W. B. (2003). Three approaches to teaching visual culture in K-12 school contexts. *Art Education, 56*(2), 44–51.

Koster, R. (2005). *A theory of fun for game design*. Scottsdale, AZ: Paraglyph Press.

Kutner, L., & Olsen, C. K. (2008). *Grand theft childhood: The surprising truth about violent video games and what parents can do*. New York, NY: Simon & Schuster.

Lenhart, A., Kahne, J., Middaugh, E., Macgill, A.R. Evans. C, Vitak, J. (2008). *Teens, video games, and civics: Teen's gaming experiences are diverse and include significant social interaction and civic engagement*. Pew Charitable Trust and McAruthur Foundation.

McLellan, H. (1996). "Being digital": Implications for education. *Educational Technology, 36*(6), 5–20.

Morrison, G. R., Lowther, D. L., & DeMeulle, L. (1999). *Integrating computer technology into the classroom*. Upper Saddle River, NJ: Prentice Hall.

National Center for Children Exposed To Violence Website. (2012). Retrieved April 5, 2012, from http://www.nccev.org/resources/statistics.html#media & http://www.nccev.org/violence/media.html

Oblinger, D. G. (2006). Games and learning: Digital games have the potential to bring play to the learning experience. *EDUCAUSE Quarterly, 29*(3), 5–7.

Ohio Department of Education. (2010). *Academic content standards for visual art: Alignment by standard*. Retrieved from http://www.ode.state.oh.us/GD/Templates/Pages/ODE/ODEDetail.aspx?page=3&TopicRelationID=1700&ContentID=1388&Content=88231

Prensky, M. (2006). *"Don't bother me Mom, I'm learning!": How computer and video games are preparing your kids for twenty-first century success and how you can help!* St. Paul, MN: Paragon House.

Prensky, M. (2010). *Teaching digital natives: Partnering for real learning.* Thousand Oaks, CA: Sage.

Probart, C., McDonnell, E., Lachterberg, C., & Anger, S. (1997). Evaluation of implementation of an interdisciplinary nutrition curriculum in middle schools. *Journal of Nutrition Education, 29*(4), 203–209. doi:10.1016/S0022-3182(97)70199-7

Rice, J. (2007). New media resistance: Barriers to implementation of computer video games in the classroom. *Journal of Educational Multimedia and Hypermedia, 16*(3), 249–261.

Rogers, P. L. (1995). Towards a language of computer art: When paint isn't paint. *Art Education, 48*(5), 17–22. doi:10.2307/3193529

Salen, K. (2007). Gaming literacies: A game design study in action. *Journal of Educational Multimedia and Hypermedia, 16*(3), 301–322.

Salen, K., & Zimmerman, E. (2003). *Rules of play: Game design fundamentals.* Cambridge, MA: MIT Press.

Squire, K. (2008). Video game literacy: A literacy of expertise. In Coiro, J., Knobel, M., Leu, D., & Lankshear, C. (Eds.), *Handbook of research on new literacies.* New York, NY: MacMillan.

Squire, K. D. (2011). *Video games and learning: Teaching and participatory culture in the digital age.* New York, NY: Teachers College Press.

Steinkuehler, C. (2010). Video games and digital literacies. *Journal of Adolescent & Adult Literacy, 54*(1). doi:10.1598/JAAL.54.1.7

Thai, A. M., Lowenstein, D., Ching, D., & Rejeski, D. (2009). *Game changer: Investing in digital play to advance children's learning and health* [policy brief]. The Joan Ganz Cooney Center at Sesame Workshop. Retrieved from http://www.joanganzcooneycenter.org/Reports-abc.html

Wellings, J., & Levine, M. H. (2009). *The digital promise: Transforming learning with innovative uses of technology: A white paper on literacy and learning in a new media age* [white paper]. The Joan Ganz Cooney Center at Sesame Workshop. Retrieved from http://www.joanganzcooneycenter.org/Reports-abc.html

Werner, L., & Freeman, C. J. (2001). *Arts for academic achievement: arts integration—A vehicle for changing teacher practice*. Minneapolis Public Schools.

Williams, D. (2006). A brief social history of game play. In Vorderer, P., & Jennings, B. (Eds.), *Playing video games: Motives, responses, and consequences* (pp. 197–212). Mahwah, NJ: Lawrence Erlbaum Associates.

Chapter 15
Using Game Design as a Means to Make Computer Science Accessible to Adolescents

Roxana Hadad
Northeastern Illinois University, USA

EXECUTIVE SUMMARY

In this case, the author discusses using game design and community-building as methods for increasing interest and knowledge of computer science for students from underrepresented populations. Students in a six-week Upward Bound Math and Science (UBMS) summer program learned game design alongside programming basics, while they spoke to programming industry experts. For four weeks, students focused on the design concepts in different games they had played and with which they were familiar. They recreated these games by programming them using MIT's Scratch software. In the remaining two weeks, students created their own game using the concepts and skills they had learned. Some students chose to program their games to use the Xbox 360® Kinect™ controller as a way for the player to interact with their game using their whole body. Programmers spoke to the students weekly, both online and in person, answering questions about the field and the work that they do. Students shared their work with one another and the instructors in a Virtual Learning Environment (VLE).

DOI: 10.4018/978-1-4666-2848-9.ch015

ORGANIZATION BACKGROUND

The Chicago Teachers' Center at Northeastern Illinois University (CTC@NEIU) is a division of the College of Education. CTC@NEIU has worked to improve urban education through collaborative partnerships with K-12 schools, universities, and arts and community organizations since 1978. CTC@NEIU's 80 full-time and 200 part-time professionals have extensive expertise in working with all of the stakeholders that make up a school community, including students, teachers, parents, administrators, and staff from community agencies, universities, arts and cultural organizations, and businesses. CTC@NEIU's work to improve outcomes for K - 12 students is funded by various federal, state, and private grants. Northeastern Illinois University is the only four-year public Hispanic-Serving Institution (HSI) in the Midwest, and is ranked top both for being the most ethnically diverse university and for having students with the least amount of debt upon graduation in the Midwest region according to *U.S. News & World Report's* Best Colleges (2011).

SETTING THE STAGE

Though CTC@NEIU is composed of various grant-funded programs, these programs are united by a common vision of (1) increasing access to education, (2) building learning communities, and (3) transforming education practices. All CTC@NEIU programs, including the UBMS program, see computational literacy and the effective implementation of technology in educational practices as instrumental in accomplishing this vision.

As Director of Math, Science, and Technology at CTC@NEIU, I am charged with increasing interest in knowledge of science, technology, engineering and math (STEM) among the students with whom we work. At CTC@NEIU, we reach out to Chicagoland area middle and high schools in communities with high percentages of low socioeconomic status and underrepresented minorities. As Chicago grows as a technology hub, my research interest is how to increase interest and knowledge in computational fields to provide more opportunities for our students.

CASE DESCRIPTION

Because of my role to promote STEM at CTC@NEIU, I belong to various educational technology organizations, including Adobe Education Leaders (AEL). It was through the AEL program that I met an assistant principal who taught at a large state-run secondary school in a suburb of London, England. When I met him, this teacher had just asked his students what they were most interested in so that they could focus on it in class. Almost in unison, the students called out that they loved playing video games. The teacher responded that he was not interested in having his students play video games all day; as an art teacher, he was more interested in having them create rather than consume media. What if they made games, instead? The students thought that would be fantastic. Soon after, the assistant principal hired me to teach game design to his high school students. Through the AEL community, he learned that I had studied game design and had some experience developing educational games. He thought that the fact that I lived in Chicago and his students were in England was irrelevant. With videoconferencing and asynchronous virtual learning environments, students could learn from anyone, anywhere in the world. Because we were using videoconferencing to meet, he and I agreed that we should capitalize on the opportunity and include industry professionals from all over the world in the course, exposing students to practitioners and their professional lives. Soon, the interaction with industry practitioners became the most popular part of the course, and the coursework began to revolve around those interactions.

Due to this initial class, I came to believe that through both design and development, the creation of video games leads to a better understanding of computational and design thinking. In addition, video games provide unparalleled engagement and a common media touchstone for people of various backgrounds. Building on my experience with the English students, I worked with CTC@NEIU's Upward Bound Math and Science (UBMS) six-week summer program to provide students with a game design workshop within a community of programmers. UBMS students are low-income, first-generation college-bound, and academically-challenged high school students. All of the students participating in the summer game design class were of Hispanic ethnicity, and almost half were female. Having industry professionals interact with students throughout the course, answering their questions about the field and providing input on their project, included students in the programming community of practice. This integration of the industry in the classroom supported the goal to move minority and female students from having a passing interest in games to having a deep interest and knowledge in computer programming. Because of my work with the English students, I had a better sense of what worked well and what did not. This experience, combined with knowledge of current cognitive theories of how students learn, led to a more thoughtful design that better addressed the needs of the UBMS students whom I was trying to introduce to the field of computer science.

LITERATURE REVIEW

According to the National Center for Women & Information Technology, by 2018 there will be 1.4 million computer specialist jobs (2009). Unfortunately, universities will only generate one third of the graduates needed to fill these positions (NCWIT, 2009). The fact that most women and underrepresented minorities are not even considering computer science as a college or career choice is a major source of this problem. Underrepresented minorities receive only 10.6 percent of undergraduate, 4.8 percent of Master's, and 3.6 percent of Doctoral degrees in computing (Zweben, 2011). The number of women and underrepresented minorities obtaining associate's, bachelor's, master's, or doctoral degrees in computer science fell by 4 percent between 1986 and 2005. During this same period, the number of other STEM degrees rose for this group (with the exception of mathematics, which fell by 2 percent). With women obtaining 59 percent, Blacks 10 percent, and Hispanics 8 percent of bachelor's degrees in 2009 (NCES, 2010), there is a large portion of the population that could be included in computer science education, but are not.

Preliminary trials of using game development as a means of introducing students to ideas in computer sciences have shown some initial success (Bayliss and Strout, 2006; Parberry, Kazemzadeh and Roden, 2006). However, I wanted to be more structured and use a theoretical framework, specifically the Model of Domain Learning (MDL) (Alexander, 1997), so that I could assess our outcomes. According to the MDL, learning is contained in both stages and phases. Stages are age-related and step-like (acclimation, competence, and proficiency/expertise) while phases (i.e., subject-matter knowledge, learner interest, and general strategic processing), flow throughout the stages. Based on the MDL, the goal of our game design course was to increase students' knowledge and interest from acclimation to competence (Alexander, 1997). Games in the class served as *situational interests* for the students, that is, the lure of video games for a course of a few weeks is interesting for the short-term, "marginally influencing an individual's knowledge and values" (Hidi, 1990). Students are exposed to game design concepts (rules, boundaries, challenge, etc.) as well as programming concepts (forever loops, if/then statements, messaging, etc.) in order to give them the foundation to create their own games. These game design concepts provide the students with the language to describe what they already know, give voice to their prior knowledge, and acknowledge the expertise they already have (Bransford, Brown, & Cocking, 1999, p. 10) (e.g. *"Call of Duty* is fun because the level of challenge is hard enough to be exciting but not so hard that it is frustrating"). By combining the design concepts with programming concepts ("To make the game we are designing fun, we should adjust the obstacles with a *variable*, in order to get the right level of challenge"), we hoped to parlay the *situational interest* of games design into an *individual interest* - a deep-seated investment in and the pursuit of knowledge or skills related to a particular domain or topic area (Lawless & Kulikowich, 2006). This *individual interest* is meant to be one that moves beyond a general interest toward a professional interest, a "specialized, goal-oriented interest aligned with vocational activities" (Alexander, 2003, p. 11). The idea was then to take advantage of this *personal interest* to move students' fragmented knowledge into a knowledge base that is more "cohesive and principled in structure" (Alexander, 2003, p. 12). To do this, we employed *legitimate peripheral participation* (LPP) (Lave & Wenger, 1991). LPP is based on the conception of the intrinsically social and experiential nature of learning. It describes how a community of practice brings in new members by familiarizing them through low-risk tasks (i.e. the new members are on the *periphery* of the community). The tasks increase with complexity as the new members become more acclimated to the community, and in doing so, the new members become more familiar with the culture of the community (Lave & Wenger, 1991).

Including students in the programming community of practice is vital because feelings of belonging have shown to lead to greater interest in academics (Goodenow, 1993), and are especially important for underrepresented populations. Cheryan (2009) has shown that even an ambient sense of belonging gives women greater interest in computer science. Belonging is an aspect of identity that is crucial for feelings of self-efficacy. These feelings of inclusion often lead to greater feelings of self-efficacy, which according to O'Brien, Martinez-Pons, and Kopala, is the only predictor for interest in science (1999). In addition, participating in the community of practice gives students a better sense of the reality of a programmer. Unclear perceptions about what is involved in a career in the field of computer science leads many students to choose different careers (Biggers, Brauer, & Yilmaz, 2008; Ross, 2007).

By having a greater sense of belonging and self-efficacy, as well as having a clearer sense of what it means to be a programmer, it was my hope that students would be more motivated to pursue computer science-related activities. Motivation, as part of the MDL, is an attitude that demonstrates that students have reached the stage of competency. Once students' "base of domain knowledge becomes more coherent and richer, their intrinsic motivation to learn may become stronger, and as a consequence, their strategic processing becomes more effortful, planful, and effective" (Alexander, Jetton, & Kulikowich, 1995, p. 560). Motivation moves interest to action, and students are encouraged to take more coursework and network with people they feel could help them be a part of the programming community. Through interacting with and mentoring by these game design and programming professionals, our hypothesis was that students would feel part of (or join) the programming community, become acculturated into its vocabulary and work practices, and therefore, feel less isolated in the field.

PRACTICALITIES OF RUNNING THE COURSE

The course was composed of three elements (1) instruction on elements of game design; (2) instruction in programming; and (3) interaction with game designers and programmers.

The 2011 summer school class took place during a six-week summer UBMS session in Chicago, during which students spent an hour and a half every Monday, Tuesday, and Wednesday on the north campus of Northeastern Illinois University. I wanted to introduce students to programming software that they would be able to use during the times we were not meeting. I could not expect the students to purchase and be able to use an expensive and large software package at home. I selected MIT's Scratch (http://www.scratch.mit.edu), which is free and can be used on any operating system. It also gives an easy introduction to programming through block programming, which allows for an understanding of concepts (forever loops, variables, etc.) in a visual way without having to worry about syntax errors, as shown in Figure 1.

Two colleagues, who are experienced programmers based in Chicago, found a driver that assisted the interaction between Scratch and the XBox 360® Kinect™ (http://scratch.saorog.com/), created by Stephen Howell at the Institute of Technology in Tallaght, Ireland. The Kinect™ is a device that senses motion and allows for the ability to control a game without having to hold a controller. I saw the Kinect™ making the Scratch interface even more engaging and exciting for the students. I asked these programmer friends to help teach the programming sections of the UBMS class and they readily agreed.

On the Monday of each week, we focused on game design. I would ask the students to focus on the formal and dramatic elements that make up a game; elements the students should be considering when designing their own game (rules, boundaries, challenge, story, etc.). I would generally bring up a concept and then ask for examples that the students were familiar with about that concept ("Why are boundaries important in games? How do boundaries work in soccer? In tag? In 'Angry Birds'?"). On Tuesdays, we focused on programming. The first four weeks were devoted to making one small game each week focusing on a particular programming concept. In the last two weeks, students focused on using the game design concepts and programming they had learned to make their own games. On Wednesdays, we invited a guest speaker from the game design/programming community to speak to the students. Two of the presenters spoke to the class in person while the other three joined the class through an online classroom using Adobe Connect (http://www.adobe.com/products/adobeconnect.html). The students prepared some questions ahead of time to ask the presenters in addition to asking impromptu questions

Figure 1. Example of blocks in a Scratch program of Pong

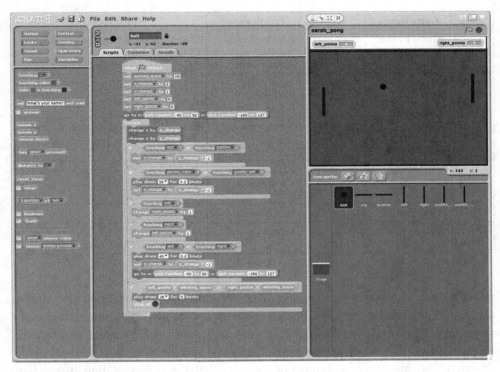

based on the presentation. The students also showed their work to the presenters for feedback. When the guest speakers joined us online, students used text chat to communicate with them.

One of the comments made by the English students in the online class I taught earlier was that they saw the game design and the programming as two completely separate classes. In response to this feedback, in designing the UBMS we attempted to inform the game design with the programming and vice versa to and to make the course as seamless as possible by fitting the game design lessons in with the programming lessons, as shown in Table 1.

During the first week, we discussed what a game was, what made a good game, and what made a bad game. We showed an example of a bad game, Atari's infamous 'E.T.', and talked about what made it a bad game. We had a long discussion about rules, the backbone of games, and how manipulating them changes the player experience. We also talked about the design process, learned what iterative design was, and talked about the steps involved in making a game: brainstorming, storyboarding, prototyping, and production. We used Pong (http://www.ponggame.org/) as a focus that week. Pong was a good game to start with because it allowed us to

Table 1. Syllabus for the game design and development class

Week	Game Design	Game	Programming	Guest speaker
1	What is a game? Design process Rules	Pong	Intro to Scratch Variables Forever loops	Chair of local Game Design organization / Chair of Code Academy
2	Characters Worlds	Robot Unicorn	Random Operators Collision detection	N/A
3	Conflict Challenge Boundaries	Asteroids	Message passing	Programmer for large Chicago company
4	Storyboarding	Drawing	Using Kinect™ Understanding sensors	Programmer for museum installations
5	Production	N/A	Production	Web programmer
6	Production	N/A	Production	Stephen Howell Presentation to family and friends

give a history lesson on video games and how far they have come. Pong also allows for a good introduction to game design concepts as well as programming due to its simplicity. We introduced Scratch that week and went over variables and forever loops and how they work in programs. Our guest speaker was chair of local game design organization and the founder of a non-profit that provided coding instruction. He was a good first guest speaker because he himself was fairly new to the programming community and was able to talk about how and why he decided to involve himself with programming and its promotion. He was also an African-American from the South Side of Chicago, and spoke a bit about being an underrepresented minority in the field of computing.

The second week, we used Robot Unicorn Attack (http://games.adultswim.com/robot-unicorn-attack-twitchy-online-game.html) as the anchoring game to teach the lessons. We talked about characters and worlds and how they change the nature of the gameplay (e.g. comparing Robot Unicorn Attack to Pong). We explored how different games have different kinds of characters (e.g. round vs. flat) and how game worlds are characters themselves. Based on this idea, we introduced randomness and operators to programming in order for students to make their characters and worlds as predictable (or unpredictable) as they liked. We also introduced collision detection, to help characters navigate good and bad parts of the game worlds. Due to the Independence Day holiday, we had no guest speaker that week.

In the third week, we focused on Asteroids (http://www.play.vg/games/4-Asteroids.html). In design class, we discussed the ideas of conflict and challenge and how boundaries affect them, using Asteroids as an example. In programming, the focus was on message passing, where objects can send messages to other objects or processes, allowing for better synchronization. That week, we had a Latino programmer from a large software company in Chicago as the guest speaker. He spoke a bit about how when he was not programming, he was playing music for a heavy metal band, and the flexibility and pay of being a programmer allowed for this.

In the fourth week, the students were introduced to the Kinect™ and how it worked with Scratch. The programming instructors made a simple drawing program using both Scratch and Kinect™ (http://scratch.mit.edu/projects/sarahgray/1930973), where a bouncing ball could be retained by a line drawn with the player's right hand and erased with the left hand. Students learned how to calibrate the Kinect™ and how to connect it to their program. They were then paired off (they could pick their own partner). By working in pairs, the UBMS students mirrored the agile software development technique of paired programming. Agile development is a programming methodology that focuses on iterative design. In paired programming, one programmer takes control of the coding ("drives"), while the other observes and points out any mistakes or offers alternative solutions (Williams, 2001). In this way, we were able to expose students to a type of workflow used in the software development industry.

Students then began brainstorming for their game. To help them generate ideas, I used a method similar to that of the Boardgame Remix Kit (http://boardgame-remix-kit.com/), and I asked the students to come up with two of their favorite games and then break them up into separate elements. For instance, Pac-Man, (1) is a maze, (2) is from a bird's eye perspective, (3) requires the player to eat all of the pellets before you move to the next stage, (4) enemies cannot hurt you for a brief period of time after you eat power pellets, (5) if you make contact with an enemy when you have not eaten a power pellet, you lose a life, etc. DOOM (1) has a maze-like quality, (2) is from a first-person perspective, (3) requires the players to get to the exit before being killed by an enemy, (4) the player starts with a handgun, but can acquire bigger and better weapons throughout the game, etc. Then, they were encouraged to mix and mash the elements from these two games (e.g. By combining elements of Pac-Man and DOOM, they could create a first-person maze game where one has to eat all of the items in the maze before being able to see the exit to the next level).

If the students were going to use the Kinect™ as a controller (only three of the six teams wanted to use the Kinect™), they could incorporate an action that they wanted as part of their player experience goal. That is, if they wanted their player to be more active, then their action could be "jumping" and they could make that an element of the game. Once they had an idea of what they were going to do, they had to create a storyboard of the game using Google Presentation to share with the other students and the instructors. The speaker that week programmed installations in museums.

During the next two weeks, the students worked on their games. They also created posters, as seen in Figure 2, promoting their games and a slide show presentation, as seen in Figure 3, that doubled as a document. The poster served as a sort of marketing device, providing screenshots of the game and a short description. The presentation/design document went over how they conceived of the idea and how they created the game. The evening of the final day of class, the students presented their games to an audience of their family and friends at Northeastern Illinois University. The posters were displayed and the students gave short presentations about their work using the slideshows they created. After each presentation they asked for a volunteer from the audience to approach the stage and play their game.

TECHNOLOGY COMPONENTS

For UBMS, we wanted to provide students with software they could use on their own. Free and easily downloaded to any computer, MIT's Scratch was a great resource. The block-based approach to programming allowed students to play with programming concepts without having to concern themselves with simple syntax errors. In addition, because my focus was on having students learn through communities of practice, Scratch was attractive because of its social nature. Students are able to upload their work to the Scratch site and have it evaluated by their peers.

Figure 2. Game poster a pair of students made to describe their game

Figure 3. Google Presentation students made for their talk on their game

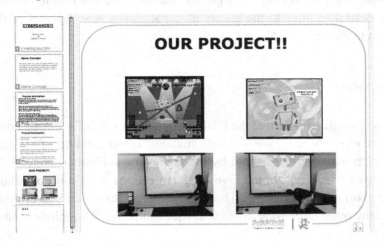

They can also download the Scratch programs made by their peers and modify them in a way that suits them. The UBMS students took to it quite easily, although some were disappointed with the limitations of the graphics.

To add interest to the Scratch programming, we introduced the students to Kinect™, a driver to assist the interaction between Scratch and the XBox 360® Kinect™. Kinect™ allows players to control a game through body movement. This added element encouraged students to focus on "player experience goals" (Fullerton, 2008), designing backwards from what they wanted their audience to experience when playing their game. Because one needs Kinect™ for the full body interaction with the students' games, we recorded videos of the students playing their own games and asked them to compare their actions that they saw on the video with the player experience goals they determined at the beginning of creating their game.

Students used Google Apps for Education to assist with their game design and presentation. They used Google Documents to organize their brainstorming sessions, Google Drawings for the posters to advertise their work, and Google Presentations to organize their demonstrations to their family and friends. The course also used Google Sites as a type of Virtual Learning Environment (VLE), posting the slideshows for each class, links to every student's Scratch profile and games, and information on each guest presenter. At the end of the six weeks, students presented their games and their process to an auditorium filled with their friends and families. They used their Google slideshows to organize their presentations. A Google Apps for Education domain was established for the UBMS students, so we used that as the VLE for our students. Google Sites served as the main structure, providing a place for the Google Documents, Google Drawings, and Google Presentations that they had made supporting their games. We provided information on the guest speakers, as well as links to the games of the students. A screenshot of the VLE can be seen in Figure 4.

EVALUATION

To evaluate the effectiveness of the UBMS course in terms of acquired knowledge in computer programming, we assessed students' understanding of programming concepts by pre-and post-tests and by the games the students produced. The test was composed of six questions. Five of the questions were multiple-choice and one was a short answer question. Three of the questions concerned programming terms, and the other three were application questions. Table 2 includes some of the questions in the knowledge test.

There were only twelve (12) valid response sets for the pre- and post-test and the survey assessments (of the fourteen students, one was not available for the pre-test, and another was not available for the post-test). Due to the low number, no statistical significance could be conducted, but the means are shown to demonstrate the improvement from the pre-test to the post-test. As shown in Table 3, the mean score improved after the six weeks.

A rubric, shown in Table 4, was adapted from one created by Patten and found on Rubistar (2011). It was used to determine the quality of the games the students produced. The course was a summer program, so the students did not directly receive a score.

Figure 4. Virtual learning environment created with Google Sites

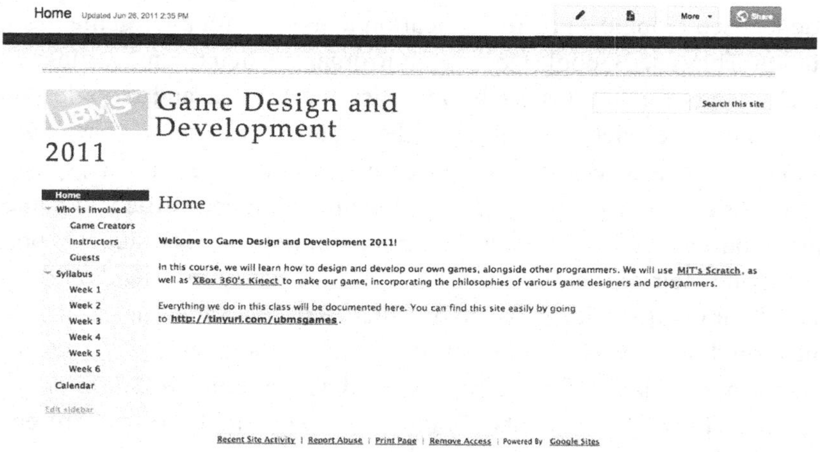

Table 2. Sample of the programming knowledge pre- and post-test questions

Q1.	What is a good use for a list in programming? a. When you have lots of something and want to keep them together - Correct Answer b. When you have one of something and want to keep it separate c. When you need to write a list of objects d. When you need to do something multiple times
Q2.	If you wanted to have a character say "huzzah" every time they scored a point, and be silent every time they fail to score a point, what structure would you use to tell the character when to speak? a. An 'if/else' block - Correct Answer b. A 'while' loop c. A 'Forever if true' block d. A 'timeout'
Q3.	As a game designer you want one character (sprite), a cat, to hiss every time a dog, another character, comes into its basket. How would you set up a program for a cat to hiss every time the dog approached? Students should: 1. mention forever loop 2. mention if statement 0 points - mentions 0/2 1 point - mentions 1/2 2 points - mentions 2/2

Table 3. Sample questions from the programming knowledge pre- and post-test results

	Question	$\bar{x}$	s
Q1.	What is a good use for a list in programming? (Pre-test)	.33	.492
	What is a good use for a list in programming? (Post-test)	.58	.515
Q2.	… what structure would you use to tell the character when to speak? (Pre-test)	.42	.515
	…what structure would you use to tell the character when to speak? (Post-test)	.67	.492
Q3.	How would you set up a program for a cat to hiss every time the dog approached? (Pre-test)	.50	.674
Q3.	How would you set up a program for a cat to hiss every time the dog approached? (Post-test)How would you set up a program for a cat to hiss every time the dog approached? (Pre-test)	.75.50	.622.674
	How would you set up a program for a cat to hiss every time the dog approached? (Post-test)	.75	.622

Three groups created games using the Kinect™, and three did not. Of the groups using the Kinect™, one group created a dancing game, requiring the player to move their hands and feet to corresponding symbols on the screen. As seen in Figure 5, another group created a paddle ball game that required the player to bounce a character to the other side of a wall. Of the groups not using the Kinect™, one group created a complex game that required the player to shoot at flying mice and collect money, and with enough points, move onto defeat a boss character.

Table 4. Games rubric

CATEGORY	Excellent (3)	Good (2)	Fair (1)	Poor (0)
Game Purpose	Player was clear from the beginning about the purpose of the game and how to win or lose.	Player was somewhat clear about the purpose of the game and how to win or lose.	Player was often unclear about the purpose of the game and how to win or lose.	Player was always unclear about the purpose of the game and had no idea how to win or lose.
Code Execution	Code was complex, well written and had no bugs.	Code was advanced, well written and had minimal bugs.	Code was simple, worked fairly well and had a few bugs.	Code was very simple, did not work for much of the time and made the game play difficult.
User Interface	The game was clear, well designed and easy to use. The player knew what to do immediately.	The game was relatively clear, but at times the player did not know what to do.	The game was somewhat unclear. The player was able to finish but struggled with how to play the game.	The game was confusing and difficult to use. The player could not complete the game because he/she didn't know what to do.
"Fun" Quotient	The game was fun to play and enticed the user to play multiple times.	The game was fun to play once.	The game was confusing and a bit boring and the player quickly lost interest.	The game was confusing to the user, incomplete or caused the player to lose interest immediately.
Student Engagement/ Effort	Student consistently put forth his/her best effort throughout this project.	Student made a good effort throughout the project.	Student was sometimes engaged and did fairly good work.	Student was not engaged in the project and did not put forth his/her best effort.

*Figure 5. Game created by UBMS students using both Scratch and the Xbox 360®
KinectTM where the player must use their body to control a paddle*

To determine any change in interest, we examined results in a pre- and post-survey examining feelings of belonging, perception of the computer sciences professions, and motivation to pursue their interests in the computer sciences. The survey contained eight questions. Students were asked to score each statement on a scale of 1 (Strongly Disagree) to 5 (Strongly Agree). Table 5 includes some of the questions from the pre- and post- survey, as well as the results. Once again, due to the low number of participants (N=12), I could only use descriptive statistics for the results. There was an increase in the mean of the students' feelings of belonging, perception of the computer sciences professions, and motivation to pursue their interests in the computer sciences.

CHALLENGES

To prepare for the interactions with the professionals, the students were given a suggested list of questions to begin conversations. However, the students generally asked questions of their own. The most commonly asked questions were the following:

1. How much money do you make?
2. What video game are you playing now?
3. What's your favorite video game?
4. What job would you like to do if you weren't doing what you do now?
5. Would you encourage your children to do what you do for a living?
6. Is your job stressful?
7. What sports do you play?
8. What do you do when you are not at work?

Table 5. Sample questions from the programming interest pre- and post-survey results

	Question	$\bar{x}$	s
Q1.	I plan to become a programmer when I graduate school. (Pre)	3.08	1.17
	I plan to become a programmer when I graduate school. (Post)	3.33	1.23
Q2.	When I graduate, I would like to work with people who program software. (Pre)	3.08	1.24
	When I graduate, I would like to work with people who program software. (Post)	3.42	1.31
Q3.	I look forward to taking more programming courses.	3.67	1.16
	I look forward to taking more programming courses.	3.92	0.10

The salary question was asked of every presenter, and at first, I was admittedly horrified and embarrassed and I scolded the students for asking it once we logged off with the presenters. They asked why they could not ask that, and I said because it was just too personal and one just does not ask strangers those types of questions. They argued that they were concerned with salary and they did not want to waste their time pursuing a career that did not pay for the hard work they invested. I said that happiness was not all about making money, and they countered that it was a large part of it. As the weeks wore on (and they continued to ask the presenters the salary question, despite my pleas not to), I began to realize how much a determinant salary was for students, and it was ridiculous of me not to respect that, as it was a question based in the reality of making a living for oneself and one's family. They just wanted to know if this career would support the kind of lifestyle they would hope to have. My desire for them to pursue their life's passion regardless of income disregarded their practical outlook. Some presenters refused to answer the question, but others acquiesced and gave the students a salary range. Also, questions like "Would you encourage your children to do what you do for a living?", "Is your job stressful?", "What sports do you play?" and "What do you do when you are not at work?" underscored that the students were not only concerned about money but life-style as well.

As for finding presenters, ever since the first class for the school in England, it has been a challenge finding women to speak in front of a class. I have found several who would have been perfect, but many felt they were not qualified to speak to the students, for whatever reason. We had no female speakers for the UBMS class, although I hope to find more in the future.

One challenge in teaching a course using this structure is being able to teach good game design alongside good programming. In our first iteration of the course (in school), students started seeing the two kinds of lessons as two different kinds of courses.

As much as I like to mirror the iterative design process of an actual game design studio, it is difficult in an abbreviated class structure. One part of the process I eliminated in the UBMS class was paper prototyping. This would require the students to create their game ideas physically. What I like about it is that it requires the students to focus on the mechanics of their game and the player experience goals, instead of the programming. However, I have found that students spend too much time on the aesthetics of their paper prototype and have trouble translating their gameplay to the physical world. If there was more time, I would certainly include physical prototypes.

It was also sometimes difficult to provide access to adequate technology. The schools may have computers that are older and lack the proper software/updates to allow students to create proper games and/or effectively interact with the guest speakers using videoconferencing software. Also, access to proprietary software can be very limited so that students could not work on their games at home.

It has proven difficult to fully create a community of practice that employs legitimate peripheral participation, as industry professionals are generally very busy with their jobs, and are unsure what their role is when interacting with students.

SOLUTIONS AND RECOMMENDATIONS

Before having the students meet with the presenters, I would ask them what kind of questions they would like to ask, and then have them elaborate on why they would ask a particular question. Then, I would give the presenters a list of the types of questions the students might ask, with the understanding that they could let the students know if they were not interested in answering the question, along with the answer of why not. This would give students a sense of an informational interview.

Finding female developers that are willing to speak to a class may be as simple as reaching out to online communities that employ LPP and mentorship, like DevChix (http://www.devchix.com/). These communities are devoted to help diversify the field through personal support, and are made of individuals who may not be reluctant to talk about the field to a class

To better unify the game design and programming aspects of the course, we are in the process of redesigning the curriculum so that the lesson on a specific programming concept was aligned with a related game design concept (e.g. we teach collision detection while we teach challenge). Teaching the elements of the same game throughout the week, for both design and programming, may prove to be helpful as well.

In order for the community of practice to work as legitimate peripheral participation, the guest speakers must be well integrated into the course design. Their interaction with the students should involve the relevant lesson at the time. It is important for them to have access to documentation of the interactions of previous presenters and to build upon those lessons. In addition, students should be prepared to present their work-in-progress to the guest speakers and to ask focused questions in order to generate critiques of what they are doing.

SUMMARY

Our game design courses engaged students, developed students' ability to collaborate and utilize critiques, and increased their knowledge of programming. We used game design and development as a platform for students to experiment with design and programming, and representatives from the industry helped them to delve deeper into these areas. We were quite surprised at how quickly students began to play with the ideas they learned and the innovative products they were able to produce. By acknowledging students' prior knowledge and interest in games, while integrating them into the game industry's community of practice, we followed John Dewey's advice that schools lessen their isolation through close contact with the business, academic, and cultural worlds (1915).

However, although the evidence is positive in respect with how much students are gaining in knowledge and interest, much more research needs to be done. First, I would like to more closely study if these types of interventions address the needs of minorities and women, two groups that are small in numbers in the programming community. I also hope to conduct further research with a much larger sample size of students. Furthermore, it remains to be seen whether these types of interventions result in students actually following through on a path toward a computer programming career, so I would like to develop a longitudinal study.

Finally, I believe the assessments in place could have been stronger. The students should be made aware of the rubrics and they should be employed throughout the course; i.e. each weekly game assignment should have a rubric attached. The knowledge pre- and post- test should focus less on vocabulary (e.g. "what is a variable?") and more on what the students actually learned in the course (e.g. how to write a script that would need a variable). I recorded audio of the students throughout the class to measure their use of programming vocabulary, but realized that once they were more skilled, they stopped asking questions using the vocabulary and started typing it, so I would no longer be able to hear once they grasped the concept. If I wanted to hear them using more programming language, I would have to have a structured time where there is a programming problem and I would need them to solve it aloud as a class.

NOTE

The contents of this chapter were developed under a grant, #P047M080103, from the Department of Education. However, those contents do not necessarily represent the policy of the Department of Education, and you should not assume endorsement by the Federal Government.

REFERENCES

Abraham, L. B., Morn, M. P., & Vollman, A. (2010). *Women on the Web: How women are shaping the internet*. comScore, Inc. Retrieved April 10, 2012, from http://www.iab.net/media/file/womenontheweb.pdf

Alexander, P. A. (1997). Mapping the multidimensional nature of domain learning: The interplay of cognitive, motivational, and strategic forces. In Maehr, M. L., & Pintrich, P. R. (Eds.), *Advances in motivation and achievement* (*Vol. 10*, pp. 213–250). Greenwich, CT: JAI Press.

Alexander, P. A. (2003). The development of expertise: The journey from acclimation to proficiency. *Educational Researcher, 32*(8), 10–14. doi:10.3102/0013189X032008010

Alexander, P. A., Jetton, T. L., & Kulikowich, J. M. (1995). Interrelationship of knowledge, interest, and recall: Assessing a model of domain learning. *Journal of Educational Psychology, 87*(4), 559. doi:10.1037/0022-0663.87.4.559

America's Best Colleges. (2011). Washington, DC. *U.S. News & World Report*.

Bayliss, J. D., & Strout, S. (2006). *Games as a "flavor" of CS1*. Paper presented at SIGCSE'06, Houston, Texas, USA.

Beck, K., Beedle, M., van Bennekum, A., Cockburn, A., Cunningham, W., & Fowler, M. Thomas, D. (2001). *Manifesto for agile software development*. Agile Alliance. Retrieved April 14, 2012, from http://agilemanifesto.org/

Biggers, M., Brauer, A., & Yilmaz, T. (2008). Student perceptions of computer science: A retention study comparing graduating seniors vs. CS leavers. *SIGCSE Bulletin, 40*(1), 402–406. doi:10.1145/1352322.1352274

Bransford, J., Brown, A. L., Cocking, R. R., & Educational Resources Information Center (U.S.). (1999). *How people learn: Brain, mind, experience, and school*. Washington, DC: National Academy Press.

Bureau of Labor Statistics. (2010). *Overview of the 2008-18 projections*. Washington, DC: Author. Retrieved February 13, 2012, from http://www.bls.gov/oco/oco2003.htm#occupation_d

Cheryan, S., Plaut, V. C., Davies, P. G., & Steele, C. M. (2009). Ambient belonging: How stereotypical cues impact gender participation in computer science. *Journal of Personality and Social Psychology, 97*(6), 1045–1060. doi:10.1037/a0016239

Dewey, J. (1915). *The school and society*. Chicago, Ill: The University of Chicago Press.

Fullerton, T. (2008). *Game design workshop: A playcentric approach to creating innovative games*. Amsterdam, The Netherlands: Elsevier Morgan Kaufmann.

Goodenow, C. (1993). Classroom belonging among early adolescent students: Relationships to motivation and achievement. *The Journal of Early Adolescence, 13*(1), 21. doi:10.1177/0272431693013001002

Hidi, S. (1990). Interest and its contribution as a mental resource for learning. *Review of Educational Research, 60*(4), 549–571.

Hidi, S., & Anderson, V. (1992). Situational interest and its impact on reading and expository writing. In Renninger, K. A., Hidi, S., & Krapp, A. (Eds.), *The role of interest in learning and development* (pp. 215–238). Hillsdale, NJ: Lawrence Erlbaum Associates.

Lave, J., & Wenger, E. (1991). *Situated learning: Legitimate peripheral participation*. Cambridge, UK: Cambridge University Press. doi:10.1017/CBO9780511815355

Lawless, K. A., & Kulikowich, J. M. (2006). Domain knowledge and individual interest: The effects of academic level and specialization in statistics and psychology. *Contemporary Educational Psychology, 31*(1), 30–43. doi:10.1016/j.cedpsych.2005.01.002

Lenhart, A., Jones, S., & Macgill, A. R. (2008). *Video games: Adults are players too*. Pew Internet and American Life Project. Retrieved April 12, 2012, from http://pewresearch.org/pubs/1048/

National Center for Education Statistics (NCES). (2010). *Degrees conferred by sex and race*. Retrieved April 12, 2012, from http://nces.ed.gov/fastfacts/display.asp?id=72

National Center for Women & Information Technology (NCWIT). (2009). *By the numbers*. Retrieved April 12, 2012, from http://www.ncwit.org/pdf/BytheNumbers09.pdf

O'Brien, V., Martinez-Pons, M., & Kopala, M. (1999). Mathematics self-efficacy, ethnic identity, gender, and career interests related to mathematics and science. *The Journal of Educational Research, 92*(4), 231. doi:10.1080/00220679909597600

Palaigeorgiou, G. E., Siozos, P. D., Konstantakis, N. I., & Tsoukalas, I. A. (2005). A computer attitude scale for computer science freshmen and its educational implications. *Journal of Computer Assisted Learning, 21*(5), 330–342. doi:10.1111/j.1365-2729.2005.00137.x

Parberry, I., Kazemzadeh, M. B., & Roden, T. (2006). *The art and science of game programming.* Paper presented at SIGCSE'06, Houston, Texas, USA.

Patten. (2008). *Final project - Creating a game in Scratch.* Retrieved from http://rubistar.4teachers.org/index.php?screen=ShowRubric&rubric_id=2063440&

Ross, J. (2007). Perhaps the greatest grand challenge: improving the image of computing. *Computing Research News, 19*(5). Retrieved February 12, 2012, from http://www.cra.org/resources/crn-archive-view-detail/perhaps_the_greatest_grand_challenge_improving_the_image_of_computing/

Trefry, G. (2010). *Casual game design: Designing play for the gamer in all of us.* Burlington, MA: Morgan Kaufmann.

Vygotsky, L. S. (1978). *Mind and society: The development of higher mental processes.* Cambridge, MA: Harvard University Press.

Williams, L. (2001). *Integrating pair programming into a software development process.* Paper presented at the Fourteenth Conference on Software Engineering Education and Training.

Zweben, S. (2011). *Taulbee survey report: 2009-2010.* Washington, DC: Computing Research Association.

ADDITIONAL READING

Boardgame Remix Kit. (n.d.). Retrieved from http://boardgame-remix-kit.com/

Create Compete Collaborate. (2009). Retrieved from http://www.createcompetecollaborate.org.uk/get_involved/wheels_of_glory.html

Fullerton, T., Swain, C., & Hoffman, S. (2008). *Game design workshop: A playcentric approach to creating innovative games.* Amsterdam, The Netherlands: Elsevier Morgan Kaufmann.

Gutnick, A. L., Bernstein, L., & Levine, M. H. (2011). *Always connected: The new digital media habits of young children.* New York, NY: The Joan Ganz Cooney Center at Sesame Workshop.

Kuruvada, P., Asamoah, D., Dalal, N., & Kak, S. (2010). *The use of rapid digital game creation to learn computational thinking.*

Rosenzweig, G. (2008). *ActionScript 3.0 game programming university.* Indianapolis, IN: Que.

Salen, K., & Zimmerman, E. (2003). *Rules of play: Game design fundamentals.* Cambridge, MA: MIT Press.

Scratch. (n.d.). Lifelong Kindergarten Group, MIT Media Lab. Retrieved from http://scratch.mit.edu

Trefry, G. (2010). *Casual game design: Designing play for the gamer in all of us.* Burlington, MA: Morgan Kaufmann.

KEY TERMS AND DEFINITIONS

Agile Software Development: A method of software development that is evolutionary in nature, depending on iterative processes that reveal an appropriate structure by which to organize and develop code (Kent et al., 2001).

Community of Practice: A group that engage in activities or discussions around a shared domain of interest in which they are all active practitioners (Lave & Wenger, 1991).

Individual Interest: A personal relationship between a person and a specific topic.

Legitimate Peripheral Participation (LPP): Interaction within a community of practice where newcomers are brought into the practices of the community by engaging in low-risk tasks that encourage communication with more senior members (Lave & Wenger, 1991).

Model of Domain Learning (MDL): A framework that delineates the path to expertise through knowledge, interest, and strategic processing (Alexander, 1997).

Pair Programming: A technique that employs two programmers working side-by-side at one workstation. Often used as part of agile software development, the structure encourages one programmer to write code while the other programmer observes and reviews. These roles can switch back and forth (Williams, 2001).

Situational Interest: The appeal an activity has for an individual, instead of the individual seeking out the activity because of his/her personal interest (Hidi & Anderson, 1992).

Virtual Learning Environment: An online site that facilitates interaction and discussion between peers, instructors, and mentors around specific material.

Section 5
Games for Teacher Education

Chapter 16
3D GameLab:
Quest-Based Pre-Service Teacher Education

Chris Haskell
Boise State University, USA

EXECUTIVE SUMMARY

Games and gaming constructs have emerged as a tantalizing and often provocative tool for instructional delivery. Methods and pedagogy for effectively employing games, like quest-based learning, as educational tools are developing. This chapter explores the use of game-based pedagogy for a pre-service teacher education course, as well the development of a quest-based learning management system (3D GameLab) to support the class. The chapter is grounded in design-based research, and discusses four phases of development and theory generation. In each of these phases, the quest-based learning management system, course curriculum, and game-based pedagogy were subject to the same iterative process to test and generate new theory toward game-based/quest-based learning.

INTRODUCTION

The purpose of this chapter was to identify the characteristics of attractive quest-based learning activities as evidenced by learner selection and completion. Guiding questions for this study included: (1) What characteristics are common in those quests most selected by students in a quest-based learning environment? (2) What characteristics are evident in those quests that are completed?

The following methods provided the strategy for answering this and the related research questions and provided rationale for the procedures that were used. These

DOI: 10.4018/978-1-4666-2848-9.ch016

methods also identify the participants used in the study and their characteristics, demographics, and sample orientation. The measures and instruments used are also clearly outlined and detailed.

Case Design

This case study utilized a quantitative research design to identify the characteristics of attractive quest-based learning. This was done by employing data-mining techniques and tools SAS Enterprise Miner version 6.2 using data captured from the 3-D GameLab learning management system. Fayyad, Piatetsky-Shapiro, & Smyth (1996a) offer data mining as a process of Knowledge Discovery in Databases (KDD) through (1) data selection, (2) data cleaning, (3) data transformation, (4) data mining, and (5) results evaluation and interpretation. This process was used to find quantitative evidence.

Characteristics of this quantitative research design included descriptive statistics. These descriptive statistics guided the process of data mining. This was done to identify patterns in the data that might not be otherwise observable. Analysis was focused on a large volume of LMS interactions collected from 98 students.

The survey instrument was validated using the SPSS. Martin (2010) submits that the use of un-validated instruments or techniques in the classroom is problematic. He suggests that evidence-based pedagogy and practice are critical. This is necessary to avoid what Yates (2005) describes as "illusory correlations and fundamental computational bias." In inferential statistics, many suggest that research producing strong reliable evidence should be conducted such that a high degree of importance is placed on effect size, statistical power, confidence intervals, reliability and validity coefficients, and a randomization where possible (Horn et al., 2009 ; Shelby & Vaske, 2008, Smith, Levine, & Lachlan, 2002; Zientek, Capraro, & Capraro, 2008). However, the whole data set was collected and analyzed, an inferential measure of reducing the error were not necessary (Fayyad, Piatetsky-Shapiro, & Smyth, 1996b).

Participants and Sample

The research was conducted using four face-to-face sections of an introductory educational technology course for pre-service teachers enrolled at a university in the northwest United States. The course focused on the use of productivity and Internet tools for teachers in a classroom setting. It provided practical skills and methodological/pedagogical strategies for the implementation of word processing, presentation, spreadsheet, and Internet technologies for teaching and learning. The course was offered as one of two pre-requisites for admission to upper-division education courses. For this reason, students often take it in their second year of undergraduate studies.

Course

The participants from this introductory educational technology course for pre-service teachers met twice weekly for 85 minutes during a16-week course in the Fall 2011 semester. The course used the 3-D GameLab Quest-based learning management tool that allowed students the opportunity to participate in as many as 66 quests in six categories: context (18), presentations (5), portfolio (9), spreadsheets (4), web tools (23), and word processing (7).

These educational quests were the basic units of progress within the larger scope of the quest-based curriculum (Barab & Dede, 2007) similar to assignments, projects, readings, and other educational interactions in traditional academic settings. Participants in this course selected activities from a pool of available quests. Each quest was also aligned to one of the primary curricular categories and corresponding International Society for Technology in Education National Educational Technology Standards for Teachers (ISTE NETS-T).

Each quest had an associated experience point (XP) value that contributed to an accumulating overall score. The XP value for each quest varied and was set by the instructor/course designer ranging from 10 to 100. Each student's XP accumulated toward a winning condition, a course completion of 2,000 points and submission of a completed portfolio of work. Unlike traditional assignments and activities that offer flexible grading, quests had fixed XP values, which were absolute. If students submitted a quest that did not fully meet the expectations, it was returned by the instructor with notes and modifications. Students could resubmit a quest as many times as was necessary to perfect it without penalty.

As student XP accumulated throughout the course, progress was gaged by advancement through 11 ranks (See Figure 1). Ranks were set at predetermined fixed intervals and served as prerequisites for many quests. Of the 65 quests available to students throughout the course, only seven were initially visible and selectable. All others were subject to prerequisites including ranks, quests, badges, and XP. The winning condition of the course was set at a completed portfolio and 2000+ XP for an A. Other grades were available at 1750+ (B), 1500+ (C), 1250 (D), and 1249 (F). The number of quests required to meet the winning condition varied ($\mu = 39.31$, SD = 2.51).

Class sessions were comprised of seven mandatory teacher-led full group quests, 10 optional teacher-led small group quests, and 21 student-directed open lab sessions. Because students in the EDTECH-202 course (See Figure 2) had the ability to choose their activities from multiple options, students pursued activities that

Figure 1. Screenshot of the back to school presentation quest from EDTECH-202

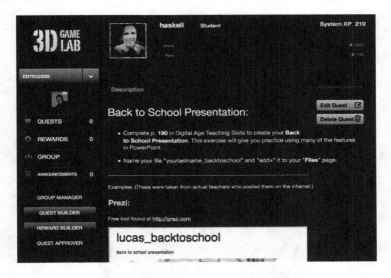

interested them the most. This student choice allowed for the testing of the attractive characteristics of the quests themselves.

Measures

Human Participants

This research was subject to the review of the Boise State University Institutional Review Board (IRB). In compliance with the Department of Health and Human Services (DHHS) regulations for research involving human participants, the IRB (Assurance Number: #FWA00000097; IORG0000591) reviews all research to protect the welfare and rights of human subjects who participate in research conducted at or through the university. All research involving human subjects conducted by researchers at the University must be reviewed by the IRB in compliance with Federal, state, and university regulations. The study was conducted entirely by using existing data mined from the 3-D GameLab learning management system and from the results of a technology use and proficiency survey titled, "Examining Preservice Teachers Technology Competencies" (Haskell & Pollard, 2008) used for course improvement. Before extracting or extrapolating any data, a research proposal was presented and approved by Boise State University IRB (#EX- 104-SB12-006) and is referenced in Appendix C.

Figure 2. Course Ranks for EDTECH-202

Security and Privacy

Preserving the privacy of research subjects is the first priority of the researcher. The 3D GameLab system has been designed to reflect guidelines set forth by the Family Educational Rights and Privacy Act (FERPA) and Children's Online Privacy Protection Act (COPPA). Compliance with these acts ensures that personal or identifiable student information is not unwittingly shared with other users or made public. All participants selected for the study are over the age of 18. Student identities have and will remain masked with a student-selected GamerTag (or nickname). Individual student experiences are detailed or highlighted in the reporting. The technology use and proficiency survey did produce personally identifiable information and only serves to provide general demographic and descriptive findings.

Procedure

The sample size for this study utilized the navigational and decision data of 98 participants enrolled in four sections of the introductory educational technology course for pre-service teachers. Due to the relatively small number of students participating in a specific treatment, all student navigational and decision data was included as a purposive sample (Godambe, 1978) thus avoiding the pitfalls of selection bias, Type-I (or II) error, or other inferential measurement errors.

Consent

Under the guidelines of the governing university institutional review board (IRB) and in compliance with Title 45, part 46, Protection of Human Subjects, research was conducted using existing data collected "in such a manner participants cannot be identified, directly or though identifiers linked to the participants" (Moreno, Caplan, & Wolpe, 1998; OHRP, 2009). Aligned with the Basic HHS Policy for Protection of Human Research Subjects (Federal policy for the protection of human subjects; notices and rules, 1991), existing data can be used provided that "research is conducted in established and commonly accepted educational settings, involving normal educational practices such as…research on regular instructional strategies." The research focused on the characteristics of the quests or activities that students interacted with, not the students individually. At no point were students identified as individuals. For these reasons, subject consent was not sought to use this information after the fact.

Instruments

The study utilized data previously collected from an instrument titled *Technology Proficiency and Use Survey* developed by Haskell and Pollard (2008) to provide demographic and technology fluency data of the sample population, but was not directly correlated to the data mining (Appendix A; Haskell & Pollard, 2008). The tool was originally developed to discern the characteristics of undergraduate preservice teacher candidates engaged in an introductory educational technology course. Data collected from the self-report online survey was used to develop a profile of the population students entering the pre-service course for teachers. It was designed to identify the following information:

- **Background:** Demographic data including gender, years out of high school, university academic program, teaching emphasis, and technology use in high school by application type.
- **Usage:** Weekly hours dedicated to specific technology-mediated interactions (e-mail, social networking, games, etc.).
- **Proficiency:** Self-reported skill in a broad range of technologies (file management, word processing, spreadsheets, etc.).

The instrument (Appendix A) used a 4-point scale (1 = often, 4 = never) to determine technology usage by type of respondents while in high school. The tool used 6-point scales (1 = none, 6 = 8-10 hours per week) that measure use of communication tools, gaming activities, and digital entertainment and leisure practices. It also used a 5-point scale (1 = no experience, 5 = very strong) that measures self-reported skill in file management, word processing, presentation software, spreadsheet software, Internet, Youtube, text chat, email, social networking, computer and console gaming, and others. This instrument was used to provide additional demographic, descriptive, and comparative data to supplement the data mining. The instrument has not been validated.

It is important to note that this instrument cannot be correlated to data mining results as it does not identify individuals. As such, it only provides an overview of the participant's profile.

Procedures

In order to accurately prepare the existing data for data mining prior to extraction, it was necessary to perform cleaning, coding, and organizing data in the 3-D GameLab system. This allowed for alignment of quest characteristics more amenable to effective analysis. The following procedures were necessary to prepare the data.

1. A taxonomy was developed and standardized that identified key quest types and characteristics.
2. 3-D GameLab quests tags were modified to include these characteristics.
3. Unnecessary or confusing tags were removed.

These procedures are outlined more specifically in the following sections.

Coding for Taxonomy

Coding quest types and characteristics to determine an educational quest taxonomy was performed. The purpose of this step was to code characteristics of quests for the purpose of tagging for analysis and data mining, which required uniformity. No such educational quest taxonomy was discovered. The coding scheme was developed using the educational taxonomy and learning object classification schemes adapted from Redeker (2003), McGreal (2004), and/or Wiley (2000) with those game-based taxonomies of Bateman and Nacke (2010) and Ashmore & Nitche (2007). This framework was not fully developed and needed to be supplemented and filled out at the beginning of the analysis phase of the study. It supported the identification and tagging of 5 primary areas for each quest.

1. What *Knowledge Objects* were present? Digital text, image, video, embedded object, etc., in three different categories: static, dynamic, and interactive (McGreal, 2004; Redeker, 2003; Wiley, 2000).
2. What organizational features were employed within the quest description? Headings, bullets, numbers, lines or separators, etc.
3. Is the quest goal-based or task-based (Sullivan et al., 2009)?
4. What digital tools can the student interact with (word processing, video production, animation, etc.)?
5. What is the deliverable (blog, document, presentation, no deliverable, etc.)?
6. Additional characteristics (Redeker, 2003).

Once the basic quest taxonomy was been adapted from the above, a systematic review of all quests in the targeted course was completed to determine if the quest taxonomy was sufficient to proceed to tagging. Once the comprehensive quest taxonomy was created, it was used to generate tags to the quests to assist in the data mining and analysis.

Digital Learning Objects

Wiley (2000) describes *digital learning objects* (DLO) as any digital resource that can be reused to support learning. They are small units of instructional components applicable to multiple learning contexts. Learning objects are also defined, not just as bundles of learning materials, but as "interactive web-based tools that support the learning of specific concepts by enhancing, amplifying, and/or guiding the cognitive processes of learners" (Kay & Knaack, 2008, p. 147). A DLO centered around the American civil rights movement might include knowledge units such as a news article about the Freedom Riders, Martin Luther King's "I have a dream" video, and an image of segregated drinking fountains, etc. Individually, these elements or *Knowledge Units* (or knowledge objects) can be applied to other courses of study like journalism, forensics, or photography (Redeker, 2003). Their value as learning objects is in their construction and application. A DLO can be constructed with individual or combinations of *Knowledge Units* (KU) that make up a single unit of study.

DLOs are stored in a digital, often web-based, repository and can be brought together to form lessons, activities, or units of instruction (McGreal, 2004). In this way, educational quests and DLOs are similar and can share classifications. For continuity, types of KUs adapted for the quest classification include small bits of text, digital images or photos, live data feeds (like stock tickers), live or prerecorded video or audio snippets, animations, and smaller web-delivered applications. These are defined below and detailed in Table 1.

Knowledge Units Types

Specific knowledge units were identified in the taxonomy and displayed in the quest tags. In future versions of the 3-D GameLab software, the system will likely identify these knowledge unit components and automatically tag them. Table 1 is a list of knowledge units originally identified by McGreal (2004) and supplemented to reflect emerging knowledge unit types and those observed in the 3D GameLab quests.

Organizational Elements

Identification of organizational characteristics provided insight into quest attractiveness. Fleming and Levie (1993) assert clearer visual organization as essential characteristics of effective instructional message design. A reasonable and open-text display supported by appropriate organizational characteristics serves to gain and maintain learner attention, and thus attractive design (Fleming & Levie, 1993). The following characteristics were added as tags to quests when present: Headings, bullets, numbers, accents (bold, italics, underline, strike through), procedures, and line/separator.

Tools Used by Students

Different digital tools can be attractive and engaging to different users (Wiley, 2000). Identification of these tools in quest tags served as an additional variable for attractiveness. Like knowledge types and organizational elements, tools used by students were listed in the tags of the quest in which they were found for the purpose of classification and data mining. Table 2 is a list of tools used in 3D GameLab.

Deliverable Type

Students may be attracted to different types of artifacts or interactions in quests or learning objects (Sullivan et al., 2009). For example, a quest that requires a participant to write a paper may be less attractive than one that requires the student to create a short video. Including these characteristics in a quest's tags allowed for classification and data mining. The quest tags often included more than one type. Deliverables were specifically identified from the following list in Table 3.

Table 1. Knowledge unit types

text	video desription*
image	video content
table	video tutorial*
hyperlinks	embedded object-static*
resource	embedded object-interactive*
example	narrative/role-play*

Note: *Indicates expansion of existing KU classification.

Table 2. Tools used by students

• apps store	• ARIS	• Blogger
• Google doc	• Google Site	• iPod touch
• Camtasia	• Cinch	• email
• games	• presentation software	• SmartBoard
• spreadsheet	• survey	• twitter
• video camera	• video production tools	• video streaming
• voicethread	• Voki	• Webquest
• webquest	• word processor	• word processor
• YouTube	• mobile device	• none

Task or Goal-Oriented Quests

Sullivan et al. (2009) described two distinct quest structures: task-based and goal-based. Task-based quests include an inflexible list of tasks designed to be completed in a specific order. Goal-based quests establish an objective with a clear end point and the student chooses how to complete it. A simple identification of task-oriented or goal-oriented disposition added to the quest tags allowed for classification and data mining to be performed. As such, the above described game-based approach was applied using the following two definitions adapted for the educational quest taxonomy.

- **Task-Based Quest:** A detailed list of procedures that produce a uniform product.
- **Goal-Based Quest:** Activities that provide an outline of the deliverable with freedom to embellish or create.

Table 3. Student deliverables

• account creation	• animated object	• blog posts
• Google doc	• Google Site	• iPod touch
• choice	• Cinch object	• cooperative product
• digital text	• document-stylized	• document-text
• embed/link	• embedded object	• evaluation
• participation	• presentation	• reflection
• spreadsheet	• video	• video walk-through
• VoiceThread participation	• Webpage	• wiki

Additional Data

In addition to the tag data described above, data about four other characteristics was also available. This data was automatically recorded through user interactions and was leveraged as additional dependent variables. They include the XP value of the quest, average time to complete (as reported by students), average user rating, and category. These values were included in the data set and used for categorization and data mining.

Later Research

Although considered for this original taxonomy, some areas of quest characteristics were removed. Wiley (2000) proposed that quests (or learning objects) are defined by depth of interaction. These areas were defined as fundamental, combined-closed, combined-open, generative-presentation, and others. In much the same way as Bloom's taxonomy, identification of quests as they relate to demonstrating higher order thinking skills proved problematic.

Redeker (2003) suggests identifying the learner's role in the classification of digital learning objects. This learner's role is respective to the interaction the learner will have. These primary areas include the learner's role as a receptive, internally interactive, and cooperative. While these were compelling ways of looking at these initial quests, difficulty in identifying these characteristics in both coding and identification by students make it problematic.

Quest Tags

All quests in the 3D GameLab system include a field for alphanumeric tags. This allows users to search for quests in the system by keywords. The quest tags in the study group have not been standardized to allow for appropriate analysis. Standardization of keywords is a critical step to ensure patterns are detectable in data mining (Fayyad, Piatetsky-Shapiro, & Smyth, 1996a). Using the coding of the quest taxonomy, all quests in the course system were tagged with the appropriate tags. All other descriptive tags were either made uniform or were removed. This prepared and cleaned the data for data mining.

Descriptive Analysis

As the 3D GameLab system records all actions, views, clicks, and user events, over 100,000 data records exist for the analysis. The statistical analysis software tool JMP SAS 9 and Enterprise Miner 6.2 were used to perform the majority of the analysis on the data collected in four primary areas: user profiling, quest profiling, survey results, and predictive modeling. User, quest, and activity data was collected from 3D GameLab within the date range of course activity.

The descriptive analysis included demographic data collected from both the 3D GameLab tool (age, occupation, location) and from the survey instrument (gender, teaching emphasis, technology skill, and practice). It is important to note, quest behavior data by student was not correlated to results from the survey because the instrument does not collect identity. Additional group and user behaviors are described in Chapter 4, including login frequencies, total XP earned, quest related XP vs reward XP, quests completed, quests dropped or left unfinished, average time reported, as well as badges, awards, and achievements earned.

Quest data was also described, including average and range of XP, average completion time, user rating, category, completed, not completed, dropped, and average completion window. Using an algorithm described below, quest-specific data supported the creation of multiple attractiveness scores, which combined with tag data to determine attractive characteristics.

Data Mining

Data mining is a technique ideal for identifying pathways to success and failure within a system of many complex decisions (Fayyad, Piatetsky-Shapiro, & Smyth, 1996c) and is ideally suited for analysis of large quantities of data. The data mining was performed using statistical analysis SAS Enterprise Miner version 6.2. It illuminated student participation patterns and associations. Behavioral inferences were drawn from meta-patterns related to what they viewed and how long as well as which quests were attempted, completed, or dropped, in that order. Recordable behaviors in the 3D GameLab system are listed in Table 4.

Table 4. Detectable behaviors

Click/View Dispositions (recorded by system)	Explanation
Add quest feedback	Submitting a quest for approval (text is required)
Browse groups	Looking at groups that are available to join
Comment on a quest attempt	Leaving a public comment available to other users
Drop a quest attempt	Removing a quest from the users "in progress" list
Expanded a quest to view more info	Expanding a quest to view more info
List quests in group	Selecting "Quests" button showing all "available", "in progress", and completed quests
Load quest feedback form	Clicking the "Complete" button in an active quest
Quest submitted for approval	Finalizing the quest submission process
Start a new quest attempt	Selecting the "Start Quest" button
Switch to group	Switching to a group the user belongs to
Updated a student	Saving edits to a users playercard and account details
View a group's announcements	Viewing group announcements
View a quest's details	Viewing an "in progress" quest
View group dashboard	Selecting the "group" button.
View playercard	Selecting the "GamerTag" to view student playercard
View quest attempt	Selecting and viewing a "completed" quest
View reward	Selecting a reward from the rewards page to show details
View rewards	Selecting the "reward" button
Viewed an announcement marking it read	Selecting and viewing an individual announcement

Navigational pattern analysis was also conducted using sequential association rules to analyze the activity logs. Path analysis was conducted to show the relationship between key behaviors. Table 5 shows the specific analysis applied to each research question.

Predictive modeling was conducted using several analyses. Decision trees were used to predict a student performance under similar circumstances (Fayyad, Piatetsky-Shapiro, & Smyth, 1996a). Decision trees (by anonymous individuals and groups) were generated using dependent variables, including frequency of login, XP, number of attempts, returned quests (failed attempts), success rate, individual quest completion time, rewards, quest characteristics, quest rating, demographic factors, and other variables.

Table 5. Research questions and analysis techniques

Research Question	Analysis	Data Sets/Variables
1. What are the characteristics of educational quests as they currently exist?	Descriptive statistics and cluster analysis	Quest details and Tags
2. What is the taxonomy of quest characteristics (including combinations) currently used in the test group?	Descriptive statistics and cluster analysis	Quest details and Tags
3. What different types of quest construction (goals, activities, context, deliverable, organization) exist?	Descriptive statistics and cluster analysis	Quest details and Tags
4. What combinations of variables produce more attractive quests visible through learner selection, completion and rating?	Descriptive, classification, clustering, segment profiling, regression, text-mining	Quest details, tags, Attraction score, interest score, success score, completion score, user comments
5. Based on qualitative and quantitative measures, which design variables are most likely to contribute to the attractiveness of a quest, and thus, learner selection, completion and rating?	Descriptive, classification, clustering, segment profiling, regression, text-mining	Quest details, tags, Attraction score, interest score, success score, completion score, user comments

Quantifying Attractiveness

In an effort to determine what attractive variables or characteristics exist in educational quests, it was necessary to determine if, in fact, they were quantifiably attractive to the student or not. The study identified the characteristics that lead a student to "select" a quest. While initial attraction might be valuable in selecting some quests, as the student selects more quests, additional factors likely contributed to the selection of future quests. Three significant events occurred within the 3D GameLab system that helped to identify whether or not a quest was attractive to the user. Distinct decisions were made by the user and recorded by the system that helped to determine attractiveness as follows:

1. **Interest:** After viewing the quest details, did the student start the quest?
2. **Completion:** After starting the quest, did the students complete, drop, or leave the quest unfinished?
3. **Experience:** After completing the quest, how did the student rate it?

Quantifying interest alone was likely not enough to determine overall attractiveness. It was possible that the initial student interest could be high because of certain characteristics (i.e., embedded video, opportunity for collaboration, etc.). However, if the student failed to complete the quest because it proved difficult, uninteresting, or otherwise unmanageable, this would not be reflected in its "attractiveness." Furthermore, it is reasonable to assume that the student would be less likely to engage in a similar type of quest in the future. Since the purpose of the research is ultimately to identify characteristics of attractive quest-based learning, quantifying the interest (at the point of selection) and completion experience is required. Use of the students selected user rating served as a descriptive element.

After thorough research, no studies were uncovered that combined the elements necessary to utilize an instrument for quantifying the attractiveness of educational quests. The following was selected as a method for combining all three phases into a single attractiveness score.

For the purposes of this study, overall quest "attractiveness" is defined as the operational relationship of three components: capturing one's interest, sustaining one's effort, and resulting in a meaningful, personally relevant (highly rated) learning experience (See Figure 3). By this definition, it is possible to quantitatively characterize the student experience through the use of recordable variables.

Interest can be quantified by students viewing and choosing quests. In the system, students could view a list of available quests that show the quest icon image, quest name, XP, average time, user rating, category, and due date if applicable (Figure 4).

Users could "click" on an individual quest to see an expanded view of an individual quest that includes a short description, tags, public comments, and the ability to start the quest (Figure 5). This additional information may compel a student to start the quest or dissuade from proceeding.

As navigational and decision-making data was recorded by the 3-D GameLab system, the number of times each quest was *expanded* vs. *started* by each user was mined from the system and a value created for comparison. Rather than a ratio, a conversion percentage was generated and expressed as a decimal value. This value was used so that it could be averaged with the other points of attraction. The formula for calculating interest is found in Figure 6.

Figure 3. Quest attractiveness diagram

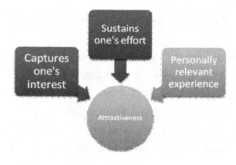

3D GameLab

Figure 4. 3D GameLab available quest menu

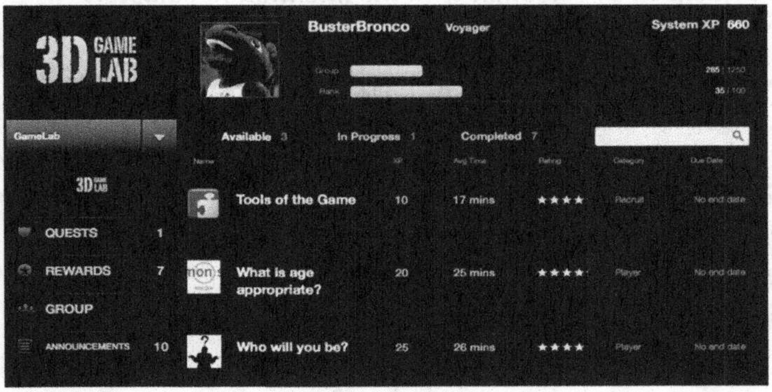

Figure 5. Expanded quest view in 3-D GameLab quest menu

The attractiveness of a quest was also quantified by its ability to hold the student's interest. Thus, sustaining one's efforts can be quantified by quest *completion*. 3D GameLab recorded each occurrence of quests being selected, dropped, or left unfinished. This was quantified using the formula in Figure 7 and stated as a conversion percentage expressed as a decimal value.

User rating also served as a possible way to quantify meaningful and personally relevant learning experiences. At the completion of a quest, students are asked to rate the quest using a five-star system (Lowest = 1 star, highest = 5 stars). The students also reported completion time for the purpose of an aggregated average completion time visible to other users and comments available to potential users (Figure 8).

Figure 6. Formula for quantifying quest "interest" or the initial attractiveness of the quest as evidenced by selection with the intention to complete

$$\text{Interest} = \frac{\text{Quest Started}}{\text{Quest Expanded View}} = \text{(i.e.)} .454$$

Figure 7. Formula for quantifying quest "completion" or the attractiveness of the quest as evidence by its completion

$$\text{Completion} = \frac{\text{Quest Completed}}{\text{Quest Started}} = \text{(i.e.)} .812$$

The user experience cannot be expressed in the same way a conversion %. It is an average of values selected between one and five. In order to express it similarly, as value between .001 and 1, it was necessary to divide the average user rating by the possible rating of 5 as seen in Figure 9.

It was proposed that the average of these three attraction values could lead to an overall attractiveness score representing all three phases of student interaction with the quest. These are outlined in Table 6.

While these areas of attraction proved initially promising to generate an overall attractiveness score, concerns about inconsistencies in user rating yielded a comprehensive attractiveness score including only selection and completion. This is referenced and detailed in Chapter 4.

Figure 8. Quest completion and rating screen

Figure 9. Formula for quantifying quest "experience" or attractiveness of the quest as evidenced by user rating

$$\text{Completion} = \frac{\text{User Rating}}{\text{Rating Possible (5)}} = (\text{i.e.}).812$$

Text Mining

The final step of the analysis was text mining (Baker & Yacef, 2009). Tan (1999, N.P.) describes text mining or text data mining as "knowledge discovery from textual databases" and refers to the process of "extracting interesting and non-trivial patterns or knowledge from text documents." It was applied to analyze ratings and text comments of individual quests as well as high, medium, and low rated quests. The Gini gain formula was used which can determine parameters for ratings. Text mining analysis was applied to areas of quest tags, users generated comments, and users question submissions.

Results and Implications

This section organizes and delivers the results of the data analysis explicitly while using the primary guiding research questions as a framework. The primary research questions that guided this study included: 1) What characteristics are common in those quests most selected by students in a quest-based learning environment?, 2) What characteristics are present in those quests that are completed?, and 3) What characteristics exist in quests more highly rated by students?

Table 6. Formulas for the areas of attraction

Area of Attractiveness	Formula	Evidenced By
Capturing one's interest	$= \dfrac{\text{Quest Started}}{\text{Quest Expanded View}}$	Selection
Sustaining one's effort	$= \dfrac{\text{Quest Completed}}{\text{Quest Started}}$	Completion
Personally relevant learning experience	$= \dfrac{\text{User Rating}}{\text{Rating Possible (5)}}$	User Rating
Overall attractiveness	Average of all three	Average of all three

These questions were investigated by studying quests designed in the 3-D GameLab quest-based learning platform and were restricted to those characteristics that could be controlled and quantified. Primary guiding questions related to the overarching research question are listed below.

Guiding Question #1

The research was able to answer primary guiding question: (1) What are the characteristics of educational quests as they currently exist in the 3D GameLab? Quest analysis, that utilized new and a priori coding, produced 73 separate characteristics in 5 categories: Knowledge objects (14), organizational features (6), goal-based/task-based (2), digital tools (28), and deliverables (23).

The most common characteristics used in knowledge object construction included text (in 65 quests), hyperlinks (32), and video tutorials (12). Organizational characteristics of quests included accents like bold, italicized, or underlined text (40), section headings (37), and bullets and numbering (31). The combination of these two categories of characteristics created a uniform design, with many quests displaying a similar visual layout.

More than two thirds of the quests followed the task-based design principle, which focuses on a specific set of detailed procedural instructions to yield a specific product. 45 of the 66 quests selected for this analysis were task-based. The remaining 21 quests were identified as goal-based, which describe a general final product without explicit instructions (McGreal, 2004). Goal-based quests allow for student freedom and creativity (Charsky, 2010; Sullivan & Mateas, 2009).

A number of digital tools were employed in quest design that participants interacted with. The most commonly occurring of these tools were Google Sites (22), blogger (11), spreadsheets (9), word processors (8), and games (7). Participants also had the opportunity to interact with other web-based digital productivity and creativity tools including Voki, Voicethread, Youtube, Vimeo, Skype, uStream, Animoto, Cinch, and others.

Quests included a broad range of student deliverables, or product options. The most common were reflections (16), various forms of digital text including blog posts (13), embedded or linked objects (7), and other digital documents including spreadsheets, presentations, videos, etc. In all, 23 different deliverable types were available.

The implications of these findings show that the characteristics of quest-based learning design include a relatively broad set of variables. Rather than relatively minimal set of characteristics, the quests utilized in this study contained a variety of media, design, tools, and deliverables.

As such, it is possible for quest-based design to offer flexibility to both teacher and learner based on need, mandate, and/or preference. While the guiding question was to determine the breadth of these characteristics to identify variables for data mining, an unintended realization was that quest-based design can offer a wide variety of choices and combinations. This can contribute to the attractiveness.

Guiding Question #2

After identifying what characteristics existed, the research was able to identify commonly occurring characteristics to support the identification of a taxonomy. The research was able to address and answer question (2), What is the taxonomy of quest characteristics (including combinations) currently used in the test group? A total of eight taxonomic clusters were reported as a result of cluster analysis. These clusters are detailed below.

Cluster 1: (N=10 quests, 15% of total quests) Was comprised of quests where students interacted with the game and reflected on that experience using a blog. Quest designs and layouts consistently utilized headings and bullets, among other design elements.

Cluster 2: (N=2, 3%) Included only text, images, accents, and hyperlinks and asked the student to produce a text-based product.

Cluster 3: (N=3, 5%) Used VoiceThreads as a means of both interaction and deliverable.

Cluster 4: (N=10, 15%) Focused on the creation of portfolio elements utilizing digital text in their Google Site portfolio page.

Cluster 5: (N=7, 11%) Were tutorial and procedure-based quests to assist students in developing stylized spreadsheets.

Cluster 6: (N=18, 27%) Included text content, resources, videos, and other embedded objects to information didactically. These quests were all found in the Context category.

Cluster 7: (N=10, 15%) Was associated with the creation of word processor documents.

Cluster 8: (N=6, 9%) Utilized presentation software to both learn about and create presentations.

Although many quests contained unique characteristics, all fit into one of these taxonomic clusters. Analysis of these clusters show that #4 and #6 were the most attractive while #7 and #8 were the least attractive to students. The characteristics of these taxonomic clusters and their attractiveness based on detailed analysis will be discussed as they relate to guiding questions 4 and 5. All implications associated with these clusters and their attractiveness will be addressed in that section.

Guiding Question #3

Originally, the hope was to differentiate the taxonomies further with guiding question 3), What different types of quest construction (goals, activities, tools, deliverable, organization) exist? However, guiding question #1 and #2 provided the necessary data to understand the types of quests, characteristics, taxonomy, and quest construction that existed within the sample set. The research and subsequent data mining and analysis sufficiently rounded out the understanding in this area.

Guiding Questions #4 and #5

The final two guiding questions address the variables of attractive quests design. The research contributed to the answer of question 4), What combinations of variables produce more attractive quests visible through learner selection, completion, and rating? It also provided evidence for question 5), Based on qualitative and quantitative measures, which design variables are most likely to contribute to the attractiveness of a quest, and thus, learner selection, completion and rating? As they are related, answers to both guiding questions are paired below.

Task-Based Design is More Attractive

Attractive quest design favors a task-based design approach in that students are more likely to select quests that offer a clear path to completion. The data showed that task-based quests were more attractive than the goal-based quests by being more likely to capture the students interest and sustain their efforts to completion. Task-based quests contained tutorial videos, step-by-step instruction, and utilized procedural content.

Students rated the goal-based quests more highly, however. Because of the nature of the 5-star rating system, it is unclear whether this score is indicative of quest design, tools used, deliverable type, goal-based/task-based design, or any number of other variables. A quest pool that contains both task-based and goal-based versions of quests might be a valuable future consideration.

Further text mining and decision tree analysis in this area might yield additional tags and characteristics of task-based and goal-based quest design worthy of investigation. The depth of this study did not allow for a more direct comparison or clustering by participant. The possibility exists that certain participants might favor goal-based over task-based quests. These patterns were not available in this research design.

Quests Contributing to the Final Product Are Attractive

Interactions suggest that participants were attracted to quests related to portfolio creation, which served as the final product of the course. These quests were built around the creation of pages for a personal learning portfolio utilizing Google Sites. Each quest asked students to produce digital texts and reflections using the wiki features of the site.

Quests associated with the portfolio were clustered with those of high interest (HI) and high completion (HC). These HI-HC pair clusters containing quests include "Reflection: Fundraiser Spreadsheet," "Reflection: Standards Update," "Portfolio: Future Goals," "Portfolio: Role of Technology," "Social Software Webpage," "Reflection: M&M Spreadsheet," and "Portfolio: About Me." In fact, all quests in the "Portfolio" category were presented in the HI cluster and all but 2 in the HC cluster. The remaining two were in the MC cluster, both were reflection quests. None of the Portfolio category quests were included in either the LI or LC clusters.

The implications are that educational quests that are connected directly to a final product are attractive both in high initial interest and high completion scores. Quests that might be viewed by students as clearly representing progress toward the winning condition, as "jewels in a crown," may be more attractive.

Embedded Video Doesn't Automatically Make Quests Attractive

While some of the most attractive quests did contain embedded video, even more quests with mid to low attraction scores also contained embedded video. The characteristic of embedded video alone did not lead to quantifiable student attraction. While embedded video may support attractive quest design, other characteristics related to the video may also impact attractiveness.

The study had no way to identify or catalogue the quality, length, or number of video elements embedded in a single quest. It is possible that a single, high impact, professionally produced video would be more attractive than a number of variable combinations of video design and implementation. It is also possible that different types of video content might be attractive to different students. This could be a compelling area of future research in quest-based learning design.

Web Tools Are Attractive

Students selected quests that utilized unique web tools like VoiceThread, Cinch, Prezi, Voki, iPod touch, uStream, Blogging, Aris, and other web-based and app-based productivity and creativity tools. However, not all of the quests that were quickly and easily selected were completed with the same regularity. Many continued to be attractive after selection while others were not. The study showed the use of Web-based tools including those that are novel, interactive, embedded, or visually appealing can influence the initial attractiveness of an educational quest. But utilizing web tools does not assure the quest will remain attractive and compelling to students through completion.

Although the study design did not allow for differentiation of Web-based tool characteristics beyond tags, possible explanations for why some web tools lacked attractiveness through completion exist. It is possible that some participants found the Web-based tools initially attractive but difficult to use or understand. Experience with these types of web-based applications may also impact their attractiveness through completion as students may have a schema that can support their implementation and use.

Word Processing and Spreadsheet Quests May Be Less Attractive

Completion scores for word processing and spreadsheet related quests were lower than other categories. Tag cluster analysis showed other tools were more attractive to users. Independent of other quests, it is possible that these tools and their related quests would be attractive. However, in a learning environment where students may choose between activities, these were less attractive.

Other tools deemed more attractive by this comparison include video games, wikis, blogs, web-based presentation software, and web-based animation tools. Although these tools were not individually identified or clustered as part of the cluster analysis, they were present in many of the quests identified as more attractive through the analysis.

Comments Predict Attractiveness

Quest with higher numbers of user comments were more attractive by completion score. One implication is that attractive quest activities elicit more positive feedback and those that were less attractive did not. This information can be valuable to teachers and designers as formative evaluation in addition to user rating and comments. One implication is that it may be possible to utilize this information and data value in an algorithm, which draws attention to the quest beyond simple performance. Teachers and designers may benefit from an early warning to potential attractiveness of a quest. If necessary, an intervention could be put in place to increase the attractiveness of the quest.

Shorter Quests Garner More Interest

Decision tree analysis demonstrated that quests with a lower student reported completion time were more attractive in terms of initial interest. Quests averaging lower than 49 minutes in average completion time were more attractive than those that took longer. As a predictor of interest score, these results are instructive and offer meaningful inferences.

First, implications of these results offer a pedagogical consideration useful in the design of new curriculum. Designing quests that can be completed in shorter amounts of time are more attractive. Higher initial attractiveness is beneficial to students by increasing motivation. Teachers and designers who focus on shorter, more compact quests should see higher learner interest.

Second, these implications extend beyond the development of new curriculum. These findings also suggest one possible approach to revamping existing, possibly lower performing, quest-based curriculum. Quests that are larger could be broken into smaller, calibrated slices. These quests could then be organized in a short "pearl-chain." In this way, existing curriculum could be slightly modified to make it more attractive in terms of initial interest. Layered with other considerations, this initial interest could support overall attractiveness and effectiveness of an educational quest.

Importance of Findings

These findings are important for the advancement of our understanding of quest-based learning design. As previously referenced, student engagement is critical in the successful implementation of a curriculum (Ames, 1992; Boekaerts, 1997; Bronack et al., 2006; Dede, 2009; Eccles & Wingfield, 2002; Papert, 1998; Vaughn & Horner, 1997). Failure to attract a learner impacts student motivation and performance negatively. This section outlines the importance of these findings in terms of a student-centered focus, pedagogical considerations, and development potential of algorithms and other computer-based feedback systems.

Focuses Design on Learner Attraction

A thorough review of this research should highlight to readers the importance of a student-centered approach to quest-based curriculum design. The ways in which learners interact with quests and learning activities has a direct effect on their like-liness to select and complete them. As such, student success is influenced by an individual students attraction to learning activities.

Although there is much that can still be gleaned from this and future research, savvy teachers and designers of quest-based curriculum would do well to consider how it will be received by their students. One of the broad important findings of this research is that quest attraction influences student success in varying degrees. Designing curriculum predicated on student choice, using a quest-based approach, requires the consideration of student experience and learner attraction to quests.

Pedagogical Considerations

This research identifies the first known set of pedagogical considerations specific to quest-based learning. While not complete, these suggestions, recommendations, and approaches served to inform a growing community of quest-based learning teachers and designers. These pedagogical considerations inform the types of tools that may be more attractive to users. They identify types of media that may be effective in the construction of attractive quests including suggestions for methods to prevent it from becoming unattractive. This research provides descriptions of quest design as it exists in an active, successful curriculum. These details can be useful to designers in the development or modification of their own coursework.

Development Potential of Algorithms

As the system used to deliver quest-based learning is digital, these findings could serve to inform and instruct the development of algorithms to provide meaningful feedback in several areas.

Utilizing the results of the study, algorithms could be developed to predict student success based on the types of quests they individually find more attractive. Based on these results, algorithms could be designed to suggest quests to students based on their characteristics and various profiles created by student interactions. An individual student's interest score, completion score, and quest characteristics could be used to tailor quest content to create an approach to computer-mediated, differentiated instruction.

Algorithms could also be developed to monitor and influence quest success. Using results of this research, it would be possible to develop processes that would look for low performing characteristics. A quest-based system could then identify at-risk quests and possibly suggest pedagogical interventions to teachers and designers.

Potential Areas of Future Study

Characteristics of students who frequently drop quests might be a valuable area of future investigation. As referenced in Chapter 4, an average numbers of dropped quests indicate relative satisfaction. However, a number of outliers demonstrated a different experience. Investigating the behaviors, attitudes, dispositions, and outcomes of students who drop a high volume of quests may contribute to the understanding of effective quest-based learning design. Detailed user decision records would be necessary to conduct this research. Understanding this outlier behavior could be instructive and benefit all students.

Utilization of organizational characteristics like accents, section headings, and bullets and numbering may decrease the completion time of the quest by providing students a quest-based learning object that is less confusing. This research was not designed to answer this question but implications from other areas of attractive quest design suggest this possibility. A comparative study with several instructional message design principles applied to quest design could yield more knowledge in this area. As such, researchers could consider organizational elements and its effect on completion time and user rating in the future.

Text mining of user comments could also be a potential direction for future research related to user experience. While possible in the study, specific focus was paid to the quantitative results of user experience while the qualitative was set aside. Combining these in a mixed methods approach, utilizing text-mining strategies, may be a consideration for future investigation.

Goal-Based vs. Task-Based Quests

One of the more intriguing areas for potential future research revolves around the results of goal-based and task-based quests. Task-based quests were identified as more attractive based on their combined interest and completion scores. These quests directed participants to complete a highly specific task, often with detailed step-by-step instructions, to produce an explicit product. Although these quests allowed for some personalization of the product, the outcomes were predetermined. Task-based quests yielded a higher interest and completion score compared to goal-based quests.

Despite the high quantifiable attractiveness of task-based quests, goal-based quests yielded a higher average user rating (4.63, +.25). Although user decision data indicated higher attractiveness for task-based quests, user rating fails to support this conclusion. A possible reason for this difference could include that quests that outlined a specific path to completion were initially more attractive but those that allowed for more creativity, choice, or less restrictive completion guidelines were, in the final analysis, more compelling or perhaps personally relevant and meaningful.

Another possible explanation is that a clear path to a specific outcome appears "easier" and thus less restrictive. Although an open, goal-based, outcome might be offer fewer restrictions, it does implicitly mandate creativity. It is possible that students viewed the need to be creative as "harder" than activities that mandated the steps. As previously stated, this may be a valuable area for future consideration.

It is important to note that user rating is not specifically an indication of popularity, preference, or quality. Users were not provided a rubric of how to rate request. Thus, reasons associated with rating are determined by the user. Future research could look at user rating more explicitly. Rather than an open ended, nondescript user rating, the system could direct students to rate specific characteristics of quests to help differentiate or explain these findings.

After the Winning Condition

As previously stated, the winning condition of the course being studied was 2,000 XP and a completed portfolio. Despite a clear and finite course completion, more than half of all students continued to complete quests. In fact, 55% of students who reached the winning condition submitted 200 XP or more worth of quests.

Several questions emerge about this phenomenon. Future research would do well to investigate the characteristics of quests selected by participants after they have reached the winning condition. Do students continue to complete quest because they are selecting activities they are interested in? Do they continue for competitive reasons? Understanding why students continue to complete quests when no longer compelled by the requirements of the curriculum could lead to more attractive and meaningful quest and curriculum design.

Differences by Demographics

Because demographic data was only used to describe the participants and not leveraged against the decision data, results of data mining were not differentiated by individual users. As such, the research design did not enable organization of findings by individual, gender, age, race, or other distinguishing participant characteristics. Future research would do well to include participant demographics for consideration in the data mining and analysis.

Continued research in the attractiveness of educational quest design could explore potential differences based on these demographic details. Do participants in different age groups find certain quests more or less attractive? Are the characteristics of attractive quest design different for men and women? As data mining and analysis is a powerful tool for identifying patterns not otherwise visible, utilizing demographic data as part of the process could serve to improve our understanding.

Differences by Technology Proficiency

Participants completed a technology proficiency survey at the beginning of the course for demographic description and course improvement. It may be possible to leverage this data to create a unique user technology proficiency profile. Individual preferences, tendencies, and aversions may influence the attractiveness of certain types of quests. Future research could consider a student's technology proficiency profile in the data mining and analysis.

This line of research could give way to the development of unique and meaningful algorithms leveraging student interest, quest attractiveness (by learner), and proficiency to direct or recommend quests and learning activities ideally suited to the individual. Similar algorithms could also serve to provide the instructor or designer with information about the alignment, or goodness of fit, between curriculum and learner.

Quest Load

Another potential area of future research could delve into the area of quest load. In the current quest-based delivery structure, it is possible for students to have large numbers of quests available to choose from. While the design attempted to make no more than 5 to 10 quests available at any one time, based on a user's individual path it was possible for as many as 21 quest to be available at a given time.

Natural questions arise: do large numbers of quests affect the attractiveness? Do too many quests results in loss of novelty? Future research could consider comparisons of available quests in attractiveness. For example, of the seven quests that were available, which characteristics were evident in those selected versus not selected?

As the results of decision tree analysis showed, user comments left at quest completion lead to positive outcomes. High completion score is predicted by high numbers of student comments. One potential implication of this finding is that the system could prompt users of low performing quests, as evidenced by low comments, to answer the question "How could this quest be improved?" Identifying quests early by their low performing characteristics could serve to inform instructors and designers of curriculum. Acting on this knowledge, curriculum could be modified, enhanced, improved, or removed to improve the overall quest-based educational experience.

Using the results of this analysis, algorithms could be constructed within the system to allow it to look for and identify low-performing quests as evidenced by these predictors. Automated messages, in the form of a pop-up comment box, could collect information from the user and deliver it anonymously to the teacher or designer. This formative evaluation could serve as a real-time intervention to low performing or at risk quests.

Learning Analytics

This research may serve to inform designers of quest-based learning analytics by developing profiles of both the user and quest characteristics. Identifying an individual's experience, preferences, tendencies, and gaps in knowledge and ability represents an exciting potential area of future research. Developing learning analytics and subsequent algorithms would be a valuable next step.

This could indicate a number of broadly different things including either dissatisfaction with quest options or use of the drop feature as a means of organizing ones workload. The data does not offer a clear explanation for this difference nor suggest inferences to cause. For this reason, dropped quests will not be specifically characterized as less attractive on this data alone.

Other Considerations

This section addresses the possible explanations of the research design and explores possible alternate explanations for some findings. Similar to previously identified limitations, the following could influence the direction of future research.

Although the age of the participants varied, the majority of students were near 20 years of age. The characteristics of this group may have limited or focused the results. Attributes, habits, and attitudes of young adult students may not be consistent with that of other age groups.

The participant group was composed primarily of college education majors, a unique group of individuals. As these students had completed more than 12 years of school, the expectations, interests, and motivations may be different from other users of quest-based course materials and design. Different subjects my have yielded different results. If the study had been conducted using middle school students, high school students, or other college majors, those groups may have identified with different attractive variables, although the diversity of teaching disciplines (English, Science, Music, etc.) may have had the same effect.

Depending on the progress and path of each individual, it is possible to have between 1-20+ quests available for selection at any one time. If the quest load is larger, it's possible that students may inspect large numbers of quests to select the most attractive. The larger the number of available quests, the more previewing or expanding of available quests may take place. This creates more quest expansions recorded by the system influencing the quest attractiveness score. Attractiveness scores, specifically for interest, for quests at certain high quest load points during the course may be influenced.

Certain points may also exist within the course where the quest load is higher for all participants, thus increasing the possibility that quests that appear within a certain XP or rank range are more likely to register a higher number of quests expansions, a critical variable for calculating quest interest. For example, when students reach the rank "Learner 3" an additional 10 quests are made available and visible. If a student has 10 or more available quests before this point, the number of possible quests to select from doubles.

In the same way quest interest score may be influenced by quest load and other factors, quest completion may be influenced by factors within the organization of the course. As students approach and reach the winning condition, quests that were attractive at the point of selection are no longer needed to complete the course. While some students may complete these previously selected quests, others may not. The decision to abandon or drop selected quests would have less to do with their overall attractiveness and more to do with need. Attractiveness scores, specifically for completion, for quests that become available near the end of the course may be influenced.

Finally, future research should consider the experience of individual students rather than just that of the whole group when possible. This research focused on the mean without consideration of standard deviation as a method for looking at diversity of experience. Future research designs would do well to consider and prepare to report the possibility of outlier experiences.

REFERENCES

Aarseth, E. (2004). Beyond the frontier: Quest games as post-narrative discourse. In Ryan, M. L. (Ed.), *Narrative across media*. University of Nebraska Press.

Achterbosch, L., Pierce, R., & Simmons, G. (2007). Massively multiplayer online role-playing games: The past, present, and future. *Computers in Entertainment, 5*(4).

Ames, C. (1992). Classrooms: Goals, structures, and student motivation. *Journal of Educational Psychology, 84*, 261–271. doi:10.1037/0022-0663.84.3.261

Amory, A. (2007). Game object model version II: A theoretical framework for educational game development. *Educational Technology Research and Development, 55*(1), 51–77. doi:10.1007/s11423-006-9001-x

Anderson, C. A. (2003). Violent video games: Myths, facts, and unanswered questions. *Psychological Science Agenda: Science Briefs, 16*(5), 1–3.

Annetta, L. A., Minogue, J., Holmes, S. Y., & Cheng, M. T. (2009). Investigating the impact of video games on high school students' engagement and learning about genetics. *Computers & Education, 53*(1), 74–85. doi:10.1016/j.compedu.2008.12.020

Antonacci, D. M., & Modaress, N. (2008). Envisioning the educational possibilities of user-created virtual worlds. *AACE Journal, 16*(2), 115–126.

Ashmore, C., & Nitche, M. (2007). The quest in a generated world. *Proceedings of the 2007 Digital Games Research Association. (DiGRA) Conference: Situated Play*, (pp. 503-509). Tokyo, Japan.

Astley, R. (Performer). (1987). *Never gonna give you up* [Web]. Retrieved from http://www.youtube.com/watch?v=dQw4w9WgXcQ

Baek, Y. K. (2010). *Gaming for classroom-based learning: Digital role playing as a motivator of study*. Hershey, PA: IGI Global. doi:10.4018/978-1-61520-713-8

Baker, R. S. J. D., & Yacef, K. (2009). The state of educational data mining in 2009: A review and future visions. *Journal of Educational Data Mining, 1*(1), 3–17.

Barab, S., & Dede, C. (2007). Games and immersive participatory simulations for science education: An emerging type of curricula. *Journal of Science Education and Technology, 16*(1), 1–3. doi:10.1007/s10956-007-9043-9

Barab, S., Scott, B., Siyahhan, S., Goldstone, R., Ingram-Goble, A., Zuiker, S., & Warren, S. (2009). Transformational play as a curricular scaffold: Using videogames to support science education. *Journal of Science Education and Technology, 18*(4), 305–320. doi:10.1007/s10956-009-9171-5

Bartholow, B. D., Sestir, M. A., & Davis, E. B. (2005). Correlates and consequences of exposure to video game violence: Hostile personality, empathy, and aggressive behavior. *Personality and Social Psychology Bulletin, 31*(11), 1573–1586. doi:10.1177/0146167205277205

Bartle, R. (1996). Hearts, clubs, diamonds, spades: Players who suit MUD's. *Journal of MUD Research, 1*, 1.

Bateman, C. (2004). Demographic game design. *International Hobo*. [text file] Retrieved from http://onlyagame.typepad.com/ihobo/_misc/dgd_brochurefinal.pdf

Bateman, C., & Nacke, L. (2010). The neurobiology of play. *Futureplay '10: Proceedings of the International Academic Conference on the Future of Game Design and Technology*, Vancouver, BC, Canada.

Baxter, M. G., & Murray, E. A. (2002). Amygdala and reward. *Nature Reviews. Neuroscience, 3*, 563–573. doi:10.1038/nrn875

Becker, K. (2007). Pedagogy in commercial video games- Foreword. In Gibson, D., Aldrich, C., & Prensky, M. (Eds.), *Games and simulations in online learning: Research and development frameworks*. Hershey, PA: Information Science Publishing.

Bell, R. C. (1979). *Board and table games from many civilizations (Vol. 1-2)*. Toronto, ON, Canada: General Publishing Company.

Bellotti, F., Berta, R., Gloria, A. D., & Primavera, L. (2009). Enhancing the educational value of video games. *Computers in Entertainment, 7*(2), 1. doi:10.1145/1541895.1541903

Berridge, K. C., & Robinson, T. E. (2003). Parsing reward. *Trends in Neurosciences, 26*(9), 507–513. doi:10.1016/S0166-2236(03)00233-9

Biederman, I., & Vessel, E. A. (2006). Perceptual pleasure and the brain. *American Scientist, 94*(3), 247–253.

Bloom, B. S. (1956). *Taxonomy of educational objectives, handbook I: The cognitive domain*. New York, NY: David McKay Co.

Boekaerts, M. (1997). Self-regulated learning: a new concept embraced by researchers, policy makers, educators, teachers, and students. *Learning and Instruction, 7*(2), 151–186. doi:10.1016/S0959-4752(96)00015-1

Briggs-Myers, I. (1962). *The Myers-Briggs type indicator*. Palo Alto, CA: Consulting Psychology Press.

Bronack, S., Riedl, R., & Tashner, J. (2006). Learning in the zone: A social constructivist framework for distance education in a 3-dimensional virtual world. *Interactive Learning Environments, 14*(3), 219–232. doi:10.1080/10494820600909157

Cailois, R. (1961). *Man, play, and games* (M. Barash, Trans.). New York, NY: The Free Press. Charles, D., Charles, T., McNeill, M., Bustard, D., & Black, M. (2011). Game-based feedback for educational multi-user virtual environments. *British Journal of Educational Technology, 42*(4), 638–654. doi:doi:10.1111/j.1467-8535.2010.01068.x

Charsky, D. (2010). From edutainment to serious games: A change in the use of game characteristics. *Games and Culture, 5*(2), 177–198. doi:10.1177/1555412009354727

Chatfield, T. (2010, December 21). *7 ways to reward the brain* [Video file]. Retrieved from http://www.ted.com/talks/lang/en/tom_chatfield_7_ways_games_reward_the_brain.html

Chatfield, T. (2010a). *Fun, Inc.: Why games are the 21st century's most serious business*. Virgin Books.

Cole, J., Calmenson, S., & Tiegreen, A. (1990). *Miss Mary Mack: And other children's street rhymes*. New York, NY: Harper Collins.

Cox, A., & Campbell, M. (1994). Multiuser dungeons. *Interactive Fantasy, 2*, 15–20.

Davies, R. S., Williams, D. D., & Yanchar, S. (2008). The use of randomization in educational research and evaluation: A critical analysis of underlying assumptions. *Evaluation and Research in Education, 21*(4), 303–317. doi:10.1080/09500790802307837

Dede, C. (2005). Why design-based research is both important and difficult. *Educational Technology, 45*(1), 5–8.

Dede, C. (2009). Immersive interfaces for engagement and learning. *Science, 323*(5910), 66–69. doi:10.1126/science.1167311

Dweck, C. (1986). Motivational processes affecting learning. *The American Psychologist, 41*(10), 1040–1048. doi:10.1037/0003-066X.41.10.1040

Eccles, J. S., & Wingfield, A. (2002). Motivational beliefs, values, and goals. *Annual Review of Psychology, 53*, 109–132. doi:10.1146/annurev.psych.53.100901.135153

Fayyad, U., Piatetsky-Shapiro, G., & Smyth, P. (1996a). From data mining to knowledge discovery in databases. *AI Magazine, 17*(3), 37–54.

Fayyad, U., Piatetsky-Shapiro, G., & Smyth, P. (1996b). The KDD process for extracting useful knowledge from volumes of data. *Communications of the ACM, 39*(11), 27–34. doi:10.1145/240455.240464

Fayyad, U., Piatetsky-Shapiro, G., & Smyth, P. (1996c). Knowledge discovery and data mining: Towards a unifying framework. *Proceedings of Knowledge Discovery and Data Mining 1996*. Retrieved from http://scholar.google.com/scholar?hl=en&btnG=Search&q=intitle:Knowledge+Discovery+and+Data+Mining+:+Towards+a+Unifying+Framework#0

Federal policy for the protection of human subjects; notices and rules. (1991, June 18). *56 Federal Register 28002-28032*.

Fleming, M., & Levie, W. H. (Eds.). (1993). *Instructional message design: Principles from the behavioral and cognitive sciences* (2nd ed.). Englewood Cliffs, NJ: Educational Technology Publications.

Gee, J. P. (2005). Learning by design: Good video games as learning machines. *E-learning, 2*(1), 5–16. doi:10.2304/elea.2005.2.1.5

Gee, J. P. (2006). Why game studies now? Video games: A new art form. *Games and Culture, 1*(1), 58–61. doi:10.1177/1555412005281788

Gibson, D., Aldrich, C., & Prensky, M. (Eds.). (2006). *Games and simulations in online learning: Research and development frameworks*. Hershey, PA: Information Science Publishing. doi:10.4018/978-1-59904-304-3

Godambe, V. (1978). Estimation in survey-sampling: Robustness and optimality. *Proceedings of the International Conference on Statistics*, (pp. 14-15). Retrieved from http://www.amstat.org/sections/srms/Proceedings/papers/1981_003.pdf

Gratch, J., & Kelly, J. (2009). MMOGs: Beyond the wildest imagination. *Journal of Interactive Learning Research, 20*(2), 175–187.

Grotzer, T. A., Dede, C., Metcalfe, S., & Clarke, J. (2009, April). *Addressing the challenges in understanding ecosystems: Why getting kids outside may not be enough*. National Association of Research in Science Teaching (NARST) Conference, Orange Grove, CA, April 18, 2009.

Haskell, C., & Pollard, C. (2008). Understanding and preparing teachers of millennial learners. *Proceedings of the World Conference on E-Learning*, Las Vegas, NV.

Hinske, S., Lampe, M., Magerkurth, C., & Rocker, C. (2007). Classifying pervasive games: On pervasive computing and mixed reality. *Concepts and technologies for Pervasive Games-A Reader for Pervasive Gaming Research*, 1. Retrieved from http://citeseerx.ist.psu.edu/viewdoc/download?doi=10.1.1.66.6807&rep=rep1&type=pdf

Hirumi, A., & Stapleton, C. (2009). Applying pedagogy during game development to enhance game-based learning. In Miller, C. T. (Ed.), *Games: Purpose and potential in education*. New York, NY: Springer. doi:10.1007/978-0-387-09775-6_6

Hoffman, B., & Nadelson, L. (2009). Motivational engagement and video gaming: A mixed methods study. *Educational Technology Research and Development, 58*(3), 245–270. doi:10.1007/s11423-009-9134-9

Horn, C., Snyder, B., Coverdale, J., Louie, A., & Roberts, L. (2009). Educational research questions and study design. *Design*, (June), 261-267.

Howard, J. (2008) *Quests: Design, theory, and history in games and narratives*. Wellesley, MA: A K Peters, Ltd.

Jegers, K. (2007). Pervasive game flow: Understanding player enjoyment in pervasive gaming. *Computers in Entertainment, 5*(1). Retrieved from http://portal.acm.org/citation.cfm?id=1236238

Jensen, E. (2008). A fresh look at brain-based education. *Phi Delta Kappan, 86*(6).

Jonassen, D. H. (2000). Toward a design theory of problem solving. *Educational Technology Research and Development, 48*(4), 63–85. doi:10.1007/BF02300500

Joyce, B., Weil, M., & Calhoun, E. (2004). *Models of teaching*. Boston, MA: Allyn and Bacon.

Juul, J. (2003). *The game, the player, the world: Looking for a heart of gameness*. Keynote presentation of the Level Up Conference in Utrecht, Netherlands.

Kafai, Y. B. (2006). Playing and making games for learning: Instructionist and constructionist perspectives for game studies. *Games and Culture, 1*(1), 36–40. doi:10.1177/1555412005281767

Kay, R. H., & Knaack, L. (2008). Assessing learning, quality and engagement in learning objects: The learning object evaluation scale for students (LOES-S). *Educational Technology Research and Development, 57*(2), 147–168. doi:10.1007/s11423-008-9094-5

Ketelhut, D. J. (2007). The impact of student self-efficacy on scientific inquiry skills: An exploratory investigation in River City, a multi-user virtual environment. *Journal of Science Education and Technology, 16*(1), 99–111. doi:10.1007/s10956-006-9038-y

Ketelhut, D. J., Nelson, B. C., Clarke, J. E., & Dede, C. (2010). A multi-user virtual environment for building and assessing higher order inquiry skills in science. *British Journal of Educational Technology, 41*(1), 56–68. doi:10.1111/j.1467-8535.2009.01036.x

Koepp, M. J., Gunn, R. N., Lawrence, A. D., Cunningham, V. J., Dagher, A., & Jones, T. (1998). Evidence for striatal dopamine release during a video game. *Nature, 393*(6682), 266–268. doi:10.1038/30498

Koster, R. (2005). *A theory of fun in game design*. Paraglyph Press. Retrieved from http://portal.acm.org/citation.cfm?id=1207478

Lange, P. G. (2010). Learning real-life lessons from online games. *Games and Culture, 6*(1), 17–37. doi:10.1177/1555412010377320

Lazzaro, N. (2005). Why we play games: Four keys to more emotion without story. *Proceedings of the Game Developers Conference*. Retrieved from http://xeodesign.com/xeodesign_whyweplaygames.pdf

Lenhart, A., Jones, S., & Macgill, A. (2008). *Video games: Adults are players too*. Retrieved from http://pewresearch.org/pubs/1048/

Lenhart, A., Kahne, J., Middaugh, E., & Macgill, A. (2008). *Teens, video games, and civics*. Retrieved from http://www.pewinternet.org/PPF/r/263/report_display.asp

Lenhart, A., Ling, R., Campbell, S., & Purcell, K. (2010). *Teens and mobile phones*. Retrieved from http://www.pewinternet.org/Reports/2010/Teens-and-Mobile-Phones.aspx

Lindtner, S., & Dourish, P. (2011). The promise of play: A new approach to productive play. *Games and Culture, 6*(5), 453–478. doi:10.1177/1555412011402678

Malaby, T. M. (2009). Beyond play: A new approach to games. *Games and Culture, 2*(2), 95–113. doi:10.1177/1555412007299434

Martin, S. (2010). Teachers using learning styles: Torn between research and accountability? *Teaching and Teacher Education, 26*(8), 1583–1591. doi:10.1016/j.tate.2010.06.009

McGonigal, J. (2010). *Gaming can make a better world*. TED Talks. Retrieved from http://www.ted.com/talks/lang/eng/jane_mcgonigal_gaming_can_make_a_better_world.html

McGreal, R. (2004). Learning objects: A practical definition. *International Journal of Instructional Technology and Distance Learning, 1*(9), 21–32.

McMahan, A. (2003). Immersion, engagement and presence. In *The video game theory reader*. Retrieved from http://people.ict.usc.edu/~morie/SupplementalReadings/ch3-McMahanrev.pdf

Moreno, J., Caplan, A. L., & Wolpe, P. R. (1998). Updating protections for human subjects involved in research: Project on informed consent, human research ethics group. *Journal of the American Medical Association, 280*(22), 1951–1958. Retrieved from http://www.ncbi.nlm.nih.gov/pubmed/9851484 doi:10.1001/jama.280.22.1951

Nacke, L., Bateman, C., & Mandryk, R. (2011). *BrainHex: Preliminary results from a neurobiological gamer typology survey*. Paper presented at the 10th International Conference on Entertainment Computing, Vancouver, BC, Canada.

O'Brien, D., Lawless, K. A., & Schrader, P. G. (2010). A taxonomy of educational games. In Baek, Y. (Ed.), *Gaming for classroom-based learning: Digital role playing as a myouotivator of study* (pp. 1–23). doi:10.4018/978-1-61520-713-8.ch001

OHRP. (2009). Retrieved from http://www.hhs.gov/ohrp/humansubjects/guidance/45cfr46.html

Papastergiou, M. (2008). Digital game-based learning in high school computer science education. *Computers & Education*, *52*, 1–12. doi:10.1016/j.compedu.2008.06.004

Papert, S. (1998, June). Does easy do it? Children, games, and learning. *Game Developer*, 87-88.

Poole, S. (2000). *Trigger happy: Video games and the entertainment revolution*. New York, NY: Arcade Publishing.

Przybylski, A., Rigby, C. S., & Ryan, R. (2010). A motivational model of video game engagement. *Review of General Psychology*, *14*(2), 154–166. doi:10.1037/a0019440

Redeker, G. (2003). An educational taxonomy for learning objects. In the *Proceedings of Learning Technologies, 2003*. Retrieved from http://ieeexplore.ieee.org/xpls/abs_all.jsp?arnumber=1215068

Salen, K., & Zimmerman, E. (2003). *Rules of play: Game design fundamentals*. Cambridge, MA: MIT Press.

Shelby, L. B., & Vaske, J. J. (2008). Understanding meta-analysis: A review of the methodological literature. *Leisure Sciences*, *30*(2), 96–110. doi:10.1080/01490400701881366

Siwek, S. (2010). *Video games in the 21st century: The 2010 report*. Washington, DC: Entertainment Software Association. Retrieved from http://www.theesa.com/facts/pdfs/VideoGames21stCentury_2010.pdf

Slavin, R. E. (2008). Perspectives on evidence-based research in education—What works? Issues in synthesizing educational program evaluations. *Educational Researcher*, *37*(1), 5–14. doi:10.3102/0013189X08314117

Smith, R., Levine, T., & Lachlan, K. (2002). The high cost of complexity in experimental design and data analysis: Type I and type II error rates in multiway ANOVA. *Human Communication, 28*(4), 515-530. Retrieved from http://onlinelibrary.wiley.com/doi/10.1111/j.1468-2958.2002.tb00821.x/abstract

Squire, K. (2003). Video games in education. *International Journal of Intelligent Games & Simulation, 1*(1), 10. doi:doi:10.1145/950566.950583

Sullivan, A., Mateas, M., & Wardrip-Fruin, N. (2009). Questbrowser: Making quests playable with computer-assisted design. In *The Proceedings of Digital Arts and Culture*, Irvine, CA

Sullivan, F. R. (2009). Risk and responsibility: A self-study of teaching with Second Life. *Journal of Interactive Learning Research, 20*(3), 337–357.

Tan, A. (1999). Text mining: The state of the art and the challenges. In *Proceedings of Pacific Asia Conference on Knowledge Discovery and Data Mining PAKDD '99 Workshop on Knowledge Discovery from Advanced Databases*, pp. 65-70.

Tversky, A., & Kahneman, D. (1981). The framing of decisions and the psychology of choice. *Science, 211*(4481), 453–458. Retrieved from http://www.ncbi.nlm.nih.gov/pubmed/7455683 doi:10.1126/science.7455683

U.S. Department of Education Office of Educational Technology. (2010). *Transforming American education—Learning powered by technology (executive summary)*. Retrieved from http://www.ed.gov/sites/default/files/netp2010-execsumm.pdf

Vallerand, R. J., Fortier, M. S., & Guay, F. (1997). Self-determination and persistence in a real-life setting: Toward a motivational model of high school dropout. *Journal of Personality and Social Psychology, 72*(5), 1161–1176. doi:10.1037/0022-3514.72.5.1161

Van Eck, R. (2006). Digital game-based learning: It's not just the digital natives who are restless. *EDUCAUSE Review, 41*(2), 1–16.

Van Eck, R. (2007). The building artificially intelligent learning games. In Gibson, D., Aldrich, C., & Prensky, M. (Eds.), *Games and simulations in online learning: Research and development frameworks*. Hershey, PA: Information Science Publishing.

Vaughn, B. J., & Horner, R. (1997). Identifying instructional tasks that occasion problem behaviors and assessing the effects of student versus teacher choice among these tasks. *Journal of Applied Behavior Analysis, 30*(2), 299–312. doi:10.1901/jaba.1997.30-299

Wagner, C., & Ip, R. K. F. (2009). Action learning with Second Life: A pilot study. *Journal of Information Systems Education, 20*(2), 249–258.

Waters, J. K. (2009). A "Second Life" for educators. *T.H.E. Journal, 36*(1), 29–34.

Weber, R., Ritterfiled, U., & Mathiak, K. (2006). Does playing violent video games induce aggression? Empirical evidence of any functional magnetic resonance imaging study. *Media Psychology, 8*, 39–60. doi:10.1207/S1532785XMEP0801_4

Wentzel, K. R. (1997). Student motivation in middle school: The role of perceived pedagogical caring. *Journal of Educational Psychology, 89*(3), 411–419. doi:10.1037/0022-0663.89.3.411

Weusijana, B. K., Svihla, V., Gawel, D., & Bransford, J. (2009). MUVEs and experiential learning: Some examples. *Innovate: Journal of Online Education, 5*(5).

Wiley, D. A. (2000). *Connecting learning objects to instructional design theory: A definition, a metaphor, and a taxonomy.* Association for Instructional Technology & Association for Educational Communications and Technology. doi:10.1002/stab.200710001

Yates, G. C. R. (2005). "How obvious": Personal reflections on the database of educational psychology and effective teaching research. *Educational Psychology, 25*(6), 681–700. doi:10.1080/01443410500345180

Yee, N. (2006). The demographics, motivations and derived experiences of users of massively-multiuser online graphical environments. *Presence (Cambridge, Mass.), 15*, 309–329. doi:10.1162/pres.15.3.309

Zagal, J. P., Fernandez-Vara, C., & Mateas, M. (2008). Rounds, levels, and waves: The early evolution of gameplay segmentation. *Games and Culture, 3*(2), 175–198. doi:10.1177/1555412008314129

Zaphiris, P., & Wilson, S. (2010). Computer games and sociocultural play: An activity theoretical perspective. *Games and Culture, 5*(4), 354–380. doi:10.1177/1555412009360411

Zickuhr, K. (2011). *Generations and their gadgets.* Pew/Internet. Retrieved from http://www.pewinternet.org/Reports/2011/Generations-and-gadgets/Report/Game-consoles.aspx

Zientek, L. R., Capraro, M. M., & Capraro, R. M. (2008). Reporting practices in quantitative teacher education research: One look at the evidence cited in the AERA panel report. *Educational Researcher, 37*(4), 208–216. doi:10.3102/0013189X08319762

Chapter 17
Preparing Pre–Service Teachers for Game–Based Learning in Schools

Soojeong Lee
Kyungnam University, South Korea

EXECUTIVE SUMMARY

This chapter describes the pre-service teacher's preparation of teaching consumption education to middle school students when using Farmville, a social network-based game. Consumption education is a complex topic, involving principals such as consumers, producers, governments, etc., as well as related abstract concepts such as resource type, the management and distribution of resources, use of consumer information, consumer decision-making, et cetera. Consumer satisfaction varies based on interaction types between each factor. Because of the abstract nature of this discussion, there are many limits to teaching this topic using only theoretical classes. However, students reported that using Farmville was helpful in learning on consumption and related contents, specifically because of its ability to confirm specific results, including stream of resources management, consumption pattern by decision-making process, etc. through the process of giving and receiving resources with peers who participate in a game. Also, students understood the stream of actual market economy and realized the importance of shared consumption as an environmental factor.

DOI: 10.4018/978-1-4666-2848-9.ch017

OVERALL DESCRIPTION

Consumption behavior is very sensitive to domestic and foreign market economy. They change from time to time and the variables related to it are very diverse. Particularly, goals and types of consumption behaviors vary on based on the demographic location of the consumer, producer (company), government, etc. However, highest rate of consumer satisfaction can be maximized using interactions between each principal. Accordingly, by combining the game of *Farmville*, where various consumption principals and situation can be experienced, with a conversation on consumption, students can experience decision-making as a principal related with actual consumption, unlike in theoretical classes, and then evaluate the results.

In Korea, the topic of consumption education focuses on developing 'consumer' capabilities. Ideally, these skills will enable their user to cope with a rapidly changing the market economy in the modern society and to practice sustainable consumption behaviors. In order to accomplish this goal, it helps to learn related knowledge, understand the interactions between the consumer and the market economy, and to find opportunities for students to practice consumption-related behaviors. Further, teachers' own ability to deliver consumption education concepts must be developed, particularly for home economics pre-service teachers.

This chapter analyzes the consumption education in middle school textbooks. These textbooks are in accordance with the 2007 revised curriculum now being applied to current school fields. This chapter also describes the possibilities of a student-oriented classroom model using *Farmville* to teach on consumption, and the ways in which consumption lives are affected by domestic and foreign market economy changes, by the goals and types of consumption behaviors, and by the demographics of the consumer, producer (company), and government. Further, by allowing early career teachers to experience each stage of course design (from session design, lesson plans, and metric design) when using a social network game as a keystone of the course, teachers can experience with new types of classroom environments incorporating smart-learning, student-oriented class, etc.

Practicalities and Preparation for Game-Based Learning

The lecture is designed in 5 stages over the course of the semester of a pre-service teacher training course. In the 1st stage, pre-service teachers are asked to analyze contents of consumption education in the revised textbook which adopted revised curriculum standards in 2007. In the 2nd stage, pre-service teachers are asked to prepare a report on related factors using the analyzed textbook contents and *Farmville*. In the

3rd stage, pre-service teacher are asked to prepare a lesson plan by planning classes containing the above contents. In the 4th stage, they actually teach a practice class. In the final stage, we evaluate all class progresses and try to build up improvements.

STAGE 1. ANALYZING TEXTBOOK CONTENTS RELATED WITH CONSUMPTION EDUCATION

This stage involved analyzing contents related to consumption education within middle school technology·home economics textbooks and classified them into 6 major categories, with sub-categories in each. The 6 major categories are: Consumer Sovereignty, Resource Management, Consumer Decision-Making, Consumer Issues, Consumer information Collection and Use, and Consumption Culture.

STAGE 2. FINDING CORRELATIONS BETWEEN CONSUMPTION EDUCATION CONCEPTS AND *FARMVILLE*

1. *Farmville* Game Play

This discussion of game-play begins with Figure 1.

If a star appears over the head of an animal, that animal can be milked or harvested. As shown in Figure 2, the player can use the initial capital required when a user buy seeds or harvest or plow a field to compare the income of planting seed with that maintaining animals. Another factor would be time management. It is possible to make money by repeating the same expenses and incomes. However,

Figure 1. Notification of harvest time

Figure 2. Animals and plants

more money can be made by sowing seeds in consideration of one's own time pattern. Animals only require a few initial expenses and can be harvested continuously. But the income generated from this is small. Sowing properly and harvesting is more desirable in the long run, even though it seems animals are more profitable at first.

As shown in Figure 3, if the player puts a cursor on their crops after sowing seeds, they can see how long they have until harvest.

As shown in Figure 4 and Figure 5, by using Seeder, Harvest and Tractor, the player can harvest and plow more effectively.

As shown in Figure 6, the player can visit one neighbor a day and give fertilizer. By giving fertilizer, the withered crops of the player's neighbors can come back to life or stay healthy longer. This helps the player make money.

Figure 3. Checking the crops

Figure 4. Harvest

Figure 5. Tractor

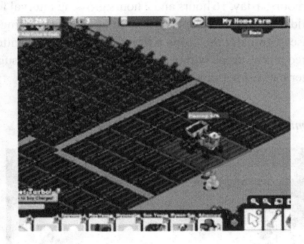

Figure 6. Transferring fertilizer to neighbors

As shown in Figure 7, the player can customize their avatar's physical attributes by clicking Facial Features. They can change their face type, hair, eye, eyelash, ear, nose, mouth, skin, cosmetics, etc. Also, there is free clothing available for the avatar. The player can choose to pay for clothing or to buy clothing.

When a user plays a fixed quantity of games, they earn a coin called 'Reward-Ville.' This coin is circled in the above Figure 8. This achievement can unlock a house or a free/cheap item. There is a display in the top of a screen indicating how many RewardVille own coins one has. If RewardVille coins are clicked, the following

In the Figure 9, the player earned a free veranda house. In the above Figure 10, marked as '1' is the veranda house, and marked as '2' is the "lighthouse cove" (earned at level 17). They are all free items.

As shown in the Figure 11, the circles in the above image highlight that there are 10 hours, 20 hours, a day, 16 hours and 2 hours growing interval for these plants. The player should harvest these plants within 20 hours after sowing those particular seeds, because eventually the crops will rot. If the player's pattern is to check on their crops frequently, crops with a longer harvest period are suggested. If not, crops with shorter harvest periods are recommended.

Figure 7. Customizing avatar

Figure 8. RewardVille

Figure 9. Veranda house as a bonus

Figure 10. Free item: a farm

Figure 11. Managing plant cultivation

2. Relevance between Categories of Consumption Education Contents and Game Activities

Table 1 shows contents of consumption education and *Farmville* factors.

3. Correlation between Consumption Education Contents Model Developed by Korea Consumer Agency (KCA)

The consumption education content model developed by the KCA is comprised of 4 large categories. These are 'Understanding the market economy', 'Rational purchase and use', 'Resolving consumer problems and preventive education', and 'New consumption culture and building education'. Each category is comprised of 2 intermediate categories and 5 small categories. If the educational factors of *Farmville* are classified based on these categories, they would be as follows.

Understanding a Market Economy: Management of Consumer Resources

Through playing *Farmville*, the meaning of high and low income and resource management method can be learned. The student-as-play can learn that energy and time worked can be reduced by purchasing different tools, (including the Seeder, Harvester and Tractor) or by using fuel to sow seeds after harvesting a lot so that the player can harvest and plow more effectively. The player can also learn the meaning resource management, as well as management methods for resources other than money (like time, various durable goods, public goods, etc.) by using Seeder, Harvester and Tractor to harvest crops directly rather than clicking on the mouse.

- **Money:** Money as a factor is found in category two, "Resource Management", under "Income management –Income, expenditure and liability management" in the above table. In *Farmville*, money is a very important resource. While expenses incur when buying seeds, income accrues by harvesting. Without it, the player can't extend or harvest their field. There are several ways of making money. A good way of making money as a low-level player is through harvesting activities and raising animals. As for a method of managing money, the player must consider their own use-time pattern, choose a harvest item and harvest that item within the applicable window of time. The user also has to consider how many of that item they can harvest in a particular time, and whether planting a particular item costs them money or makes them money.

Table 1. Relations between consumption education contents and Farmville factors

Consumption education contents			Farmville Factor
Large category	**Sub-category**	**Detailed contents**	
1. Consumer Sovereignty	1) Consumer sovereignty	•Consumerism •Understanding of consumer sovereign • Consumer rights and responsibilities • Roles of consumers	
	2) Consumer values	•Meaning of consumption •Consumer values	
	3) Consumption ethics	•Consumption ethics •Value and concept of money	
	4) Consumer civic awareness	•Participation consciousness as active consumers •Community spirits	o o
2. Resource Management	1) Market economy	•Principles of choice in the market economy •Understanding of market economy and home economy	o
	2) Income management	•understanding domestic economy •Income, expenditure and liability management •Consumer credit	o
	3) Asset management	•Principles of investment •Management of financial assets and real estates	o
	4) Life resources management	•Public goods and time management	o
3. Consumer Decision-making	1) Rational decision-making	•Rationality of consumer decision-making •Effectiveness of consumer decision-making	o o
	2) Consumer decision-making process	• Affecting factors of consumer decision-making •Consumer decision-making process by consumer issue type	o
	3) Marketing activities and consumer counterstrategy	•Understanding of consumer and market environment •Understanding of corporate activities and consumer counter plan	
4. Consumer Issues	1) Laws related with consumers	• Basic Consumer Act and laws related to consumers •Systems related with consumers	
	2) Resolving consumer issues	•Cause of consumer issues •Consumer issue types •Consumer damage prevention and remedies	

continued on following page

Table 1. Continued

Consumption education contents			*Farmville* Factor
Large category	**Sub-category**	**Detailed contents**	
5. Consumer Information Collection and Use	1) Consumer information collection	•On/off-line Consumer Information Agency • On/off-line consumer information content system • On/off-line information collection and analysis	
	2) Consumer information use	• On/off-line consumer information use • On/off-line consumer information evaluation	
6. Consumption Culture	1) Consumption	•Consumption culture phenomenon change procedure •Consumption culture characteristics by consumer group •Understanding of consumer	o
	2) Sustainable consumption	•Concepts of sustainable production and consumption •Environmental protection •Recycling and reusing	o

This is particularly relevant because if the player waits too long, the harvest item will rot and waste the player's money. Managing harvest times is a very effective way of making money and continuing to play the game.

- **Fertilizer:** Fertilizer has to do with the first category, "Consumer sovereignty," particularly the subsection "Consumer civic awareness – Community spirit" in the above table. A user can visit 'in-game neighbors' added through their social media networks and distribute fertilizers to their neighbors' crops. This exchange between neighbors links community spirit to being a consumer.

- **Farm Machines and Fuel:** Farm machines and fuel fit into the second category, "Resource Management," in subsection four, "Living resources management – public goods and time management." As harvesting and plowing a field can be accomplished more effectively using farm machines, the player can see the importance of time management and enhancing the effectiveness of one's resources.

- **Animals and Trees:** Like money, animals and trees also have to do with the category of "Resource Management," but instead fit into the subsection "Asset management." The player needs money to raise animals. The player can experience the importance of distributing resources, as they can harvest crops continuously and automatically if the correct investment is made in the first phase. Otherwise, acquiring animals, trees, equipment and money will take time.

- **Seed:** Seed fits into the sixth category, "Consumption Culture," in the sub-section "Sustainable consumption – Concepts of sustainable production and consumption" as well the third category, "Consumer Decision-making," in the subsection "Rationality/effectiveness of consumer decision-making." Through spreading seeds and repeating harvests, the player can experience sustainable production/consumption. Also, the player can experience resource management and the process of rational consumer decision-making by purchasing seeds and harvesting crops according based on the player's time and energy.

- **Clothing:** Clothing fits into the category of "Consumer decision-making" in subsection two, "Decision- making process of consumers – Effect factors of consumers' decision-making," and in the category "Consumption Culture," in subsection one, "Consumption trend and culture – consumption culture characteristics by consumer group." Because the player can purchase clothing after saving a certain amount of money, the player can experience consumption culture characteristics by participating in the process of consumption-based decision-making, and its interactions with fashion and consumers' own preference types.

- **Housing and Construction Materials:** Housing and construction materials fit into the second category, "Resource Management," in subsection one, "Market economy – principles of choice in the market economy." Although a house and construction materials can be purchased after achieving certain amount of capital, some capital should be saved for harvest, which helps the player experience principles of choice in a market economy.

- **Human Resources, Effective Time Management:** Effective time management in *Farmville* fits into category three, "Consumer Decision-making," in the section "Rational decision-making – effectiveness of consumers' decision-making." If the player is likely to check the proceedings of their game often, crops with short cultivation periods are suggested. If not, crops with long cultivation periods are recommended. By applying this strategy to real-life time management, the player can learn to manage their own time systematically and effectively.

Rational Purchase and Use: Consumer Decision-Making

The player can collect, read and analyze various consumer information about *Farmville* using the internet, newspapers, magazines, etc. The player can analyze these pieces of information by making consumption decisions based on the information about various pieces of farm equipment, farm products, animals, trees, etc., maximizing their satisfaction with the play experience. Also, the player can learn the purpose of various kinds of commercial information, such as advertising, marketing strategies, etc. and their impact on consumers' choices. When a player searches for a vehicle in the "Farm Aids" section of *Farmville*'s market, various farm machines come out. Because the user can preview various farm machines, they can learn about evaluating various pieces of information including usefulness. This can also help with teaching the player to understand and make use of various price-marking information, including standard, quality, safety, and hazard, etc.

Rational Purchase and Use: Purchase Rationale

Through playing *Farmville*, the player can practice the process of purchase decision-making process, and experience the various factors affecting the process.

The player can also experience avoiding unfair transactions after learning about proper transactions and contract methods. Lastly, a user can practicing saving, since an abundance of crops can be stored in the player's farm and used whenever necessary. The player can also understand the way purchasing fits into a larger consumption culture by paying attention to the price of the seed versus the selling price of the crop; the role of "experience points" as a status marker, and the player's own game satisfaction.

STAGE 3. PREPARING A LESSON PLAN

1. Ideas for Classroom Activity

This section focuses on designing classroom activities. *Farmville* enables the student-as-consumer to have many diverse experiences as a consumer. These include expenditure, purchase, resource management, and building community. Students will learn that acting as a consumer while managing their time effectively is useful, even when playing a game.

Combining a class on being an aware consumer with a game seems to be effective. The player can act as both consumer and producer. Through exchanging crops with neighbors, the student as player becomes aware of how they participate in consumption. Also, by exchanging crops with neighbors, community spirit can be built up. This kind of game works especially well with a class, since class members can visit farms of neighbors/classmates and share fertilizers as part of establishing a class-based community spirit. Students also become more interested in learning by planning strategies and describing their own consumption behavior within

Farmville. They can transition these skills to their daily lives by mimicking actual consumption behaviors useful within *Farmville*, such as developing an interest in saving assets and learning their own spending styles.

2. Example of a Lesson Plan

In this section of the course, we helped teachers design a lesson plan, using Table 2 as an example.

STAGE 4. LESSON PRACTICE AND DEBRIEFING

The actual lesson progressed according to above prepared lesson plan and all students participated in class discussion. The results of discussion were used to revise upcoming lesson plans.

1. Technology Components: *Farmville*

Farmville is a farming simulation social network game developed by Zynga in 2009. *Farmville* incorporates the social networking aspect of Facebook into many areas of gameplay. This consumer science was carried out during 2nd period Monday and the 3rd and 4th period Tuesday every week. Students participated through Facebook for 2 weeks in mid-September and practiced the game after making individual IDs for *Farmville*. From October 3, *Farmville* was used as a discussion prompt.

2. Computer

A class was held in a multi-media classroom. Pre-service teacher could use an individual computer.

STAGE 5. EVALUATION

Students were questioned what they thought of a lesson using a game.

1. Attitude towards the Lesson

10 students answered they joined the class with a positive attitude and only a student answered that they weren't sure. The students said they became interested in the material because of the game itself and naturally were motivated to see if they could

Table 2. Sample lesson plan

Lesson Plan
Understanding a market economy
Lesson Description
Main Category: 1. Understanding the market economy **Sub-section:** (2)Management of consumer resources **Theme:** Effective money management method for adolescents (2/3) **Type of Student:** Middle school students **Teaching media:** Textbook, audio-visual materials (video), learning activity material, ppt. and *Farmville* game **Learning type:** Practical problem-oriented lesson **Essential Question:** What should we do to manage money effectively?
Instructional Goals and Objectives
1. To be able to analyze the character of adolescent money use. 2. To own attitude towards spending money as an adolescent. 3. To learn practical strategies for effective money management.
Learning Activities
Instructional Goal/Objective 1 - Watching video clips ▪ Video clip is about 3 minutes and should contain examples of money use problems. ▪ Students should write what they feel and think when watching the video ▪ To promote learning about effective money use through watching a video clip and discussing it in simple language **Instructional Goal/Objective 2 – Analysis through a game.** ▪To draw on examples of *Farmville,* a game the class has been playing for the last week and to think over the effective game money use and prompt critical thinking. ex) T: Watch the screen! You can see your game money in the top of left side of a game. We should grow crops and buy other farm facilities and machines within a restricted budget. But let's say we spent all our monies for buying crops, and don't have anything left to plant new ones. If our present set of crops withered, then aren't we in danger of not paying our own expenses for recovery? So, money should be used after planning as well as allocated effectively. ▪ Students are to prepare a comparison of money use in the game for a week with actual money use in their daily lives, sharing their own game screens and give presentations. ▪ By comparing their own experiences with other students, students will be able to reflect on their consumption lives within the game as well as their actual lives. **Instructional Goal/Objective 3 – Application of practical strategies through a game** ▪ To help students understand effective money management by giving examples of allowance use. ▪ By suggesting 3 strategies for effective money management with PPT ▪To practice by applying strategies to a game ex) Choosing how much should be spent on crops or other farm facilities or farm machines using a restricted budget in the game
Lesson Progress Stage
1. Introductory stage 1) Greetings and learning preparation: introducing students to learning environment 2) Ask students to talk about what they already know - To remind students of earlier course content through demonstrative lesson explanations. 3) Catching student interest - Show images for time management strategies characteristic of adolescents to promote interest before getting into a main lesson. -Let students think and talk about video clip. 4) Talk about lesson objective

continued on following page

Table 2. Continued

2. Main Activities
1) Promote critical thinking
- Begin critical thinking by discussing a game students have experience with
- Students are to prepare a comparison of money use in the game for a week with their actual money use in their daily lives and give presentations.
2) Understand the principal concept
- To let them understand effective time and money management.
- To let them understand 3 strategies for considering effective money management.
3) Promote successful behaviors
- Let students practice newly learned concepts by applying what they have learned through *Farmville*
3. Conclusion
1) Summarize lesson contents
- Summarize effective money management strategies
2) Evaluate success of lesson plan
- Student will discuss remaining knowledge gaps
- Students will solve these by presenting these problems in using PPT and confirm they understand the material
-To provide feed backs for formative evaluation contents
3) Confirm information retention
4) Introduce next lesson
Notes for Lesson Study By Stage
1. Introduction
-To create a learning atmosphere
-To understand whether students learned the earlier lessons by watching them talk through what they remember
-To let students watch a video clip critically and encourage discussion
-To promote learning through a video clip
2. Main discussion
- To create atmosphere for concentrating on visual materials
- To promote using a game as a teaching tool.
- To enable to students to compare their experiences with others' experiences
- To promote critical thinking through experiences with this game
- To let students concentrate on the PowerPoint.
- To help students play a game when not focusing on the game itself instead the lesson contents
3. Conclusion
- To get feedback from students
- To allow students to make their own evaluation of lesson material

gain achievements through the process of leveling up. These factors seemed to lead to active participation in the class. As there were activities which required individual learning as well as group work, and it was a class which required participating in discussion, it is possible they actively participated naturally.

First of all, because a media or a game was applied, I had interest and was motivated. So I came to think, 'Wow, a game can be a lesson' beyond my solid understanding of studying' and began to study more actively owing to my interest than in other classes. (Student 1).

As it was very fresh, I could not help but have more concern and interest, for I had to work out ideas by discussing them with our group members, I could participate in the class with a more active attitude than just listening to lessons. I could join the class aggressively because I had to join directly, while other classes only required sitting on a chair. (Student 2)

As a result, most of students wished to continue having a game-based class.

2. Effects of Lesson

All 13 students joined in the class said the class was interesting and 10 students among them said they came to have more interest in consumption education through this class. To cite some of their replies,

It was a little bit difficult as this was new. And students could voluntarily join the class through a game, a sensational subject matter which was interesting as an educational method (use of pc and internet social networking). Participating students had increased concentration and therefore more effective learning effects were expected. (Student 1)

Based on these responses, it is useful to carry out game-based learning. Active participation can be promoted, because of the game helping rapid understanding of core concepts, raising student interest and increasing student motivation. But there are some difficulties in relating interest to the lessons and designing lessons for the applicable class years. Also, unrelated stages of game-play should be gone through to reach the concepts, the objective of lesson.

Students were asked which concepts were helpful in understanding out of contents of consumption education attending a game-based learning specifically. *Farmville* was described as helpful in learning time management, money management, consumer decision-making, information collection and analysis, consumer sovereign, basic principles of the market economy, etc.

It seems I could understand consumer agency more easily. The ultimate goal of consumption education means to realize consumer agency. So, through this game, I could understand more easily through learning the decision-making process, consumer rights, etc., which can be said to be methods of realizing consumer agency. These can be examples to suggest to the producers which things should be supplied in the game.

According to the results of the lesson, 10 students replied they could explain newly learned consumer concept to others and 8 out of them said they use consumer concepts learned in a game-base lesson in their actual lives. These concepts include money management, resources management, time management, etc. To cite answers of 3 students;

I could apply to actual life as I could use and practice proper strategies using a game and learned more deeply. (Student 1)

If a game-based lesson is carried out not once but in a cycle or in the long-term, the effects, I think, would be more maximized. (Student 2)

In fact, I could understand sustainable consumption and resource management, parts of which were hard regardless of my major, more easily through this game. So it seems to apply to actual life more easily. (Student 3)

3. Rationale for Lesson Effectiveness

We asked students which points they felt game-based consumption education communicated most effectively. In reading the answers they listed, it was useful to see that they could understand situations directly using a game and learn by applying the concepts. Because it is a game, the type of media selected raised interest; this increased concentration on the lesson, and lead to active participation. By playing a game repeatedly, students can be reminded of what they learned. Through voluntary participation and discussion, they practice critical thinking about their own lives. Using the game was good in that it meant learning activities could occur beyond class hours while students played the game. Answers about the above could be arranged into the following 5 types: Promotion of easy understanding, Repetitive learning available, Active participation through interesting-stimulation, Voluntary learning and Learning beyond class hours. To cite the answers of 2 students;

I think it is a helpful method for learning is using a game with a virtual setting in respect of learning the concepts. A game which involves carrying out missions with a limited time emphasizes time management and improves one's abilities of proper time use when carrying out your studies. (Student 1)

It was effective in that I could understand consumer science concepts easily, I got interested in learning as the game was interesting and I could apply lots of consumer problems which arose while playing the game. (Student 2)

4. Fun of Lesson

We questioned in what respects the class was more interesting than other classes. The students answered that it was more fun and useful; it was an interesting lesson, promoted easy understanding through direct and active participation in the game; using the game made learned concepts easier to memorize, and helped maintain interest and concern; students could feel proud as they learned a new strategy that could be applied to actual school subjects. To cite their answers:

Generally, a lesson learned and understood from a book is not actually understood and reached; in contrast, it was good to learn by carrying out the game or the interesting media directly. (Student 1)

If a lesson is carried out only from a textbook, it can create a somewhat hard and gloomy atmosphere. And it becomes the main method, where a teacher delivers contents and students learn by heart. But a very interesting class could be made with a natural and soft atmosphere while using game-based learning. If game-based learning is carried out in actual subjects, student participation could be maximized and the class could be very interesting. Students are likely to learn what a teacher intends to deliver, naturally, through a game. (Student 2)

5. Student Comprehension

In the above question on effectiveness and interest in the lesson, most of students answered that they understood learning contents more easily. So what about the specific content of the course? Most of students answered that course content seemed to be more easy and faster to experience through a game and that they understand consumption principal which are difficult to explain. They also said that the classes were very active owing to the combination of static and dynamic activities. Terms and concepts could be recognized naturally using the game, and rapid understanding was possible because these were all student-led activities.

To cite the answers of two students;

By applying what I learned in the class to the game, I could use practice what I learned and understand interesting concepts. This is a good example of combining lesson design with a game. Class participation was very high because the game was played as they worked through their own lesson. (Student 1)

A class carried out using a textbook is mainly a method where a teacher delivers knowledge via words and students learn by listening. But in games-based learning, students come to knowledge naturally by carrying out a game. Accordingly, I think this way can be more effective than a lecture-based lesson. And I think the class will be one in which students wait for and anticipate what to do next. (Student 2)

6. Cooperation in Class

As there are a lot of cases requiring cooperative work between group members as part of the learning process, we asked about the importance of cooperation in a game-based learning. Most of students answered that cooperation is very important in this class. The reasons they felt that cooperation was important mainly involved role distribution with group members as crucial to the process of solving tasks and sharing information necessary to progress in the game. *Farmville* is not a single-player game. It requires that the player invite friends, who then become the player's "neighbors" in the world of the game. The importance of cooperation with group members as a way to advance in the game was very clear. One student said,

It would have been very difficult to raise crops or expand my farm if I played the game alone. I could grow my farm because my group members visited my farm, gave me help and accepted my help as well since I visited the farms of group members and received gains. I could feel the importance of cooperation because of my group members' help in expanding my farm and advancing levels.

7. Direction of the Future

It was questioned whether there was any technical difficulty or problem in learning consumption education lesson through a game. 9 students said there were 'difficulty or problem' and 4 students replied there was none. To those 9 students, we specifically asked what technical difficulty or other problem they had. Several answered that it was difficult to find a relationship between game factors, education courses, and lesson design. To design a lesson using a game requires a great deal of investment on the part of the teacher. Below are some excerpts from their responses.

To teach consumption education using a game, it is required that you understand the game well and learn by combining [the game and the concept]. So it seems to be a little bit difficult. (Student 1)

It was difficult in that lots of time should be allocated to the game to apply lesson concepts to the game. (Student 2)

Because of the difficulties described above, students began developing their own ideas on what games would be effective for teaching on consumption. We asked what types of games would be especially useful. Students replied that the game should allow for students to manage, plan, and expand their resources, both monetary and material; on where critical thinking could be applied to students' everyday lives; and the game should move quickly so that students can play continuously and confirm results immediately. Most suggested games designed not much more advanced than *Farmville* type games. Some pointed out the relevance of time investment for game proceedings and others suggested an alternative type of games which improved this element.

One student said,

Lots of time is required for learning in Farmville. For this reason, if students invest more time in the game than self-study, it could cause adverse effects because of concentrating too much on the game rather than the class. So, games used in a consumption education class must be the proper type of games, where students can experience various activities without investing too much time. (Student 1)

CHALLENGES

1. Achieving the Lesson Objective

Concepts such as resource types, resource characteristics, consumer decision-making process, consumer satisfaction, etc. are hard to understand just through theoretical explanations. The lesson objectives of a consumption education course include understanding market economy principles; the roles of consumer, producer, government, etc. simultaneously; and the capabilities of independent consumers. For this, a learning environment similar to a real consumption environment is required, so that students can understand reciprocal relations between various consumption principals and consumption resources in micro or macro perspectives. At this time, *Farmville* can be an optimal lesson learning site and satisfies these demands. Namely, *Farmville* useful in achieving lesson learning objectives because students are expected to live wise consumption lives through increasing their assets by managing them, making decisions using proper consumer strategies, evaluating their own consumption types and patterns with such results, etc., all of which can be applied to their own lives

2. Self-Directed Learning

In *Farmville*, students can plan their own game play according to their schedules. Their leveling up depends on game play. *Farmville* also enables students to understand lessons through managing their farms directly and motivates them to learn more at the same time. When students make decisions related to resource management by themselves, they are carrying out self-directed learning. As they participate more in a game, student satisfaction and academic achievement increase. By performing a project with their group, they can raise fellowship and share mutually beneficial information, achieving goals by jointly managing their resources.

3. Future Improvement

To better achieve lesson objectives, consumption education content and the game should be taught simultaneously. It caused students increased workload, time and effort to get familiar with the game individually. Also some problems were found. Teachers need to prepare a lesson plan, practice an actual lesson, to use this in the school; the burden of assignment development and use will extend the entire semester. The teacher should augment the lesson with supplemental materials which students can use to understand consumption education contents when participating in a game, or manuals which can assist in understanding the contents of the game.

SUMMARY AND CONCLUSION

This chapter focused on integrating *Farmville* with lesson planning for a middle school classroom. Consumption education is a complex subject, and students can struggle with grasping such abstract concepts. According to the results of students' survey, *Farmville* was helpful in understanding consumption education concepts specifically by confirming specific results, such as the impact of resource management, consumption patterns as a decision-making process, etc. Through the process of giving and receiving resources with peers who participate in the game, students found they understand the stream of an actual market economy and realized the importance of a communal consumer culture.

REFERENCES

Hong, Y. (2010). Status and future of social network games. *Korean Contents Promotion Focus*, *18*(1), 34–37.

Hye, W.-H., & Sera, S. (2010). Analysis on user behavior of social game. *Journal of Korea Contents*, *10*(12), 137–145. doi:10.5392/JKCA.2010.10.12.137

Jeong, K.-H. (2010). The successful example of the serious game. *Korea Information Processing Society Review, 17*(1), 122–125.

Kim, Y.-C. (2011). Analysis of growth trend for social network service game market. *Korea Information Processing Society Review, 18*(6), 97–106.

Park, J.-C., Jun, S.-J., & Lee, H.-J. (2011). The effects of social network service activities in the consumers' knowledge creation and continuous intention to use. *Journal of Korea Service, 12*(4), 201–226.

Park, S.-B. (2008). Electronic games appropriated for the classrooms: A proposal of the questionnaire containing 17 questions. *International Journal of Contents, 8*(3), 156–172.

Seo, S.-P., & Kim, J.-H. (2008). Design of model for instruction based on on-line game. *Journal of Korea Information Education, 8*(1), 28–35.

KEY TERMS AND DEFINITIONS

Consumer Civic Awareness: This is related to participation consciousness as active consumers and community spirits. It contains civic capabilities to assert consumer rights and adapt to a consumer society, and actively accept consumer responsibility. It is in school that civic awareness is shaped and schools are fertile ground for molding the mind of future consumers. There is no doubt that the integration of consumption education into the formal school curriculum can be of immense benefit to societies. Students already make consumer choices in school cafeterias, canteens and local shops and kiosks. Students for example should be educated to distinguish the needs from wants, to budget their spending and to make informed choices about the goods they buy. Surely, the growing market products, services and advertising aimed.

Consumption Education: The preparation of an individual through skills, concepts and understanding that are required for everyday living to achieve maximum satisfaction and utilization of his resources. It is defined as education given to the consumer about various consumer goods and services, covering price, what the consumer can expect, standard trade practice, etc. A process of teaching, training and learning to improve knowledge and develop skills among consumers, is called as Consumption education. The Consumption education relates to imparting knowledge to and developing skills in consumers regarding consumer rights, consumer laws, product quality- standards, health aspects of various products, availabilities of various public and private services, units and measurements, redressal of consumer problems and making correct choices while buying different commodities etc.

Consumer Sovereignty: A term used in economics. It refers to consumers determining the production of goods. The term can prescribe what consumers should be permitted, or describe what consumers are permitted. The term was coined by William Hutt in his 1936 book, "Economists and the Public". To most neoclassical economists, complete consumer sovereignty is an ideal rather than a reality because of market failure. Some economists of the Chicago school and the Austrian school see consumer sovereignty as a reality in a free market economy without interference from government or other non-market institutions, or anti-market institutions such as monopolies or cartels. That is, alleged market failures are seen as the result of non-market forces.

Ethical Consumerism: The intentional purchase of products and services that the customer considers to be made ethically. This may mean with minimal harm to or exploitation of humans, animals and/or the natural environment. Ethical consumerism is practiced through 'positive buying' in that ethical products are favoured, or 'moral boycott', that is negative purchasing and company-based purchasing.

FarmVille: A farming simulation social network game developed by Zynga in 2009. Gameplay involving various aspects of farm management such as plowing land, planting, growing and harvesting crops, harvesting trees and bushes, and raising livestock. It is available as an Adobe Flash application via the social-networking website Facebook and Microsoft's MSN Games, and as an app for the iPhone, iPod Touch and iPad. The game is a freemium game, meaning there is no cost to play but players have the option of purchasing premium content.

Social Network Game: A type of online game that is played through social networks, and typically features multiplayer and asynchronous gameplay mechanics. Social network games are most often implemented as browser games, but can also be implemented on other platforms such as mobile devices. They are amongst the most popular games played in the world, with several products with tens of millions of players. While they share many aspects of traditional video games, social network games often employ additional ones that make them distinct.

Chapter 18

Death in Rome:
Using an Online Game for Inquiry-Based Learning in a Pre-Service Teacher Training Course

Shannon Kennedy-Clark
Australian Catholic University, Australia

Vilma Galstaun
University of Sydney, Australia

Kate Anderson
University of Sydney, Australia

EXECUTIVE SUMMARY

This chapter presents a case study that used an online game in a pre-service science teacher training course in the context of computer-supported inquiry learning. Numerous studies have shown that pre-service teachers complete their education with an inadequate range of skills and knowledge in the use of technology in the classroom. In this study, the authors focus on developing pre-service teachers' skills in using a game to teach students through inquiry-based learning. The game used in this study was Death in Rome, a free to access point-and-click game. In the workshop, the participants were required to complete an inquiry-based learning activity using an online game. Overall, this study shows a positive change in attitudes towards game-based learning in science education.

DOI: 10.4018/978-1-4666-2848-9.ch018

INTRODUCTION

This chapter discusses how an online game can be used to develop pre-service teachers' skills and competency in the use of computer games to teach inquiry skills. There is a growing body of research on the integration of information and communication technologies (ICTs) into pre-service teacher training programs and the varying degrees of success of these initiatives (Hu & Fyfe, 2010). Numerous studies, such as Phelps et al. (Phelps, Graham, & Watts, 2011) and Webb and Cox's (2004) literature review, have confirmed that a teacher's attitude towards technology and sustained exposure to ICTs both have a significant impact upon a teacher's decision to use ICT.

In this chapter we will focus specifically on the embedding of game-based learning technologies into the science curriculum for secondary school education through a case study. The case study used an online point and click game called *Death in Rome*. This chapter will focus on how to improve practice-based learning using online games, and will focus on developing new curriculum, embedding ICT within a content area, and developing skills necessary to source appropriate games.

PRE-SERVICE TEACHERS AND GAME-BASED LEARNING

Before moving further forward in this chapter, it is necessary to explore how pre-service teacher curricula need to change to embed ICT into content specific areas in order to be effective. After providing the background, we will describe our starting point for the studies using game-based learning.

The role of teachers in facilitating the use of ICT is pivotal in the successful implementation of selected technologies in a classroom. Advocates of the use of ICT in education foreground several benefits for the use of ICT in classroom situations. These benefits include that using ICT makes the lesson more interesting, and the novelty factor is linked with a divergence from daily teacher fronted classrooms that can invigorate students (de Winter, Winterbottom, & Wilson, 2010; Dede, Clarke, Ketelhut, Nelson, & Bowman, 2005; Goldsworthy, Barab, & Goldsworthy, 2000; Squire, Barnett, Grant, & Higginbottom, 2004). Using ICT, such as simulations and modeling, can result in better teaching outcomes as students can visualize a situation or concept that may be difficult without additional support (Brack, Elliott, & Stapleton, 2004; la Velle, Wishart, McFarlane, Brawn, & John, 2007; Lowe, 2004; M. E. Webb, 2005; Zacharia, 2003).

Student-centeredness or the development of students as individual learners is seen as a benefit in using ICT in classrooms. Pedagogical factors, such as joint task development, promoting self-management, supporting meta-cognition, fostering multiple perspectives, increased student-student and student-teacher time are seen as the benefits of technology-supported learning in science (Hennessy, Ruthven, & Brindley, 2005; M. E. Webb, 2005). However, there are also numerous barriers and problems for novice teachers and these barriers include the additional time pressure to learn new skills, teacher self-efficacy, lack of technological support within the school, and concern over the pedagogical value of the technology (Barab, Hay, & Duffy, 1998; Davis, Preston, & Sahin, 2009; Dede, 1997).

In terms of teacher training programs, there are numerous recommendations aimed at developing lifelong skills and positive attitudes towards technology enhanced learning. Firstly, teachers need well-designed, hands on tutorials and discussion in order to develop their skills (Lee, 1997). These sessions need to be developed with teachers and to focus on discipline (subject area) specific skills and technologies rather than generic computer skills workshops. Lawless and Pellegrino (2007) indicate that discipline-based training is more effective, so having professional development sessions for science teachers that are separate from English teachers may result in a customized and, consequently, more usable skills set. Webb and Cox (2004) support this premise stating that by blending ICT with discipline area expertise, teachers can plan to maximize and explain the affordances of technology to students. This enables students to be more motivated and engaged in the learning activities whilst making the most of the use of a technology. While these studies have all focused on classroom teachers, pre-service teachers also need the same exposure to ICT during their degrees.

The limited and inadequate amount of training that pre-service teachers often receive before entering a classroom means that pre-service teachers, in many cases, do not feel that they have the legitimacy to access technical support in a school. Pre-service teachers may also lack the skills and pedagogical rationale for implementing ICT in the classroom (Angeli, 2004; Lee, 1997). As Figg and McCartney (2010) clarify, novice teachers often teach the tool, rather than teaching with the tool and this is compounded by the fact that ICT is often taught as a separate generic subject that is rarely linked to discipline areas. It is suggested that to develop the appropriate knowledge and skills to use ICT in the classroom, pre-service teachers need to see the use of technology in the context of a discipline, such as science or history (Gill & Dalgarno, 2008; Mishra & Koehler, 2006). That is, pre-service teachers need to be able see the relationships that exist between ICT resources and the discipline and they also need to be able to select and evaluate resources as part of this integration (de Winter, et al., 2010).

CASE STUDY: PRE-SERVICE TEACHERS AND GAME-BASED INQUIRY LEARNING

We commenced our research from the perspective that pre-service teachers need context-specific training in the use of ICT. On the basis of our research (see, for example, (Galstaun, Kennedy-Clark, & Hu, 2011; Hu & Fyfe, 2010; Hu, Wong, Fyfe, & Chan, 2010; Kennedy-Clark, 2011)) we decided that the generic ICT skills-based unit of study was not targeted to particular discipline areas and that students needed discipline specific training with ICT to complement the generic courses. As a consequence, we extended our research into the discipline area of Science. In this study we focus on the embedding of game-based learning into a secondary (high school) science education unit of study.

The study was set in the context of a core science curriculum unit. In this unit of study, students were either completing a Master of Teaching or a combined Bachelor of Secondary Education majoring in science. The two-hour workshop focused on the integration of game-based learning into inquiry learning. 18 students participated in the workshop (11 females and seven males) with an average age of 24.4 years and a standard deviation of 5.52). These students were all majoring in science education and 10 were post-graduates and 8 were undergraduates. None of the participants had worked as a paid classroom teacher and all had completed at least one in-school practicum.

CURRICULUM CONTENT AND WORKSHOP DESIGN

Technological Pedagogical Content Knowledge (TPACK)

The workshop provided students with background information on game-based learning and virtual worlds and the technological pedagogical content knowledge (TPACK) conceptual model (Mishra & Koehler, 2006). TPACK is a framework that is used to describe teacher knowledge for the integration of technology into a classroom environment (Mishra & Koehler, 2006). The framework can be used to provide a technological solution to a pedagogical problem. TPACK is an extension of pedagogical content knowledge (PCK) (Shulman, 1986). While pedagogical content knowledge focuses on the development of understanding of how students learn specific content areas – their perceptions of the content being learned, common misconceptions that they have about the content, and teaching approaches that can maximize students learning; TPACK focuses on the "the connections, interactions, affordances, and constraints between and among content, pedagogy, and technology"

(Mishra & Koehler, 2006, p. 125). Similar conceptual models have also been put forward, such as "integration literacy", "ICT related PCK" and "electronic PCK" (Schmidt et al., 2009).

The adoption of TPACK as a conceptual model to support the integration of ICT into education has grown rapidly and has been the focus of much interest within the CSL field (Graham, 2011). There is a substantial amount of literature regarding the need for teachers to use a combination of different knowledge types when in the classroom. These knowledge types are presented as falling under the broad headings of Content, Pedagogy and Technology (Choy, Wong, & Gao, 2008; Figg & McCartney, 2010; Foster & Mishra, 2009; Graham, 2011; Mishra & Koehler, 2006; Schmidt, et al., 2009). These individual knowledge types have been combined to form a string of acronyms representing new knowledge, such as PCK (pedagogical content knowledge), TPK (technical pedagogical knowledge) and TPCK (technical pedagogical content knowledge) (Galstaun, et al., 2011; Hu & Fyfe, 2010).

TPACK emphasizes a teacher's understanding of how technologies can be used effectively as a pedagogical tool (Koehler & Mishra, 2009). Koehler and Mishra (2009) explain that technologies have their own characteristics, affordances and limitations, which may make them more suitable to certain tasks. Markauskaite (2007) found in her research with pre-service teachers and ICT literacy that being able to plan to use and evaluate different forms of ICT is as important as having the capabilities to use the ICT. According to the framework, to overlay a TPACK model on a classroom activity, teachers not only need to know how to use a computer and its associated software, but they also need to be aware of the strategies to incorporate ICT tools to enhance student understanding of a particular subject's content. Using a TPACK approach has, in preliminary studies, been shown to improve teachers' confidence and skills in the productive use of ICT in classroom situations (Hu & Fyfe, 2010).

Workshop Design

The workshop on game-based learning was arranged for week 4 of Semester 1, 2011. In week 3, students were emailed the workshop materials. Pre- and post-test questionnaires (hereafter referred to as pre-and post-tests) were administered immediately before and after the workshop. The pre- and post-test had 14 questions. The first five questions were Likert style questions and were adapted from the questionnaire used by Hu and Fyfe (2010) in their study using a cohort of pre-service teachers. Questions six to 14 were open-ended questions that were used to assess attitudes and were based on a survey used in a previous study on game-based learning in science (Kennedy-Clark, 2011).

At the beginning of the workshop we facilitated a discussion on computer games and virtual worlds: identified who played games; discussed what types of ICTs they had used in their practicum; and identified problems that the pre-service teachers encountered during their practicum. We discussed inquiry learning and what inquiry learning meant in science. Participants were introduced to the TPACK conceptual model. They then discussed the framework and how pedagogy, technology and content could be integrated in classroom situations. In Table 1, an overview of the activities that students completed is provided in respect to the TPACK conceptual model.

The workshop applied the following TPACK principles: (1) learning tasks are problem-centered, (2) skills are developed via learning-technology-by-design approach where students are provided with an overview of the principles of multimedia learning design theory (Mayer & Moreno, 2002) (3) design tasks are accomplished collaboratively, and (4) learners are encouraged to engage in reflective practice.

The students, in dyads or groups of three completed the online BBC UK historical inquiry activity *Death in Rome*. Using a think, pair, share strategy the group discussed issues such as where, how and why they would use this activity; the strengths and weaknesses of the tool; and connections to the NSW Science 7-10 Syllabus.

Death in Rome

Death in Rome, is a point and click adventure game hosted on the BBC website (http://www.bbc.co.uk/history/ancient/romans/launch_gms_deathrome.shtml). The game is set in 80AD in Ostia, a river port near Rome. In this game, students have to find and evaluate evidence in order to support a hypothesis on how Tiberius Claudius Eutychus died (Figure 1). The game was selected for use in the pre-service teacher ICT workshop because it was designed around an inquiry model.

In the game, participants are asked to solve the mystery of how Tiberius died. They are given a simulated time limit, which is until dawn of the next day, to investigate the mystery. There are several sources of data that can be accessed provid-

Table 1. Pre-service teacher workshop activities

TPACK Three Bodies of Knowledge	Activities
Pedagogical content knowledge	Design activities that support how they would use *Death in Rome* in a science inquiry lesson. Identification of year group or stage of learning, syllabus area and context.
Technological content knowledge	Evaluation of a range of online games and virtual environments. Evaluate for usability and effectiveness of software.
Technology pedagogical knowledge	In groups exploration of the affordances of the allocated online games and how they address a particular teaching/learning need.

Figure 1. Screenshot of Death in Rome

ing clues and questions to assist with inquiry and problem solving. The game works by moving a mouse over the main screen, and as students pass over an object it is illuminated as seen in Figure 2. If a student selects the object a text box appears asking whether or not they would like to investigate the clue. If they select "no", they return to the screen and can continue to investigate the room. If they select "yes" a text box opens has and a modern day expert offers opinions, set on one side of the screen and "character witnesses" who knew Tiberius during this period, on the other side. Each person that the student consults will cost them more time to solve the mystery. The modern day experts include a numismatist (coins expert), an archeologist and historian, a food historian, a medicine expert and a religion expert. The three character witnesses are Tiberius' slave, a Roman trader, and a doctor (Figure 3).

Figure 2. Selecting a clue to investigate

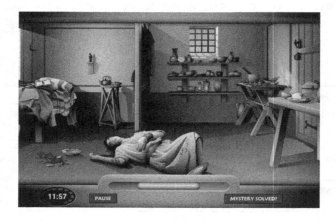

Once the student has investigated a number of clues they can then attempt to solve the mystery. They can open a text box that provides six possible causes of Tiberius's death. These causes (or hypotheses) are malaria, murdered by the doctor, murdered by the trader, suicide, lead poisoning and food poisoning (Figure 4).

After selecting a possible cause of death, the students are required to select three sources of appropriate evidence (Figure 5). If students do not have enough evidence or if they select the wrong evidence, students are directed back to Tiberius's room to investigate more clues and gather additional evidence.

Death in Rome is congruent with Bybee's (2008; Kim & Pedersen, 2011) five e-learning cycle inquiry model. This model advocates developing an inquiry that has five stages: engagement, exploration, explanation, elaboration, evaluation. *Death in Rome* works well as an online inquiry, where students are engaged in the problem, need to explore a range of clues and are required to evaluate several sources of evidence. Students cannot confirm a hypothesis unless they have selected and investigated three pieces of evidence. Ultimately, Tiberius died from malaria, but the students cannot confirm this without investigating the evidence thoroughly.

As a historical point, there is a tomb of Tiberius Claudius Eutychus in Isola Sacra, Ostia that dates from around this time. For teachers, this is a useful piece of information because it contributes to the authenticity of the game, and can be used as a segue to extension activities.

In regards to principles of design in multimedia environments proposed by Mayer and Moreno (2001), *Death in Rome*, adheres to these principles. Table 2 describes how *Death in Rome* adheres to the design principles to reduce cognitive load. The game is simple to master and users are able to navigate through the screens without difficulty.

Figure 3. Investigation area showing experts and character witness

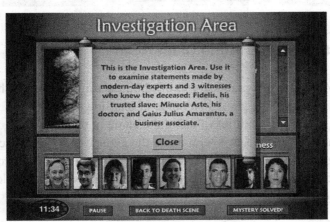

Figure 4. Causes of Tiberius's death

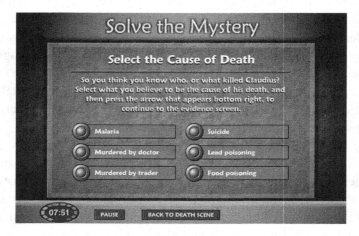

Figure 5. Selecting evidence in Death in Rome

Using *Death in Rome* in the Classroom

This section will outline the practicalities of administering the game in the classroom and strategies for using the game in a range of learning situations.

In regards to the practicalities of using the game in the classroom, we have not encountered any technical issues with using the game either in high school or university settings. We have used the game across a range of education contexts from high school science lessons, to pre-service teacher professional development, and to learning and teaching forums for university teaching staff.

Table 2. The design of Death in Rome in respect to reducing cognitive load

Design Principle	Death in Rome
I. **Off-Loading**: using narration without on-screen text to remove the need for students to read and listen to text at the same time.	Text-based material reduces the need to listen and read concurrently.
II. **Segmenting**: allowing short breaks, or pauses, between sections of a presentation.	Students can move between screens which act as a pause in the presentation of information.
III. **Pre-Training**: starting off the presentation with lessons about any terms or concepts that are new and important to what they will learn in the game.	Pre-training is provided via the two preliminary screens. Screen 1 provides the background to the problem. Screen 2 provides users with directions on how to use the game.
IV. **Weeding**: leaving out any unnecessary audio or visual elements.	The game is simple. Users can only access a limited amount of text at any one time. Users do not need to scroll down or sideways reducing the need to focus on navigation.
V. **Signalling**: using arrows, highlighting, or other cues to the viewer as a means of clarifying important points or confusing images.	Clues are highlighted only when passed over. There are clear requests to select a tab to move forward or backward in the game.
VI. **Aligning:** ensuring that on-screen text and images that rely on each other are shown physically close together.	If a clue is selected to investigate, an enlarge image of the clue is shown in the pop-up text box. This same image is used in the solving the mystery box.
VII. **Eliminating Redundancy**: removing visual elements that are duplicated by narration or graphics.	There is no replication of images or text.
VIII. **Synchronising**: maintaining a close match between narration and visual elements shown in the game.	Synchronizing is achieved whereby all text is related to a particular clue or stage of the inquiry.

The game is hosted on the BBC website, which is a 'low risk' site where content is managed via the British Broadcasting Corporation. In this respect, the site is not blocked by schooling sectors providing easy accessibility, and there is minimal (if any) possibility of harm to students as it is a single user game with no contact with outside users.

We found the game appropriate for high school students, where teachers can adopt the supporting materials to focus on different areas of the game or to suit different year groups. For example, the game could be used in either history or science; it can be used to investigate cultural practices, inquiry skills, disease epidemics and evaluation of historical sources. We have found that using the game collaboratively with two people sharing a computer works well as the students are encouraged to discuss the evidence and make decisions on which clues to investigate.

The game can be used within one classroom lesson. As it is a point and click game, no pre-training is required. The game takes approximately ten minutes to complete, but we have found that users, both university and high school students, often miss salient information on the first pass through the game. It is recommended that they access the game at least twice so that they can spend more time interacting with the resources and have the opportunity to develop a better understanding of the content and inquiry skills.

Results

The results of this study showed that there were significant shifts in the negative responses in the pre-test towards more positive responses. The tests measured prospective teachers' Technological Knowledge (TK), Technological Pedagogical Knowledge (TPK), Technology Pedagogy and Content Knowledge (TPACK) and pre-service teachers' evaluation of the workshop.

The responses to the first five questions also showed an increased confidence in pre-service teachers' knowledge to select appropriate resources and to use the resources. That is, through using a TPACK framework the pre-service teachers believe that they can use the technology effectively as a teaching tool and that their selected resource will work in a classroom.

Several questions in the pre-and post-tests focused on the use of games specifically for education. The analysis of the pre- and post-tests indicated that students' perceptions of educational games changed as a result of the dedicated workshop and showed a positive shift towards using technology in the classroom. The pre-service teachers were asked what they perceived to be the benefits of using educational games in the science classroom, and what they felt were the possible problems or issues that may arise. The results have been presented together in Table 3. It is evident from the results that the pre-service teachers in both the pre- and post-tests saw the value of using educational games in their ability to teach concepts (18.2%; 17.2%) and to engage learners (18.2%; 27.6%). Other benefits included visualization (13.6%; 6.9%) and interactivity (9.1%; 6.9%).

The main shift in the concerns about the use of game-based learning in education is evident in the results. In the pre-test, fun, but no learning (18%) was the main concern, but in the post test this had shifted to technical issues (37.1%). This may actually be a beneficial change. Many of the pre-service teachers were naïve in regards to the integration of ICTs into a classroom. This heightened concern about the technical issues is congruent with classroom teachers concerns about ICTs that were raised in the report *A review of the literature on barriers to the uptake of ICT by teachers* (British Educational Communications and Technology Agency, 2004), and shows a more realistic appraisal of using ICT.

The final question of the pre- and post-tests asked pre-service teachers if they, as teachers, would use educational games and virtual worlds in their classrooms. In the pre-test, of the 13 students that responded to the question, 61.5% (n=8) indicated that they would use games in the class for reasons that included:

Table 3. Pre-service teachers views on the potential advantages, benefits, problems and issues of using educational games in a classroom setting

Pre-Survey		Post-Survey	
Perceived Benefits of Game-based Learning			
Characteristic	**%**	**Characteristic**	**%**
Concepts application	18.2%	Engagement	27.6%
Engagement	18.2%	Concepts application	17.2%
Visualization	13.6%	Motivating	10.3%
Context	9.1%	Modern relevance	10.3%
Safety/simulation	9.1%	Visualization	6.9%
Interactivity	9.1%	Interactivity	6.9%
Problem solving	4.5%	Complex systems	6.9%
Revision	4.5%	Collaboration	3.4%
Enjoyment	4.5%	Inquiry	3.4%
Learning styles	4.5%	Problem solving	3.4%
Literacy	4.5%	Revision	3.4%
		Safety/simulation	3.4%
		Literacy	3.4%
n	22	*n*	29
Perceived Problems of Game-Based Learning			
Characteristic	**%**	**Characteristic**	**%**
Fun, but no learning	18%	Technical issues	37.1%
Lack of ICT skills	18%	Off-task/distracted	25.7%
Off-task/distracted Technical	18%	Fun, but no learning	8.6%
issues	16%	Un-reliable/not specific	8.6%
Un-reliable/not specific	16%	content	5.7%
content	8%	Time consuming Cyber	5.7%
Perpetuate misconceptions	8%	safety	2.9%
Time consuming	8%	Perpetuate misconceptions	2.9%
Cyber safety	4%	Lack of ICT skills	2.9%
Parental concern	4%	Plagiarism	
Plagiarism			
n	25	*n*	35

Yes, I see the benefit in teaching through educational games. The advantages out-weigh the disadvantages but mostly as a tool for revision.

The remaining five students (38.5%) were uncertain of whether they would use games in the classroom.

In the post-test, of the 15 students that responded to the question, 86.7% (n=13) indicated that they would use computer games in the classroom. Their explanations indicated that they are critical of the ICT resources and that the resource would need to deliver content and be reliable, for example:

Yes, but I would have to ensure that all the educational goals are met and they can be easily accessed by all students.

Yes, only appropriate games which tie in closely to curriculum content and peda-gogical orientation.

The students' responses to this question and their intention to use the games is based on the educational value and learning affordance of the tool. This suggests that by allowing students to evaluate and report to the class on their group's ICT resources enabled the development of essential skills in critically evaluating a resource on the basis of criteria such as content, ease of use, time constraints and technical limitations. These responses indicate that the pre-service teachers were considering how ICT can be used in the classroom context. This may also show a move away from teaching the tool to teaching with the tool to using ICT meaningfully.

Pre-Service Teacher Professional Development

It was shown in this case study that a pre-service teacher's attitudes to the use of game-based learning in scientific inquiry were mainly positive as a result of the dedicated workshop. This is also consistent with the results of Hu and Fyfe (2010) who found a significant change in the self-reported attitudes towards designing and using ICTs in the classroom as a result of their semester-long study. The pre-service teachers indicated in the post-test that engagement and visualization were the main learning affordances of using game-based learning in classrooms, which is consistent with other studies on these technologies (Ketelhut, Clarke, & Nelson, 2010; Watson, Mong, & Harris, 2011).

There was a significant difference between the pre-and post-tests in the barriers that might be faced by a teacher using game-based learning in a classroom. In the post-test, the pre-service teachers were more concerned about technical problems rather than the learning outcomes. This is consistent with several studies on teachers attitudes towards using ICT in classrooms (Urhahne, Schanze, Bell, Mansfield, & Holmes, 2010; M. Webb & Cox, 2004).

It should be raised here that in this study we were conscious of not over-estimating the ICT literacy of the students as our previous studies have discounted notions such as *Digital Natives* (Prensky, 2001). The stereotype of Generation Y as being digital natives does not reflect the reality that many pre-service teachers lack a basic knowledge of ICT, which is compounded by limited exposure to ICT in the context of a discipline area. Hence, although pre-service teachers may have exposure to technology, such as iPhones, laptops, iPads and game consoles, it should not be assumed that this exposure results in an understanding of how to use technology for learning and teaching. Prensky's (2001) statement that the current cohort of students are "native speakers" of the digital language is not reflected in the pre-test feedback provided by the students in the study. The overall findings indicate that pre-service teacher self-efficacy plays a pivotal role in their confidence in using ICT; however, many of the pre-service teachers do not have a strong understanding of ICTs, their affordances or their limitations. This needs to be considered when designing a curriculum that embeds ICT into content areas. Students will often need basic support in how to access, evaluate and plan to use ICT in a classroom to complement their content and pedagogical knowledge.

The results of this study showed a positive shift in pre-service teachers' understanding of how ICT can be used effectively as a pedagogical tool through using a TPACK framework. This understanding of ICT as a pedagogical tool is the basis of effective teaching with technology (Graham, 2011; Mishra & Koehler, 2006). Consequently, any training in ICT needs to provide pre-service teachers with ongoing access to ICT tools over the course of their degree program. This is in order to build a sustainable teaching practice wherein a graduating teacher can use ICT in a pedagogically sound manner. The embedding of ICT should be integrated both into coursework and as part of their professional experience.

The limitations of this study are that it was a one-off study, and this may not be sufficient to develop sustainable confidence and skills in using ICTs in the classroom. Factors such as school efficacy and pre-service teacher attitudes have a more resounding impact on a novice teacher than a brief interlude with a game-based learning workshop (M. Webb & Cox, 2004). A second limitation is that although a TPACK conceptual model was used to design the materials, at what level the TPACK framework influenced the results has not been considered. Though, there was a significant change between the pre-and the post-test in favor of game-based learning, the pre-and post-tests did not demonstrate how TPACK may have influenced the outcome of this study. Moreover, this study did not consider all of the permutations of the TPACK elements.

SUMMARY

As with many emerging technologies used in education, we run the risk when using online games and virtual worlds of throwing the technology at the students and expecting them to just learn because it is interesting. We see from the case study that professional development both for educators and pre-service teachers needs to be ongoing and carefully considered for any changes, such as embedding ICT within the curriculum areas, to be sustainable.

What has continued to come out of our research is that these experiences need to be carefully designed in order for the potential of these authentic, powerful and complex learning environments to be met. We see this as a future trend in game-based learning in science education: that the lessons we have learned from other emerging technologies and from extensive work in the learning sciences, be incorporated into the design of the curriculum so that students can actually experience the ICT resource within the context of a content area. Further studies need to be undertaken to gain a better understanding of how novice teachers use ICTs, such as computer games and virtual worlds, when they are in the classroom.

REFERENCES

Angeli, C. (2004). The effects of case-based learning on early childhood pre-service teachers' beliefs about the pedagogical uses of ICT. *Journal of Educational Media*, *29*(2), 139–151. doi:10.1080/1358165042000253302

Barab, S. A., Hay, K. E., & Duffy, T. M. (1998). Grounded constructions and how technology can help. *TechTrends*, *43*(2), 15. doi:10.1007/BF02818171

Brack, C., Elliott, K., & Stapleton, D. (2004, 5-8 December). *Visual representations: Setting contexts for learners.* Paper presented at the 21st ASCILITE Conference, Perth, WA.

British Educational Communications and Technology Agency. (2004). *A review of the literature on barriers to the uptake of ICT by teachers.* British Educational Communications and Technology Agency.

Choy, D., Wong, A., & Gao, P. (2008). *Singapore's pre-service teachers perspectives in integrating information and communication technology (ICT) during practicum.* Paper presented at the AARE 2008, Brisbane. Retrieved from http://www.aare.edu.au/08pap/cho08326.pdf

Davis, N., Preston, C., & Sahin, I. (2009). Training teachers to use new technologies impacts multiple ecologies: Evidence from a national initiative. *British Journal of Educational Technology*, *40*(5), 861–878. doi:10.1111/j.1467-8535.2008.00875.x

de Winter, J., Winterbottom, M., & Wilson, E. (2010). Developing a user guide to integrating new technologies in science teaching and learning: Teachers' and pupils' perceptions of their affordances. *Technology, Pedagogy and Education*, *19*(2), 261–267. doi:10.1080/1475939X.2010.491237

Dede, C. (1997). Rethinking: How to invest in technology. *Educational Leadership*, *55*(3), 12–16.

Dede, C., Clarke, J., Ketelhut, D. J., Nelson, B., & Bowman, C. (2005). *Fostering motivation, learning and transfer in multi-user virtual environments*. Paper presented at the American Educational Research Association, Montreal, Canada. Retrieved from http://muve.gse.harvard.edu/rivercityproject/research-publications.htm#2005

Department of Education. (2008). *Success through partnership: Achieving a national vision for ICT in schools: Strategic plan to guide the implementation of the digital education revolution initiative and related initiatives.* Employment and Workplace Relations.

Feiman-Nemser, S. (2001). From preparation to practice: Designing a continuum to strengthen and sustain teaching. *Teachers College Record, 103*(6), 1013–1055. doi:10.1111/0161-4681.00141

Figg, C., & McCartney, R. (2010). Impacting academic achievement with student learners teaching digital storytelling to others: The ATTTCSE digital video project. *Contemporary Issues in Technology & Teacher Education, 10*(1).

Foster, A. N., & Mishra, P. (2009). Games, claims, genres & learning. In Ferdig, R. E. (Ed.), *Handbook of research on effective electronic gaming in education* (pp. 33–50). Hershey, PA: Information Science Reference.

Galstaun, V., Kennedy-Clark, S., & Hu, C. (2011). *The impact of TPACK on pre-service teacher confidence in embedding ICT into the curriculum areas*. Paper presented at the ED-MEDIA 2011 World Conference on Educational Multimedia, Hypermedia & Telecommunications, Lisbon.

Gill, L., & Dalgarno, B. (2008). *Influences on pre-service teachers' preparedness to use ICTs in the classroom.* Paper presented at the Hello! Where Are You in the Landscape of Educational Technology, ASCILITE, Melbourne.

Goldsworthy, R. C., Barab, S. A., & Goldsworthy, E. L. (2000). The STAR project: Enhancing adolescents' social understanding through video-based, multimedia scenarios. *Journal of Special Education Technology, 15*(2), 13–26.

Graham, C. R. (2011). Theoretical considerations for understanding technological pedagogical content knowledge (TPACK). *Computers & Education, 57*(3), 1953–1960. doi:10.1016/j.compedu.2011.04.010

Hennessy, S., Ruthven, K., & Brindley, S. (2005). Teacher perspectives on integrating ICT into subject teaching: Commitment, constraints, caution, and change. *Journal of Curriculum Studies, 37*(2), 155–192. doi:10.1080/0022027032000276961

Hu, C., & Fyfe, V. (2010). *Impact of a new curriculum on pre-service teachers' technical, pedagogical and content knowledge (TPACK)*. Paper presented at the Curriculum, technology & transformation for an unknown future, ASCILITE Sydney 2010.

Hu, C., Wong, W. Y., Fyfe, V., & Chan, H. (2010). *Formative evaluation via technology-mediated peer assessment*. Paper presented at the World Conference on Educational Multimedia, Hypermedia and Telecommunications 2010 Toronto, Canada.

Kennedy-Clark, S. (2011). Pre-service teachers' perspectives on using scenario-based virtual worlds in science education. *Computers & Education, 57,* 2224–2235. doi:10.1016/j.compedu.2011.05.015

Ketelhut, D. J., Clarke, J., & Nelson, B. (2010). The development of River City, a multi-user virtual environment-based scientific inquiry curriculum: historical and design evolutions. In M. J. Jacobson & P. Reimann (Eds.), *Designs for learning environments of the future* (pp. 89-110). New York, NY: Springer Science + Business Media.

Kim, H. J., & Pedersen, S. (2011). Advancing young adolescents' hypothesis-development performance in a computer-supported and problem-based learning environment. *Computers & Education, 57*(2), 1780–1789. doi:10.1016/j.compedu.2011.03.014

Koehler, M. J., & Mishra, P. (2009). What is technolgical pedagogical content knowledge. *Technology and Teacher Education, 9*(1), 60–70.

la Velle, L., Wishart, J., McFarlane, A., Brawn, R., & John, P. (2007). Teaching and learning with ICT within the subject culture of secondary school science. *Research in Science & Technological Education, 25*(3), 339–349. doi:10.1080/02635140701535158

Lawless, K. A., & Pellegrino, J. W. (2007). Professional development in integrating technology into teaching and learning: Knowns, unkowns and ways to pursue better questions and answers. *Review of Research in Education, 77*(4), 575–614. doi:10.3102/0034654307309921

Lee, D. (1997). Factors influencing the success of computer skills learning among in-service teachers. *British Journal of Educational Technology, 28*(2), 139–141. doi:10.1111/1467-8535.00018

Lowe, R. (2004). Interrogation of a dynamic visualisation during learning. *Journal of Learning and Instruction, 14,* 257–274. doi:10.1016/j.learninstruc.2004.06.003

Markauskaite, L. (2007). Exploring the structure of trainee teachers' ICT literacy: The main components of, and relationships between, general cognitive and technical capabilities. *Educational Technology Research and Development, 55,* 547–572. doi:10.1007/s11423-007-9043-8

Mayer, R., & Moreno, R. (2002). Aids to computer-based multimedia learning. *Learning and Instruction, 12,* 107–119. doi:10.1016/S0959-4752(01)00018-4

Mayer, R. E., & Moreno, R. (2003). nine ways to reduce cognitive load in multimedia learning. *Educational Psychologist, 38*(1), 43–52. doi:10.1207/S15326985EP3801_6

Mishra, P., & Koehler, M. J. (2006). Technological pedagogical content knowledge: A framwork for integrating technology in teacher knowledge. *Teachers College Record, 108*(6), 1017–1054. doi:10.1111/j.1467-9620.2006.00684.x

Phelps, R., Graham, A., & Watts, T. (2011). Acknowledging the complexity and diversity of historical and cultural ICT professional learning practices in schools. *Asia-Pacific Journal of Teacher Education, 39*(1), 47–63. doi:10.1080/135986 6X.2010.541601

Prensky, M. (2001). Digital natives, digital immigrants part 1. *Horizon, 9*(5), 1–6. doi:10.1108/10748120110424816

Schmidt, D., Baran, E., Thompson, A. D., Mishra, P., Koehler, M. J., & Shin, T. S. (2009). Technological pedagogical content knowledge (TPACK): The development and validation of an assessment instrument for preservice teachers. *Journal of Research on Technology in Education, 42*(2), 123–149.

Shulman, L. (1986). Those who understand: Knowledge growth in teaching. *Educational Researcher, 15*(2), 4–14.

Squire, K. D., Barnett, M., Grant, J. M., & Higginbottom, T. (2004). *Electromagentism supercharged! Learning physics with digital simulation games.* Paper presented at the International Conference of the Learning Sciences, Los Angeles, CA. Retrieved from http://www.educationarcade.org/files/articles/Supercharged/SuperchargedResearch.pdf

Urhahne, D., Schanze, S., Bell, T., Mansfield, A., & Holmes, J. (2010). Role of the teacher in computer-supported collaborative inquiry learning. *International Journal of Science Education, 32*(2), 221–243. doi:10.1080/09500690802516967

Watson, W. R., Mong, C. J., & Harris, C. A. (2011). A case study of the in-class use of a video game for teaching high school history. *Computers & Education, 56,* 466–474. doi:10.1016/j.compedu.2010.09.007

Webb, M., & Cox, M. (2004). A review of pedagogy related to information and communications technology. *Technology, Pedagogy and Education*, *13*(3), 235–286. doi:10.1080/14759390400200183

Webb, M. E. (2005). Affordances of ICT in science learning: Implications for an integrated pedagogy. *International Journal of Science Education*, *27*(6), 705–735. doi:10.1080/09500690500038520

Zacharia, Z. (2003). Beliefs, attitudes, and intentions of science teachers regarding the educational use of computer simulations and inquiry-based experiments in physics. *Journal of Research in Science Teaching*, *40*(8), 792–823. doi:10.1002/tea.10112

ADDITIONAL READING

Barab, S. A., Dodge, T., Ingram-Goble, A., Volk, C., Peppler, K., & Pettyjohn, P. (2009). Pedagogical dramas and transformational play: Narratively-rich games for education. In Lurgel, I. A., Zagalo, N., & Petta, P. (Eds.), *Interactive storytelling* (pp. 332–335). Heidelberg, Germany: Springer. doi:10.1007/978-3-642-10643-9_42

Barab, S. A., Dodge, T., Thomas, M. K., Jackson, C., & Tuzun, H. (2007). Our designs and the social agendas they carry. *Journal of the Learning Sciences*, *16*(2), 263–305. doi:10.1080/10508400701193713

Ketelhut, D. J., Clarke, J., & Nelson, B. (2010). The development of River City, a multi-user virtual environment-based scientific inquiry curriculum: Historical and design evolutions. In M. J. Jacobson & P. Reimann (Eds.), *Designs for learning environments of the future* (pp. 89-110). New York, NY: Springer Science + Business Media.

Watson, W. R., Mong, C. J., & Harris, C. A. (2011). A case study of the in-class use of a video game for teaching high school history. *Computers & Education*, *56*, 466–474. doi:10.1016/j.compedu.2010.09.007

Section 6
Game-Based Learning in Practice

Chapter 19
Games, Models, and Simulations in the Classroom:
Designing for Epistemic Activities

Terence C. Ahern
West Virginia University, USA

Angela Dowling
West Virginia University, USA

EXECUTIVE SUMMARY

Games, models, and simulations have been suggested as an effective classroom activity for the middle school. This chapter describes the use of a teacher created simulation targeted to one unit of the science curriculum. The authors found the key feature in playing games in the classroom is for each student to commit to the effort of playing the game. Given the cultural importance of video games, students understand the underlying requirements of playing games. Once the students commit wholeheartedly to playing the game they are able to engage their imagination and creativity while understanding that "failure" is simply a part of the game. The key to the authors' success was the use of a whole class scaffolding technique that allowed the teacher and her students an opportunity to play.

DOI: 10.4018/978-1-4666-2848-9.ch019

INTRODUCTION

Scientific knowledge is a crucial skill for the 21st Century. Consider that 100 years ago swamps were viewed as a major health threat and were systematically drained. Now we know that swamps are an intrinsic part of the larger eco-system. By understanding the role that these wet lands play in the eco-system, we are able to choose a more appropriate response. Instead of gaining science knowledge, the United States is losing its edge and is falling farther behind in the highly competitive disciplines of Science, Technology, Engineering and Mathematics (STEM). The Nation's Report Card documents this decline in science knowledge among our nation's high school graduates. According to the National Assessment of Educational Progress, the nation's 12th graders are performing significantly lower than 12th graders were only a decade earlier in 1996 (NAEP, 2009). This trend is all the more troubling because the modern world demands a minimum of science literacy of all its citizens

Improving our children's grasp of scientific knowledge is difficult (See Hibert and Sigler 2004) because the predominant teaching paradigm within most classrooms today in the United States according to Schwartz, Chase, Oppezzo and Chin (2011) is *tell and practice* (T&P). T & P as an instructional delivery strategy is similar to the classic recitation model. First the teacher tells or demonstrates content and then has the students either answer questions or perform some task (Hibert and Sigler 2004, p. 13). This form of instructional delivery however, according to some researchers, hinders a deeper understanding of the problem. Catrambone writes that

"Students tend to memorize the details of how the equations are filled out rather than learning the deeper, conceptual knowledge that is implicit in the details. Thus, if they are given a new problem that seems similar to an old one—at a surface level—they will try to apply a set of steps from the old problem (1998, p335).

In contrast deVries, Lund and Baker argue that "An important goal of teaching is for students not only to be able to solve specific problems, but also for them [students] to understand the concepts and principles that underlie problem solving" (2002, p. 64). They want students to become flexible in "new situations, predicting future states of affairs, and solving types of problems that have not already been practiced" (deVries, Lund & Baker, 2002, p. 64).

Quality instruction creates opportunities for students to engage, to practice with the new knowledge or skill. Therefore, "Effective practice is deliberate. It involves attention, rehearsal and repetition and leads to new knowledge or skills that can later be developed into more complex knowledge and skills" (Brabeck & Jeffery, N.D. para. 1).

The goal, therefore, is to design learning activities that encourage students to engage in effective practice (deVires, Lund & Baker, 2002). Well designed practice is essential in providing students with the opportunity to apply not only "what" or "how" they know but also "when" to apply the new skill or knowledge. deVries, Lund & Baker concur and suggest that students should not only be " able to solve specific problems, but also for them to understand the concepts and principles that underlie problem solving" (2002, p. 64) which Ohlsson (1995) calls "practical knowledge".

Practical knowledge is a disposition to act in a particular way when pursuing a goal under certain circumstances (Ohlsson, 1995). Consider a math formula that a student has just mastered. Even though the student can execute the formula correctly they may not know *why* or *when* to apply the formula. Therefore the key to effective practice is to integrate "the knowing what" with "the knowing how". Consequently the goal is to develop learning activities that encourage epistemic development.

Epistemic activities are discursive (e.g. text writing, verbal interaction, or presentation) that operate on knowledge and understanding rather than procedures (deVries, Lund & Baker, p. 64). One way to achieve this paradigm shift is to engage today's learners with games, models and simulations. Previous research has shown that using video games in the classroom can be rewarding on many levels including academic achievement, motivation, and classroom dynamics *(Lee, 2004)*.

Games, models and simulations are terrific vehicles to create dynamic epistemic activities. However, adapting games, models and simulations for use in the typical classroom is difficult. Most commercial-off-the-shelf (COTS) games have their own internal goal structure which does not conveniently align with the intended learning objective. Squire recognized that the introduction of a game into the classroom can improve student's motivation, but can also lead to distraction from the curriculum's goals and objectives (2003, no page). However, Squire found that "roughly 25% of students in school situations complained that the game was too hard, complicated, and uninteresting. They elected to withdraw from the gaming unit (2003, para. 6)". Instead of focusing on the intended learning outcome, the students became self-absorbed and focused on the intricacies of the game. Papert (1993) recognized that even though the computer in the classroom can be used to encourage innovative thinking on the part of the student, the computer itself does not represent good teaching or learning (1993, p. xiv).

Current research on the use of games, simulations and models has bifurcated into two rival camps. According to Ke (2008), frequently-cited arguments for the success of using games and simulations include:

- Engagement in learners;
- Encouraging active learning or learning by doing;
- Enhancing learning and understanding of complex subject matter;
- Fostering collaboration among learners.

Some researchers have pointed out that there is a lack of empirical evidence in the literature supporting the use of games within the classroom (see Vogel et al, 2006).

The difficulty with the current research lies " in the lack of an empirically-grounded framework for integrating computer games into classrooms" (Ke, 2008, p. 1609). This chapter reports on an eco-simulation of a food web in a middle school science classroom. The students were successful in coming to understand the dynamics of complex eco-systems. We discuss why the project was successful and describe a design model for teachers to successfully integrate games and simulations in the classroom.

BACKGROUND

Games, models and simulations have been proposed as a dynamic addition to the more traditional classroom strategies of tell and practice. But what is a "game" and what makes it useful for schools?

A game is a rule-based activity that takes place in a defined context. Abt describes the traditional view of a game as an activity among two or more independent decision-makers seeking to achieve their objectives in some limiting context. A more conventional definition would say that a game is a context with rules among adversaries trying to win objectives (1970, p. 6)

The limiting context as suggested by Abt, defines the boundaries of the game: where it begins, where it ends and where the game is played. For most games, this limiting context is depicted by the gameboard, a tangible artifact of the game which changes over time reflecting the actions and re-actions of the players. Chess is played on a chessboard that is divided into 64 squares (eight-by-eight) of alternating color. The chessboard creates a tangible artifact which defines the context for the game.

Secondly, according to Abt's definition, a game is a rule-based activity. The rules dictate how to set-up the initial state of the game. They define the conditions for how to determine the end of the game. Finally the rules describe how each piece of the game can legally move.

Game play is iterative and continues until, by rule, the game is ended. Klopfer, Osterweil & Salen (2009) suggest that to actually play a game an individual player must exhibit four personal attributes: effort, imagination, creativity, and resilience after failure. Consider the following:

- **Effort:** In order to play, games require each player to exhibit some effort.. Because every action in the game is well defined, players know what to do in order to "play" the game. Consider the first time you learned how to play checkers with your father. He told you that you HAD to jump even though you realized at the time that he had set you up. Further, in order to play the game the player has to know what constitutes a legal move. Consider for example in chess the knight is the only piece that can jump over other pieces, or the Queen is the only piece that can move in any direction.

- **Imagination:** As a player, playing the game requires that you make your move. However, knowing which move is the best move requires imagination. In order to make the best move, given the current state of the gameboard, the player has to imagine what could happen given this move or that. Players use prior experience in juxtaposition with the current state of the gameboard. Players must weigh the consequences of any given move in order to achieve the best possible future outcome.

- **Creativity:** As we have seen, a player can imagine what will happen given a particular move. However, the only way to actually see what really happens is for the player to make the move. Creativity and experimentation are essential elements in game play. Games and simulations allow players an opportunity to experiment with "what if" problems.

- **Resilience:** The ultimate beauty of a game is that it is ok to fail. Consider that a great hitter in baseball is also a player who fails seven out of ten times. Games make it ok to fail.

Playing games is iterative and recursive. Games are iterative Given that we fail in a game more often than we succeed, the great thing about playing a game is that we get another chance. The game continues with each player getting their move until by rule the game is over.

A game is also recursive. Each player makes a move based on the current state of the gameboard. Every action is built upon a prior action. Every move in the game becomes the input for a subsequent re-action. The game changes in relationship to each move of the players. . . The gameboard is always changing and as Yogi Berra observed "the game ain't over till it's over".

INTEGRATING THE SIMULATION IN THE CLASSROOM

The science classroom is a perfect venue for integrating game play. Consider the structure of a player's typical move in a game as illustrated in Figure 1.

In playing a game, players consider the current situation as shown by the current state of the gameboard. They weigh their options for their next move. Finally they must make a decision and make the move.

The structure of a game is a very similar to what Polya (1971) suggested as a four-step procedure for solving problems:

Figure 1. Making a move

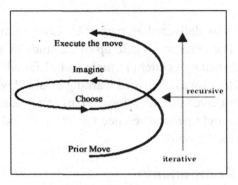

- Understand the problem;
- Devise a plan;
- Execute the plan; and
- Revise.

According to Polya you must first understand the problem. Just as in a game, the player needs to understand the current state of the game, where his pieces are in relation to the other pieces on the gameboard. Secondly, Polya wants the problem-solver to devise a plan. Similarly the game player has to evaluate the current state of the board and assess whatever options are available for the best move. Finally, just as Polya suggests the game player chooses what to do move and does it. Polya's problem solving algorithm maps closely to the making of a move within in the game.

Games provide an easy entrance into problem solving. The game focuses engagement and interest in itself; it attracts the student's attention, and increases communication while symbolizing the pursuit of a common goal (Roth, 1996, p. 148). -Everything a player needs to play the game is contained within the context of the game as realized by the gameboard. The player observes and analyzes the current state of the game as suggested by the gameboard. They make their next move as indicated by the gameboard and their experience within the game.

We were interested in investigating if a teacher-designed simulation could be more easily integrated into the middle school classroom. The rationale was that the simulation would be tailored to the specific curriculum content. Further, because it was designed and programmed by the teacher it would be easier and adapt more simply. To investigate these questions we used an exploratory case design (Yin, 1989)

Participants

The food web model was delivered as part of an ecosystem unit in an 8th grade middle school class. The class was made up of 22 students ranging from age 12 to14 and evenly distributed by gender (11 male and 11 female). Within this class 8 were academically gifted, 1 was identified learning disabled with an Individualized Education Plan and 3 received modifications as part of a Student Assistance Team's plan. The teacher has taught general science for 17 years and 8th grade science at this particular school for 16 years.

The Technology Components

The classroom was equipped with an electronic white-board which was attached to a computer. Consequently the teacher was able to demonstrate the FoodWeb for the whole class simultaneously.

The software was introduced at the end of a unit on ecosystems (biomes). The teacher started the lesson by reintroducing the students to the notion of consumer and producers. She then launched the FoodWeb and began the lesson. The teacher used StarLogo to program a simulation of a Food-Web (See Figure 2) that has three dynamic agents: rabbits, wolves and bears and one static agent, the trees. The initial state is shown in Figure 1. To set the simulation in motion the teacher simply clicks on the FOREVER button.

The agents were designed to interact with each other so, for example, the trees serve as a food source for the rabbits. If enough rabbits nibble on the same tree it dies and it is removed from the screen which reduces the overall food supply for the rabbits. The rabbit is the food source for the wolves and the bears so when a bear or wolf "bumps" into a rabbit it is "eaten".

Figure 2. Initial screen of the Food Web simulation

The model was coded with additional complexity. If the rabbits have enough food and they hit another rabbit then a baby rabbit is born. After a couple of cycles the rabbit matures. The wolves and the bears are programmed to grow old and die.

StarLogo (MIT, 2010) reduces the overhead for learning how to program end-user games, models and simulations such as the Food Web by using a puzzle piece metaphor (See Figure 3). This makes the development of the application quick but also easily adaptable.

This ease of use made it possible for the teacher and her students to modify the simulation during runtime.

Procedure

During the first few minutes of the lesson the teacher had the student recall prior concepts and notions. For example she reminded them that they had already studied the idea of a model, producers and consumers as agents in an eco-system. At this time she launched the Food-Web-model to the whole class using the white-board located at the front of the classroom. The teacher structured this learning activity much like a game with the entire class acting as a "player". Consequently, each "turn" had the students observing, evaluating, repairing and executing the model. Further the teacher established the goal for the game by posing the following question: "Can we create a balanced food web?" She then started the simulation which generated the following response:

Figure 3. Programming elements in StarLogo

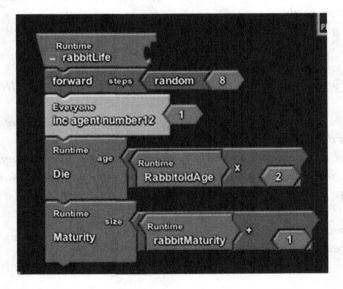

T (teacher): *This is a food web I made, OK? And in this food web we have trees that simulate producers (remember, its a model).*

C (class comments): *Look at the trees!*

T: *We talked about it at the beginning of the year. A model is a simulation of something and its really kind of not easy to work with. Here we have a model - plants -trees - something to eat all of your plants. For your consumers we have rabbits which are our herbivores, OK, we have here - you can hardly see it - its wagging its tail - its a wolf. The problem with this is, no not a problem, we have bears which can be omnivores and we have the wolves which can be carnivores, herbivores are the rabbits and we have producers with the trees.*

In this exchange the teacher starts the game. She wants the class to "observe"; to notice what the model is doing. The students respond by noticing the number of trees to which she counters that they are only one part of the model. There are other agents present in the food web model and she identifies them as a note of awareness.

The next part of a basic game move is the analysis of what the player just observed. Here the player observes or notices the current state of the gameboard. For example, does the current position of the game pieces match what the player expected or were there some surprises? The player needs to reconcile what was expected and respond to what is actually present on the gameboard. Here the students evaluate what is going on with the model

T: *And when I click on the forever button it will run ("forever" is a widget on the "runtime" window that executes the model and sets it to run). Let's see what happens.*

C: *A low murmur; oh!*

T: *You want me to slow down?*

C: *Yeah!*

A: *What do you see right now?*

C: *I see baby bunnies; a LOT of bunnies; a LOT of bunnies;AHHHHH; why are those ....*

T: *Your trees....your trees are disappearing - see your tree disappeared - a couple of trees disappeared - you have a lot of rabbits ....*

T: *The model is programmed so that if the rabbits hit the trees enough times they would "die", that is, be consumed and then leave the model. Notice that the trees are disappearing from the model due to an over population of rabbits.*

C: *Bunnies!!; even bears; bears look old.*

A: *And the bears will die.*

A: *And the bears begin to disappear.*

A: *That's because it's old and it's died.*
C: *I think another bear died.*

At this point the class is only halfway through a "move". Notice that they understand that the bears, being the highest member of the food chain simply age and die once their population is not supported by the bunnies.

Now the teacher suggests what they need to fix or repair the model in order to achieve the intended goal of creating a balanced eco-system. The students have to come up with a strategy, a solution, a plan. So she prompts them with what they already know:

T: *I can change the program ...well first of all, scientific method....what's the first thing you do when you do an experiment?*
C: *Ask a good question.......how many to change.*
C: *One.*
T: *One thing at a time ... so what do we want to change?*
C: *Maybe increase the bears; bears.*
A: *You want to increase the bears? How many bears you want? we got three.*

The teacher goes to the white board to change the initial number of bears in the program at the code level.

T: *It's a simple mouse click.*
C: *Fifteen; two; fifty; thirteen.*
T: *Let's realistically increase the bears....ten bears?*
C: *Ten; thirteen bears; doggies.*
T: *Remember, in the population yesterday with the wolves they brought ten wolves, so let's take ten bears and see what happens ok?*
C: *Yeah.*
T: *I can click on here.*
C: *You are making them to do this, your bears...(unintelligible).*

The students have developed a plan for the repair and they need to finally implement the move. She inputs the agreed upon number and executes the program.

There is a brief pause of sound everyone is watching the food web run. . . Finally the class breaks into a loud hubbub.

C: *Give... HOHOHO; bears; a little bit; laughter; rabbits; their ();*
T: *Lot of rabbits.*
A: *There's a lot of bears though.*

C: *There's a lot of bears; Too many bears! there's one rabbit HOORAY!*
T: *Are there any rabbits left?*
C: *There's one!; run bunny run!*
T: *And now he's old and died; look what happened to the rabbits.*
C: *They died.*
T: *And why would the rabbits die?*
C: *Too many bears!*
T: *So now what should we do? Hands raised!*

The simulation lasted until all of the rabbits, wolves and bears died out. All that was left standing were some of the trees. In terms of game play the class completed one complete turn from observation to interpretation to strategy to execution. Remember game play is highly iterative and the classroom activity proceeded like this for the entire period. This give and take continued for the entire 55 minutes of the period.

One feature of game play that is extremely useful for the classroom is that it is recursive. Games are constrained and self-contained activities. Everything you need to play the game is contained in the current state of the game. Consequently, when a player is choosing their next move all the information required to alter the current state of the problem is right in front of them.

Evaluation

Ke(2009) suggested that one reason for a lack of consistent success in the use of games and simulations in the classroom was due to the lack of an integrative framework. However we suggest, based on our data, that the lack of an "integrative framework" is not what is missing but a lack of understanding of how games work within the nature of play. We suggest that to use games and simulation effectively in the classroom teachers must understand the nature of play and the process of epistemic dialogue.

According to Huizinga, play takes place outside of normal reality. He describes play as "play-grounds, i.e., forbidden spots, isolated, hedged round, hallowed, within which special rules obtain. All are temporary worlds within the ordinary world, dedicated to the performance of an act apart" (Huizinga, p.10). For Huizinga this place is a magic place, a special place – a place free from normal everyday conse-quences. We can, just for a moment, imagine what it would be like to hit a Nolan Ryan fastball in the PC game Major League or conquer the world in RISK. This magic world, as Salem and Zimmer observe, "is just that—a circle—is an important feature of this concept. As a closed circle, the space it circumscribes is enclosed and separate from the real world" (2004, p. chapter 9).

Huizinga suggests the Magic Circle is where everyday objects can take on magical properties. For Huizinga play creates the possible. Within the Magic Circle the player can risk, explore, think, and act without consequence. In the magic circle it is time away.

According to Klopfer, Osterweil and Salen (2009) play provides the player with an environment where there is freedom to fail, to experiment, to imagine, to try.

The teacher in our project created just such a context where all her students felt able to participate. She translated the learning activity into a game space where they were given permission to fail with a single caveat that they needed to be creative and imaginative. The students demonstrated remarkable resilience in the face of multiple failures. She encouraged them. Further the simulation itself was essential in that it provided immediate response to the suggested changes (see Roth, 1996). The students were able to track the outcomes of their previous suggestions. The simulation functioned as the gameboard that provided an instant update to the current state of the model.

Secondly as Squire (2005) pointed out many students become discouraged in using games at school. They cannot figure out the purpose of the game play and loose interest. However our teacher was able to further enhance the learning experience by scaffolding game play through an epistemic dialogue (See Figure 4). She helped them observe, evaluate, repair and execute. She made it "fun" while maintaining the learning outcome.. These tasks were done collaboratively in a whole class environment.

She would show the model and prompt the students to observe the changes. She then posed questions to help them refine their observation and interpretation. Next she gave them suggestions as to what they could do within the model and then

Figure 4. Epistemic dialogue

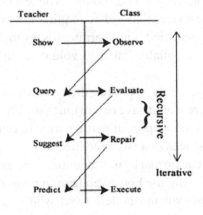

helped them predict what might happen when they executed the revised model. One element of playing the game was it was fun and that the students were willing to play – to enter the magic circle.

SUMMARY AND CHALLENGES

The key to effectively using games in the classroom is an understanding of the nature of play and the specific epistemic objective. Games provide the opportunity for students to apply what they know in unique and dynamic situations. Consequently, the epistemic or the practical knowledge element is crucial. The data shows that the students were able to collectively observe, analyze, repair and execute the model of the food web.

In conjunction with scaffolding of the play by the teacher the students could apply all the knowledge and skill that they learned concerning eco-systems and food webs prior to engaging the computer model. The teacher for her part also participated in the game playing by making sure that the students stayed on task. Secondarily she would prompt or point out elements in the model that worked or did not work.

The simulation was iterative – she and the students worked on the model in an attempt to create homeostasis. Even though the class never really got the desired outcome the entire class remained engaged in the process.

The primary element was that they engaged in the recursive process by remembering what changes they as a group had already suggested and executed. In the end they made the rather insightful comment that they would never create homeostasis by simply concentrating on a single variable or agent but would need to simultaneously modify each of the agents either through simple numbers or through a redesign of the various behaviors.

These students were able to risk and experiment without having to worry about whether or not the day's activity would "count". The teacher embedded the simulation activity into a "game space" that had no requirements other than to participate. The students who were identified with learning disabilities and IEP as well as the more gifted students were equally liable to volunteer an answer. The game is a powerful environment.

However, if the magic circle is broken then everything counts. If the activity becomes "work" then there would have been a much different outcome. The brighter students would be more circumspect in participation because they understand that this activity has consequences in a larger context.

However this does not mean that by not "counting" the game activity that learning is lost. We argue that by using the FoodWeb learning was reinforced. The students were willing to experiment with the model – to see what might happen if they simply changed one thing. They were able to build on those elements of the unit that they had already completed. The game allowed them to explore some of the concepts in a fun and non-threatening environment. Our data suggests that to better use games in the classroom the teacher should be willing to maintain the magic circle unbroken.

REFERENCES

Abt, C. C. (1970). *Serious games*. New York, NY: Viking Press.

Ahern, T. C. (2009). *Bridging the gap: Cognitive scaffolding to improve computer programming for middle school teachers*. Frontiers in Education 39th ASEE/IEEE, M1H-1-6. Retrieved from http://fie-conference.org/fie2009/

Braebeck, M., & Jeffery, J. (n.d.). *Practice for knowledge acquisition (not drill and kill)*. Retrieved from http://www.apa.org/education/k12/practice-acquisition.aspx

Catrambone, R. (1998). The subgoal learning model: Creating better examples so that students can solve novel problems. *Journal of Experimental Psychology. General, 127*(4), 355–376. doi:10.1037/0096-3445.127.4.355

deVries, E., Lund, K., & Baker, M. (2002). Computer-mediated epistemic dialogue: Explanation and argumentation as vehicles for understanding scientific notions. *Journal of the Learning Sciences, 11*(1), 63–103. doi:10.1207/S15327809JLS1101_3

Heibert, J., & Stigler, J. W. (2004). A world of difference: Classrooms abroad provide lessons in teaching math and science. *Journal of Staff Development, 24*(4), 10–15.

Huizinga, J. (2002). *Homo Ludens: A study of the play element in culture*. New York, NY: Routledge.

Ke, F. (2008). A case study of computer gaming for math: Engaged learning from game play? *Computers & Education, 51*, 1609–1620. doi:10.1016/j.compedu.2008.03.003

Klopfer, E., & Begel, A. (2003). StarLogo under the hood and in the classroom. *Kybernetes, 32*(1-2), 15–37. doi:10.1108/03684920310452328

Klopfer, E., Osterweil, S., & Salen, K. (2009). *Moving learning games forward: Obstacles, opportunities & openness*. MIT Press: The Education Arcade.

Lee, J., Luchini, K., Michael, B., Norris, C., & Soloway, E. (2004). More than just fun and games: Assessing the value of educational video games in the classroom. *Proceedings of CHI 2004, Association of Computing Machinery* (pp. 1375-1378).

Ohlsson, S. (1995). Learning to do and learning to understand. In Reiman, P., & Spada, H. (Eds.), *Learning in humans and machines* (pp. 37–62). New York, NY: Elsevier Science Inc.

Papert, S. (1993). *Mindstorms: Children, computers and powerful ideas* (2nd ed.). New York, NY: Basic Books.

Polya, G. (1971). *How to solve it: A new aspect of mathematical method.* Princeton, NJ: Princeton University Press.

Roth, W.-M. (1966). Art and artifact of children's designing: A situated cognition perspective. *Journal of the Learning Sciences, 5*(2), 129–166. doi:10.1207/s15327809jls0502_2

Salen, K., & Zimmerman, E. (2004). *Rules of play: Game design fundamentals.* Retrieved from http://common.books24x7.com.www.libproxy.wvu.edu/toc.aspx?bookid=7016

Schwartz, D. L., Chase, C. C., Oppezzo, M. A., & Chin, D. B. (2011). Practicing versus inventing with contrasting cases: The effects of telling first on learning and transfer. *Journal of Educational Psychology, 103*(4), 759–775. doi:10.1037/a0025140

Shafer, D. W. (2005). Epistemic games. *Innovate: Journal of Online Education, 6*(1). Retrieved from http://www.innovateonline.info/index.php?view=article&id=79

Squire, K. (2005). Changing the game: what happens when video games enter the classroom? *Innovate: Journal of Online Education, 1*(6). Retrieved from http://www.innovateonline.info/index.php?view=article&id=82

StarLogo. (2010). *Computer program.* MIT: Schneller Teacher Education Program.

U.S. Department of Education, Institute of Education Sciences, National Center for Education Statistics. (2009). *National assessment of educational progress (NAEP), 2009 science assessment.* Retrieved from http://www.nagb.org/publications/frameworks/science-09.pdf

Vogel, J. J., Vogel, D. S., Cannon-Bowers, J., Bowers, C. A., Muse, K., & Wright, M. (2006). Computer gaming and interactive simulations for learning: A meta-analysis. *Journal of Educational Computing Research, 34*(3), 229–243. doi:10.2190/FLHV-K4WA-WPVQ-H0YM

Yin, R. K. (1989). *Case study research: Design methods* (revised ed.). Newbury Park, CA: Sage.

KEY TERMS AND DEFINITIONS

Eco-System: The study of the interrelated biological systems.

Epistemic Activity: Activities that are not just learning what but also how to use that prior knowledge in unique situations.

Game: A game is a rule-based activity that has a beginning, middle and an end. The rules specify how to set-up the game, how to play the game and how to end the game.

Gameboard: The gameboard is a dynamic artifact that depicts the context for playing the game.

Magic Circle: According to Huizinga the Magic Circle is a place for an individual to play without consequence.

Play: Play is an "act" apart that has no intrinsic value.

Problem Solving: The ability to apply prior knowledge to unique situations.

StarLogo: A simulation programming environment that was created at MIT.

Chapter 20

The Role of Animations and Manipulatives in Supporting Learning and Communication in Mathematics Classrooms

Lida J. Uribe-Flórez
New Mexico State University, USA

Jesús Trespalacios
New Mexico State University, USA

EXECUTIVE SUMMARY

This chapter describes the use of a computer-based animation and manipulatives to support learning and communication of mathematical thinking in a fourth-grade classroom. The educational animation called Overruled, part of the Math Snacks project (mathsnacks.com), was utilized to address the concept of length units. The animation describes a story in which the king and the queen from two different kingdoms (Kingopolis and Queentopia) fell in love and wanted to unite their territories by constructing a bridge. Engineers from each kingdom were responsible for building their side of the bridge. However, each kingdom has its own length unit. Authors follow research based recommendations to use the Overruled animation in mathematics activity with fourth-grade students.

DOI: 10.4018/978-1-4666-2848-9.ch020

1. OVERALL DESCRIPTION

A wide range of tools can be utilized to support communication in mathematics classrooms. For instance, teachers can utilize computer-based animations as tools to introduce students to a specific math concept while promoting classroom discussions. Manipulatives are other tools that, when appropriately used, could also support communication and learning in mathematics classrooms.

The Principles and Standards for School Mathematics guidelines consider communication as a relevant activity in learning mathematics. Specifically, in grades 3-5, " … communication should include sharing, thinking, asking questions, and explaining and justifying ideas. Students should be encouraged to express and write about their mathematical conjectures, questions, and solutions" (National Council of Teachers of Mathematics (NCTM), 2000, p. 194). In addition, the Common Core State Standards for Mathematics (CCSS-M) emphasize the need for students to "justify their conclusions, communicate them to others, and respond to the arguments of others" (CCSSI, n.d., p. 6-7).

This chapter illustrates a short case in which educational animation and manipulatives were utilized to support communication and learning of mathematical concepts during an after-school program. There were twelve fourth-grade students with a score below proficiency in mathematics based on the standardized state test. Five of the students participating in this case were native Spanish speakers. The authors utilized a computer-based educational animation that involves the concept of length measurement, and a broken ruler as a manipulative to help students learn about measuring objects while communicating mathematically.

2. LITERATURE REVIEW

In a position statement about technology and math education, NCTM (2008) indicates technology is an essential tool for learning mathematics in the 21st century, and all schools must ensure that all their students have access to technology. Effective teachers maximize the potential of technology to develop students' understanding, stimulate their interest, and increase their proficiency in mathematics. (p. 1)

Even though, in mathematics education, technology is usually related to calculators and interactive mathematical software, instructional animations are also great technological tools that teachers can use to foster students' understanding and interest in mathematics. These animations have been increasingly popular in computer-based education (Hasler, Kersten & Sweller, 2007). Animated materials have the potential to support students' learning based on their capacity to depict dynamic situations explicitly (Betrancourt, 2005; Lowe, 2004). However, research has failed to provide enough evidence of the benefits of using computer-based animations in education (Ayres & Paas, 2007).

Based on multimedia learning theory (Mayer, 2005, 2009) and cognitive load theory (Plass, Moreno & Brünken, 2010; Sweller, Ayres & Kalyuga, 2011), Ayres, Kalyuga, Marcus and Sweller (2005) summarized specific instructional strategies that may improve the effectiveness of instructional animations. These authors recommend: (1) acquiring sufficient prior knowledge; (2) keeping the information longer on the screen; (3) controlling the pace of the animation; (4) segmenting the animation in parts; (5) presenting statics before animations; (6) increasing interactivity; and (7) predicting situations in the animation.

Another tool that has been proposed to support students' mathematics learning and understanding is manipulatives (Hiebert et al., 1997). Learning occurs not just by using the manipulatives (Ball, 1992; Clements & McMillen, 1996), but it also happens when students reflect on what they are doing with these objects (Baroody, 1989; Hull, Balka & Miles, 2011). Therefore, the impact of manipulative use on learning depends on the instructional strategies implemented in mathematics classrooms. Moreover, manipulatives could support communication in a mathematics classroom. According to Kosko and Wilkins (2010), manipulative use and communication in mathematics classrooms are related. To impact learning, manipulatives should be used in ways that support students' engagement in communicating their ideas from reflecting on the manipulation of objects and connecting those actions to the mathematical content.

There are some manipulatives used to understand measurement of length. Clements (1999) suggested specific strategies for using manipulatives to help children's communication and learning of this concept. For younger students, Clements (1999) recommends that teachers should allow learners to interact with rulers along with manipulable units such as centimeters cubes. This manipulation allows students to create their own rulers, helping students connect their experiences and ideas. For older students, activities that require standard units are needed.

3. PRACTICALITIES OF RUNNING THE GAME

In the case discussed in this chapter, we utilized the animation *Overruled,* which is related to measurement, specifically, the concept of length units. This animation was one of the three prepared activities that support students' understanding of the concept. First, the students were involved in an activity using manipulatives (wood pieces) to identify differences between units; students then participated in the discussion involving the animation; and finally, students participated in another activity involving the use of another manipulatives (broken rulers) to reinforce the concept.

During the first activity, students were involved in a task that requires measuring edges of different prisms. We asked students to measure three different edges of the prisms using one-centimeter wood pieces and after that, using one-inch wood pieces. Our goal was to help students develop the concept of unit by repeatedly using an identical unit (Lehrer, Jaslow, & Curtis, 2003; Lehrer, 2003). In addition, this activity provided students experiences with the concept of length measurement which, in turn, helped them understand the ideas in the instructional animation.

For the second activity, the animation was presented to the students. *Overruled* is a six-minute animation created by *Math Snacks* project (mathsnacks.com) at New Mexico State University that involves the concept of length units. This animation describes a story in which the king of "Kingopolis" and the Queen of "Queentopia" fell in love and wanted to unite their kingdoms by constructing a bridge between their territories. Engineers from both kingdoms met and decided that the bridge should be "twelve noble feet high," describing *noble feet* as the size of the kingdom leader's foot. Engineers from each kingdom began the bridge at their territory and agreed to build it until the middle meeting point. Troubles started when engineers found that the two halves of the bridge were of different heights. The video also implements the use of ratios, proportions, and measurement conversions to solve the problems. Implicitly, the story in the animation is divided into five parts: (1) introducing the animation's main characters; (2) building a bridge to connect both kingdoms; (3) facing the problem based on the heights of the two bridge halves; (4) finding the origin of the problem; and (5) solving the problem.

During the final activity, we wanted students to reinforce that concept by using a different manipulative. This time, they used the broken ruler. The aim of the activity was to have students identify the units included in rulers, as well as generate a discussion on length measurement using different broken rulers. Students were confident when they measured each side of a shape drawn on a piece of paper using a whole ruler (which includes the 0). However, students were challenged when measuring the sides of those shapes using a broken ruler. They needed to analyze where to start, as well as how they were going to count the units, either centimeters or inches, to calculate the length of what they are measuring.

4. DETAILS OF USING GAMES FOR TEACHING, LEARNING AND ASSESSMENT

We presented the *Overruled* animation using a laptop and a computer projector. The animation was projected on a white screen placed in the front of the room. Students were seated at their tables with a clear view to the screen. Instructors were either seated around the projector (while playing the animation) or in front of the class (while interacting with students). While presenting the animation, the instructors followed the seven recommendations proposed by Ayres et al. (2005).

Acquiring sufficient prior knowledge. The students were involved in activities related to measurement and length units. As has been described, students were asked to measure edges of different prisms using one-centimeter and one-inch wood pieces. This activity provided them with the idea of length unit and the need for having same units when measuring distance.

Presenting statics before the animation. Before starting the animation, we presented the first screen that appears before starting the animation. In this animation, there are three people: one female and two males (See Figure 1). The female and one of the males have crowns indicating they are the queen and the king of the story. Viewers can identify differences between the queen's and the king's foot sizes. Next, the instructors explained that they were going to present a short video that starts with that snapshot. Students then were asked what they thought the animation was about and what they could see in that picture.

While watching the animation, the instructors followed the other five recommendations. The animation was stopped several times; first, after the context of the situation was presented; second, after the problem was presented; and the final time, when the problem was solved. Each time the animation was stopped, the instructors asked several questions and promoted interaction between students. Students' interaction and discussion allow instructors to assess their understanding of the situations and their ideas about measurement and length units.

After the animation set the context of the situation and before beginning discussion of the problem, instructors stopped the video and asked the students what the animation was about, who were the characters in the animation, and what was

Figure 1. Overruled animation main characters

happening to the different characters. These questions provided students with the opportunity to communicate their ideas about the animation and allow instructors to know whether or not students were following the story. In this case, we wanted to be sure that the English language learner students in the group were able to follow the animation. We could observe that all students were interested in the animation, and they were willing to share their ideas and understanding of the story. For instance, after the second part of the video (building the bridge) the instructor asked: "What are they trying to do?" One student answered, "They are trying to build a bridge so they [the King and the Queen] can keep in touch" (See Figure 2).

After the presentation of the problem, we stopped the animation once again and asked students what problem the animation was presenting? Why the bridge didn't connect? For instance, one student said, "it depends on the foot, and so the Queen's foot is bigger and the King's smaller." Before the animation identified the solution to the problem, the instructor asked the students what solutions they suggested for solving the problem (See Figure 3). The instructors observed that the students utilized their previous knowledge and suggested options, including measuring the King and Queen's feet, and identifying who has the "right foot" (twelve inches long). In a similar solution, one student suggested using a ruler to determine which foot is 12 inches long. This discussion helped instructors assess understanding of conversion between inches and feet, and students were using their previous knowledge on measurement based on the comparison of lengths and the need to have an object with numbers (Barrett, Jones, Thornton & Dickson, 2003).

For the last part of the animation (solving the problem), the pedicurist discovers the difference between the loyal feet and found that two Queen's feet are equal to three King's feet. With this equivalence, they were able to solve the problem using

Figure 2. Overruled animation context

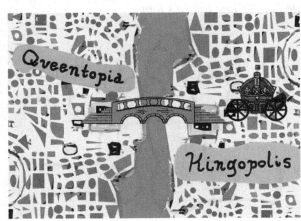

Figure 3. Overruled animation problem

conversion of measures. By asking students about the solution of the problem, they understood how the pedicurist solves the problem using ratios between the foot sizes (See Figure 4). Summarizing, students indicated that the problem was that engineers from different kingdoms were using different units to measure the height of the bridge, and when building or measuring objects it is important to use the same unit.

While interacting with the students, instructors kept the snapshots of the main parts of the animation related to the discussion that students were answering. Therefore, the information, in snapshot representation, was presented on the screen for students to use and refer to while presenting their ideas.

Figure 4. Overruled king's and queen's foot

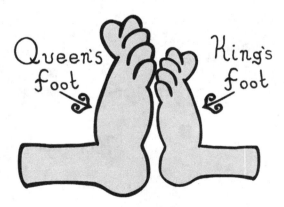

5. TECHNOLOGY COMPONENTS AND CHALLENGES

To develop our activity of the measurement concept, the instructors used a computer projector and a laptop with Internet access to display the *Overruled* animation. This is a flash animation designed by the NSF funded *Math Snacks* project at New Mexico State University. The animation and educational materials designed for students and teachers are available for free at www.mathsnacks.org.

Since there were not enough computers to let each student interact with the animation, instructors decided to show the animation to the whole class using one laptop, a computer projector, and a white screen. In this setting, students do not have the chance to interact with or manipulate the animation on their own, but it allows a better interaction among the whole class. Instructors were in charge of manipulating the animation and deciding the pace of halting and continuing the animation based on students' interactions and discussions. In addition, the quality of the animation and the stop points (predefined by the instructors to promote discussion among the students), allow a relevant educational environment where students communicate their ideas based on the educational animation.

6. SUMMARY

Although research on instructional animations does not show convincing results, multimedia learning and cognitive load theories have demonstrate that these can be useful resources. The instructors believe that well-designed educational animations such as *Overruled* are important technological tools that can be easily integrated in the curriculum to introduce specific concepts to students. Instructional animations with multimedia capabilities have the potential to help students to visualize situations that otherwise might be difficult to understand. Moreover, each educational animation from *Math Snacks* has a learners' guide that students can use to practice the concepts, and so be able to transfer conceptual understanding to math problem solving.

7. LESSONS LEARNED/TIPS FOR PRACTITIONERS

Technology is changing education. Educators need to become familiar with these tools, but, more importantly, they should to modify their teaching styles in order to use the technological tools in ways that support student learning. If educators accommodate technology to the same teaching style, we are limiting the power of technology. Educators can modify their lesson plans and teaching styles to incorporate more problem-based learning, in which students have the opportunity to explore these new technological resources where they learn from solving problems, working collaboratively, and communicating ideas. Computer-based animations and manipulatives are just two examples of technological tools that can help educators create problem-based environments that promote communication between students when working in pairs, or with the whole class. The instructors utilized computer-based animations and manipulatives with teaching strategies that complemented the use of these tools. An effective strategy is to discuss a problem with the class, then ask children to work in pairs, and finally have the children share the solutions strategies with the group (Sarama & Clements, 2009). Computer-based animations can be a tool to support learning, but it is important to know how to use this tool effectively in the classroom. Simply having the technology in the classroom does not necessarily support learning, therefore activities that include this tool should provide students with the opportunity to reflect, think, and discuss the content presented, as ways for them to be able to construct their knowledge.

NOTE

This material is based on work supported by the National Science Foundation (NSF) under Grant No. 0918794. Any opinions, findings, and conclusions or recommendations expressed in this material are those of the author and do not necessarily reflect the views of the NSF.

REFERENCES

Ayres, P., Kalyuga, S., Marcus, N., & Sweller, J. (2005). *The conditions under which instructional animation may be effective*. Paper presented at an International Workshop and Mini-conference, Open University of the Netherlands: Heerlen, The Netherlands.

Ayres, P., & Paas, F. (2007). Making instructional animations more effective: A cognitive load approach. *Applied Cognitive Psychology, 21*, 695–700. doi:10.1002/acp.1343

Ball, D. L. (1992). Magical hopes: Manipulatives and the reform of math education. *American Educator, 16*(2), 14–18, 46–47.

Barlow, A. T., & McCroy, M. R. (2011). Strategies for promoting math disagreements. *Teaching Children Mathematics, 17*(9), 530–539.

Baroody, A. J. (1989). One point of view: Manipulatives don't come with guarantees. *The Arithmetic Teacher*, *37*, 4–5.

Barrett, J. E., & Dickson, S. (2003). Broken rulers: Teaching notes. In Bright, G. W., & Clements, D. H. (Eds.), *Classroom activities for learning and teaching measurement* (pp. 11–14). Reston, VA: National Council of Teachers of Mathematics.

Barrett, J. E., Jones, G., Thornton, C., & Dickson, S. (2003). Understanding children's developing strategies and concepts for length. In Clements, D. H. (Ed.), *Learning and teaching measurement* (pp. 17–30). Reston, VA: National Council of Teachers of Mathematics.

Betrancourt, M. (2005). The animation and interactivity principles in multimedia learning. In Mayer, R. E. (Ed.), *The Cambridge handbook of multimedia learning* (pp. 287–296). New York, NY: Cambridge University Press. doi:10.1017/CBO9780511816819.019

Clements, D. H. (1999). Teaching length measurement: Research challenges. *School Science and Mathematics*, *99*(1), 5–11. doi:10.1111/j.1949-8594.1999.tb17440.x

Clements, D. H., & McMillen, S. (1996). Rethinking concrete manipulatives. *Teaching Children Mathematics*, *2*(5), 270–279.

Clements, D. H., & Sarama, J. (2007). Early childhood mathematics learning. In Lester, F. K. (Ed.), *Second handbook of research on mathematics teaching and learning* (pp. 461–555). Reston, VA: National Council of Teachers of Mathematics.

Common Core State Standards Initiative. (2010). *Common core state standards for mathematics*. Retrieved from http://www.corestandards.org/assets/CCSSI_Math%20Standards.pdf

Hasler, B. S., Kersten, B., & Sweller, J. (2007). Learner control, cognitive load and instructional animation. *Applied Cognitive Psychology*, *21*, 713–729. doi:10.1002/acp.1345

Hiebert, J., Carpenter, T. P., Fennema, E., Fuson, K. C., Wearne, D., & Murray, H. Human, P. (1997). *Making sense: Teaching and learning mathematics with understanding*. Portsmouth, NH: Heinemann.

Hull, T. H., Balka, D. S., & Miles, R. H. (2011). *Visible thinking in the K–8 mathematics classroom*. Thousand Oaks, CA: Corwin.

Kebritchi, M., & Hynes, M. (2010). Games for mathematics education. In Hirumi, A. (Ed.), *Playing games in school: Video games and simulations for primary and secondary education* (pp. 119–145). Eugene, OR: International Society for Technology in Education.

Lehrer, R. (2003). Developing understanding of measurement. In Kilpatrick, J., Martin, W. G., & Schifter, D. (Eds.), *A research companion to principles and standards for school mathematics* (pp. 179–192). Reston, VA: National Council of Teachers of Mathematics.

Lehrer, R., Jaslow, L., & Curtis, C. (2003). Developing and understanding of measurement in the elementary grades. In Clements, D. H. (Ed.), *Learning and teaching measurement* (pp. 100–121). Reston, VA: National Council of Teachers of Mathematics.

Mayer, R. E. (Ed.). (2005). *The Cambridge handbook of multimedia learning*. New York, NY: Cambridge University Press. doi:10.1017/CBO9780511816819

Mayer, R. E. (2009). *Multimedia learning* (2nd ed.). New York, NY: Cambridge University Press. doi:10.1017/CBO9780511811678

National Council of Teachers of Mathematics. (2000). *Principles and standards for school mathematics*. Reston, VA: National Council of Teachers of Mathematics.

Plass, J. L., Moreno, R., & Brünken, R. (Eds.). (2010). *Cognitive load theory*. New York, NY: Cambridge University Press.

Sarama, J., & Clements, D. H. (2009). Teaching math in the primary grades: The learning trajectories approach. *Young Children, 64*(2), 63–65.

Sweller, J., Ayres, P., & Kalyuga, S. (2011). *Cognitive load theory*. New York, NY: Springer. doi:10.1007/978-1-4419-8126-4

Yin, R. K. (2009). *Case study research: Design and methods* (4th ed.). Thousand Oaks, CA: SAGE.

Chapter 21
It's All in How You Play the Game:
Increasing the Impact of Gameplay in Classrooms

Shani Reid
ICF International, USA

Helene Jennings
ICF International, USA

Scot Osterweil
The Massachusetts Institute of Technology, USA

EXECUTIVE SUMMARY

The purpose of this chapter is to describe a study of the online learning game Lure of the Labyrinth. The game is unique in that it is based on a model for how learning games can be effectively used in classroom settings. Key components of the model include identifying games appropriate for the classroom, incorporating the game in a way that maximizes instructional time, and reconstructing the role of the teacher in game play lessons. The model was tested by 29 teachers in 80 middle school classroom, where 1,549 students were exposed to the game and its associated resources. In a quasi-experimental study of the impact of the game on student outcomes it was determined that students in school districts that more closely followed the game implementation model performed better than their comparison group.

DOI: 10.4018/978-1-4666-2848-9.ch021

OVERALL DESCRIPTION

Lure of the Labyrinth is a digital game for middle school pre-algebra students. It includes a wealth of intriguing math-based puzzles wrapped into an exciting narrative game that evolves over time. In the story, the player's avatar (the representation of the player in the game world) works to find their lost pet in a mysterious place called the Tasti Pet Factory, which is populated by monsters. By the end of the game, the player would have recovered his pet, freed other kidnapped pets, and destroyed the factory. The development of the game was funded by a U.S. Department of Education (ED) Star Schools grant awarded to Maryland Public Television (MPT). Key partners in the project were the Education Arcade at the Massachusetts Institute of Technology (MIT), FableVision, and ICF International.

Lure of the Labyrinth is a long-form game that might take students as long as 15 hours to complete. Throughout the game, players earn tokens that they can use to free pets. The game keeps track of players' progress and saves their place in the game on exit so they can continue exactly where they left off the next time. The game consists of 27 puzzles that teach students proportions, variables and equations, and number and operations—typical pre-algebra content.

One puzzle that teaches students proportions is the Employee Cafeteria. In this puzzle, students meet four monsters seated at a cafeteria table with partially filled trays in front of them. The items on the trays have numbers inserted. Through trial and error, students discover that (1) by pushing a button a new food item with a number value appears; (2) they can move the food item to any monster's tray; (3) if they move the item to the correct tray the monster responds favorably and they earn tokens; and (4) if they move it to the incorrect tray, the monster complains and the food is moved to the correct tray, but they lose several lights on their play counter. Once all the play counter lights are extinguished, the game ends.

Through puzzle play students eventually learn that there is a proportional relationship between the food items on each tray that players must determine (e.g., there must always be twice as much drumsticks than sushi on each tray), and a proportional relationship among the monsters' trays (e.g., Monster A eats half as much as Monster B). Tokens students accumulate throughout the game can be used for their pet rescue attempts. Students must successfully complete each puzzle three times to be able to move to the next, more challenging level (See Figure 1).

Lure of the Labyrinth is not only a learning game, but is a game based on a specific model for the effective implementation of games in classroom settings. In this chapter, we present a description of this model and describe how teachers implemented it in 80 middle school classrooms (grades 6 through 8). We then look at the effect the implementation had on student performance. The discussion of student performance is based on a quasi-experimental study conducted by ICF Interna-

Figure 1. Screenshot of the employee cafeteria puzzle

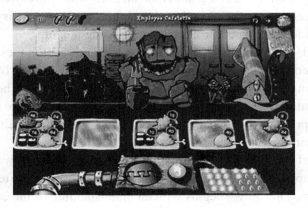

tional that examined the impact of the game on students' scores on standardized math tests. Twenty-nine middle school mathematics teachers in Maryland volunteered to integrate the game into their lessons. Over the course of the study 1,549 students in grades 6 through 8 were introduced to the game.

LITERATURE REVIEW

For several decades, educators have debated the value of using games in schools—some have argued based on educational philosophy, some share anecdotes, and some argue using data they have obtained to prove or disprove the benefit of games. However, beyond the question of whether to include games in educational settings lies the bigger questions of "which" games and "how" games. In this chapter, we argue that for educators to truly understand "why" they should use a game in school requires that they understand "which" games are appropriate for school, and "how" to use them. We see these as important questions, because educators' preconceived notions of what gaming will look like in their classroom will influence their decision to use them.

As stated previously, the "which" centers on which games are most appropriate for inclusion in educational settings. Klopfer, Osterweil, and Salen (2009) note that there are two main perspectives on "which" games. One perspective advocates for the use of commercial, off-the-shelf (COTS) games. Proponents of this perspective support COTS games because they feel that through these games students develop the 21st century skills (The Partnership for 21st Century Skills, 2011) that are needed in the "real world." This group values the learning that takes place through games as more relevant to a students' future than the learning that occurs in classrooms. The second perspective advocates for games that integrate well with current instructional practices—games that can be played in short bursts of time, are easy to grasp, and are directly connected to specific content skills being taught.

Klopfer et al. conclude that "[i]f the first group embraces games and abandons schools, this second group often embraces school to the detriment of anything that looks like gaming" (p. 2). These researchers go on to argue that the two perspectives are not mutually exclusive. Games can be developed that are both engaging and retain the principles of what makes gameplay fun, while being specifically applicable to learning that occurs within classrooms.

The "how" of games is more complex. Here, the focus is on how a teacher, who has selected an appropriate learning game, makes the most effective use of that game in the classroom. The "how" begins with an understanding of the concerns teachers face when asked to use games. Perhaps one of the loudest concerns is whether the teacher will be able to cover all required curriculum material *and* play games. In essence, will the game detract from the "real work" of school (Jenkins, 2002; Squire, 2003). This is especially problematic in content areas such as math, where student performance is examined annually on standardized tests and where teachers may be required to follow a "pacing guide" indicating the math topic to be covered each day or in a series of days. In fact, in recruiting for this case study, we talked with several teachers who were interested in using the game but were told by their administration that they could not because of this exact concern. We anticipate that navigating this roadblock will prove even more challenging in an era where student performance is factored into teachers' compensation.

The "how" also relates to teachers understanding their role in a gaming classroom. Prensky (2001) identifies several roles for teachers in this new world. Teachers are *motivators*, finding ways to engage students in gameplay. They are *structurers*, creating learning opportunities at the intersection of the game and the curriculum. They are *debriefers*, creating space for students to reflect on gameplay and apply their gameplay knowledge and skills to traditional classroom assignments. They are *tutors*, serving as guides and coaches to students as they engage in gameplay.

In essence, a successful "how" is one that provides strategies to incorporate the game that maximizes the use of instructional time, and one that provides techniques for teachers to play the multiple roles that are essential to successful learning through gameplay.

The design of *Lure of the Labyrinth* is based on the "which" and the "how." It fulfills the "which" through a design that retains all the key gaming elements while delivering pre-algebra content. It fulfills the "how," through a plethora of resources developed specifically for the game that are housed on the game's publicly available site at http://labyrinth.thinkport.org. These resources include suggestions on how teachers can motivate students. They also include detailed lessons plans that tie the game to the state curriculum and contain follow-up activities to tie the game to traditional assessments.

We propose that the combination of these resources gives the *Lure of the Labyrinth* the potential to be very effective in classroom settings. The game is not designed to be used in isolation, but to be used along with the resources provided or other teacher-developed resources. The development team explicitly states that playing the game is not sufficient. It is the reflection that occurs after play where the most effective instruction occurs. This idea is supported in Squire (2003) and Thiagarajan (1998). Although directly referencing simulations, the concept is also true of games.

[S]imply using a simulation does not ensure that learners will generate the kinds of understandings that educators might desire. Rather, learners need opportunities to debrief and reflect, and the amount of time spent on reflection should equal the amount of time spent engaging in the game or simulation. Instructors play an important role in this process fostering collaboration, promoting reflection, and coordinating extension activities. (Squire, 2003, p. 6)

PRACTICALITIES OF RUNNING THE GAME

Lure of the Labyrinth is designed to be completely embedded in the culture of a pre-algebra classroom. This means that the most effective implementation of the game begins before students even enter the classroom. Teachers are encouraged to consider their state standards and curriculum, and identify where the standards and curriculum intersect with the concepts the game is designed to teach. Next, teachers are encouraged to identify times where students can play the game at school. This can be times in or out of class (e.g., near the end of class when students have finished assigned tasks or during lunch). These brief moments of in-school play are, in part, designed to motivate students to keep playing at home; where all they need is internet access to continue the game.

Introducing the game to students and getting them involved in gameplay is encouraged at the beginning of the year, prior to any lesson being taught. Throughout the year, teachers continue to encourage students to play the game and provide time for them to do so. Once teachers reach a point where the game intersects with the curriculum, they then use specific puzzles in the game to support targeted instruction.

In order to participate in the ICF study, middle school teachers had to agree to teach a minimum of three game lessons to two of their math classes in which pre-algebra content is covered. At the start of the study, participating teachers were required to attend a 3-hour orientation in their home district. During the orientation, teachers were introduced to the variety of resources that they could access on the game website, and were provided demonstrations of several useful game features, some of which are described below.

Administrator Tool

The administrator tool permits teachers to set up their class lists and divide each class into teams. In this area, teachers create unique usernames and passwords for each student. This allows students' game usage to be tracked and reported. Teachers can generate reports on the number of times each student attempted each puzzle, how many of those attempts were successful, and the length of time the student spent playing the game and each puzzle.

Game Mode vs. Puzzle Mode

There are two ways to use the game with students. In Game Mode, students can access the game story. The game story mirrors many of the commercial games available and is designed to encourage students to keep playing. To advance to the next chapter in the story, they must successfully complete the game in the present chapter. In Game Mode, students have access to puzzles in sequence (i.e., level 2 of a puzzle cannot be accessed unless level 1 has been successfully mastered). In Puzzle Mode, students have access to all 27 puzzles, but they do not have access to the game story. Puzzle Mode is primarily designed so that teachers can readily include individual puzzles into their lessons. So, if there is a particular concept a teacher wishes to focus on that is in level 2 of a puzzle, she can have all students directly access that puzzle, even if they do not yet have access in Game Mode.

Tasti-Pet Communicator (TPC)

The TPC is only available in Game Mode. Through the TPC, players are provided with information on how to play the game, including hints on how to find puzzle rooms, and recaps of the game story they have accessed so far. It is also used as a communication tool through which students on the same team can leave messages for each other about how to solve specific puzzles. Because each instance of the game is played with randomly generated numbers, leaving the specific answer to a puzzle does not help students. They must leave messages that include the *strategy* they used to solve the puzzle. Teachers can monitor communication on the TPC and leave their own messages.

Website Resources

The development of *Lure of the Labyrinth* occurred along with development of a wealth of resources to support teacher use of the game. The website (http://labyrinth. thinkport.org/www/) contains resources for educators and families. These include lesson plans that are aligned to Maryland's Voluntary State Curriculum, an overview of game features, a summary of the storyline, graphic organizers to be used in instruction, and a quick start guide.

During the orientation, a model for classroom implementation was also discussed. It was recommended that teachers do the following:

- Spend sufficient time playing the game themselves so they could understand the puzzles (We found that teachers had significant variations in experience in playing games for their own enjoyment).
- Provide their students immediate access to the game and over the course of the study encourage gameplay in and outside of the classroom.
- Before teaching the lesson in class, require students to spend time playing the puzzle on which a particular lesson was based.
- Allow time for in-class puzzle play before and after the lesson.
- Make use of follow-up activities after the lessons that connect the math in puzzle play to traditional math assessments.

By the end of the study, the 29 teachers had taught 269 game-related lessons to 1,549 students. The extent to which teachers followed the recommended model varied widely:

- We measured how much time teachers spent playing the game by counting the number of puzzle attempts they made. This ranged from 4 to 200 attempts.
- We measured how much time students spent playing the game by counting the number of puzzle attempts they made. This ranged from 0 to 421 attempts.
- We measured how much lead time teachers gave students to play the puzzle on which a specific lesson was based. Fifty percent of all students had little or no lead time as they were told to play the specific puzzle the same day the lesson was taught.
- Half of all students spent less than 1 hour in in-class puzzle play per lesson.
- Most students (89%) participated in some sort of follow-up activity related to the lesson.

TECHNOLOGY COMPONENTS

Lure of the Labyrinth is developed in Flash, and served over the web. It can be played on any reasonably updated computer with internet access, a web browser, and the Flash Player plugin. In preparing for this study, we noted that although all participating schools had existing equipment on which they could play the game, the majority had to install the Flash Player plug-in. In some cases, this had to be done by the school's technology administrator as students and teachers did not have permission to install software.

A few schools had difficulty accessing a reliable internet connection. While the school did have internet access, the network might be down, or the quality of the connection deteriorated once all students had connected to the game site.

Teachers were free to organize gameplay in different ways to suit the technology they had in their classrooms. The *Lure of the Labyrinth* website included notes on how to play the game if they (1) had a one computer classroom with an LCD projector, (2) had several computers in their classroom, or (3) used a computer lab or laptop cart where there were sufficient computers for each student.

EVALUATION

Collecting feedback from teachers was a critical component of the ICF study. Overall, teachers were very positive about the game. All teachers returning to teach middle school math the year after the study said they would use the game in the future. As one enthusiastic teacher expressed,

I am very excited to use these lessons from the start of the year. I have recommended this site to other educators. I tell them how wonderful it was to include technology like this in my classes.

All teachers said it was a useful teaching tool, and nearly half said they felt it was especially effective at motivating and engaging students. They liked how it allowed students to learn about math in a different way and offered an appropriate challenge to students at different levels of understanding in math. A few teachers commented,

It is a good way to get students engaged. Sometimes, the kids didn't even seem to realize they were using math!

Students are a lot more engaged when Labyrinth is in the background of the lesson. They bring some of the excitement they have about the game into the formal lesson.

Students were much more engaged while using the computer game to learn this topic than they were when we taught it the first time in class.

When asked what aspects of the game students seemed to find the most engaging, the most common response (38%) was that students really enjoyed playing the game once they figured out the strategies they needed to navigate the game world and attempt the puzzles. One-third of teachers said their students most enjoyed various game elements (e.g., the storyline, graphics, and creating an avatar). Some teachers (21%) said that their students enjoyed the challenge of applying the lower-level approaches to solving the harder puzzles. As one teacher noted:

After learning how to play the first level, they liked seeing how those rules applied to the higher levels of each game.

Several teachers mentioned students were also engaged in using the message board to communicate with their teammates. A number of teachers noted that students enjoyed being able to choose the level of difficulty at which they wanted to play the puzzle (this was only possible in Puzzle Mode), because they could choose to engage in what they most enjoyed or understood.

The summative evaluation of this project also included a quasi-experimental study, where ICF examined the extent to which the game improved student achievement on state standardized tests. For this study the treatment group was identified as students taught by teachers implementing the game as part of their instruction (1,549 students), while the comparison group was students taught by teachers of similar courses using the resources they would typically use in instruction (1,654 students). Treatment and comparison students were enrolled in different schools to minimize the risk that comparison students would become exposed to the game. The evaluation was originally designed to be a yearlong experimental study. However, due to a change in Star Schools funding, the evaluation was modified to a shorter quasi-experimental study.

Four school districts accepted our invitation to participate in the study. Each district coordinator was asked to identify one or two middle schools that would implement the game. These schools needed to have at least two teachers who would volunteer to be included in the study. Additionally, these two teachers had to teach at least two sections of a math course with pre-algebra content. Once treatment schools were selected, the district math coordinator recommended matched schools and classrooms within these schools that would serve as the comparison group. The students participating in the study were a cross-section of middle school students in the state (Table 1).

Students' scores on the state's standardized test were first analyzed at each of the three grades (6–8) included in the study. This analysis found that students at the sixth-grade level who played the game scored on average half a standard deviation (0.5 SD) higher than students who did not play the game. At the seventh-grade level, there was no difference in the performance of students who played the game and students who did not play the game. At the eighth-grade level, students who played the game scored an average of four-tenths of a standard deviation (0.4 SD) lower those who did not play the game.

More importantly, we found differences across school districts at these different grade levels. We analyzed the data by school district within each grade level. Only two districts had participating sixth-grade classes (Districts A and B). Students in District A scored an average one standard deviation (1.0 SD) higher than students in the comparison group. However, there was no difference in the performance of treatment and comparison students in District B. Three districts had participating seventh-grade classes (Districts B, C, and D). There was no difference in the perform`nce of treatment and comparison students in District B, treatment students in District C scored an average of half a standard deviation (0.5 SD) lower than comparison students, and treatment students in District D scored an average of three-tenths of a standard deviation (0.3 SD) higher than students in the comparison group. Three districts participated in the eighth-grade study (Districts A, B, and C). There was no difference in the performance of treatment and comparison students in Districts A and B. Students in District C scored an average of six-tenths of a standard deviation unit (0.6 SD) lower than students in the comparison group.

Table 1. Description of student participants

Characteristic	Treatment		Comparison	
Gender	N	%	N	%
Male	774	50%	844	51%
Female	775	50%	810	49%
Special Education Student	108	7%	111	7%
Eligible for Free and Reduced Meals	650	42%	651	41%
English Language Learners	31	2%	32	2%
Ethnicity				
Asian	47	3%	33	2%
Black	341	22%	413	25%
Hispanic	77	5%	83	5%
White	1,084	70%	1,125	68%

In an attempt to explore reasons why there were such wide discrepancies at each grade level between districts, we began looking at how teachers implemented the game. Although most teachers followed instructions regarding the minimum number of game lessons they should teach, we noted significant differences across districts in the nature of their implementation; specifically, the degree to which they followed the recommended implementation procedures. For example, when the game database was checked, we noted that in District B (the district that reflected no differences between treatment and comparison groups), only a few students had even logged into the game. 2

We then analyzed more closely how well teachers in each district followed the implementation model with which they were presented at the orientation. For each district, we developed a rating system to measure the degree to which the recommended model was followed. For example, on the first dimension, the district with the highest median number of teacher puzzle attempts was assigned a rank of 4, while the district with the lowest median number of teacher puzzle attempts was assigned a rank of 1. A summary of how the four districts ranked on five dimensions of implementation fidelity is presented in Table 2.

We then compared these ratings with student's performance on the standardized tests. We observed that students in districts that scored higher on adherence to the implementation model (and the underlying game design) (District A and District D) were more likely than students in districts that scored lower on adherence (District B and District C) to outperform students in their comparison group.

CHALLENGES

As a part of the evaluation of the project, teachers were asked to identify the challenges they faced in using the game with their students. Teachers were given a list of challenges they could select and given the option to write in other challenges.

Table 2. Summary of the degree of adherence to the recommended implementation model

Model Dimension	District A	District B	District C	District D
Teacher time playing the game	4	3	1	2
Encourage students to spend time playing the game	3	1	4	2
Try the puzzle before the lesson	2	1	3	4
In-class puzzle play	1	3	2	4
Follow-up activities	4	2	1	4
Total	14	10	11	16

The most frequent challenges selected were encouraging gameplay outside of class (76%), making connections between the math in the puzzle and traditional math assessments (66%), making efficient use of in-class puzzle play time (41%), and inadequate time to develop the topic fully (41%).

All of these challenges were anticipated by the game designers, and resources on how to meet the challenges are included on the *Lure of the Labyrinth* website. For example, to encourage gameplay, the designers recommend that teachers do the following:

- Be enthusiastic about *Lure of the Labyrinth* and talk to your kids about your experiences playing the game (and yes, that means it's a great idea to play the game yourself ... at least, a little). Let students see you playing and enjoying *Lure of the Labyrinth*.
- Talk to your students about their game-playing experiences; encourage them to discuss their game strategies with their teammates, both within *Lure of the Labyrinth* and outside *Lure of the Labyrinth* (in-person conversations and brainstorming sessions).
- Schedule as many opportunities as possible for your students to play *Lure of the Labyrinth*—during class, after class or school, and during lunch or free time.
- Refer to *Lure of the Labyrinth* often during your more formal pre-algebra instruction as an example of how students can, have, and will use the math they're learning.
- Display posters of characters and/or scenes from the game to entice students to want to enter the world of *Lure of the Labyrinth* and to spend time there (http://labyrinth.thinkport.org/www/educators/before/yourrole.php).

Unfortunately, due to the condensed timeframe in which the study had to be conducted, it is possible that teachers did not have the time to implement the strategies suggested or may have simply forgotten they were there as they hurried to fulfill the other requirements of the study.

Teachers were also asked to identify their students' greatest challenge with the game. Seventy-nine percent of teachers said that students were frustrated with the game because there were no hints or directions for completing the puzzles. Several teachers also said that their students would often give up after unsuccessful attempts at solving the puzzles.

...For about 20 minutes I wanted [the student] to try to play the game, and between him and [me] we couldn't even get out of the first room...

The game, however, is intentionally designed to provide only a limited number of hints for several reasons: (1) to maintain the look and feel of traditional online games which in fact do not contain a lot of hints; (2) to encourage students to discuss strategies with their teammates either in person or over the TPC; and (3) the game lesson itself, when it is introduced, is the ultimate "cheat" resource as students learn the math behind the game.

SUMMARY

Lure of the Labyrinth is a digital game for use by middle school math students. Its design, development, and subsequent testing in classrooms sheds light on some critical questions about game use in schools today. Can gameplay in school be fun? Can games designed to teach have the look and feel of games teens play in their free time? Can games be linked to the curriculum? How can teachers implement games in their instruction without consuming too much classroom time? And, in the end, does the use of games (at least in math) make a difference on students' understanding of critical concepts and on their performance on standardized tests?

The Education Arcade at MIT has worked on design principles that focus on assumptions about play and learning. They emphasize the following:

- Choosing for the classroom games that are both truly games and truly deliver targeted content.
- Breaking the mold for where educational games are played—playing them outside of class and then discussing them in school.

Games developed with these elements in mind require teachers to develop a modified perception of their role in the classroom; one that perhaps goes against their innate desire to always be providing instructions or directions, and against their students' desires to always being told what to do. But exploration and discovery can hook students into the story and the challenge of figuring out a solution. These engaging experiences aid students' understanding and transfer to higher levels of problem solving.

The ICF study was able to answer the critical question of how games affect student learning. Although the quasi-experimental study was of limited duration, analysis of performance on standardized tests for over 3,000 treatment and comparison students in four different school districts yielded mixed results. In some districts, treatment students performed better; in others, they performed worse. However, more significantly, students in districts that were more deliberate in implementation and in support of the design assumptions of the game had better student outcomes than those in the comparison classrooms.

REFERENCES

Jenkins, H. (2002). Game theory. *Technology review.* Retrieved April 25, 2005, from www.technologyreview.com

Klopfer, E., Osterweil, S., & Salen, K. (2009). *Moving learning games forward: Obstacles, opportunities & openness.* The Education Arcade, MIT. Retrieved January 20, 2012 from http://education.mit.edu/papers/MovingLearningGames-Forward_EdArcade.pdf

Prensky, M. (2001). *Digital game-based learning.* New York, NY: McGraw-Hill.

Squire, K. (2003). Video games in education. *International Journal of Intelligent Simulations and Gaming, 2*(1).

The Partnership for 21st Century Skills. (2011). *P21 common core toolkit: A guide to aligning the common core state standards with the framework for 21st century skills.* Retrieved April 30, 2012, from http://www.p21.org/storage/documents/P21CommonCoreToolkit.pdf

Thiagarajan, S. (1998). The myths and realities of simulations in performance technology. *Educational Technology, 38*(5).

KEY TERMS AND DEFINITIONS

Avatar: The player's representation of themselves in the game world.

Implementation Fidelity: The extent to which a program or intervention has been delivered as intended.

Long-Form Game: A game designed to be completed over multiple sessions.

Pre-Algebra: A course commonly taken in grade 6, 7, or 8 to prepare students for algebra. The course typically includes topics such as variables and equations, proportions, and some aspects of geometry.

Quasi-Experimental Study: A study designed to examine the impact of an intervention on participants. The main distinction between quasi-experimental studies and experimental studies is participants are not randomly assigned to the treatment and control groups.

Star Schools Program: A federally funded program to support distance education projects that encourage improved instruction in mathematics, science, foreign languages, and other subjects and serve underserved populations. This program was last funded in 2007.

Summative Evaluation: A study conducted to determine how well a program achieved its stated objectives.

Chapter 22
Challenges of Introducting Serious Games and Virtual Worlds in Educational Curriculum

C. Ribeiro
Instituto Superior Técnico, Technical University of Lisbon, Portugal

C. Calado
Akademia, Portugal

J. Pereira
Instituto Superior Técnico, Technical University of Lisbon, Portugal

C. Ferreira
Akademia, Portugal

EXECUTIVE SUMMARY

Although the impact that Virtual Worlds and Serious Games can have on learning efficacy and efficiency has been recognized, there is still many open questions related to this issue. Specifically there aren't guidelines or standards to help practitioners introduce this kind of technologies in a learning environment. In this chapter, the authors describe two experiments involving virtual worlds and serious games in a learning environment. These experiments allowed the authors to understand the real potential of this kind of technology, but also some of the difficulties one can come across. The authors hope that the experiments described in this chapter can serve as a basis for similar experiments done by other practitioners. Finally, some of the pitfalls that should be avoided are described as a set of lessons learnt at the end of the chapter.

DOI: 10.4018/978-1-4666-2848-9.ch022

INTRODUCTION

It is unanimously acknowledged that we are living in the information age, taking part in the information society (Reigeluth 1996; Bates 1999). What makes these two emerging concepts possible is technology, or rather, the rate of progress that has been achieved in technology over the past 50 or so years (Molenda & Sullivan 2003). Throughout this period, technology has been both the generator and the transmitter of information with an increasingly faster speed and wider audience. It now dominates most facets of our lives penetrating into the conduct of normal daily life.

The field of education is not an exception in the permeation of technology. Nevertheless, the high expectations regarding the revolutionary impacts of technology on education has not yet been realized. As Bates et al. argue (1999), the current instructional technology methods are insufficient to meet the consequences of the paradigm shift from industrial age to information age. Consequently, instructional designers are faced with the challenge of forcing learning situations to fit an instructional design method rather than selecting an appropriate method to fit the needs of varying learning situations (Gustafson & Branch 2002).

These radical changes in learning and technology are fuelling a transition in modern learning in the era of the Internet, commonly referred to as e-learning. Zhang et al. (2004) explore the recent advances in e-learning technology and practice, and present experimental results that compare the effectiveness of e-learning and conventional classroom learning. Another novelty in instructional methods is the use of games. Indeed, it may possibly be wrong to call games a novelty since young children, by nature, begin to learn through games and playing since their earliest years (Rieber 1996). The use of games as a way of enhancing learning dates back to 3.000 BC where games where applied mainly to battle planning, trade accounting, fortune telling and religious divination. Although it may seem strange to look at fortune telling and religious divination as learning areas they were the equivalent to the use of mathematics and science in that era as they help people to rationalize a complex universe and to make intelligent decisions.

Recognizing the importance and the impact that Virtual Worlds and Serious Games can have on learning efficacy and efficiency we have devised two experiments in order to study the real impacts of introducing this kind of technologies in education curriculum. With this intent, two groups of studies were conducted involving teachers, psychologists and learners in an educational setting. The first involved using Virtual Worlds for distance learning and the second involved using off-the-shelf games to assess learners learning strategies profile.

The first set of studies consisted in comparing the effectiveness of learning in a Virtual World developed in INESC-ID[1], the Blackboard Platform[2] and a traditional classroom.

The second set of studies had the purpose of assessing leaners learning strategies when using off-the-self brain games such as the ones provided by the Lumosity platform[3] as complementary to the traditional learning mediums.

In the remainder of the chapter we present a desk review on Virtual Worlds and Serious Games for teaching, learning and assessment. Also, a desk review about assessment methodologies to evaluate learning and memory retention and learning strategies profiles is presented. Next, the contexts, research methodologies and results for both experiences are described. Finally, the lessons learned during this process are presented as well as the conclusions, which summarize the main points of the work carried out.

SETTING THE STAGE

Serious Games and Virtual Worlds in Education Settings

Education has always been considered as potentially one of the most productive breeding grounds for technology, where it would perhaps find its finest resonances and lead to revolutionary effects. Yet, high expectations regarding the revolutionary impacts of technology on education have hardly been realized so far. This relative ineffectiveness of instructional technology can be strongly related with the application of the same old methods in new educational media, *"New wine was poured, but only into old bottles"* (Cohen & Ball, 1990).

E-learning and on-line courses can be created and designed using several tools namely, Learning Management Systems (LMS), Learning Content Systems (LCS), Web 2.0 tools or a mixture of the previous. Nevertheless these options have several limitation regarding communication and interaction levels that can be achieved between students. Specifically, most learning systems are asynchronous and don't allow an effective real-time interaction, collaboration and cooperation (Loureiro, 2011). Whilst they typically have synchronous chats and white-boards, these capabilities are often sterile and don't stimulate the appropriate interactions that enhance learning.

The past few years have seen a surge of interest in Multi-User Virtual Environments (MUVEs) and virtual worlds - such as Second Life and World of Warcraft (WoW) - especially in terms of unique affordances these worlds potentially offer in education (Lim, 2009). Virtual worlds can offer both synchronous chat and white-boards but also new ways of interacting with the learning content in real-time and in a collaborative way. In addition, these platforms usually provide support for a wide range of user-based adaptation mechanisms, reinforcing a more personalized learning tailored to the individual learner's needs (de Freitas & Yapp 2005; West-Burmham 2005) and therefore allowing a greater learner autonomy (Field 2007).

Due to its characteristics, virtual worlds are nowadays adopted in a wide variety of contexts, from pre-school to university or business. There are already a large number of universities using Second Life both for teaching as an extra-curricular tool. In those contexts, virtual worlds are normally used to represent a real life environment. For example, the Harvard Law School created Harvard Extension School's moot court, where students learn about court proceedings using Second Life (Nolan 2006). Another example is the Theatron 3 Project where replicas of European theatres were built in a virtual world aiming at students of an architecture course (The Higher Education Academy English Subject Centre 2006).

At this time, hundreds of educational institutions of higher education and individual educators are active in virtual learning environments, supporting the study of things such as: group behaviour, economics and video game development (Foster 2005; Foster 2007).

Due to geographical dispersion of its human resources, companies are also becoming more and more interested in the use of virtual worlds, in order to support some of their business processes such as: distance training, supporting meetings and holding company events. Virtual worlds offer, in this context, a significantly cheaper solution than video conferencing, e-learning development and traveling to instructor-led events but still provide an engaging and enjoyable learning medium. Studies have shown that engaging experiences are required in adult learners aiming at improving retention.

Learning in a 3D environment allows enhanced interaction with content and other individuals and provide a notion of "advanced presence" (feeling like you are really there) and engagement, motivating a "collective learning". Perhaps the most direct application of virtual worlds in education is related with distance education. Today millions of students are taking virtual world based courses using its capabilities to complete assignments, communicate with their peers and instructors and support a set of secretarial processes such as classes registrations and access to educational content (Allen & Seaman 2008; National Center for Education Statistics 2003).

Although these platforms suggest clear benefits and improvements in the educational processes, their adoption requires a major rethink in the curriculum structure. This is essential in order to take full advantage of these virtual worlds. There are a huge number of solutions in the market, finding the best mediums for each context can be difficult, but choosing the right one can make a tremendous difference in student satisfaction and learning (Baggerly 2002; McKeachie 2006; Peters 2003; Sherry 1996).

The stakeholders involved in introducing these technologies into the classrooms or curriculums are also of key importance. The school management, teachers, students and parents play an important role in the success of the application of these technologies. In the majority of these situations, if not all, the teachers are not digital natives, which means that their ability to manipulate these kind of tools are obviously limited and sometimes even inadequate.

For all the reasons presented above, we can conclude that the success of integrating virtual worlds in the classrooms is very dependent on choosing the best solution taking into account the context, and on aligning the expectations of the different stakeholders towards that process. Although the current solutions offer a wide range of services and functionalities there is still a lack of integration methodologies and standards which makes a wider adoption of such platforms difficult.

Assessing Learning in Serious Games and Virtual Worlds

A learning process is the basis of human development and depends on the integration of life experiences and on the improvement of cognition (Kolb & Kolb 2009; Zull 2002). Due to its central role in a person´s life, its construction and its requirements constitute the basis of a broad research field where several models and assessments were developed.

A learning process can be defined in terms of the amount of information required to make a reasonable cognitive map and establish or applying relationships between concepts and representations (Kolb 1984).

Mayes and de Freitas (2004; 2006) based on the categorization of learning models, theories and approaches, defined this process as a "cycle" of learning (Greeno, Collins & Resnick 1996; Mayes & de Freitas 2007) that can be subdivided into three different domains: associative learning which involves activities through structured tasks, situated learning which is related with social practice, and cognitive learning which depends on experience, reflection, abstraction and experimentation.

Based upon cognitive processing, experiential learning provides the conceptual underpinning for a holistic interpretation of learning process (Dillon 2007) connecting the outer world and inner worlds experiences of the learner (Burns 1998).

Kolb (1984, p.41) defines learning as "*the process whereby knowledge is created through the transformation of experiences. Knowledge results from the combination of grasping and transforming experience*". Ten years later, Abbot (1994) argues that "*Learning ... [is a] reflective activity which enables a learner to draw upon previous experience to understand and evaluate the present, so as to shape future action and formulate new knowledge*", adding some key elements, which have individual and social implications for educational context.

Nowadays, the definition of learning includes an active process in which the learner integrates new experiences giving them meaning, and may accommodate and assimilate these new ideas; connects past, present and future with the assumption that un-learning and re-learning may be implied; recognizes that previous learning influences the individual action in future situations. In other words, learning means to integrate the new information on previous person´s mental schemes through its cognitive mechanisms, in a dynamic way (Kolb 2009).

Based on meta cognition ideas, Kolb (2009), formulated his Experience Learning Theory, describing the process of constructing knowledge based on a tension among the four learning modes portrayed as an idealized learning cycle: Concrete Experience (CE), Abstract Conceptualization (AC), Reflective Observation (RO) and Active Experimentation (AE). This process involves experiencing, reflecting, thinking, and acting on a learning situation. Kolb´s theory provides a holistic model of the learning process and a multilinear model of development, accentuating the central role that experience plays in the learning progress (Kolb, Richard, Boyatzis, Charalampos, & Mainemelis 2000) and suggesting that people acquire new knowledge and skills learning by thinking, feeling and doing. Therefore, one of the basic presupposes is that they needed to be involved in the learning process to improve it (Beard, Wilson & McCarter 2007; Heron 2001).

This theory conceptualizes learning based on six fundamental characteristics: learning is a process and not an outcome, it derives from experience, it requires an individual to resolve dialectically opposed modes of adaptation, it is a holistic integrative process, it requires the interplay between a person and the environment, and it results in knowledge creation (Kolb 1984; Kayes 2002).

Some researchers (MacMillan, Alexander, Weil, & Littleton 2005) claim that this theory should be the basis of the curriculum development and the integration of specific didactics in learning environment to improve learning process. Based on the ideas of this theory (such as collaborative learning, experiential based learning, active participating and content creation) some of the new educational strategies are being improved in educational contexts (Bransford, Brown, & Cocking 2000; Gütl 2010).

The Experiential Learning Theory is the foundation for best practices and it´s crucial as a role of debriefing in the learning spiral as a task of simulation/gaming (Crookall 2011). As de Freitas and Oliver (2006) said, *"General trends in the research indicate the increasing popularity amongst learners for using serious games and simulations to support curricular objectives"*.

Game-Based Learning pretends to embed students in a set of activities and processes according to some pedagogical approach – experiential or problem-based (Kolb 1984). Games allow players to experience, to try, to improve skills, to learn content and to practice strategy (Arts 2005) using interactive learning techniques such as learning by doing, learning from mistakes, goal-oriented learning, role playing, constructivist learning, adaptive learning and feedback (Prensky 2001). Games can be used as metaphors, as tools, as therapy and as rehearsal of skills, supporting higher cognition in micro worlds and as open spaces for experimentation (Prensky 2001).

Serious games have become an important topic in the recent history of education as special tool in learning environment (Prensky 2001), pretend to address both the cognitive and affective dimensions of learning (O'Neil, Wainess & Baker 2005), to enable learners to adapt learning to their cognitive needs and to provide motivation for learning (Malone 1981). Therefore, serious games provide a powerful and effective learning environment and capture the student's attention, engaging them in the curricular content (Kirriemuir & MacFarlane 2004; Mayo 2007).

The potential of serious games to improve the effectiveness of learning has been a subject of study over recent years because of the increasing use in educational context. Some of the main reasons outlined to explain this increase applied to learning contexts are the use of actions rather than explanations, the creation of personal motivation and satisfaction, the accommodation of multiple learning styles and abilities, and the fostering of decision-making and problem-solving activities in a virtual setting (Garris, Ahlers & Driskell 2002; Mayo 2007; Wrzesien & Alcañiz Raya 2010). Greitzer, Kuchar and Huston (2007), argued that the cognitive principles can be applied to serious games to improve the training effectiveness, stimulating semantic knowledge, managing the learner's cognitive load, immersing the learner in problem-solving activities, emphasizing interactive experiences, and engaging the learner.

According to experiential learning models, immersive learning context as 3D environments permit access to richer interfaces and develops new capabilities for supporting enriched social interactions with peers (de Freitas, & Neumann 2010). Mueller (2008) defend that simulating real-life learning environments provide students with the opportunity to apply, analyse, synthesize, and evaluate concepts immersed in real-life activities and to enhance several skills (Karet & Hubbell 2003) such as encouraging them to be more reflective about their experience, the context and the consequences of their actions within the artificial social network of a computer game (Hamlen 2011; Stewar 2011). This process allows students to make sense of activities performed in the immersive world and improve their relevance with real or lived world tasks (Lynch and Tunstall 2006), concerning learning as trial of specialized skills, based upon experiences, interactions and interchanges.

Nowadays, literature (de Freitas & Levene 2004; Garris et al. 2002) indicates that technology based on simulations and game environments are accelerating learning progress, increasing motivation and supporting the development of cognitive thinking skills, specifically immersive virtual games are becoming more effective in learning practice (de Freitas & Oliver 2006).

New researches on this area attest the improvement of games and virtual world applications and compare the efficacy of this approach with face-to-face training approaches and other e-learning approaches putting on evidence the clear benefits of learning in immersive worlds and through 3D visualizations (e.g. de Freitas 2006; de Freitas et al. 2006).

Assessing Students Competency Profile

The impact of an individual's learning style towards an individual's performance in learning situations has been explored by many authors over the last few years (Kolb 1985; Honey & Mumford 1992; Riding 1991, 1997; Ford 2000). Even recognizing that students learning styles have a large influence on their cognitive process (Gardner 1983), only a few systems try to profile users and to adapt the educational content accordingly with individual's learning strategies.

Tennant's (1988) defines cognitive style as *"an individual's characteristic and consistent approach to organizing and processing information"* that are central and an unchanging part of *"a fixed characteristic of an individual"* (Riding 1991, 1996). Sadler-Smith (1996) considers cognitive and learning styles as *"fundamentally quite distinct and having different but complementary implications for the design of teaching"* and when comparing them, the first one has a lower level of variance over time and space (Valley 1997).

According with Reiff (1992), learning styles have three essential aspects: cognitive (remembering, problem solving and perceiving think), physiological (environment, gender and nutrition) and affective (personality, motivations and social interaction), that serve as relatively stable indicators of how learners perceive, interact with, and respond to the learning environment (Felder 2010; Keefe 1979). Coffield, Moseley, Hall and Ecclestone, (2004) stated that *"learning styles are different ways that a person can learn. It's commonly believed that most people favour some particular method of interacting with, taking in, and processing stimuli or information."*

The difference between individual's learning styles has been recognized by educators and learners but only few educational systems use this knowledge to personalize and enrich interactive day-to-day applications. Learning strategies should be designed to meet the needs of students in a way to improve learning effectiveness in different learning situations through life span (Felder 1996; Schmeck 1988).

According with the ideas of the Experiential Learning Theory, Kolb's (1984) learning styles model, attests: *"Experience as the source of learning and development"*. To evaluate the combination of the individual's preferred approaches Kolb (1984) created a learning styles inventory that allows students to designate how they like to learn, providing results which show the student's preferred learning style, strategies for learning styles and allows student involvement in the learning process.

More recently, Gardner (1999), corroborates Kolb's, exposing the theory of multiple intelligences, that emphasize the existence of different learning styles and the impact on the way that each student assimilates experiences and knowledge. Gardner (1983) introduced the principle of multiple intelligences, attesting that individuals have natural predispositions to understand and to process information according to their learning or cognitive styles. When learning environment match with individual's learning style, the interest in the topic taught and the motivation can be increased (Lambert et al. 2002) resulting in an improvement of educational outcomes (Levine 1999; Green et al. 2006).

Over the last years, some researches continued studying the impact of learning styles in a learning process. Cognitive Styles Analysis test (Riding & Read 1996; Pillay 2002) have been done on a variety of age groups and in different settings and suggested that the learning style of an individual can affect learning performance (Pillay 1998); preferred mode of working (Riding & Read 1996); and the effectiveness of book or hypertext (Wilkinson, Crerar & Falchikov 1997).

There are many advantages to understand the most efficient way in which each student processes information such as academic advantages (maximize learning potential; succeed on all educational levels; improve the best study and the better grades on tests; reduce frustration and stress levels and expand learning strategies), personal advantages (improve self-confidence and self-esteem; learn how to best use the brain; learn how to enjoy learning; develop motivation for learning and maximize natural abilities and skills) and professional advantages (manage teams in a more effective manner; improve skills and increase power).

Further work relates cognitive and learning styles to developments on the Internet (Riding & Rayner 1995) and technology-based training (Riding 1996, 2001). These two points are an important factor to organize learning environments and help students to learn more effectively by locating and processing information in a more efficient manner.

Online algorithms analyse a student's performance and reorganize the levels depending on which specific performance the learner shows. According with Felicia and Pitt (2007), *"User profiling is a growing research field that aims to categorize the players and find ways to predict their actions, preferences or needs"*. The use of cognitive styles and learning strategies combined with interfaces can facilitate the achievement of individual goals. Therefore, providing interfaces which can be readjusted according to the different user needs allows the identification of relevant and useful information about students (Ray Webster 2001).

If some psychologists have proposed several complementary taxonomies of learning styles, other psychologists and neuroscientists have questioned the scientific basis for learning style theories arguing that learning style models have no sound theoretical basis and that the instruments used to assess learning styles profile have not been appropriately validated (Coffield, Moseley, Hall & Ecclestone 2004; Massa & Mayer 2006). To improve the understanding of learning strategies, it will be necessary to conduct more studies about the impact of learning styles on student´s ways to learn.

CASE DESCRIPTION

Using Virtual Worlds for Teaching, Learning, and Assessment

Context

The first phase of the project unfolded over 6 days and each session had a duration of 5 hours. Each session consisted in three lectures, one in a classroom, one in the Blackboard platform and one in the virtual world. The Blackboard platform is a learning management system that includes several functionalities that enhances the traditional face-to-face lectures with online and multimedia content. Specifically, it includes a learning system that provides online course delivery and management for institutions, a community and portal system for use in creating online campus communities, a content management system for centralized control over course content and a system to record and analyse student assessment results.

After and before each lecture the students did a set of questionnaires in order to evaluate previous knowledge about the topic and the knowledge apprehended after the lectures. The organization of each day is represented in Table 1.

The lectures consisted of a set of slides previously prepared by a teacher, which covered 45 minutes of learning material on a specific topic. The topics were grouped into three main areas: mathematics, portuguese and natural sciences. The instruments used in this study were applied during the summer vacations in an institution denominated Akademia which organizes after school activities for pupils in primary and secondary education, attending the 5th to 10th grade of public and private schools in academic time granted for this purpose. Each main topic was therefore organized according to the grade of each group of student. For 5th grade students

Table 1. Organization of a project day

	Day1 ... Day6
Activity	Questionnaires (socio demographic, knowledge about lectures, computer usage)
	Lecture A in virtual world based lecture Questionnaire about lecture A *10m break* Lecture B in face-to-face lecture Questionnaire about lecture B *10m break* Lecture C in e-learning lecture Questionnaire about lecture C Questionnaire (Evaluation)
Duration	5h

the topic concerning mathematics was geometry, concerning Portuguese was narrative text and concerning natural sciences was the cell. For 6th grade students was isometrics, summaries and blood, respectively, and so on. Depending on the grade level the subject of each main area varied in order to be adequate to the expected learning ability of the experimental group.

Akademia has children with age raging from 3 to 17 years old and besides the normal activities also includes a program for supporting the students with their homework after school hours. Akademia has a number of educators but also psychologists that are specialized in accompanying the students in this kind of activities.

In order to perform this experiment a set of computers were setup with the specific software (virtual world, blackboard, etc.) and hardware (headphones, microphones, etc.). The computers were spread out in four different rooms: one for a teacher to give a lecture using the virtual world; one for a teacher to give a lecture in the blackboard platform and two different rooms for the students. There was also another room for a teacher to give a face-to-face lecture in a normal classroom with just tables and chairs and a whiteboard.

Weeks before the experiment was carried out, parents were given a consent form to authorize the participation of their respective children and a schedule when the experiment was supposed to take place.

Methodology

This research project is a qualitative study inspired by experiment research design whose purpose is to evaluate the effectiveness of three different learning strategies after the attendance of different signatures (face-to-face lecture, an e-learning lecture, and virtual world based lecture). In experiment research design the investigators deliberately control and manipulate the conditions, which determine the events in which they are interested, introduce an intervention and measure the difference that it makes (Cohen et al, 2010). An experiment involves making a change in the value of one variable – the independent variable – and observing the effect of that change on another variable – called the dependent variable.

The purpose of this experiment was to observe the effect of changing the signature (face-to-face lecture, an e-learning lecture, and virtual world based lecture) on the level of learning. Therefore, the independent variable was the signature and the dependent variable was the level of learning. The study design results were accomplished through the evaluation of questionnaires (pretest and posttest) done before and after each lecture. The pretest results are concerned with the previous knowledge student had about the topics. The posttest results are concerned with the knowledge the student acquired after having a lecture in each of the different signatures. Finally the retest was done two weeks after the experiment and its results are concerned with the knowledge that was actually retained regarding the topics taught during the experiment. To examine these propositions we use a sample of 91 students.

Each day was dedicated to students of a specific grade, so on day one only 5th grade students were tested, on day two 6th grade students were tested and so on. Before any test started the students were submitted to a questionnaire about the topics that were to be taught. According to the results of this questionnaire the students were divided in three groups. In this manner, the students were organized in groups that had the same level of previous knowledge.

After this questionnaire and for the next 2.30h approximately each group was submitted to their designated lectures (portuguese, mathematics and biology). It was randomly chosen which group and which lectures (portuguese, mathematics and biology) were to start in a virtual world based lecture, or e-learning lecture or face-to-face lecture, but all would have to participate once in each different signature. This means that if a student had mathematics in a face-to-face lecture he would have, for example, Portuguese in the Blackboard platform and biology in the virtual world. There were no repetition between lectures and signatures. After each lecture the students group was submitted to a questionnaire previously prepared by the teacher of that specific topic in order to evaluate the acquired knowledge. This questionnaire consisted in a total of 20 questions of either true/false or fill in the blanks.

At the end of the lectures the students were submitted to one more questionnaire about their general appreciation of the experience. With this questionnaire we tried to understand what their preference in terms of signature was. All the questionnaires were identified with the student name, therefore allowing us to later correlate this preference with their level of learning in each of the signatures.

After each project day an informal discussion with the involved teachers was carried out in order to understand what were their personal impressions regarding the adoption of these kind technologies as a complementary learning strategy.

The statistical analyse was performed using the statistical package Statistical Package for Social Sciences (SPSS - version 19.0). The results obtained using SPSS were analysed according to two fundamental dimensions. One of the dimensions was concerned with learning strategies and their respective learning effectiveness. The other dimension was concerned with the personal experience of both students and learners towards the different technologies used during the test. It was important to observe the studies according to both dimensions because although certain factors may have constraint the statistical learning results, divergent personal experience results might still provide sufficient strength to support the adoption to these kinds of technologies.

On the learning dimension the main purpose was to understand if the research results confirmed the null hypothesis or not. Our null hypothesis stated that there was no substantial difference between the efficiency of knowledge acquisition and retention between the different learning strategies after the attendance of different signatures. On the personal experience dimension the main purpose was to understand what were the learners' impression regarding their level of knowledge acquisition, level of fun, personal choice and level of interest for each attended signature.

Results

The purpose of the described study was to evaluate the effectiveness of three different learning strategies after the attendance of different signatures (face-to-face lecture, an e-learning lecture, and a virtual world based lecture) as stated by our null hypothesis. Also, it was equally important to understand what was the position of the teachers and psychologists involved regarding the introduction of such technologies in educational curriculums. Therefore, when analysing the results we tried to answer the following research questions:

Question 1: Is the virtual world technology an appropriate and efficient learning strategy in terms of knowledge acquisition compared with a face-to-face or e-learning lecture?

Question 2: Is the virtual world technology an appropriate and efficient learning strategy in terms of knowledge retention compared with a face-to-face or e-learning lecture?

Question 3: Are the teachers and learners' open to use virtual world or e-learning technologies in the classroom?

The results of each of the test are summarized in Figure 1. According to the results the signature that had better results concerning knowledge acquisition was the face-to-face lecture in classroom with just a whiteboard. Both the blackboard platform and Virtual world obtained identical results, meaning that regardless of using any of the referred platforms the efficiency of learning should be the same (de Freitas 2006; de Freitas & Levene 2004; de Freitas & Olive 2006). It should be noted that the backboard platform besides being a commercial stable platform it was in previous occasions used by both students and teachers, therefore having clear advantages concerning the virtual world platform which was a prototype software version unknown to both students and teachers.

However, the retest had quite different results. Although the face-to-face lecture still presented in general better results for mathematics, for natural sciences and portuguese topics all the platforms had similar results. This indicates that for these

Figure 1. Knowledge acquired about the topics concerning each signature and each test (pretest, posttest, and retest)

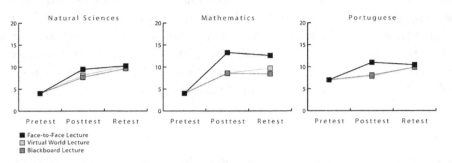

particular topics the level of knowledge retention is equally good for all the different signatures. This results leads to believe that the kind of topic and material used (technical vs. non-technical) can have an impact on the learning efficiency of the chosen technology (Collis and Moonen 2001; de Freitas, Jarvis 2006).

Regarding the last research question as described in the methodology section informal discussions were carried out with the involved teachers. From these discussions several mixed feelings and perceptions emerged. In general all teachers were enthusiastic and interested in how new technologies could be used to improve the efficiency of learning. Nevertheless all were new when it came to their practical usage, which resulted in the demonstration of technical difficulties and a limited used of the potential provided specifically by the virtual world platform. By limited used, we mean a limited used of the potentialities and functionalities offered by the virtual world.

Regarding the learners personal impressions, a questionnaire was conducted at the end of the project day that basically intended to capture the their personal opinions regarding their level of knowledge acquisition, level of fun, personal choice and level of interest for each attended signature (Kirriemuir & MacFarlane 2004; Mayo 2007). The results of this questionnaire are presented in Figure 2.

In general all learners agreed that having a lecture in a virtual world platform was more fun, interesting and therefore it would be their personal choice. Nevertheless, regarding the "impression" of having learned was attributed to the face-to-face lecture. This could be concerned with a social idea of how a lecture or knowledge transfer is usually done. Also, the fact that in a classroom there is a physical professor present with which learners interact might be a strong fact that could induce the "impression" of learning more.

Figure 2. Preferences of the students

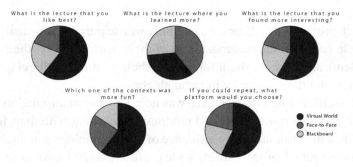

Using Serious Games for Teaching, Learning, and Assessment

Context

The second phase of the study spread-out over one week with 4 sessions per day (one in the morning and three in the afternoon). Each session consisted in playing games that were specifically tailored to train a set of cognitive areas, namely attention, memory, problem solving and math accuracy. At the end of each session the scores where recorded for every learner. These score were then used to grade the learners and potentially to extract meaningful information about their particular ability of the referred cognitive areas.

Each learner only participated in one session and played one game from each of the considered categories, which had a total of 20 minutes. The organization of the day is displayed in Table 2.

The games used in this study were applied during the Christmas vacations in an institution denominated Akademia which organizes after school activities for children and youth, in academic time granted for this purpose. A group of 71 adolescents, males and females, with 10 to 13 years old, were part of the same after school tutoring service mentioned in the above. During game play, the students were organized in groups of 4, where each used an individual laptop. The instructor was responsible for explaining the gaming activity and also to support the learners during game play.

Table 2. Organization of a project day

	Attention	**Memory**	**Problems Solving**	**Math Accuracy**
Time	5 minutes	5 minutes	5 minutes	5 minutes
Score	0-10	0-10	0-10	0 – 10

Methodology

This research project is a qualitative case study whose purpose is to analyse learners learning style based on the understanding of their work memory, their capacity to solve problems and process the information, their aptitude to direct and maintain their attention and their accuracy in basic algebra.

In experiment research design there was no control or manipulation of the conditions. The 71 learners were selected randomly, according with their free time.

This study aimed to analyse the influence of new technologies, namely computer games, to assess each learner learning style profile. Therefore, we used four games from different cognition areas (attention, memory, problems solving and math accuracy) in order to be able to assess their learning styles.

In each game they had to do different tasks according with the cognition area under study. In the game devoted to test attention skills, the player had to feed some fishes that were in constant movement. Depending on the performance of the player, the complexity of the game increased – the number of fishes increased and their movements become more complex. In the memory test game, the player had to memorize a route and then go to a specific location without hitting any of the monsters spread out along the way. The difficulty of the route and the number of monsters also depended on the player's performance. This means that, just like in the previous game, the difficulty of the game increased with the improvement of the performance. The problem solving game consisted in find a way out of a maze. During the game and according with the player's performance, the route gets more complex and the maze starts spinning, which further difficult the task of the player. To evaluate maths accuracy, each player had to solve a sequence of equations as quickly as he can.

Each student had the opportunity to play each of the game and there wasn't any time limitation. During the gameplay one of the psychologists participating in the experience observed each student and also provided a briefing concerning each game goals and gameplay before each game session.

Results

The purpose of the described study was to analyse learners learning styles profile, using virtual games and explore if virtual activities are as effective as manual ones to evaluate students efficiently. Therefore, when analysing the results we tried to answer the following research questions:

Question 1: Are virtual activities as effective as manual ones to evaluate learners efficiently?

Question 2: Are these games appropriated to evaluate learners' profile?

During the profile evaluations the students were motivated and all of them played the games in an amused mode – they are involved in the current tasks. These effects corroborate Mayo´s research (2007), indicating that serious games provide a powerful and effective learning environment and capture the learners' attention, engaging them in the curricular content. In this way, using games to evaluate their profile promote higher levels of engagement and, consequently, the result will be more effective.

According with games accuracy and learners final levels it´s possible to conclude that games are a great tool to evaluate specific individual areas, using online algorithms to analyse the student's performance and reorganize the levels depending on which specific performance the learner shows. With online algorithms it´s possible to readjust the games according with the different needs of users (Ray Webster 2001).

On the other hand, the results of these games were not effective to identify learners learning styles. Some of the reasons to explain the difficulty to evaluate learners learning styles were related to the difficulty of measuring factors that influence learning and the instability of personal learning styles over the time (Brown et al. 2006). At the same time, the games used in this research weren't created for this purpose, and we considered that they are not adjusted and as extensive as it will be necessary to collect all relevant information about each learners learning style.

Lessons Learned/Tips for Practitioners

Lesson 1: Don't underestimate the technical challenges associated with getting 3D virtual world environment software to run on participants' computers and enabling participants to get network access to run the software. Hardware and firewall issues should be dealt with as early as possible in the deployment process. A good way to do this is to run a small pilot program to test the access to the environment. These proof-of-concept "dry runs" are invaluable in identifying technical problems early. Don't wait until you start running your experiment to find out you can't play audio on learner's machines or that they don't support the graphics.

Lesson 2: Be aware of the differences between using open-source software and commercial software. Open-source software might be easier to adapt to your needs and requirements but also the probability of being faulty is bigger. Moreover, open-source software is not tested against the same benchmarking as commercial software, therefore interaction metaphors, functionalities, etc. might not be laid out in the most appropriate way. This obviously has impacts on the level of acceptance and immersion of both learners and teachers.

Lesson 3: Don't assume that what works in the classroom or in traditional events translates to the virtual environment. Learning in virtual worlds is more experiential, action-oriented, and social. Focus must be placed on function and interactivity when preparing a lecture to be taught inside a virtual world. Also be sure to allow plenty of time for unstructured interaction. Encourage informal social interaction.

Lesson 4: When using off-the-self games be aware that although they might seem the most appropriate for the purpose of your study, it often turns out that these games have several limitations and/or inadequacies concerning the debriefing information you require to draw conclusions or even fail to cover some of the fundamental areas related to learning goals.

Lesson 5: When using only virtual games to profile students´ learning styles be aware that it´s possible to evaluate the emotional and the relational areas and not just the cognition. The student performance depends on his capacities, his motivation and his relation with school (teachers and other students).

CONCLUSION

This chapter aimed to provide an overview of some of the pedagogic theories that support the use of computer games in learning contexts, and to discuss the value of serious games to improve the efficacy and efficiency of learning. Although there are different views about Game-Based Learning, there is an agreement that computer games can be used as a tool for supporting learning processes based on the findings from early studies on Game-Based Learning.

To evaluate the impact of serious games on learning efficacy and efficiency we have devised two experiments in order to study the influence of this kind of technologies in education curriculum. With this intent, two groups of studies were conducted involving teachers, psychologists and learners in an educational setting.

The first set of studies consisted in comparing the effectiveness of learning in a Virtual World developed in INESC-ID, the Blackboard Platform and a face-to-face lecture. According to the results there are no statistical differences between the contexts, demonstrating that the efficiency of learning it´s the same regardless the learning context. In general all learners demonstrate higher levels of interest, motivation and engagement when having a lecture in a virtual world platform. The second set of studies had the purpose of assessing students´ learning strategies using brain games in a way to profile learning styles and organize strategies to improve their study. During the evaluations, the students were motivated and involved in the tasks demonstrating that games are a powerful tool to capture attention and to promote higher levels of engagement, and, consequently, a more effective result.

Also, games use algorithms to analyze the student's performance and to reorganize the levels depending on the learner's performance facilitating the accuracy of the results. In the other way, it's necessary to develop specific games for this propose in a way to get more specific information from them.

These studies have revealed that Virtual Worlds and Serious Games can be beneficial for improving learning outcomes based on student engagement and on the higher level of motivation that they demonstrated while playing virtual games. It has shown that the engagement that students demonstrate can benefit learning. Overall it suggests that virtual games can help to find their preferences and learning styles in a way to improve learning processes.

More research into the potential and limitations of Game-Based Learning is required to develop a greater understanding on the efficacy of the techniques and its impact on learning processes.

As de Freitas (2007) said, *"the key challenge for effective learning with games is for the learner to be engaged, motivated, supported and interested but also importantly for the learning to be undertaken in relation to clear learning outcomes as well as being made relevant to real-world contexts of practice.*

ACKNOWLEDGMENT

This project is partially funded under the European Community Seventh Framework Programme, through the GALA Network of Excellence in Serious Games (FP7-ICT-2009-5-258169)

REFERENCES

Abbot, J. (1994). Learning makes sense: Re-creating education for a changing future. Letchworth, UK. *Education*, 2000.

Allen, I. E., & Seaman, J. (2008). *Staying the course: Online education in the United States, 2008*. The Sloan Consortium.

Baggerly, J. (2002). Pratical technological application to promote pedagogical principles and active learning in counselor education. *Journal of Technology in Counseling*, 2(2).

Bates, J. (1992, January). Virtual reality, art, and entertainment. *Presence (Cambridge, Mass.)*, *1*, 133–138.

Beard, C., Wilson, J. P., & McCarter, R. (2007). Towards a theory of e-learning: Experiential e-learning. *Journal of Hospitality, Leisure, Sport and Tourism Education, 6*(2), 3–15. doi:10.3794/johlste.62.127

Bransford, J. D., Brown, A. L., & Cocking, R. R. (2000). *How people learn: Brain, mind, experience, and school.* Washington, DC: National Academy Press.

Coffield, F., Moseley, D., Hall, E., & Ecclestone, K. (2004). *Learning styles and pedagogy in post-16 learning. A systematic and critical review.* London, UK: Learning and Skills Research Centre.

Cohen, L., Manion, L., & Morrison, K. (2010). *Research methods in education.* Routledge.

Collis, B., & Moonen, J. (2001). *Flexible learning in a digital world.* London, UK: Kogan-Page.

Crookall, D. (2011). Serious games, debriefing, and simulation/gaming as a discipline. *Simulation & Gaming, 41*, 898–920. doi:10.1177/1046878110390784

de Freitas, S. (2004). *Learning styles and e-learning. Technical report: 0014.* London, UK: Birkbeck.

de Freitas, S., & Jarvis, S. (2006). *A framework for developing serious games to meet learner needs.* I/ITSEC Conference, Florida, December.

de Freitas, S., & Levene, M. (2004). *An investigation of the use of simulations and video gaming for supporting exploratory learning and developing higher-order cognitive skills.* IADIS International Conference in Cognition and Exploratory Learning in the Digital Age, 15-17 December, 2004. Lisbon, Portugal.

de Freitas, S., & Neumann, T. (2009). The use of exploratory learning for supporting immersive learning in virtual environments. *Computers & Education, 52*(2), 343–352. doi:10.1016/j.compedu.2008.09.010

de Freitas, S., & Oliver, M. (2006). How can exploratory learning with games and simulations within the curriculum be most effectively evaluated? *Computers & Education, 46*, 249–264. doi:10.1016/j.compedu.2005.11.007

de Freitas, S., & Yapp, C. (2005). *Personalizing learning in the 21st century.* Stafford, UK: Network Education Press.

de Freitas, S. I. (2006). Using games and simulations for supporting learning. *Learning, Media and Technology, 31*(4), 343–358. doi:10.1080/17439880601021967

Dillon, P. (2007). *A pedagogy of connection and boundary crossings: Methodological and epistemological transactions in working across and between disciplines.* Paper presented at Creativity or Conformity? Building Cultures of Creativity in Higher Education, University of Wales and the Higher Education Academy, Cardiff, 8-10 January.

Felder, R. M. (1996). Matters of style. *ASEE Prism, 6*(4), 18–23.

Felder, R. M. (2010). *Are learning styles invalid?* North Carolina State University.

Felicia, P., & Pitt, I. J. (2007). *The PLEASE model: An emotional and cognitive approach to learning in video games.* International Technology Education and Development Conference (INTED), Valencia, Spain, 8-10 March.

Field, J. (2007). Looking outwards, not inwards. *ETL Journal, 61*(1), 30–38.

Ford, N. (2000). Cognitive styles and virtual environments. *Journal of the American Society for Information Science American Society for Information Science, 51*(6), 543–557. doi:10.1002/(SICI)1097-4571(2000)51:6<543::AID-ASI6>3.0.CO;2-S

Foster, A. L. (2006). Harvard to offer law course in "virtual world". *The Chronicle of Higher Education, 53*(3), A.29.

Foster, A. L. (2007). Virtual worlds as social-science labs. *The Chronicle of Higher Education, 53*(44), A.29.

Gardner, H. (1983). *Frames of mind: The theory of multiple intelligences.* New York, NY: Basic Books.

Gardner, H. (1999). *The disciplined mind: What all students should understand.* New York, NY: Simon and Schuster.

Garris, R., Ahlers, R., & Driskell, J. E. (2002). Games, motivation, and learning: A research and practice model. *Simulation & Gaming, 33*(4), 441–467. doi:10.1177/1046878102238607

Green, H., Facer, K., & Rudd, T. (2006). *Personalisation and digital technologies.* Future Lab.

Greeno, J. G., Collins, A. M., & Resnick, L. (1996). Cognition and learning. In Berliner, D. C., & Calfee, R. C. (Eds.), *Handbook of educational psychology.* New York, NY: Simon & Schuster Macmillan.

Greitzer, F., Kuchar, O., & Huston, K. (2007). Cognitive science implications for enhancing training effectiveness in a serious gaming. *Journal of Educational Resources in Computing, 7*(3). doi:10.1145/1281320.1281322

Griebel, T. (2006). Self-portrayal in a simulated life: projecting personality and values in The Sims2. *International Journal of Computer Game Research*, *6*(1).

Gustafson, K., & Branch, R. (2002). *Survey of instructional development models.* Eric Clearinghouse on Information.

Gütl, C. (2011). The support of virtual 3D worlds for enhancing collaboration in learning settings. In Pozzi, F., & Persico, D. (Eds.), *Techniques for collaboration in online learning communities: Theoretical and practical perspectives* (pp. 278–299). doi:10.4018/978-1-61692-898-8.ch016

Hamlen, K. (2011). Stochastic frontier estimation of efficient learning in video games. *Computers & Education*, *58*(1), 534–541. doi:10.1016/j.compedu.2011.09.006

Hawk, T., & Shah, A. (2007). Using learning style instruments to enhance student learning. *Decision Sciences Journal of Innovative Education*, *5*(1), 1–19. doi:10.1111/j.1540-4609.2007.00125.x

Honey, P., & Mumford, H. (1992). *The manual of learning styles* (rev. ed.). Maidenhead, UK: Peter Honey.

Hopko, D. R., Ashcarft, M. H., & Gute, J. (1998). Mathematics anxiety and working memory: Support for a deficient inhibition mechanism. *Journal of Anxiety Disorders*, *12*, 343–355. doi:10.1016/S0887-6185(98)00019-X

Karet, N., & Hubbell, E. R. (2003). Authentic assessment: Current trends and issues in instructional technology.

Kayes, C. D. (2002). Experiential learning and its critics: Preserving the role of experience in management learning and education. *Academy of Management Learning & Education*, *1*, 137–149. doi:10.5465/AMLE.2002.8509336

Keefe, J. W. (1979). Learning style: An overview. In *NASSP's student learning styles: Diagnosing and proscribing programs* (pp. 1–17). Reston, VA: National Association of Secondary School Principles.

Kirriemuir, J., & McFarlane, A. (2004). *Report 8: Literature review in games and learning*. Futurelab Series.

Kolb, A. Y., & Kolb, D. A. (2009). The learning way: Meta-cognitive aspects of experiential learning. *Simulation & Gaming*, *40*(3), 297–327. doi:10.1177/1046878108325713

Kolb, D. A. (1984). *Experiential learning*. Englewood Cliffs, NJ: Prentice Hall.

Kolb, D. A. (1985). *Learning style inventory and technical manual*. Boston, MA: McBer.

Kolb, D. A., Boyatzis, R. E., & Mainemelis, C. (2000). Experiential learning theory: Previous research and new directions. In Sternberg, R. J., & Zhang, L. F. (Eds.), *Perspectives on cognitive learning and thinking styles*. Lawrence Erlbaum.

Lambert, N. M., & McCombs, B., L. (2002). *How students learn: Reforming schools through learner-centered education*. Washington, DC: American Psychological Association.

Lazzaro, N. (2004). Four keys to more emotions in games.

Levine, J. (1999). *The Enneagram intelligences: understanding personality for effective teaching and learning*. Bergin and Garvey Publishers.

Lynch, M., & Tunstall, R. (2008). When worlds collide: Developing game-design partnerships in universities. *Simulation & Gaming, 39*, 379–398. doi:10.1177/1046878108319275

MacMillan, J., Alexander, A., Weil, S., & Littleton, B. (2005). *DARWARS: An architecture that supports effective experiential training*. Cambridge, UK: BBN Technologies.

Malone, T. (1981). Toward a theory of intrinsically motivating instruction. *Cognitive Science, 4*, 333–369. doi:10.1207/s15516709cog0504_2

Massa, L. J., & Mayer, R. E. (2006). Testing the ATI hypothesis: Should multimedia instruction accommodate verbalizer-visualizer cognitive style? *Learning and Individual Differences, 16*, 321–336. doi:10.1016/j.lindif.2006.10.001

Mayes, T., & de Freitas, S. (2007). Learning and e-learning: The role of theory. In Beetham, H., & Sharpe, R. (Eds.), *Rethinking pedagogy in the digital age*. London, UK: Routledge.

Mayo, M. J. (2007). Games for science and engineering education. *Communications of the ACM, 50*(7), 31–35. doi:10.1145/1272516.1272536

McKeachie, W. J. (2006). *McKeachie's teaching tips: Strategies, research, and theory for college and university teachers*. Boston, MA: Houghton Mifflin.

Molenda, M., & Sullivan, M. (2003). *Issues and trends in instructional technology: Treading water*. Libraries Unlimited.

Mueller, J. (2008). Authentic assessment toolbox. Retrieved December 8, 2008, from http://jonathan.mueller.faculty.noctrl.edu/toolbox/index.htm.

National Centre for Education Statics. (2003). *Distance education at degree-granting postsecondary institutions: 2000-2001*. NCES.

Neisser, U. (2009). Cognitive psychology. In *Grolier multimedia encyclopedia*.

Nolan, R. B. (2006). At law school, "Second Life", in the cards, and the course catalogue. *The Harvard Crimson: Online Edition*.

O'Neil, H. F., Wainess, R., & Baker, E. L. (2005). Classification of learning outcomes: Evidence from the computer games literature. *Curriculum Journal, 16*, 455–474. doi:10.1080/09585170500384529

Peters, O. (2003). Learning with new media in distance education. In Moore, M. G., & Abderson, W. G. (Eds.), *Handbook of distance education* (pp. 87–112). Mahwah, NJ: Lawrence Erlbaum Associates.

Pillay, H. (2002). An investigation of cognitive processes engaged in by recreational computer game players: An implication for skills of the future. *Journal of Research on Technology in Education, 34*, 336–350.

Prensky, M. (2001). *Digital game-based learning*. New York, NY: McGraw-Hill.

Reiff, J. C. (1992). *Learning styles*. Washington, DC: National Education Association.

Reigeluth, C. (1996). A new paradigm of ISD? *Educational Technology, 36*, 13–20.

Riding, R. (2002). *School learning and cognitive style*. London, UK: David Fulton.

Riding, R. J. (1991). *Cognitive styles analysis*. Birmingham, UK: Learning and Training Technology.

Riding, R. J. (1996). *Learning styles and technology-based training. OL244*. Sheffield: Department for Education and Employment.

Riding, R. J. (1997). On the nature of cognitive style. *Educational Psychology, 17*, 29–50. doi:10.1080/0144341970170102

Riding, R. J., & Ashmore, I. (1980). Verbaliser-imager learning style and children's recall of information presented in pictorial versus written form. *Educational Psychology, 6*, 141–145.

Riding, R. J., & Mathias, D. (1991). Cognitive Styles and preferred learning mode, reading attainment and cognitive ability in 11-year-old children. *Educational Psychology, 11*, 383–393. doi:10.1080/0144341910110312

Riding, R. J., & Read, G. (1996). Cognitive style and pupil learning preferences. *Educational Psychology, 16*(1), 81–106. doi:10.1080/0144341960160107

Riding, R. J., & Wigley, S. (1997). The relationship between cognitive style and personality in further education students. *Personality and Individual Differences, 23*, 379–389.

Rieber, L. (1996). Seriously considering play: Designing interactive learning environments based on the blending of microworlds, simulations, and games. *Educational Technology Research and Development, 44*, 43–58. doi:10.1007/BF02300540

Sadler-Smith, E. (1996). Learning styles and instructional design. *Innovations in Educational and Training Technology, 33*(4).

Salen, K., & Zimmerman, E. (2003). *Rules of play*. Cambridge, MA: MIT Press.

Schmeck, R. R. (1988). *Learning strategies and learning styles*. New York, NY: Plenum Press.

Sherry, L. (1996). Issues in distance learning. *International Journal of Educational Telecommunications, 1*(4), 337–365.

Tennant, M. (1988). *Psychology and adult learning*. Routledge. doi:10.4324/9780203441619

The Higher Education Academy English Subject Centre. (2006, 11th December, 2007). *Theatron 3 – Educational undertakings in Second Life*.

Valley, K. (1997). Learning styles and the design of courseware. *ALT-J Association for Learning Technology Journal, 5*(2), 42–51. doi:10.1080/0968776970050205

Wilkinson, S., Crerar, A., & Falchikov N. (1997). *Book versus hypertext: exploring the association between usability and cognitive style.*

Wrzesien, M., & Alcañiz Raya, M. (2010). Learning in serious virtual worlds: Evaluation of learning effectiveness and appeal to students in the E-Junior project. *Computers & Education, 55*(1), 178–187. doi:10.1016/j.compedu.2010.01.003

Zull, J. (2002). *The art of changing the brain: Enriching the practice of teaching by exploring the biology of learning*. Sterling, VA: Stylus Publishing.

ADDITIONAL READING

de Freitas, S., & Veletsianos, G. (2010). Crossing boundaries: Learning and teaching in virtual worlds. *British Journal of Educational Technology, 41*(1), 3–9. doi:10.1111/j.1467-8535.2009.01045.x

Klopfer, E., Osterweil, S., Groff, J., & Haas, J. (2009). *Using the technology of today, in the classroom of today: The instructional power of digital games, social networking, simulations and how teachers can leverage them* [white paper]. The Education Arcade, MIT.

Palmer, P. J. (2007). *The courage to teach. Exploring the inner landscape of a teacher's life*. San Francisco, CA: Jossey-Bass.

Prensky, M. (2010). *Teaching digital natives: Partnering for real learning*. Thousand Oaks, CA: Sage.

Shaffer, D. W. (2007). *How computer games help children learn*. New York, NY: Palgrave.

Squire, K.D. (2011). *Video games and learning: Teaching and participatory culture in the digital age*. New York, NY: Teachers College Press.

ENDNOTES

[1]   http://tvnet.sapo.pt/noticias/video_detalhes.php?tv=2&id=67748
[2]   http://www.blackboard.com/
[3]   http://www.lumosity.com/

Section 7
Researching Games and Learning

Chapter 23

Serious Games for Reflective Learning:
Experiences from the MIRROR Project

L. Pannese
imaginary srl, Italy

A. Ascolese
imaginary srl, Italy

M. Prilla
imaginary srl, Italy

D. Morosini
imaginary srl, Italy

EXECUTIVE SUMMARY

This chapter describes some of the work carried out in the MIRROR project, which focuses on reflective learning where adults' motivation to learn and reflect through games is being researched. It briefly introduces the project and the theoretical framework, and then describes the serious game that was created for research in detail. The last part of this chapter focuses on users' evaluations and describes some lessons learned about the importance of guidance and of a de-briefing session, thus highlighting the potential of serious games for collaborative knowledge construction.

DOI: 10.4018/978-1-4666-2848-9.ch023

1. THE MIRROR PROJECT: SCENARIO AND THEORETICAL FRAMEWORK

Reflecting on our personal experiences and emotions can be a great mechanism for learning how to behave and react in certain specific situations. Unfortunately there are many such situations that people either never encounter or avoid in their daily lives. This limits the opportunity to learn through such personal experiences but with new tools like serious games it is now possible to create 'real new learning experiences' in a safe virtual environment. In this way, serious games can provide these missing learning opportunities because they allow people to access a potentially unlimited pool of environments through which they can experience those situations in a risk-free way and thereby enlarge the spectrum of their knowledge. Furthermore, well developed serious games have the potential to induce in players a state of flow in which they are so involved in the game activity that nothing else seems to matter (Csikszentmihalyi, 1990). When players reach this state they are more motivated to learn and, by reflecting on their actions and consequences within the serious game, players can translate the knowledge acquired in this virtual environment into the real world.

'MIRROR-Reflective learning at work' (http://www.mirror-project.eu/) is a Seventh Framework Programme project with the aim of encouraging human resources to reflect on previous experiences at the workplace and learn from them. The focus of MIRROR is the creation of a set of applications ('Mirror apps') that enable employees to learn lessons from their own experiences (as well as experiences of others) and thereby improve their future performance. One kind of apps envisioned in this context is serious games. A prerequisite for exploring innovative solutions in this context is the reliance on our ability to efficiently and effectively learn directly from tacit knowledge, without the need for making it explicit.

Among all the techniques explored by MIRROR, serious games have a special role as they provide virtual experiences to reflect upon. One of the main objectives of this project is to investigate how serious games can contribute to triggering reflection on one's own experiences as well as supporting a willingness to share these experiences of reflection within a team.

Before describing the serious game that is being developed in this context, it is important to underline what serious games are and why they can be considered a great tool for triggering reflection. It is also important to describe in depth the meaning of the term 'reflection' and more specifically the concept of 'reflection at work' in the context of the MIRROR project.

1.1 Serious Game as a Tool for Reflection

Today, a consistent and generally accepted definition of the term 'serious game' has not yet been agreed upon. However, in general, a serious game can be defined as an interactive simulation which has the look and feel of a game but is actually a simulation of real-world events or processes or represents these in the form of a metaphor (Micheal & Chen, 2005; De Freitas, 2010). As one of the first to attempt a definition, Abt writes in 1970 of 'serious games in the sense that these games have an explicit and carefully thought-out educational purpose and are not intended to be played primarily for amusement'. Although in this definition the entertainment aspect is put in the background, it is not said that serious games must not be entertaining. Fun elements are in fact a key component of a serious game: they are the source of positive emotions as well as the engine of motivation. Furthermore, entertaining elements can capture users' interest and curiosity, speed up the acquisition of content and skills and motivate learners to engage themselves in activities in which they have little or no previous experience (Shaffer, 2005; De Freitas & Griffith, 2009; Breuer & Bente, 2010).

An approach which most notably accommodates the idea of gaming and already describes the potential areas of application of serious games comes from Zyda (2005). He defines serious games as a 'mental contest, played with a computer in accordance with specific rules that uses entertainment to further government or corporate training, education, health, public, policy, and strategic communication objectives' (Zyda, 2005, p.25-32). According to this definition, the main intent of a serious game is imparting knowledge or skills through direct experience of carrying out a task ('learning by doing'). Furthermore, serious games can support contemporary learning activities and foster intellectual growth (Prensky, 2007).

Thanks to these researchers it is possible to understand why, in recent years, the use of serious games has become increasingly popular. In fact generally speaking, a serious game always has one or more of the following main goals (Micheal & Chen, 2005):

1. To train and educate;
2. To inform;
3. To change attitude and behaviour.

Also, as previously stated, well-developed serious games have the potential to induce in players a state of flow in which they are so involved in the game activity that nothing else seems to matter. Csikszentmihalyi (1990) described the positive experience of being fully engaged in an activity as a state of 'flow'. Thus, flow represents an optimal state of performance at a task, a sense of enjoyment and control, where an individual's skills are matched to the faced challenges. This state derives from activities that are optimally challenging and in which there are clear goals and feedback, concentration is intensely focused, there is a high degree of control, and users are absorbed to the extent that they lose a sense of time and self. Csikszentmihalyi's research (1990) identified eight major components of flow: a challenging activity requiring skill, a merging of action and awareness, clear goals, direct and immediate feedback, concentration on the task, a sense of control, loss of self-consciousness and an altered sense of time.

The concept of flow provides one perspective on the feelings of enjoyment and engagement that can be experienced by game users and this can be considered one of the main elements that can contribute to triggering reflection. At least it is possible to identify some key aspects that are very important to our understanding of how serious games could be considered as a new important way to support reflection:

1. A simulated environment, system or a realistically recreated role play scenario can allow learners to experience something that is too costly, too risky or even physically impossible to achieve in the real world, the so-called 'experimenting with alternatives' approach (van Woerkom et al., 2008).
2. Repeatability or learning by trial and error is also a key strength of a game or simulation-based approach. Learners can play out a particular strategy or adopt a certain approach. If they fail or do not quite deliver the desired outcome, then they can try again with a modified approach.
3. A serious game has to be considered as an experience because it allows people to live and experiment within real situations in a safe virtual environment. For these reasons, games engage people psychologically (they can be very emotional experiences) and also physiologically.

Reflective learning in the workplace entails a 'there-and-then' reflection intertwined with the work as well as reflection at some distance from the work, exemplifying the reflection-in-action and reflection-on-action observed by Schön (1983). A serious game provides unique opportunities to pace the simulated work process and the reflection sessions so as to achieve a good combination of reflection and action based on the learner's needs. The next paragraph describes how a serious game is used in the frame of the MIRROR project as a tool for triggering reflection.

1.2 Theory Reflection Model

The understanding of the process of reflective learning, in the frame of the MIRROR project, is based on the model of Boud (1985), shown in Figure 1, in which the learner re-evaluates past experience by attending to its various aspects (including affective ones) and thereby produces outcomes.

Figure 1. A model of the reflective process (Boud et al, 1985)

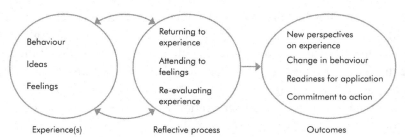

According to this model, a key aspect in making a reflective process happen is the presence of triggers that can be defined as unexpected situations, disturbances and perception of uncertainty but also positive situations like surprising success. In general, reflection seems to be triggered by awareness of discrepancy between expectations and the current experience. Specifically this process might be triggered by an external event or agent or might develop from one's own thinking of a whole series of occurrences over time as an inner need to reflect. Furthermore reflection can occur incidentally or intentionally but most authors (Krogstie, 2009) agree that in both cases reflection is a conscious evaluation of experience that leads to a better understanding of the experience and allows for drawing conclusions that guide future behaviour. Of course, in order to reach this level, learners need to develop the ability to generalise and form abstractions from concrete experience.

Moreover reflection can take place individually and/or collaboratively (Krogstie, 2009), either of which provide certain advantages and disadvantages and entail different needs of support. For reflection to be collaborative, the participants need to share experiences and relate to the experiences of others in their own reflection. The different characteristics of individual and collaborative reflection typically make it useful to combine both in workplace learning. For all these reasons the outcome of reflection can include cognitive, affective, and/or behavioural consequences.

With reference to the model of Boud et al. (1985), serious games provide particularly good opportunities to help a learner return to (and reconstruct) experience, the environment of the experience being captured within the game environment, and the events of the experience (e.g. the steps chosen by the learner) which are normally stored and available for replay. Re-evaluation of experience involves considering the experience in the light of alternatives and in the game environment there will be alternative options already incorporated in the game as well as the possibility to capture and replay the choices made by other learners. Work settings may entail situations that are emotionally challenging to handle. Returning to these emotional aspects is an important element of the reflective process (Boud et al., 1987). A serious game which successfully captures the aspects of work in a way that makes the user react emotionally in a similar way to that of the real work situation thereby holds the potential to support important aspects of reflection. In this way the serious game also serves as a tool for learners to come to terms with the emotional aspects of the job and understand their own reactions, in this way becoming more prepared to meet them in the real life situation.

For all these reasons, serious games can be considered a useful way to trigger and support reflection.

2. THE CLinIC SERIOUS GAME: EXPERIENCES FROM THE MIRROR PROJECT

Working with these theoretical backgrounds within the framework of the MIRROR project, the first serious game to foster reflection in learning and around learning at work and dealing with the topic 'complex dialogues' was developed for a hospital in Germany (Neurological Clinic Bad Neustadt). All the different phases and elements of the CLinIC serious game: the preparation, the structure, the reflection session and the evaluation are described in depth below.

2.1 Preparation of the CLinIC Serious Game

Building the prototype of the MIRROR serious game 'CLinIC' for the hospital in Germany was a very intensive activity distributed over a long period of time and characterised by a high interaction with the test bed.

This "point and click" serious game is focused on difficult communication between nursing staff and patients and aims to foster reflection around different dialogues. Nurses in fact underlined the necessity to improve their ability to deal with complex situations and reflect about their own work behaviours and having the opportunity to experiment with different approaches and to share their experiences with peers.

As shown in Figure 2, the structure of the serious game is based on a branching story that was designed with a so-called 'mind-map' (representing the structure of the contents graphically). The game consists of 23 different scenes, 2 of which are descriptive and 21 of which ask the player to make a decision between different options, all of which are never obvious or evident. Overall, there are 71 different options. Every scene is determined by the previous choice, or sometimes randomly picked from a pool of possibilities, to make the user engage with the story even when playing again. For the graphics of this serious game the hospital wanted to have a realistic environment as an adequate frame for a realistic virtual experience. Therefore, they asked a professional photographer to take pictures of their hospital

Figure 2. Particular of the CLinIC mind-map

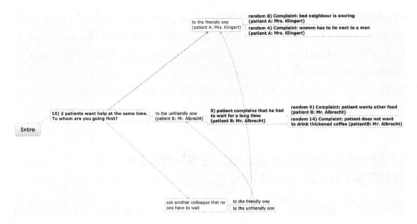

Figure 3. Pictures of the hospital graphically treated

and some of these were chosen for the game and had to be graphically treated to be embedded as gaming scenario (See Figure 3).

2.2 Structure of the CLinIC Serious Game to Trigger Reflection

Figure 4 shows the structure of the serious game in which users have the opportunity to experience different scenes of daily life at work. Nurses in a hospital have to deal with different patients, choose how to react to strange requests and balance their time and interventions among concurrent calls and needs.

Figure 4. Structure of the MIRROR serious game about complex dialogues

A 'mood map', based on the 'Circumplex model of affect' (Russel, 1989), was introduced into the serious game to capture the mood of players at various moments in time, typically at the beginning and at the end of the game. According to the chosen model, emotional experiences depend on two major dimensions, the degree of arousal and the degree of pleasure. During the game, whenever users feel it is relevant, they can record their emotional state (an icon to access the mood map is always displayed). Furthermore, in a couple of carefully chosen key situations of the game, users are invited to record their emotions in those specific moments, allowing the development of a user's 'emotional path'. The mood map works as an element able to trigger reflection: stopping for a short break during the flow experience, users are able to be aware of their emotional state and start to reflect on why they are experiencing that emotional state and how it relates to the ongoing situation. In this specific situation it is fundamental to record users' emotions for at least three reasons:

1. The flow experience is strictly linked to positive emotions;
2. Revising the experience together with the emotions connected to the specific action is a trigger for reflection after the game experience;
3. Reflecting on the emotional path allows players to analyse relationships between emotions and behaviours.

Due to the lack of an automatic system to recognise users' emotions, this tool was chosen as being the least invasive towards the flow. To maintain flow in these games, reflection sessions were avoided. Instead it was decided to have a larger reflection session at the end of the dialogue. The reflection session is organised as follows.

459

2.3 Reflection Session after the Game Play

Once the game is over, users have to do a self-evaluation based on pre-defined parameters (*Patient satisfaction, Quality of response, Response in relation to the patient, Time management*). Feedback based on the same parameters then comes from the system and a spider-web graph comparing the two (self-evaluation and feedback) is displayed. Finally, in order to be able to better reflect on the differences between the system and self-evaluations and on the experience, users are able to review the dialogues, where the thoughts of the patient are shown as well (these are not displayed while playing the game).

This structure contains different elements which help to facilitate the reflective process:

- Through feedback, users can check their behaviour during the game experience and reflect on it (See Figure 5);
- With self-evaluation processes users are motivated to reflect on their actions and reactions during the game (See Figure 6);

Figure 5. Feedback

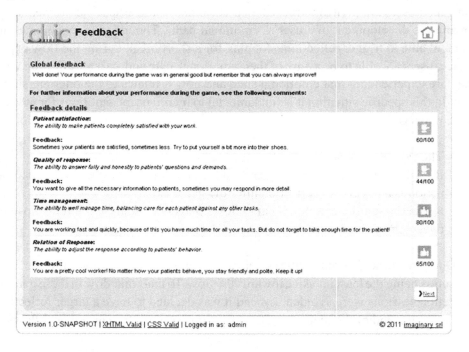

Figure 6. Self-evaluation

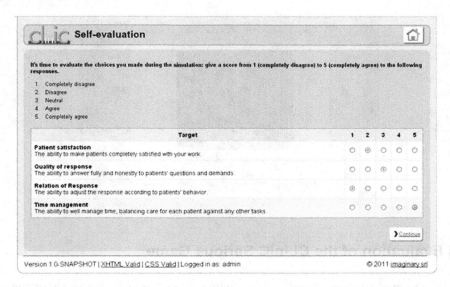

Figure 7. Thoughts of the patient

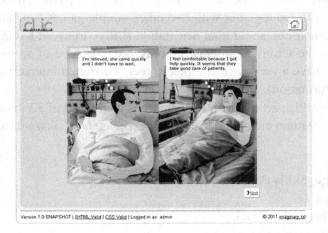

- The opportunity to see the thoughts of the patient allows users to compare different points of view (See Figure 7);
- Through different data sources, e.g. coming from the mood map, users can check their behaviour and reflect on it (See Figure 8);
- Final reports which help users to reflect on the whole experience they had during the game.

Figure 8. Emotional state

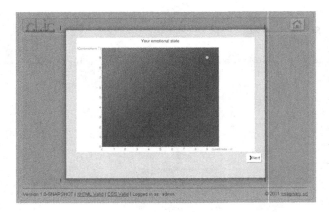

2.4 Evaluation of the CLinIC Serious Game

In order to evaluate the CLinIC serious game, a short questionnaire about 'game, motivation and reflection' was developed and administered to 11 nurses in the hospital.

The first part of the questionnaire is about the flow experience: the CLinIC game described was offered together with two other sample games (one about safety at the workplace and one about goal orientation skills), to avoid having non-expert users perceive the CLinIC game as the only possible type of serious game (the other 2 games have a very different look & feel, a different interaction and way of presenting information).

In particular this part of the questionnaire is composed of 32 items that aim to investigate the 9 main elements of the flow experience (Csikszentmihalyi, 1990), namely:

1. Challenge–Skills Balance
2. Clear Goals
3. Unambiguous Feedback
4. Action-Awareness Merging
5. Concentration on Task at Hand
6. Paradox of Control
7. Loss of Self-Consciousness
8. Transformation of Time
9. Autotelic Experience

Table 1. Average of NBN answers (N=11) in a scale with 1 min flow and 5 max flow

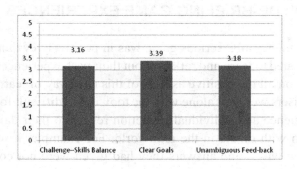

In analysing the collected results, attention was focused particularly on the first three of the nine features, as these three characteristics can be considered key elements in the study of motivation related to serious games.

Analysing the data from our sample of 11 subjects on a scale of 1 (min flow) to 5 (max flow) the following mean scores emerged (See Table 1):

- Challenge – Skills Balance $\rightarrow$ $M^1 = 3.16$; $SD^2 = 1.40$
- Clear Goals $\rightarrow$ $M = 3.39$; $SD = 1.06$
- Unambiguous Feedback $\rightarrow$ $M = 3.18$; $SD = 1.10$

This data show how in general users evaluate the experience with game as an experience able to trigger flow.

The second part of the questionnaire consisted of 18 open-ended questions. The questions were designed to investigate in more detail the whole experience with the serious game and underlined how positive and relevant this experience was. Majority of the users claimed to have experienced pleasure, regardless of the consequences and the potential rewards for their decisions. Also, almost all of the game player indicated that learning with a game that is strongly related to their working environment was preferable to a metaphorical one with a high level of abstraction.

Another important element relates to the topic 'challenge and skills'. All users stated that their skills were sufficient to face the challenge of the game but most of them suggested that a more difficult challenge would have increased their commitment to the game. Some users also felt the need for greater support in terms of clearer feedback as well as a better introductory description of the goals.

In conclusion, the data shows how users generally tend to evaluate the experience with serious games as positive and pleasant; the scores of the quantitative part of the questionnaire, slightly over average, are somehow reinforced by the results of the qualitative part.

3. SERIOUS GAMES AS A BASIS AND TRIGGER FOR REFLECTION: DE-BRIEFING GAME EXPERIENCES

As already said, the CLinIC serious game was in positively evaluated. Individual users were motivated to learn and reflect about their past experiences at work. They also commented on all the positive aspects of this new way of learning.

However, if users were left alone with the tool, it was difficult for them to relate the virtual experience and individual reflection results to their daily work and to their cooperation with others in the real world. For example, it was difficult for individuals to see why some answers they had given were not correct and what they could have done better.

Game debriefing has been found to be a viable mechanism of connecting experiences made in a game to real world contexts (Peters & Vissers, 2004), as learners can use debriefing sessions to engage in discussions and make sense of games experiences together (Ravenscroft, Wegerif, & Hartley, 2007). Adapting this concept to post-game reflection as the task for debriefing, a debriefing session was conducted at the hospital to collaboratively reflect on the experiences encountered in the game and to explore how the reflection within games can be connected to real world reflection. In particular, the aim was to explore whether games may trigger collaborative reflection and learning processes about work and whether reflection then relates solely to the game experience or also to real world practice.

3.1 Setting and Course of the Debriefing

The debriefing session was conducted with five participants. Among them there was the head physician of the ward the game was tested in, two head nurses and two normal nurses of the same ward. These participants were asked to engage in both individual and collaborative reflection of five scenes (see the guiding questions below for an overview of individual and collaborative parts) from the game which had been perceived as particularly important for the hospital, or especially interesting due to the variety of answers given in the game. Table 2 gives an overview of the scenes used.

The debriefing explicitly included collaborative reflection for two reasons. First, group interaction has been found to be beneficial when it comes to connecting experiences from games to the real world (Peters & Vissers, 2004; Ravenscroft et al., 2007;). Second, collaborative reflection has advantages over individual reflection in that is enables a group to include several experiences and perspectives into reflection and thus create a shared understanding (Hoyrup, 2004). This, in turn, most likely leads to collective knowledge such as norms and rules for individual and cooperative behaviour (Daudelin, 1996; Prilla, Herrmann, & Degeling, 2012).

Table 2. Scenes used as a basis and trigger for reflection in the debriefing session

Scene	Name	Content
1	Loud neighbour	A patient complains that the patient in the other bed of this rooms snores during the night.
2	Swallowing problems	As is quite common after a stroke, a patient has swallowing problems and is thus given a thickened drink. She complains because she wants a normal drink.
3	Angry patient	When the nurse enters a patient's room, he immediately snarls at her, because in his eyes she is late.
4	Unknown nurse	When the nurse enters the patient's room, the patient does not recognize her and asks who she is.
5	Lost valuables	The patient complains that he is missing the money in his purse and that he had it before he came into the hospital.

Putting this into the context of nurses reflecting on treating patient, collaborative reflection is beneficial to agree on common ways to approach and interact with patients for (Forneris & Peden-McAlpine, 2006).

In order to explore collaborative reflection on experiences from these scenes, participants were asked to conduct a series of simple tasks such as commenting on the practical occurrence of scenes from the CLinIC game, tell stories in which they encountered similar situations, discuss each other's statements and derive solutions or actions to be applied in these situations. In particular, this was supported by a set of three guiding assignments, which were used iteratively for each scene:

1. Think about this situation: have you ever been in such as situations and if so, how many times did that happen and what did you do? (Relation to real life, individual task).
2. Tell a story you remember from such a situation to your colleagues and write down on a paper card how you reacted in this story and why you reacted this way (Individual, sharing with others).
3. Discuss the scene and your stories and tell the facilitator one or more correct reactions for this scene. Give reasons for your choice based on your stories. You may choose from the answers already existing in the game, but you may also provide new ones (Collaborative task).

In order to avoid external influences, the project manager of the hospital facilitated the workshop. He explained the overall task, took care of the time for answering the questions and structured the following discussions. To relate the articulations of participants stemming from answering these questions directly about the scenes discussed, the scenes were printed out and pinned to boards in the workshop room. Then all articulations of participants were written down by them on paper cards

Figure 9. Results from collaborative reflection on a scene from the CLinIC game

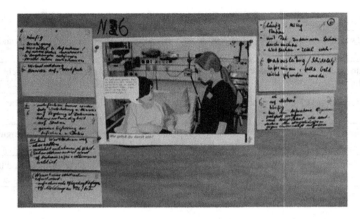

and pinned to the scene printout they belonged to (See Figure 9 for an example). In addition, notes were taken on everything that was not written down on cards but was interesting such as e.g. interaction among people and arguments exchanged.

3.2 Reflection and Learning Effects of Collaborative Game Debriefing

Results from the workshop indicate that both the CLinIC game and the approach of debriefing have the potential to trigger and support collaborative reflection: participants overall assessed the scenes to be relevant for their daily practice, they told many stories related to the scenes and discussed each scene intensively even based on the guiding questions given by the facilitator. As a result, the participants identified new solutions for three of five scenes and brought up additional issues related to three scenes. Table 3 gives an overview of the activities and results from the debriefing session.

Table 3. Results of the debriefing/reflection workshop of CLinIC at the hospital

Scene	No. cards	No. answers	New answers	Discussions/(new) solutions	Stories shared	Broader discussions
1	8	5	3	1 / 2	2	0
2	8	6	3	2 / 3	0	2
3	10	2	0	3 / 2	3	1
4	5	2	0	2 / 2	3	0
5	10	7	3	4 / 4	5	1
Total (avg.)	41 (8.2)	22 (4.4)	9 (1.8)	12 (2.4) / 11 (2.2)	3 (0.6)	13 (2.6)

Table 3 shows the results from collaboratively reflecting the scenes of the CLinIC game and also contains strong indicators of learning. For example, the number of stories related to the game scenes (especially scenes 3 to 5) shows that the participants perceived them to be relevant for their daily work and that they were able to relate real world experiences to them. In addition, the participants arrived at many new and agreed upon answers and solutions for the scenes discussed (1,8 new answers and 2,2 new solutions in). This was even present in cases in which they did not find new answers to questions in the game but where they intensively discussed details of the scenes (see the discussions and solutions shown for scenes 3 and 4 in Table 3). This shows that not only their experiences but also the resolutions found were applicable to their daily practice. Moreover, the discussions of scenes were not only focused on the scenes displayed. For four of five scenes, reflection on other related issues was triggered as well. For example, during the work on scene 3 ('Angry patient'), participants started to reflect on generally appreciated and polite behaviour on the ward. Likewise, during the discussion of scene 2 ('Swallowing problems'), they reflected on how to support patients in asking the right questions during the ward round when a physician is present in order for the physician to clarify questions on swallowing problems.

Altogether, these observations show that the reflection triggered by scenes from the games did not stay within the game, but was related to real life context and resulted in ideas for changes for daily work. In addition, it also invoked discussions on details of the problems and on related issues. Therefore, it is strongly proposed that serious games and collaborative debriefing form an approach provoking fruitful reflection and learning on daily work.

3.3 Effects of Guidance and Collaboration for Game Debriefing

The description given above shows that relating real world experiences to scenes from games has huge potential to bridge the gap between the virtual ground of games and real life reflection. However, this might not happen on its own in the debriefing session. It needed a set of questions guiding the reflection process and triggering it. The description of the workshop also shows that this is not complex: three basic questions and material common to most organizations was used. In addition, the workshop was run by an internal project manager, which shows that it is easily applicable to other organizations as well. As an alternative, tools using prompts for users can also provide similar questions and assignments automatically and without a human facilitator. Whether this also produces the effects described above, however, is subject to further research.

The debriefing experiment also shows the advantage of collaboration – conforming existing work (e.g. Peters & Vissers, 2004; Ravenscroft et al., 2007) and extending it to the domain of reflective learning from games – in reflection on the scenes as it included results that can only be achieved together:

- **Mutual Self-Assurance:** When discussing scene 5 ('Lost valuables'), the nurses told each other that 'the introduction of badges for the suitcases of patients was successful'[3] in terms of locating the patients' property.
- **Insights on the Importance of Agreed Upon Behaviour:** During the discussion of scene 3 ('Angry patient'), the nurses realised that besides avoiding mistakes they needed to support each other: 'Mistakes also happen without influence of staff. Therefore, mutual safeguarding and control among colleagues is even more important!'.
- **Different Options when Dealing with Problems**: In some discussions (e.g. scenes 3 and 5), the participants shared different stories and thus broadened the spectrum of possible reactions in the scene discussed by combining their experiences.

From these examples, it is obvious that the level of certainty and agreement among colleagues could not have been reached with every participant reflecting individually and only exchanging their individual results. Therefore, reflection through serious games should also be supported by creating opportunities to comparing players' own experiences with that of others in the games, for example by showing the answers (and possibly comments on them) by others during and after gaming.

In addition to the guiding force of comparison with other data, situations were also observed in the debriefing session that led to the conclusion that more guidance needs to be given when serious games are used as a reflection aid. For example, in the discussion of scene 5 ('Lost valuables'), one of the nurses stated: 'There is a quality management standard for dealing with patients' valuables'. Others stated that they were not aware of this standard or did not have it in mind during the game. As a result, the resolutions found were agreed to be preliminary and needed to be checked against the standard. This, and other examples, indicates that there is a need to make people aware of other resources to be taken into account during and after playing a serious game in order to make the reflection on experiences from the games more helpful and realistic. This might also apply for access to other tools being used in an organisation.

Besides guidance to take into account existing resources and tools, hints on helpful guidance were also found during the games. For example, two nurses who were not familiar with scene 4 ('Unknown nurse') benefited a lot from the other two sharing their experiences on the corresponding situation with them. In addition, three nurses perceived scene 5 ('Lost valuables') to happen often, while one thought it was rather seldom. Collaboratively contextualizing and reflecting on these scenes helped a lot in the debriefing session and are therefore considered to be integrated in a policy for game debriefing to be part of a serious game.

3.4 Potential of Collaborative Game Debriefing Experiences and their Support

Serious games, as described above, provide virtual situations likely to happen in real life and enable people to playfully and safely simulate them. This can be helpful in individual reflection, but as was experienced from our debriefing session with players, the game provide most benefit when reflection is collaborative. This has two reasons which were also visible in the session described above:

- First, people made sense of the situation they encountered virtually and critically evaluated both the underlying scenario and the answers available in the game according to its importance for their daily work. This can be seen in the multitude of alternative resolutions collected in the debriefing session and in the surprising assessments of the scenarios being part of the debriefing. The result of this step then provides the basis for and supports the choice of scenarios for in-depth reflection of certain situations.
- The second reason for collaborative reflection of experiences from a serious game like CLinIC can be found in the virtuality of situations encountered in games: in the debriefing experiments, participants often felt the need to contextualize scenarios by providing corresponding stories from real life experience. In addition, some situations in the game included to-be scenarios and thus their resolution included plans for future behaviour, as can be seen from the description above. The intertwining of real and virtually acquired experience as well as the planning aspects of game reflection can therefore clearly benefit from multiple perspectives being available in collaborative reflection sessions.

Therefore, it is proposed that collaborative debriefing with a focus on reflecting experiences encountered in a game can enhance and should therefore be an integral part of the usage of serious games in organizations. As we found feedback pointing to the need of more guidance during games and their reflection and realized that this guidance can be decisive or at least helpful in many situations, a focus for further development will be set to establishing this guidance. On an organizational and facilitation level, this can be provided by a small set of guiding questions and should focus on certain scenes from a game – experiences from the debriefing session show that three questions were sufficient to produce good results. On a socio-technical level, as an extension of the situation applied in our experiment, it is planned to include usage data from the game such as individual and aggregated decisions in scenes into the reflection process, as they may support people in articulating their rationales for decisions and thus support the collaborative reflection process. Likewise, games will be connected to real world data such as the quality management documentation mentioned above and to applications available in the organization in order to better support players in intertwining real and game experiences.

4. SUMMARY

Serious games are an innovative concept for learning on the job, and usually unknown to the target groups. In addition, understanding serious games as an enabler to acquire experiences in a virtual world and reflect on such experiences in the context of the real world is an entirely new approach for learning at the workplace. This makes carrying out studies with serious games in this context a complex task and as such, studies need to promote a new concept among potential users who might be sceptical as to whether gaming can improve their job performance, to evaluate the relevance of games for real work, and to explore the effects that game play actually have on daily work. However, the task is at the same time interesting and stimulating as it opens up new possibilities for individual and collaborative learning at the workplace – either directly from playing or from sharing experiences gained during game play.

In the study described in this chapter, after an initial phase of explaining and negotiating the utility of the games with the nurses participating in the study, it was found that the game was perceived positively: users in general evaluated the experience that they had with the CLinIC serious game as a 'flow experience' and this means that CLinIC was able to motivate people to learn and reflect. Analysing the collected data, it can be concluded that nurses are in general motivated to experiment learning with serious games and to reflect upon these learning experiences both as individuals and in a team. In addition, the study showed that an appropriate and well-organized debriefing session after playing the game can be a good way to transfer what the users have learned in the game into the real life and help them to reflect about this.

From the results described above, it can be concluded that serious games are a tool for allowing users to enjoy experiences in a safe virtual environment and to transfer these experiences to the real world. This can support reflection, leading to a better understanding of and support for different situations that users have to deal with. However, sometimes this connection is not immediate and it is not easy to bridge the gap between the virtual ground of games and real life reflection. As was illustrated in this chapter, there are two reasons for this. First, there is a tension between flow in the game and the step back needed for reflection: both individual and collaborative reflection breaks the flow and thus might spoil the game experience. Thus the challenge is to combine flow and reflection in games in a non-obtrusive manner that thereby retains the advantages of the game-reflection combination shown in this chapter. Secondly, players are experiencing difficulties in establishing and sustainably keeping up a relationship between games and the real world context. Therefore, a focus of further work will be set to better connect these two worlds on a data level as well as with guidance within and after the game.

Another focus within the frame of the MIRROR project will be to make the user as independent as possible within the serious games in order to reduce the need for external consulting and coaching support. The idea is to more deeply integrate coaching and guidance into the serious games with a 'buddy-learning companion' that supports users in the game experience. Furthermore investigation should be carried out into the role of collaboration and guidance within a multi-player game in which users have the opportunity to simulate a real meeting in a virtual environment and discuss important topics related to the experience that they have already had with game.

REFERENCES

Abt, C. (1970). *Serious games*. New York, NY: Viking Press.

Aldrich, C. (2004). *Simulations and the future of learning*. San Francisco, CA: John Wiley and Sons.

Aldrich, C. (2005). *Learning by doing*. San Francisco, CA: Pfeiffer.

Alvarez, J., & Michaud, L. (2008). *Serious games: Advergaming, edugaming, training and more*. Montpellier, France: IDATE.

Barrett, L. F., & Russell, J. A. (2009). The circumplex model of affect . In Sanders, D., & Scherer, K. (Eds.), *Oxford companion to emotion and the affective sciences*. New York, NY: Oxford University Press.

Boud, D. (1985). Promoting reflection in learning: A model . In Boud, D., Keogh, R., & Walker, D. (Eds.), *Turning experience into learning*. London, UK: Routledge Falmer.

Breuer, J., & Bente, G. (2010). Why so serious? On the relation of serious games and learning. *Journal for Computer Game Culture*, 4(1), 7–24.

Csikszentmihalyi, M. (1990). *Flow: The psychology of optimal performance*. New York, NY: Cambridge University Press.

Csikszentmihalyi, M. (1997). *Finding flow*. New York, NY: Basic.

Csikszentmihalyi, M., Abuhamdeh, S., Nakamura, J. E., Andrew, J., & Dweck, C. S. (Eds.). (2005). *Handbook of competence and motivation* (pp. 598–608). New York, NY: Guilford Publications.

Csikszentmihalyi, M., & Csikszentmihalyi, I. (Eds.). (1988). *Optimal experience*. Cambridge, UK: Cambridge University Press.

Daudelin, M. W. (1996). Learning from experience through reflection. *Organizational Dynamics*, *24*(3), 36–48. doi:10.1016/S0090-2616(96)90004-2

de Freitas, S. (2006). *Learning in immersive worlds: A review of game-based learning*. London, UK: JISC e-Learning Programme.

de Freitas, S. (2006). Using games and simulations for supporting learning. *Learning, Media and Technology Special Issue on Gaming*, *31*(4), 343–358.

de Freitas, S., & Griffiths, M. D. (2008). The coverage of gaming practices with other media forms: What potential for learning? A review of the literature. *Learning, Media and Technology*, *33*(1), 11–20. doi:10.1080/17439880701868796

de Freitas, S., & Neumann, T. (2009). The use of 'exploratory learning' for supporting immersive learning in virtual environments. *Computers & Education*, *52*(2), 343–352. doi:10.1016/j.compedu.2008.09.010

de Freitas, S., & Veletsianos, G. (2010). Crossing bounderies: Learning and teaching in virtual worlds. *British Journal of Educational Technology*, *41*(1), 3–9. doi:10.1111/j.1467-8535.2009.01045.x

Forneris, S. G., & Peden-McAlpine, C. J. (2006). Contextual learning: A reflective learning intervention for nursing education. *International Journal of Nursing Education Scholarship*, *3*(1), 1–17. doi:10.2202/1548-923X.1254

Hoyrup, S. (2004). Reflection as a core process in organisational learning. *Journal of Workplace Learning*, *16*(8), 442–454. doi:10.1108/13665620410566414

Jackson, S., & Csikszentmihalyi, M. (1999). *Flow in sports: The keys to optimal experiences and performances*. Champaign, IL: Human Kinetics.

Jackson, S., & Marsh, H. (1996). Development and validation of a scale to measure optimal experience: The flow state scale. *Journal of Sport & Exercise Psychology*, *18*, 17–35.

Jackson, S. A., & Eklund, R. C. (2004). La flow state scale-2 e la dispositional flow scale-2 . In Muzio, M. (Ed.), *Sport: Flow e prestazione eccellente*. Milano, Italy: Franco Angeli.

Jefferies, L. N., Smilek, D., Eich, E., & Enns, J. T. (2008). Emotional valence and arousal interact in the control of attention. *Psychological Science, 19*(3), 290–295. doi:10.1111/j.1467-9280.2008.02082.x

Kolb, D. A., Boyatzis, R. E., & Mainemelis, C. (2000). Experiential learning theory: Previous research and new directions . In Sternberg, R. J., & Zhang, L. E. (Eds.), *Perspectives on cognitive, learning and thinking styles* (pp. 227–247). Mahwah, NJ: Lawrence Erlbaum.

Krogstie, B. (2009). A model of retrospective reflection in project based learning utilizing historical data in collaborative tools. In U. Cress, V. Dimitrova, & M. Specht (Eds.), *EC-TEL 2009, LNCS 5794*. Berlin, German: Springer.

Micheal, D., & Chen, S. (2005). *Serious games: Games that educate, train and inform*. New York, NY: Muska & Lipman.

Pappa, D., Dunwell, I., Protopsaltis, A., & Pannese, L. (2011). Game-based learning for knowledge sharing and transfer: the e-VITA approach for intergenerational learning. In Felicia, P. (Ed.), *Handbook of research on improving learning and motivation through educational games: Multidisciplinary approaches*. Hershey, PA: IGI Global. doi:10.4018/978-1-60960-495-0.ch045

Peters, V. A. M., & Vissers, G. A. N. (2004). A simple classification model for debriefing simulation games. *Simulation & Gaming, 35*(1), 70–84. doi:10.1177/1046878103253719

Prensky, M. (2002). The motivation of game play. *Horizon, 10*(1), 1–14.

Prensky, M. (2007). *Digital game based learning*. Minneapolis, MN: Paragon House.

Prilla, M., Herrmann, T., & Degeling, M. (2012). Collaborative reflection for learning at the healthcare workplace . In Goggins, S., Jahnke, I., & Wulf, V. (Eds.), *CSCL@ Work: Case studies of collaborative learning at work*. Springer.

Protopsaltis, A., Hetzner, S., Pappa, D., & Pannese, L. (2011). *Serious games and formal and informal learning*. eLearning Papers, nr 25, July 2011.

Ravenscroft, A., Wegerif, R., & Hartley, R. (2007). *Reclaiming thinking: Dialectic, dialogic and learning in the digital age. BJEP Monograph Series II, Number 5-Learning through Digital Technologies (Vol. 1*, pp. 39–57). British Psychological Society.

Ritterfeld, U., Cody, M., & Vorderer, P. (2009). *Serious games: Mechanisms and effects*. New York, NY: Routledge.

Shaffer, D. W. (2005). Epistemic games. *Innovate: Journal of Online Education, 1*(6).

Van Woerkom, M., & Croon, M. (2008). Operationalising critically reflective work behavior. *Personnel Review, 37*(3), 317–331. doi:10.1108/00483480810862297

Zyda, M. (2005). From visual simulation to virtual reality to games. *IEEE Computer, 38*(9).

KEY TERMS AND DEFINITIONS

Collaborative Reflection: It is a mechanism to support a holistic learning experience. It enables a group to include several experiences and perspectives into reflection and thus create a shared understanding.

Flow: It represents an optimal state of performance at a task, a sense of enjoyment and control, where an individual's skills are matched to the faced challenges.

MIRROR Project: Is a Seventh Framework Programme (FP7) project with the aim of encouraging human resources to reflect on previous experiences at the workplace and learn from them.

Motivation: It is the willingness or desire to engage in a task. More specifically, motivation refers to an individual's choice to engage in an activity and the intensity of effort or persistence in that activity.

Reflection Learning: It is the ability to return to experience through which the experience is re-evaluated in order to promote continuous learning.

Serious Game: It is an interactive virtual simulation which looks like a game, but has a serious objective.

Technology Enhanced Learning (TEL): It is a research field that refers to the technological support of any pedagogical approach that utilizes technology.

ENDNOTES

[1]   Mean
[2]   Standard Deviation
[3]   The statements were translated from German by the authors

Chapter 24
Evaluating Games in Classrooms:
A Case Study with DOG*eometry*

Günter Wallner
University of Applied Arts Vienna, Institute of Art & Technology, Austria

Simone Kriglstein
University of Vienna, Faculty of Computer Science Austria

Johannes Biba
University College of Teacher Education Vienna/Krems, Austria

EXECUTIVE SUMMARY

Educational games have gained wide acceptance over the years and have found their way into many classrooms. Numerous evaluations of such games have been published, but mostly evaluations were carried out in controlled environments, with a small sample size or over a short period of time. However, the particular context where playing takes place has been established as a critical factor for game-based learning. Moreover, educational games are often considered as black box, measuring only input and output variables but neglecting the intermediate process. Many researchers have therefore argued that evaluations of educational games have to go beyond testing the learning outcomes only and should also show how and why it works. In this chapter the authors describe the evaluation of the game DOGeometry, which was carried out in a classroom environment over a four month period. They report the development process, the design of the evaluation, results, challenges, and problems faced.

DOI: 10.4018/978-1-4666-2848-9.ch024

OVERALL DESCRIPTION

The motivation to find alternative teaching methods to break through the traditional lecture format – where students are passively siting in classrooms – has increased in recent years. Digital technologies enable interactive learning environments with a high pedagogical potential (Foreman, 2003). Today's children grow up with digital technologies and digital games are one of the top activities in their life (Annetta et al., 2006; The Henry J. Kaiser Family Foundation, 2002). Several studies, such as (Kumar & Lightner, 2007; Tan, Ling & Ting 2007; Greenblat & Duke, 1981), found that the usage of games, animations and other multimedia elements are valuable methods to motivate student positively and to open new ways of offering learning support. For example, Mayo (2009) shows that digital games can help to increase the learning outcome positively in comparison with a lecture on the same material in a classroom. Although educational games cannot solve all problems with education, it opens new opportunities to engage students with their learning and to motivate them to devote more, than is prescribed in a course.

A successful acceptance of a game depends strongly on if it meets learners' needs to deal with the learning content in such a way that the game can support them to learn the subject matter without being discouraged. Therefore, it is not only necessary to evaluate learning outcomes of educational games but also to make sure that the game provides a satisfactory experience for the learner and to identify problems regarding gameplay or design. However, the testing sessions of such games are primarily conducted in controlled environments, with small sample sizes or over short time periods. Controlled studies are often preferred over field studies because they are easier to control and to reproduce. Although controlled studies usually use a test environment with a realistic setting (e.g., in a usability lab), the classroom environment plays an essential role, because challenges and interesting insights (e.g., about social interactions between children) can occur which cannot be tested in an isolated controlled environment within a short time frame. For example, it is interesting to observe how children accept and use a game over a longer period of time.

In this chapter we present a case study that illustrates the evaluation of the educational game DOG*eometry*. The evaluation was carried out in nine classes divided into control and experimental group over a four month period. The game should help elementary school children to learn and understand the basic concepts of geometric transformations (e.g., rotations, translation, and reflection) by solving different tasks (puzzles and creation of objects). We will describe the development and evaluation process as well as the design of the pre- and post-test, address practical challenges we encountered and report on the feedback received from pupils and teacher surveys. Furthermore, the value of visualizations in analyzing gameplay data in addition to statistical analysis is highlighted.

LITERATURE REVIEW

Game-based learning gained more and more acceptance over the years and games made their way into contemporary classrooms. Many educational games have been developed and their evaluations have been published in various conference proceedings, journals, and books. Sometimes the evaluations were carried out with small sample sizes or over a short period of time neglecting long-term benefits that may result from playing a game. Other cases studies were conducted in a controlled environment, neglecting the particular context for which the game is intended. However, as Defreitas and Oliver (2006) emphasize, context (e.g., classroom based, access to equipment, etc.) has been established as a critical factor for effective use of e-learning tools. Yet, to our best knowledge, there exist only few case studies on evaluating games in a school environment and all of them have been published in the last few years.

For example, Malliet, Quinten, and Van der Sluys (2010) used collaborative design methods and qualitative user experience tests to evaluate small educational games in a classroom context. The games were tested in three classrooms with a total of 57 pupils. They report on practical challenges encountered due to the testing in a school environment and formulated practical guidelines for using such qualitative evaluation methods. Vankúš (2008) conducted a control group study with two fifth grade classes to assess the impact of didactical games on the attitude of pupils toward mathematics and its teaching as well as the effect on children's knowledge. The experiment was conducted over 17 lessons and in the experimental group geometry was taught with five different educational games. The author reports an improvement of pupils' attitudes towards mathematics. However, statistically no difference in knowledge was observable between experimental class and control class. Unfortunately, the author did not report on practical challenges faced during the study. The work of Sedig (2008) also includes the evaluation of an educational mathematics game in a school environment, which was carried out during lessons when children were scheduled to learn mathematics. However, children played the game not in their classroom but in a separate room set up specifically for the study. The author reports improvements after interaction with the educational game for each of the treatment groups and a strong positive response from the children towards the game. Again, no discussion of encountered issues as a result of the school context is included in the article.

Not an evaluation of a game itself but also interesting with regard to classroom evaluations is the work of Kirriemuir and McFarlane (2003). They report the results of two informal surveys of how and why games are used in formal classroom learning, obstacles to their usage and about emerging trends in their employment. It should be noted that the report only considered *pure entertainment games* and did not include educational games and therefore some of their findings do not necessarily apply to education-oriented games.

Furthermore, as some researchers, like Kriz and Hense (2006) argued, evaluations of game-based learning applications should not only consider testing of learning outcomes but should also reveal "how and why it works (or fails to work) in a given context" (p. 270). Game companies on the other hand have begun to use visual data mining to analyze automatically collected instrumentation data in addition to *traditional methods* such as observational studies of players, interviews, thinking aloud, or playability testing. However, almost all of the published work concentrates on gameplay visualization for *entertainment games*. Examples, to name a few, include Data Cracker (Medler, John, & Lane, 2011), developed at Electronics Arts to monitor player behavior in Dead Space 2, the seminal work of Hoobler, Humphreys, and Agrawala (2004) who presented a visualization system to analyze behavior patterns of players in the game Return to Castle Wolfenstein: Enemy Territory or the TRUE system (Kim et al., 2008) from Microsoft Game Studios which combines behavioral instrumentation with Human Computer Interaction methods.

With regard to analyzing educational games the work of Andersen et al. (2010) is worth mentioning. Andersen et al. (2010) analyzed an abstract educational puzzle game by visualizing transitions through game states with a node-link representation. They used their approach to identify common points of confusion in the game and were able to detect some unexpected solutions. In our previous work (Wallner & Kriglstein, 2011) we used our gameplay visualization tool – described in (Wallner & Kriglstein, 2012) – to verify if the learning curve of DOG*eometry* is appropriate for the intended age group.

GAME DESIGN

DOG*eometry* is an educational game which teaches basic concepts of geometric transformations – namely, translation, rotation and reflection – and concepts about object hierarchy. It is intended for children between eight and ten years old and was designed to engage the children with geometry rather than to replace the traditional teaching. The game is split into two main parts: problem solving tasks (puzzles) and content creation. An example of a puzzle is shown in Figure 1. The goal of the puzzles is to construct a path for the dog such that it can get to the veterinarian. To accomplish this task a limited set of tiles has to be placed on a grid. Once placed, the tiles have to be rearranged and duplicated with a limited set of transformations. Obstacles, like lakes or molehills restrict the placement of the tiles in order

Figure 1. An example of a more advanced puzzle. Tiles can be dragged from the left onto the grid. Once placed they can be rearranged and duplicated with a limited set of transformations. Currently translation is active.

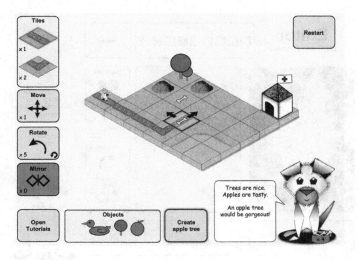

to increase the level of difficulty. Following Gee's multiple routes principle (Gee, 2004) some puzzles can be solved in different ways. However, children can collect rewards in the form of bones if they solve a puzzle with a more complex solution. The purpose of the bones is twofold. First, children with more bones are ranked higher in the high-score table in order to encourage friendly competition. Second, bones can be exchanged for hints if players get stuck in a level. Levels increase gradually in difficulty and concepts learned in earlier levels have to be applied in later levels in order to "lead players to form hypotheses that work well for later, harder problems" (Gee, 2005, p. 7).

From time to time the dog will request new objects (for example, in the level depicted in Figure 1, the dog would like to have an apple tree). Such objects have to be created in the object editor, as shown in Figure 2. An animation shows the player how the object can be constructed. Afterward, the player has to recreate the object by arranging and transforming given shapes. To give an example, an ellipse can be created by scaling a circle. Once the finish button is pressed the dog will rate the object with regard to how well it matches the reference object (shown in grey in the drawing area, cf. Figure 2). For very well made objects a gold goblet is awarded, otherwise a silver goblet. Players with more gold goblets are ranked higher in the high-score table. A more thorough description of the game concept can be found in (Wallner & Kriglstein, 2011).

Figure 2. A screenshot of the object editor. Children have to recreate the object shown on the left by arranging and transforming basic geometric shapes. Part of the flower has already been constructed.

PRACTICALITIES OF RUNNING THE GAME AND TECHNOLOGY COMPONENTS

The game was implemented using Adobe Flash, the server side programming was done in PHP and a MySQL database is used to store the player information, such as password, current level, number of collected bones and more. Furthermore, we added instrumentation to the game to automatically record all player interactions to text log-files. Each time a player interacts with the game a PHP script is called to write the information about the event, along with a timestamp, into a log-file on the server. The collected data is later used as input to our gameplay visualization system.

We decided to implement DOG*eometry* as a browser-based game in order to ensure that the game is able to run on the school equipment. Many contemporary games require special hardware like modern 3D graphics cards which are not available in many schools. Furthermore, as studies – such as the one from Kirriemuir and McFarlane (2003) – have shown teachers often spent more time solving technical or compatibility problems than they find acceptable. For this reason, the game was hosted at our own webserver and therefore no installation was required from the schools IT department, except unblocking the game's webpage and creating a shortcut on the desktop. Each classroom was equipped with two PCs. In addition a computer room with 12 PCs (Intel Dualcore E5400, 2 GB Ram, onboard graphics card, Windows 7) was made available to children were they could play during some lessons.

DEVELOPMENT AND EVALUATION PROCESS

The development and evaluation process for the educational game is based on the human centered design process (International Organization for Standardization, 1999) which is a well-known approach in the Human Computer Interaction community for designing useful and usable user interfaces. The motivation to adapt the human centered design process was because it considers the users (the players in our case) already early in the development process in order to get feedback about the design idea and to identify problems regarding gameplay or design. Figure 3 gives an overview of our employed development and evaluation process which is divided into two parts: part (a) and part (b). Although part (a) was already described in detail in the work of Wallner and Kriglstein (2011) we will also include it here briefly to make the chapter self-contained. Part (b) was carried out in spring 2011 in two elementary schools over a four-month period and will be the main focus of this chapter.

Part A: Development and Pre-Evaluation

Our process started by understanding the game context and with the specification of the game requirements because the success of an educational game strongly depends on its tasks and goals. Therefore, we began by analyzing the content of the curriculum associated with geometry teaching in elementary schools. We concluded

Figure 3. Overview of the development and evaluation process: part (a) covers the development and a first pre-evaluation to verify the appropriateness for the intended target group and part (b) concentrates on a thorough evaluation in a classroom context

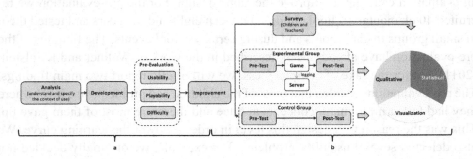

that an educational game would be helpful to support children to understand the basics of geometric transformations. Based on this outcome we defined the following requirements which we wanted to consider in the design of the game:

1. Children should arrange shapes in space by using basic transformations (translation, rotation and reflection).
2. Children should create and arrange shapes by using combinations of multiple transformations (e.g., every rotation can alternatively be performed with two reflections).
3. Children should recognize shapes which have reflective and rotational symmetry.
4. Children should use geometric shapes to create familiar objects.
5. The game should prepare children for secondary school were topics like recognizing structures and properties of geometric shapes, recognizing relationships between geometric primitives, and modeling objects with transformations are part of the curriculum.

Based on these requirements we developed DOG*eometry* with the basic concept to combine problem-solving tasks (puzzles) with artistic expression (object creation). Evaluating the game is an important step because, as pointed out by Isbister, Flanagan, and Hash (2010), the reason why many educational games fail is that too little effort is dedicated to testing. According to (Tan et al., 2007) educational games can be evaluated in two different ways: (1) evaluation of the pedagogical components and (2) game design components. Whereas the evaluation of pedagogical components concentrates on issues such as how well the game supports learners in their learning process, the evaluation of game design components focuses on issues such as if the game is understandable for the learners (Tan et al., 2007). However, a poor game design can negatively influence the learning curve and therefore it is advisable to evaluate the usability, playability and difficulty of the game before evaluating the pedagogical effectiveness (Wallner & Kriglstein, 2011). Therefore, we conducted a pre-evaluation of the game design components before starting with the evaluation of the educational impact of the game. The gained insights of such an evaluation can help to improve the game design. For the pre-evaluation we recruited 40 elementary school children between eight and ten years and tested them in small groups in classrooms and during certain school events. The findings of the pre-evaluation have already been described in the work of Wallner and Kriglstein (2011), but for the sake of completeness, we will briefly report two main findings. The pre-evaluation revealed that most of the children had problems in a level where they had to learn too many concepts at once and therefore most of them gave up. This was the reason to redesign this level in order to lower the learning curve. We also detected several usability problems. For example, we originally decided not to include an undo function to avoid that children try to solve a puzzle by trial and error without thinking about possible solutions. However, the results of the pre-evaluation showed us that they got frustrated if they solved most of the puzzle and then accidentally performed a wrong move due to the interface design. Therefore, we included an undo function to reverse the last move.

Part B: Evaluation in Classrooms

After the improvements of the game design were successfully finished, we evaluated the game in a school environment. The goal of the evaluation was to measure whether the game DOG*eometry* improves the understanding of geometry, in particular transformations (translation, rotation and reflection), and whether recognition of the relationships of geometric figures in objects is improved. Furthermore, we wanted to find out how the game was accepted by the children. One hundred and ninety-nine elementary school children between eight and ten years old from two local elementary schools participated in the evaluation. The schools were chosen because of the number of teachers willing to participate in the study and because of having the same curriculum and similar demographics.

One school constituted the experimental group with 115 children in five classrooms at different grade levels and the other school served as control group with 84 children in four classrooms at different grade levels. All teachers in the experimental group had already used other games in class as part of regular lessons and had a positive attitude toward game-based learning. Both groups (experimental and control) had to take the same pre- and post-test which were conducted – in the presence of the teacher – by the same researcher to ensure that all groups are treated the same. Testing sessions took about 45 minutes (corresponds to one lesson). In contrast to the control group, children from the experimental group had the possibility to play the game in their classrooms. Children were not forced to play the game but could do so voluntarily in breaks and during after school care. Playing the game did not replace the typical curriculum about the subject, but one teacher also used it as part of a lesson. The physical separation of the control group and experimental group ensured that the control group could not get access to the game. It was important for us that the teaching quality standard of both schools was equal to ensure that the children have the same previous knowledge about the subject matter.

In addition to the pre- and post-tests, we conducted surveys with teachers and pupils to get feedback about DOG*eometry* and to find out what impressions teachers gained while they observed the children with the game. However, surveys are often subjective and therefore all interactions of the children with the game were logged. Every time a player performed an action (e.g., clicking on a button, dragging a tile, coloring a shape) an entry was written automatically to a text file. Each entry includes a timestamp, the type of action and, depending on the action, some supplementary information (e.g., location where a tile was placed, which kind of tile was placed, etc.). This allowed us to get more detailed information about the players' behavior. The next step in the process was the qualitative and quantitative analysis of the collected data. For the analysis of the automatically created log-files we used visualizations – an example of which is shown in Figure 6 – which allowed us to inspect the gameplay data in more detail. For example, visualizations gave us an overview about the different ways how the children solved the different levels. However, before the data could be analyzed it was first necessary to prepare the raw data, because it can often contain missing values or errors (Card, Mackinlay, & Shneiderman, 1999). We only analyzed data from children if they participated in the pre- and post-test. Furthermore, children in the experimental group were taken into account only if they actually played the game. The final datasets are based on 80 children in the experimental group and 74 children in the control group.

Pre/Post Test Design

In creation of the pre- and post-tests, consideration was initially given to which items could be utilized for the evaluation. Based on the primary school curriculum, the items were to come in part from the children's specific world of experience[1] (e.g., recognizing the geometric shape *square* or *circle* in photos of a building facade), while abstract shapes should also be used[2].

Included in these considerations was the fact that Thurstone, as quoted by Damm (2007, p. 6), lists *spatial visualization* and *spatial relation* among the *primary mental abilities*. It was therefore clear that the recognition of rotation and reflection must also be tested on the basis of abstract figures.

Another argument for using abstract figures in addition to concrete objects for testing the understanding of geometric concepts in primary school is offered by Innerhofer and Klipcera (1988). In their *theory of logical forms*, they assume three modes of information processing. One of these information processing modes is the *V-Schema*. Innerhofer and Klicpera (1988) define this *V-Schema* as a "logical form that is not represented by language" (p. 32). This form therefore cannot be referred to as verbal. This form can only be conceived of as an internal mental image.

Therefore, six subtests consisting of four to twelve items each were used. The individual subtests tested the following skills:

1. Recognizing geometric shapes (rectangle, square, triangle, circle) in photos of real buildings.
2. Identifying object constancy in the rotation of abstract images.

3. Checking for the *closure* construct on the basis of *embedded figures* (according to (Thurstone, as quoted by Damm, 2007; Horn, 1962; Horn et al., 2002)). In other words, recognizing geometric figures in abstract images.
4. Recognition of object constancy in the mirroring of a real object (giraffe).
5. Recognition of object constancy in the mirroring of abstract images.
6. Locating the axis (or axes) of symmetry in real objects.

RESULTS

In this section we present the findings and insights from the questionnaires, briefly report results from the pre- and post-tests, and show exemplarily the usefulness of visualizations for the analysis of gameplay data.

Questionnaire

We received 57 statements from the children (35 from males, 22 from females) in response to the question what they liked about DOG*eometry* and the by far most frequent response was "creating the objects" which was stated by 20 children. In contrast, six children liked solving the puzzles. Male and female equally stated that they liked the dog or that they had to help the dog (seven statements).

Five children responded that they enjoyed that the game was tricky and not too easy. The level of difficulty was an issue raised by a teacher during the pre-questionnaire who was concerned that some of the levels might be too complex for children aged eight to ten years. However, children were very eager to solve the puzzles. Some of them needed more than 20 attempts for a single level and still did not give up as long as they had the impression they are making progress and the puzzle is actually solvable. Figure 4 lists the six most frequently named aspects what the children liked about the game.

When asking about issues they disliked about the game, we received 22 replies (12 from males, 10 from females). Four children (3 female, 1 male, all in the same class) said that some of the levels were somewhat difficult. Although not directly connected to the game itself but nevertheless interesting, three girls replied that they were disappointed that they could only play rarely. Figure 5 lists the negative statements children made about the game.

78.21% from 78 children responded that they were motivated by the high-score table. Although children who noted that they felt motivated by the table collected on average the same amount of bones (4.73) as children who were not motivated (4.44 bones on average), they used them more sparingly (0.71 bones on average in contrast to 1.50 bones).

Figure 4.The six most frequent statements from children what they liked about the game

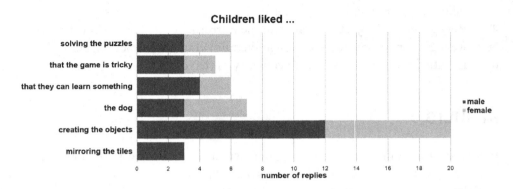

Figure 5. The six most frequent statements from children what they disliked about the game

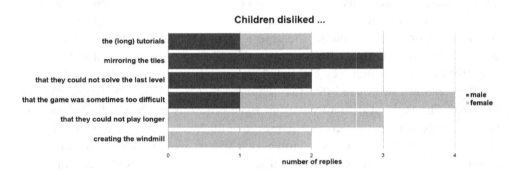

Four of five teachers responded to our post-test survey and three of those reported that DO*Geometry* was as well or better received by the children than previously used games. One teacher responded that the initial enthusiasm faded soon. Interestingly, this was in the same class were four children replied that the game was too hard for them. All four teachers reported that children were talking with each other about the game, like which level was already reached or how they solved a particular puzzle. This shows us that the game not only was played but also influenced children's social interactions with their peers. Social interactions are an important aspect for learning because they allow to reflect on topics. A meta-analysis by (Lou, Abrami, & d'Apollonia, 2001) evaluated the positive effect of social context when students learn with the help of computer technology.

Figure 6. Visualizations of gameplay data from Level 6 (left) and Level 10 (right). Both levels can be solved with the same path (solution A) but the available transformations are different. The player icon depicts the number of the players who attempted the level.

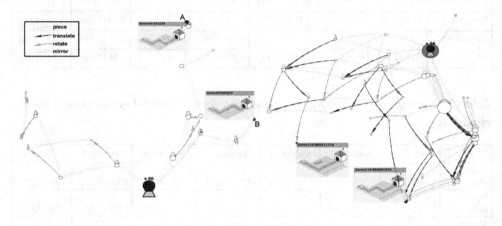

Pre/Post Test Results

Two interesting aspects were observed in the evaluation. The first aspect was that two subtests were clearly too easy and were already solved correctly by almost all participants during the pre-test. One was subtest 3, recognizing geometric shapes in abstract images. The other was subtest 4, recognizing mirroring based on a real figure (a giraffe constructed of cubes). The second interesting aspect of the evaluation was that the game hardly improved geometric comprehension at all among eight-year-olds. An improvement could only be verified as of ages nine and ten. An explanation for this could be found in Piaget's Stage Theory of Cognitive Development. Piaget (2010) says that children of ages seven to eight are only just developing an understanding for the recognition of body shapes. Only afterward does the understanding of symmetry, space and congruence develop.

Average gain scores for experimental group and control group can be found in Table 1 and Table 2. An interesting point that we want to highlight is the remarkable total gain score of 3.30 of eight year old children in the control group (cf. Table 2). Analysis of the data from the two classes with eight year old pupils showed that especially the children from one class improved considerably. It seems they were learning for the test, although we asked the teachers not to do so.

Table 1. Average gain score for each question for the experimental group (standard deviation is given in parenthesis)

	Subtest 1	Subtest 2	Subtest 3	Subtest 4	Subtest 5	Subtest 6	Total
8-year-olds	0.75 (2.54)	0.09 (1.92)	0.06 (0.62)	0.19 (0.59)	0.00 (1.59)	-0.06 (1.16)	1.03 (4.16)
9-year-olds	0.60 (2.48)	0.69 (1.41)	0.03 (0.95)	0.03 (0.66)	1.17 (2.16)	0.54 (1.79)	3.06 (4.06)
10-year-olds	1.15 (2.19)	0.23 (1.17)	-0.15 (0.69)	0.00 (0.00)	0.38 (2.90)	1.23 (1.36)	2.85 (3.85)
all	0.75 (2.44)	0.38 (1.61)	0.01 (0.79)	0.09 (0.58)	0.58 (2.14)	0.41 (1.55)	2.21 (4.13)

Table 2. Average gain score for each question for the control group (standard deviation is given in parenthesis)

	Subtest 1	Subtest 2	Subtest 3	Subtest 4	Subtest 5	Subtest 6	Total
8-year-olds	1.60 (1.78)	0.70 (1.42)	0.60 (1.26)	-0.10 (0,32)	-0.10 (1,29)	0.60 (2.12)	3.30 (3.27)
9-year-olds	0.41 (2.37)	0.38 (1.96)	0.25 (0.62)	0.19 (0.59)	0.13 (1.54)	0.16 (1.22)	1.50 (3.87)
10-year-olds	0.65 (2.17)	0.35 (1.69)	0.41 (1.05)	-0.03 (0.30)	0.71 (1.77)	0.21 (1.07)	2.29 (3.35)
all	0.67 (2.22)	0.41 (1.76)	0.37 (0.92)	0.05 (0.46)	0.36 (1.63)	0.24 (1.29)	2.09 (3.57)

Visualizations

Beside statistical analysis we used graph-based visualizations of the logged gameplay data in order to better understand the player behavior. In many cases evaluations of educational games measure only the impact of the artifact on the learning outcome. However, researchers, like Kriz and Hense (2006) or Defreitas and Oliver (2006), have argued that it is equally important to observe the intermediate relationships to show how and why something works. By visualizing the tracked gameplay data we were able to detect common solutions and to examine if the players solved the levels in the intended way.

Two examples of such visualizations are shown in Figure 6. A node in the graph corresponds to a specific arrangement of the tiles on the grid. For the embedding of the nodes multidimensional scaling (Kruskal & Wish, 1978) – a technique for exploring similarities in data – is used. This way, nodes representing similar configurations of the grid are placed near to each other. Edges show transitions between nodes by performing an action, like placing, translating, or rotating a tile. The size of a node reflects the number of players who arrived at this node and similarly the thickness of an edge corresponds to the number of players who performed this particular move. Edges are colored according to the action they represent. In case of Figure 6 white arrows show a placement of a tile, dark gray depicts a translation, medium gray a rotation and light gray a reflection. Black nodes represent solutions, gray nodes are starting nodes and all other nodes are colored white. A complete description of the visualization system can be found in (Wallner & Kriglstein, 2012).

Figure 6 compares the gameplay data from Level 6 with Level 10. Both levels can be solved with the same solution. In Level 6 one straight tile and three turns can be placed whereas in Level 10 one straight tile but only one turn is available. Three rotations are available in Level 6 in contrast to Level 10 which allows two translations, one rotation and four reflections. The graph of Level 6 is well-arranged and the principal direction toward the goal state *A* is clearly visible. Some children opted for solution *B* (nodes on the way to *B* are smaller and arrows thinner) but the majority chose solution *A*. The graph for Level 10 is a bit more cluttered which indicates that the children were not so sure how to approach the level. There was some disagreement among the children about the best order in which to perform the transformations. This fact is also reflected in the number of attempts children needed on average to solve the level (2.21 attempts for Level 6 and 7.67 attempts for Level 10). Nonetheless, the principal direction is still noticeable which shows us that the children were not lost and managed to solve the puzzle eventually.

CHALLENGES

Setting up the evaluation in the school required more time than we initially expected. We wanted to perform the pre- and post-tests in all classes in the same week such that all groups have approximately the same time-span between pre- and post-test. This was not so easy to achieve because of the differing time-tables. Furthermore, getting the permissions from the education authority and the consents of the parents also required a lot of time.

As the post-test survey revealed, many girls were disappointed that they could not play very often because the computers were "always occupied by the boys". One of the five teachers solved this problem by allocating one computer for girls only. One teacher also noted that next time she will take care that all children can play equally long rather than letting them play on a first-come, first-serve basis.

Since the game is web-based it can be quitted anytime by closing the browser window without exiting it properly. It may also stay open in the background while the user is browsing other websites. This caused some problems with the log-files because they can end anytime or the tracked time-stamps are not meaningful. In addition, events were sometimes not logged in the correct order. If, for example, an event *A* occurred before event *B* in the game it could happen that *B* appeared before *A* in the log-file. This was most probably due to TCP[3] packets to be delivered out of order. Although this occurred rarely, we had to reorder some events by hand because the causal relationships were not captured properly. A better way would be to use the ActionScript socket class to open a continuous TCP/IP connection to the server because this way packets are guaranteed to arrive in the right order. Setting up a server to allow socket connections may be more challenging for the developer, but it does not require additional support from the IT personnel at school.

SUMMARY

In this chapter we presented the design of the development and evaluation process of the educational game DOG*eometry*. We discussed results, challenges, and problems we faced. The evaluation of the game was conducted in nine classes in two elementary schools divided into control and experimental group over a four month period.

Although the conditions are not easily controllable and access to the equipment can be a critical factor for an effective use of the game, we decided to conduct the evaluation in classroom environments and not in a controlled environment (e.g., in a usability lab) in order to evaluate the game for a longer period of time in the environment it will finally be used. This also allowed us to gain valuable insights about social interactions between children and about their *natural* play behavior, which is not possible in a laboratory setting. In addition to the statistical analysis we used visualizations of gameplay data to get deeper information about player behavior that allowed us to go beyond testing of learning outcomes and players' feedback. The visualizations helped us to identify the different ways how the children solved the different levels and gave us valuable insights were particular problems occurred.

Overall, the evaluation showed us that the game was well received by the children and most of them were motivated to play the game in their classrooms. Especially, the high-score table was an incentive for children to play the game over a longer period of time which encouraged a friendly competition between the children. For example, one child stated that "I play as long until I'm number one". Another interesting observation was that the game was not only played but also a popular topic in the classrooms and influenced children's social interaction with each other. For example, children were discussing which level they reached.

In conclusion, the analysis of the gameplay data and the feedback of the children and teachers showed us that the pre-evaluation was really important in order to ensure that the game was well-balanced. Although the evaluation went well we would invest even more effort in the design of the pre- and post-test for subsequent evaluations to adapt the difficulty better to the target audience.

REFERENCES

Andersen, E., Liu, Y.-E., Apter, E., Boucher-Genesse, F., & Popovic, Z. (2010). Gameplay analysis through state projection. In *Proceedings of the Fifth International Conference on the Foundations of Digital Games*. ACM Press.

Annetta, L. A., Murray, M. R., Laird, S. G., Bohr, S. C., & Park, J. C. (2006). Serious games: Incorporating video games in the classroom. *EDUCAUSE Quarterly, 29*(3), 16–22.

Card, S., Mackinlay, J. D., & Shneiderman, B. (1999). *Readings in information visualization: Using vision to think*. Morgan Kaufmann.

Damm, D. (2007). *Die Förderung des räumlichen Vorstellungsvermögens durch den handelnden Umgang mit Würfelbauten*. Norderstedt, Germany: Grin Verlag.

Defreitas, S., & Oliver, M. (2006). How can exploratory learning with games and simulations within the curriculum be most effectively evaluated? *Computers & Education, 46*(3), 249–264. doi:10.1016/j.compedu.2005.11.007

Foreman, J. (2003). Next-generation educational technology versus the lecture. *EDUCAUSE Review, 38*(4), 13–22.

Gee, J. P. (2004). *What video games have to teach us about learning and literacy*. New York, NY: Palgrave Macmillan. doi:10.1145/950566.950595

Gee, J. P. (2005). *Good video games and good learning*. Retrieved November 10, 2011, from www.academiccolab.org/resources/documents/Good_Learning.pdf

Greenblat, C. S., & Duke, R. D. (1981). *Principles and practices of gaming-simulation*. Sage Publications.

Hoobler, N., Humphreys, G., & Agrawala, M. (2004). Visualizing competitive behaviors in multi-user virtual environments. In *Proceedings of IEEE Visualization 2004*, IEEE Computer Society.

Horn, W. (1962). *Leistungsprüfsystem L-P-S*. Göttingen, Germany: Verl. f. Psychologie Hogrefe.

Horn, W., Lukesch, H., Kormann, A., & Mayrhofer, P. (2002). *Prüfsystem für Schul- und Bildungsberatung für 4. bis 6. Klassen - revidierte Fassung (PSB-R 4-6)*. Göttingen, Germany: Hogrefe.

Innerhofer, P., & Klicpera, C. (1988). *Die Welt des frühkindlichen Autismus*. München, Germany: Reinhard.

International Organization for Standardization. (1999). [Human-centered design processes for interactive systems.]. *ISO, 13407*, 1999.

Isbister, K., Flanagan, M., & Hash, C. (2010). Designing games for learning: Insights from conversations with designers. In *Proceedings of the 28th International Conference on Human Factors in Computing Systems*, ACM Press.

Kim, J. H., Gunn, D. V., Schuh, E., Phillips, B., Pagulayan, R. J., & Wixon, D. (2008) Tracking real-time user experience (TRUE): A comprehensive instrumentation solution for complex systems. In *Proceedings of the 26th Annual SIGCHI Conference on Human Factors in Computing Systems*. ACM Press.

Kirriemuir, J., & McFarlane, A. (2003). Use of computer and video games in the classroom . In *Proceedings of Level Up: The Digital Games Research Conference*. University of Utrecht.

Kriz, W. C., & Hense, J. U. (2006). Theory-oriented evaluation for the design of and research in gaming and simulation. *Simulation & Gaming, 37*(2), 268–283. doi:10.1177/1046878106287950

Kruskal, J. B., & Wish, M. (1978). *Multidimensional scaling*. Beverly Hills, CA: Sage Publications.

Kumar, R., & Lightner, R. (2007). Games as an interactive classroom technique: Perceptions of corporate trainers, college instructors and students. *International Journal of Teaching and Learning in Higher Education, 19*(1), 53–63.

Lou, Y., Abrami, P. C., & d'Apollonia, S. (2001). Small group and individual learning with technology: A meta-analysis. *Review of Educational Research, 71*(3), 449–521. doi:10.3102/00346543071003449

Malliet, S., Quinten, N., & Van der Sluys, V. (2010). Evaluating educational game experiences in a classroom context implications for qualitative research. In *Proceedings of the Fun and Games 2010 Workshop*. NHTV Expertise Series.

Mayo, M. J. (2009). Video games: A route to large-scale stem education? *Science, 323*(89).

Medler, B., John, M., & Lane, J. (2011) Data Cracker: Developing a visual game analytic tool for analyzing online gameplay. In *Proceedings of the 29th Annual SIGCHI Conference on Human Factors in Computing Systems*. ACM Press.

Piaget, J. (2010). *Meine Theorie der geistigen Entwicklung*. Weinheim, Germany: Beltz.

Sedig, K. (2008). From play to thoughtful learning: A design strategy to engage children with mathematical representations. *Journal of Computers in Mathematics and Science Teaching, 27*(1), 65–101.

Tan, P., Ling, S., & Ting, C. (2007). Adaptive digital game-based learning framework. In *Proceedings of the 2nd International Conference on Digital Interactive Media in Entertainment and Arts*. ACM Press.

The Henry J. Kaiser Family Foundation. (2002). *Children and video games*. Retrieved January 04, 2012, from http://www.kff.org/entmedia/3271-index.cfm

Vankúš, P. (2008). Games based learning in teaching of mathematics at lower secondary school. *Acta Didactica Universitatis Comenianae - Mathematics, 8,* 103-120.

Wallner, G., & Kriglstein, S. (2011). Design and evaluation of the educational game DOGeometry - A case study. In *Proceedings of the 8th International Conference on Advances in Computer Entertainment Technology*. ACM Press.

Wallner, G., & Kriglstein, S. (2012). A spatiotemporal visualization approach for the analysis of gameplay data. In *Proceedings of the 30th Annual SIGCHI Conference on Human Factors in Computing Systems*. ACM Press.

KEY TERMS AND DEFINITIONS

Browser Game: A game which can be played over the internet using a web-browser.

DOG*eometry*: An educational game for children to teach the concepts of transformation geometry.

Educational Game: A game designed to teach people about a certain topic or to assist them in their learning.

Gameplay Visualization: A visualization to enhance the understanding of the complex data collected during gameplay.

Human Centered Design Process: A general process defined in ISO 13407 which includes users in the development of products.

Pre-Post Test Design: A method which can be used to assess the effectiveness of an intervention.

Survey: A research method to collect information from a number of individuals.

ENDNOTES

[1] Federal Law Gazette No. 134/1963 as amended by Federal Law Gazette II No. 402/2010: Primary School Curriculum, Vienna, 2010, p. 23

[2] Federal Law Gazette No. 134/1963 as amended by Federal Law Gazette II No. 402/2010: Primary School Curriculum, Vienna, 2010, p. 161

[3] TCP/IP, short for Transmission Control Protocol (TCP) and Internet Protocol (IP), is the common communication protocol for the internet.

Chapter 25
Learning with the Support of a Digital Game in the Introduction to Finance Class:
Analysis of the Students' Perception of the Game's Ease of Use and Usefulness

M. Romero
ESADE Law & Business School, Spain

M. Usart
ESADE Law & Business School, Spain

EXECUTIVE SUMMARY

This chapter aims to introduce the case of the eFinance Game (eFG), from the Serious Games' design to an analysis of the learning experience resulting from the use of the game, as well as its use in the context of the Introduction to Finance course in ESADE Law and Business School. After an overall description of the game, the chapter turns attention to the Serious Games (SG) learning experience, considering students' perception of both ease of use and usefulness, but also the implications for teaching and learning assessment that arise with the utilization of this game. Considering the students' performance and their perception of the game, the chapter then analyzes the current challenges and transfers the knowledge generated by this case to practitioners aiming to design, develop, and use digital games in their schools.

DOI: 10.4018/978-1-4666-2848-9.ch025

OVERALL DESCRIPTION

Practicing the basic concepts through a finance game could be perceived as a challenge for most students without a previous knowledge of the field. Considering the diversity of the post-secondary students' profiles and their different levels of literacy in finance, the identification of their previous knowledge level and the monitoring of the learning progression should be among the major objectives of the teacher, whilst taking into account the fact that students don't make their prior knowledge explicit in a lecture-based class in a natural way. In addition, it could be a challenge to monitor the students' learning progression over the course of a lecture-based class as, in this kind of environment, the interaction between teacher and students does not properly ensure the participation of every student in the class; more active students tend to participate to a greater degree, while others only play a very limited role, for the most part remaining passive and merely listening to the lecture. In order to ensure that students are learning, teachers should reconsider their lecture-based classroom in favour of an activity-oriented class (Foreman, 2003; Lederman & Abd-El-Khalick, 1998) where students play a central role. From the teacher's perspective, it is necessary to design learning activities that allow students to make their prior knowledge explicit, but which also assess the students' knowledge progression over the course of the session to allow the teacher to better-adjust their teaching activity. In order to achieve these requirements and propose engaging situations which constitute a challenge for all the students, the methodology chosen for the instructional redesign of the activity was that of Game Based Learning (GBL).

The Game Based Learning (GBL) methodology has been of particular interest in recent decades, and is still a prolific field of research in education (Pivec, Koskinen & Tarín, 2011). Researchers and educators have observed that GBL can be defined as the use of pedagogically designed or adapted games for learning purposes. It has been asserted that game scenarios can help players in the active construction of understanding (Klopfer & Yoon, 2005), while well-designed games could allow for both individual and group interpretations of given information, thereby permitting students to collaborate (Jacques, 1995). According to Prensky (2001), effective Serious Game (SG) design must achieve a balance between fun and educational value. GBL is a pedagogical methodology enhancing the engagement of students in active learning situations where they have to apply their knowledge and competencies in scenario-based problem-solving and decision-making environments (Gee, 2007; Kiili, 2005; Prensky, 2001).

We chose to situate our experience of the GBL methodology, and especially the collaborative GBL approach, in an environment where students play in small groups or dyads in order to try to reach their objectives. This, together with the opportunities generated by computer-based environments for collecting data concerning the students' activities before, during and after the game, led us to design a digital game for the introductory course in finance, called 'eFinance Game' (Romero, Usart, Almirall, 2011; Usart, Romero & Almirall, 2011). The eFG game involves a declaration of the previous knowledge of, and experience in, finance by the students, and allows an evaluation of their performance when choosing between assets and liabilities which have been explained by the professor in the first part of the Introduction to Finance course. The game presents both individual and collaborative (dyad) phases in order to ensure individual accountability in the collaboration process (Slavin, 1989), but also to take advantage of the benefits of creating collaborative gaming experiences that facilitate mutual understanding, contribute to teamwork orientation (Dieleman & Huisingh, 2006) and develop the ability to learn with others (Whitton & Hollins, 2008) in a safe environment. In particular, with reference to cognitive and metacognitive processes involved in learning, some authors affirm that dyad training may be an effective method for practicing some specific competences (Crook & Beier, 2010). Following Dillenbourg (2006), this blend of individual and collaborative (dyad) activities in a computer-based environment is called integrated learning. This scenario facilitates discussion among peers by solving cognitive conflicts which appear because of the different points of view of each member of the dyad.

The GBL approach entails continuing professional development in a Lifelong Learning environment. It is necessary both for individuals who need to achieve a specific grade in competences and for organizations who wish to have an updated workforce (Wall & Ahmed, 2008). Present management education is shifting towards blended learning models that could both lead to the increased engagement of students, and create the conditions for constructing a stronger sense of community among participants (Rovai & Jordan, 2004). Focusing on the collaborative aspect, Joiner, Nethercott, Hull and Reid (2006) investigated motivation factors and saw that a spontaneous balance of competition and collaboration happened inside teams. This is an important aspect for management students; professionals should learn to collaborate in a competitive environment.

PRACTICALITIES OF RUNNING THE GAME

The eFinance Game (eFG) was designed in collaboration with an experienced professor of the Department of Finance in ESADE. Involving the professor throughout the process of designing and developing the game was intended to ensure the development of an authentic and relevant activity in the field of finance, as well as to permit the professor to gain confidence in the use of the game in the classroom. This first release of the eFG is designed to be played in the classroom under the supervision of the Finance professor. For this reason, the professor's involvement in the design of the game aided the avoidance of any possible stumbling blocks could have arisen whilst using the game (Baek, 2008). The game was designed with the aim of improving and optimizing an activity that the professor usually performed in the first, introductory class, the objective of which was to make sure that the students had correctly learnt, and were able to apply the knowledge of, the difference between assets and liabilities. In this class dynamic, the teacher asked students to enumerate different assets and liabilities. As we have previously pointed out, only more active students participated, and little collaboration among students could be observed.

The paper-based game starts with the individual phase, where students play alone. After this phase, they are invited to collaborate in dyads, with another student, for the second and third phases of the game. At the end of the game, the students receive feedback on their performance as a team and can observe, in a ranked scoreboard, their level of achievement in relation to the other dyads in their class. We decided to make groups of only two students in order to better observe and assess individual students' performances. Dyads are created with the professor's advice, bearing in mind that two students who are in total accord from the beginning could potentially collaborate less and will, therefore, probably present lower cognitive gains (Dillenbourg, 2006). Each member of the dyad has a different set of items in the individual and correction phases but the same items in the third phase. The gaming activity was first designed in a paper-based support. Figure 1 shows the two different panels that were designed and printed for the gaming experience.

Each panel had one side that was devoted to explaining the game and collecting both the previous experience and literacy in finance of each student, along with their names and ages. The other side of the panel was the game zone. It had three columns which corresponded to three stages or phases. The first was individual, and required players to decide which of the six different items shown were assets and which liabilities. The second column corresponded to the correction phase, in which students classified another six items individually, but armed with information concerning their peer's performance and level of certainty about those items. The final column, along with a chat space, was devoted to the collaborative phase. In this space, dyads could discuss and

Figure 1. Screenshot of the paper-based game panel

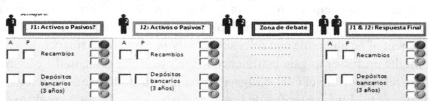

Table 1. Overview of the distribution of items across the panels

Panel	High-difficulty items	Medium-difficulty items	Discussion zone
Panel 1	2a,5a	1a,3a.4a.6a	3rd column
Panel 2	2b,5b	1b,3b.4b.6b	3rd column

write down their final answer as a team and definitively choose the category for each of the twelve items. In summary, the two panels had the same twelve items, but placed in different columns. All panels showed items with two levels of difficulty. The selection of the items was carried out by an experienced professor with more than 30 years experience of teaching finance in the same context and with similar target students. The objective of combining medium-difficulty items with high-difficulty items is to observe differences among the students' level of learning. The finance professor selected a number of items large enough to suggest different panels to each student, in order to avoid each member of the dyad ending up with the same items. In order to maintain a homogeneous level of difficulty, each panel proposed 2 high-difficulty items and 4 medium-difficulty items, appearing always in the same panel positions (Table 1).

The dyad that performs better, that is, the team with a higher level of correctly classified items, wins the game. If there is more than one dyad with the same score, the time spent by the dyad in solving the game is the tiebreaker.

After this first, paper-based experience, the game was developed as a computer-based game (Padrós, Romero, Usart, 2011). We firstly revised and extended the list of items for the game. With the teacher's help, a library of items with two different levels of difficulty was implemented. Secondly, we changed the level of certainty tool from the 3-graded widget of the paper-based version to a more accurate, 10-graded Likert scale tool. The next step was to design the game screens with the same structure as the panels of the paper-based game and to augment these with an in-game guide for players. This guide was present on every screen, showing the players the phase of the game they were playing at that moment (Figure 2).

A third version of the computer-based game (eFG V1.5) has recently been developed and implemented. This version has an improved 2D graphical design, which is better adapted to the average Esade student, with a more professional design. In addition, the eFG V1.5 also includes a link to the previous knowledge test and the number of screens has been reduced to facilitate engagement; instructions are now more precise and are shown before each phase shown in Figure 3.

Figure 2. Peer-correction phase in the computer-based game V1.1

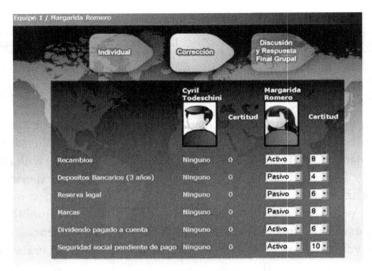

Figure 3. Example of eFG V1.5 Instructions screen before correction phase

Table 2. Overview of the differences between the computer-based eFG versions

	Language	Time Out	Design	Avatar
eFG 1.1	Spanish	No	Simple	Standard
eFG 1.5	Spanish English	Yes	Professional, 2d graphics	Personalized (uploadable)

Another new element in the 1.5 version of the eFG (Table 2) is the analysis of user experience through the TAM questionnaire (Davis, 1989). Students are invited to fill in this survey at the end of the game. TAM aims to study the acceptability of a computer-based environment, according to user-Perceived Usefulness (PU) and user-Perceived Ease of Use (PEU), as we will see in more detail.

In this process of transforming a class activity into a computer-based game, there are different challenges that have to be faced. Computer Based Collaborative Learning (CSCL), and especially collaborative GBL, should be designed in light of the knowledge that the expected users have different levels of ICT literacy. A useful computer-based environment should be both easy to use and relevant to the purposes of all possible players. In the case of collaborative GBL, this environment should also permit communication, provide a clear understanding of how to play and assess players in order to achieve their learning goals. For this purpose, a multidisciplinary approach, both from the pedagogical and the technological point of view, was used to ensure both the learning experience and the learning efficiency of the new GBL environment (Burgos et al., 2007).

After the game, the students' learning experience in the use of the eFG is analyzed, both from the learning performance perspective and taking into account the usability-, acceptability-, and utility-perception of the digital game. There are different models available to evaluate the degree of adoption of the ICT by the users in computer-based environments. Among these, we can find the Technology Acceptance Model (TAM) (Davis, 1989), the System Usability Scale (SUS) (Slater, Usoh & Steed, 1994), and others which are modifications or developments of these models. Although Albert, Tullis and Tedesco (2010) observed that SUS (with only a 10-item rating scale) yielded among the most reliable results across sample sizes compared with other models, we assume that, for educational contexts, the Technology Acceptance Model could be a useful aid in the process of implementation in computer-based activities (El-Gayar, Moran & Hawkes, 2011).

The TAM aims to predict the acceptability of a computer-based environment, according to the user-Perceived Usefulness (PU) and user-Perceived Ease of Use (PEU). PU is defined as being the degree to which users think that the IT system will improve their performance. PEU refers to users' perception of the IT's facility of use. The use of the TAM for evaluating the digital game is starting to be considered as an important factor in understanding the students' acceptance of digital games for educational purposes (Yusoff, Crowder & Gilbert, 2010). In order to better understand the students' perception of the computer-based activity, the TAM questionnaire was augmented with two questions, the first being about perceived ICT self-efficacy (ICT-SE), and the second asking players to compare the computer-based game with a paper-based activity.

USING GAMES FOR TEACHING, LEARNING, AND ASSESSMENT

The eFinance Game (eFG) is an instructional activity with two main learning objectives; firstly, the evaluation of two basic financial concepts, assets and liabilities, which have been introduced by the teacher during the lecture session; secondly, practice of the collaboration competence through collaborative decision-making related to the financial concepts of assets and liabilities. In this sense, the eFG is a Collaborative game (or GBL environment) that aims to promote collaborative learning by allowing students to observe their peer's answers, correct them, and finally, to discuss the collaborative decision making before reaching a consensus on the joint answer to the assets/liabilities evaluation.

The eFG assessment has been designed with the following three levels in mind: firstly, the teacher can observe the individual answers for each of the students, and the overall individual performance; secondly, he can also observe the peer evaluation for each student dyad; finally, he can observe the collaborative decision making of the dyad in relation to the previous individual and peer evaluation answers. To implement eFG in the classroom, the teacher shoud introduce the players in a web-based form and define the items that will be proposed to the students' to classify during the individual and collective level of the game.

In order to monitor all the processes and collect the students' performances for further analysis, two improvements were made in the 1.5 version. Firstly, to give each dyad a specific task-focused space for discussion of the final answers, a synchronous communication tool (chat) was added to the learning platform and linked to the collaborative phase screen. Students were able to interact with their team-peers during this final phase to reach an agreed answer. Furthermore, chat cues were registered for further analysis. In addition to this, the application allowed the teacher to analyze the pairs' dynamics, and their interaction, for further research. In addition, a database was designed and implemented in MySQL. This database stores players' actions while gaming, actions including performance and confidence level for each item and phase, as well as total time spent playing.

With this purpose, a complete gaming experience was finally implemented in real class environments. All players who participated in the game experiences, from the paper-based version to the present eFG version 1.5, were students in management courses. The average player was an adult manager with little experience in finance. In order to correctly assess this assumption, at the beginning of the game each player was invited to make explicit both his experience and literacy in finance. Therefore, using the eFinance Game (eFG) in class, a teacher can have a clear idea of his students' literacy of, and previous experience in, finance, as well as evaluate their understanding of the subject after the first lecture session.

The eFG is played in the first lecture class of an introductory course on finance. In the first part of the session, the professor explains the basic finance concepts and the difference between assets and liabilities. After this theoretical introduction, students are grouped in dyads in order to play the eFG. The entire activity lasts a maximum of 40 minutes, with ten minutes for the individual phase, ten for correction, and 20 for the collaborative discussion and final answer.

After playing the last version (V1.5) of the game, students were invited to fill in the TAM questionnaire along with the two new questions added by the researchers. For the experience reported in this chapter, all students in the first context (n=24) participating in the gaming activity completed the TAM questionnaire. A second context with n=20 students, used the second release of the game and completed the TAM after the game.

TECHNOLOGY COMPONENTS

The eFinance Game is being developed in an iterative prototyping approach that has been progressively refined from a paper-based prototype (eFG 1.0, January 2011), which was tested in a class of n=18 students until the present computer-based collaborative GBL activity, based in a graphic scenario (eFG V1.5, September 2011 that has been called MetaVals), performed in another course, of n=20 students. In order to facilitate navigation in the computer-based releases, the different screens have been designed and reviewed to better access each of the stages of the eFG. The present progressive display of the screens fosters the scaffolding of the individual and the collaborative dynamics of the eFG. The separation of the content in different screens has been discussed by Lee, Plass and Homer (2006) as a way to facilitate comprehension of the activity and reduce the cognitive load associated with the use of a computer-based learning environment.

Each of the four prototypes of the game was tested with real students in authentic classroom situations and the feedback on the TAM (1989) was analyzed after the first computer-based releases. The TAM results on the first computer-based release (n=24) allowed us to observe a high score on the Perceived Ease of Use (PEU, m=5.9 on a 7 point scale) but a lower Perceived Usefulness (PU, m=4.7 on a 7 points scale).

The second data retrieval of the TAM survey was conducted among students of an English EMMS program, who had previously played the eFG 1.5. The TAM results on this second computer-based release (n=20) allowed us to observe a lower score on the Perceived Ease of Use (PEU, m=4.48 on a 7 point scale), but a similar Perceived Usefulness (PU, m=4.48 on a 7 point scale). The results of both experiences are shown in Table 3.

Table 3. Average and standard deviation for the TAM questionnaire on the eFG 1.1 vs. the 1.5

Results of the TAM questionnaire	ICT-SE M SD	PEU M SD	PU M SD
V1.1	4.56 (1.18)	5.22 (0.78)	4.88 (2.29)
V1.5	5.45 (1.44)	4.48(1.62)	4.48(1.38)

We can observe the differences in the TAM results for participants in the two versions of the game (Figure 4).

These results allow us to think about the next steps that could be implemented in the design of the eFG.

CHALLENGES

Despite a high Perceived Ease of Use (PEU) for the eFG V1.1, and an acceptable score on the eFG V1.5, the students consider its Perceived Usefulness (PU) an aspect that could be improved. We discuss this result in two ways. The first one can be understood as the lack of appreciation that students displayed during the collaborative learning phases of the game. One of the objectives of the eFG is to allow the students to engage in better decision-making together in the collaborative phases of the game. However, students participating in the survey do not appreciate specifically this collaboration as useful for their learning. This could be due to the fact that students had to use an external communication tool, which probably hampered the collaborative gaming process by forcing them to constantly change applications; communication in the final phase was therefore slow and interrupted, communicating to the participants a sense of difficulty, which could also be related to the lower PEU in the second sample.

Figure 4. Average and standard deviation for the TAM questionnaire on the eFG 1.1 vs. the 1.5

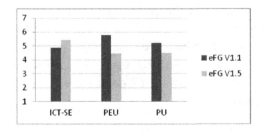

The second way to view the improvable PU, is to consider that the game is too oriented to individual and team-based assessment, and does not provide the students with useful knowledge acquisition; it is an environment where students practice what they have previously learnt. The eFG is a computer-based game allowing the identification of Assets and Liabilities after the teacher's lecture on the topic. In addition, the game was pedagogically designed to permit the elicitation of each player's certainty level in order to minimize the "trial and error" effect (Keith & Frese, 2008). However, the eFG does not provide any additional, new finance content that could help the students to improve their learning.

In summary, the high degree of technology acceptance that students displayed in the TAM questionnaire for the eFG gives us cause to consider the potential interest in computer-supported collaborative GBL, not only in the context of finance and management education, but also with the aim of adapting the method to different fields and levels of study where the collaborative process could be scripted as an individual activity followed by a collaborative activity. With this aim in mind, the eFG is being adapted for a statistics course in the University of the West of Scotland (UWS). This project aims to study the possibilities of the game in another context, namely, in evaluating the acquisition of statistics knowledge during a psychology course for degree students.

GBL environments enable students to perform in a real-time and authentic scenario; a good learning strategy of the eFG could be to promote competition among the members of the class while, at the same time, permitting them to work in dyads to collaboratively win a game. Management collaborative GBL contexts, in which individuals cooperate as a group or dyad and compete against other groups, can result in high learning performance (Ke & Grabowski, 2007). However, in light of the TAM results, there is a need to implement a communication tool within the game that permits more fluent communication among peers in the third phase. Synchronous collaborative games in the field of education are not usual, and these knowledge-supporting widgets still pose a challenge for the game designers. Further longitudinal experiences with the new version of the eFG (1.5) will be developed in order to study the stability of these results and to test it on a greater number of players.

NOTE

This chapter is submitted as part of the research program developed by the Esade Law & Business School Department of Learning Innovation and Academic Quality (DIPQA) within the framework of the FP7 Network of Excellence (NoE) Game and Learning Alliance (GaLA) and the FP7 NoE Stellar GEL Theme.

REFERENCES

Albert, B., Tullis, T., & Tedesco, D. (2010). *Beyond the usability lab: Conducting large-scale user experience studies*. San Francisco, CA: Morgan Kaufmann.

Baek, Y. K. (2008). What hinders teachers in using computer and video games in the classroom? Exploring factors inhibiting the uptake of computer and video games. *Cyberpsychology & Behavior*, *11*, 665–671. doi:10.1089/cpb.2008.0127

Burgos, D., Tattersall, C., & Koper, R. (2007). Re-purposing existing generic games and simulations for e-learning. *Computers in Human Behavior*, *23*, 2656–2667. doi:10.1016/j.chb.2006.08.002

Crook, A. E., & Beier, M. E. (2010). When training with a partner is inferior to training alone: The importance of dyad type and interaction quality. *Journal of Experimental Psychology. Applied*, *16*(4), 335–348. doi:10.1037/a0021913

Davis, F. D. (1989). Perceived usefulness, perceived ease of use, and user acceptance of information technology. *Management Information Systems Quarterly*, (September): 318–340.

Dieleman, H., & Huisingh, D. (2006). Games by which to learn and teach about sustainable development: Exploring the relevance of games and experiential learning for sustainability. *Journal of Cleaner Production*, *14*, 837–847. doi:10.1016/j.jclepro.2005.11.031

Dillenbourg, P. (2006). The solo/duo gap. *Computers in Human Behavior*, *22*(1), 155. doi:10.1016/j.chb.2005.05.001

El-Gayar, O., Moran, M., & Hawkes, M. (2011). Students acceptance of tablet PCs and implications for educational institutions. *Journal of Educational Technology & Society*, *14*(2), 58–70.

Foreman, J. (2003). Next-generation educational technology versus the lecture. *EDUCAUSE Review*, *38*(4), 12.

Gee, J. P. (2007). *What video games have to teach us about learning and literacy* (2nd ed.). Cambridge, MA: New Riders. doi:10.1145/950566.950595

Jacques, D. (1995). Games, simulations and case studies. A review. In D. Saunders (Ed.), *The simulation and gaming yearbook, Vol. 3: Games and simulations for business*. London, UK: Kogan Page.

Joiner, R., Nethercott, J., Hull, R., & Reid, J. (2006). Designing educational experiences using ubiquitous technology. *Computers in Human Behavior, 22*(1), 67–76. doi:10.1016/j.chb.2005.01.001

Ke, F., & Grabowski, B. (2007). Gameplaying for maths learning: Cooperative or not? *British Journal of Educational Technology, 38*(2), 249–259. doi:10.1111/j.1467-8535.2006.00593.x

Keith, N., & Frese, M. (2008). Effectiveness of error management training: A meta-analysis. *The Journal of Applied Psychology, 93*, 59–69. doi:10.1037/0021-9010.93.1.59

Kiili, K. (2005). Digital game-based learning: Towards an experiential gaming model. *The Internet and Higher Education, 8*(1), 13–24. doi:10.1016/j.iheduc.2004.12.001

Klopfer, E., & Yoon, S. (2005). Developing games and simulations for today and tomorrows tech savvy youth. *TechTrends, 49*(3), 33–41. doi:10.1007/BF02763645

Lederman, N. G., & Abd-El-Khalick, F. (1998). Avoiding de-natured science: Activities that promote understandings of the nature of science. In McComas, W. F. (Ed.), *The nature of science in science education: Rationales and strategies* (pp. 83–126). Dodrecht, The Netherlands: Kluwer. doi:10.1007/0-306-47215-5_5

Lee, H., Plass, J. L., & Homer, B. D. (2006). Optimizing cognitive load for learning from computer-based science simulations. *Journal of Educational Psychology, 89*, 902–913. doi:10.1037/0022-0663.98.4.902

Padrós, A., Romero, M., & Usart, M. (2011). Developing serious games: From face-to-face to a computer-based modality. *Elearning Papers, 25*, 1–12.

Pivec, M., Koskinen, T., & Tarín, L. (2011). Game-based learning: New practices, new classrooms [Editorial]. *eLearning Papers, 25*, 1-6.

Prensky, M. (2001). *Digital game-based learning.* New York, NY: McGraw-Hill.

Romero, M., Usart, M., & Almirall, E. (2011). Serious games in a finance course promoting the knowledge group awareness. *EDULEARN11 Proceedings*, (pp. 3490-3492).

Romero, M., Usart, M., & Todeschini, C. (2011). *A serious game for individual and cooperative learning activities.* Retrieved November 22, 2011, from http://serious.gameclassification.com/EN/games/18150-MetaVals/index.html

Rovai, A. P., & Jordan, H. M. (2004). Blended learning and sense of community: A comparative analysis with traditional and fully online graduate courses. *International Review of Research in Open and Distance Learning, 5*(2).

Slater, M., Usoh, M., & Steed, A. (1994). Depth of presence in virtual environments. *Presence (Cambridge, Mass.), 3*, 130–144.

Usart, M., Romero, M., & Almirall, E. (2011). Impact of the feeling of knowledge explicitness in the learners participation and performance in a collaborative game based learning activity. *Lecture Notes in Computer Science, 6944*, 23–35. doi:10.1007/978-3-642-23834-5_3

Wall, J., & Ahmed, V. (2008). Use of a simulation game in delivering blended lifelong learning in the construction industry - Opportunities and challenges. *Computers & Education, 50*(4), 1383–1393. doi:10.1016/j.compedu.2006.12.012

Whitton, N., & Hollins, P. (2008). Collaborative virtual gaming worlds in higher education. *Association for Learning Technology Journal, 16*(3), 221–229. doi:10.1080/09687760802526756

Yusoff, A., Crowder, R., & Gilbert, L. (2010) Validation of serious games attributes using the technology acceptance model. In *The 2nd International IEEE Conference on Serious Games and Virtual Worlds for serious applications* (VSGAMES 2010), March 25-26, 2010, Braga, Portugal, (pp. 45-51).

Chapter 26
Racing Academy:
A Case Study of a Digital Game for Supporting Students Learning of Physics and Engineering

Richard Joiner
University of Bath, UK

Ben Drew
University of West of England, UK

Ioanna Iacovides
University College London, UK

John Duddley
Barnfield Further Education College, UK

Jos Darling
University of Bath, UK

Martin Owen
Medrus, UK

Andy Diament
Penwith Further Education College, UK

Carl Gavin
Manchester Business School, UK

EXECUTIVE SUMMARY

Racing Academy is a digital game, which is specifically designed to engage and motivate students in science and engineering. The aim of this chapter is to report a case study where the authors evaluated how effective Racing Academy is at supporting students' learning of science and engineering. The study involved 219 students from five different courses in three further and higher educational institutions. They were given a pre-test a week before they started using Racing Academy. It consisted of an assessment of the students' knowledge of engineering or physics and motivation towards engineering or physics. A week after they had used Racing Academy, they were given a post-test, which was the same as the pre-test, but it also included a measure of how motivating they found Racing Academy. The project found that after playing Racing Academy there is an increase in students' knowledge and

DOI: 10.4018/978-1-4666-2848-9.ch026

understanding in all five of the courses in which Racing Academy was used. The students found Racing Academy motivating to play, and 95% thought that Racing Academy was successful. The implications of these findings and the lessons learnt are discussed.

INTRODUCTION

Science, technology engineering and mathematics (STEM) is seen by the USA and by the UK as essential for their long term economic futures (DfEL, 2009; Engineering UK, 2009; US NSB, 2007), which has led to a drive to improve STEM education (National Research Council, 2010; National Science Board, 2010). In pursuit of this aim, there has been considerable interest in using digital games for supporting STEM education for a number of reasons. First, a number of reports have shown that digital games have become an integral part of life for children and adolescents. In a recent survey of US adolescents, 98% of teenagers played digital games (Lenhert, Kahne, Middaugh, Macgill, Evans & Vitak, 2008) regularly at least once a week.

Second, well designed digital games can provide powerful learning environments (Gee 2005, FAS 2006, Mayo 2007, 2009). The Federation of American Scientists (FAS, 2006) identifies the following reasons why digital games could facilitate students' learning in STEM.

- They are highly motivating (Kafai, 2001) and research has consistently shown that high levels of motivation leads to high learning outcomes.
- They provide clear learning goals and players know why they are learning something.
- Players are presented with a range of experiences and practice opportunities.
- They are learning in a complex challenging simulated world rather than learning a set of abstract facts devoid of real world context.
- The lessons can be practiced over and over again.
- Video games continually monitor player's progress and provide feedback which is clear and often immediate.
- Video games move at a rate that keeps players at the edge of his or her capabilities moving to higher challenges when mastery is acquired.
- They are infinitely patient and can offer scaffolding, providing learners with cues, prompts, hints and partial solutions to keep them progressing through learning until they are capable of directing and controlling their own learning path.
- They encourage inquiry and questions and respond with answers that are appropriate to the leaner and context.

510

Furthermore, Gee (2003, 2005) and Shaffer, Squire, Halverson & Gee (2005) both argue that digital games have the potential of placing students in simulated environments where they face authentic, open ended challenges similar to those faced by actual professionals. Gee (2005) argues that when individuals play these type of digital games experience first hand how members of a profession think, behave and solve problems, thus they are engaged in a deep, meaningful learning experience. Shaffer et al., (2005) argue that too much of classroom learning is about understanding symbols divorced from the concrete reality of those symbols. In the virtual worlds of games learners experience the concrete realities of what those words and symbols represent. They can understand complex concepts without losing the connection between the abstract ideas and the real problems they can be used to solve. Shaffer et al., (2005) conclude that one reason computer games are powerful learning environments is because they make it possible to develop situated understanding.

Recent research appears to confirm the benefits of digital games for supporting situated learning. Coller & Scott (2009) developed a racing car game which they used to support students learning of numerical methods in an undergraduate mechanical engineering course. They found that students taking the game based course spend roughly twice as much time, outside of class, on their course work. They showed greater depth of understanding of the relationship between concepts and they were very interested in a further follow up course. Mayo (2009) reports that digital games can increase learning in STEM between 7% to 40% compared to traditional lecture based courses.

The aim of this chapter is to report a case study which investigated the use of a digital game, called Racing Academy, to support students' learning of engineering and physics in further and higher education. We evaluated the effectiveness of Racing Academy and interviewed both the students and the lecturers to explore their experiences of using a digital game for supporting their learning and teaching. The analysis of the interviews led us to identify a number of challenges faced by both the students and lecturers which impacted on the effectiveness of Racing Academy. Finally we discuss the lessons learnt from this case study.

PRACTICALITIES OF RUNNING RACING ACADEMY

Racing Academy was specifically designed to engage and motivate students in science and engineering. It aimed to achieve this by engaging them in tasks that were authentic, that involve real practice and through which they can see the effects of their choices, interventions and actions. It is based on a real-time vehicle dynamics simulation system, which is capable of recreating the experience of driving any automobile. It accurately models in real-time how cars behave and react. The games engine has the capacity to allow users to manipulate over 1,000 vehicle parameters, which is particularly important because it enables the students to change the vehicle parameters (such as the engine, transmission, tires and suspension) in order to optimize vehicle performance. Through this optimization process the students get a better understanding of the system dynamics that influence behaviour. Players must engage with the underlying physics and work as a member of a team where practice arises out of real physics and involves the social negotiation of understanding.

The game has three levels and a race level. In the first three levels, players race a computer controlled opponent ("the AI driver") along a quarter mile drag strip (See Figure 1). Every time they beat the AI driver they move on to the next level and the races typically last between 11-15 seconds.

In level 1 the player is given the choice of changing the controls, changing the color of the car and a choice of one of six engines. In level 2 the players have a choice of tires and in level 3 the players can change the gear ratios. After level 3, the students can access the Race level. The Race level has a test circuit and a skid-pan. The skid pan was designed to test the handling characteristics of the car, in particular under steer and over steer (See Figure 2).

At this level, the students can change 12 different characteristics of the car, as well as the engine, the tires and the gear ratios. On the test circuit, they compete against themselves to obtain the quickest time around the test circuit. Racing Academy can be downloaded free from the following website: www.racing-academy.org

DETAILS OF USING RACING ACADEMY FOR TEACHING AND LEARNING

At the start of the project, we held a design workshop with the lecturers and the Racing Academy Design Team. The outcome of this meeting was a number of suggested modifications to Racing Academy. Racing Academy was used in two further education colleges and one university. At Barnfield Further Education College, it was used in the IMI Nationals: Motor Vehicle Engineering course. Fifteen students took this course and they were all male and had an average age of 17 years. It was also used in a BTECH Motor Vehicle engineering course. Eighteen students (17 males and 1 female) took this course, their average age was 19.0. At Penwith Further Education College, Racing Academy was used to support 15 students' learning on the AS/A2 level courses in Physics. There were, all male and they had an average age of 17 years. At the University of Bath, it was used to support two courses in

Figure 1. Drag strip

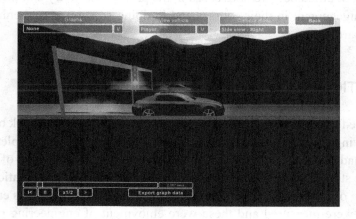

the Department of Mechanical Engineering: a first year course on solid mechanics (average age 19, 143 males and 15 females) and a final year course on Vehicle Dynamics (average age 22, 14 males and 1 female).

Racing Academy was used as part of the students' course and the students were organised into racing teams consisting of 3 to 5 students. The teams designed a racing car in Racing Academy which was used to compete in the drag race for the best time. Each team had their own private discussion forum, where they could discuss how best to set up their car. Engineering support was provided through an open discussion forum. The project lasted two weeks and at the end of two weeks there was a grand final where the teams raced against each other and there was a prize for the winning team.

Figure 2. Skidpan

The aim of all the lecturers involved in the project was to try and increase their students' engagement in their courses and in doing so support and enhance their students' learning.

EVALUATION

We evaluated Racing Academy by using a pre-test administered a week before they started playing with Racing Academy and a post-test the students completed a week after they had finished using Racing Academy. The pre-test consisted of an assessment of the students' knowledge of engineering or physics and motivation towards engineering or physics. Three different aspects of motivation towards engineering or physics were measured and these were enjoyment of engineering or physics, perceived competence in engineering or physics and how important engineering or physics was to them personally. Students answered the questions using a five point Likert scale ranging from 1 strongly disagree to 5 extremely agree.

The post-test was exactly the same as the pre-test, but it also included a measure of how motivating they found Racing Academy. We asked them how much they enjoyed playing Racing Academy, how good they were at playing Racing Academy, how much effort they put into playing Racing Academy and how valuable playing Racing Academy was in their studies. The students answered it using a five point Likert scale, ranging from 1 strongly disagree to 5 extremely agree. Finally we asked the students how often in the previous week they had played Racing Academy, how often they read the message boards and how frequently they posted messages on the message boards. The students answered this with a five point scale ranging from, 0 never to 4 several times a day.

First, we looked at how frequently students played with Racing Academy. They were playing it at least once a week at Barnfield and several times a week at Penwith (See Table 1). We found that students were playing Racing Academy more at college than at home. The message boards were not being used so frequently, with the exception of the students at Penwith Further Education College.

There is a big difference how frequently students use Racing Academy between the two courses at the University of Bath (See Table 2). Students were playing Racing Academy several times a week in Solid mechanics and less than once a week in Vehicle Dynamics.

The questionnaire for the courses at Bath did not distinguish between playing Racing Academy at Home and at College

Next we evaluated how much students learnt from playing Racing Academy. We measured learning in terms of the difference between the number of questions they answered correctly on the pre and post-test measures (See Table 3). There were

Table 1. Frequency of playing Racing Academy at Penwith and Barnfield

	At College		At Home		Reading message board		Posting Messages	
	M	SD	M	SD	M	SD	M	SD
Barnfield IMI Nationals	1.2	0.4	0.7	0.4	0.7	0.4	0.4	0.5
Barnfield BTECH	1.3	0.6	0.5	0.6	1.0	0.6	0.4	0.6
Penwith AS/A2 Level Physics	2.0	0.0	0.4	0.5	1.5	0.5	1.0	0.6

Table 2. Frequency of playing Racing Academy at Bath

	Play Racing Academy		Reading message board		Posting Messages	
	M	SD	M	SD	M	SD
Bath Solid Mechanics	2.1	0.8	1.5	0.8	0.5	0.8
Bath Vehicle Dynamics	0.5	0.5	1.0	0.7	0.5	0.5

Table 3. Pre-test and post-test scores for the 5 courses

	Pre-test		Post-test			
	M	SD	M	SD	t	
Barnfield IMI Nationals	21.4	7.3	22.7	5.5	1.6	
BarnfieldBTECH	16.5	4.6	20.3	5.5	2.0	*
Bath Solid mechanics	7.7	2.5	9.2	2.8	9.1	*
Bath Vehicle Dynamics	2.7	1.5	3.9	1.7	3.0	*
Penwith AS/A2 Level Physics	7.9	2.8	10.6	2.1	4.7	*

* $P < 0.05$

statistically significant improvements in solid mechanics, vehicle dynamics, BTECH motor vehicle engineering and AS/A2 level Physics. There was an improvement in the IMI Nationals vehicle engineering course, but this was not statistically significant.

One of the key aims of the project was to encourage and motivate engineering and science students. Before the students played Racing Academy we measured 3 different aspects of motivation towards physics or engineering. These were how much students enjoyed physics or engineering, how competent they perceived themselves at physics or engineering and how important physics or engineering was in their life. We also measured their motivation after they had finished using Racing Academy for their courses (See Table 4).

We found no significant improvement in students' motivation towards physics or engineering (See Table 4), however it is evident from the means that the students already had high levels of motivation even before the project started.

We assessed how motivating students found Racing Academy by using the following four scales: (1) how much they enjoyed playing Racing Academy, (2) how good they were at playing Racing Academy, (3) how much effort they put into playing Racing Academy and (4) how valuable playing Racing Academy was.

There were a number of similarities and differences between the four courses concerning how motivating Racing Academy was to play (See Table 5). Students in all the courses found Racing Academy enjoyable to play. Students at Penwith, Barnfield (IMI Nationals & BTECH) and Bath (Solid Mechanics) felt they were competent at playing Racing Academy. Students at Penwith, Barnfield (IMI Nationals) and Bath (Solid Mechanics) felt that playing Racing Academy was worth the effort. Students at Penwith and Barnfield (IMI Nationals) course thought that Racing Academy was a valuable exercise.

Table 4. Pre and post-test measures of motivation for engineering and physics

	Enjoyment		Importance to self		Perceived Competence	
	Pre	Post	Pre	Post	Pre	Post
BarnfieldIMI Nationals	6.4	6.1	6.0	5.9	5.3	5.1
Barnfield BTECH	5.4	5.3	5.5	5.3	4.6	4.5
Bath Solid mechanics	5.2	5.1	5.0	5.0	5.6	5.6
Bath Vehicle Dynamics	5.1	5.1	5.2	5.0	4.4	4.2
Penwith AS/A2 Level Physics	5.3	5.4	4.9	5.0	4.1	4.0

Table 5. Racing academy and motivation

	Enjoyment		Competence		Effort		Value	
	M	SD	M	SD	M	SD	M	SD
Barnfield IMI Nationals	5.2	0.6	5.2	0.6	4.6	0.8	4.7	0.7
Barnfield BTECH	4.5	1.2	4.6	0.7	3.9	1.2	4.1	1.1
Bath Solid mechanics	4.4	0.5	4.2	0.6	4.1	0.7	4.1	0.6
Bath Vehicle Dynamics	4.5	0.7	4.2	0.6	3.7	0.7	4.6	0.7
Penwith AS/A2 Level Physics	5.2	0.7	4.8	0.7	4.6	0.5	4.6	0.5

Another measure of the impact of Racing Academy on students learning is how successful they felt Racing Academy was in supporting their learning. We assessed this by asking the students the following question 'Racing Academy was specifically designed to support your learning on your course. Do you think it was successful? Table 6 shows that ninety five percent of students thought it was successful at supporting their learning.

The students where also asked to explain why they thought Racing Academy was successful or not. Table 7 shows that 103 students said something positive, 73 said something negative, while 17 had either neutral comments or suggestions.

The comments were grouped into positive, negative and neutral comments. Table 7 shows that 76% of the students made a positive comment about the success of Racing Academy.

Example 1: "It explains scientific methods in an easier form, it is fun and enjoyable and it allows you to see the changes your making and the effects" (Barnfield IMI Nationals Student).

Example 1 illustrates a number of reasons given by students for why Racing Academy was successful. Fifty percent of students said that it increased their understanding. In Example 1, it increased the student's understanding of the scientific method. Seventeen percent of students, like the student above, thought that the learning by doing method was an effective teaching method and thought Racing Academy was fun (10%).

Example 2: "Because I was using graphs on my performance, it helped to understand how to get better performance out of the car and this was by using the physics in the graphs to improve, so this benefitted me with my physics" (Penwith AS/A2 student).

Ten percent of students commented on the usefulness of the graphs generated by the game and how the graphs helped their learning (See Example 2).

Table 7 shows less than 50% of the students made a negative comment. Fifteen percent of students' felt Racing Academy was not successful because it did not provide sufficient information about how to improve the car's performance (See Example 3).

Example 3: "It had some relevance to the course, however it did not help with improving my mechanics. There was very little theory as such" (Bath Solid Mechanics Student).

Table 6. Perceived success of Racing Academy

	Percentage Number of Students			
	Not at all successful	A little bit successful	Quite successful	Very successful
Barnfield IMI Nationals	0.0	35.7	64.3	0.0
BarnfieldBTECH	11.1	44.4	38.9	5.6
Bath Soli mechanics	5.4	48.3	44.9	1.4
Bath Vehile Dynamics	6.7	26.7	53.3	13.3
Penwith A/A2 Level Physics	0.0	30.8	53.8	15.4
Overall	4.6	37.2	51.0	7.1

Table 7. Positive and negative comments

	Positive		Negative		Neutral	
	N	%	N	%	N	%
Barnfield IMI Nationals	10/14	71.4%	7/14	50.0%	1/15	7.1%
BarnfieldBTECH	16/18	88.9%	7/18	38.9%	2/18	11.1%
Bath Soli mechanics	103/140	73.6%	73/140	52.1%	17/140	12.1%
Bath Vehile Dynamics	11/15	73.3%	2/15	13.3%	10/15	66.7%
Penwith A/A2 Level Physics	12/13	92.3%	8/13	61.5%	2/13	15.4%
Overall	152/199	76.0%	97/199	48.5%	32/199	16.0%

Fifteen percent of student felt that it was not relevant to their courses (See Example 4).

Example 4: "Didn't learn anything from it, the whole process was trial and error for getting the fastest time down the track. Had no relation to what we are doing in the courses" (Bath Solid Mechanics Student).

Fourteen percent of students thought that the learning by doing method was not as effective as more traditional methods (See Example 5).

Example 5: "Some bits, like looking at the graph, were helpful, but on the whole I think I learn better from the board and listening" (Penwith AS/A2 student).

In summary, we found that most students found Racing Academy motivating and they did learn from their experience with Racing Academy. The vast majority of students thought Racing Academy was successful. When asked why? The reasons given were as follows; (1) it increased their understanding, (2) they thought learning by doing was effective method of teaching, (3) it was fun, and (4) they thought the graphs generated by Racing Academy were useful for their learning. A minority of students felt Racing Academy was not successful. The reasons they gave was because (1) a lack of information concerning how to improve the car's performance, (2) it was not relevant to the course and (3) felt traditional methods were a more efficient method of teaching.

LESSONS LEARNED

One important lesson we learnt from this project was the importance of involving both lecturers and students in the design process. Even though Racing Academy had been used before to support younger children's learning it became quickly apparent in the initial design workshops that the software required certain modifications which led to the development of the software which was more suited to the needs of the lecturers and further and higher education students. For example, it was quickly apparent that the students were using different computers and not the same computer as initially assumed, thus it was important that they had a simple way to move their design from one machine to the next. The designers quickly came up with racing car design file which stored all the design information and could be transferred from one machine to the next.

The findings from the evaluation also revealed a number of important lessons for the use of digital games for supporting learning. The first is that it is important to make sure that the game content is closely couple to the curriculum content of the course. It was apparent from the open ended comments that Racing Academy was more closely coupled to the engineering courses than the physics course. Even the representation of the car was not appropriate for the curriculum content of the AS/A2 physics course. The representation of the car in Racing Academy is a realistic representation, whereas in the AS/A2 physics course they use a point to represent the motion of an object.

The second lesson is that it is important to provide some material at the appropriate level which provides information concerning how to improve the performance of the car. The aim at the outset was for the students to search for this information online, but this proofed difficult for most of the students. The problem with providing appropriate information is that each course would require different information which would be costly to produce and maintain. One possible solution would be to set up a game website where the players of the game and lecturers who use the game can provide useful information for other players and lecturers.

A third lesson concerned the best ways to organise teams. The competition was judged on the basis of the quickest car in the team, which meant that if one member had a very quick car the other members of the team did not have to develop their own car. A more pedagogically effective organisation which would have probably led to more constructive collaboration between team members would have been to have judged the team either on the basis of their average race times or the time of the slowest member of the team. The latter may have been better because it might have resulted in the more able members supporting and giving instructions to the less able members of the team.

A fourth lesson was the overly fierce competition between the teams, which was not conducive to a more collaborative atmosphere. The competition at the end of Racing Academy may have been responsible for this overly fierce competition between some teams, which led to some students stealing over teams designs. One possible solution would be to have arranged awards based on the team's performance rather than the team's position. For example if you were awarded prizes for reaching set performance goals. For example achieving certain times (e.g. for going under 11 seconds) and/or for consistency (going under 12 second in 3 drag races in a row).

The above lesson is related to next, which concerns the individuals' motivation to play the game. Once the students had beaten the AI driver and they felt they could not compete against some of the best students they lacked motivation to carry on playing. Again one possible solution would be to have more rewards in the game. The students could be awarded medals, or laurel leaves, which may be more appropriate for a racing car game, for achieving performance goals.

Another issue was the limited use of the online forums, especially the student forums. This was particularly the case for students who saw each other regularly face to face, although the forums were used significantly more in Penwith, which was because the lecturer was a frequent contributor to the forums and responded quickly to the students' questions and comments.

A final issue concerns gender. Some students commented that Racing Academy may not be as motivating for females as Males. We have compared males and females playing Racing Academy and found that there was no gender difference in the beneficial effect of Racing Academy. In fact, there was some evidence that, female students found Racing Academy more motivating than male students (Joiner et al., 2011).

CONCLUSION

Therefore in summary, Racing Academy was successfully implemented in five courses, in two further education colleges and one university, to support the learning of physics and engineering. We found evidence that students found playing Racing Academy motivating and that it did support students' learning. The majority of students thought Racing Academy was successful because playing Racing Academy increased their understanding, (2) learning by doing was effective method of teaching, (3) it was fun, and (4) the graphs generated by Racing Academy were useful. A minority of students felt Racing Academy was not successful. The reasons they were because (1) there was a lack of information concerning how to improve the car's performance, (2) it was not relevant to the course and (3) felt traditional methods were a more efficient method of teaching. From these findings a number of lessons were discussed. These findings are consistent with previous research which has also found that playing digital games can facilitate students learning in STEM subjects in higher education (Coller, & Scott, 2009). It extends this research by showing that it can also facilitate learning in STEM subjects in further education, although the findings also show that these benefits are not universal with some students feeling it was not successful. Some of these difficulties could be overcome by providing more background material and explaining the relevance of playing the game for their course. In conclusion, this case study shows the potential of digital games for supporting students learning in STEM subjects.

REFERENCES

Barab, S., & Dede, C. (2007). Games and immersive participatory simulations for science education: An emerging type of curricula. *Journal of Science Education and Technology*, *16*(1), 1–3. doi:10.1007/s10956-007-9043-9

Barab, S., Dodge, T., Tuzun, H., Job-Sluder, K., Jackson, C., & Arici, A. Heiselt, C. (2007). The Quest Atlantis Project: A socially-responsive play space for learning. In B. E. Shelton & D. Wiley (Eds.), *The educational design and use of simulation computer games* (pp. 159-186). Rotterdam, The Netherlands: Sense Publishers.

Coller, B. D., & Scott, M. J. (2009). Effectiveness of using a video game to teach a course on mechanical engineering. *Computers & Education*, *53*, 900–912. doi:10.1016/j.compedu.2009.05.012

Dede, C., & Barab, S. (2009). Emerging technologies for learning science: A time of rapid advance. *Journal of Science Education and Technology, 18*(4), 301–304. doi:10.1007/s10956-009-9172-4

Dede, C., Nelson, B., & Ketelhut, D. J. (2004). *Design-based research on gender, class, race, and ethnicity in a multi-user virtual environment.* Paper presented at the Meeting of the American Educational Research Association, San Diego, CA.

Department for Employment and Learning. (2009). *Report of the STEM Review.* Retrieved January 15, 2010, from http://www.delni.gov.uk/index/publications/pubs-successthroughskills/stem-review-09.htm

Engineering, U. K. (2009). *Engineering UK 2009/10.* Retrieved January 15, 2012, from http://www.engineeringuk.com/what_we_do/education_&_research/engineering_uk_2009/10.cfm

Federation of American Scientists. (2006). *Summit on Educational Games: Harnessing the power of video games for learning.* Retrieved January 15, 2010, from http://www.fas.org/gamesummit/

Gee, J. (2003). *What videogames have to teach us about learning and literacy.* New York, NY: Palgrave.

Gee, J. P. (2005). What would a state of the art instructional video game look like? *Innovate, 1*(6). Retrieved January 15, 2012, from http://www.innovateonline.info/index.php?view=article&id=80

Joiner, R., Iacovides, J., Owen, M., Gavin, C., Clibbey, S., Darling, J., & Drew, B. (2011). Digital games, gender and learning in engineering: Do females benefit as much as males? *Journal of Science Education and Technology, 20*(2), 178–185. doi:10.1007/s10956-010-9244-5

Kafai, Y. (2001). *The educational potential of electronic games: From games-to-teach to games-to-learn.* Retrieved January 15, 2012, from http://culturalpolicy.uchicago.edu/conf2001/papers/kafai.html

Lenhart, A., Kahne, J., Middaugh, E., Rankin Macgill, A., Evans, C., & Vitak, J. (2008). *Teens, video games and civics.* Pew Internet and Life Project. Retrieved January 15, 2012, from http://www.pewinternet.org/Reports/2008/Teens-Video-Games-and-Civics.aspx

Mayo, M. J. (2007). Games for science and engineering education. *Communications of the ACM, 50*(7), 31–35. doi:10.1145/1272516.1272536

Mayo, M. J. (2009). Video games: A route to large-scale STEM education? *Science*, *323*(79), 79–82. doi:10.1126/science.1166900

McFarlane, A., Sparrowhawk, A., & Heald, Y. (2002). *Report on the educational use of games*. Retrieved January 15, 2010, from http://www.teem.org.uk/publications/teem_gamesined_full.pdf

National Research Council. (2010). *Rising above the gathering storm, revisited: Rapidly approaching category 5. 2005 "Rising Above the Gathering Storm" Committee; Prepared for the Presidents of the National Academy of Sciences, National Academy of Engineering, and Institute of Medicine*. Washington, DC: National Academies Press.

National Science Board. (2007). *A national action plan for addressing the critical needs of the US science technology, engineering and mathematics engineering system*. (National Science Foundation NSB/HER-07-9). Retrieved January 15, 2010, from http://nsf.gov/nsb/edu_com/report.jsp

National Science Board. (2010). *Preparing the next generation of STEM innovators: Identifying and developing our nation's human capital. (NSF Publication NSB1033)*. Arlington, VA: Author.

National Science Foundation, Division of Science Resources Statistics. (2009). *Women, minorities, and persons with disabilities in science and engineering: 2009*. (NSF 09-305). Arlington, VA: Author. Retrieved January 15, 2010, from http://www.nsf.gov/statistics/wmpd/

Nelson, B. (2007). Exploring the use of individualized, reflective guidance in an educational multi-user virtual environment. *Journal of Science Education and Technology*, *16*(1), 83–97. doi:10.1007/s10956-006-9039-x

Rideout, V., Roberts, D. F., & Foehr, U. G. (2005). *Generation M: Media in the lives of 8–18 year-olds* [executive summary]. Retrieved January 15, 2010, from http://www.kff.org/entmedia/upload/Executive-Summary-Generation-M-Media-in-the-Lives-of-8-18-Year-olds.pdf

Roberts, D. F., Foehr, U. G., & Rideout, V. (2005). *Generation M: Media in the lives of 8–18 year-olds*. Kaiser Family Foundation Study. Retrieved January 15, 2010, from http://www.kff.org/entmedia/upload/Generation-M-Media-in-the-Lives-of-8-18-Year-olds-Report.pdf

Shaffer, D. W., Squire, K. A., Halverson, R., & Gee, J. P. (2005). Video games and the future of learning. *Phi Delta Kappan*, *87*(2), 104–111.

Compilation of References

30 *Great Games Outdoor Fun* [Computer software]. (2009). Los Angeles, CA: D3 Publisher of America.

9 *05* [Computer software]. (2000). Retrieved January 8, 2011 from http://adamcadre.ac/content/905.zip

Aamodt, A., & Plaza, E. (1994). Case-based reasoning: Foundational issues, methodological variations and system approaches. *AI Communications, 7*(1), 39-59. Retrieved January 26, 2006, from http://www.idi.ntnu.no/emner/it3704/lectures/papers/Aamodt_1994_Case.pdf

Aarseth, E. (1997). *Cybertext: Perspectives on ergodic literature* (p. 3). Baltimore, MD: Johns Hopkins University Press.

Aarseth, E. (2004). Beyond the frontier: Quest games as post-narrative discourse. In Ryan, M. L. (Ed.), *Narrative across media*. University of Nebraska Press.

Abbot, J. (1994). Learning makes sense: Re-creating education for a changing future. Letchworth, UK. *Education*, 2000.

Abraham, L. B., Morn, M. P., & Vollman, A. (2010). *Women on the Web: How women are shaping the internet.* comScore, Inc. Retrieved April 10, 2012, from http://www.iab.net/media/file/womenontheweb.pdf

Abt, C. (1970). *Serious games.* New York, NY: Viking Press.

Achterbosch, L., Pierce, R., & Simmons, G. (2007). Massively multiplayer online role-playing games: The past, present, and future. *Computers in Entertainment, 5*(4).

Adams, D. M., Mayer, R. E., MacNamara, A., Koenig, A., & Wainess, R. (2012). Narrative games for learning: Testing the discovery and narrative hypotheses. *Journal of Educational Psychology, 104*(1), 235–249. doi:10.1037/a0025595

AERO Social Studies Curriculum Framework. (n.d.) Retrieved from http://www.projectaero.org/ss/socialstudies.pdf

Ahern, T. C. (2009). *Bridging the gap: Cognitive scaffolding to improve computer programming for middle school teachers.* Frontiers in Education 39th ASEE/IEEE, M1H-1-6. Retrieved from http://fie-conference.org/fie2009/

Ahmed, S. (2006). *Queer phenomenology: Orientations, objects, others.* Durham, NC: Duke University Press.

Albert, B., Tullis, T., & Tedesco, D. (2010). *Beyond the usability lab: Conducting large-scale user experience studies.* San Francisco, CA: Morgan Kaufmann.

Compilation of References

Aldrich, C. (2004). *Simulations and the future of learning*. San Francisco, CA: John Wiley and Sons.

Aldrich, C. (2005). *Learning by doing*. San Francisco, CA: Pfeiffer.

Alexander, A. L., Brunye, T., Sidman, J., & Weil, S. A. (2005). *From gaming to training: A review of studies on fidelity, immersion, presence, and buy-in and their effects on transfer in pc-based simulations and games*. DARWARS Training Impact Group. Retrieved June 9, 2008, from http://www.darwars.com/downloads/DARWAR%20Paper%2012205.pdf.

Alexander, P. A. (1997). Mapping the multidimensional nature of domain learning: The interplay of cognitive, motivational, and strategic forces. In Maehr, M. L., & Pintrich, P. R. (Eds.), *Advances in motivation and achievement* (*Vol. 10*, pp. 213–250). Greenwich, CT: JAI Press.

Alexander, P. A. (2003). The development of expertise: The journey from acclimation to proficiency. *Educational Researcher*, *32*(8), 10–14. doi:10.3102/0013189X032008010

Alexander, P. A., Jetton, T. L., & Kulikowich, J. M. (1995). Interrelationship of knowledge, interest, and recall: Assessing a model of domain learning. *Journal of Educational Psychology*, *87*(4), 559. doi:10.1037/0022-0663.87.4.559

Al-Khalifa, H. S. (2011). An m-learning system based on mobile phones and quick response codes. *Journal of Computer Science*, *7*(3), 427-430. Retrieved 14th January, 2012, from http://www.doaj.org/doaj?func=abstract&id=803858

Allen, I. E., & Seaman, J. (2008). *Staying the course: Online education in the United States, 2008*. The Sloan Consortium.

Ally, M. (2004). Foundations of educational theory for online learning. In Anderson, T., & Elloumi, F. (Eds.), *Theory and practice of online learning*. Athabasca University.

Alvarez, J., & Michaud, L. (2008). *Serious games: Advergaming, edugaming, training and more*. Montpellier, France: IDATE.

America's Best Colleges. (2011). Washington, DC. *U.S. News & World Report*.

Ames, C. (1992). Classrooms: Goals, structures, and student motivation. *Journal of Educational Psychology*, *84*, 261–271. doi:10.1037/0022-0663.84.3.261

Amory, A. (2007). Game object model version II: A theoretical framework for educational game development. *Educational Technology Research and Development*, *55*(1), 51–77. doi:10.1007/s11423-006-9001-x

Amory, K. (2001). Building an educational adventure game: Theory, design and lessons. *Journal of Interactive Learning Research*, *12*, 249–263.

Amory, K., Naicker, J. V., & Adams, C. (1999). The use of computer games as an educational tool: Identification of appropriate game types and game elements. *British Journal of Educational Technology*, *30*, 311–321. doi:10.1111/1467-8535.00121

Andersen, E., Liu, Y.-E., Apter, E., Boucher-Genesse, F., & Popovic, Z. (2010). Gameplay analysis through state projection. In *Proceedings of the Fifth International Conference on the Foundations of Digital Games*. ACM Press.

Anderson, C. A. (2003). Violent video games: Myths, facts, and unanswered questions. *Psychological Science Agenda: Science Briefs*, *16*(5), 1–3.

Angeli, C. (2004). The effects of case-based learning on early childhood pre-service teachers' beliefs about the pedagogical uses of ICT. *Journal of Educational Media, 29*(2), 139–151. doi:10.1080/13581650420 00253302

ANMC. (2006). *National competency standards for the registered nurse*. Australian Nursing and Midwifery Council. Retrieved from http://www.anmc.org.au/userfiles/file/competency_standards/Competency_standards_RN.pdf

Annetta, L. A. (2008). Video games in education: Why they should be used and how they are being used. *Theory into Practice, 47,* 229–239. doi:10.1080/00405840802153940

Annetta, L. A., Minogue, J., Holmes, S. Y., & Cheng, M. T. (2009). Investigating the impact of video games on high school students' engagement and learning about genetics. *Computers & Education, 53*(1), 74–85. doi:10.1016/j.compedu.2008.12.020

Annetta, L. A., Murray, M. R., Laird, S. G., Bohr, S. C., & Park, J. C. (2006). Serious games: Incorporating video games in the classroom. *EDUCAUSE Quarterly, 29*(3), 16–22.

Antonacci, D. M., & Modaress, N. (2008). Envisioning the educational possibilities of user-created virtual worlds. *AACE Journal, 16*(2), 115–126.

Are you smarter than a 5th grader? (Version Wii Platform) (2008). [Computer software]. Agoura Hills, CA: THQ, Inc.

Ashmore, C., & Nitche, M. (2007). The quest in a generated world. *Proceedings of the 2007 Digital Games Research Association. (DiGRA) Conference: Situated Play,* (pp. 503-509). Tokyo, Japan.

Astley, R. (Performer). (1987). *Never gonna give you up* [Web]. Retrieved from http://www.youtube.com/watch?v=dQw4w9WgXcQ

AUQA. (2008). *Good practice principles for english language proficiency for international students in Australian universities – Final report.* Australian Universities Quality Agency. Retrieved from http://www.deewr.gov.au/HigherEducation/Publications/Documents/Final_Report-Good_Practice_Principles.pdf

Austin, T. X., & the The New Media Consortium. Retrieved January 8, 2011, from http://wp.nmc.org/horizon2011/

Australian Government Department of Families, Housing, Community Services and Indigenous Affairs. (n.d.). Retrieved on August 19, 2010, from http://www.fahcsia.gov.au/sa/families/progserv/communitieschildren/Pages/default.aspx

Australian Government Department of Health and Ageing. (n.d.). Retrieved on August 20th 2010 from http://www.health.gov.au/internet/main/publishing.nsf/Content/phd-nutrition-childrens-survey-userguide

Avedon, E. M., & Sutton-Smith, B. (Eds.). (1971). *The study of games.* New York, NY: John Wiley & Sons, Inc.

Ayres, P., Kalyuga, S., Marcus, N., & Sweller, J. (2005). *The conditions under which instructional animation may be effective.* Paper presented at an International Workshop and Mini-conference, Open University of the Netherlands: Heerlen, The Netherlands.

Ayres, P., & Paas, F. (2007). Making instructional animations more effective: A cognitive load approach. *Applied Cognitive Psychology, 21,* 695–700. doi:10.1002/acp.1343

Badman, T., Badman, C., & DeNote, M. (2012, January 3). *Gaming in the classroom.* Retrieved January 14, 2012, from www.gamingintheclassroom.com

Baek, Y. K. (2008). What hinders teachers in using computer and video games in the classroom? Exploring factors inhibiting the uptake of computer and video games. *Cyberpsychology & Behavior, 11*, 665–671. doi:10.1089/cpb.2008.0127

Baek, Y. K. (2010). *Gaming for classroom-based learning: Digital role playing as a motivator of study.* Hershey, PA: IGI Global. doi:10.4018/978-1-61520-713-8

Baggerly, J. (2002). Pratical technological application to promote pedagogical principles and active learning in counselor education. *Journal of Technology in Counseling, 2*(2).

Bagherkazemi, M., & Alemi, M. (2010). Literature in the EFL/ESL classroom: Consensus and controversy. *LIBRI, 1*(1), 1–12.

Baker, R. S. J. D., & Yacef, K. (2009). The state of educational data mining in 2009: A review and future visions. *Journal of Educational Data Mining, 1*(1), 3–17.

Ball, D. L. (1992). Magical hopes: Manipulatives and the reform of math education. *American Educator, 16*(2), 14–18, 46–47.

Bandai. (2012). *Tamagotchi town.* Retrieved 26 January, 2012, from http://www.bandai.com/tamagotchi/

Bang, M., Gustafsson, A., & Katzeff, C. (2007). Promoting new patterns in household energy consumption with pervasive learning games. *Proceedings of the Second International Conference on Persuasive Technology, Lecture Notes in Computer Science.* Berlin, Germany: Springer.

Barab, S., Dodge, T., Tuzun, H., Job-Sluder, K., Jackson, C., & Arici, A. Heiselt, C. (2007). The Quest Atlantis Project: A socially-responsive play space for learning. In B. E. Shelton & D. Wiley (Eds.), *The educational design and use of simulation computer games* (pp. 159-186). Rotterdam, The Netherlands: Sense Publishers.

Barab, S. (2006). Design-based reearch: A methodological toolkit for the learning scientist. In Sawyer, R. K. (Ed.), *The Cambridge handbook of the learning sciences* (pp. 153–169). New York, NY: Cambridge University Press.

Barab, S. A., Gresalfi, M., & Ingram-Goble, A. (2010). Transformational play. *Educational Researcher, 39*(7), 525. doi:10.3102/0013189X10386593

Barab, S. A., Hay, K. E., Barnett, M., & Squire, K. (2001). Constructing virtual worlds: Tracing the historical development of learner practices. *Cognition and Instruction, 19*(1), 47–94. doi:10.1207/S1532690XCI1901_2

Barab, S. A., Hay, K. E., & Duffy, T. M. (1998). Grounded constructions and how technology can help. *TechTrends, 43*(2), 15. doi:10.1007/BF02818171

Barab, S. A., Warren, S. J., & Ingram-Goble, A. (2008). Academic play spaces. In Ferdig, R. (Ed.), *Handbook of research on effective electronic gaming in education.* Hershey, PA: Idea Group Reference.

Barab, S., & Dede, C. (2007). Games and immersive participatory simulations for science education: An emerging type of curricula. *Journal of Science Education and Technology, 16*(1), 1–3. doi:10.1007/s10956-007-9043-9

Barab, S., Scott, B., Siyahhan, S., Goldstone, R., Ingram-Goble, A., Zuiker, S., & Warren, S. (2009). Transformational play as a curricular scaffold: Using videogames to support science education. *Journal of Science Education and Technology, 18*(4), 305–320. doi:10.1007/s10956-009-9171-5

Barab, S., & Squire, K. (2004). Design-based research: Putting a stake in the ground. *Journal of the Learning Sciences, 13*, 1–14. doi:10.1207/s15327809jls1301_1

Barab, S., Thomas, M., Dodge, T., Carteaux, R., & Tuzun, H. (2005). Making learning fun: Quest Atlantis, a game without guns. *Educational Technology Research and Development, 53*, 86–107. doi:10.1007/BF02504859

Barab, S., Zuiker, S., Warren, S., Hickey, D., Ingram-Goble, A., & Kwon, E.-J. (2007). Situationally embodied curriculum: Relating formalisms and contexts. *Science Education, 91*, 750–782. doi:10.1002/sce.20217

Barlow, A. T., & McCroy, M. R. (2011). Strategies for promoting math disagreements. *Teaching Children Mathematics, 17*(9), 530–539.

Baroody, A. J. (1989). One point of view: Manipulatives don't come with guarantees. *The Arithmetic Teacher, 37*, 4–5.

Barrett, T. (n.d.). *EDTE.CH inspire connect engage create*. Retrieved January 14, 2012, from http://edte.ch/blog/

Barrett, J. E., & Dickson, S. (2003). Broken rulers: Teaching notes. In Bright, G. W., & Clements, D. H. (Eds.), *Classroom activities for learning and teaching measurement* (pp. 11–14). Reston, VA: National Council of Teachers of Mathematics.

Barrett, J. E., Jones, G., Thornton, C., & Dickson, S. (2003). Understanding children's developing strategies and concepts for length. In Clements, D. H. (Ed.), *Learning and teaching measurement* (pp. 17–30). Reston, VA: National Council of Teachers of Mathematics.

Barrett, L. F., & Russell, J. A. (2009). The circumplex model of affect. In Sanders, D., & Scherer, K. (Eds.), *Oxford companion to emotion and the affective sciences*. New York, NY: Oxford University Press.

Barrows, H. S. (1986). A taxonomy of problem based learning methods. *Medical Education, 20*, 481–486. doi:10.1111/j.1365-2923.1986.tb01386.x

Barrows, H. S., & Tamblyn, R. M. (1980). *Problem-based learning. An approach to medical education*. New York, NY: Springer.

Bartholow, B. D., Sestir, M. A., & Davis, E. B. (2005). Correlates and consequences of exposure to video game violence: Hostile personality, empathy, and aggressive behavior. *Personality and Social Psychology Bulletin, 31*(11), 1573–1586. doi:10.1177/0146167205277205

Bartle, R. (1996). Hearts, clubs, diamonds, spades: Players who suit MUD's. *Journal of MUD Research, 1*, 1.

Barton, D., & Hamilton, M. (1998). *Local literacies*. New York, NY: Routledge.

Bateman, C. (2004). Demographic game design. *International Hobo*. [text file] Retrieved from http://onlyagame.typepad.com/ihobo/_misc/dgd_brochurefinal.pdf

Bateman, C., & Nacke, L. (2010). The neurobiology of play. *Futureplay '10: Proceedings of the International Academic Conference on the Future of Game Design and Technology*, Vancouver, BC, Canada.

Compilation of References

Bates, J. (1992, January). Virtual reality, art, and entertainment. *Presence (Cambridge, Mass.), 1*, 133–138.

Baxter, M. G., & Murray, E. A. (2002). Amygdala and reward. *Nature Reviews. Neuroscience, 3*, 563–573. doi:10.1038/nrn875

Bayliss, J. D., & Strout, S. (2006). *Games as a "flavor" of CS1*. Paper presented at SIGCSE'06, Houston, Texas, USA.

Baym, N. (2003). I think of them as friends: Joining online communities. In Dines, G., & Humez, J. M. (Eds.), *Gender, race, class, and media* (2nd ed., pp. 488–495). Thousand Oaks, CA: SAGE Publications.

Beard, C., Wilson, J. P., & McCarter, R. (2007). Towards a theory of e-learning: Experiential e-learning. *Journal of Hospitality, Leisure, Sport and Tourism Education, 6*(2), 3–15. doi:10.3794/johlste.62.127

Beck, K., Beedle, M., van Bennekum, A., Cockburn, A., Cunningham, W., & Fowler, M. Thomas, D. (2001). *Manifesto for agile software development*. Agile Alliance. Retrieved April 14, 2012, from http://agile-manifesto.org/

Becker, K. (2007). Digital game-based learning once removed: Teaching teachers. *British Journal of Educational Technology, 38*(3), 478–488. doi:10.1111/j.1467-8535.2007.00711.x

Becker, K. (2007). Pedagogy in commercial video games- Foreword. In Gibson, D., Aldrich, C., & Prensky, M. (Eds.), *Games and simulations in online learning: Research and development frameworks*. Hershey, PA: Information Science Publishing.

Becker, K. (2010). Distinctions between games and learning: A review of current literature on games in education. In Van Eck, R. (Ed.), *Gaming and cognition: Theories and practice from the learning sciences* (pp. 22–54). Hershey, PA: Information Science Reference. doi:10.4018/978-1-61520-717-6.ch002

Bellotti, F., Berta, R., Gloria, A. D., & Primavera, L. (2009). Enhancing the educational value of video games. *Computers in Entertainment, 7*(2), 1. doi:10.1145/1541895.1541903

Bell, R. C. (1979). *Board and table games from many civilizations (Vol. 1-2)*. Toronto, ON, Canada: General Publishing Company.

Berridge, K. C., & Robinson, T. E. (2003). Parsing reward. *Trends in Neurosciences, 26*(9), 507–513. doi:10.1016/S0166-2236(03)00233-9

Betrancourt, M. (2005). The animation and interactivity principles in multimedia learning. In Mayer, R. E. (Ed.), *The Cambridge handbook of multimedia learning* (pp. 287–296). New York, NY: Cambridge University Press. doi:10.1017/CBO9780511816819.019

Betrus, A. K., & Botturi, L. (2010). Principles of playing games for learning. In Hirumi, A. (Ed.), *Playing games in school: Video games and simulations for primary and secondary education* (pp. 33–56). Eugene, OR: International Society for Technology in Education.

Biederman, I., & Vessel, E. A. (2006). Perceptual pleasure and the brain. *American Scientist, 94*(3), 247–253.

Big Brain Academy Wii degree. [Computer software]. (2007). Redmond, WA: Nintendo of America Inc.

Biggers, M., Brauer, A., & Yilmaz, T. (2008). Student perceptions of computer science: A retention study comparing graduating seniors vs. CS leavers. *SIGCSE Bulletin, 40*(1), 402–406. doi:10.1145/1352322.1352274

Biggs, J. (1999). What the student does: Teaching for enhanced learning. *Higher Education Research & Development, 18*(1), 57–75. doi:10.1080/0729436990180105

Björk, S., & Holopainen, J. (2005). *Patterns in game design*. Hingham, MA: Charles River Media.

Blackman, I., & Hall, M. (2009). Estimating the complexity of applied English language skills. In Matthews, B. (Ed.), *The process of research in education: A Festschrift in honour of John P Keeves AM* (pp. 167–183). Adelaide, Australia: Shannon Research Press.

Bloom, B. S. (1956). *Taxonomy of educational objectives, handbook I: The cognitive domain*. New York, NY: David McKay Co.

Boekaerts, M. (1997). Self-regulated learning: a new concept embraced by researchers, policy makers, educators, teachers, and students. *Learning and Instruction, 7*(2), 151–186. doi:10.1016/S0959-4752(96)00015-1

Boellstroff, T. (2008). *Coming of age in Second Life*. Princeton, NJ: Princeton University Press.

Bogost, I. (2005). The rhetoric of exergaming. In *Proceedings of the Digital Art & Culture (DAC) Conference 2005*, Copenhagen, November 30th – December 3rd 2005. Retrieved 14th January, 2012, from http://www.bogost.com/downloads/I.%20Boogst%20The%20Rhetoric%20of%20Exergaming.pdf

Bolkan, J. V. (2010). Playing games and the NETS. In Hirumi, A. (Ed.), *Playing games in school: Video games and simulations for primary and secondary education* (pp. 33–56). Eugene, OR: International Society for Technology in Education.

Boström, L. (2011). Students' learning styles compared with their teachers' learning styles in secondary schools. *Institute for Learning Styles Research Journal, 1*, 16–38.

Boud, D. (1985). Promoting reflection in learning: A model. In Boud, D., Keogh, R., & Walker, D. (Eds.), *Turning experience into learning*. London, UK: Routledge Falmer.

Boud, D., Cohen, R., & Sampson, J. (2001). *Peer learning in higher education: Learning from and with each other*. London, UK: Kogan.

Boyce, A., & Barnes, T. (2010). BeadLoom Game: Using game elements to increase motivation and learning. In *Proceedings of the Fifth International Conference on the Foundations of Digital Games* (FDG '10), (pp. 25-31). New York, NY: ACM.

Boyer, D. M., & Akcaoglu, M. (2009). The Zon project: Creating a virtual environment for learning Chinese language and culture. In T. Bastiaens, et al., (Eds.), *Proceedings of World Conference on E-Learning in Corporate, Government, Healthcare, and Higher Education 2009* (pp. 2389-2393). Chesapeake, VA: AACE.

Brack, C., Elliott, K., & Stapleton, D. (2004, 5-8 December). *Visual representations: Setting contexts for learners*. Paper presented at the 21st ASCILITE Conference, Perth, WA.

Compilation of References

Braebeck, M., & Jeffery, J. (n.d.). *Practice for knowledge acquisition (not drill and kill)*. Retrieved from http://www.apa.org/education/k12/practice-acquisition.aspx

Bransford, J. D., Brown, A. L., & Cocking, R. R. (2000). *How people learn: Brain, mind, experience, and school*. Washington, DC: National Academy Press.

Breuer, J., & Bente, G. (2010). Why so serious? On the relation of serious games and learning. *Journal for Computer Game Culture*, *4*(1), 7–24.

Briggs-Myers, I. (1962). *The Myers-Briggs type indicator*. Palo Alto, CA: Consulting Psychology Press.

British Educational Communications and Technology Agency. (2004). *A review of the literature on barriers to the uptake of ICT by teachers*. British Educational Communications and Technology Agency.

Bronack, S., Riedl, R., & Tashner, J. (2006). Learning in the zone: A social constructivist framework for distance education in a 3-dimensional virtual world. *Interactive Learning Environments*, *14*(3), 219–232. doi:10.1080/10494820600909157

Brown, H. J. (2008). *Videogames and education*. New York, NY: M.E. Sharpe.

Brown, J. S., Collins, A., & Duguid, P. (1989). Situated cognition and the culture of learning. *Educational Researcher*, *18*, 32–42.

Bruning, R. H., Schraw, G. J., & Norby, M. M. (2011). *Cognitive psychology and instruction* (5th ed.). Boston, MA: Pearson.

Buckingham, D., & Burn, A. (2007). Game literacy in theory and practice. *Journal of Educational Multimedia and Hypermedia*, *16*(3), 323–349.

Bureau of Labor Statistics. (2010). *Overview of the 2008-18 projections*. Washington, DC: Author. Retrieved February 13, 2012, from http://www.bls.gov/oco/oco2003.htm#occupation_d

Burgos, D., Tattersall, C., & Koper, R. (2007). Re-purposing existing generic games and simulations for e-learning. *Computers in Human Behavior*, *23*, 2656–2667. doi:10.1016/j.chb.2006.08.002

Cailois, R. (1961). *Man, play, and games* (M. Barash, Trans.). New York, NY: The Free Press.

Card, S., Mackinlay, J. D., & Shneiderman, B. (1999). *Readings in information visualization: Using vision to think*. Morgan Kaufmann.

Carr, D., Buckingham, D., Burn, A., & Schott, G. (2006). *Computer games: Text, narrative and play*. Polity Press.

Catrambone, R. (1998). The subgoal learning model: Creating better examples so that students can solve novel problems. *Journal of Experimental Psychology. General*, *127*(4), 355–376. doi:10.1037/0096-3445.127.4.355

Chaffin, A., & Barnes, T. (2010). Lessons from a course on serious games research and prototyping. In *Proceedings of the Fifth International Conference on the Foundations of Digital Games* (FDG '10) (pp. 32-39). New York, NY: ACM.

Chang, E. (2008).Gaming as writing, or, World of Warcraft as world of wordcraft [Electronic version]. *Computers and Composition: An International Journal.* Retrieved February 2, 2012, from http://www.bgsu.edu/cconline/gaming_issue_2008/Chang_Gaming_as_writing/index.html

Charles, D., Charles, T., McNeill, M., Bustard, D., & Black, M. (2011). Game-based feedback for educational multi-user virtual environments. *British Journal of Educational Technology, 42*(4), 638–654. doi:doi:10.1111/j.1467-8535.2010.01068.x

Charsky, D. (2010). From edutainment to serious games: A change in the use of game characteristics. *Games and Culture, 5*(2), 177–198. doi:10.1177/1555412009354727

Charsky, D., & Mims, C. (2008). Integrating commercial off-the-shelf video games into school curriculums. *TechTrends, 52*(5), 38–44. doi:10.1007/s11528-008-0195-0

Chatfield, T. (2010, December 21). *7 ways to reward the brain* [Video file]. Retrieved from http://www.ted.com/talks/lang/en/tom_chatfield_7_ways_games_reward_the_brain.html

Chatfield, T. (2010). *Fun, Inc.: Why games are the 21st century's most serious business.* Virgin Books.

Cheryan, S., Plaut, V. C., Davies, P. G., & Steele, C. M. (2009). Ambient belonging: How stereotypical cues impact gender participation in computer science. *Journal of Personality and Social Psychology, 97*(6), 1045–1060. doi:10.1037/a0016239

Cheung, A., & Harrison, C. (1992). Microcomputer adventure games and second language acquisition: A study of Hong Kong tertiary students. In Pennington, M. C., & Stevens, V. (Eds.), *Computers in applied linguistics: An international perspective.* Clevedon, UK: Multilingual Matters Ltd.

Choy, D., Wong, A., & Gao, P. (2008). *Singapore's pre-service teachers perspectives in integrating information and communication technology (ICT) during practicum.* Paper presented at the AARE 2008, Brisbane. Retrieved from http://www.aare.edu.au/08pap/cho08326.pdf

Christensen, C., Johnson, C. W., & Horn, M. B. (2008). *Disrupting class: How disruptive innovation will change the way the world learns.* New York, NY: McGraw-Hill.

Clark, R. E. (1983). Reconsidering research on learning from media. *Review of Educational Research, 53*(4), 445–459.

Clark, R., & Mayer, R. E. (2008). *E-learning and the science of instruction* (2nd ed.). San Francisco, CA: Jossey-Bass.

Clements, D. H. (1999). Teaching length measurement: Research challenges. *School Science and Mathematics, 99*(1), 5–11. doi:10.1111/j.1949-8594.1999.tb17440.x

Clements, D. H., & McMillen, S. (1996). Rethinking concrete manipulatives. *Teaching Children Mathematics, 2*(5), 270–279.

Clements, D. H., & Sarama, J. (2007). Early childhood mathematics learning. In Lester, F. K. (Ed.), *Second handbook of research on mathematics teaching and learning* (pp. 461–555). Reston, VA: National Council of Teachers of Mathematics.

Cobb, P., Confrey, J., DiSessa, A., Lehrer, R., & Schauble, L. (2003). Design experiments in educational research. *Educational Researcher*, *32*(1), 9–13. doi:10.3102/0013189X032001009

Coffield, F., Moseley, D., Hall, E., & Ecclestone, K. (2004). *Learning styles and pedagogy in post-16 learning. A systematic and critical review*. London, UK: Learning and Skills Research Centre.

Cohen, L., Manion, L., & Morrison, K. (2010). *Research methods in education*. Routledge.

Cole, J., Calmenson, S., & Tiegreen, A. (1990). *Miss Mary Mack: And other children's street rhymes*. New York, NY: Harper Collins.

Coller, B. D., & Scott, M. J. (2009). Effectiveness of using a video game to teach a course on mechanical engineering. *Computers & Education*, *53*, 900–912. doi:10.1016/j.compedu.2009.05.012

Collins, A., & Halverson, R. (2009). *Rethinking education in the age of technology*. New York, NY: Teachers College Press. doi:10.1007/978-3-540-69132-7_1

Collis, B., & Moonen, J. (2001). *Flexible learning in a digital world*. London, UK: Kogan-Page.

Common Core State Standards Initiative. (2010). *Common core state standards for mathematics*. Retrieved from http://www.corestandards.org/assets/CCSSI_Math%20Standards.pdf

Connolly, T. M., Stansfield, M. H., & Boyle, L. (Eds.). (2009). *Games-based learning advancements for multi-sensory human computer interfaces: Techniques and effective practices*. Hershey, PA: IGI Global. doi:10.4018/978-1-60566-360-9

Cook, A. (2006). Induction: A formal initiation into a position or office. In A. Cook, K. A. Macintosh, & B. S. Rushton (Eds.), *Supporting Students: Early Induction* (pp. 7-12). Coleraine, UK: University of Ulster. Retrieved 14th January, 2012, from http://www.ulster.ac.uk/star/resources/%28D%29%20Supporting%20Students%20-%20Early%20Induction.pdf

Cook, D. (2006). *What are game mechanics?* Retrieved December 13, 2010, from http://lostgarden.com/2006_10_01_archive.html

Cornillie, F., Jacques, I., De Wannemacker, S., Paulussen, H., & Desmet, P. (2011). Vocabulary treatment in adventure and role-playing games: A playground for adaptation and adaptivity. In S. De Wannemacker, G. Clarebout, & P. De Causmaecker (Eds.), *Interdisciplinary approaches to adaptive learning: A look at the neighbours: The First International Conference on Interdisciplinary Research on Technology, Education and Communication, Revised Selected Papers, ITEC 2010, Kortrijk, Belgium, May 25-27, 2010*, (pp. 132-148). Springer.

Cox, A., & Campbell, M. (1994). Multiuser dungeons. *Interactive Fantasy*, *2*, 15–20.

Crook, A. E., & Beier, M. E. (2010). When training with a partner is inferior to training alone: The importance of dyad type and interaction quality. *Journal of Experimental Psychology. Applied*, *16*(4), 335–348. doi:10.1037/a0021913

Crookall, D. (2011). Serious games, debriefing, and simulation/gaming as a discipline. *Simulation & Gaming*, *41*, 898–920. doi:10.1177/1046878110390784

Csikszentmihalyi, M. (1990). *Flow: The psychology of optimal performance*. New York, NY: Cambridge University Press.

Csikszentmihalyi, M., Abuhamdeh, S., Nakamura, J. E., Andrew, J., & Dweck, C. S. (Eds.). (2005). *Handbook of competence and motivation* (pp. 598–608). New York, NY: Guilford Publications.

Csikszentmihalyi, M., & Csikszentmihalyi, I. (Eds.). (1988). *Optimal experience*. Cambridge, UK: Cambridge University Press.

Damm, D. (2007). *Die Förderung des räumlichen Vorstellungsvermögens durch den handelnden Umgang mit Würfelbauten*. Norderstedt, Germany: Grin Verlag.

Daudelin, M. W. (1996). Learning from experience through reflection. *Organizational Dynamics*, *24*(3), 36–48. doi:10.1016/S0090-2616(96)90004-2

Davies, R. S., Williams, D. D., & Yanchar, S. (2008). The use of randomization in educational research and evaluation: A critical analysis of underlying assumptions. *Evaluation and Research in Education*, *21*(4), 303–317. doi:10.1080/09500790802307837

Davis, F. D. (1989). Perceived usefulness, perceived ease of use, and user acceptance of information technology. *Management Information Systems Quarterly*, (September): 318–340.

Davis, N., Preston, C., & Sahin, I. (2009). Training teachers to use new technologies impacts multiple ecologies: Evidence from a national initiative. *British Journal of Educational Technology*, *40*(5), 861–878. doi:10.1111/j.1467-8535.2008.00875.x

de Freitas, S. (2008). Emerging trends in serious games and virtual worlds. *Emerging Technologies for Learning*, 3.

de Freitas, S., & Jarvis, S. (2006). *A framework for developing serious games to meet learner needs*. I/ITSEC Conference, Florida, December.

de Freitas, S., & Levene, M. (2004). *An investigation of the use of simulations and video gaming for supporting exploratory learning and developing higher-order cognitive skills*. IADIS International Conference in Cognition and Exploratory Learning in the Digital Age, 15-17 December, 2004. Lisbon, Portugal.

de Freitas, S. (2004). *Learning styles and e-learning. Technical report: 0014*. London, UK: Birkbeck.

de Freitas, S. (2006). *Learning in immersive worlds: A review of game-based learning*. London, UK: JISC e-Learning Programme.

de Freitas, S. (2006). Using games and simulations for supporting learning. *Learning. Media and Technology Special Issue on Gaming*, *31*(4), 343–358.

de Freitas, S., & Griffiths, M. D. (2008). The coverage of gaming practices with other media forms: What potential for learning? A review of the literature. *Learning, Media and Technology*, *33*(1), 11–20. doi:10.1080/17439880701868796

de Freitas, S., & Neumann, T. (2009). The use of exploratory learning for supporting immersive learning in virtual environments. *Computers & Education*, *52*(2), 343–352. doi:10.1016/j.compedu.2008.09.010

de Freitas, S., & Oliver, M. (2006). How can exploratory learning with games and simulations within the curriculum be most effectively evaluated? *Computers & Education*, *46*, 249–264. doi:10.1016/j.compedu.2005.11.007

de Freitas, S., & Veletsianos, G. (2010). Crossing bounderies: Learning and teaching in virtual worlds. *British Journal of Educational Technology, 41*(1), 3–9. doi:10.1111/j.1467-8535.2009.01045.x

de Freitas, S., & Yapp, C. (2005). *Personalizing learning in the 21ˢᵗ century*. Stafford, UK: Network Education Press.

de Haan, J. W. (2005). Learning language through video games: A theoretical framework, an evaluation of game genres and questions for future research. In Schaffer, S., & Price, M. (Eds.), *Interactive convergence: Critical issues in multimedia* (pp. 229–239). The Inter-Disciplinary Press.

de Winter, J., Winterbottom, M., & Wilson, E. (2010). Developing a user guide to integrating new technologies in science teaching and learning: Teachers' and pupils' perceptions of their affordances. *Technology, Pedagogy and Education, 19*(2), 261–267. doi:10.1080/1475939X.2010.491237

Dede, C. (2005). Planning for neomillennial learning styles: Implications for investments in faculty and technology. In D. Oblinger & J. Oblinger (Eds.), *Educating the net generation* (pp. 15.1–15.22). Boulder, CO: EDUCAUSE. Retrieved 14th January, 2012, from http://www.educause.edu/educatingthenetgen

Dede, C., Clarke, J., Ketelhut, D. J., Nelson, B., & Bowman, C. (2005). *Fostering motivation, learning and transfer in multi-user virtual environments*. Paper presented at the American Educational Research Association, Montreal, Canada. Retrieved from http://muve.gse.harvard.edu/rivercityproject/research-publications.htm#2005

Dede, C., Nelson, B., & Ketelhut, D. J. (2004). *Design-based research on gender, class, race, and ethnicity in a multi-user virtual environment*. Paper presented at the Meeting of the American Educational Research Association, San Diego, CA.

Dede, C. (1997). Rethinking: How to invest in technology. *Educational Leadership, 55*(3), 12–16.

Dede, C. (2005). Why design-based research is both important and difficult. *Educational Technology, 45*(1), 5–8.

Dede, C. (2009). Immersive interfaces for engagement and learning. *Science, 323*(5910), 66–69. doi:10.1126/science.1167311

Dede, C., & Barab, S. (2009). Emerging technologies for learning science: A time of rapid advance. *Journal of Science Education and Technology, 18*(4), 301–304. doi:10.1007/s10956-009-9172-4

DEEWR. (2007). *National code of practice for registration authorities and providers of education and training to overseas students*. Australian Government Department of Education Employment and Workplace Relations. Retrieved from http://www.aei.gov.au/AEI/ESOS/NationalCodeOfPractice2007/National_Code_2007_pdf.pdf

Defreitas, S., & Oliver, M. (2006). How can exploratory learning with games and simulations within the curriculum be most effectively evaluated? *Computers & Education, 46*(3), 249–264. doi:10.1016/j.compedu.2005.11.007

del Blanco, Á., Torrente, J., Moreno-ger, P., & Fernández-Manjón, B. (2011). Enhancing adaptive learning and assessment in virtual learning environments with educational games. In Jin, Q. (Ed.), *Intelligent learning systems and advancements in computer-aided instruction: Emerging studies* (pp. 114–163). Hershey, PA: IGI Global. doi:10.4018/978-1-61350-483-3.ch009

DeNote, M. (n.d.). *New ideas?* Retrieved January 14, 2012, from http://teach-n-learn. blogspot.com/

Department for Employment and Learning. (2009). *Report of the STEM Review*. Retrieved January 15, 2010, from http://www.delni.gov. uk/index/publications/pubs-successthroughs-kills/stem-review-09.htm

Department of Education. (2008). *Success through partnership: Achieving a national vision for ICT in schools: Strategic plan to guide the implementation of the digital education revolution initiative and related initiatives*. Employment and Workplace Relations.

Derryberry, A. (2008). *Serious games - Online games for learning*. Retrieved from http://www.adobe.com/resources/elearning/pdfs/serious_games_wp.pdf

Design-Based Research Collective. (2003). Design-based research: An emerging paradigm for educational inquiry. *Educational Researcher*, *32*(1), 5–8. doi:10.3102/0013189X032001005

Desilets, B. (1999). Interactive fiction vs. the pause that distresses: How computer-based literature interrupts the reading process without stopping the fun. *Currents in Electronic Literacy, 1*. Retrieved January 8, 2011, from http://www.cwrl.utexas.edu/currents/spr99/desilets.html

Desilets, B. (1989). Reading, thinking, and interactive fiction. *English Journal*, *78*(3), 75–77. doi:10.2307/819460

Devaney, L. (2008, April 22). *Gaming helps students hone 21st-century skills*. Retrieved November 28, 2011, from http://www.es-choolnews.com/2008/04/22/gaming-helps-students-hone-21st-century-skills/

deVries, E., Lund, K., & Baker, M. (2002). Computer-mediated epistemic dialogue: Explanation and argumentation as vehicles for understanding scientific notions. *Journal of the Learning Sciences*, *11*(1), 63–103. doi:10.1207/S15327809JLS1101_3

Dewey, J. (1915). *The school and society*. Chicago, Ill: The University of Chicago Press.

Dickey, M. D. (2006). *Ninja looting for instructional design: The design challenges of creating a game-based learning environment*. Paper presented at the ACM SIGGRAPH 2006 Conference, Boston.

Dickey, M. D. (2006). Game design narrative for learning: Appropriating adventure game design narrative devices and techniques for the design of interactive learning environments. *Educational Technology Research and Development*, *54*, 245–263. doi:10.1007/s11423-006-8806-y

Dickey, M. D. (2007). Game design and learning: A conjectural analysis of how massively multiple online role-playing games (MMOR-PGs) foster intrinsic motivation. *Educational Technology Research and Development*, *55*, 253–273. doi:10.1007/s11423-006-9004-7

Dieleman, H., & Huisingh, D. (2006). Games by which to learn and teach about sustainable development: Exploring the relevance of games and experiential learning for sustainability. *Journal of Cleaner Production*, *14*, 837–847. doi:10.1016/j.jclepro.2005.11.031

Compilation of References

Dillenbourg, P. (2006). The solo/duo gap. *Computers in Human Behavior*, *22*(1), 155. doi:10.1016/j.chb.2005.05.001

Dillon, P. (2007). *A pedagogy of connection and boundary crossings: Methodological and epistemological transactions in working across and between disciplines*. Paper presented at Creativity or Conformity? Building Cultures of Creativity in Higher Education, University of Wales and the Higher Education Academy, Cardiff, 8-10 January.

Dondlinger, M., & Warren, S. J. (2009). *The global village playground: A qualitative case study of designing an ARG as a capstone learning experience*. PhD Dissertation, Denton, Texas: University of North Texas.

Dondlinger, M. J. (2006). Educational video game design: A review of the literature. *Journal of Applied Educational Technology*, *3*(1), 21–31.

Dror, I. E. (2008). Technology enhanced learning: The good, the bad, and the ugly. *Pragmatics & Cognition*, *16*, 215–223.

Duffy, T. M., & Cunningham, D. J. (1996). Constructivism: Implications for the design and delivery of instruction. In Jonassen, D. H. (Ed.), *Handbook of research for educational communications and technology*. New York, NY: Macmillan.

Dweck, C. (1986). Motivational processes affecting learning. *The American Psychologist*, *41*(10), 1040–1048. doi:10.1037/0003-066X.41.10.1040

Dyer, R. (1999). Making 'white' people white. In Mackenzie, D., & Wacjman, J. (Eds.), *The social shaping of technology* (pp. 134–140). Ann Arbor, MI: Open University Press.

Eccles, J. S., & Wingfield, A. (2002). Motivational beliefs, values, and goals. *Annual Review of Psychology*, *53*, 109–132. doi:10.1146/annurev.psych.53.100901.135153

Education International. (2009). *The global economic crisis and its impact on education*. Brussels, Belgium: Education International. Retrieved 14th January, 2012, from http://download.ei-ie.org/Docs/WebDepot/Report_of_the_EI_Survey_on_the_Impact_of_the_Global_Economic_Crisis_on_Education_en.pdf

Edward, N. S. (2003). First impressions last. An innovative approach to induction. *Active Learning in Higher Education*, *4*(3), 226–242. doi:10.1177/14697874030043003

Egenfeldt-Nielsen, S. (2005). *Beyond edutainment*. Unpublished dissertation, University of Copenhagen. Copenhagen, Denmark.

El-Gayar, O., Moran, M., & Hawkes, M. (2011). Students acceptance of tablet PCs and implications for educational institutions. *Journal of Educational Technology & Society*, *14*(2), 58–70.

Endless Ocean [Computer software]. (2008). Redmond, WA: Nintendo of America.

Engineering, U. K. (2009). *Engineering UK 2009/10*. Retrieved January 15, 2012, from http://www.engineeringuk.com/what_we_do/education_&_research/engineering_uk_2009/10.cfm

Entertainment Software Association Website. (2012). Retrieved, January 2, 2012 from http://www.theesa.com/facts/index.asp

European Universities Association. (2011). *Impact of the economic crisis on European universities*. Brussels, Belgium: Author.

Facer, K., Ulicsak, M., & Sandford, R. (2007). Can computer games go to school? *Emerging Technologies for Learning, 2*, 47-63. Retrieved from http://www.mmiweb.org.uk/publications/ict/emerging_tech02.pdf

Fayyad, U., Piatetsky-Shapiro, G., & Smyth, P. (1996). Knowledge discovery and data mining: Towards a unifying framework. *Proceedings of Knowledge Discovery and Data Mining 1996.* Retrieved from http://scholar.google.com/scholar?hl=en&btnG=Search&q=intitle:Knowledge+Discovery+and+Data+Mining+:+Towards+a+Unifying+Framework#0

Fayyad, U., Piatetsky-Shapiro, G., & Smyth, P. (1996). From data mining to knowledge discovery in databases. *AI Magazine, 17*(3), 37–54.

Fayyad, U., Piatetsky-Shapiro, G., & Smyth, P. (1996). The KDD process for extracting useful knowledge from volumes of data. *Communications of the ACM, 39*(11), 27–34. doi:10.1145/240455.240464

Federal policy for the protection of human subjects; notices and rules. (1991, June 18). *56 Federal Register 28002-28032.*

Federation of American Scientists. (2006). *Summit on Educational Games: Harnessing the power of video games for learning.* Retrieved January 15, 2010, from http://www.fas.org/gamesummit/

Feiman-Nemser, S. (2001). From preparation to practice: Designing a continuum to strengthen and sustain teaching. *Teachers College Record, 103*(6), 1013–1055. doi:10.1111/0161-4681.00141

Felder, R. M. (1996). Matters of style. *ASEE Prism, 6*(4), 18–23.

Felder, R. M. (2010). *Are learning styles invalid?* North Carolina State University.

Felicia, P., & Pitt, I. J. (2007). *The PLEASE model: An emotional and cognitive approach to learning in video games.* International Technology Education and Development Conference (INTED), Valencia, Spain, 8-10 March.

Field, J. (2007). Looking outwards, not inwards. *ETL Journal, 61*(1), 30–38.

Figg, C., & McCartney, R. (2010). Impacting academic achievement with student learners teaching digital storytelling to others: The ATTTCSE digital video project. *Contemporary Issues in Technology & Teacher Education, 10*(1).

Finocchiaro, M., & Brumfit, C. (1983). *The functional-notional approach.* Oxford, UK: Oxford University Press.

Fleming, M., & Levie, W. H. (Eds.). (1993). *Instructional message design: Principles from the behavioral and cognitive sciences* (2nd ed.). Englewood Cliffs, NJ: Educational Technology Publications.

Ford, N. (2000). Cognitive styles and virtual environments. *Journal of the American Society for Information Science American Society for Information Science, 51*(6), 543–557. doi:10.1002/(SICI)1097-4571(2000)51:6<543::AID-ASI6>3.0.CO;2-S

Foreman, J. (2003). Next-generation educational technology versus the lecture. *EDUCAUSE Review, 38*(4), 12.

Foreman, J. (2004). Game-based learning: How to delight and instruct in the 21st century. *EDUCAUSE Review*, 50–66.

Forneris, S. G., & Peden-McAlpine, C. J. (2006). Contextual learning: A reflective learning intervention for nursing education. *International Journal of Nursing Education Scholarship*, *3*(1), 1–17. doi:10.2202/1548-923X.1254

Forrester, G., Motteram, G., Parkinson, G., & Slaouti, D. (2004). *Going the distance: Students' experiences of induction to distance learning in higher education.* Paper presented at the British Educational Research Association Annual Conference, University of Manchester, 16–18 September, 2004. Retrieved 14th January 2012 from http://www.leeds.ac.uk/educol/documents/00003849.htm

Foster, A. L. (2006). Harvard to offer law course in "virtual world". *The Chronicle of Higher Education, 53*(3), A.29.

Foster, A. L. (2007). Virtual worlds as social-science labs. *The Chronicle of Higher Education, 53*(44), A.29.

Foster, A. (2008). Games and motivation to learn science: Personal identity, applicability, motivation, and meaningfulness. *Journal of Interactive Learning Research*, *19*(4), 597–614.

Foster, A. N., & Mishra, P. (2009). Games, claims, genres & learning. In Ferdig, R. E. (Ed.), *Handbook of research on effective electronic gaming in education* (pp. 33–50). Hershey, PA: Information Science Reference.

Freedman, K. (1997). Visual art/virtual art: Teaching technology for meaning. *Art Education*, *50*(4), 6–12. doi:10.2307/3193647

French, S. A., Story, M., & Perry, C. L. (1995). Self-esteem and obesity in children and adolescents: A literature review. *Obesity Research*, *3*(5), 479–490. doi:10.1002/j.1550-8528.1995.tb00179.x

Fullerton, T. (2008). *Game design workshop: A playcentric approach to creating innovative games*. Amsterdam, The Netherlands: Elsevier Morgan Kaufmann.

Fullerton, T., Swain, C., & Hoffman, S. (2004). *Game design workshop: Designing, prototyping and playtesting games (Gama Network Series)*. San Francesco, CA: CMP Books.

Galstaun, V., Kennedy-Clark, S., & Hu, C. (2011). *The impact of TPACK on pre-service teacher confidence in embedding ICT into the curriculum areas*. Paper presented at the ED-MEDIA 2011 World Conference on Educational Multimedia, Hypermedia & Telecommunications, Lisbon.

Games, I. (2009). *21st century language and literacy in Gamestar Mechanic: Middle school students' appropriate through play of the discourse of computer game designers.* PhD Dissertation, University of Wisconsin-Madison, Madison, WI.

Games, I. A. (2008). Three dialogs: A framework for the analysis and assessment of twenty-first-century literacy practices, and its use in the context of game design within *Gamestar Mechanic. E-learning*, *5*(4), 396–417. doi:10.2304/elea.2008.5.4.396

Gardner, H. (1983). *Frames of mind: The theory of multiple intelligences*. New York, NY: Basic Books.

Gardner, H. (1999). *The disciplined mind: What all students should understand*. New York, NY: Simon and Schuster.

Gardner, H. (2009). Multiple approaches to understanding. In Illeris, K. (Ed.), *Contemporary theories of learning* (pp. 106–115). Oxon, UK: Routledge.

Garris, R., Ahlers, R., & Driskell, J. E. (2002). Games, motivation, and learning: A research and practice model. *Simulation & Gaming, 33*(4), 441–467. doi:10.1177/1046878102238607

Gartner. (2011). *Gartner says 428 million mobile communication devices sold worldwide in first quarter 2011, a 19 percent increase year-on-year*. Stanford, CA: Author. Retrieved 14th January, 2012, from http://www.gartner.com/it/page.jsp?id=1689814

Gauntlett, D. (2011). *Making is connecting. The social meaning of creativity, from DIY and knitting to YouTube and Web 2.0*. Cambridge, UK: Polity Press.

Gee, J. P. (2005). *Good video games and good learning*. Retrieved November 10, 2011, from www.academiccolab.org/resources/documents/Good_Learning.pdf

Gee, J. P. (2005). What would a state of the art instructional video game look like? *Innovate, 1*(6). Retrieved January 15, 2012, from http://www.innovateonline.info/index.php?view=article&id=80

Gee, J. P. (2003). *What video games have to teach us about learning and literacy*. New York, NY: Palgrave Macmillan. doi:10.1145/950566.950595

Gee, J. P. (2004). *Situated language and learning: A critique of traditional schooling*. London, UK: Routledge.

Gee, J. P. (2005). Learning by design: Good video games as learning machines. *E-learning, 2*(1), 5–16. doi:10.2304/elea.2005.2.1.5

Gee, J. P. (2006). Why game studies now? Video games: A new art form. *Games and Culture, 1*(1), 58–61. doi:10.1177/1555412005281788

Gee, J. P., & Hayes, E. R. (2010). *Women and gaming: The Sims and 21st century learning*. New York, NY: Palgrave Macmillan.

Gee, J. P., & Shaffer, D. W. (2010). Looking where the light is bad: Video games and the future of assessment. *Edge, 6*(1), 1–19.

Gershenfeld, A. (2011, September/October). Leveling up from player to designer. *Knowledge Quest, 40*(1), 55–59.

Gibson, D., Aldrich, C., & Prensky, M. (Eds.). (2006). *Games and simulations in online learning: Research and development frameworks*. Hershey, PA: Information Science Publishing. doi:10.4018/978-1-59904-304-3

Gibson, D., & Baek, Y. (2009). *Digital simulations for improving education: Learning through artificial teaching environments* (1st ed., p. 514). Hershey, PA: Information Science Reference. doi:10.4018/978-1-60566-322-7

Gill, L., & Dalgarno, B. (2008). *Influences on pre-service teachers' preparedness to use ICTs in the classroom*. Paper presented at the Hello! Where Are You in the Landscape of Educational Technology, ASCILITE, Melbourne.

Godambe, V. (1978). Estimation in survey-sampling: Robustness and optimality. *Proceedings of the International Conference on Statistics*, (pp. 14-15). Retrieved from http://www.amstat.org/sections/srms/Proceedings/papers/1981_003.pdf

Goldsworthy, R. C., Barab, S. A., & Goldsworthy, E. L. (2000). The STAR project: Enhancing adolescents' social understanding through video-based, multimedia scenarios. *Journal of Special Education Technology, 15*(2), 13–26.

Compilation of References

Goodenow, C. (1993). Classroom belonging among early adolescent students: Relationships to motivation and achievement. *The Journal of Early Adolescence, 13*(1), 21. do i:10.1177/0272431693013001002

Gove, P. B. (Ed.). (1986). *Webster's third new international dictionary of the English language, unabridged.* Springfield, MA: Merriam-Webster.

Grabe, M., & Dosmann, M. (1988). The potential of adventure games for the development of reading and study skills. *Journal of Computer-Based Instruction, 15*(2), 72–77.

Graham, C. R. (2011). Theoretical considerations for understanding technological pedagogical content knowledge (TPACK). *Computers & Education, 57*(3), 1953–1960. doi:10.1016/j.compedu.2011.04.010

Gratch, J., & Kelly, J. (2009). MMOGs: Beyond the wildest imagination. *Journal of Interactive Learning Research, 20*(2), 175–187.

Gredler, M. (2004). Games and simulations and their relationships to learning. In Jonassen, D. (Ed.), *Handbook of research on educational communications and technology* (pp. 571–581). Mahwah, NJ: Erlbaum.

Greenblat, C. S., & Duke, R. (1981). *Principles and practices of gaming-simulation.* Beverly Hills, CA: Sage Publications.

Green, H., Facer, K., & Rudd, T. (2006). *Personalisation and digital technologies.* Future Lab.

Greeno, J. G., Collins, A. M., & Resnick, L. (1996). Cognition and learning. In Berliner, D. C., & Calfee, R. C. (Eds.), *Handbook of educational psychology.* New York, NY: Simon & Schuster Macmillan.

Greenwood-Ericksen, A. (2008). *Learning African American history in a synthetic learning environment.* Doctoral dissertation, University of Central Florida, Florida.

Greitzer, F., Kuchar, O., & Huston, K. (2007). Cognitive science implications for enhancing training effectiveness in a serious gaming. *Journal of Educational Resources in Computing, 7*(3). doi:10.1145/1281320.1281322

Griebel, T. (2006). Self-portrayal in a simulated life: projecting personality and values in The Sims2. *International Journal of Computer Game Research, 6*(1).

Gros, B. (2007, Fall). Digital games in education: The design of games-based learning environments. *Journal of Research on Technology in Education, 40*(1), 23-38. ERIC database (EJ826060).

Grotzer, T. A., Dede, C., Metcalfe, S., & Clarke, J. (2009, April). *Addressing the challenges in understanding ecosystems: Why getting kids outside may not be enough.* National Association of Research in Science Teaching (NARST) Conference, Orange Grove, CA, April 18, 2009.

Grubby Games. (2010). *The amazing brain train (Version WiiWare)* [Computer software]. Orem, Utah: NinjaBee.

Guetzkow, H. (1963). *Simulation in international relations.* Prentice-Hall.

Guhde, J. A. (2003). English-as-a-second language (ESL) nursing students: Strategies for building verbal and written language skills. *Journal of Cultural Diversity, 10*(4), 113–117.

Gustafson, K., & Branch, R. (2002). *Survey of instructional development models.* Eric Clearinghouse on Information.

Gütl, C. (2011). The support of virtual 3D worlds for enhancing collaboration in learning settings. In Pozzi, F., & Persico, D. (Eds.), *Techniques for collaboration in online learning communities: Theoretical and practical perspectives* (pp. 278–299). doi:10.4018/978-1-61692-898-8.ch016

Habermas, J. (1984). The theory of communicative action: *Vol. 1. Reason and the rationalization of society*. Boston, MA: Beacon Press.

Habermas, J. (1987). The theory of communicative action: *Vol. 2. Lifeworld and system*. Boston, MA: Beacon Press.

Habermas, J. (1998). *On the pragmatics of communication*. Cambridge, MA: The MIT Press.

Hamlen, K. (2011). Stochastic frontier estimation of efficient learning in video games. *Computers & Education*, *58*(1), 534–541. doi:10.1016/j.compedu.2011.09.006

Haraway, D. (1988). Situated knowledges: The science question in feminism and the privilege of partial perspective. *Feminist Studies*, *14*, 575–599. doi:10.2307/3178066

Haskell, C., & Pollard, C. (2008). Understanding and preparing teachers of millennial learners. *Proceedings of the World Conference on E-Learning*, Las Vegas, NV.

Hasler, B. S., Kersten, B., & Sweller, J. (2007). Learner control, cognitive load and instructional animation. *Applied Cognitive Psychology*, *21*, 713–729. doi:10.1002/acp.1345

Hassanien, A., & Barber, A. (2007). An evaluation of student induction in higher education. *International Journal of Management Education*, *6*(3), 35-43. Retrieved 14th January, 2012, from http://www-new1.heacademy.ac.uk/assets/bmaf/documents/publications/IJME/Vol6No3/IJME6380pageHassanien-Barber.pdf

Hawk, T., & Shah, A. (2007). Using learning style instruments to enhance student learning. *Decision Sciences Journal of Innovative Education*, *5*(1), 1–19. doi:10.1111/j.1540-4609.2007.00125.x

Hayot, E., & Wesp, E. (2009). Towards a critical aesthetic of virtual world geographies. *Game Studies*, *9*. Retrieved February 2, 2012, from http://gamestudies.org/0901/articles/hayot_wesp_space

Heibert, J., & Stigler, J. W. (2004). A world of difference: Classrooms abroad provide lessons in teaching math and science. *Journal of Staff Development*, *24*(4), 10–15.

Hennessy, S., Ruthven, K., & Brindley, S. (2005). Teacher perspectives on integrating ICT into subject teaching: Commitment, constraints, caution, and change. *Journal of Curriculum Studies*, *37*(2), 155–192. doi:10.1080/0022027032000276961

Herrig, B. (2009, Winter). Thinking like a programmer. *TEAP Journal*, *57*(4), 9–17.

Hidi, S. (1990). Interest and its contribution as a mental resource for learning. *Review of Educational Research*, *60*(4), 549–571.

Compilation of References

Hidi, S., & Anderson, V. (1992). Situational interest and its impact on reading and expository writing. In Renninger, K. A., Hidi, S., & Krapp, A. (Eds.), *The role of interest in learning and development* (pp. 215–238). Hillsdale, NJ: Lawrence Erlbaum Associates.

Hiebert, J., Carpenter, T. P., Fennema, E., Fuson, K. C., Wearne, D., & Murray, H. Human, P. (1997). *Making sense: Teaching and learning mathematics with understanding.* Portsmouth, NH: Heinemann.

Hill A., Morton N., Lawton R., & Hemingway A. (2007, January). *Enhancing employability through games and simulations.* Creativity or Conformity? Building Cultures of Creativity in Higher Education Conference, University of Wales Institute, Cardiff.

Hinske, S., Lampe, M., Magerkurth, C., & Rocker, C. (2007). Classifying pervasive games: On pervasive computing and mixed reality. *Concepts and technologies for Pervasive Games-A Reader for Pervasive Gaming Research*, 1. Retrieved from http://citeseerx.ist.psu.edu/viewdoc/download?doi=10.1.1.66.6807&rep=rep1&type=pdf

Hirumi, A., & Stapleton, C. (2009). Applying pedagogy during game development to enhance game-based learning. In Miller, C. T. (Ed.), *Games: Purpose and potential in education.* New York, NY: Springer. doi:10.1007/978-0-387-09775-6_6

Hişmanoğlu, M. (2005). Teaching English through literature. *Journal of Language and Linguistic Studies, 1*(1), 53-66. Retrieved January 8, 2011, from http://jlls.org/Issues/Volume1/No.1/murathismanoglu.pdf

Hoffman, B., & Nadelson, L. (2009). Motivational engagement and video gaming: A mixed methods study. *Educational Technology Research and Development, 58*(3), 245–270. doi:10.1007/s11423-009-9134-9

Hoffman, J. (1999). Writers, texts, and writing acts. In Mackenzie, D., & Wajcman, J. (Eds.), *The social shaping of technology* (pp. 222–228). Philadelphia, PA: Open University Press.

Honey, P., & Mumford, H. (1992). *The manual of learning styles* (rev. ed.). Maidenhead, UK: Peter Honey.

Hong, Y. (2010). Status and future of social network games. *Korean Contents Promotion Focus, 18*(1), 34–37.

Hoobler, N., Humphreys, G., & Agrawala, M. (2004). Visualizing competitive behaviors in multi-user virtual environments. In *Proceedings of IEEE Visualization 2004*, IEEE Computer Society.

Hopko, D. R., Ashcarft, M. H., & Gute, J. (1998). Mathematics anxiety and working memory: Support for a deficient inhibition mechanism. *Journal of Anxiety Disorders, 12*, 343–355. doi:10.1016/S0887-6185(98)00019-X

Horn, C., Snyder, B., Coverdale, J., Louie, A., & Roberts, L. (2009). Educational research questions and study design. *Design*, (June), 261-267.

Horn, W. (1962). *Leistungsprüfsystem L-P-S.* Göttingen, Germany: Verl. f. Psychologie Hogrefe.

Horn, R. (1977). *The guide to simulations/games for education and training (Vol. 1)*. Crawford, NJ: Didactic Systems. doi:10.1177/1046878195264008

Horn, W., Lukesch, H., Kormann, A., & Mayrhofer, P. (2002). *Prüfsystem für Schul- und Bildungsberatung für 4. bis 6. Klassen - revidierte Fassung (PSB-R 4-6)*. Göttingen, Germany: Hogrefe.

Howard, J. (2008) *Quests: Design, theory, and history in games and narratives*. Wellesley, MA: A K Peters, Ltd.

Hoyrup, S. (2004). Reflection as a core process in organisational learning. *Journal of Workplace Learning, 16*(8), 442–454. doi:10.1108/13665620410566414

Hu, C., & Fyfe, V. (2010). *Impact of a new curriculum on pre-service teachers' technical, pedagogical and content knowledge (TPACK)*. Paper presented at the Curriculum, technology & transformation for an unknown future, ASCILITE Sydney 2010.

Hu, C., Wong, W. Y., Fyfe, V., & Chan, H. (2010). *Formative evaluation via technology-mediated peer assessment*. Paper presented at the World Conference on Educational Multimedia, Hypermedia and Telecommunications 2010 Toronto, Canada.

Hudson, T. (1998). The effects of induced schemata on the "short circuit" in L2 reading: Non-decoding factors in L2 reading performance. In Carell, P. L., Devine, J., & Eskey, D. E. (Eds.), *Interactive approaches to second language reading* (pp. 183–205). Cambridge, UK: Cambridge University Press.

Huizinga, J. (2002). *Homo Ludens: A study of the play element in culture*. New York, NY: Routledge.

Hull, T. H., Balka, D. S., & Miles, R. H. (2011). *Visible thinking in the K–8 mathematics classroom*. Thousand Oaks, CA: Corwin.

Hunicke, R., LeBlanc, M., & Zubek, R. (2004). MDA: A formal approach to game design and game research. In *Proceedings of the Challenges in Game AI Workshop, 19th National Conference on Artificial Intelligence AAAI '04*, San Jose, CA. AAAI Press.

Huynh-Kim-Bang, B., Labat, L.-M., & Wisdom, J. (2011). *Design patterns in serious games: A blue print for combining fun and learning*. Retrieved December 13, 2011, from http://seriousgames.lip6.fr/DesignPatterns/designPatternsForSeriousGames.pdf

Hye, W.-H., & Sera, S. (2010). Analysis on user behavior of social game. *Journal of Korea Contents, 10*(12), 137–145. doi:10.5392/JKCA.2010.10.12.137

Hymes, D. (1974). *Foundations in sociolinguistics: An ethnographic approach*. Philadelphia, PA: University of Pennsylvania Press.

Ingleby, E., Joyce, D., & Powell, S. (2010). *Learning to teach in the lifelong learning sector*. New York, NY: Continuum International Publishing Group.

Ingold, J. (2009). Thinking into the box: On the use and deployment of puzzles. In K. Jackson-Mead & J. R. Wheeler (Eds.), *IF theory reader* (pp. 229-247). Retrieved January 8, 2011, from http://www.lulu.com/items/volume_71/11643000/11643447/1/print/10228464_IFTheoryBookv2.pdf

Compilation of References

Innerhofer, P., & Klicpera, C. (1988). *Die Welt des frühkindlichen Autismus*. München, Germany: Reinhard.

International Organization for Standardization. (1999). [Human-centered design processes for interactive systems.]. *ISO, 13407*, 1999.

International Society for Technology in Education (ISTE). (2007). *Standards for students*. Retrieved August 10, 2010, from http://www.iste.org/Content/NavigationMenu/NETS/ForStudents/2007Standards/NETS_for_Students_2007_Standards.pdf

Isbister, K., Flanagan, M., & Hash, C. (2010). Designing games for learning: Insights from conversations with designers. In *Proceedings of the 28th International Conference on Human Factors in Computing Systems*, ACM Press.

Ito, M., Baumer, S., Bittanti, M., Boyd, D., Cody, R., & Herr-Stephenson, B. Tripp, L. (2009). *Hanging out, messing around, and geeking out: Kids living and learning with new media* (John D. and Catherine T. MacArthur Foundation Series on Digital Media and Learning, 1 edition). Cambridge, MA: The MIT Press.

Jackson, S. A., & Eklund, R. C. (2004). La flow state scale-2 e la dispositional flow scale-2. In Muzio, M. (Ed.), *Sport: Flow e prestazione eccellente*. Milano, Italy: Franco Angeli.

Jackson, S., & Csikszentmihalyi, M. (1999). *Flow in sports: The keys to optimal experiences and performances*. Champaign, IL: Human Kinetics.

Jackson, S., & Marsh, H. (1996). Development and validation of a scale to measure optimal experience: The flow state scale. *Journal of Sport & Exercise Psychology, 18*, 17–35.

Jacques, D. (1995). Games, simulations and case studies. A review. In D. Saunders (Ed.), *The simulation and gaming yearbook, Vol. 3: Games and simulations for business*. London, UK: Kogan Page.

Järvinen, A. (2008). *Games without frontiers: Theories and methods for game studies and design*. Doctoral dissertation, Tampere University, Tampere, Finland.

Jefferies, L. N., Smilek, D., Eich, E., & Enns, J. T. (2008). Emotional valence and arousal interact in the control of attention. *Psychological Science, 19*(3), 290–295. doi:10.1111/j.1467-9280.2008.02082.x

Jegers, K. (2007). Pervasive game flow: Understanding player enjoyment in pervasive gaming. *Computers in Entertainment, 5*(1). Retrieved from http://portal.acm.org/citation.cfm?id=1236238

Jenkins, H. (2002). Game theory. *Technology review*. Retrieved April 25, 2005, from www.technologyreview.com

Jenkins, H., Clinton, K., Purushotma, R., Robison, A., & Weigel, M. (2006). *Confronting the challenges of participatory culture: Media education for the 21st century*. Chicago, IL: The MacArthur Foundation. Retrieved April 16, 2007, from http://digitallearning.macfound.org/atf/cf/%7b7e45c7e0-a3e0-4b89-ac9c-e807e1b0ae4e%7d/jenkins_white_paper.pdf

Jenkins, H. (2006). *Convergence culture.* New York, NY: New York University Press.

Jensen, E. (2008). A fresh look at brain-based education. *Phi Delta Kappan, 86*(6).

Jeong, K.-H. (2010). The successful example of the serious game. *Korea Information Processing Society Review, 17*(1), 122–125.

Johnson, L., Smith, R., Levine, A., & Haywood, K. (2010). *The 2010 horizon report: K-12 edition.* Retrieved March 12, 2011, from http://www.nmc.org/pdf/2010-Horizon-Report-K12.pdf

Johnson, L., Smith, R., Willis, H., Levine, A., & Haywood, K. (2011). *The 2011 horizon report.*

Joiner, R., Iacovides, J., Owen, M., Gavin, C., Clibbey, S., Darling, J., & Drew, B. (2011). Digital games, gender and learning in engineering: Do females benefit as much as males? *Journal of Science Education and Technology, 20*(2), 178–185. doi:10.1007/s10956-010-9244-5

Joiner, R., Nethercott, J., Hull, R., & Reid, J. (2006). Designing educational experiences using ubiquitous technology. *Computers in Human Behavior, 22*(1), 67–76. doi:10.1016/j.chb.2005.01.001

Jonassen, D. H. (2000). Toward a design theory of problem solving. *Educational Technology Research and Development, 48*(4), 63–85. doi:10.1007/BF02300500

Jonassen, D. H. (2011). *Learning to solve problems: A handbook for designing problem-solving learning environments.* New York, NY: Routledge.

Joyce, B., Weil, M., & Calhoun, E. (2004). *Models of teaching.* Boston, MA: Allyn and Bacon.

Ju, E., & Wagner, C. (1997). Personal computer adventure games: Their structure, principles and applicability for training. *The Data Base for Advances in Information Systems, 28,* 78–92. doi:10.1145/264701.264707

Just Dance [Computer software]. (2009). San Francisco, CA: Ubisoft.

Juul, J. (2003). *The game, the player, the world: Looking for a heart of gameness.* Keynote presentation of the Level Up Conference in Utrecht, Netherlands.

Kafai, Y. (2001). *The educational potential of electronic games: From games-to-teach to games-to-learn.* Retrieved January 15, 2012, from http://culturalpolicy.uchicago.edu/conf2001/papers/kafai.html

Kafai, Y. B. (2006). Playing and making games for learning: Instructionist and constructionist perspectives for game studies. *Games and Culture, 1*(1), 36–40. doi:10.1177/1555412005281767

Karet, N., & Hubbell, E. R. (2003). Authentic assessment: Current trends and issues in instructional technology.

Kayes, C. D. (2002). Experiential learning and its critics: Preserving the role of experience in management learning and education. *Academy of Management Learning & Education, 1,* 137–149. doi:10.5465/AMLE.2002.8509336

Kay, R. H., & Knaack, L. (2008). Assessing learning, quality and engagement in learning objects: The learning object evaluation scale for students (LOES-S). *Educational Technology Research and Development, 57*(2), 147–168. doi:10.1007/s11423-008-9094-5

Kaywa. (2012). *QR-code generator.* Retrieved 27 January, 2012, from http://qrcode.kaywa.com/

Compilation of References

Kebritchi, M., & Hynes, M. (2010). Games for mathematics education. In Hirumi, A. (Ed.), *Playing games in school: Video games and simulations for primary and secondary education* (pp. 119–145). Eugene, OR: International Society for Technology in Education.

Keefe, J. W. (1979). Learning style: An overview. In *NASSP's student learning styles: Diagnosing and proscribing programs* (pp. 1–17). Reston, VA: National Association of Secondary School Principles.

Kee, K., Vaughan, T., & Graham, S. (2010). The haunted school on horror hill: A case study of interactive fiction in the classroom. In Baek, Y. (Ed.), *Gaming for classroom-based learning: Digital role playing as a motivator of study* (pp. 113–124). Hershey, PA: IGI Global. doi:10.4018/978-1-61520-713-8.ch007

Ke, F. (2008). A case study of computer gaming for math: Engaged learning from game play? *Computers & Education, 51,* 1609–1620. doi:10.1016/j.compedu.2008.03.003

Ke, F., & Grabowski, B. (2007). Gameplaying for maths learning: Cooperative or not? *British Journal of Educational Technology, 38*(2), 249–259. doi:10.1111/j.1467-8535.2006.00593.x

Keifer-Boyd, K. (2005). Children teaching children with their computer game creations. *Visual Arts Research, 31*(160), 117–128.

Keifer-Boyd, K., Amburgy, P. M., & Knight, W. B. (2003). Three approaches to teaching visual culture in K-12 school contexts. *Art Education, 56*(2), 44–51.

Keith, N., & Frese, M. (2008). Effectiveness of error management training: A meta-analysis. *The Journal of Applied Psychology, 93,* 59–69. doi:10.1037/0021-9010.93.1.59

Keller, D. (2007). Reading and playing: what makes interactive fiction unique. In Williams, J. P., & Smith, J. H. (Eds.), *The players' realm: Studies on the culture of video games and gaming* (pp. 276–298). Jefferson, NC: McFarland & Co.

Keller, J. M. (1987). Development and use of the ARCS model of motivational design. *Journal of Instructional Development, 10*(3), 2–10. doi:10.1007/BF02905780

Kelly, J., Turner, J. J., & McKenna, K. (2006). What parents think: Children and healthy eating. *British Food Journal, 108*(5), 413–432. doi:10.1108/00070700610661376

Kennedy-Clark, S. (2011). Pre-service teachers' perspectives on using scenario-based virtual worlds in science education. *Computers & Education, 57,* 2224–2235. doi:10.1016/j.compedu.2011.05.015

Ketelhut, D. J., Clarke, J., & Nelson, B. (2010). The development of River City, a multi-user virtual environment-based scientific inquiry curriculum: historical and design evolutions. In M. J. Jacobson & P. Reimann (Eds.), *Designs for learning environments of the future* (pp. 89-110). New York, NY: Springer Science + Business Media.

Ketelhut, D. J. (2007). The impact of student self-efficacy on scientific inquiry skills: An exploratory investigation in River City, a multi-user virtual environment. *Journal of Science Education and Technology, 16*(1), 99–111. doi:10.1007/s10956-006-9038-y

Ketelhut, D. J., Nelson, B. C., Clarke, J. E., & Dede, C. (2010). A multi-user virtual environment for building and assessing higher order inquiry skills in science. *British Journal of Educational Technology, 41*(1), 56–68. doi:10.1111/j.1467-8535.2009.01036.x

Kiili, K. (2005). Digital game-based learning: Towards an experiential gaming model. *The Internet and Higher Education, 8*(1), 13–24. doi:10.1016/j.iheduc.2004.12.001

Kim, J. H., Gunn, D. V., Schuh, E., Phillips, B., Pagulayan, R. J., & Wixon, D. (2008) Tracking real-time user experience (TRUE): A comprehensive instrumentation solution for complex systems. In *Proceedings of the 26th Annual SIGCHI Conference on Human Factors in Computing Systems*. ACM Press.

Kim, H. J., & Pedersen, S. (2011). Advancing young adolescents' hypothesis-development performance in a computer-supported and problem-based learning environment. *Computers & Education, 57*(2), 1780–1789. doi:10.1016/j.compedu.2011.03.014

Kim, Y.-C. (2011). Analysis of growth trend for social network service game market. *Korea Information Processing Society Review, 18*(6), 97–106.

Kirriemuir, J., & McFarlane, A. (2004). *Report 8: Literature review in games and learning*. Bristol, UK: Nesta Futurelab Series. Retrieved from http://www.futurelab.org.uk/resources/documents/lit_reviews/Games_Review.pdf

Kirriemuir, J., & McFarlane, A. (2003). Use of computer and video games in the classroom. In *Proceedings of Level Up: The Digital Games Research Conference*. University of Utrecht.

Kirriemuir, J., & McFarlane, A. (2004). *Literature review in games and learning (No. 8)*. Bristol, Canada: Nesta Futurelab.

Kleinsasser, A. (2000). Researchers, reflexivity, and good data: Writing to unlearn. *Theory into Practice, 39*(1), 155–162. doi:10.1207/s15430421tip3903_6

Klopfer, E., Osterweil, S., & Salen, K. (2009). *Moving learning games forward: Obstacles, opportunities & openness*. MIT Press: The Education Arcade.

Klopfer, E., & Begel, A. (2003). StarLogo under the hood and in the classroom. *Kybernetes, 32*(1-2), 15–37. doi:10.1108/03684920310452328

Klopfer, E., & Yoon, S. (2005). Developing games and simulations for today and tomorrows tech savvy youth. *TechTrends, 49*(3), 33–41. doi:10.1007/BF02763645

Koehler, M. J., & Mishra, P. (2009). What is technolgical pedagogical content knowledge. *Technology and Teacher Education, 9*(1), 60–70.

Koepp, M. J., Gunn, R. N., Lawrence, A. D., Cunningham, V. J., Dagher, A., & Jones, T. (1998). Evidence for striatal dopamine release during a video game. *Nature, 393*(6682), 266–268. doi:10.1038/30498

Kolb, A. Y., & Kolb, D. A. (2009). The learning way: Meta-cognitive aspects of experiential learning. *Simulation & Gaming, 40*(3), 297–327. doi:10.1177/1046878108325713

Kolb, D. A. (1984). *Experiential learning*. Englewood Cliffs, NJ: Prentice Hall.

Kolb, D. A. (1985). *Learning style inventory and technical manual*. Boston, MA: McBer.

Kolb, D. A., Boyatzis, R. E., & Mainemelis, C. (2000). Experiential learning theory: Previous research and new directions. In Sternberg, R. J., & Zhang, L. F. (Eds.), *Perspectives on cognitive learning and thinking styles*. Lawrence Erlbaum.

Compilation of References

Koster, R. (2005). *A theory of fun for game design*. Scottsdale, AZ: Paraglyph Press.

Kriz, W. C., & Hense, J. U. (2006). Theory-oriented evaluation for the design of and research in gaming and simulation. *Simulation & Gaming, 37*(2), 268–283. doi:10.1177/1046878106287950

Krogstie, B. (2009). A model of retrospective reflection in project based learning utilizing historical data in collaborative tools. In U. Cress, V. Dimitrova, & M. Specht (Eds.), *EC-TEL 2009, LNCS 5794*. Berlin, German: Springer.

Kruskal, J. B., & Wish, M. (1978). *Multidimensional scaling*. Beverly Hills, CA: Sage Publications.

Kumar, R., & Lightner, R. (2007). Games as an interactive classroom technique: Perceptions of corporate trainers, college instructors and students. *International Journal of Teaching and Learning in Higher Education, 19*(1), 53–63.

Kutner, L., & Olsen, C. K. (2008). *Grand theft childhood: The surprising truth about violent video games and what parents can do*. New York, NY: Simon & Schuster.

la Velle, L., Wishart, J., McFarlane, A., Brawn, R., & John, P. (2007). Teaching and learning with ICT within the subject culture of secondary school science. *Research in Science & Technological Education, 25*(3), 339–349. doi:10.1080/02635140701535158

Lambert, N. M., & McCombs, B., L. (2002). *How students learn: Reforming schools through learner-centered education*. Washington, DC: American Psychological Association.

Lancy, D. F., & Hayes, B. L. (1988). Interactive fiction and the reluctant reader. *English Journal, 77*(7), 42-66. Retrieved January 8, 2011, from http://www.jstor.org/stable/818936

Land, S., & Zembal-Saul, C. (2003). Scaffolding reflection and articulation of scientific explanation in a data-rich, project-based learning environment: An investigation of progress portfolio. *Educational Technology Research and Development, 51*, 65–84. doi:10.1007/BF02504544

Lange, P. G. (2010). Learning real-life lessons from online games. *Games and Culture, 6*(1), 17–37. doi:10.1177/1555412010377320

Lave, J., & Wenger, E. (1991). *Situated learning: Legitimate peripheral participation*. Cambridge, UK: Cambridge University Press. doi:10.1017/CBO9780511815355

Law, C., & So, S. (2010). QR codes in education. *Journal of Educational Technology Development and Exchange, 3*(1), 85-100. Retrieved 14th January, 2012, from http://libir1.ied.edu.hk/pubdata/ir/link/pub/7-So.pdf

Lawless, K. A., & Kulikowich, J. M. (2006). Domain knowledge and individual interest: The effects of academic level and specialization in statistics and psychology. *Contemporary Educational Psychology, 31*(1), 30–43. doi:10.1016/j.cedpsych.2005.01.002

Lawless, K. A., & Pellegrino, J. W. (2007). Professional development in integrating technology into teaching and learning: Knowns, unkowns and ways to pursue better questions and answers. *Review of Research in Education, 77*(4), 575–614. doi:10.3102/0034654307309921

Lazzaro, N. (2004). Four keys to more emotions in games.

Lazzaro, N. (2005). Why we play games: Four keys to more emotion without story. *Proceedings of the Game Developers Conference*. Retrieved from http://xeodesign.com/xeodesign_whyweplaygames.pdf

Lederman, N. G., & Abd-El-Khalick, F. (1998). Avoiding de-natured science: Activities that promote understandings of the nature of science. In McComas, W. F. (Ed.), *The nature of science in science education: Rationales and strategies* (pp. 83–126). Dodrecht, The Netherlands: Kluwer. doi:10.1007/0-306-47215-5_5

Lee, J., Luchini, K., Michael, B., Norris, C., & Soloway, E. (2004). More than just fun and games: Assessing the value of educational video games in the classroom. *Proceedings of CHI 2004, Association of Computing Machinery* (pp. 1375-1378).

Lee, D. (1997). Factors influencing the success of computer skills learning among in-service teachers. *British Journal of Educational Technology*, *28*(2), 139–141. doi:10.1111/1467-8535.00018

Lee, H., Plass, J. L., & Homer, B. D. (2006). Optimizing cognitive load for learning from computer-based science simulations. *Journal of Educational Psychology*, *89*, 902–913. doi:10.1037/0022-0663.98.4.902

Lee, K. M., Park, N., & Jin, S. A. (2006). Narrative and interactivity in computer games. In Vorderer, P., & Bryant, J. (Eds.), *Playing video games: Motives, responses, and consequences* (pp. 259–274). New Jersey: Lawrence Erlbaum Associates.

Lehrer, R., Jaslow, L., & Curtis, C. (2003). Developing and understanding of measurement in the elementary grades. In Clements, D. H. (Ed.), *Learning and teaching measurement* (pp. 100–121). Reston, VA: National Council of Teachers of Mathematics.

Lenhart, A., Jones, S., & Macgill, A. (2008). *Video games: Adults are players too.* Retrieved from http://pewresearch.org/pubs/1048/

Lenhart, A., Kahne, J., Middaugh, E., & Macgill, A. (2008). *Teens, video games, and civics.* Retrieved from http://www.pewinternet.org/PPF/r/263/report_display.asp

Lenhart, A., Ling, R., Campbell, S., & Purcell, K. (2010). *Teens and mobile phones.* Retrieved from http://www.pewinternet.org/Reports/2010/Teens-and-Mobile-Phones.aspx

Levine, J. (1999). *The Enneagram intelligences: understanding personality for effective teaching and learning*. Bergin and Garvey Publishers.

Lindtner, S., & Dourish, P. (2011). The promise of play: A new approach to productive play. *Games and Culture*, *6*(5), 453–478. doi:10.1177/1555412011402678

Lost Pig [Computer software]. (2007). Retrieved January 8, 2011 from http://www.grunk.org/lostpig/

Lou, Y., Abrami, P. C., & d'Apollonia, S. (2001). Small group and individual learning with technology: A meta-analysis. *Review of Educational Research*, *71*(3), 449–521. doi:10.3102/00346543071003449

Lowe, R. (2004). Interrogation of a dynamic visualisation during learning. *Journal of Learning and Instruction*, *14*, 257–274. doi:10.1016/j.learninstruc.2004.06.003

Lynch, M., & Tunstall, R. (2008). When worlds collide: Developing game-design partnerships in universities. *Simulation & Gaming, 39*, 379–398. doi:10.1177/1046878108319275

MacMillan, J., Alexander, A., Weil, S., & Littleton, B. (2005). *DARWARS: An architecture that supports effective experiential training.* Cambridge, UK: BBN Technologies.

Magerkurth, C., Cheok, A., Mandryk, R., & Nilsen, T. (2005). Pervasive games: Bringing computer entertainment back to the real world. *ACM Computers in Entertainment, 3*(3), 1–19.

Malaby, T. M. (2009). Beyond play: A new approach to games. *Games and Culture, 2*(2), 95–113. doi:10.1177/1555412007299434

Malliet, S., Quinten, N., & Van der Sluys, V. (2010). Evaluating educational game experiences in a classroom context implications for qualitative research. In *Proceedings of the Fun and Games 2010 Workshop.* NHTV Expertise Series.

Malone, T. (1981). Toward a theory of intrinsically motivating instruction. *Cognitive Science, 4*, 333–369. doi:10.1207/s15516709cog0504_2

Malone, T. W., & Lepper, M. R. (1987). Making learning fun: A taxonomy of intrinsic motivations for learning. In Snow, R. E., & Farr, M. J. (Eds.), *Aptitude, learning and instruction: III- Conative and affective process analyses* (pp. 223–253). Hillsdale, NJ: Erlbaum.

Markauskaite, L. (2007). Exploring the structure of trainee teachers' ICT literacy: The main components of, and relationships between, general cognitive and technical capabilities. *Educational Technology Research and Development, 55*, 547–572. doi:10.1007/s11423-007-9043-8

Marsh, T. (2010). Activity-based scenario design, development and assessment in serious games. In Eck, R. V. (Ed.), *Gaming and cognition: Theories and practice from the learning sciences* (pp. 214–227). Hershey, PA: IGI Global. doi:10.4018/978-1-61520-717-6.ch010

Martin, A., & Chatfield, T. (2006). Alternate reality games. In A. Martin (Ed.), *White paper - IGDA ARG SIG* (pp. 82). Mt. Royal, NJ: International Game Developers Association.

Martin, S. (2010). Teachers using learning styles: Torn between research and accountability? *Teaching and Teacher Education, 26*(8), 1583–1591. doi:10.1016/j.tate.2010.06.009

Massa, L. J., & Mayer, R. E. (2006). Testing the ATI hypothesis: Should multimedia instruction accommodate verbalizer-visualizer cognitive style? *Learning and Individual Differences, 16*, 321–336. doi:10.1016/j.lindif.2006.10.001

Mawer, K., & Stanley, G. (2011). *Digital play Computer games and language aims.* Delta Publishing.

Mayer, R. E. (2009). *Multimedia learning* (2nd ed.). New York, NY: Cambridge University Press. doi:10.1017/CBO9780511811678

Mayer, R. E. (Ed.). (2005). *The Cambridge handbook of multimedia learning.* New York, NY: Cambridge University Press. doi:10.1017/CBO9780511816819

Mayer, R. E., & Moreno, R. (2003). nine ways to reduce cognitive load in multimedia learning. *Educational Psychologist, 38*(1), 43–52. doi:10.1207/S15326985EP3801_6

Mayer, R., & Moreno, R. (2002). Aids to computer-based multimedia learning. *Learning and Instruction, 12*, 107–119. doi:10.1016/S0959-4752(01)00018-4

Mayes, T., & de Freitas, S. (2007). Learning and e-learning: The role of theory. In Beetham, H., & Sharpe, R. (Eds.), *Rethinking pedagogy in the digital age*. London, UK: Routledge.

Mayo, M. (2009). Want to truly scale a learning program? Try gaming. *Kaufmann Thoughtbook, 3*. Ewing Marion Kauffman Foundation. Retrieved from http://www.kauffman.org/education/try-gaming.aspx

Mayo, M. J. (2007). Games for science and engineering education. *Communications of the ACM, 50*(7), 31–35. doi:10.1145/1272516.1272536

Mayo, M. J. (2009). Video games: A route to large-scale stem education? *Science, 323*(89).

McFarlane, A., Sparrowhawk, A., & Heald, Y. (2002). *Report on the educational use of games*. Retrieved January 15, 2010, from http://www.teem.org.uk/publications/teem_gamesined_full.pdf

McGinnis, J. M., Gootman, J., & Kraak, V. I. (2006). *Food marketing to children and youth: Threat or opportunity?* Washington, DC: The National Academies Press.

McGonigal, J. (2010). *Gaming can make a better world*. TED Talks. Retrieved from http://www.ted.com/talks/lang/eng/jane_mcgonigal_gaming_can_make_a_better_world.html

McGreal, R. (2004). Learning objects: A practical definition. *International Journal of Instructional Technology and Distance Learning, 1*(9), 21–32.

McHaney, R. (1991). *Computer simulation: A practical perspective*. San Diego, CA: Academic Press.

McInnes, C., James, R., & McNaught, C. (1995). *First year on campus: Diversity in the initial experiences of Australian undergraduates*. Canberra, Australia: AGPS.

McKeachie, W. J. (2006). *McKeachie's teaching tips: Strategies, research, and theory for college and university teachers*. Boston, MA: Houghton Mifflin.

McLellan, H. (1996). "Being digital": Implications for education. *Educational Technology, 36*(6), 5–20.

McLouglin, C., & Oliver, R. (1998). Maximising the language and learning link in computer learning environments. *British Journal of Educational Technology, 29*(2), 125–136. doi:10.1111/1467-8535.00054

McMahan, A. (2003). Immersion, engagement and presence. In *The video game theory reader*. Retrieved from http://people.ict.usc.edu/~morie/SupplementalReadings/ch3-McMahanrev.pdf

Medler, B., John, M., & Lane, J. (2011) Data Cracker: Developing a visual game analytic tool for analyzing online gameplay. In *Proceedings of the 29th Annual SIGCHI Conference on Human Factors in Computing Systems*. ACM Press.

Meyer, J. H. F., & Land, R. (2003) Threshold concepts and troublesome knowledge: linkages to ways of thinking and practising, In C. Rust (Ed.), *Improving student learning - Theory and practice ten years on*, (pp. 412-424). Oxford, UK: Oxford Centre for Staff and Learning Development (OCSLD).

Micheal, D., & Chen, S. (2005). *Serious games: Games that educate, train and inform*. New York, NY: Muska & Lipman.

Mishra, P., & Koehler, M. J. (2006). Technological pedagogical content knowledge: A framwork for integrating technology in teacher knowledge. *Teachers College Record*, *108*(6), 1017–1054. doi:10.1111/j.1467-9620.2006.00684.x

Molenda, M., & Sullivan, M. (2003). *Issues and trends in instructional technology: Treading water*. Libraries Unlimited.

Montana, M. (2011). A lulogical view on the pervasive mixed-reality game research paradigm. *Personal and Ubiquitous Computing*, *15*, 3–12. doi:10.1007/s00779-010-0307-7

Montfort, N. (2003). *Twisty little passages: An approach to interactive fiction*. London, UK: MIT Press.

Moon, J. (2010). *Using story in higher education and professional development*. Oxon, UK: Routledge.

Moreno-Ger, P., Burgos, D., Sierra, J. L., & Fernández-Manjón, B. (2008). Educational game design for online education. *Computers in Human Behavior*, *24*(6), 2530–2540. doi:10.1016/j.chb.2008.03.012

Moreno-Ger, P., Torrente, J., Bustamante, J., Fernández-Galaz, C., Fernández-Manjón, B., & Comas-Rengifo, M. D. (2010). Application of a low-cost web-based simulation to improve students' practical skills in medical education. *International Journal of Medical Informatics*, *79*, 459–467. doi:10.1016/j.ijmedinf.2010.01.017

Moreno, J., Caplan, A. L., & Wolpe, P. R. (1998). Updating protections for human subjects involved in research: Project on informed consent, human research ethics group. *Journal of the American Medical Association*, *280*(22), 1951–1958. Retrieved from http://www.ncbi.nlm.nih.gov/pubmed/9851484doi:10.1001/jama.280.22.1951

Morrison, G. R., Lowther, D. L., & DeMeulle, L. (1999). *Integrating computer technology into the classroom*. Upper Saddle River, NJ: Prentice Hall.

Mueller, J. (2008). Authentic assessment toolbox. Retrieved December 8, 2008, from http://jonathan.mueller.faculty.noctrl.edu/toolbox/index.htm.

Müller, A. (2011). Addressing the English language needs of international nursing students. *Journal of Academic Language & Learning*, *5*(2), A14–A22.

Muller, A. (2012). Improving the identification of medication names by increasing phonological awareness. In Arnab, S., Dunwell, I., & Debattista, K. (Eds.), *Serious games for healthcare: Applications and implications*. Hershey, PA: IGI Global. doi:10.4018/978-1-4666-1903-6.ch014

Nacke, L., Bateman, C., & Mandryk, R. (2011). *BrainHex: Preliminary results from a neurobiological gamer typology survey*. Paper presented at the 10th International Conference on Entertainment Computing, Vancouver, BC, Canada.

Nakamura, L. (2007). *Digitizing race*. Minneapolis, MN: University of MN Press.

National Center for Children Exposed To Violence Website. (2012). Retrieved April 5, 2012, from http://www.nccev.org/resources/statistics.html#media & http://www.nccev.org/violence/media.html

National Center for Education Statistics (NCES). (2010). *Degrees conferred by sex and race*. Retrieved April 12, 2012, from http://nces.ed.gov/fastfacts/display.asp?id=72

National Center for Women & Information Technology (NCWIT). (2009). *By the numbers*. Retrieved April 12, 2012, from http://www.ncwit.org/pdf/BytheNumbers09.pdf

National Centre for Education Statics. (2003). *Distance education at degree-granting postsecondary institutions: 2000-2001*. NCES.

National Council of Teachers of Mathematics. (2000). *Principles and standards for school mathematics*. Reston, VA: National Council of Teachers of Mathematics.

National Research Council. (2010). *Rising above the gathering storm, revisited: Rapidly approaching category 5. 2005 "Rising Above the Gathering Storm" Committee; Prepared for the Presidents of the National Academy of Sciences, National Academy of Engineering, and Institute of Medicine*. Washington, DC: National Academies Press.

National Science Board. (2007). *A national action plan for addressing the critical needs of the US science technology, engineering and mathematics engineering system*. (National Science Foundation NSB/HER-07-9). Retrieved January 15, 2010, from http://nsf.gov/nsb/edu_com/report.jsp

National Science Board. (2010). *Preparing the next generation of STEM innovators: Identifying and developing our nation's human capital. (NSF Publication NSB1033)*. Arlington, VA: Author.

National Science Foundation, Division of Science Resources Statistics. (2009). *Women, minorities, and persons with disabilities in science and engineering: 2009*. (NSF 09-305). Arlington, VA: Author. Retrieved January 15, 2010, from http://www.nsf.gov/statistics/wmpd/

Nation, I. S. P. (2010). *Learning vocabulary in another language*. Cambridge, UK: Cambridge University Press.

Neisser, U. (2009). Cognitive psychology. In *Grolier multimedia encyclopedia*.

Nelson, B. (2007). Exploring the use of individualized, reflective guidance in an educational multi-user virtual environment. *Journal of Science Education and Technology, 16*(1), 83–97. doi:10.1007/s10956-006-9039-x

Neville, D., Shelton, B. E., & McInnis, B. (2009). Cybertext redux: Using DGBL to teach L2 vocabulary, reading and culture. *Computer Assisted Language Learning, 22*(5), 409–424. doi:10.1080/09588220903345168

Niesz, A. J., & Holland, N. N. (1984). Interactive fiction. *Critical Inquiry Chicago, 11*(1), 110–129. doi:10.1086/448277

Nolan, R. B. (2006). At law school, "Second Life", in the cards, and the course catalogue. *The Harvard Crimson: Online Edition*.

Northrup, P. T. (2007). *Learning objects for instruction: design and evaluation*. Hershey, PA: Information Science Publishing. doi:10.4018/978-1-59904-334-0

Nunan, D. (1991). *Language teaching methodology.* London, UK: Prentice Hall International.

Nunan, D. (2004). *Task-based language teaching.* Cambridge, UK: Cambridge University Press. doi:10.1017/CBO9780511667336

Nutbeam, D. (2000). Health literacy as a public goal: A challenge for contemporary health education and communication strategies into the 21st century. *Health Promotion International, 15*(3), 259–267. doi:10.1093/heapro/15.3.259

O'Brien, D., Lawless, K. A., & Schrader, P. G. (2010). A taxonomy of educational games. In Baek, Y. (Ed.), *Gaming for classroom-based learning: Digital role playing as a myouotivator of study* (pp. 1–23). doi:10.4018/978-1-61520-713-8.ch001

O'Neil, H. F., Wainess, R., & Baker, E. L. (2005). Classification of learning outcomes: Evidence from the computer games literature. *Curriculum Journal, 16*, 455–474. doi:10.1080/09585170500384529

Oblinger, D. G. (2003). Understanding the new students: Boomers, Gen-Xers, Millennials. *Educause Review, 38*(4). Retrieved 14th January, 2012, from http://net.educause.edu/ir/library/pdf/erm0342.pdf

Oblinger, D. G., & Oblinger, J. L. (Eds.). (2005). *Educating the net generation.* Washington, DC: Educause. Retrieved 14th January, 2012, from http://www.educause.edu/educatingthenetgen

Oblinger, D. G. (2006). Games and learning: Digital games have the potential to bring play to the learning experience. *EDUCAUSE Quarterly, 29*(3), 5–7.

O'Brian, P. (1993). *Interactive fiction and reader response criticism.* Unpublished paper, University of Colorado, Boulder. Retrieved January 8, 2011 from http://spot.colorado.edu/~obrian/ifrrc.txt

O'Brien, V., Martinez-Pons, M., & Kopala, M. (1999). Mathematics self-efficacy, ethnic identity, gender, and career interests related to mathematics and science. *The Journal of Educational Research, 92*(4), 231. doi:10.1080/00220679909597600

Ogden, C. L., Carroll, M. D., & Flegal, K. M. (2008). High body mass index for age among US children and adolescents, 2003–2006. *Journal of the American Medical Association, 299*(20), 2401–2405. doi:10.1001/jama.299.20.2401

Ohio Department of Education. (2010). *Academic content standards for visual art: Alignment by standard.* Retrieved from http://www.ode.state.oh.us/GD/Templates/Pages/ODE/ODEDetail.aspx?page=3&TopicRelationID=1700&ContentID=1388&Content=88231

Ohlsson, S. (1995). Learning to do and learning to understand. In Reiman, P., & Spada, H. (Eds.), *Learning in humans and machines* (pp. 37–62). New York, NY: Elsevier Science Inc.

OHRP. (2009). Retrieved from http://www.hhs.gov/ohrp/humansubjects/guidance/45cfr46.html

Overmars, M. (1999-2009). *GameMaker* (Version 8.0 Pro) [Computer software and manual]. YoYoGames Ltd.

Pace, T. (2008). *Can an orc catch a cab in Stormwind?* Conference presentation. Retrieved February 12, 2012, from http://www.chi2008.org/altchisystem/index.php?action=showsubmission&id=156

Padrós, A., Romero, M., & Usart, M. (2011). Developing serious games: From face-to-face to a computer-based modality. *Elearning Papers*, *25*, 1–12.

Palaigeorgiou, G. E., Siozos, P. D., Konstantakis, N. I., & Tsoukalas, I. A. (2005). A computer attitude scale for computer science freshmen and its educational implications. *Journal of Computer Assisted Learning*, *21*(5), 330–342. doi:10.1111/j.1365-2729.2005.00137.x

Palmberg, R. (1988). Computer games and foreign-language vocabulary learning. *English Language Teaching Journal*, *42*(4), 247–252. doi:10.1093/elt/42.4.247

Palmer, P. J. (2007). *The courage to teach. Exploring the inner landscape of a teacher's life*. San Francisco, CA: Jossey-Bass.

Panichi, L., Deutschmann, M., & Molka-Danielsen, J. (2010). Virtual worlds for language learning and intercultural exchange: Is it for real? In Guth, S., & Helm, F. (Eds.), *Telecollaboration 2.0: Languages, literacies and intercultural learning in the 21st century* (pp. 165–195). Bern, Switzerland: Peter Lang.

Papastergiou, M. (2008). Digital game-based learning in high school computer science education. *Computers & Education*, *52*, 1–12. doi:10.1016/j.compedu.2008.06.004

Papert, S. (1998, June). Does easy do it? Children, games, and learning. *Game Developer*, 87-88.

Papert, S. (1993). *Mindstorms: Children, computers and powerful ideas* (2nd ed.). New York, NY: Basic Books.

Pappa, D., Dunwell, I., Protopsaltis, A., & Pannese, L. (2011). Game-based learning for knowledge sharing and transfer: the e-VITA approach for intergenerational learning. In Felicia, P. (Ed.), *Handbook of research on improving learning and motivation through educational games: Multidisciplinary approaches*. Hershey, PA: IGI Global. doi:10.4018/978-1-60960-495-0.ch045

Parberry, I., Kazemzadeh, M. B., & Roden, T. (2006). *The art and science of game programming*. Paper presented at SIGCSE'06, Houston, Texas, USA.

Pardew, L., Nunamaker, E., & Pugh, S. (2004). *Game design for teens. Premier Press Game Development Series*. Premier Press.

Park, J.-C., Jun, S.-J., & Lee, H.-J. (2011). The effects of social network service activities in the consumers' knowledge creation and continuous intention to use. *Journal of Korea Service*, *12*(4), 201–226.

Park, S.-B. (2008). Electronic games appropriated for the classrooms: A proposal of the questionnaire containing 17 questions. *International Journal of Contents*, *8*(3), 156–172.

Partnership for 21st Century Skills (2004). *The intellectual and policy foundations of the 21st century skills framework*. Retrieved July 9, 2009, from http://www.21stcenturyskills.org/route21/images/stories/epapers/skillsfoundationsfinal.pdf

Patten. (2008). *Final project - Creating a game in Scratch*. Retrieved from http://rubistar.4teachers.org/index.php?screen=ShowRubric&rubric_id=2063440&

Pereira, J. (2011). *The AVALON project and Second Life - The analysis and selection of a virtual world for language learning and teaching*. Retrieved January 8, 2011 from http://avalon.humanities.manchester.ac.uk/wpcontent/uploads/2010/11/AVALON_Second_Life_Report.pdf

Pereira, J. (2011). A narrative at war with a crossword - An introduction to Interactive Fiction. In H. Görür-Ataba\u015f & S. Turner (Eds.), *Expectations eclipsed in foreign language education: Learners and educators on an ongoing journey* (pp. 87-96). İstanbul, Turkey: Sabancı Üniversitesi. Retrieved January 8, 2011, from http://digital.sabanciuniv.edu/ebookacik/3011200000287.pdf

Pereira, J. (in press). Using Interactive Fiction for digital game-based language learning. In Garton, S., & Graves, K. (Eds.), *International perspectives in ELT materials*. Palgrave MacMillan.

Pernsteiner, S. M., Boyer, D. M., & Akcaoglu, M. (2010). Understanding player activity in a game-based virtual learning environment: A case for data-driven instructional design. *World Conference on E-Learning in Corporate, Government, Healthcare, and Higher Education 2010* (p. 763). Chesapeake, VA: AACE.

Peters, O. (2003). Learning with new media in distance education. In Moore, M. G., & Abderson, W. G. (Eds.), *Handbook of distance education* (pp. 87–112). Mahwah, NJ: Lawrence Erlbaum Associates.

Peters, V. A. M., & Vissers, G. A. N. (2004). A simple classification model for debriefing simulation games. *Simulation & Gaming, 35*(1), 70–84. doi:10.1177/1046878103253719

Phelps, R., Graham, A., & Watts, T. (2011). Acknowledging the complexity and diversity of historical and cultural ICT professional learning practices in schools. *Asia-Pacific Journal of Teacher Education, 39*(1), 47–63. doi:10.1080/1359866X.2010.541601

Piaget, J. (2010). *Meine Theorie der geistigen Entwicklung*. Weinheim, Germany: Beltz.

Piatt, K. (2010). Who is Herring Hale? In Whitton, N. (Ed.), *Learning with digital games: A practical guide to engaging students in higher education* (pp. 167–171). Oxon, UK: Routledge.

Pillay, H. (2002). An investigation of cognitive processes engaged in by recreational computer game players: An implication for skills of the future. *Journal of Research on Technology in Education, 34*, 336–350.

Piper, A. (1986). Conversation and the computer. A study of the conversational spin-off generated among learners of English as a foreign language working in groups. *System, 4*(2), 187–198. doi:10.1016/0346-251X(86)90008-4

Pivec, M., Koskinen, T., & Tarín, L. (2011). Game-based learning: New practices, new classrooms [Editorial]. *eLearning Papers, 25*, 1-6.

Pivec, M., & Pivec, P. (2011). Digital games: Changing education, one raid at a time. *International Journal of Game-Based Learning, 1*(1), 1–18. doi:10.4018/ijgbl.2011010101

Plass, J. L., Moreno, R., & Brünken, R. (Eds.). (2010). *Cognitive load theory*. New York, NY: Cambridge University Press.

Plotkin, A., & Albaugh, L. (2010). *IF-for-beginner's card*. Retrieved January 8, 2011, from http://pr-if.org/doc/play-if-card/

Polsani, P. R. (2003). Use and abuse of reusable learning objects. *Journal of Digital Information, 3*(4), 164.

Polya, G. (1971). *How to solve it: A new aspect of mathematical method.* Princeton, NJ: Princeton University Press.

Poole, S. (2000). *Trigger happy: Video games and the entertainment revolution.* New York, NY: Arcade Publishing.

Prensky, M. (2008, January 13). *Programming is the new literacy.* Retrieved April 9, 2012, from http://www.edutopia.org/programming-the-new-literacy

Prensky, M. (2001). *Digital game-based learning.* New York, NY: McGraw-Hill.

Prensky, M. (2001). Digital natives, digital immigrants part 1. *Horizon, 9*(5), 1–6. doi:10.1108/10748120110424816

Prensky, M. (2002). The motivation of game play. *Horizon, 10*(1), 1–14.

Prensky, M. (2006). *"Don't bother me Mom, I'm learning!": How computer and video games are preparing your kids for twenty-first century success and how you can help!* St. Paul, MN: Paragon House.

Prensky, M. (2010). *Teaching digital natives: Partnering for real learning.* Thousand Oaks, CA: Sage.

Prilla, M., Herrmann, T., & Degeling, M. (2012). Collaborative reflection for learning at the healthcare workplace. In Goggins, S., Jahnke, I., & Wulf, V. (Eds.), *CSCL@Work: Case studies of collaborative learning at work.* Springer.

Probart, C., McDonnell, E., Lachterberg, C., & Anger, S. (1997). Evaluation of implementation of an interdisciplinary nutrition curriculum in middle schools. *Journal of Nutrition Education, 29*(4), 203–209. doi:10.1016/S0022-3182(97)70199-7

Protopsaltis, A., Hetzner, S., Pappa, D., & Pannese, L. (2011). *Serious games and formal and informal learning.* eLearning Papers, nr 25, July 2011.

Przybylski, A., Rigby, C. S., & Ryan, R. (2010). A motivational model of video game engagement. *Review of General Psychology, 14*(2), 154–166. doi:10.1037/a0019440

Raiha, T., Tossavainen, K., & Turunen, H. (2006). Adolescents' nutrition health issues: Opinions of Finnish seventh-graders. *Health Education, 106*(2), 114–132. doi:10.1108/09654280610650954

Ramsden, P. (2003). *Learning to teach in higher education.* Oxon, UK: RoutledgeFalmer.

Ravenscroft, A., Wegerif, R., & Hartley, R. (2007). *Reclaiming thinking: Dialectic, dialogic and learning in the digital age. BJEP Monograph Series II, Number 5-Learning through Digital Technologies* (Vol. 1, pp. 39–57). British Psychological Society.

Ray, B., & Coulter, G. A. (n.d.). Perceptions of the value of digital mini-games: Implications for middle school classrooms. *Journal of Digital Learning in Teacher Education, 28*(3), 92-99.

Redeker, G. (2003). An educational taxonomy for learning objects. In the *Proceedings of Learning Technologies, 2003.* Retrieved from http://ieeexplore.ieee.org/xpls/abs_all.jsp?arnumber=1215068

Compilation of References

Reiff, J. C. (1992). *Learning styles*. Washington, DC: National Education Association.

Reigeluth, C. (1996). A new paradigm of ISD? *Educational Technology*, *36*, 13–20.

Reinders, H., & Wattana, S. (2011). Learn English or die: The effects of digital games on interaction and willingness to communicate in a foreign language. *Digital Culture and Education*, *3*(1), 4–28.

Rice, J. (2007). New media resistance: Barriers to implementation of computer video games in the classroom. *Journal of Educational Multimedia and Hypermedia*, *16*(3), 249–261.

Richards, J. C., & Rodgers, T. S. (2001). *Approaches and methods in language teaching* (2nd ed.). New York, NY: Cambridge University Press. doi:10.1017/CBO9780511667305

Rideout, V., Roberts, D. F., & Foehr, U. G. (2005). *Generation M: Media in the lives of 8–18 year-olds* [executive summary]. Retrieved January 15, 2010, from http://www.kff.org/entmedia/upload/Executive-Summary-Generation-M-Media-in-the-Lives-of-8-18-Year-olds.pdf

Riding, R. (2002). *School learning and cognitive style*. London, UK: David Fulton.

Riding, R. J. (1991). *Cognitive styles analysis*. Birmingham, UK: Learning and Training Technology.

Riding, R. J. (1996). *Learning styles and technology-based training. OL244*. Sheffield: Department for Education and Employment.

Riding, R. J. (1997). On the nature of cognitive style. *Educational Psychology*, *17*, 29–50. doi:10.1080/0144341970170102

Riding, R. J., & Ashmore, I. (1980). Verbaliser-imager learning style and children's recall of information presented in pictorial versus written form. *Educational Psychology*, *6*, 141–145.

Riding, R. J., & Mathias, D. (1991). Cognitive Styles and preferred learning mode, reading attainment and cognitive ability in 11-year-old children. *Educational Psychology*, *11*, 383–393. doi:10.1080/0144341910110312

Riding, R. J., & Read, G. (1996). Cognitive style and pupil learning preferences. *Educational Psychology*, *16*(1), 81–106. doi:10.1080/0144341960160107

Riding, R. J., & Wigley, S. (1997). The relationship between cognitive style and personality in further education students. *Personality and Individual Differences*, *23*, 379–389.

Rieber, L. (1996). Seriously considering play: Designing interactive learning environments based on the blending of microworlds, simulations, and games. *Educational Technology Research and Development*, *44*, 43–58. doi:10.1007/BF02300540

Ritterfeld, U., Cody, M., & Vorderer, P. (2009). *Serious games: Mechanisms and effects*. New York, NY: Routledge.

Ritterfield, U., & Weber, R. (2005). Video games for entertainment and education. In Vorderer, P., & Bryant, J. (Eds.), *Playing video games: Motives responses and consequences* (pp. 399–414). Mahwah, NJ: Erlbaum.

Roberge, G. D., Gagnon, L. L., & Oddson, B. E. (2011). The ideal classroom: A comparative study of education and nursing student learning and psychosocial environmental preferences. *Institute for Learning Styles Research Journal*, *1*, 1–16.

Roberts, D. F., Foehr, U. G., & Rideout, V. (2005). *Generation M: Media in the lives of 8–18 year-olds*. Kaiser Family Foundation Study. Retrieved January 15, 2010, from http://www.kff.org/entmedia/upload/Generation-M-Media-in-the-Lives-of-8-18-Year-olds-Report.pdf

Roberts, E., & Gallagher, P. S. (2010). Challenges to SCORM. In Jesukiewicz, P., Kahn, B., & Wisher, R. (Eds.), *Learning on demand: ADL and the future of e-learning* (pp. 49–70). Alexandria, VA: Advanced Distributed Learning.

Rogers, P. L. (1995). Towards a language of computer art: When paint isn't paint. *Art Education, 48*(5), 17–22. doi:10.2307/3193529

Romero, M., Usart, M., & Almirall, E. (2011). Serious games in a finance course promoting the knowledge group awareness. *EDULEARN11 Proceedings*, (pp. 3490-3492).

Ross, J. (2007). Perhaps the greatest grand challenge: improving the image of computing. *Computing Research News, 19*(5). Retrieved February 12, 2012, from http://www.cra.org/resources/crn-archive-view-detail/perhaps_the_greatest_grand_challenge_improving_the_image_of_computing/

Roth, W.-M. (1966). Art and artifact of children's designing: A situated cognition perspective. *Journal of the Learning Sciences, 5*(2), 129–166. doi:10.1207/s15327809jls0502_2

Rouse, R. (2005). *Game design: Theory and practice* (2nd ed.). Sudbury, MA: Wordware Publishing, Inc.

Rovai, A. P., & Jordan, H. M. (2004). Blended learning and sense of community: A comparative analysis with traditional and fully online graduate courses. *International Review of Research in Open and Distance Learning, 5*(2).

Ryan, M. (2006). *Avatars of story*. Minneapolis, MN: University of Minnesota Press.

Sadler-Smith, E. (1996). Learning styles and instructional design. *Innovations in Educational and Training Technology, 33*(4).

Sadoski, M., & Paivio, A. (2004). A dual coding theoretical model of reading. In Ruddell, R. B., & Unrau, N. J. (Eds.), *Theoretical models and processes of reading* (5th ed., pp. 1329–1362). Newark, DE: International Reading Association. doi:10.1598/0872075028.47

Salen, K., & Zimmerman, E. (2004). *Rules of play: Game design fundamentals*. Retrieved from http://common.books24x7.com.www.libproxy.wvu.edu/toc.aspx?bookid=7016

Salen, K. (2007). Gaming literacies: A game design study in action. *Journal of Educational Multimedia and Hypermedia, 16*(3), 301–322.

Salen, K., Torres, R., Wolozin, L., Rufo-Tepper, R., & Shapiro, A. (2011). *Quest to learn: Developing the school for digital kids*. Cambridge, MA: MIT Press.

Salen, K., & Zimmerman, E. (2003). *Rules of play: Game design fundamentals*. Cambridge, MA: MIT Press.

Sarama, J., & Clements, D. H. (2009). Teaching math in the primary grades: The learning trajectories approach. *Young Children, 64*(2), 63–65.

Sardone, N. B., & Devlin-Scherer, R. (2010). Teacher candidate responses to digital games: 21st-century skills development. *Journal of Research on Technology in Education, 42*(4), 409-425. ERIC database (EJ895055).

Savery, J. R., & Duffy, T. M. (1995). Problem based learning: An instructional model and its constructivist framework. *Educational Technology, 35*, 31–38.

Schank, R., & Abelson, R. (1977). *Scripts, plans, goals, and understanding: An inquiry into human knowledge structures*. Hillsdale, NJ: Lawrence Erlbaum.

Schmeck, R. R. (1988). *Learning strategies and learning styles*. New York, NY: Plenum Press.

Schmidt, D., Baran, E., Thompson, A. D., Mishra, P., Koehler, M. J., & Shin, T. S. (2009). Technological pedagogical content knowledge (TPACK): The development and validation of an assessment instrument for preservice teachers. *Journal of Research on Technology in Education, 42*(2), 123–149.

Schmitt, N. (2008). Review article: Instructed second language vocabulary learning. *Language Teaching Research, 12*(3), 329–363. doi:10.1177/1362168808089921

Schwartz, D. L., Chase, C. C., Oppezzo, M. A., & Chin, D. B. (2011). Practicing versus inventing with contrasting cases: The effects of telling first on learning and transfer. *Journal of Educational Psychology, 103*(4), 759–775. doi:10.1037/a0025140

Scottish Qualifications Authority. (2003). *Core skills framework: An introduction*. Glasgow, UK: Author. Retrieved 14th January, 2012, from http://www.sqa.org.uk/files_ccc/Core%20skills%20combined%20241106.pdf

Sedig, K. (2008). From play to thoughtful learning: A design strategy to engage children with mathematical representations. *Journal of Computers in Mathematics and Science Teaching, 27*(1), 65–101.

Seo, S.-P., & Kim, J.-H. (2008). Design of model for instruction based on on-line game. *Journal of Korea Information Education, 8*(1), 28–35.

Settles, D. (2011, September/October). Gaming and core content: Conjoined twins. *Knowledge Quest, 40*(1), 70–72.

Shaffer, D. W. (2005). Epistemic games. *Innovate: Journal of Online Education, 1*(6).

Shaffer, D. W., Squire, K. D., Halverson, R., & Gee, J. P. (2005). Video games and the future of learning. *Phi Delta Kappan, 87*(2), 105–111.

Shane, G. P. (2010). The development of SCORM. In Jesukiewicz, P., Kahn, B., & Wisher, R. (Eds.), *Learning on demand: ADL and the future of e-learning* (pp. 49–70). Alexandria, VA: Advanced Distributed Learning.

Shelby, L. B., & Vaske, J. J. (2008). Understanding meta-analysis: A review of the methodological literature. *Leisure Sciences, 30*(2), 96–110. doi:10.1080/01490400701881366

Sherry, L. (1996). Issues in distance learning. *International Journal of Educational Telecommunications, 1*(4), 337–365.

Show King, T. V. 2 [Computer software]. (2009). New York, NY: Gameloft.

Shulman, L. (1986). Those who understand: Knowledge growth in teaching. *Educational Researcher, 15*(2), 4–14.

Shute, V. J., Ventura, M., Bauer, M. I., & Zapata-Rivera, D. (2009) Melding the power of serious games and embedded assessment to monitor and foster learning. In U. Ritterfeld, M. J. Cody, & P. Vorderer (Eds.), *Serious games: Mechanisms and effects* (pp. 295-321). Philadelphia, PA: Routledge.

Sicart, M. (2008). Designing game mechanics. *International Journal of Computer Game Research, 8*(2). Retrieved from gamestudies.org/0802/articles/sicart

Silver Tree Media (Design Studio). (2008). *Pixie hollow* [MMOG]. United States: Disney.

Siwek, S. (2010). *Video games in the 21st century: The 2010 report*. Washington, DC: Entertainment Software Association. Retrieved from http://www.theesa.com/facts/pdfs/VideoGames21stCentury_2010.pdf

Slater, M., Usoh, M., & Steed, A. (1994). Depth of presence in virtual environments. *Presence (Cambridge, Mass.), 3*, 130–144.

Slavin, R. E. (2008). Perspectives on evidence-based research in education—What works? Issues in synthesizing educational program evaluations. *Educational Researcher, 37*(1), 5–14. doi:10.3102/0013189X08314117

Smith, R., Levine, T., & Lachlan, K. (2002). The high cost of complexity in experimental design and data analysis: Type I and type II error rates in multiway ANOVA. *Human Communication, 28*(4), 515-530. Retrieved from http://onlinelibrary.wiley.com/doi/10.1111/j.1468-2958.2002.tb00821.x/abstract

Squire, K. (2005). Changing the game: what happens when video games enter the classroom? *Innovate: Journal of Online Education, 1*(6). Retrieved from http://www.innovateonline.info/index.php?view=article&id=82

Squire, K. (2008). Video game-based learning: An emerging paradigm for instruction. *Performance Improvement Quarterly, 2*(2).

Squire, K. D., Barnett, M., Grant, J. M., & Higginbottom, T. (2004). *Electromagentism supercharged! Learning physics with digital simulation games*. Paper presented at the International Conference of the Learning Sciences, Los Angeles, CA. Retrieved from http://www.educationarcade.org/files/articles/Supercharged/SuperchargedResearch.pdf

Squire, K., & Steinkuehler, C. (2005, April 15). Meet the gamers. *The Library Journal*. Retrieved March 14, 2010, from http://www.the library journal.com

Squire, K. (2003). Video games in education. *International Journal of Intelligent Simulations and Gaming, 2*(1).

Squire, K. (2004). *Replaying history: Learning world history through playing Civilization III. (Ph.D.)*. Bloomington, IN: Indiana University-Bloomington.

Squire, K. (2005). Changing the game: What happens when video games enter the classroom. *Innovate: Journal of Online Education, 1*(6), 25–49.

Compilation of References

Squire, K. (2008). Video game literacy: A literacy of expertise. In Coiro, J., Knobel, M., Leu, D., & Lankshear, C. (Eds.), *Handbook of research on new literacies*. New York, NY: MacMillan.

Squire, K. (2011). *Video games and learning: Teaching and participatory culture in the digital age*. New York, NY: Teachers College Press.

Squire, K. D. (2008, Mar-Apr). Video games and education: Designing learning systems for an interactive age. *Educational Technology Magazine: The Magazine for Managers of Change in Education, 48*, 17–26.

Squire, K., & Durga, S. (2008). Productive gaming: The case for historiographic game play. In Ferdig, R. (Ed.), *Handbook of research on effective electronic gaming in education*. Hershey, PA: Information Science Reference.

Squire, K., & Jenkins, H. (2004). Harnessing the power of games in education. *Insight (American Society of Ophthalmic Registered Nurses), 3*(1), 5–33.

Squire, K., & Steinkuehler, C. (2005). Generating cyberculture's: The case of Star Wars Galaxies. In Gibbs, D., & Krause, K.-L. (Eds.), *Cyberlines 2.0: Languages and cultures of the Internet* (2nd ed., *Vol. 1*, pp. 177–198). Albert Park, Australia: James Nicholas Publishers.

Stănescu, I. A., Ştefan, S., & Roceanu, I. (2011). Interoperability in serious games. In *Proceedings of the 7th International Scientific Conference "eLearning and Software for Education"*, (pp. 28-29). April 2011, Romania.

StarLogo. (2010). *Computer program*. MIT: Schneller Teacher Education Program.

Steinkuehler, C. (2008). Cognition and literacy in massively multiplayer online games. In J. Coiro, K. C., C. Lanskear, & D. Leu (Eds.), *Handbook of research on new literacies* (pp. 611-634). Mahwah, NJ: Erlbaum.

Steinkuehler, C. (2006). Massively multiplayer online video gaming as participiation in a discourse. *Mind, Culture, and Activity, 13*, 38–52. doi:10.1207/s15327884mca1301_4

Steinkuehler, C. (2010). Video games and digital literacies. *Journal of Adolescent & Adult Literacy, 54*(1). doi:10.1598/JAAL.54.1.7

Steinkuehler, C., & King, B. (2009). Digital literacies for the disengaged: Creating after school contexts to support boys' game-based literacy skills. *Horizon, 17*(1), 47–59. doi:10.1108/10748120910936144

Sullivan, A., Mateas, M., & Wardrip-Fruin, N. (2009). Questbrowser: Making quests playable with computer-assisted design. In *The Proceedings of Digital Arts and Culture*, Irvine, CA

Sullivan, F. R. (2009). Risk and responsibility: A self-study of teaching with Second Life. *Journal of Interactive Learning Research, 20*(3), 337–357.

Sweller, J. (2010). Element interactivity and intrinsic, extraneous, and germane cognitive load. *Educational Psychology Review, 22*(2). doi:10.1007/s10648-010-9128-5

Sweller, J., Ayres, P., & Kalyuga, S. (2011). *Cognitive load theory.* New York, NY: Springer. doi:10.1007/978-1-4419-8126-4

Taguchi, E., Gorsuch, G., & Sasamoto, E. (2006). Developing second and foreign language reading fluency and its effect on comprehension: A missing link. [from http://www.readingmatrix.com/articles/taguchi_gorsuch_sasamoto/article.pdf]. *The Reading Matrix, 6*(2), 1–17. Retrieved January 8, 2011

Takatalo, J., Hakkinen, J., Kaistinen, J., & Nyman, G. (2011). User experience in digital games: Differences between laboratory and home. *Simulation & Gaming, 42*(5), 656–673.

Tan, A. (1999). Text mining: The state of the art and the challenges. In *Proceedings of Pacific Asia Conference on Knowledge Discovery and Data Mining PAKDD'99 Workshop on Knowledge Discovery from Advanced Databases*, pp. 65-70.

Tan, P., Ling, S., & Ting, C. (2007). Adaptive digital game-based learning framework. In *Proceedings of the 2nd International Conference on Digital Interactive Media in Entertainment and Arts.* ACM Press.

Tennant, M. (1988). *Psychology and adult learning.* Routledge. doi:10.4324/9780203441619

Thai, A. M., Lowenstein, D., Ching, D., & Rejeski, D. (2009). *Game changer: Investing in digital play to advance children's learning and health* [policy brief]. The Joan Ganz Cooney Center at Sesame Workshop. Retrieved from http://www.joanganzcooney-center.org/Reports-abc.html

The Amazing Race [Computer software]. (2010). San Francisco, CA: Ubisoft.

The Entertainment Software Association (ESA). (2011). *Essential facts about the computer game industry, 2011.* Retrieved January 8, 2011, from http://www.theesa.com/facts/pdfs/ESA_EF_2011.pdf

The Henry J. Kaiser Family Foundation. (2002). *Children and video games.* Retrieved January 04, 2012, from http://www.kff.org/entmedia/3271-index.cfm

The Higher Education Academy English Subject Centre. (2006, 11th December, 2007). *Theatron 3 – Educational undertakings in Second Life.*

The Horizon Report. (2007). *EDUCAUSE learning initiative: The New Media Consortium.* Retrieved January 8, 2011, from http://www.nmc.org/pdf/2007_Horizon_Report.pdf

The Oregon Trail [Computer software]. (2011). Mechanicville, NY: SVG Distribution.

The Partnership for 21st Century Skills. (2011). *P21 common core toolkit: A guide to aligning the common core state standards with the framework for 21st century skills.* Retrieved April 30, 2012, from http://www.p21.org/storage/documents/P21CommonCoreToolkit.pdf

Thiagarajan, S. (1998). The myths and realities of simulations in performance technology. *Educational Technology, 38*(5).

Thorne, S., Wheatley, J., & Purushotma, R. (2009). *10 key principles for designing video games for foreign language learning.* Retrieved January 8, 2011 from http://lingual-games.wordpress.com/article/10-key-principles-for-designing-video-27mkxqba7b13d-2/

Compilation of References

Thorne, S. L. (2008). Transcultural communication in open internet environments and massively multiplayer online games. In Magnan, S. (Ed.), *Mediating discourse online* (pp. 305–327). Amsterdam, The Netherlands: John Benjamins.

Torrente, J., del Blanco, Á., Marchiori, E. J., Moreno-Ger, P., & Fernández-Manjón, B. (2010). <e-Adventure>: Introducing educational games in the learning process. *Proceedings of the IEEE EDUCON 2010 Conference (Special issue e-Madrid)*, 14-16 April 2010, Madrid, Spain.

Torrente, J., Moreno-Ger, P., Martínez-Ortiz, I., & Fernández-Manjón, B. (2009). Integration and deployment of educational games in e-learning environments: The learning object model meets educational gaming. *Journal of Educational Technology & Society*, *12*(4), 359–371.

Torres, R. (2009). *Learning on a 21st century platform: Gamestar Mechanic as a means to game design and systems-thinking sklils within a nodal ecology*. (PhD Dissertation), New York University, New York.

Towne, M. D. (1995). *Learning and instruction in simulation environments*. Englewood Cliffs, NJ: Educational Technology Publications.

Trefry, G. (2010). *Casual game design: Designing play for the gamer in all of us*. Burlington, MA: Morgan Kaufmann.

Tversky, A., & Kahneman, D. (1981). The framing of decisions and the psychology of choice. *Science*, *211*(4481), 453–458. Retrieved from http://www.ncbi.nlm.nih.gov/pubmed/7455683doi:10.1126/science.7455683

U.S. Department of Education Office of Educational Technology. (2010). *Transforming American education—Learning powered by technology (executive summary)*. Retrieved from http://www.ed.gov/sites/default/files/netp2010-execsumm.pdf

U.S. Department of Education, Institute of Education Sciences, National Center for Education Statistics. (2009). *National assessment of educational progress (NAEP), 2009 science assessment*. Retrieved from http://www.nagb.org/publications/frameworks/science-09.pdf

UK Dept of Health. (2011). *Obesity – Public health*. Retrieved 26 January, 2012, from http://www.dh.gov.uk/en/Publichealth/Obesity/index.htm

Urhahne, D., Schanze, S., Bell, T., Mansfield, A., & Holmes, J. (2010). Role of the teacher in computer-supported collaborative inquiry learning. *International Journal of Science Education*, *32*(2), 221–243. doi:10.1080/09500690802516967

Usart, M., Romero, M., & Almirall, E. (2011). Impact of the feeling of knowledge explicitness in the learners participation and performance in a collaborative game based learning activity. *Lecture Notes in Computer Science*, *6944*, 23–35. doi:10.1007/978-3-642-23834-5_3

Vallerand, R. J., Fortier, M. S., & Guay, F. (1997). Self-determination and persistence in a real-life setting: Toward a motivational model of high school dropout. *Journal of Personality and Social Psychology*, *72*(5), 1161–1176. doi:10.1037/0022-3514.72.5.1161

Valley, K. (1997). Learning styles and the design of courseware. *ALT-J Association for Learning Technology Journal*, *5*(2), 42–51. doi:10.1080/0968776970050205

Van Eck, R. (2006). Digital game-based learning: It's not just the digital natives who are restless. *EDUCAUSE Review, 41*(2), 1–16.

Van Eck, R. (2007). The building artificially intelligent learning games. In Gibson, D., Aldrich, C., & Prensky, M. (Eds.), *Games and simulations in online learning: Research and development frameworks*. Hershey, PA: Information Science Publishing.

Van Merriënboer, J. J. G., & Kester, L. (2005). The four-component instructional design model: Multimedia principles in environments for complex learning. In Mayer, R. E. (Ed.), *Cambridge handbook of multimedia learning* (pp. 71–93). Cambridge, UK: Cambridge University Press. doi:10.1017/CBO9780511816819.006

Van Woerkom, M., & Croon, M. (2008). Operationalising critically reflective work behavior. *Personnel Review, 37*(3), 317–331. doi:10.1108/00483480810862297

Vankúš, P. (2008). Games based learning in teaching of mathematics at lower secondary school. *Acta Didactica Universitatis Comenianae - Mathematics, 8,* 103-120.

Vaughn, B. J., & Horner, R. (1997). Identifying instructional tasks that occasion problem behaviors and assessing the effects of student versus teacher choice among these tasks. *Journal of Applied Behavior Analysis, 30*(2), 299–312. doi:10.1901/jaba.1997.30-299

Vogel, J. J., Vogel, D. S., Cannon-Bowers, J., Bowers, C. A., Muse, K., & Wright, M. (2006). Computer gaming and interactive simulations for learning: A meta-analysis. *Journal of Educational Computing Research, 34*(3), 229–243. doi:10.2190/FLHV-K4WA-WPVQ-H0YM

Vygotsky, L. S. (1978). *Mind and society: The development of higher mental processes*. Cambridge, MA: Harvard University Press.

WA Dept of Health. (2011). *Healthy options WA: Food and nutrition policy for WA health services and facilities*. Retrieved 15 September, 2001, from http://www.healthyoptions.health.wa.gov.au/visitors/traffic_light.cfm

Wagner, C., & Ip, R. K. F. (2009). Action learning with Second Life: A pilot study. *Journal of Information Systems Education, 20*(2), 249–258.

Wakefield, J. S., Warren, S. J., & Alsobrook, M. (2012). Learning and teaching as communicative actions: Tweeting global policy challenges. *Knowledge Management & E-Learning: An International Journal, 3*(4), 563–584.

Wall, J., & Ahmed, V. (2008). Use of a simulation game in delivering blended lifelong learning in the construction industry - Opportunities and challenges. *Computers & Education, 50*(4), 1383–1393. doi:10.1016/j.compedu.2006.12.012

Wallner, G., & Kriglstein, S. (2011). Design and evaluation of the educational game DOGeometry - A case study. In *Proceedings of the 8th International Conference on Advances in Computer Entertainment Technology*. ACM Press.

Wallner, G., & Kriglstein, S. (2012). A spatiotemporal visualization approach for the analysis of gameplay data. In *Proceedings of the 30th Annual SIGCHI Conference on Human Factors in Computing Systems*. ACM Press.

Compilation of References

Warren, S. J. (2010). *Broken Window codex* (3rd ed. Vol. 2). Denton, TX: ThinkTank-Two@UNT.

Warren, S. J. (2005). *Archfall (Vol. 1)*. Bloomington, IN: Quest Atlantis Publishers.

Warren, S. J., Dondlinger, M., McLeod, J., & Bigenho, C. (2011). Opening the door: An evaluation of the efficacy of a problem-based learning game. *Computers & Education, 58*, 1–15.

Warren, S. J., & Jones, G. (2008). Yokoi's theory of lateral innovation: Applications for learning game design. *I-Manager's Journal of Educational Technology, 5*, 32–43.

Warren, S. J., & Lin, L. (2012). Ethical considerations in the design and use of educational games. In Yang, H. H., & Yuen, S. C.-Y. (Eds.), *Handbook of research on practices and outcomes in virtual worlds and environments* (1st ed., *Vol. 1*, pp. 1–18). Hershey, PA: IGI Global.

Warren, S. J., & Stein, R. (2008). Simulating teaching experience with role-play. In Gibson, D., & Baek, Y. (Eds.), *Digital simulations for improving education: Learning through artificial teaching environments* (*Vol. 1*). Hershey, PA: IGI Global.

Warren, S. J., Stein, R., Dondlinger, M. J., & Barab, S. (2009). A look inside a design process: Blending instructional design and game principles to target writing skills. *Journal of Educational Computing Research, 40*(3), 295–301. doi:10.2190/EC.40.3.c

Warschauer, M., Meskill, C., & Rosenthal, J. W. (2000). Technology and second language teaching. In Rosenthal, J. (Ed.), *Handbook of undergraduate second language education*. Mahwah, NJ: Lawrence Erlbaum.

Waters, J. K. (2009). A "Second Life" for educators. *T.H.E. Journal, 36*(1), 29–34.

Watson, W. R. (2010). Games for social studies education. In Hirumi, A. (Ed.), *Playing games in school: Video games and simulations for primary and secondary education* (pp. 33–56). Eugene, OR: International Society for Technology in Education.

Watson, W. R., Mong, C. J., & Harris, C. A. (2011). A case study of the in-class use of a video game for teaching high school history. *Computers & Education, 56*, 466–474. doi:10.1016/j.compedu.2010.09.007

Webb, M. E. (2005). Affordances of ICT in science learning: Implications for an integrated pedagogy. *International Journal of Science Education, 27*(6), 705–735. doi:10.1080/09500690500038520

Webb, M., & Cox, M. (2004). A review of pedagogy related to information and communications technology. *Technology, Pedagogy and Education, 13*(3), 235–286. doi:10.1080/14759390400200183

Webb, N., Nemer, K., & Ing, M. (2006). Small-group reflections: Parallels between teacher discourse and student behavior in peer-directed groups. *Journal of the Learning Sciences, 15*, 63–119. doi:10.1207/s15327809jls1501_8

Weber, R., Ritterfiled, U., & Mathiak, K. (2006). Does playing violent video games induce aggression? Empirical evidence of any functional magnetic resonance imaging study. *Media Psychology, 8*, 39–60. doi:10.1207/S1532785XMEP0801_4

Wellings, J., & Levine, M. H. (2009). *The digital promise: Transforming learning with innovative uses of technology: A white paper on literacy and learning in a new media age* [white paper]. The Joan Ganz Cooney Center at Sesame Workshop. Retrieved from http://www.joanganzcooneycenter.org/Reports-abc.html

Wentzel, K. R. (1997). Student motivation in middle school: The role of perceived pedagogical caring. *Journal of Educational Psychology, 89*(3), 411–419. doi:10.1037/0022-0663.89.3.411

Werner, L., & Freeman, C. J. (2001). *Arts for academic achievement: arts integration—A vehicle for changing teacher practice.* Minneapolis Public Schools.

Westera, W., Nadolskl, R. J., Hummel, H. G. K., & Woperels, I. G. J. H. (2008). Serious games for higher education: A framework for reducing design complexity. *Journal of Computer Assisted Learning, 24,* 420–432. doi:10.1111/j.1365-2729.2008.00279.x

Weusijana, B. K., Svihla, V., Gawel, D., & Bransford, J. (2009). MUVEs and experiential learning: Some examples. *Innovate: Journal of Online Education, 5*(5).

Whelchel, A. (2003). Using civilization simulation video games in the world history classroom. *World History Connected, 4*(2), Retrieved from http://worldhistoryconnected.press.illinois.edu/4.2/whelchel.html

Whitton, N. (2007). *An investigation into the potential of collaborative computer game-based learning in higher education.* PhD Thesis, Napier University, Edinburg, UK. Retrieved January 8, 2011, from http://playthinklearn.net/?page_id=8

Whitton, N. (2008). *Alternate reality games for developing student autonomy and peer learning.* Paper presented at LICK 2008. Edinburgh. Retrieved 14th January, 2012, from http://www2.napier.ac.uk/transform/LICK_proceedings/Nicola_Whitton.pdf

Whitton, N. (2010). *Learning with digital games.* New York, NY: Routledge.

Whitton, N., & Hollins, P. (2008). Collaborative virtual gaming worlds in higher education. *Association for Learning Technology Journal, 16*(3), 221–229. doi:10.1080/09687760802526756

Wii Fit [Computer software]. (2008). Redmond, WA: Nintendo of America.

Wii Sports [Computer software]. (2006). Redmond, WA: Nintendo of America Inc.

Wii Sports Resort [Computer software]. (2009). Redmond, WA: Nintendo of America.

Wiley, D. A. (2000). *Connecting learning objects to instructional design theory: A definition, a metaphor, and a taxonomy.* Association for Instructional Technology & Association for Educational Communications and Technology. doi:10.1002/stab.200710001

Wiley, D. A. (2007). The learning objects literature. In Spector, M. J., Merrill, D. M., & Merrienboer, V. J. (Eds.), *Handbook of research on educational communications and technology* (pp. 345–353). New York, NY: Lawrence Erlbaum Associates.

Wilkinson, S., Crerar, A., & Falchikov N. (1997). *Book versus hypertext: exploring the association between usability and cognitive style.*

Williams, L. (2001). *Integrating pair programming into a software development process*. Paper presented at the Fourteenth Conference on Software Engineering Education and Training.

Williams, D. (2006). A brief social history of game play. In Vorderer, P., & Jennings, B. (Eds.), *Playing video games: Motives, responses, and consequences* (pp. 197–212). Mahwah, NJ: Lawrence Erlbaum Associates.

Williamson, B. (2009). *Computer games, schools and young people: A report for educators on using games for learning*. Bristol, UK: Futurelab. Retrieved 14th January, 2012, from http://archive.futurelab.org.uk/resources/documents/project_reports/becta/Games_and_Learning_educators_report.pdf

Wilson, B., & Cole, P. (1991). A review of cognitive teaching models. *Educational Technology Research and Development*, *39*(4), 47–64. doi:10.1007/BF02296571

Winn, W. (2002). Current trends in educational technology research: The study of learning environments. *Educational Psychology Review*, *14*(3), 331–351. doi:10.1023/A:1016068530070

Winter Sports. (2007). *The Ultimate Challenge* [Computer software]. Santa Monica, CA: Conspiracy Entertainment.

Wong, W. L., Shen, C., Nocera, L., Carriazo, E., Tang, F., & Bugga, S. Ritterfeld, U. (2007). *Serious video game effectiveness*. Paper presented at the ACE '07.

WordJong Party [Computer software]. (2008). Plymouth, MN: Destineer.

World Health Organisation. (2012). *Childhood overweight and obesity*. Retrieved 26 January, 2012, from http://www.who.int/dietphysicalactivity/childhood/en/

Wrzesien, M., & Alcañiz Raya, M. (2010). Learning in serious virtual worlds: Evaluation of learning effectiveness and appeal to students in the E-Junior project. *Computers & Education*, *55*(1), 178–187. doi:10.1016/j.compedu.2010.01.003

Yates, G. C. R. (2005). "How obvious": Personal reflections on the database of educational psychology and effective teaching research. *Educational Psychology*, *25*(6), 681–700. doi:10.1080/01443410500345180

Yee, N. (2005). Motivations of play in MMORPGs. *Proceedings of International DiGRA Conference*. Vancouver.

Yee, N. (2006). The demographics, motivations and derived experiences of users of massively-multiuser online graphical environments. *Presence (Cambridge, Mass.)*, *15*, 309–329. doi:10.1162/pres.15.3.309

Yin, R. K. (2009). *Case study research: Design and methods* (4th ed.). Thousand Oaks, CA: SAGE.

Yu, T. (2009). Learning in the virtual world: The pedagogical potentials of massively multiplayer online role playing games. *International Education Studies, 2*.

Yusoff, A., Crowder, R., & Gilbert, L. (2010) Validation of serious games attributes using the technology acceptance model. In *The 2nd International IEEE Conference on Serious Games and Virtual Worlds for serious applications* (VSGAMES 2010), March 25-26, 2010, Braga, Portugal, (pp. 45-51).

Zacharia, Z. (2003). Beliefs, attitudes, and intentions of science teachers regarding the educational use of computer simulations and inquiry-based experiments in physics. *Journal of Research in Science Teaching*, *40*(8), 792–823. doi:10.1002/tea.10112

Zagal, J. P., Fernandez-Vara, C., & Mateas, M. (2008). Rounds, levels, and waves: The early evolution of gameplay segmentation. *Games and Culture*, *3*(2), 175–198. doi:10.1177/1555412008314129

Zaphiris, P., & Wilson, S. (2010). Computer games and sociocultural play: An activity theoretical perspective. *Games and Culture*, *5*(4), 354–380. doi:10.1177/1555412009360411

Zhao, Y., & Lai, C. (2009). Massively multiplayer online role playing games (MMORPGS) and foreign language education. In Ferdig, R. E. (Ed.), *Handbook of research on effective electronic gaming in education* (pp. 402–421). New York, NY: IDEA Group.

Zickuhr, K. (2011). *Generations and their gadgets*. Pew/Internet. Retrieved from http://www.pewinternet.org/Reports/2011/Generations-and-gadgets/Report/Game-consoles.aspx

Zientek, L. R., Capraro, M. M., & Capraro, R. M. (2008). Reporting practices in quantitative teacher education research: One look at the evidence cited in the AERA panel report. *Educational Researcher*, *37*(4), 208–216. doi:10.3102/0013189X08319762

Zimmerman, E., & Salen, K. (2003). *Rules of play: Game design fundamentals*. Cambridge, MA: The MIT Press.

Zollinger, S. W., & Martinson, B. (2010). Do all designers think alike? What research has to say. *Institute for Learning Styles Research Journal*, *1*, 1–15.

Zon. (2011). *About Zon*. Retrieved January 5, 2012, from http://enterzon.com/#about

Zull, J. (2002). *The art of changing the brain: Enriching the practice of teaching by exploring the biology of learning*. Sterling, VA: Stylus Publishing.

Zweben, S. (2011). *Taulbee survey report: 2009-2010*. Washington, DC: Computing Research Association.

Zyda, M. (2005). From visual simulation to virtual reality to games. *IEEE Computer*, *38*(9).

Zylka, J., & Nutzinger, H. P. (2010). Educational games in formal education – Results of an explorative study using an educational game in school. *Proceedings of the International Conference on Computer-aided Learning 2010 (ICL 2010)*, (pp. 954-963). 15-17 September, Hasselt, Belgium.

About the Contributors

Youngkyun Baek is a Professor and Director of Game Studio at Department of Educational Technology at Boise State University. With a background in both computing and education, he is interested in research and design of educational games, especially mobile games. His research focuses on the design, implementation, and evaluation of games of learning.

Nicola Whitton is a Research Fellow at Manchester Metropolitan University. With a background in both computing and education, she is interested innovative ways in which to engage students in learning, particularly in the context of Higher Education. Her research focuses on the design, implementation, and evaluation of games for learning, the use of technologies to support learning, and the used of student-centered and play-based learning methods.

* * *

Terence Ahern is an Associate Professor in Instructional Design and Technology in the College of Human Resources and Education at West Virginia University. He received his doctorate from Penn State. His research interests are in the use of instructional technology in the classroom. He has published extensively in the areas of distance education and social network media. Further, he is a Software Engineer and has created the IdeaWeb and RedPencil Web-based applications. He has researched these applications and is interested in the use of the technology to further collaboration and foster interaction within learning environments. Currently, he is using his expertise in instructional design and programming to create game-based learning environments for the middle school classroom.

Mete Akcaoglu is a Ph.D. student at the Educational Psychology and Educational Technology Program at Michigan State University. His current research interests include, but are not limited to, gaming in education, distance education theories and their practical applications, educational policy, and comparative international education research. Previously, he worked with a team of creative individuals on creating an online MMORPG, Zon, which aims to teach Chinese to learners from all over the world. Recently, he is interested in using object-oriented game design platforms (i.e. Microsoft Kodu) as a scaffold for fostering higher order thinking skills (i.e. problem solving) in middle school settings. To this end, he both worked at summer and after school camps in the US, and created an academic summer camp teaching kids how to design games in Turkey.

Kate Anderson is a Lecturer in Science Education at the University of Sydney. She was also involved as an ICT Pedagogy Officer on the Australian Teaching Teachers for the Future Project. Prior to her role at Sydney University, Kate worked as a Head Teacher of Science and she has extensive experience as a secondary science teacher. Kate's areas of research lie in science education, inquiry-based learning and pre-service teacher training. Her Doctoral research focuses on the nature of science and inquiry learning.

Stănescu Ioana Andreea is a Researcher at the Advanced Distributed Learning Partnership Laboratory established at CAROL I National Defence University in Bucharest. She also works as a Project Manager at Advanced Technology Systems, Romania. Her research focuses on game ecosystems, game-based learning, interoperability and semantics, decision support systems, knowledge management, mobile technologies, translation software, and creative learning. She is an ICT evaluator within the Joint Call SEE-ERA.NET PLUS and a member of the European Association for Language Testing and Assessment (EALTA). Since 2009 she is the Manager of the eLearning Think Tank Initiative that reunites over 25 researchers that operate at international level in the field of educational technology. She has been involved in the development and management of national and international RDI initiatives and currently activates within several European projects: the European Game and Learning Alliance (GaLA) Network – leading the technical Committee on Interoperability and Semantics; Game-Enhanced Learning (GEL).

Antonio Ascolese earned a PhD in "Subjective well-being, health, and cross cultural communication" at Milano-Bicocca University. He graduated in Developmental and Communication Psychology (Master's degree) in 2006 at the Catholic University of Milan. He completed a post-doc as Researcher on serious games at CESCOM (Centre for Research in Communication Science) at Milano-Bicocca University. Presently, he's working at Imaginary SRL, as Project Manager on serious games. His research interests include positive psychology, psychology of nonverbal communication, psychology of emotion, and learning processes in simulated environments. He is a Chartered Psychologist since 2007.

Michelle Aubrecht is a game based learning specialist. She is making a multi-disciplinary educational video game about the Newark Earthworks. On this project, she is the coordinator and environment artist and part of the game development team. This project is funded by the National Endowment for the Humanities. In addition, she is the project coordinator for Earthworks Badges. In conjunction with Digital Watershed, she is developing an interactive badge system and website funded by HASTAC Digital Media and Learning competition 4. She also designed and hosted the game-based learning area for eTech Ohio's 2012 conference.

R.S. Aylett has actively researched Artificial Intelligence for 20 years, starting at the AI Applications Institute at University of Edinburgh in 1989. She researches architectures for virtual agents, with particular emphasis on affective components. Professor Aylett coordinated the highly successful EU IST Framework V project VICTEC and currently coordinates the FP6 IST project eCIRCUS. She also co-ordinated the EU Asia-Europe IT&C project ELVIS – Empathic Learning with Virtual Interactive Synthetic characters. Professor Aylett has over 130 publications in journals, book chapters, and refereed conferences, and is the co-chair of the international workshop Intelligent Virtual Agents.

Christina Badman is the Dean of Curriculum and Middle School Language Arts Teacher (6th-8th grade) for Sacred Heart Interparochial School in Pinellas Park, Florida. She has her Bachelor's degree in Elementary Education from Wright State University in Dayton, Ohio and her Master's degree in Curriculum and Instructional Technology from Grand Canyon University in Phoenix, Arizona. Christina has been teaching for sixteen years and is always looking for ways to improve and further guide students through the learning process. She has been integrating the Wii gaming system into her curriculum for the past two years and is constantly amazed by the increased student engagement, excitement, and achievement the game lessons and units yield. Christina and co-presenter, Matthew DeNote, have presented about the topic using games in the classroom at both the Florida Educational Technology Conference in January 2012 and the 4T Virtual Conference in May of 2012.

Johannes Biba worked several years as primary school teacher after finishing his studies to obtain a degree as primary school teacher. Then he started his studies at the University of Vienna in Psychology and Pedagogy. After finishing his Dissertation, he is working now as a psychologist and professor at the University College of Teacher Education Vienna and lecturer at the Private University of Health Sciences, Medical Informatics and Technology, UMIT.

Catarina Calado received her degree in Psychological Sciences from Faculdade de Psicologia e Ciências da Educação, Universidade de Coimbra, in 2008. Subsequently, she defended her Master's of Psychology on the topic of vocational identity at the University of Coimbra, in 2010. Presently, she works as a Psychologist in Akademia. Research interests are in experiential learning, cognitive science, and neuropsychological bases of learning.

Jos Darling is a Senior Lecturer and the Department of Mechanical Engineering Director of Learning and Teaching. His research is in the area of vehicle dynamics and engineering education, specialising in three-wheeled vehicle dynamics and game-based learning.

Matthew DeNote is the Director of Technology for Espiritu Santo Catholic School in Safety Harbor, Florida. He has a Bachelor's degree in Elementary Education from Barry University in Miami, Florida and his Master's degree in Curriculum and Instructional Technology from University of Florida in Gainesville, Florida. Matthew has been teaching and facilitating the integration of technology in schools for nineteen years and is currently focusing on implementing a 1 to 1 program at his school with middle school students. He has been utilizing the Nintendo Wii gaming system into multiple curriculums for the past three years and has been successful in integrating this gaming platform into different school environments. Matthew and co-presenter, Christina Badman, have presented about the topic using games in the classroom at both the Florida Educational Technology Conference in January 2012 and the 4T Virtual Conference in May of 2012.

Andy Diament is a Senior Lecturer of AS/A2 physics at Penwith College of Further Education. Andy Diament and is also an experienced user and deliverer of e-learning.

Angela Dowling, originally from Racine, Wisconsin, earned a BS in Life Sciences from the University of Wisconsin. She also attended West Virginia University where she earned a MA in Secondary Education and an EdD in Instructional Design and Technology. She currently is in her 19th year at Suncrest Middle School in Morgantown, WV and teaches 8th Grade Science. Dowling has collaborated in the writing of several grants including a $30,000 Tech Connect grant and a $10,000 Toyota Tapestry grant. Dowling has presented at various state and national level educational conferences, including the West Virginia Science Teachers Association Conference, the West Virginia State Technology Conference, the International Society for Technology in Education Conference, and the Society for Information Technology in Teacher Education Conference.

Benjamin Drew is a Senior Lecturer in Mechanical and Motorsport Engineering at the University of the West of England, in Bristol.

John Dudley is Manager of the Motor Vehicle College of Vocational Education. He teaches science and maths to engineering students. He has received funding from Eduserv to review resources for motor vehicle tutors and to publish web based tutor guides relating to a number of vocational courses.

Cristina Ferreira received her degree on Comunication Sciences from Faculdade de Ciências Sociais e Humanas at Universidade Nova de Lisboa, in 2000. Subsequently she defended her post graduate on education sciences, on the topic of analysis and intervention in education, at the University Nova de Lisboa, in 2008. Presently she works as Pedagogical Director in Akademia. Research interests are in the impact of virtual environments in learning contexts. Some current work includes the development of an online study platform.

Vilma Galstaun is a Lecturer in ICT in the Bachelor of Education and Master of Teaching programs at the University of Sydney. In recent years, she has systematically redesigned core technology units to capture some of the essential qualities of knowledge required by teachers for technology integration in their teaching. Prior to her appointment at the University of Sydney, Vilma was Senior Curriculum Officer for Primary Education at the NSW Board of Studies. She is a former primary school teacher with a broad range of leadership experience in primary education and professional learning. She is currently completing her PhD studies at Macquarie University. Vilma's Doctoral research investigates curriculum development processes and the role of stakeholders.

Carl Gavin is a Senior Lecturer and Deputy Director of the Managing Projects executive education programme at Manchester Business School. He founded Lateral Visions, a Serious Games software company that developed 'Racing Academy' and was Managing Director of the company for nine years.

Roxana Hadad, as Director of Math, Science, and Technology at the Chicago Teacher's Center at Northeastern Illinois University (CTC@NEIU), designs, develops, and implements STEM (science, technology, engineering, and math) program services for Chicago-area students and teachers. She is currently a Doctoral student in Educational Psychology at the University of Illinois at Chicago. Her research focuses on increasing the number of students from underrepresented populations in the field of computer science. Roxana received her Master's degree in Interactive Telecommunications from New York University's Tisch School of the Arts and has a Bachelor's degree in English and Spanish from the University of Illinois at Urbana-Champaign. She has been named an Adobe Education Leader, a Google Certified Teacher, an NYU Graduate and Professional Opportunity Fellow, and a National Hispanic Foundation for the Arts Fellow.

Chris Haskell, with experience as a Music Educator, an M.S. in Educational Technology (Boise State, 2008), and an Ed.D. in Education, Curriculum and Instruction, Foundational Studies (Boise State, 2012), Dr. Chris Haskell has been teaching as a Clinical Assistant Professor in the Department of Educational Technology at Boise State University since 2007. In addition to teaching, he is an active presenter at conferences throughout the West sharing his knowledge and interest in online learning and education through social networks, virtual worlds, and gaming.

Brian Herrig is a seventh and eighth grade Technology Education teacher at Canonsburg Middle School, a 2011 Pennsylvania Don Eichhorn and National Schools to Watch middle school located in Canonsburg, Pennsylvania. He earned his Bachelor of Science in Education from California University of Pennsylvania in 2003 and his Master of Arts Teaching from California University of Pennsylvania in 2012. His research interests include cyber safety and middle level education. His publications and presentations include the incorporation of programming into middle level Technology Education and the implications of cyber safety for students and parents.

Danielle Herro is an Assistant Professor of Digital Media and Learning at Clemson University; she was formerly an Instructional Technology Administrator in the Oconomowoc Area Schools in Wisconsin. Danielle has worked as classroom teacher, Technology Resource Teacher, and Coordinator. Her research interests involve examining the influence of social media, games, and emerging technologies on learners and finding ways to help teachers and students connect relevant, engaging tools to learning. Danielle has extensive experience writing, implementing, and evaluating content-focused technology curriculum in K-12 schools. She recently served as chair of Wisconsin's Department of Education Curriculum and Assessment Digital Advisory Committee and as a lead participant in the Consortium for School Networking (CoSN) Leading Edge Schools cadre.

Christopher Horne is currently a Lecturer at Forth Valley College, a Further Education college located in Central Scotland. He has been working within Further Education for the past 10 years, where he specialises in Sport and Fitness studies. Previously, Chris worked as a Web Developer and Animator for a number of international blue chip clients. He recently graduated from Edinburgh Napier University with an MSc in Blended and Online education, and during those studies developed a keen interest in combining both elements of both aforementioned vocations in order to help foster the encouragement of utilising Technology Enhanced Learning within non-classroom based educational environments. This has led him to focus to his current academic study and development within the fields of blended learning, mobile learning, exergaming, and games based learning.

Ioanna Iacovides is currently working on a project investigating ways to improve the safety of interactive medical devices. Her research is focused on understanding errors that occur when using devices such as infusion pumps and developing methods to evaluate usability in this context. Previously, she has been involved in researching digital games with respect to considering how learning and involvement come together in practice.

Helene Jennings is a Senior Fellow at ICF International, responsible for conducting and overseeing research and evaluation studies. She has over 25 years of professional experience, carrying out projects in a diverse set of areas including literacy, STEM (science, technology, engineering, and mathematics), educational technology, design education, and international studies. Additionally, she has directed many community service, welfare-related research, and technical assistance assignments. She has conducted numerous education studies using randomized controlled trials (RCTs) and is also skilled in both survey and case study methodologies. A former teacher, she has led a number of studies designed to reach a broad set of learners through technology and games and simulations. She has focused on producing final reports in engaging and audience-appropriate formats. She has a MA from Stanford University.

Richard Joiner is a Senior Lecturer in the Department of Psychology at the University of Bath. His main area of research is the use of digital technology to support learning. He has long term interests in the use of digital games for supporting students learning and computer supported collaborative learning, with a particular interest in the role of technology for supporting the resolution of inter-individual conflict.

Shannon Kennedy-Clark is a Senior Lecturer in Academic Development at Australian Catholic University. In this role, she works across the University to embed academic and ICT literacy into degree programs. Prior to this position, Shannon was an ICT Pedagogy Officer on the Australian Teaching Teachers for the Future Project. Shannon has worked as a Lecturer in Education and Academic Communication both in Australia and overseas. Her PhD is on the use of computer games in computer-supported inquiry learning. Her research interests lie in game-based learning, discourse analysis, and pre-service teacher training.

Simone Kriglstein, studied Computer Science at the Vienna University of Technology and graduated with honors in 2005. Her diploma thesis was about "Visual Perception and Interface Design." She received her doctoral degree (Dr. techn., Computer Science, with honors) from the University of Vienna in 2011. In her Doctoral thesis she described an approach to the development process for ontology visualizations through the help of the human centered design approach. Since 2007, she is a Lecturer at the University of Vienna for the courses Visualization, Human Computer Interaction and Psychology, and Database Systems and also participated as a reviewer for several conferences (e.g., "CHI" and "VAST"). From 2007-2011 she worked at the University of Vienna as research assistant and teaching staff (Faculty of Computer Science, Research Group Workflow Systems and Technology). Since 2011, she works for several projects at the University of Vienna and the Vienna University of Technology.

Soojeong Lee is a Professor of Home Economics Education at Kyungnam University in South Korea. She is interested in the research on curriculum, teaching & learning, and evaluation in home economics education. Especially, her interest is in describing and analyzing the actual scene of teaching through both qualitative and quantitative research. Now, she is Director of the Korean Association of Home Economics Education, Director of the Korean Association of Practical Arts Education, Director of the Korean Association of Population Education, and a member of AERA. She serves as an Editor of the Society of Korean Practical Arts Education and an Editor of the Korean Society for the Vocational Education.

Theodore Lim is an active member within the Digital Tools Group; part of the EPSRC-funded Innovative Manufacturing Research Centre (IMRC) at Heriot-Watt University (www.smi.hw.ac.uk). As both an academic and researcher with considerable industrial experience, he has been instrumental in the research, analysis, and development of virtual engineering environments in a variety of product engineering domains and now focuses his work on the acquisition of engineering knowledge information management systems within all aspect of product engineering, with a particular emphasis on conceptual design. He has also implemented game-based learning methods in design and manufacturing taught courses. With over 40 international publications, a book, and the successful commercialisation of his novel feature recognition algorithms, he is now applying his knowledge and expertise to the domain of serious games, gameware, and computational biometrics for next generation engineering applications.

Sandy Louchart is a Lecturer in Human Computer Interaction and Interaction Design in the School of Mathematical and Computer Sciences (MACS) at Heriot-Watt University. His PhD, awarded by the University of Salford in 2007, explored the domain of interactive storytelling (IS) via the development of the emergent narrative concept. The work was conducted in the domains of artificial intelligence, synthetic characters, and interactive narratives, and involved the design of autonomous synthetic characters and their affect-based action/selection mechanisms to simulate characterisation within an interactive drama scenario. The research led to the development of a novel approach to synthetic character action/selection mechanisms featuring projection-based affective planning so as to select dramatically intense actions and events for interaction; the double appraisal action/selection mechanism. His work has been published internationally in intelligent agents, virtual reality, game, and interactive storytelling journals and conferences.

Iván Martínez-Ortiz is an Associate Professor in the Computer Science Studies at UCM and a member of the e-UCM research group. His research interests include e-learning technologies and the integration of educational modeling languages, serious games, and e-learning standardization. Within the group, he has led the development of tools to support diverse IMS educational specifications including the integration of games in the learning flow. He has contributed more than 40 academic publications in topics related to games based learning and technology enhanced learning. He is part of the e-learning CTN71/SC36 technical committee under the Spanish Standard Organization AENOR.

Gregory Mathews is the Media Designer in the Learning Design Development Unit at the School of Nursing & Midwifery, Flinders University, where he has been working since 2007. He previously worked as a professional multimedia designer, jointly fronting a multimedia business working in health education and gaming. Gregory has a keen interest in using affective design to motivate and engage students in blended learning. He is also interested in creating novel, active learning experiences, such as case-based learning environments and serious games. His co-work on "Vital Essence – Lymphoedema" was a finalist in the education category in the Australian Animation and Effects festival awards, he received a Silver Serif award from the Australian Institute of Professional Communicators for work on Adage Hypertension, and was the multimedia designer on the team that won an ALTC citation in 2011 for the Clinical Communication Program.

Mark McMahon is an Associate Professor and Director of Teaching and Learning in Edith Cowan University's School of Communications and Arts. He is responsible for its Creative Industries programs and coordinates the Games Design and Culture course. He has previously worked as a multimedia developer and instructional designer. Mark's PhD was in exploring approaches to developing metacognitive skills through learning technologies. His research interests are in the area of interface, information, and experiential design for elearning and serious games. He consults to industry in elearning and instructional design on projects such as the Australian Flexible Learning Framework – where he mentored the development of over 40 toolboxes of elearning for Australia's vocational education and training sector.

Pablo Moreno-Ger is an Associate Professor in the Dep. of Software Engineering and Artificial Intelligence. From a research perspective, he has a broad research experience on Web-based learning, adaptive learning, and educational games. He also has experience with educational standards and his research interests include many approaches to technology-enhanced learning. He was the original creator of the eAdventure project, a platform for the development of web-oriented educational adventure games. He has contributed more than 40 academic publications in topics related to games based learning and technology enhanced learning.

Dalia Morosini, Psychologist, graduated with honors in 2010 in Developmental and Communication Psychology at the Università Cattolica of Milan. During her studies she was particularly interested in issues such as: communication psychology, new media psychology and learning psychology. At present, she is involved in conceiving, designing, and writing contents of the serious games in the context of European research projects.

Amanda Müller's professional qualifications include a Doctor of Philosophy in English, a Graduate Certificate in Teaching English as a Second/Other Language, and a Graduate Certificate in Higher Education. Her research interests include educational gaming, computer-assisted language learning, cognition-based instructional design, second language acquisition, inter-language transfer, and applied linguistics. Her language-based interests include Japanese, German, Spanish, Scots, non-Standard English, and nonverbal communication. She currently provides English for specific purposes support to over 500 international students in the School of Nursing & Midwifery at Flinders University. Dr Müller is keen to collaborate with other international researchers and welcomes any opportunity to be involved with language-based projects.

Anjum Najmi is a Teaching Fellow in the Learning Technologies Department at the University of North Texas. She is working on her PhD. in Educational Computing through the College of Information, Library Science, and Technologies. Her research interests are problem-based learning, games and simulations, and distributed learning.

Chrissi Nerantzi is an Academic Developer at the University of Salford in the United Kingdom. She is leading the multi-disciplinary Postgraduate Certificate in Academic Practice Programme, a recognised teaching qualification in Higher Education for academics and professionals who support learning within the institution. Chrissi's background is in teaching Modern Foreign Languages and Translation. She has worked in educational institutions in Greece, Germany, and for the last 12 years, in the United Kingdom. After arriving in the UK, she continued her postgraduate studies and gained a Master's in Learning and Teaching in Higher Education and a Master's in Blended and Online Education, as well as additional postgraduate qualifications in Coaching and Mentoring in Education. Chrissi has been working since 2007 in teacher education and academic development in adult, further, and higher education. She is a passionate lifelong and lifewide learner and her approach to learning and teaching is experimental. Her current research interests are game-based learning, social media e-portfolios for professional development, open learning, peer observation, as well as mobile learning.

Scot Osterweil is the Creative Director of the MIT Education Arcade and a Research Director in the MIT Comparative Media Studies Program. He is a designer of award-winning educational games, working in both academic and commercial environments, and his work has focused on what is authentically playful in challenging academic subjects. He has designed games for computers, handheld devices, and multi-player on-line environments. Scot is the creator of the acclaimed *Zoombinis* series of math and logic games, and has led a number of projects in the Education Arcade, including *Vanished: The MIT/Smithsonian Curated Game* (environmental science), *Labyrinth* (math), *Kids Survey Network* (data and statistics), *Caduceus* (medical science), and *iCue* (history and civics). He is a founding member and Creative Director of the Learning Games Network (www.learninggamesnetwork.org) where he leads the Gates Foundation's *Language Learning Initiative* (ESL).

Martin Owen is an Independent Researcher and Developer in applying technology to support learning. He was formerly Director of Learning at Futurelab, researcher, teacher educator, and school teacher. He has specific interests in social & collaborative media, games for assessment & learning, how to invent and innovate, mobile & location technologies, using and designing smart objects, and designing learning.

Lucia Pannese graduated in Applied Mathematics, has extended experience in research projects with special attention to technology enhanced learning solutions, particularly based on the use of serious games. After working for more than 10 years in mainly technology companies with training and research/innovation responsibilities, in February 2004 she founded Imaginary S.R.L, a company belonging to the Innovation Network of the university Politecnico di Milano. Imaginary specialises in the design and development of serious games and virtual worlds. At present, she is covering the position of CEO and manager for international (research) activities. In October 2008 she founded Games2Growth Ltd based at the Serious Games Institute, Coventry University Technology Park, another SME specialising in the design and development of serious games and virtual worlds. With numerous Italian and international publications and presentations about serious games, learning, and training, she is often invited to international conferences dealing with the serious games and storytelling topic.

Joe Pereira teaches English as a Foreign Language at the British Council in Porto, Portugal. He holds an MA in Educational Technology & TESOL from The University of Manchester, where he focused his research on digital game-based language learning in virtual worlds. He has participated in projects involving digital game-based learning and virtual instruction in Second Life for the British Council, and was a Tutor and Researcher for the EU-funded AVALON project. Currently, his research interests have moved away from 3D virtual worlds to the completely text-based worlds of interactive fiction, which he considers to be the perfect digital game-based language learning tool.

João Pereira is Associate Professor at the Computer Science Department of the Technical University of Lisbon (Instituto Superior Técnico - IST/UTL) of the Technical University of Lisbon, Portugal, where he teaches Computer Graphics. João Pereira holds a PhD in Electrical and Computers Engineering (Computer Graphics) from IST/UTL, Technical University, earned in December 1996. He received also an MSc and a BsEE degree in Electrical and Computers Engineering from IST/UTL in 1989 and 1984, respectively. He coordinates the Visualization and Simulation action line of the VIMMI group at INESC-ID (Computer Systems Engineering Institute).

Michael Prilla is a Post-Doc Researcher at the Infomation and Technology Management working group at the University of Bichum, Germany. He holds a Diploma degree in Computer Science and a PhD in Engineering. Michael's work is focused on cooperation research, including fields such as computer supported cooperative work (CSCW), human computer interaction (HCI), computer supported collaborative learning (CSCL), and technology enhanced learning (TEL), as well as business process management (BPM). His special interest is the merging of digital and real world communication and cooperation, especially concerning the access to cooperation infrastructures. In the MIRROR project funded by the EC (http://www.mirror-project.eu/), Michael is responsible for a joint work package on collaborative knowledge creation. He has (co-) authored more than 50 national and international papers in books, conferences, and journals.

Shani Reid is a Technical Specialist at ICF International where she manages evaluation and research projects in the field of education. Her work has included evaluation and research in the areas of teacher professional development, mathematics education, reading, arts education, college and career readiness, online learning, and learning games. In addition to managing projects, Dr. Reid also often serves as the Lead Quantitative Analyst on studies. She has designed and conducted several quasi-experimental studies that examine the effect of a variety of interventions on student outcomes. Dr. Reid is a former middle and high school computer science teacher, and is an adjunct at The George Washington University's Graduate School of Education and Human Development where she also obtained her Doctorate in Curriculum and Instruction.

Claudia Ribeiro received her BsCS and MsC in Information Systems and Computer Engineering from the Technical University of Lisbon (Instituto Superior Técnico - IST/UTL), Portugal. Presently, she works as a Researcher in the Visualization and Intelligent Multimodal Interfaces Group in INESC-ID where she is doing her PhD. She has also participated in several European founded projects focusing on: serious games, virtual environments, artificial intelligence and digital storytelling. Since 2007, she lectures several courses of the BsCS and MSc in Information Systems and Computer Engineering at IST/UTL, addressing topics such as: artificial intelligence, simulation and game development, and databases. Research interests are in Agent-based modelling, game theory, simulations, artificial intelligence, and serious games.

J.M. Ritchie specialises in design, manufacturing, and manufacturing management. With over 150 publications, recent research interests include product development applications including the use of virtual reality in design and manufacture, rapid prototyping, design process capability analysis and mechanical engineering knowledge and information capture. He has applied game concepts in engineering manufacturing taught courses. He has been involved in a large number of UK-funded research projects and Knowledge Transfer Partnerships (KTPs) with industry, as well as EU-funded work. He is a leading member of Heriot-Watt University's IMRC and heads the Institute of Manufacturing, Process, and Energy Engineering.

Ion Roceanu is Director of Advanced Distributed Learning Department, Member of the Romanian Scientists Academy, and Member of the Advanced Distributed Learning Work Group of NATO and Partnership for Peace Consortium; he is also Member of the NATO ADL Advisory Team which is in charge for consulting and supporting national ADL capabilities at level of the MoD in NATO and PfP countries, Director for two research projects: Security and crises management e-learning Pilot Centre; M-Learning environment for real time course content access, and experts in others. He has published papers and books with e-Learning as a central subject.

Margarida Romero earned European Ph.D. in Psychology from UMR CNRS (France) and Universitat Autonoma de Barcelona (Extraordinary Ph.D. Award in Psychology). She is Associate Director of E-learning in ESADE Law & Business School and Associate Professor of Psychology in UAB and e-learning in UOC. She was awarded with the 3rd prize on Technology Transfer from the EU NoE Kaleidoscope in 2007, and the 1st prize of the Artificial Intelligence French Association Award in 2006. Her research aims to advance the understanding of the time factor in computer supported collaborative learning in the contexts of online learning and serious games.

Solomon Senrick has been teaching Middle School Social Studies for 10 years, including classes in American and Indian History, Civics, Global Studies, and Beliefs and Culture. Sol's interest and passion for professional learning, project facilitation, and technology integration are foundational to his practice. Sol is the leader of the 21st Century Skills Taskforce and an active member of the Game Based Learning task force at the American School of Bombay (ASB). Sol presented "Gaming with the End in Mind: Digital Games for Learning" at ASB's Unplugged Conference in 2012, and co-authored a chapter for ASB's Evolutions. Sol currently uses digital games in various units of instruction, on topics including general history, colonization and imperialism, geography, and government.

Neil Suttie is a PhD student in Artificial Intelligence at the University of Heriot-Watt, Edinburgh. He received his BSc with honours in Computer Science in 2010, with his honours dissertation investigating autonomous story presentation in interactive narrative. His research interests include artificial intelligence, affective computing, games design, interactive narrative, and serious games. He is currently exploring the application of psychophysiological inference for intelligent agents in the context of game based learning environments.

Jesús Trespalacios is a college Assistant Professor in the Curriculum and In-struction Department at New Mexico State University, where he teaches graduate courses on learning technologies. He earned his PhD in Learning Sciences and Technologies from Virginia Tech. With almost fifteen years of teaching experience at different levels and countries, he is interested in teacher preparation and the use of technology in mathematics classrooms at K-12 level. For the last two years, he has been part of the Learning Games Lab at New Mexico State University, exploring the design of serious games and their implementation in the classroom.

Mireia Usart earned her M.Sc.in E-Learning from Universitat Oberta de Cata-lunya (UOC), and is PhD candidate in the eLearn Center (UOC). Her PhD paper was awarded with first prize in eLSE 2012 conference. She did her Fellowship in the Direction of Educational Innovation and Academic Quality in ESADE Law & Business School. She is Member of the Institute of Educational Sciences (ICE) in the Universitat de Barcelona (UB), and she collaborates in the research and innovation task group for secondary education methodology programs. Her research aims to advance the understanding of the time factor, concretely time perspective, in game based learning in the contexts of blended learning.

Lida J. Uribe-Flórez is an Assistant Professor in the Curriculum and Instruc-tion Department at New Mexico State University. She teaches different course in education, including Mathematics Methods courses for Elementary and Secondary pre-service teachers. She earned her Ph.D. in Mathematics Education from Virginia Tech. With mathematics teaching experience at elementary, secondary, and university level, one of her areas of research is mathematics teaching and learning at K-12 grade level. More specifically, she is interested in the use of tools, in mathematics classrooms, to support learning. During the three years that she has been in Las Cruces, NM, she has been involved working with schools of the area.

Maria Velazquez is a Doctoral candidate at the University of Maryland, Col-lege Park. Her research interests include constructions of race, class, gender, and sexuality in contemporary media, as well as community-building and technology. She served on the board of Lifting Voices, a District of Columbia-based nonprofit that helped young people in DC discover the power of creative writing. She blogs for The Hathor Legacy (www.thehathorlegacy.com), a feminist pop culture blog, and recently received the Winnemore Dissertation Fellowship from the Maryland Institute for Technology in the Humanities. She has also received a fellowship from the Consortium on Race, Gender, and Ethnicity's Interdisciplinary Scholars Program. Maria is a Ron Brown Scholar and an alumna of Smith College.

Günter Wallner, studied Computer Science at the Vienna University of Technology and obtained his Diploma degree with honors in 2005. He earned a Doctoral degree with honors in Natural Sciences at the University of Applied Arts Vienna in 2009 where he currently works as Senior Scientist at the Institute of Art & Technology, Department of Geometry. Since 2008 he works as External Lecturer at the University of Vienna. His research interests include computer graphics and rendering, GPU programming, and visualization, as well as the design, development, and evaluation of digital games.

Scott Waren designs and conducts research on digital experiences at the University of North Texas, ranging from alternate reality games to ethical and moral concerns related to the use of games and simulations for educational purposes. He seeks to improve student literacy in all subject areas, but especially reading and writing. He believes that it is important to examine the role of play in developing learning experiences in a systematic manner in order to create replicable instructional designs for use in learning environments from K-20. In short, he is a Researcher, Instructor, Instructional Designer, and Writer.

Index